GLOBAL PROBLEMS AND THE
CULTURE OF CAPITALISM

THIRD EDITION

GLOBAL PROBLEMS AND THE CULTURE OF CAPITALISM

RICHARD H. ROBBINS

State University of New York at Plattsburgh

Boston ■ New York ■ San Francisco
Mexico City ■ Montreal ■ Toronto ■ London ■ Madrid ■ Munich ■ Paris
Hong Kong ■ Singapore ■ Tokyo ■ Cape Town ■ Sydney

Series Editor: *Jennifer Jacobson*
Series Editorial Assistant: *Emma Christensen*
Marketing Manager: *Kris Ellis-Levy*
Senior Production Editor: *Annette Pagliaro*
Editorial Production Service: *Omegatype Typography, Inc.*
Composition Buyer: *Linda Cox*
Manufacturing Buyer: *Megan Cochran*
Cover Administrator: *Kristina Mose-Libon*
Photo Research: *Laurie Frankenthaler*
Electronic Composition: *Omegatype Typography, Inc.*

For related titles and support materials, visit our online catalog at www.ablongman.com.

Copyright © 2005, 2002, 1999 Pearson Education, Inc.

All rights reserved. No part of the material protected by this copyright notice may be reproduced or utilized in any form or by any means, electronic or mechanical, including photocopying, recording, or by any information storage and retrieval system, without written permission from the copyright owner.

To obtain permission(s) to use material from this work, please submit a written request to Allyn and Bacon, Permissions Department, 75 Arlington Street, Boston, MA 02116 or fax your request to 617-848-7320.

Between the time Website information is gathered and published, some sites may have closed. Also, the transcription of URLs can result in typographical errors. The publisher would appreciate notification where these occur so that they may be corrected in subsequent editions.

Library of Congress Cataloging-in-Publication Data

Robbins, Richard Howard
 Global problems and the culture of capitalism / Richard H. Robbins.—3rd ed.
   p. cm.
 Includes bibliographical references and index.
 ISBN 0-205-40741-2
   1. Economics history—1990– 2. Social problems. 3. Capitalism. 4. Consumption (Economics) 5. Poverty. I. Title.

HC59.15 R63 2005
330.12'2—dc22
                                                                2004044692

Printed in the United States of America
10 9 8 7 6 5 4 3 2   09 08 07 06 05 04

Credits appear on page 432, which constitutes a continuation of this copyright page.

CONTENTS

CHAPTER THREE

The Rise of the Merchant, Industrialist, and Capital Controller   65

CHAPTER FOUR

The Nation-State in the Culture of Capitalism   108

PREFACE

Over the past 400 to 600 years, a culture and society, originating for the most part in Europe and dedicated to the idea of trade and consumption as the ultimate source of well-being, began to expand to all parts of the globe. In many ways it is the most successful culture and society the world has ever seen, its technology, wealth, and power monuments to its success; however, accompanying its expansion have been problems—growing social and economic inequality, environmental destruction, mass starvation, and social unrest. Most members of this society and culture perceive these problems as distant from themselves or as challenges for them to meet. However, there is the possibility that these problems, which threaten to negate everything this culture has accomplished, are intrinsic to the culture itself. That is the possibility explored in this book.

The outline of this book emerged when, a few years ago, my colleagues at the State University of New York at Plattsburgh, James Armstrong and Mark Cohen, and I began developing a course on global problems. We wanted to create a course that would help students understand the major global issues that they confront in the mass media—problems such as the so-called population explosion, famine and hunger, global environmental destruction, the emergence and spread of new diseases, so-called ethnic conflict and genocides, terrorism, and social protest. We learned quickly that to make the course successful we had to overcome the often-ethnocentric perspectives of the students, perspectives that were often reinforced by media coverage of global affairs. We needed also to compensate for the students' lack of backgrounds in anthropology, history, and economics, all crucial for understanding the roots of the problems we would examine. Finally, we needed to illustrate that the problems we examined were relevant to the students, that the problems would affect them either directly or indirectly, and that their actions now or in the future would determine the extent to which the origins of these problems could be acknowledged, let alone ever addressed. The form of this book emerged from our efforts at dealing with these pedagogical issues and the classroom interactions that these efforts stimulated.

THE FOCUS OF THIS BOOK

We can summarize our approach in this book as follows: There has emerged over the past five to six centuries a distinctive culture or way of life dominated by a belief in trade and commodity consumption as the source of well-being. This culture flowered in Western Europe, reached fruition in the United States, and spread to much of the rest of the world, creating what some anthropologists, sociologists, and historians call the world system. People disagree on the critical factors in the development of this system and even whether it was unique historically, although most agree on certain basic ideas. Among the most important are the assumptions that the driving force behind the spread of the contemporary world system was industrial and corporate capitalism, and that the spread of the world system is related in some way to the resulting division of the world into wealthy nations and poor nations or into wealthy core, developed, or industrialized areas and dependent, peripheral, undeveloped, or nonindustrialized areas.

The spread of the capitalist world system has been accompanied by the creation of distinctive patterns of social relations, ways of viewing the world, methods of food production, distinctive diets, patterns of health and disease, relationships to the environment, and so on. However, the spread of this culture has not gone uncontested; there has been resistance in the form of direct and indirect actions—political, religious, and social protest and revolution. How and why capitalist culture developed and the reasons why some groups resisted and continue to resist its development are among the questions posed in this book.

The answers to these questions are based on specific assumptions. First, a central tenet of anthropology is that personal, social, cultural, and historical factors determine the point of view any person might have regarding a certain phenomenon. No less is true of those participating in the culture of capitalism who have created a view of global events that we share. Consequently, these views tend to be, to one extent or another, ethnocentric; that is, people describe, evaluate, and judge events solely from a specific cultural perspective. Among the major purposes of anthropology is to teach ways to avoid ethnocentrism and appreciate the importance of understanding the beliefs and behaviors of others from their perspectives rather than from our own, a view anthropologists refer to as *cultural relativism.* To some extent ethnocentrism is unavoidable, and the job of the person who interprets global events—whether a journalist, economist, sociologist, or anthropologist—is to make those events comprehensible to those people for whom that person is writing. Our assumption is that to minimize cultural bias we must recognize that our views of events are partially influenced by our culture and, for that reason, we must make our own culture an object of analysis.

Second, we assume that an understanding of global events requires us to recognize that no contemporary culture or society exists independent of what anthropologists refer to as the *world system,* and that each falls within either the core or the periphery of that system. Using this terminology to refer to different parts of the world permits us to avoid the more value-laden distinctions implicit in the use of terms such as *developed* or *undeveloped, modern* or *traditional, First, Second,* or *Third World.* World system theorists often include a third category, semiperiphery, to denote those nation-states or regions that are moving toward the core or that have moved out of the core. These distinctions help people recognize that countries can move from one category to another. For example, the three nation-states world system theorists consider to have been dominant in the past four centuries—the Netherlands, the United Kingdom, and the United States—all began as semiperipheral to the world system.

Third, we assume that global events and actions cannot be adequately understood without considering the events that preceded them; we must develop a historical perspective. For example, we live in a period of human history largely defined by a sequence of events that began some 400 to 500 years ago, loosely termed the *industrial revolution.* Because each of us has lived during only a particular phase of that history, we tend to take it for granted that the world has always been as it is today. Yet the modern industrial world order is, in historical terms, a very recent event. We are deceived by our biology, by our limited life span, into thinking of sixty, seventy, or eighty years as a long time, but in the perspective of human history it is a fleeting moment. Human beings have, for most of their existence, lived as bands of gatherers and hunters, for a shorter time as agriculturists and farmers, and only recently as industrialists and wage laborers. Yet the industrial revolution transformed the world and human societies as did no other event in history. We cannot understand the events, issues, and problems of today's world without understanding the hows and whys of the industrial revolution.

It will be clear that the emergence of capitalism represents a culture that is in many ways the most successful that has ever been developed in terms of accommodating large numbers of individuals in relative and absolute comfort and luxury. It has not been as successful, however, in integrating all in equal measure, and its failure here remains one of its major problems. It has solved the problems of feeding large numbers of people (although certainly not all), and it has provided unprecedented advances in health and medicine (but, again, not for all). It has promoted the development of amazingly complex technological instruments and fostered a level of global communication without precedent. It has united people in common pursuits as no other culture has. Yet it remains to be seen when the balance sheet is tallied whether capitalism represents the epitome of "progress" that some claim.

ACKNOWLEDGMENTS

Many people contributed to the writing of this book. I have already mentioned my colleagues James Armstrong and Mark Cohen. Others include Alfred Robbins, Michael Robbins, Rachel Dowty, Tom Moran, Philip Devita, Gloria Bobbie, Douglas Skopp, Edward Champagne, Vincent Carey, Larry Soroka, Ellen Fitzpatrick, Ann Kimmage, Michael Miranda, John Hess, Jan Rinaldi, Tina Charland, Tim Harnett, Daphne Kutzer, Monica van Beusekom, Russell Kleinbach, Peggy Lindsey, Art Orme, Sam Baldwin, and Mary Turner. I also thank members of the e-mail list H-World, particularly its moderator Patrick Manning; Richard Winkel, moderator of the e-mail list Activ-L (aml@webmap.missouri.edu), and its many contributors; and many of the students who used one or another version of this book and who provided invaluable feedback. I would also like to thank the reviewers for this edition: Vaughn M. Bryant, Jr., Texas A&M University; Clifford E. Griffin, North Carolina State University; David Howes, Concordia University; and Stephen Wooten, University of Oregon. Reviewers of the first edition were John L. Aguilar, Charles O. Ellenbaum, Cynthia Mahmood, Richard Moore, Jon Olson, and Dave Winther. Reviewers of the second edition were Elliot Fratkin, Smith College; James Loucky, Western Washington University; and Luis A. Vivanco, University of Vermont.

I owe a special debt of gratitude to Sylvia Shephard for her support of the project; to Sarah Kelbaugh, Jennifer Jacobson, and Annette Pagliaro of Allyn and Bacon for guiding the project through to its present edition; as well as to Louis C. Bruno, Jr., whose copyediting makes reading the book far easier than it would be otherwise. And special thanks go to Amy and Rebecca, who tolerated with unusual understanding my periods of self-imposed isolation. Needless to say, the final form of the book, for better or worse, is the result of my own decisions.

I welcome from readers any comments, suggestions, or questions. I can be reached via e-mail at richard.robbins@plattsburgh.edu or through the Web site devoted to the book at http://www.plattsburgh.edu/legacy or http://faculty.plattsburgh.edu/richard.robbins/legacy.

THE CONSUMER, THE LABORER, THE CAPITALIST, AND THE NATION-STATE IN THE SOCIETY OF PERPETUAL GROWTH: INTRODUCTION

*[W]hat difference it would make to our understanding
if we looked at the world as a whole, a totality, a system, instead of as
a sum of self-contained societies and cultures; if we understood better how
this totality developed over time; if we took seriously the admonition to think
of human aggregates as "inextricably involved with other aggregates, near
and far, in weblike, netlike, connections."*
—Eric Wolf, *Europe and the People without History*

On or about December 1910, wrote novelist Virginia Woolf, human character changed.[1] On his repeated visits to the United States, Frenchman André Giegfried noted much the same thing: "A new society has come to life in America," he said. "It was not clear in 1901 or 1904; it was noticeable in 1914, and patent in 1919 and 1925" (cited Leach 1993:266). Samuel Strauss, a journalist and philosopher writing in the 1920s, suggested the term *consumptionism* to characterize this new way of life that, he said, created a person with

> a philosophy of life that committed human beings to the production of more and more things—"more this year than last year, more next year than this"—and that emphasized the "standard of living" above all other values.

[1]The quote, which has been widely used (see, e.g., Fjellman 1992:5; Lears 1983) appeared in an essay, "Mr. Bennett and Mrs. Brown," in *The Captain's Death Bed and Other Essays,* but was originally part of a paper Woolf read to the Heretics, Cambridge on May 18, 1924. "On or about December 1910 human character changed.... The change was not sudden and definite.... But a change there was nevertheless, and since on must be arbitrary, let us date it about the year 1910."

"From a moral point of view," Strauss continued,

> ...it is obvious that Americans have come to consider their standard of living as a somewhat sacred acquisition, which they will defend at any price. This means that they would be ready to make many an intellectual or even moral concession in order to maintain that standard. (cited Leach 1993:266)

There is no question that in America at least the half-century from 1880 to 1930 marked a major transition in the rate and level of commodity consumption—the purchase, use, and waste of what comedian George Carlin called "stuff." Food production grew by almost 40 percent from 1899 to 1905; the production of men's and women's ready-made clothing, along with the production of costume jewelry, doubled between 1890 and 1900; glassware and lamp production went from 84,000 tons in 1890 to 250,563 tons in 1914. In 1890, 32,000 pianos were sold in the United States; by 1904, the number sold increased to 374,000 (Leach 1993:16).

During this period the perfume industry became the country's tenth largest; at one department store, sale of toiletries rose from $84,000 to $522,000 between 1914 and 1926. The manufacture of clocks and watches went from 34 million to 82 million in ten years. By the late 1920s, one of every six Americans owned an automobile.

Of course these figures are dwarfed by what Americans and others around the world consume today. World and national consumption expanded at an unprecedented pace during the twentieth century, with private and public consumption expenditures reaching $24 trillion in 1998, twice the level of 1975 and six times that of 1950. In 1900, real consumption expenditure was barely $1.5 trillion (United Nations Human Development Programme 1998). Today there are as many cars in the United States, for example, as there are persons with drivers' licenses, and the rest of the world is doing everything that it can to catch up.

However, although consumption rates were not nearly as high as they are today, the early twentieth century is notable because it marked the early phase of what Ernest Gellner (1983:24) called the *society of perpetual growth* and the creation of a new type of culture: consumer capitalism.

The emergence of the society of perpetual growth and the culture of capitalism marked a new stage in an ongoing global historical process that began (to the extent that it can be said to have a beginning) anytime from the fifteenth to the early nineteenth centuries. The creation of the human type that characterizes this stage, the consumer, followed soon after the emergence of two other historically unique categories of human being: the capitalist and the laborer. Merchants had existed, of course, for thousands of years, and people had always labored to produce goods and, in a fashion, consume what they'd produced. But never before in history has there existed a society founded on these categories of people: the capitalist, whose sole purpose is to invest money and accumulate profit; the laborer, whose sole means of support comes from the sale of his or her labor; and the consumer, whose sole purpose is to purchase and consume ever-increasing quantities of goods and services.

Virtually all Americans, at some point in their lives, play the roles of consumer, laborer, or capitalist; as consumers they buy things; as laborers, they work for wages; and as capitalists they invest money in banks, insurance policies, pension plans, stocks (slightly more than half of American families participate in the stock market, either directly or through investment accounts), education, or other enterprises from which they expect to profit. What ties together these roles, and indeed the entire culture, is money.

Every culture has its distinct style or elements, rituals or ritual objects, that define for its members what is most important in life. The Dogon of West Africa define their existence through art; the Balinese of Indonesia, through drama and music. The Trobriand Islanders engaged in the accumulation of yams and the ritual exchange of shell necklaces and bracelets; the ancient Aztecs of Mexico in human sacrifice. For the indigenous peoples of the American Plains, the key element of cultural life was the buffalo. For members of the culture of capitalism the key element is money. Consumers want to spend as much money as they can, laborers want to earn as much as possible, and capitalists want to invest it so that it can return more. Money, as Jack Weatherford (1997:11) notes, defines relationships, not only between buyers and sellers in the marketplace or between employers or laborers in the workplace but also

> relationships between parent and child, among friends, between politicians and constituents, among neighbors, and between clergy and parishioners. Money forms the central institutions of the modern market and economy, and around it are grouped the ancillary institutions of kinship, religion, and politics. Money is the very language of commerce for the modern world.

"Other than love and fear," writes economist Robert Guttmann (1994:xvii), "there is probably no more powerful motivating force in our lives than money." It is the only way that we have to lawfully obtain goods, services, and assets, and, to the extent that we spend it, we must compete with each other to replenish it.

We can perhaps best conceptualize the working of the culture of capitalism as sets of relations between capitalists, laborers, and consumers, tied together by the pursuit of money, each depending on the other, yet each placing demands on, and often conflicting with, the others. In this cultural scheme, the nation-state serves as, among its other functions, a mediator, controlling the creation and flow of money and setting and enforcing the rules of interaction. (Figure I.1 is a highly simplified model, but it serves to underline the key features and unique style of the culture of capitalism.)

Money, however, is, obviously, the key to understanding this culture. In another time and place, Jacob Needleman (1991:40–41) wrote

> not everyone has wanted money above all else; people have desired salvation, beauty, power, strength, pleasure, prosperity, explanations, food, adventure, conquest, comfort. But now and here, money—not necessarily even the things money can buy, but money—is what everyone wants. The outward expenditure of mankind's energy now takes place in and through money.... Therefore, if one wished to understand life, one must understand money in this present phase of history and civilization.

Money is needed as a means of exchange and, for the system to function, must constantly increase in supply; that is, it must perpetually grow. Why this is so is not immediately apparent, even to many economists; but should the money supply cease to grow, the whole system could collapse in economic, political, and social chaos. Virtually all of the issues discussed in this book relate in one way or another to money and people's efforts to acquire it.

Part One of the book is devoted to outlining the interaction of consumer, laborer, capitalist, and nation-state, and how each must function if our society is to work. In Part

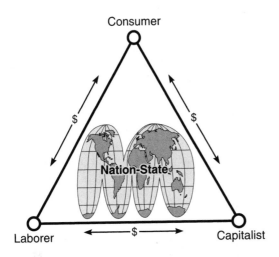

FIGURE I.1   Patterns of Relations in the Culture of Capitalism

Two we examine what economists call market externalities, that is, some of the unintended consequences that result in the interaction between consumer, laborer, capitalist, and nation-state. Finally in Part Three we explore the range of resistance to these externalities.

But first, given its central role in the working of the entire society, let's begin with a brief primer on the nature of money and an exploration of how money has assumed its importance and how it determines how we live our lives.

A PRIMER ON MONEY

It is common to see money simply as a standardized means of exchange; that is, money is a substance with which the value of goods and services can be compared and traded, a tool, so to speak. But to view money only in that way diminishes its true importance. Money might better be considered a modern-day philosopher's stone. Magicians or alchemists of old sought the philosopher's stone because it was thought to have the power to magically transmute base metals into gold, to take something that was considered worthless and convert it into something of value.

To appreciate the magic of money, the most important thing to consider is that *the prime directive of the culture of capitalism is that it must maintain economic growth.* People must buy, produce, invest, and profit more this year than last and more next year than this. Failure to maintain growth would threaten the economic, social, and political foundations and stability of our entire society. People would be unable to repay debts, banks would fail, millions would lose their jobs, and millions of businesses would go bankrupt, to name only a few of the obvious consequences. Aside from a few notable periods of economic contraction, such as the periodic depressions of the nineteenth century, the great worldwide depression of the 1930s, the recession of the early 1980s, and the

Alchemists believed that the philosopher's stone, newly popularized in the Harry Potter series of books, could convert worthless metal into gold, something worthless into something of value. By adopting paper money as a medium of exchange, the culture of capitalism has invented a new philosopher's stone—one every bit as powerful as that sought by magicians of another time.

Asian financial collapse of 1997, the world has, overall, done a reasonable job at growing the economy, although some areas have historically done a better job than others.

Economic growth is traditionally measured by the growth of gross domestic product (GDP)—a measure of the money value of all goods and services produced and sold in a given time period. Table I.1 and Figure I.2 portray the yearly growth of global GDP during the past two millennia.

Over the long term, but particularly over the past two centuries, the growth of GDP in the global economy, especially among European offshoots (e.g., the United States and Australia) and Japan, has been spectacular: a 300-fold increase in the amount of goods consumed, the number of goods produced, and the fortunes that have been made. A global citizen of today is almost nine times as wealthy as his or her counterpart some 200 years ago, and in some areas of the world the average citizen has increased her or his wealth almost twenty-five times over the same period.

These increases could only occur with a steady increase in the money supply. Without the increase, people would not have the means to buy more, employers would not have the

TABLE I.1   Level and Rate of Growth of GDP per Capita: World and Major Regions, 0–1998

REGION	0	1000	1820	1998	0– 1000	1000– 1820	1820– 1998
	Level of Growth (1990 international dollars)				*Annual Average Compound Growth Rate*		
Western Europe	450	400	1,232	17,921	−0.01	0.14	1.51
Western offshoots (e.g., United States, Australia, etc.)	400	400	1,201	26,146	0.00	0.13	1.75
Japan	400	425	669	20,413	0.01	0.06	1.93
Latin America	400	400	665	5,795	0.00	0.06	1.22
Eastern Europe and former USSR	400	400	667	4,354	0.00	0.06	1.06
Asia (excluding Japan)	450	450	575	2,936	0.00	0.03	0.92
Africa	425	416	418	1,368	0.00	0.00	0.67
World	444	435	667	5,709	0.00	0.03	0.95

Adapted from Angus Maddison, *The World Economy: A Millennial Perspective*. Development Centre of the Organization for Economic Co-operation and Development, Paris, 2003:28.

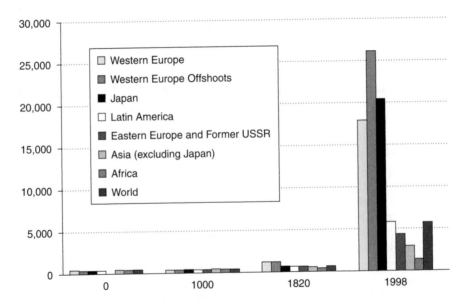

FIGURE I.2   Rate of per Capita GDP Growth by Region, 0–1998

means to pay more, and capitalists would not be able to profit more. *But how does the money supply increase? Where does money come from and what or who provides its magical power?* There were three steps to the emergence of money as a modern philosopher's stone.

STEP 1: THE DEVELOPMENT OF COMMODITY MONEY

The use of objects as a medium of exchange is likely as old as trade. The use of shells, furs, and other items of value as money are known in small-scale societies throughout the world. The use of precious metals as a medium of exchange can be traced back 5,000 years to Mesopotamia and coins to the seventh century B.C. These are examples of "commodity money." Commodity money is money that has some value in itself beyond its exchange value. Thus, precious metals used for making coins can be used for making jewelry or other objects of art. Generally, the value of the coins are equal to the value of the metals used. As such, the use of coins for trade involves the exchange of one thing of value (e.g., a shirt) for another thing of equivalent value (e.g., an equal amount of gold).

But coins had a big disadvantage; they were difficult to store and to transport. Furthermore, it was not uncommon for people to melt down the coins and use them for some

The issuing of paper money was a huge step in helping to accelerate economic growth.

other purpose, thus removing them from circulation. This is where the first bit of magic comes in; people began to substitute paper for coins. "Exchange" or "demand" notes—paper certificates that could be exchanged for a valuable commodity, generally gold or silver—were first used in China in the twelfth century and became common in Europe in the fourteenth and fifteenth centuries (Willliams 1997). Thus, a trader in Milan might buy textiles from someone in Bruges and pay with a paper note backed by gold that the seller could retrieve from a third party. Generally, banks or governments issued exchange notes or paper money, but virtually anyone could do it. The key was that, theoretically, these notes represented a specific amount of some valuable metal—usually gold or silver—that could be retrieved on demand by the holder of the note.

The issuing of paper money was a huge step in helping to accelerate economic growth because, potentially, there was no limit to the amount of money that could be created. This was the first step in money magic: Paper, which was essentially worthless, now had the same value as gold, silver, or other precious metals. In a wonderful book called *Magic and Money: A Critique of the Modern Economy in the Light of Goethe's Faust* economist Hans Binswanger (1994) describes how Johann Wolfgang von Goethe, who served as finance minister at the Weimar court, used his classic work *Faust* (published in two parts in 1808 and 1832) for a commentary on the industrial economy, and, more specifically, on the nature of money. The original Faust, on whom the story is based, was a magician, an alchemist. In Goethe's book Faust makes a bargain with Mephistopheles—the devil—who together create a new society based on paper money. Binswanger suggests the alchemist's attempts to convert lead into gold were abandoned

> not because they were futile, but because alchemy in another form has proved so successful that the arduous production of gold in the laboratory is no longer necessary. It is not vital to alchemy's aim, in the sense of increasing wealth, that lead actually be transmuted into gold. It will suffice if a substance of no value is transformed into one of value: paper, for example, into money. (Binswanger 1994:9).

There were, however, some problems with commodity money. First, there was no guarantee that the commodity being used was valued equally in different places. Thus, gold might be worth one amount in one area but a different amount in another area. Second, theoretically, anyone could produce currency. In the United States in the nineteenth century, for example, there were some 30,000 different currencies in circulation, issued by institutions from banks to drug stores. The problem was that the worth and reliability of these currencies was not guaranteed, and they often proved worthless, thus undermining people's faith in paper money altogether.

Third, although banks or other entities that issued money were, of course, under obligation to have on hand an amount of gold or silver equivalent to the amount of paper money issued, they rarely did. In fact, to profit all banks issued currencies in the form of loans well in excess of the deposits that they held. This was an especially common practice when trade and commerce thrived and it worked perfectly well as long as everyone with a deposit didn't demand their gold at the same time. Banks profited from the interest on the loans and people had more money to spend. The problems occurred when, after an economic boom, the economy slowed down and depositors demanded their gold. Unable to pay all their depositors because they had issued notes in excess of the amount of gold they had on hand, banks failed and people lost their savings.

Thus, tying paper money to a specific commodity had its drawbacks: There were thousands of different, sometimes incompatible currencies, banks failed when people rushed to convert paper into gold, and there were unacceptable fluctuations in the money supply. Furthermore, if money was strictly tied to a specific commodity, the money supply (and hence the economy) could grow only if the supply of the commodity grew.[1] Given the prime directive of perpetual economic growth, there is, consequently, a real problem with commodity money.

The U.S. government tried to address some of these problems by creating the Federal Reserve Bank in 1913 to control and stabilize the money supply. Paper money was still tied to gold and a person could retrieve paper for gold, but the Federal Reserve could ensure that banks had enough gold on hand, or could quickly acquire it, to honor withdrawals. The rule was that banks had to have on hand an amount of gold equal to 10 percent of what is actually owed. In that way, banks could honor requests for gold but be able to create new money by making loans. Thus, for every dollar deposited, banks and other lending institutions could lend out and, in effect, create nine dollars of new money. But the Federal Reserve could still not address the limitations imposed on economic growth by tying money to a fixed commodity. Solving that problem required another bit of magic and another government decree.

STEP 2: THE SHIFT FROM COMMODITY TO FIAT OR CREDIT MONEY

The next stage in the evolution of money occurred in 1931 when the United States stopped allowing people in the United States to convert paper money into gold. The value of money was still tied to the value of gold, and exchanges with foreign governments still occurred in gold, but even this was stopped in 1971 when U.S. dollars were no longer backed by gold at all. This marked the final shift from commodity to fiat or credit money, paper that was used as evidence of a claim to economic value but that, legally, was not redeemable for anything.

As might be expected, with dollars backed by nothing, the money supply could rapidly grow, and theoretically could then match or exceed the growth or potential growth of the economy. More importantly, the Federal Reserve in the United States and central banks in other countries could develop ways to control the money supply, ensuring that it grew fast enough to keep up with economic growth but not so fast that inflation resulted. Inflation would occur when the amount of money exceeded the value of goods and services that people demanded, thus driving up the prices as buyers competed for scarce resources. If, however, the supply of goods and services exceeded the money supply, prices would decline as sellers competed for limited dollars, which leads to deflation. Thus, balancing the amount of money in circulation with the goods and services that could be purchased was a major challenge for central banks, such as the U.S. Federal Reserve.

When we think of money, we think of bills and coins. But that is only a small part (5 to 10 percent) of the money supply. The rest exists only as figures on paper (or in computers) in banks and in the records of other financial institutions. Credit money, for example,

---

[1]The money supply could also grow if the value (price) of the commodity (e.g., gold) grew. However, there were real limits on the value of the commodity and the other uses to which it could be put.

TABLE I.2   Money Supply by Type in the United States, 1959, 1971, 1985, 2004 (in billions)*

	M1: the most narrowly defined measure, consists of the most liquid forms of money, namely currency and checkable deposits				M2 (includes M1): the non-M1 components of M2 are primarily household holdings of savings deposits, small time deposits, and retail money market mutual funds	M3: (includes M1 and M2): the non-M2 components of M3 consist of institutional money funds and certain managed liabilities of depositories, namely large time deposits, repurchase agreements, and eurodollars	
	Currency						
YEAR	AMOUNT	% OF TOTAL MONEY SUPPLY	SAVINGS, CHECKING DEPOSITS AND OTHER	TOTAL M1		TOTAL MONEY SUPPLY	% INCREASE IN TOTAL MONEY SUPPLY
1959	28.5	9.9	110.4	138.9	286.6	288.8	—
1971	48.9	7.1	166.5	215.4	632.8	685.4	137
1985	167.7	5.2	450.3	619.1	2494.9	3207.6	368
2004	662.0	7.5	597.7	1258.7	6070.0	8861.0	176

*M1 is included in M2 and M2 is included in M3

Adapted from *Federal Reserve Statistical Release: Historical Data* (2004). http://www.federalreserve.gov/releases/h6/hist/

is simply that; it represents a promise by the borrower of money to repay it at some future date. Table I.2 shows the kinds of money, or money stocks in circulation, along with their growth since 1959.

As you can see the money supply in 2004 was thirty times larger than it was in 1959. You can perhaps begin to see why money represents a magical process. Because *fiat* or *credit* money is backed up by nothing other than the legal power of the nation-state, but can be converted into all kinds of goods and services, we have further succeeded in the alchemists goal of taking something that is essentially worthless (paper) and turning it into objects of value (whatever we can obtain with this paper).

But, as Faust learned in his bargain with the devil, there is often a price to pay for access to the philosopher's stone. That takes us to the third step in our alchemical exercise.

STEP 3: THE NECESSARY CONVERSION OF NONMONETARY INTO MONETARY CAPITAL

Having removed money from anything of worth, one other problem remained: the natural limit on things into which money can be converted. Although the money supply might be unlimited, the goods and services that people can buy with their money is not. But if economic growth (and the supply of money) must increase every year (and must increase at a rate of at least 3 percent to maintain a healthy economy), then so must the things that money can buy. When money was tied to and limited by a commodity such as gold, the money supply was constantly trying to keep up with the goods and services available. However, once money was uncoupled from anything of value and could infinitely grow, the situation was reversed and goods and services began to chase the money supply. Thus, where we used to have a situation in which we needed more and more gold to grow, now we simply need more and more stuff. In other words, *the money supply must grow if the economy is to remain healthy, and, for the money supply to grow, there must be a steady increase in the things or services that money can buy.* It is from this simple fact that many of the problems we discuss in this book derive.

For example, for economic growth to continue (more money and more things), there must be a constant conversion of things that have no money value into things that do; that is, there must be constant commodification because money can only grow through a process whereby nonmonetary goods or values are converted into things of monetary worth (see, e.g., Bourdieu 1986:243). In this conversion process lies the genius of capitalism. In it also lies the secret of our Faustian bargain. Through the operation of a myriad of rules, regulations, values, and laws, the culture of capitalism encourages the conversion of items and activities that have no intrinsic monetary worth, but are nevertheless valuable and even necessary in other ways, into items and activities that can be bought and sold in the marketplace. Thus, trees, lakes, and mountains must be converted into things that can be sold in the marketplace; activities once associated with family life and given freely, such as child care, food preparation, and education, must be converted into monetary activities; freedom itself can be exchanged for money (see Figure I.3)

We discuss this process of capital conversion in Chapter 13 in more detail, but for now it is sufficient to understand why this conversion is necessary to fulfill the prime directive of perpetual economic growth.

In sum, then, our culture works largely on a magical principle in which money, an item of no intrinsic value, perpetually increases in quantity while, at the same time, we work to convert more and more nonmonetary capital into things that this money can buy. Of course, this is a simplification of everything that has to be done to keep the system working and in next four chapters we describe how the consumer, laborer, capitalist, and nation-state operate to maintain this magic act.

The emergence of the culture of capitalism has left little in our lives untouched—it has affected our material, spiritual, and intellectual life; it has reshaped our values; and, as we shall see, it has largely dictated the direction that every institution in our society has taken. It has produced wave after wave of consumer goods, revolutionized food production, and prompted previously unimagined developments in technology, communications, and medicine. Most dramatically, at least from the anthropological point of view, "feeding" the consumer has required a level of global integration unmatched in human history. The clothes we wear more often than not are produced in whole or in part by people in Malaysia, Hong Kong, or El Salvador; workers in Brazil probably cut the sugarcane that became the sugar that sweetens our soft drinks; our morning coffee began as coffee beans in the highlands of Colombia; the oranges we eat may have been grown in Spain, packed in cardboard boxes made of Canadian pulpwood, wrapped in plastic produced in New Jersey, and transported on trucks made in France with Italian, Japanese, and American parts. Our radios,

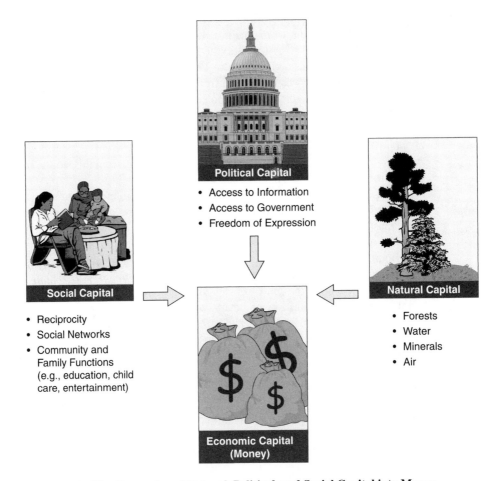

FIGURE I.3   The Conversion of Natural, Political, and Social Capital into Money

televisions, and VCRs are most likely assembled by workers in Mexico, Haiti, or Indonesia; and our automobiles, of course, may have been produced at least in part in Japan, Taiwan, or Korea.

Furthermore, the culture of capitalism is being exported to all parts of the globe. Yet few people are aware of how the culture works and how it affects our lives and those of people all over the world—how American consumption, labor, and investment patterns relate to wages paid to women in Indonesia, the destruction of the rain forests in Paraguay, or the use of water on the American Plains. This is not necessarily the fault of the individual, for, as we shall see, the culture of capitalism purposefully masks from its members the problems that result from its maintenance and spread.

CHAPTER ONE

CONSTRUCTING THE CONSUMER

The consumer revolution is a strange chapter in the ethnographic history of the species. For what may have been the first time in its history, a human community willingly harbored a nonreligious agent of social change, and permitted it to transform on a continual and systematic basis virtually every feature of social life.
—Grant McCracken, *Culture and Consumption*

The…metamessage of our time is that the commodity form is natural and inescapable. Our lives can only be well lived (or lived at all) through the purchase of particular commodities. Thus our major existential interest consists of maneuvering for eligibility to buy such commodities in the market. Further, we have been taught that it is right and just—ordained by history, human nature, and God—that the means of life in all its forms be available only as commodities…. Americans live in an overcommodified world, with needs that are generated in the interests of the market and that can be met only through the market.
—Stephen Fjellman, *Vinyl Leaves*

The culture of capitalism is devoted to encouraging the production and sale of commodities. For capitalists, the culture encourages the accumulation of profit; for laborers, it encourages the accumulation of wages; for consumers, it encourages the accumulation of goods. In other words, capitalism defines sets of people who, behaving according to a set of learned rules, act as they must act.

There is nothing natural about this behavior. People are not naturally driven to accumulate wealth. There are societies in which such accumulation is discouraged. Human beings do not have an innate drive to accumulate commodities; again, there are plenty of societies in which such accumulation is discouraged. People are not driven to work; in fact, contrary to popular notions, members of capitalist culture work far more than, say, people who live by gathering and hunting (see, e.g., Shor 1993). *How does culture, as anthropologists use the term, encourage people to behave in some ways and not in others? Specifically, how does the culture of capitalism encourage the accumulation of profit, wages, and commodities? How does it, in effect, encourage perpetual growth and what amounts to perpetual change?*

It is not easy to describe the effects of culture on people's lives; anthropologists have noted that culture consists of all learned beliefs and behaviors, the rules by which we order our lives, and the meanings that human beings construct to interpret their universes and their places in them. Yet, using these abstract descriptions, it is difficult to understand how pervasive our culture can be in determining our view of the world. It may help, therefore, to provide a metaphor for culture in the form of a belief and practice of another culture: the sandpaintings of the Navajo of the American Southwest.

Among the Navajo people, there is a healing practice in which a curer draws on the ground a miniature representation of the universe, using colored sand, cornmeal, or other bits of material. Although there are perhaps a thousand versions of these drawings, each contains vital elements of what, for the Navajo, defines the general conditions of existence. Navajo conceptions of space are indicated by symbols of the world's directions; conceptions of social life are indicated by the distribution of Navajo houses (*hogans*) and mythic beings; values are represented in the stories and chants associated with each sandpainting; material items critical to Navajo existence (e.g., horses or ritual items) are also portrayed. Once the work is completed, the patient sits on or in the sandpainting, and a curing ceremony, accompanied by chanting and prayer, proceeds. Illness, the Navajo claim, is the result of persons' losing their proper places in the world; the aim of the ceremony is to restore the patient to that place. When the ceremony is completed and harmony restored, the sandpainter destroys the painting.

Navajo sandpainting contains all the elements of what anthropologists often mean by the term culture. Like the sandpainting, a culture serves to define the universe as it is supposed to exist for a people. The sandpainting contains the key elements and symbols that people use to locate themselves in physical and social space. It affirms the place of the person in the created world and the values that govern people's lives. Like the sandpainting, particular cultural representations serve as therapeutic frames that communicate to us who and what we are and how we figure in the larger order of things. These representations are therapeutic because they help people resolve the contradictions and ambiguities that are inherent in any cultural definition of reality and self.

Furthermore, every society has its sandpainters, those individuals who are given or who take responsibility for representing the universe to others and who have the power to define those elements that are essential for others in locating and defining their identities. In some societies, as among the Navajo, it is the curer, shaman, mythmaker, or storyteller; in others, it is the priest, poet, writer, artist, singer, or dancer. In capitalism, the sandpainter works in churches, synagogues, or mosques, and in theaters, in front of television sets, at sporting events, or in the shopping malls that reaffirm the vision of abundance central to the consumers' view of the world. Contemporary sandpainters, who include marketing specialists, advertisers, government agents, corporate public relations specialists, entertainers, and journalists, among others, "spin" a vision of the world designed to maximize the production and consumption of goods. They have helped to create a culture in which the prime elements are commodities, and in which the consumer's first duty is to buy (or "Shop till you drop," as a popular bumper sticker advises). It is a culture in which virtually all our everyday activities—work, leisure, the fulfillment of social responsibilities, and so

Navajo sandpaintings serve as therapeutic stages on which a person's place in the universe is defined and ritually enacted.

on—take place in the context of commodities, and in which shopping, like the sandpainting cure, serves as a therapeutic activity. These contemporary sandpainters construct for us a culture in which at one time or another every individual enacts the identity of consumer. The question we need to explore first is, *how was the universe of the consumer and the consumer itself created?*

REMAKING CONSUMPTION

The consumer did not, of course, appear full blown in the United States of the early twentieth century. Even in the eighteenth century, merchants in Great Britain, France, and elsewhere were concerned that more goods were being produced than could be sold. But merchants generally paid little attention to how goods were marketed or presented, assuming that when people needed their products, they would buy them. It was this attitude in the United States of a century ago that was to undergo a profound change.

The change did not occur naturally. In fact, the culture of nineteenth-century America emphasized not unlimited consumption but moderation and self-denial. People, workers in particular, were expected to be frugal and save their money; spending, particularly on luxuries, was seen as "wasteful." People purchased only necessities—basic foodstuffs, clothing, household utensils, and appliances—or shared basic items when they could. If we look at a typical inventory of the possessions of an American family of 1870–1880, we find a pattern very different from that of today. In 1870, 53 percent of the population lived and worked on farms and produced much of what they consumed. One Vermont farm wife recorded making 421 pies, 152 cakes, 2,140 doughnuts, and 1,038 loaves of bread in one year (Sutherland 1989:71). Household items were relatively simple—a dinner table, wooden chairs, beds, perhaps a carpet or rug. There were few appliances to aid housework—cookstoves, eggbeaters, apple parers, pea shellers, and coffee mills, but most other housework required muscle; even hand-cranked washing machines were not available until the late 1870s. Although only the poorest or most isolated families did not buy some ready-made clothing, most of the items people wore were made at home and were largely functional. Furthermore, because the vast majority of American families lived on farms, most of the family capital was invested in farming tools and implements. There were, of course, exceptions. The wealthy members of society competed with each other in the ostentatious display of wealth and luxury, as they had for centuries. But they represented a small percentage of the population.

Of course, Americans did not yet have electricity, the automobile had yet to be invented, and the money supply was far more limited than it is today. Nevertheless, to transform buying habits, luxuries had to be transformed into necessities. In America, this was accomplished largely in four ways: a revolution in marketing and advertising, a restructuring of major societal institutions, a revolution in spiritual and intellectual values, and a reconfiguration of space and class.

Marketing and Advertising

First, there was a major transformation of the meaning of goods and how they were presented and displayed. For most of the eighteenth and nineteenth centuries, retailers paid little attention to how goods were displayed. The first department store—Bon Marché—opened in Paris in 1852, allowing people to wander through the store with no expectations that they make a purchase. Enterprises such as Bon Marché were devoted to "the arousal of free-floating desire," as Rosalind Williams put it (cited McCracken 1988:25). The displays of commodities helped define bourgeois culture, converting the culture, values, attitudes, and aspirations of the bourgeoisie into goods, thus shaping and transforming them (Miller 1994).

But Bon Marché was an exception. In stores in the United States, most products were displayed in bulk, and little care was taken to arrange them in any special way. Prepackaged items with company labels did not even exist until the 1870s, when Ivory Soap and Quaker Oats appeared (Carrier 1995:102). Shop windows, if they existed, were simply filled with items that had been languishing in back rooms or warehouses for years. Even the few large department stores of the mid-nineteenth century, such as that of Alexander Turney Stewart, the Marble Palace in New York, paid little attention to display. It was not until the 1890s and the emergence of the department store in the United States as a major retail establishment that retailers began to pay attention to how products were presented to the public.

The department store evolved into a place to display goods as objects in themselves. When Marshall Field's opened in Chicago in 1902, six string orchestras filled the various floors with music and American Beauty roses along with other cut flowers and potted palms bedecked all the counters. Nothing was permitted to be sold on the first day, and merchants in the district closed so that their employees could visit Field's. Later, elaborate theatrical productions were put on in the stores, artworks were displayed, and some of the most creative minds in America designed displays that were intended to present goods in ways that inspired people to buy them. The department store became a cultural primer telling people how they should dress, furnish their homes, and spend their leisure time (Leach 1993).

Advertising was another revolutionary development that influenced the creation of the consumer. The goal of advertisers was to aggressively shape consumer desires and create value in commodities by imbuing them with the power to transform the consumer into a more desirable person. Before the late 1880s, advertising was looked down on and associated with P. T. Barnum-style hokum. In 1880, only $30 million was invested in advertising in the United States; by 1910, new businesses, such as oil, food, electricity, and rubber, were spending $600 million, or 4 percent of the national income, on advertising. By 1998, the amount spent globally on advertising reached $437 billion, a figure that rivals the $778 billion spent on weapons.

By the early twentieth century, national advertising campaigns were being initiated and celebrities were being hired to offer testimonials to their favorite commodities. Advertising cards, catalogs, and newspaper ads became a regular feature of American life. Outdoor advertising—billboards, signs, and posters—appeared everywhere. Electrical advertising—neon and flashing signs—were marketed, and Broadway became famous as the "Great White Way." Today, advertising plays such a ubiquitous part in our lives that we scarcely notice it, even when it is engraved or embroidered on our clothing.

Another boon to merchandising was the idea of fashion: the stirring up of anxiety and restlessness over the possession of things that were not "new" or "up-to-date." Fashion pressured people to buy not out of need but for style—from a desire to conform to what others defined as "fashionable."

It is hardly surprising then that the garment industry in America led the way in the creation of fashion; its growth in the early 1900s was two or three times as great as any other industry. By 1915, it ranked only behind steel and oil in the United States. Fashion output in 1915 was in excess of $1 billion; in New York alone, 15,000 establishments made women's clothes. New fashion magazines—*Vogue, Cosmopolitan,* and *The Delineator*—set fashion standards and defined what the socially conscious woman should wear, often using royalty, the wealthy, and celebrities as models. The fashion show was introduced in the United States by Ehrich Brothers in New York City in 1903; by 1915, it was an event in virtually every U.S. city and town. Relying on this popularity, the first modeling agency was founded in New York by John Powers in 1923 (Leach 1993:309). The entertainment industry contributed by making its own major fashion statements as American women of 1920s sought to imitate stars such as Clara Bow.

Another addition to the marketing strategy was service, which included not only consumer credit (charge accounts and installment buying) but also a workforce to fawn over customers. Customers became guests.

William Leach suggested that service may have been one of the most important features of the new consumer society. It helped, he said, mask the inequality, poverty, and labor conflicts that were very much a part of the United States at this point in its history. If one wanted to understand how consumer society developed, Leach said, one could look at the rise of service. As economic inequality rose in America, and as labor conflict increased, Americans associated service with the "promise of America." Service conveyed to people the idea that everything was all right, that they had nothing to worry about, and that security and service awaited them. Service expressed what economists then and now would refer to as

> the "benevolent side" of capitalism, that is, the side of capitalism that gave to people in exchange for a dependable flow of profits—a better, more comfortable way of life. In this view, capitalism did not merely "strive for profits" but also sought "the satisfaction of the needs of others, by performing service efficiently." "Capital," said one turn-of-the-century economist, "reigns because it serves." (Leach 1993:146–147)

The Transformation of Institutions

The second way in which American buying habits were changed was through a transformation of the major institutions of American society, each redefining its function to include the promotion of consumption. Educational and cultural institutions, governmental agencies, financial institutions, and even the family itself changed their meaning and function to promote the consumption of commodities.

Before 1900, the contributions of universities to the capitalist economy largely dealt with how to "make" things, that is, with the production of commodities. Virtually no attention was paid to selling or keeping track of what was sold. For example, there was no systematic examination of mass retailing, credit systems, or banking offered by America's schools or universities. In the twentieth century, however, that began to change. For example, in New York City there was the good-design or arts-in-industry movement; schools, such as the Pratt Institute and the New York School of Fine and Applied Arts (now Parsons School of Design), developed and began to prepare students to work in the emerging sales and design industries and in the large department stores. The University of Pennsylvania's Wharton School for Business and the Harvard School for Business introduced programs in accounting (virtually nonexistent before then), marketing, and sales. In 1919, New York University's School of Retailing opened; in the mid-1920s, Harvard and Stanford established graduate business schools as did such schools as Northwestern, Michigan, California, and Wisconsin soon after. Today, there are virtually no two-year or four-year colleges that do not offer some sort of business curriculum.

Museums also redefined their missions to accommodate the growth of the consumer culture. The American Museum of Natural History and the Metropolitan Museum of Art in Manhattan, the Brooklyn Museum, and the Newark Museum, all heavily endowed by wealthy patrons such as J. P. Morgan, began to make alliances with business. Curators lectured to designers on Peruvian textiles or primitive decorative art. The head of the American Museum of Natural History, Morris D'Camp Crawford, assisted by the head of the anthropology department, Clark Wissler, urged businesspeople and designers to visit the museum. Special exhibits on the history of fashion and clothing were arranged, and Wissler even borrowed the window display techniques of New York department stores for his exhibits (as window display designers had borrowed the idea of the mannequin from anthropologist Franz Boas's display of foreign cultures at the 1893 World's Columbian Exposition in Chicago). The editor of *Women's Wear* magazine praised the museum for being "the most progressive force in the development of the designer" (Leach 1993:166).

The second set of institutions to aid in the development of consumer culture were agencies of the local and federal governments. The state, as an entity, had long taken a lively interest in commerce within its borders (as we'll see when we examine the history of global capitalist expansion in Chapter 3). But prior to the twentieth century, the state's concerns focused largely on the manufacture of commodities, the organization of business, the control of labor, and the movement of goods. It wasn't until the twentieth century that state agencies began to concern themselves with the consumption end of the business cycle. In fact, it may not be an exaggeration to say that the government did more to create the consumer than did any other institution.

Nothing better represents the increasing role of the federal government in the promotion of consumption than the growth of the Commerce Department under Herbert Hoover, who served as its head from 1921 until his election as president in 1928. When the Commerce Building opened in Washington in 1932, it was the biggest office structure in the world (and was not surpassed in size until the Pentagon was built a decade later). At the time, it brought together in one building virtually all the government departments that had anything to do with business, from the Patent Office to the Bureau of Foreign and Domestic Commerce (BFDC), then the most important agency of the department. From 1921 to 1930, the congressional appropriation for the BFDC rose from $100,000 to more than $8 million, an increase of 8,000 percent. The number of BFDC staff increased from 100 to 2,500.

Hoover clearly intended the Department of Commerce to serve as the handmaiden of American business, and its main goal was to help encourage the consumption of commodities. For example, between 1926 and 1928 the BDFC, under Hoover's direction, initiated the Census of Distribution (or "Census of Consumption," as it was sometimes called) to be carried out every ten years. (It was unique at that time; Britain and other countries did not initiate government-sponsored consumer research until the 1950s). It detailed where the consumers were and what quantities of goods they would consume; it pointed out areas where goods were "overdeveloped" and which goods were best carried by which stores. The Commerce Department endorsed retail and cooperative advertising and advised merchants on service devices, fashion, style, and display methods of all kinds. The agency advised retail establishments on the best ways to deliver goods to consumers, redevelop streets, build parking lots and underground transportation systems to attract consumers, use colored lights, and display merchandise in "tempting ways." The goal was to break down "all barriers between the consumers and commodities" (Leach 1993:366).

Hoover also emphasized individual home ownership. In his memoirs he wrote that "a primary right of every American family is the right to build a new house of its heart's desire at least once. Moreover, there is the instinct to own one's own house with one's own arrangement of gadgets, rooms, and surroundings" (cited Nash 1988:7). The Commerce Department flooded the country with public relations materials on "homebuying" ideas, producing a leaflet entitled *Own Your Own Home,* along with a film, *Home Sweet Home.* They advocated single-dwelling homes over multiunit dwellings and suburban over urban housing. The leaflet recommended a separate bedroom for each child, saying it was "undesirable for two children to occupy the same bed—whatever their age." Regardless of the reasons for these recommendations, the materials produced by the Commerce Department all promoted maximum consumption. Thus, the government responded, as much as did educational institutions, to the need to promote the consumption of commodities.

Another step in creating a consumer economy was to give the worker more buying power. The advantage of this from an economic perspective is not easy to see. From the point of view of an industrialist or an employer, the ideal situation would be to pay as low a wage as possible to keep production costs down and increase profits. However, each producer of goods would prefer other producers to pay high wages, which would allow the other producers' workers to buy more products. The ideas that higher wages would serve as an incentive for laborers to work harder or that higher wages might allow the worker to become a consumer, occurred relatively late to factory owners and investors. The working class, they assumed, would work only as hard as they needed to get their basic subsistence, and to pay them more would only result in their working less. And when an occasional economic boom gave workers the spending power to consume at a higher level, the middle and upper classes would condemn them for their lack of thrift.

The economic power derived from turning workers into consumers was realized almost by accident. As industry attempted to increase efficiency, it developed new methods. Henry Ford introduced the assembly line, one of the apparently great innovations, to the manufacturing of automobiles. Workers occupied positions on the line from which they did not move ("Walking," Ford said, "is not a remunerative activity") and from which they would perform a single task. It was a process that required almost no training and that "the most stupid man could learn within two days," as Ford said. In essence, each worker had to repeat the same motion every ten seconds in a nine-hour workday.

Workers resisted this mind-numbing process. When Ford introduced his assembly line, absenteeism increased and worker turnover was enormous. In 1913, Ford required 13,000 to 14,000 workers to operate his plant, and in that year 50,000 quit. But Ford solved the problem: He raised wages from the industry standard of two to three dollars per day to five dollars, and he reduced the working day to eight hours. Soon labor turnover fell to 5 percent, and waiting lines appeared at Ford hiring offices. Furthermore, production costs for Ford's Model-T fell from $1,950 to $290, reducing the price to consumers. Most importantly, the rise in wages made Ford workers consumers of Ford automobiles, and, as other manufacturers followed suit, the automobile industry grew. By 1929, there were 23 million automobiles in the United States; by 1950 there were more than 40 million. Today, including light trucks, there are 1.3 cars for every individual.

In addition to the money coming from higher wages, buying power was increased by the expansion of credit. Credit, of course, is essential for economic growth and consumerism because it means that people, corporations, and governments can purchase goods and services with only a promise to pay for them at some future date. Furthermore, whenever credit is extended—whether it be by a store, a bank, a corporation, a person, or a government—in effect, money has been created, and more buying power has been introduced into the economy. Buying things on credit—that is, going into debt—has not always been acceptable in the United States. It was highly frowned on in the nineteenth century. It was not fully socially acceptable until the 1920s (Calder 1999), at which time it promoted the boom in both automobile and home buying.

The increased ease of obtaining home mortgages was a key to the home building boom of the 1940s, 1950s, and 1960s, a boom that in turn fueled subsidiary industries—appliances, home furnishings, and road construction. By 1960, 62 percent of all Americans could claim to own their own home up from 44 percent in 1940. By 2002, U.S. homeowners owed more than $6 trillion in mortgages. Home mortgages had the further function of disciplining the workforce by forcing it to work to make credit payments. At the same time, homeowners gained a capital asset that served as a hedge against inflation. Automobile loans also added to consumer debt and, similarly, fueled subsidiary economic growth—malls, highways, vacation travel, and so on. Credit cards gave holders a revolving line of credit with which to finance purchases. In 2002, U.S. household debt reached $8.5 trillion, and 20 percent of American households have more debt than assets, or 40 percent when real estate is factored out. This debt represents enormous confidence in the future of the economy because this money does not exist. Lenders in our economy simply assume that the money will exist when it comes time for people to repay their debts.

None of this would have been possible without a government financial policy that put limits on interest rates ("usury ceilings"), passed "truth-in-lending" laws, made it easier for certain groups (women and minorities) to borrow, and offered subsidized student loans. Thus, credit increased consumer debt while creating a "mass market" for consumer goods, which served further to stimulate economic growth (see Guttman 1994).

In addition to changes in the way workers were viewed and the expansion of credit, there had to be a change in the way retail establishments were organized. The emergence of the consumer was accompanied by an enormous growth in retail chain stores. Until this point, distribution of goods was primarily controlled by small stores or large family-owned department stores. The 1920s saw the rise of the large retail conglomerates. In 1886, only two chains operated more than five stores; in 1912, 177 companies operated 2,235 stores; by 1929, nearly 1,500 companies were doing business in 70,000 outlets.

The Transformation of Spiritual and Intellectual Values

In addition to changing marketing techniques and modified societal institutions that stimulated consumption, there had to be a change in spiritual and intellectual values from an emphasis on such values as thrift, modesty, and moderation toward a value system that encouraged spending and ostentatious display. T. J. Jackson Lears argued that, from 1880 to 1930, the United States underwent a transformation of values from those that emphasized frugality and self-denial to those that sanctioned periodic leisure, compulsive spending, and individual fulfillment (Lears 1983). This shift in values, said Lears, was facilitated in American life by a new therapeutic ethos, an emphasis on physical and psychological health. This shift was promoted in part by the growth of the health professions and the popularity of psychology, along with the increasing autonomy and alienation felt by individuals as America ceased being a land of small towns and became increasingly urban. Advertisers capitalized on these changes by altering the way products were advertised; rather than emphasizing the nature of the product itself, they began to emphasize the alleged effects of the product and its promise of a richer, fuller life. Instead of simply being good soap, shoes, or deodorant, a product would contribute to the buyer's psychological, physical, or social well-being (Lears 1983:19).

Clothing, perfumes, deodorant, and so on would provide the means of achieving love; alcoholic beverages would provide the route to friendship; the proper automobile tires or insurance policy would provide the means of meeting family responsibilities. Commodities would be the source of satisfaction and a vital means of self-expression. Ponder, for example, the following description by a forty-year-old man of the relationship between himself and his expensive Porsche:

> Sometimes I test myself. We have an ancient, battered Peugeot, and I drive it for a week. It rarely breaks, and it gets great mileage. But when I pull up next to a beautiful woman, I am still the geek with glasses. Then I get back into my Porsche. It roars and tugs to get moving. It accelerates even going uphill at 80. It leadeth trashy women…to make pouting looks at me at stoplights. It makes me feel like a tomcat on the prowl…. Nothing in my life compares—except driving along Sunset at night in the 928, with the sodium vapor lamps reflecting off the wine-red finish, with the air inside reeking of tan glove-leather upholstery and the…Blaupunkt playing the Shirelles so loud that it makes my hairs vibrate. And with the girls I will never see again pulling up next to me, giving the car a once-over and looking at me as if I was a cool guy, not worried, instead of a 40-year-old schnook writer. (cited Belk 1988:148)

In the late nineteenth century, a series of religious movements emerged that became known as *mind cure religions.* William James, in his classic 1902 book, *Varieties of Religious Experience,* drew attention to the mind cure movements, although he was not the first to use the term. These movements—New Thought, Unity, Christian Science, and Theosophy, among others—maintained that people could simply, by an act of will and conviction, cure their own illnesses and create heaven on earth. These movements were, as William Leach (1993:225) phrased it, "wish-oriented, optimistic, sunny, the epitome of cheer and self-confidence, and completely lacking in anything resembling a tragic view of life." There was no sin, no evil, no darkness, only, as one mind curer said, "the sunlight of health."

These movements held that salvation would occur in this life and not in the afterlife. Mind cure dismissed the ideas of sin and guilt. God became a divine force, a healing power. Proponents argued that Americans should banish ideas of duty and self-denial. As one early twentieth-century advocate said,

> If you want to get the most out of life, just make up your mind that you were made to be happy, that you are a happiness machine, as well as a work machine. Cut off the past, and do not touch the morrow until it comes, but extract every possibility from the present. Think positive, creative, happy thoughts, and your harvest of good things will be abundant. (cited Leach 1993:229)

These new religions made fashionable the idea that, in the world of goods, men and women could find a paradise free from pain and suffering; they could find, as one historian of religion put it, the "good" through "goods."

Popular culture also promoted the mind cure ideology. As examples, there were L. Frank Baum's *The Wonderful Wizard of Oz,* which Leach characterized as "perhaps the best mind cure text ever written," and the Billikens doll, a squat Buddha-like figure, sometimes male and sometimes female, which represented the "god of things as they ought to be." Its success was without parallel in the toy trade and helped incite the doll craze in America. Billikens, it was said, would drive away petty annoyances and cares. One contemporary put it this way: "An atmosphere of gorged content pervades Billikens. No one can look at him [or her] and worry."

The popularity of the Billikens doll signaled change in spiritual values: It was now permissible to seek self-fulfillment in this life and find elements of satisfaction in manufactured commodities. The world was a good place: There was no misery; poverty, injustice, and inequities were only in the mind. There was enough for everyone.

These changes were not unique to America. Many of the same changes occurred in other nations, most notably Great Britain, Germany, and France (Carrier 1995). The consumer revolution of the early twentieth century was not the first of its kind either; but it happened with the most intensity and rapidity in America.

Thus by the 1930s, the consumer was well entrenched in the United States, complete with a spiritual framework and an intellectual rationalization that glorified the continued consumption of commodities as personally fulfilling and economically desirable and a moral imperative that would end poverty and injustice.

The Elmo dolls, so popular with young children and their parents, are direct descendants of the Billikens Doll, a figure designed to drive away worries and cares and convey to people that the world was a good place with plenty for everyone.

The Reconfiguration of Space and Class

The creation of the consumer did not stop in 1930. Since that time, the institutions of our society, particularly those of corporate America, have become increasingly more adept at creating sandpaintings in which people inhabit worlds whose very nature requires the continuous consumption of goods. The need to consume has reordered our living space, created new spaces for the encouragement of consumption, and altered the ways that we view each other. Home ownership, for example, particularly of the product-greedy single-family home, cast people out from city centers into the sprawling suburbs, which necessitated new roads, more cars, and virtually destroyed public transportation. Retailers and developers quickly realized the possibilities inherent in these new communities; people, they reasoned, had an endless desire to consume. "Our economy," said Macy's board chairman Jack Isodor Straus, "keeps on growing because our ability to consume is endless. The consumer goes on spending regardless of how many possessions he had. The luxuries of today are the necessities of tomorrow" (cited in Cohen 2003:261). But it was also believed that suburbanites were growing reluctant to travel to urban centers to shop. The solution was to bring the market to the people, and retailers and developers relocated shopping areas from city centers to spacious shopping centers and malls. Consumers gave various reasons for shifting their shopping from downtown to shopping centers, but the most important issues seemed to involve convenience—easy accessibility (malls and shopping centers were always constructed adjacent to new highways), easy parking, improved store layouts, increased self-service, simplified credit with charge plates, and greater availability of products. Market researchers concluded that shoppers were attracted to the ease and "progressiveness" of shopping center shopping. Consumers seemed to share the developers' sense that shopping centers were the modern way to consume (Cohen 2003:268).

The new ease of shopping, however, came with some costs. Shopping centers and malls were, unlike city centers, private spaces in which owners could control political activities. They were also easily accessible only to people with automobiles, thus removing from the suburban landscape those shoppers at the low end of the social ladder. And they redefined the nature of social interaction; shopping malls, as Zygmunt Bauman put it

> are so constructed as to keep people moving, looking around, keep them diverted and entertained no end—but in no case looking too long—by any of the endless attractions; not to encourage them to stop, look at each other, think of, ponder, and debate something other than the objects on display—not to pass their time in a fashion devoid of commercial value.... Hence a territory stripped of public space provides little chance for norms being debated, for values to be confronted, to clash and to be negotiated. (Bauman 1998:25)

In addition to defining the spaces in which we live and shop, marketers also redefined categories of people. In the early days of advertising, and up until the 1960s, manufacturers and retailers pitched their products and services to the mass market, continually stimulating demand by offering new products, changing styles, and so forth. But in the 1950s a new theory of marketing gained acceptance; rather than marketing products and services to a vast, undifferentiated middle class, sellers would differentiate or segment the market, appealing to the desires and needs of each special group. A new field, psychographics, emerged that became so sophisticated that the chief executive of Spiegel Company would boast that armed to the teeth with information, the marketer was "the friend who knows them [consumers] as well as—perhaps better than—they know themselves" (Cohen 2003:299). Target marketing singled out children and minorities for pointed appeals; marketers used "lifestyle" branding"—selling products by attracting consumers to a particular way of life rather than the good itself. Advertisers segmented by class and income, and then by gender and then age. They categorized consumers with statistical precision and gave them labels such as "blue blood estates," "shoguns and pickups," and "hispanic mix residents," singling these groups out for direct marketing, telemarketing, and Internet shopping solicitation. "Rather than sell commodities in as much volume as possible to the masses," says Lizabeth Cohen (2003:299), "modern-day marketers, equipped with advanced psychographic tactics, identify clusters of customers with distinctive ways of life and then set out to sell them idealized lifestyles constructed around commodities." Magazines probably represent the clearest example of segmentation—note the shift from the dominant magazines of the 1930s, 1940s and 1950s (*Life, Look, Saturday Evening Post*) and examine a typical magazine rack today. We might ask ourselves to what extent has the market segmentation created or exaggerated social and cultural divisions that might otherwise not exist, leaving people with less and less to share.

As Lizabeth Cohen (2003:318) points out, if any kind of segmentation epitomized the goals of marketers and advertisers, it was segmenting by age. First targeting teenagers and then children, they succeeded, with the help of governments, schools, and other institutions, in redefining childhood itself.

KINDERCULTURE IN AMERICA: THE CHILD AS CONSUMER

The Role of Children in Capitalism

Anthropology teaches us that, much like the rest of our culture, childhood is socially created. That is, childhood and the ways that it is defined vary from society to society and from era to era. Childhood in nineteenth-century America was very different from what it is today. Prior to the nineteenth century, the major role of children in a capitalist economy was as workers (Lasch 1977:14ff). There were few industries that did not employ children at some level, and there were few families whose children did not contribute economically through either farm or factory labor. In twentieth-century America, this began to change. Social movements that for decades worked to restrict child labor finally convinced state and federal legislatures to pass laws making child labor illegal. These developments signaled a transformation of children from workers to consumers. Although this may not have been the intent of the reformers, children were to contribute far more to the national economy as consumers than they ever did as laborers.

It wasn't until the beginning of the twentieth century that retailers began to target children as a discrete group of consumers. As late as 1890, there was not a children's market worth considering; children ate, wore, and played with what their parents made for them. Germany was by far the largest producer of children's toys, and there were few, if any, factories in the United States producing children's clothing. Nor was there any market for infants' or children's foods. Yet by 1915, the baby clothing industry was one of the largest in the United States, with seventy-five factories operating in New York state alone. Toy production increased by 1,300 percent between 1905 and 1920. One reason was the destruction of the German toy industry during World War I. Another was the development of new toys in the United States that became international sensations, such as the racist Alabama Coon Jigger, a laughing, prancing, mechanical Negro male. But, most importantly, retailers were beginning to appreciate the profits that could be made from children's commodities.

Retailers also began to take note of psychologists' discovery of the "natural desire" of "little people" for goods and toys, heeding the psychologists' advice that "every attention shown the child binds the mother to the store," or the observation that if they cultivated consumers "as kids [they would] have them as customers for a lifetime." Santa Claus became one of the major vehicles for selling toys; his commercialization hit its peak in the 1920s.

Child psychologists and home economists also advised parents that children needed toys for exercise and toys to relax; children, they said, should have their own playrooms. These same experts lectured at department stores, advising parents of the educational values of toys. With this new emphasis on the child as consumer, by 1926, America had become the greatest producer of toys and playthings in the world. There were toys for the backyard, camping, the beach, and the "little private room which every child desperately needs to fulfill his or her individuality." Play, said the experts, "is the child's business; toys the material with which he works" (Leach 1993:328).

The federal government played a major role in redefining childhood. In 1929, Herbert Hoover sponsored a White House Conference on Child Health and Protection. The conference report, *The Home and the Child,* concluded that children were independent beings with particular concerns of their own. The child, the report said,

> is often an alien in his home when it comes to any consideration of his special needs in the furnishings and equipment of the home. He belongs nowhere. He must accommodate himself to an adult environment—chairs and tables are too big and too high for him; there is no suitable place for his books and his toys. He moves in a misfit world with nothing apportioned to his needs. Often this results in retarding his physical, mental, and social development. (White House 1931)

The report advised parents to give their children their own "furniture and eating equipment" suitable to each child's age and size; it further advised parents to provide playrooms inside the house and to fill the backyard with "toys, velocipedes, sawhorses, wagons, wheelbarrows, slides, and places to keep pets." "Generally a sleeping room for each person is desirable," it noted. As a child grows "older and becomes more social he wants games and toys that he can share with his friends." When the family decides on "the purchase of a piece of furniture or a musical instrument" of common interest, it is important to consult the children. Take them shopping for their own "things and let them pick them out by themselves."

> Through such experiences personality develops.... [These] experiences have the advantage also of creating in the child a sense of personal as well as family pride in ownership, and eventually *teaching him that his personality can be expressed through things.* (White House 1931 [emphasis added]; see also Leach 1993:371–372)

Thus, in the space of some thirty years, the role of children in American life changed dramatically; they became, and remain, pillars of the consumer economy, with economic power rivaling that of adults. Children have become a main target of advertisers; as one marketing specialist told the *Wall Street Journal,* "Even two-year-olds are concerned about their brand of clothes, and by the age of six are full-out consumers" (Durning 1992:120). Marketing researchers estimate that children ages two to fourteen directly influence $188 billion of parental spending, indirectly influence another $300 billion, and spend themselves some $25 billion. Teen spending alone jumped from $63 billion in 1994 to $94 billion in 1998 (see McNeal 1999; Zollo 1999).

Advertisers and marketing specialists, including anthropologists and psychologists, devise all sorts of campaigns to appeal to children and are often criticized for the messages they communicate. But some advertising executives are quite candid in their objectives. As one said, "No one's really worrying about what it's teaching impressionable youth. Hey, I'm in the business of convincing people to buy things they don't need" (*Business Week,* August 11, 1997:35). Advertisers work on such things as the "nag factor," explaining to clients that children's nagging inspires about a third of a family's trips to a fast-food restaurant, video store, or children's clothing store (Ruskin 1999). Advertisers explicitly work on a child's desire to be accepted and on their fear of being "losers." As one ad agency president put it:

> Kids are very sensitive to that. If you tell them to buy something, they are resistant. But if you tell them that they'll be a dork if they don't, you've got their attention. You open up emotional vulnerabilities, and it's very easy to do with kids because they're the most emotionally vulnerable. (Harris 1989)

As colleges and universities adapted to the need to persuade people to consume with new academic courses and programs, primary and secondary schools were adapting by providing marketers with access to children. Channel One is a marketing company that provides ten minutes a day of TV news to some 8 million students in 12,000 schools, provided students also watch two minutes of advertising. "The biggest selling point to advertisers," says Joel Babbit, former president of Channel One, lies in "forcing kids to watch two minutes of commercials." As Babbit (cited Ruskin 1999) put it,

> [T]he advertiser gets a group of kids who cannot go to the bathroom, who cannot change the station, who cannot listen to their mother yell in the background, who cannot be playing Nintendo, who cannot have their headsets on.

The Social Construction of Childhood

Retail establishments in the early part of the twentieth century, particularly the new department stores, took the lead in redefining the world of children. They produced their own radio programs for children and put on elaborate shows. Macy's, which by the late 1920s had the largest toy department in the world, put on playlets for children in makeshift theaters or in store auditoriums. The most popular department store show was *The Wizard of Oz;* when the show was put on at Field's in Chicago, the children wore green-tinted glasses to better appreciate the "Emerald City."

In this era, the event that most symbolized the reconstruction of childhood was Christmas. Christmas became a time of toy giving in America in the 1840s. The Christmas holiday was appropriated by retail establishments as a way to sell goods by the 1870s; people at that time had already begun to complain that Christmas was becoming overcommercialized (Carrier 1995:189). But it wasn't until the early twentieth century that retail establishments turned Christmas into a spectacle that appealed to children especially. By the mid-1920s, nearly every city in America had its own "radio" Santa Claus. Gimbel's in New York received thousands of letters addressed to Santa Claus; each was carefully answered by staff and signed "Santa," with the name of each child carefully indexed for future use (Leach 1993:330). In 1924, Macy's inaugurated its Thanksgiving Day parade, which ran from 145th Street to West 34th Street and culminated with the appearance of Santa Claus standing on Macy's 34th Street marquee waving to the throngs below.

Thanksgiving also came to mark the beginning of the Christmas buying season, a time when Americans spend some 4 percent of their income on Christmas gifts, and when department stores sell 40 percent of their yearly total of toys and 25 percent of their candy, cosmetics, toiletries, stationery, greeting cards, and books. (By the early 1990s, Americans were spending about $37 billion on Christmas gifts, a sum greater than the gross national product (GNP) of all but forty-five countries in the world [see Restad 1995:160].) The government did its part in defining the Christmas buying season when Fred Lazarus Jr., who was to become president of Ohio's Federated Department Stores, persuaded President Franklin Roosevelt in 1939 to move Thanksgiving Day from November 30, its traditional date, to November 23 to add one more week to the Christmas buying season. Congress made that official in 1941 when it moved the Thanksgiving celebration from the last Thursday in November to the fourth Thursday. The government thus ensured that it could fall no later than November 28, guaranteeing a minimum four-week shopping spree (Restad 1995:162).

Santa Claus represents one of the more elaborate ways in which the culture of capitalism shields its members, particularly children, from some of its less savory features. The story of Santa Claus represented a world in which consumer, capitalist, and laborer were idealized: Commodities (toys) were manufactured by happy elves, working in Santa's workshop (no factories at the North Pole, and certainly no Chinese assembly plants) and distributed, free of charge, to good boys and girls by a corpulent, grandfatherly male in fur-trimmed clothes. It is perhaps ironic that when political cartoonist Thomas Nast created what has become the contemporary image of Santa Claus in 1862, he modeled Santa's costume after the fur-trimmed clothes worn by the wealthy Astor family (Carrier 1995:189).

Nast also created Santa's workshop, perhaps in nostalgic remembrance of prefactory production. Writers as early as the 1870s recognized the irony of this idealized version of Christmas and toy production. One magazine editorial in 1873, commenting on a picture of Santa's elves working gaily in some magical workplace, turning out dolls, boats, tops, and toy soldiers, compared it with the reality of the poor, working six days a week in factories (Restad 1995:149). William Waits in his book, *The Modern Christmas in America* (1992), suggested that Santa's major role was to "decontaminate" Christmas gifts, removing the stigma of factory industry (p. 25).

Others, of course, played a major role in transforming childhood, but we can do no better than to trace the trajectory of this transformation from its beginning—L. Frank Baum and his Emerald City—to its logical culmination in Walt Disney World.

The Appropriation of Childhood, Part I, Baum's Emerald City.   Pre-1900 children's stories were very different from those common today. The most famous were the stories of Jacob and Wilhelm Grimm. The Grimm brothers took traditional European folktales, most of which contained fairly gruesome and bizarre plots (cannibalism, incest, murder, etc.), and rewrote them so that they could be used as tools for the socialization of children. Each rewritten tale contained a moral lesson. But, as with nineteenth-century religion, government, and economic institutions, these stories lacked the power to produce the necessary mind cure impulse to consume. Consequently, there emerged new kinds of stories in which the world was cleansed of the darkness of the Grimm's stories and presented as a happy place full of desirable things. The leader in this reconstruction of the child's universe was L. Frank Baum.

Baum came from a well-to-do New York state family and had moved with his wife Maud Gage (whose mother, Matilda Joslyn Gage, was a leading nineteenth-century feminist leader) in the late 1880s to Aberdeen, South Dakota, where he opened a large retail store (Baum's Bazaar). In 1891, economic depression hit Aberdeen, and Baum went broke. He moved his family to Chicago, where he began to write the stories that would make him famous. In addition, he took a lively interest in the art of window display, becoming an advisor to some of the largest department stores in the city.

The Wonderful Wizard of Oz, *similar to the store display windows that Baum designed was filled with all the good things in life, assuring the reader that the world is full of things to consume and enjoy.*

Baum had always loved the theater, and he combined that with his interest in business to make window displays into theatrical productions, showing off retail goods to their best advantage. The quality of the goods mattered little to Baum; how they looked, their "selling power," was what mattered. He soon founded the National Association of Window Trimmers and developed a manual and later a journal, *The Show Window*, devoted to window displays. (The journal changed its title to *Display World* in the 1920s; it exists today as *Visual Merchandising*.) Baum's general message was to "use the best art to arouse in the observer the cupidity and longing to possess the goods" (Leach 1993:60).

Baum's personal philosophy was compatible with the various mind cure movements of the late nineteenth and early twentieth centuries. "People do not sin and should not feel guilt," he wrote in 1890 in the *Aberdeen Saturday Pioneer*, "the good things in life are given to be used." The "rainy day" theory of saving was all right, according to Baum, as long as it wasn't used as an excuse to deny oneself comforts. Who, he asked,

> will be the gainer when Death calls him to the last account—the man who can say "I have lived!" or the man who can say "I have saved?"... To gain all the meat from the nut of life is the essence of wisdom. Therefore, "eat, drink, and be merry—tomorrow you die." (cited Leach 1993:247)

Baum's books were filled with goods and mechanical inventions, landscapes of edible fruits, cakes, cookies, all intended to assure readers that the world was a good place. They were, said William Leach, affirmative, Americanized fairy tales. In fact Baum's explicit goal was to revolutionize children's literature. In his introduction to the first edition of *The Wonderful Wizard of Oz*, Baum wrote,

> The time has come for a series of newer "wonder tales" in which the stereotyped genie, dwarf and fairy are eliminated, together with all the horrible and blood-curdling incidents devised by their authors to point to a fearsome moral to each tale.... *The Wonderful Wizard of Oz* was written solely to please children of today. It aspires to being a modernized fairy tale, in which the wonderment and joy are retained and the heartaches and nightmares are left out. (cited Leach 1993:251)

The story of the *Wizard of Oz* can be interpreted as a tribute to our ability to create illusions and magic, to make people believe in spite of themselves. In Baum's stories, the Wizard is exposed as a charlatan, a "common man" with no special powers; but he is powerful because he can make others do what he wants, make them believe in the unbelievable. He is a confidence man. People adored him even as he escaped from Oz in a balloon and was remembered as the man who "built for us this beautiful Emerald City." Baum, said William Leach, created a benign trickster, consumer society's version of the capitalist. *The Wizard of Oz* represented a new spiritual–ethical climate that modeled itself on a version of the child's world in which dreams of self-fulfillment through consumption were legitimized and any negative consequences of consumption were banished. In brief, Baum's work represented but one of the sandpaintings of capitalism, one that appropriates childhood to represent a world in which the purpose of life is to consume.

Yet, as sophisticated as Baum was in creating an ethos that encouraged people to buy, the master of the art was to be Walt Disney.

The Appropriation of Childhood, Part II, Walt Disney and the Creation of Disney World.   It is difficult to say when the child's universe, created to turn children into consumers, began to be used to entice adults. Perhaps the glorification of "youth" in advertising and the upward extension of childhood to include the teens were manifestations of this phenomenon. Regardless, the appropriation of childhood as a vehicle to encourage consumption at all ages and rationalize capitalism culminated in the creation of Walt Disney World. Disney and other major American corporations have created what Shirley Steinberg and Joseph Kincheloe (see Kincheloe 1997) call kinderculture, the promotion of an ethos of pleasure for the purpose of enticing adults as well as children to consume.

Walt Disney World is the ultimate sandpainting of the culture of capitalism. Instead of a single sandpainter using bits of colored sand and grain to create a picture barely large enough to contain a single person, a corporation has used millions of tons of concrete, wood, plastic, and glass to create the "home of childhood," a miniature universe that promotes innocence and trust, that allows people to leave the "real world" behind, and that encourages (in fact, insists) that participants put themselves in the hands of Disney. However, as Stephen Fjellman (1992:13) warned,

> These hands bear watching, for in their shaping of things lies danger. It is not just that our movements are constrained with the promise, usually fulfilled, of rewards. What is important is that our thoughts are constrained. They are channeled not only in the interests of Disney itself, but also in the interests of the large corporations with which Disney has allied itself, the system of power they maintain, and the world of commodities that is their life's blood.

Like the work of the sandpainters, Walt Disney World is a kind of ritual setting where participants are returned to childhood to be reborn as Disney adults. It is a respite from the anxieties and fears of everyday life; at Walt Disney World we can walk in the roads, the place is clean, it is safe, everyone is polite, it is air-conditioned, and the trains run on time.

But if we look beyond the pleasantries, said Fjellman, we find that the environment is totally controlled and that there is a degree of discipline at work in this model world that rivals the discipline of a fascist state. And the control is real. In creating Walt Disney World, the Disney corporation secretly bought up forty square miles of central Florida real estate (twice the size of Manhattan) and was granted almost feudal powers over the land by the state. Disney World has its own government, it sets the rules, and it controls the message. But what is the message of the Disney World sandpainting? To answer this question, let's examine two aspects of Disney World: its depiction of American history and its representation of progress and the future.

History, or distory, as Mike Wallace (1985) called it, is everywhere at Walt Disney World, appropriated, like childhood, in the service of the Disney message. The history, of course, is highly idealized. Thus, when Williamsburg was first opened, it omitted any reminder of the slaves who made up 50 percent of the colonial population. At Disney World, historical figures are used as spokespersons for Disney, lending to its message the authority of their reputations. We meet presidents and listen to Thomas Edison and Davy Crockett. Benjamin Franklin and Mark Twain are tour guides. Fragments of Abraham Lincoln's speeches, most often taken out of context, are read to us by robots; and Leonardo Da Vinci, the Disney model of the prophetic visionary, is everywhere. At Disney World, there is a conscious attempt to present the history of capitalism without the warts. Disney World designers are quite forthright and unapologetic about their intent. As one Disney spokesperson explained, "we are not telling history like it really was but as it should have been" (Fjellman 1992:31). Another Disney "imagineer," as the designers are called, explains "Disney realism" as a "sort of utopian nature, where we program out all the negative, unwanted elements and program in the positive elements" (cited Wallace 1985:35).

The center of Disney World (and the original Disneyland in California) is Main Street, a highly idealized, turn-of-the-century remodeling of life as it should have been, a consumer's paradise, scaled down to five-eighths of actual area. The street or square is filled with shops and taverns; people are defined by what they sell. Main Street cultivates a nostalgia for an imagined past without classes, crime, or conflict—a time of continuous consumption, "a supermarket of fun."

On one level, Disney World is an extension of the shop windows designed by L. Frank Baum in the 1890s; on another it serves as an explicit model for the modern shopping mall. Urban planner James Rouse based a number of his town designs and historical shopping malls (Faneuil Hall in Boston, Harborplace in Baltimore, and South Street Seaport in New York) on Disney's Main Street (Wallace 1985:42; see also Kowinski 1985).

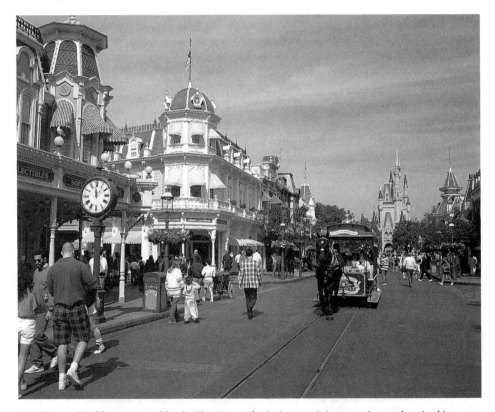

Walt Disney World represents, like the Navajo sandpainting, a miniature universe that, in this case, serves to define for its visitors their place in a world as consumers of commodities.

At the Hall of Presidents, Disney takes viewers through U.S. history in twenty-nine minutes flat. Disney does recognize, in a fashion, that U.S. history was not all that perfect. After all, the average adult visitor to Disney World is a well-educated professional who could not have been ignorant of the historical injustices in the United States's past. Consequently, Disney World provides Frederick Douglass to speak to the oppression of Blacks, Chief Joseph represents indigenous peoples, Susan B. Anthony speaks about the concerns of women, and John Muir serves to remind visitors that progress often came at the expense of the environment. However, each is a highly sanitized symbol of opposition to racism, sexism, and environmental devastation. In "distory," these figures do not remind us of persistent problems in the social fabric, rather they are presented as opportunities to overcome barriers. This is also bad, if not outright false, history.

For example, Disney appropriates for its version of indigenous people in American history the story of Chief Joseph and the Nez Percé. In 1877, the U.S. government, largely at the insistence of settlers who wanted the land, revised previous treaty commitments and attempted to resettle all Nez Percé in the Walla Walla Valley of Washington on smaller reservations. One group, led by Chief Joseph and the war chief Looking Glass, refused and, after some young warriors killed a trader accused of selling bad whiskey to the Indians, fled the area, heading east into Idaho, Wyoming, and Montana in an attempt to reach Canada. They were pursued by the command of General Oliver O. Howard, who Joseph's band defeated in battle or consistently outmaneuvered. The campaign, one of the most bloody and heroic of the Indian wars, ended when Joseph and the remnants of his band were finally surrounded by one of the three army commands that had set out to intercept them. In blizzard conditions on October 5, 1877, only forty miles from the Canadian border, Joseph met with the army's commanders to surrender. His surrender speech, among the most famous speeches in American history, was written down by an army lieutenant. At Walt Disney World, Chief Joseph, in robot form, once again delivers his speech; the Disney version is as follows (cited Fjellman 1992:104):

> Enough, enough of your words.
> Let your new dawn lead to the final sunset on my
> people's suffering.
> When I think of our condition, my heart is sick.
> I see men of my own race treated as outlaws, or shot
> down like animals.
> I pray that all of us may be brothers, with one country
> around us, and one government for all.
> From where the sun now stands, I will fight no more
> forever.

However, except for the famous final line, that was not what Joseph said. Here is the original speech as recorded that day in 1877 (cited in Beal 1963:229):

> Tell General Howard I know his heart. What he told me before I have in my heart. I am tired of fighting. Our chiefs are killed. Looking Glass is dead. The old men are all killed. It is the young men who say yes or no. He who led the young men is dead. It is cold and we have no blankets. The little children are freezing to death. My people some of them have run away to the hills and have no blankets, no food; no one knows where they are, perhaps freezing to

death. I want time to look for my children and see how many of them I can find. Maybe I will find them among the dead. Hear me my chiefs, I am tired; my heart is sick and sad. From where the sun now stands, I will fight no more forever.

There is a significant difference between the Disney version and the one recorded on the battlefield. Instead of freezing children, the death of the elderly, and a military campaign that ended only after the deaths of hundreds of American and Nez Percé soldiers, Joseph's surrender speech has been turned by Disney into a testimonial to brotherhood and the nation-state.

In telling history "as it should have been," Disney paints a picture of an American past of which people can be proud, while subtly justifying whatever excesses may have been committed. As in the land of Oz, everything has happened for the better.

EPCOT (Experimental Prototypical Community of Tomorrow) is a more adult attraction than Fantasyland or some of the other venues of Disney World. EPCOT was Walt Disney's pet project until his death in December 1966. EPCOT was to be a utopian city, of 20,000-plus residents, that would attract urban planners and experimenters from all over the world. But Walt Disney died and corporate Disney turned the project into a gigantic, corporate advertisement, using the 1939 World's Fair in New York as its guide, and having pavilions depict the corporate version of the history of progress. Thus, at EPCOT, Exxon presents the history of energy, while AT&T does communications. Transportation is presented by General Motors, the land by Kraft, the home by General Electric, and imagination by Kodak. Perhaps even more interesting, at the heart of each corporate pavilion is a ride, a setting much like a sandpainting, in which seated passengers travel through tunnels that open to huge dioramas filled with robots, videos, holograms, and other technological marvels.

Throughout the EPCOT pavilions there is this message: Technology equals progress, and progress is natural—and perhaps even American. There have been some problems along the way, the corporate exhibits tell us. "We" have made mistakes—but "we" (corporations) are working to solve those problems. "We" polluted the air, "we" abused the environment. Thus, the imagineers admit that there were problems in the past but reject corporate responsibility for them, putting the corporations at the forefront of the ecology movement. History is defined for us as "a record of the invention of commodities which allow man to master his environment" (Wallace 1985:44). Progress is defined as the availability of emancipatory consumer goods. The World of Tomorrow promotes capitalist development as inevitable, spreading the message that history was made by inventors and businesspeople, and that the corporations are the legatees of this past. It tells us, as Mike Wallace (1985:47) observed, that "citizens can sit back and consume."

But who is Disney World for? It is supposed to be for children, but it really represents the appropriation of childhood to encourage the consumption of commodities and, more importantly, once again to shield the consumer from the negative side of capitalism. Walt Disney World is now the single biggest tourist attraction in the entire world. Approximately one-tenth of the population of the U.S. travels there each year. But it is not a universal attraction. By and large it attracts people of relatively high incomes, 75 percent of whom are professionals or managers. Only 3 percent are Black and 2 percent Hispanic. Seventy-one percent are from outside Florida. As Wallace (1985:53) said,

A process of class self-affirmation seems to be at work. Certainly, Disney World seems intent on providing reassurance to this class, on presenting it with its own pedigree. EPCOT's seventies-style liberal corporatism seems tailor-made for professionals and technocrats. It's calibrated to their concerns—nothing on labor, heavy on ecology, clean, well-managed, emphasis on individual solutions, good restaurants—and it provides just the right kind of past for their hippier sensibilities. *Perhaps, therefore, professionals and managers (many of whom, after all, function as subalterns of capital) flock there because it ratifies their world.* Perhaps they don't want to know about reality—past or present—and prefer comforting and plausible stereotypes. [emphasis added]

Or as O'Toole Fintan (1998:21) put it:

Places like Disney World grapple with the problem of an audience that already knows about the exploitation and violence that its way of life requires for maintenance, but that needs, for its own well-being, to maintain a civilized distance from that knowledge.

Walt Disney World is only one manifestation of the tendency or necessity in capitalism to mask the unpleasant side effects of capitalist production and consumption. People may choose to do something that is harmful to others, but they do so according to a cultural logic that makes it the "right" choice. Our culture makes choosing even easier by masking the sometimes devastating consequences of our choices. Thus, the process of insulating the consumer from truths that might reduce consumption is built into the culture of capitalism; denial is as much a part of it as is consumption. Furthermore, this denial—this part of the culture of capitalism—determines in many ways how we view the world. Put another way, the world as seen from the point of view of the consumer is very different from the world as seen from the perspective of worker, capitalist, or people of other cultures around the world. One of the tasks of this book is to try to help the reader appreciate these other points of view.

EXPORTING THE CONSUMER

The construction of the consumer in the Western industrial countries took a century to accomplish. In the rest of the world it is taking less than a decade. According to recent studies, some 1.7 billion people, 27 percent of the world's population, can be counted as members of the consumer society, 270 million in the United States and Canada, some 350 million in Western Europe, and 120 million in Japan. The rest live in developing countries, 240 million in China, and 120 million in India alone. In China, automobile sales increased by 60 percent in 2002 and 80 percent in the first half of 2003. If growth continues at that pace, by 2015 China will have more automobiles on the road that the United States (Halweil and Mastny 2004:xvii, 3). Capitalism, writes William Leach (1993:388), "had achieved a new level of strength and world influence, especially in the wake of the collapse of communism." It also, he concluded,

appears to have a nearly unchallenged hold over every aspect of American life, from politics to culture, so much so that the United States looks like a fashion bazaar to much of the rest of the world. For some Americans the continued power of consumerism has led to further degradation of what it means to be an American or of what America is all about. For others, this evolution has only enhanced the country's appeal, making it appear more than ever an Emerald City, a feast, a department store to which everyone is invited and entitled. Just as cities in the United States once operated as generators of consumer desire for internal markets, today America functions similarly on a global scale.

The phenomenon by which people around the world want to emulate consumer capitalism represents what Joseph Nye (2003) calls "soft power." We see this power in Hollywood, which dominates the cultural industries. Countries such as India and Hong Kong try to emulate Hollywood's style while modeling for their audiences lifestyles and values that they seek to acquire. Information industries around the world are dominated by Anglo American news. People know what happens in the world because they get the news from AP or Reuters, CNN or NBC (Sisci 2002).

The rapidity of this global consumer transformation is most evident in India and China, the two most populous countries in the world, with more than one-third of the total global population. Take the case of Rajesh Julka, a thirty-four-year-old resident of the Indian city of Kolkata. In 1996, Julka couldn't afford to replace his ten-year-old television. His father had just retired and his mother was trying to run a beauty parlor from one of the rooms in their congested ground-floor apartment. Julka was unemployed, and trying to establish a sari-making operation. But by 2003, within the space of seven years, he had turned into what Indrajit Basu (2003) calls an "Indian yuppie." He married, had a child, and has since acquired a $100,000 condominium while replacing his cellphone every three months. He bought three new cars during the past four years, and recently bought a $2,500 notebook PC during his July holiday to Singapore. "I can't resist buying newer models of electronic goodies," he says. He now also owns three televisions.

Rajesh Julka represents a burgeoning consumer-conscious Indian middle class that demographers estimate will grow to some 445 million by 2006, larger than the entire population of the United States. This middle class is developing new spending patterns; from 1999 to 2002 they spent 4 percent less of their income on groceries, and almost 5 percent more on eating out and taking vacations. Spending during the same period on personal care went up 2.5 percent, whereas saving and investing went down almost 7 percent. And because more than 45 percent of India's population is under nineteen years of age, consumption levels are likely to increase at a far faster rate than in industrial countries. Between 2001 and 2002 consumer spending in India increased by 130 percent for gifts, 108 percent for mobile phones, and 68 percent for movies. The Indian consumer spent 58 percent more on clothing, 55 percent more on eating, and 22 percent more on vacations—in a single year. Furthermore, economic analysts expect household consumption to double in the next five years (Bidwai 2003).

And the most prominent symbols of consumer culture are the glitzy, air-conditioned, chrome-and-glass malls, replete with boutiques, restaurants, discos, bars, and theaters that are appearing in India. In addition to the 20 already existing, some 240 mega-malls are under construction, 43 of them in one of the wealthy suburbs of Delhi (Bidwai 2003).

What is happening in India is also happening to the most populous country in the world, China. China has averaged GDP growth around 8 percent for more than a decade.

GDP for 2003 is expected at about U.S.$1.3 trillion, slightly more than a tenth of the United States's $12 trillion economy. Nonetheless, growth is soaring upward and is evident in increased consumer spending. According to China's National Statistics Bureau, retail sales of social consumables reached 3.27 trillion yuan, (U.S.$395 million) up by 8.6 percent year-on-year in the first three quarters of 2003. Retail sales of cars, were up 77.5 percent, communications equipment up 74 percent, construction and decorative materials up 46.6 percent, petroleum and petroleum products up 38.7 percent, and sales of commercial housing up 35.9 percent (Berthelsen 2003).

The same tools that functioned to construct the consumer in the United States are at work in China. In 2002, advertising in China amounted to $11.2 billion, an increase of 16 percent during 2001. As Americans did in the 1950s, Chinese are becoming homeowners. Housing reforms turned over vast amounts of state-owned housing to the people who lived in them at discounts of up to 80 percent. Other laws ensured private property ownership. Home ownership is transforming asset-poor renters into homeowners, and driving the purchases of refrigerators, stoves, air-conditioners, and cars.

As in the United States, the Chinese consumer is being leveraged through mortgages, auto loans, credit cards, and consumer finance. Credit cards are in their absolute infancy. By 2003 about a million credit cards has been issued—one for every 1,300 people. Mortgages were made available only in 2000, auto loans in 2001. But credit card usage is on the rise. One national bank project in China expects to issue 200 million credit and cash cards by 2005 to a total urban population of about 300 million people in 400 cities nationwide (Berthelsen 2003). Auto ownership, fueled by credit, exploded upward in 2002. Production doubled in only the first four months of 2003 after soaring upward 60 percent in 2002. China had only two cars per 1,000 people in 1997; it has since doubled to four per 1,000 persons (compared to 481 per 1,000 in the United States).

In the cases of both China and India, one factor in the rising wave of consumption is the same baby boomers (people born at the end of World War II) that have fueled consumption in the United States, except in the case of Asia there are 1 billion of them. In addition, just as children began to move from their parent's homes after 1950 in the United States, they are leaving their parents in Asia. These new households require refrigerators and stoves, pots and pans, toasters and stereos (Berthelsen 2003).

The response to these trends are the same as they were in the United States; they have encouraged the growth of consumer spending and the spread of supermarkets, chainstores, and malls. Wal-Mart and the French Carrefour chain now have nearly fifty stores in China. That is already beginning to wreak damage on mom-and-pop operations across Asia. Thailand has begun to experience protests against big-box operators such as Walmart, similar to the protests the United States experienced for a decade (Berthelsen 2003).

CONCLUSION

A couple of days after al Qaeda operatives crashed two planes into the World Trade Center and another into the Pentagon on September 11, 2001, U.S. congressional members met to plan a message to the stunned public. "We've got to give people confidence to go back out and go to work, buy things, go back to the stores—get ready for Thanksgiving, get ready for Christmas," said one member of Congress, echoing the message of the president. "Get out," he said, "and be active, participate in our society" (CNN 2001). The fact that after one of the most shocking events in U.S. history government officials were urging citizens, above all, to shop and work is ample testimony of the significance of consumption in the effective working of our economy, and, indeed, for our whole society. It is to the consumer that government and business look to supply the impetus for the continued expansion of the economy and the accumulation of capital.

We mentioned earlier that consumption on the scale evident in capitalist culture is unprecedented and is not natural. That is, there is no innate desire in human beings to acquire an ever-greater quantity of stuff. In truth, not everyone agrees with that assumption. Scholars, such as James B. Twitchell (2002; 2004) argue that human beings, throughout history, have sought material luxury, and that although overconsumption does indeed have its dark side, it has its light side as well, that "getting and spending," as he puts it (2004:17), "have been the most passionate, and often the most imaginative, endeavors of modern life." By emulating the consumption-driven lifestyle of capitalist culture, he says, people around the world are being drawn closer together.

Twitchell's defense of luxury is well argued, and, insofar as luxury is attainable by all, perhaps something to be considered. But that is a problem: Can the level of wealth enjoyed by members of capitalist culture (remembering that it is twenty-five times greater, on average, than that enjoyed by citizens of two centuries ago) be attained by all but a very few? And if it can be attained, what is the cost for everything else that we must sacrifice? Francesco Sisci (2002) expresses the dilemma well:

> The American victory in the soft war creates the desire of the citizens of the world to become American, with its values, wealth and security umbrella. However, it is impossible for America to grant the American dream to all people who dream it, either in the U.S. or abroad. The danger of creating a desire that cannot be satisfied—whether desire for a certain product or a certain civilization—is the backlash that will follow: waves of protest and dissatisfaction that will translate into a wish to return to one's own history.

CHAPTER TWO

THE LABORER IN THE CULTURE OF CAPITALISM

I have read in E. P. Thompson's "The Making of the English Working Class" that the first man who attempted to establish a labor union in England at the end of the 18th century was arrested, tried for sedition, found guilty, drawn and quartered in a public square by attaching draft horses to each of his arms and legs and pulling him apart. He was then disemboweled and his guts were burned. Then they hanged what was left of him. One gathers from this that the properted classes were slow to accept the idea of organized labor.
—Robert Hass, *Washington Post,* September 5, 1999

The capitalist system makes it very much easier for people not to realize what they are doing, not to know about the danger and hardship, the despair and humiliation, that their way of life implies for others.
—Edmund Wilson, *The Shores of Light*

The consumer may drive the culture of capitalism, but without the laborer there would be no commodities to consume. Yet the emergence of the laborer—the person who survives by selling labor—is a recent historical phenomenon. In past centuries most people had access to land on which to grow their own food, selling whatever surplus they produced, or they owned tools—implements for weaving, metalworking, or producing other objects for sale or trade. Thus, to understand capitalism it is necessary to examine why people choose or are forced to sell their labor. Before beginning this examination, it is necessary to have a fundamental understanding of the workings of the capitalist economy.

Capitalism is not an easy term to define. Pierre Proudhon, who first used the term in 1861, called it "an economic and social regime in which capital, the source of income, does not generally belong to those who make it work through their labor" (cited Braudel 1982:237). The term *capitalism* does not appear in the writings of Karl Marx and did not gain currency until 1902, when the German economist Werner Sombart used it to denote the opposite of socialism. But definitions alone won't help us to understand fully the dynamics of something as complex as a capitalist economy. We need to understand the major characteristics of capitalism to appreciate how it has permeated our lives as an economic and a cultural system.

Few people will deny that the genius of capitalism lies in its ability to produce goods—commodities for people to buy and consume. Let's start our excursion into capitalism with a

Part of the genius of the culture of capitalism is its ability to produce vast quantities of goods, such as these Nike products, that consumers all over the world clamor to buy.

product, beginning with something nearly all of us buy at one point or another—sneakers—and examine, briefly, the largest manufacturer of sneakers, Nike, Inc. Today most of the sneakers—and clothes—we wear are assembled overseas because large corporations, such as Nike, have increasingly relocated assembly factories from their home countries to countries on the periphery. Consequently, the clothes we wear; the TVs, stereos, and compact discs (CDs) we listen to; and the computers we use are at least partly produced by a person in another part of the world. This situation creates a clash of cultures that can be illuminating for what they tell us about other cultures and what they may tell us about ourselves. The effects that these factories have on other countries highlight the distinctive features of the capitalist economy and perhaps approximate the impact of early capitalism on our own society. But first let us digress briefly to an understanding of the economic logic of capitalism and, particularly, the role of labor within this economic system.

A PRIMER ON THE ECONOMIC ELEMENTS OF CAPITALISM

Let's run through a quick primer on the economics of capitalism and its development. Briefly stated, the economics of capitalism grew out of the interactions of the following five items:

1. Commodities (C). There are basically two types of commodities: capital goods and consumer goods. Capital goods, such as land, raw materials, tools, machines, and factories, are used to produce consumer goods (e.g., television sets, VCRs, computers, houses) to be sold to others.
2. Money (M). Money serves as a standardized means of exchange. It reduces all goods and commodities to a standard value. By putting a monetary value on something (e.g., a forest), it can be compared with any other commodity (e.g., government bonds). Money, thus, greatly facilitates the exchange of commodities.
3. Labor power (lp). Labor power is the work that is needed to transform one type of commodity into another (e.g., steel into an automobile).
4. Means of production (mp). Another term for capital goods, that is, the machines, land, and tools with which other commodities are produced.
5. Production (P). The combination of lp and mp to produce commodities.

In precapitalist societies or noncapitalist production, as in capitalist production, people either make or obtain commodities—food, clothing, shelter, and the like—to use. These commodities have what economists call *use value.* If someone needs a shirt, they make it; if they need food, they gather, hunt, or grow it. Occasionally, they may trade for what they need or even buy it. Thus, a farmer might barter some corn (C) in exchange for a shirt (C′) or use money to purchase it, but the object is always to obtain something for use. We can diagram this type of exchange as follows:

$$C \rightarrow C' \quad \text{or} \quad C \rightarrow M \rightarrow C'$$

In capitalism, people produce or obtain goods not for their use, but for the purpose of exchange. That is, their object is to produce or obtain commodities (C) not to obtain another commodity (C′) but to get capital or money (M). The goods have what is called *exchange value.* Thus, in a business transaction, when a person buys a commodity at one price and sells it at a higher price, the commodity is said to have an *exchange value.*

$$M \rightarrow C \rightarrow M'$$

Some people might argue that this exchange is capitalism, although most would call it *mercantile exchange,* suggesting that the formula for capitalism is incomplete. You still need one more development: to combine labor and the means of production in a unique way. From this perspective, fully developed capitalism looks like this:

$$M \rightarrow C \rightarrow P \rightarrow C' \rightarrow M'$$

or

$$M \rightarrow C \rightarrow \frac{mp}{lp} \rightarrow C' \rightarrow M'$$

Thus, a manufacturer or producer has money (M) to buy commodities (C; e.g., raw material, machines, and labor) that are then combined (mp/lp) to manufacture commodities that carry a value greater than C (C′). The sale of these commodities permits the producer to receive a sum of money greater than M (M′) that constitutes profit. Note that at this point, labor is considered a commodity to be purchased or rented, in the same ways that raw materials, machines, factories, or land are purchased or rented. Labor becomes a factor of production in the same way that raw materials, land, or machines are factors of production. In addition, at this point the accumulation of wealth comes to consist increasingly of productive capital (raw materials, machines, factories).

Let's apply the formula to our sample capitalist enterprise, the Nike Corporation. Nike invests money (M) to buy commodities (C), consisting of such things as leather, rubber, machines to make textiles, and factories (mp), which they combine with labor (lp), the people who design, produce, and assemble the commodity—sneakers—(C') that they then sell for money (M'). The object of this entire process is to get M' to exceed M as much as possible. That constitutes the profit—the bottom line, so to speak.

Furthermore, Nike doesn't simply keep M'—it reinvests it in commodities and recombines it with mp and lp in order to repeat the process and earn/accumulate still more money and profits. (Figure 2.1 is a diagram of the cyclical nature of capitalist production.)

However, in the real world of finance there are other factors to consider. For example, producers of commodities do not often have the money (or capital) to start the production cycle on their own; they have to borrow money from banks or sell stock to investors to raise money to obtain the means of production and pay the labor power to produce goods. Consequently, some of the profits take the form of principal and interest to repay investors' loans. The higher the rate of interest that the manufacturer offers investors, the easier it is to obtain loans. Moreover the producer, for example, Nike, doesn't have to put its profits back into producing more sneakers. It may invest that money elsewhere with the possibility of earning greater profits; in other words the manufacture and sale of sneakers may produce a profit of 10 percent, but if those profits can be reinvested elsewhere at 12 percent, so much the better.

This reveals one dilemma that Nike and other producers of commodities face: Making a profit is not enough. They must give their investors (the banks, stockholders, and so on) who supplied the money or capital to start the cycle of production enough of a return on their money so that they do not take it elsewhere. If they go elsewhere (and investors in today's world, as we shall see, have an enormous number of investment options), Nike may

FIGURE 2.1   Cycle of Capitalist Production

find it harder to locate investors and put together the money necessary to restart the cycle. Consequently, they may have to pay higher interest rates and charge more for their products. In that case, however, they might not sell as many units, especially if Adidas or Reebok can sell their sneakers for less.

In order to make a profit, it is imperative to keep the money spent on factories, machines (mp), and labor (lp) as low as possible. In fact, according to some economists, the ability to minimize the production costs of mp and lp will determine the success or failure of the company. (We will return to that in a moment.)

It soon becomes apparent that the capitalist production process is very much a money-making game: Investors and manufacturers put money in at one end of the production process and get more money out of the other end in the form of profits or interest. It is very much like a hypothetical device that engineers call a "black box." Engineers assume that the black box produces something, but for the purposes of design and planning they do not concern themselves with how things are produced, that is, with the internal functioning of the box. They simply assume that if they put something into it—fuel, electricity, and so on—they will get something out (e.g., power, movement).

For most capitalist producers or investors, capitalism or capitalist enterprises, such as corporations, banks, bonds, or stocks, are like black boxes: You put money in one end and get more money out the other (see Figure 2.2). It is, of course, a highly complex business to know where to put the money, how much to invest, and so forth. But it is the amount of the return rather than the way that it is generated that is uppermost in importance.

Nevertheless, it is in the black box that commodities are produced and consumed. It is also in the black box that we find the patterns of social, political, economic, ecological, and ideological life that either promote or inhibit the conversion of money into more money.

Thus, capitalism is more than an economic system; its operation has far-reaching consequences for almost all aspects of our existence. Most of us order our lives in some way to produce and consume commodities that generate the profits and interest that make the capitalist system work. But although most people who invest money do not concern themselves with how it is produced, others who are affected by this almost magical transformation often conceptualize the process in profound ways. For example, peasant farmers in Colombia have a way of conceptualizing capitalist exchange that may help us understand its essential elements and its cost.

The Baptism of Money

After losing their land to large farmers and being forced to supplement their farming activities with wage labor, peasants in the lowlands of Colombia developed the practice of illicitly

The Black Box

FIGURE 2.2   The Black Box

baptizing money in a Catholic Church—instead of baptizing a newborn child. When presenting a child to the priest to be baptized, a peasant would hold a peso note that he or she believed received the priest's blessing instead of the child. The note, thus magically transformed and given the name of the child, would, it was believed, continually return to and enrich its owner by bringing with it other notes. In other words, the note would become interest-bearing capital that continued to generate more and more money. Peasants tell stories of such notes disappearing from cash registers, carrying with them all the other notes, and of the store owner who saved his money only because he heard two baptized notes fighting for possession of the drawer's contents.

The idea that money is animate, that it can magically bring back more money, may at first seem strange to us, but Michael Taussig (1977) argued that the Colombian view of money is very close to our own—the major difference having to do with their conception of the black box.

The major feature of capitalism is that money can be used to make more money. To do so, the money must be invested in goods that must be sold, or invested in factories in which people work to make goods to be sold, and so on. Yet, we often talk as if it is the money itself that makes the money, or as if money somehow has a life of its own. We speak of "the *sagging* dollar," "cash *flows*," or "putting our money to *work*." The news will report that "earnings have *surged* ahead" or that we have "*climbing* interest rates." Factories are even referred to as "*plants*" where our "money *grows*."

In other words, our language conveys the notion that capital has an innate property of self-expansion. It is talked about as if it were a living being that reproduces itself (just as the Colombian peasant believes baptized money has a life of its own and can reproduce itself).

The belief that money has a life of its own is beautifully illustrated in Benjamin Franklin's classic work, *Advice to a Young Tradesman* (1748). Here is Franklin's advice:

> Remember, that money is of the prolific, generating nature. Money can beget money, and its offspring can beget more, and so on. Five shillings turned is six, turned again it is seven and three pence and so on, till it becomes a hundred pounds. The more there is of it, the more it produces every turning, so that the profits rise quicker and quicker. He that kills a breeding-sow, destroys all her offspring to the thousandth generation. (cited Taussig 1977:140)

The attitude expressed by Benjamin Franklin and expressed daily in our own lives is one that Karl Marx called *commodity fetishism*. Fetishism attributes life, autonomy, and power to inanimate objects—dolls, sticks, places, or, in capitalism, money or other commodities. But commodity fetishism also performs another function. By attributing animate life to money, by speaking of it as if the money itself produces money, we mask and hide the actual manner in which money begets money—the exploitation of labor, land, and people. In this magical way of thinking, we begin to think of money as being able to generate value and yield interest in the same way that pear trees bear fruit or pigs bear piglets. The whole process of capital investment, making a profit, finding the cheapest labor, and so on, comes to appear natural because the real source of profits and the noneconomic consequences of capitalism are largely hidden from view.

Money, however, does not produce money by itself. It requires other things, and this is where the Colombian peasant belief about the baptism of money is quite profound. Colombian peasants' practice of baptizing money so that it brings back more money is a rational interpretation of our own view of money but with one addition: For the Colombian peasant the process is immoral. It is immoral because it is money rather than the child that is baptized; profit can come only at the cost of the child's soul. In this way, the Colombian peasant is offering a critique of the capitalism that has been imposed on his society in the past century by the expanding world system.

These peasants are also posing key questions: *How does capitalism perform its magic, converting money into more money, and do we pay a price for that conversion?*

THE CONSTRUCTION AND ANATOMY
OF THE WORKING CLASS

As noted in Chapter 1, capitalism involves interactions among three sets of people: consumers, laborers, and capitalists, each doing what it is supposed, indeed has, to do. The construction of the consumer took place largely in the twentieth century. The nineteenth century witnessed the development of the working class. Although the flowering of the consumer occurred largely in the United States, the laborer was largely a creation of the British economy, a creation that gradually migrated from Great Britain to the rest of the world.

Characteristics of the Working Class

The new working class was unlike any that had existed before. Four characteristics of this new category of persons stand out: (1) Members of this class were by necessity mobile, free to move to wherever workers were needed, unhampered by property or family connections; (2) they were segmented or divided by race and ethnicity, age, and gender; (3) they were subject to new kinds of discipline and control; and (4) they were militant, often protesting the conditions in which they were placed. Let's examine each of these characteristics in turn.

Labor Mobility.   First, the new laborers were remarkably geographically mobile, moving temporarily or permanently to sources of employment. Most were mobile because they had been forced off their land or because the products they produced were no longer in demand. Take the situation of the Italian worker, for example. Beginning in the 1870s in Italy, the sale of public domain and church lands created a situation that allowed large landholders to add to their land, whereas small landholders were squeezed out as prices for agricultural products declined, in part because of the importation of Russian wheat. A blight destroyed many vineyards, and cheap imported goods disrupted local handicrafts. In the 1860s, some 16,000 people emigrated permanently from Italy; in the 1870s, the number grew to 360,000; between 1881 and 1901, the number rose to 2 million, 80 percent of whom were agricultural laborers.

The countries to which these Italian migrants scattered, including Australia, Canada, and most often the United States, quickly utilized the cheap labor in factories, railroads, mines, stockyards, and oil fields. In the period between 1820 and 1860, the main contingents of immigrants came from Ireland (2 million), southwestern Germany (1.5 million), and the British Isles (750,000). More English, Swedes, and Germans arrived between 1860

Geographic mobility is one characteristic of the laborer in the culture of capitalism. Here Chinese boys await medical examinations at Angel Island immigration station in San Francisco around 1910.

and 1890; again they were mainly displaced agriculturists driven off their land by the importation of cheap American and Russian wheat (as Mexican farmers are currently being displaced by the importation of cheap American corn).

In 1890, the source of the new immigration shifted to southern and eastern Europe and consisted largely of displaced peasants from Italy, the Austro-Hungarian Empire, the Balkans, and Poland, along with Jews from Russia.

Coal miners in Pennsylvania had been British, Irish, and German prior to 1890, but after that time they were increasingly Poles, Slovaks, Italians, and Hungarians. The textile mills of New England that had been run by French-Canadians, English, and Irish were, after 1890, run by Portuguese, Greeks, Poles, and Syrians. In the garment trades Russians, Jews, and Italians replaced Germans, Czechs, and Irish.

Some 90,000 indentured Chinese laborers were sent to Peru between 1849 and 1874; more than 200,000 were sent to the United States between 1852 and 1875 where they were employed in fruit growing, processing and panning for gold, and railroad construction. Some 10,000 to 14,000 Chinese were used in the construction of the Central Pacific Railroad of California.

Segmentation.   A second characteristic of the working class was that they were divided, or segmented, by race, religion, ethnicity, age, and gender. The new working class split into two broader categories: a labor aristocracy better able to defend its prerequisites through union organization and political influence, and workers who had to accept lower wages and less secure jobs. These divisions were often reinforced by the use of racial or ethnic distinctions that relegated certain groups such as Blacks and, earlier in the century, the Irish to only the lowest-paying jobs. Capitalism did not create these racial and ethnic distinctions, but it did help in defining and reinforcing them and their economic consequences (Wolf 1982:380).

Ironically, the ethnic identities of new immigrants rarely coincided with their self-identification. They first thought of themselves as Hanoverians or Bavarians rather than Germans; as members of a village parish (*okolica*) rather than Poles; as Sicilians, Neapolitans, and Genoans rather than Italians; and as Tonga or Yao rather than "Nyasalanders." In effect, migrants had to be socialized to see themselves as members of particular ethnic groups. They were, as Wolf (1982:381) said, "historical products of labor market segmentation under the capitalistic mode."

The ethnic or racial groupings created or reinforced by capitalist culture often came into conflict with each other as they competed for scarce jobs and resources. The case of the Irish in England and the United States is telling. In the mid-nineteenth century, Karl Marx (1972:293–294) made the following observation about the relationship between English workers and newly arrived Irish laborers:

> Every industrial and commercial center in England now possess a working class divided into two hostile camps, English proletarians and Irish proletarians. The ordinary English worker hates the Irish as a competitor who lowers his standard of life. In relation to the Irish worker he feels himself a member of the ruling nation and so turns himself into a tool of the aristocrats and capitalists of his own country against Ireland, thus strengthening their domination over himself. He cherishes religious, social, and national prejudices against the Irish worker. His attitude towards him is much the same as "poor whites" to the "niggers" of the former slave states of the USA. The Irishman pays him back with interest in his own money. He sees the English worker at once the accomplice and the stupid tool of the English domination in Ireland.... This antagonism is the secret of the impotence of the English working class, despite their organization.

In the United States, the same degree of ethnic antagonism developed, particularly between the Irish and Blacks. Irish leaders in the early nineteenth century generally were strong critics of slavery and supporters of its abolition. However, once the Irish emigrated to the United States, they, who in their own country were treated almost as badly by British rulers as African Americans were in the United States by Whites, became strongly pro-slavery and anti-Black. What accounted for this change in attitude?

Noel Ignatiev (1995), in his book, *How the Irish Became White,* maintained that during the first half of the nineteenth century in America, free African Americans competed successfully in the North for relatively good jobs. Before the Irish arrived in large numbers in the United States, the distinction between freedom and slavery was blurred by such intermediate conditions as chattel slavery, indentured servitude, and imprisonment for debt. But the American Revolution had eliminated these intermediate economic categories and reinforced the tendency to equate slavery with blackness and freedom with whiteness. If Blacks, then, were allowed to work in the same jobs as Irish, the Irish would be assigned to the same social category as Blacks. In fact, the Irish risked being considered lower in status than

Blacks, largely because as slaves Blacks had value that the Irish did not. As one official of an Alabama stevedoring company put it, "The niggers are worth too much to be risked here; if the Paddies are knocked overboard, or get their backs broke, nobody loses anything" (Ignatiev 1995:109). Consequently, the Irish did all they could to distance themselves from Blacks, including supporting slavery. But the major task of the Irish was to ensure that Blacks did not have access to the same jobs that they did.

Gradually, by taking the menial jobs that had been done by Blacks, as they were encouraged to do by priests, the Irish began to dominate the ranks of the unskilled laborer—by 1855, the Irish made up 87 percent of New York City's 23,000 unskilled laborers. In 1851, The *African Repository,* a magazine devoted to African American concerns, wrote (cited Ignatiev 1995:111) that

> in New York and other Eastern cities, the influx of white laborers has expelled the Negro almost en masse from the exercise of the ordinary branches of labor. You no longer see him work upon buildings, and rarely is he allowed to drive a cart or public conveyance. White men will not work with him.

"White men will not work with him," became the rallying cry of labor in elbowing out Blacks from jobs that were then taken over by Irish; as Frederick Douglass said, "In assuming our avocation [the Irishmen] has assumed our degradation."

The key to the distinction between White and Black became work; White meant doing "White man's work," whereas Black meant doing "Black man's work." The distinction was arbitrary because many jobs that became White man's work when reserved for the Irish had been performed by Blacks earlier. "White," Ignatiev pointed out, was not a physical description, but rather a term of social relations. This distinction resulted, then, in a situation in which to be "White" the Irish had to work in the jobs from which Blacks were excluded (Ignatiev 1995:111). Thus, a division of labor was hardened into a distinction of race and ethnicity.

The workforce was segmented in other ways, most notably by gender and age, with women and children assigned to the lowest-paying and most menial jobs. (A discussion of that development in more detail follows later.)

Discipline.   The new working class was mobile and divided by race, ethnicity, gender, and age. In addition, it had to be disciplined. Central to this process was the factory. The factory is a relatively recent historical phenomenon, having developed largely in the late eighteenth and early nineteenth centuries in Europe (although factory production in textiles may have existed as early as the fifteenth century). Prior to its development, most work (e.g., weaving, spinning, pottery making) was done in homes or small shops. The first factories were modeled on penal workhouses and prisons. Spinning mills were built and installed in brick buildings four or five stories high and employed several hundred workers. The iron and cast iron mills of the metal industry brought together several blast furnaces and forges and a large workforce (Beaud 1983:66). These settings may have increased the efficiency of production, but the new job discipline required of workers also created tensions between workers and their employers that, at various points in the years to follow, would result in situations approaching civil war.

The factory setting, for example, necessitated workers being disciplined to accept a new conception of time. Time, another of the things we take for granted, is subject to cultural definition. Our time is dictated, by and large, by our means of measuring it—clocks

and watches. Time in other societies tends to be task oriented or dictated by natural phenomena: In Madagascar, it might be measured by rice cooking (about one-half hour); in
seventeenth-century Chile, the time needed to cook an egg was the time it took to say an
Ave Maria aloud; in Burma, monks rose when there was enough light to see the veins in
their hands; in oceanside communities, the social patterning of time depends on the ebb
and flow of tides. British anthropologist E. E. Evans-Pritchard (1940:103), in his classic
account of the life of the Nuer of the Sudan, noted that

> the Nuer have no expression equivalent to "time" in our language, and they cannot, there-
> fore, as we can, speak of time as though it were something actual, which passes, can be
> wasted, can be saved, and so forth. I don't think they ever experience the same feeling of
> fighting against time because their points of reference are mainly the activities themselves,
> which are generally of a leisurely character. Events follow a logical order, but they are not
> controlled by an abstract system, there being no autonomous points of reference to which
> activities have to conform with precision. Nuer are fortunate.

Historian E. P. Thompson (1967) noted that until the institution of modern notions of
time, work patterns were characterized by alternating bouts of intense labor and idleness,
at least whenever people were in control of their own working lives. He has even suggested
that this pattern persists today but only among some self-employed professionals, such as
artists, writers, small-farm owners, and college students.

This is not to say that preindustrial work was easy. Thompson (1967:58) described
the typical day of a farm laborer in 1636: He rose at 4 A.M., and cared for the horses, ate
breakfast at 6 A.M., plowed until 2 or 3 P.M., ate lunch, attended to the horses until 6 in the
evening, ate supper, did other chores till 8 P.M., cared for the cattle, and then retired. However, this was during the height of the laboring year on the farm, and it was probably the
laborer's wife, says Thompson, who labored the hardest.

It is difficult to say precisely when the Western concept of time and work began to
change. Clocks were not widespread in Europe until the seventeenth century, although
most towns probably had a church clock. But by the early 1800s, our present sense of time
was well established.

Time was an entity that should not be wasted. "Time," as Benjamin Franklin wrote in
Poor Richard's Almanac, "is money." At about the same period, the idea that idleness was
wicked began to gain currency. As *Youth's Monitor* phrased it in 1689, time "is too precious
a commodity to be undervalued.... This is the golden chain on which hangs a massy eternity;
the loss of time is insufferable, because irrecoverable" (quoted Thompson 1967:58). Leisure
time, in general, was attacked; in some religious circles seeking amusement was considered
to be sinful. Anything that did not contribute to production was discouraged.

At about the same time the school was being used to teach a new time and work discipline. Social reformers in the late eighteenth century suggested that poor children be sent
at the age of four to workhouses where they would work and be given two hours schooling
each day. As one person said,

> There is considerable use in their being somehow or other, constantly employed at least
> twelve hours a day, whether they can earn their living or not; for by these means, we hope
> that the rising generation will be so habituated to constant employment that it would at
> length prove agreeable and entertaining to them. (cited Thompson 1967:84)

Thus, by the middle of the nineteenth century, through the supervision of labor, fines, bells and clocks, money incentives, preaching, and schooling, a new time discipline was imposed on society at large and on the laborer in particular.

Resistance.   Finally, in addition to its mobility, segmentation, and discipline, the new working class was characterized by a new militancy that would lead to the closest thing the world has seen to a "world revolution." Early in 1848, the French political thinker and chronicler of American democracy, Alexis de Tocqueville, addressed the French Chamber of Deputies, saying what many Europeans feared. "We are sleeping," he said, "on a volcano.... Do you not see that the earth trembles anew? A wind of revolution blows, the storm is on the horizon" (cited Hobsbawm 1975:9).

At about the same time, the thirty-year-old Karl Marx and his twenty-eight-year-old friend Friedrich Engels were drafting the *Manifesto of the Communist Party,* which appeared in London in February 1848. Perhaps within days, revolutionaries in France declared the establishment of a new republic; by March the revolution had moved into Germany, Hungary, and Italy; within weeks the governments of an area today encompassing France, Germany, Austria, Italy, Czechoslovakia, Hungary, part of Poland, Belgium, Switzerland, Denmark, and the old Yugoslavia were all overthrown. However, within six months of the outbreak the movement faltered, and within eighteen months only the new government of France remained, and it was trying to put distance between itself and the insurrectionists. The only long-lasting change was the abolition of serfdom in what had been the Hapsburg Empire.

Although they had the support of moderates and liberals in the various countries, they were, nevertheless, "social revolutions of the labouring poor," as Hobsbaum (1975:15) put it. The revolutions were an expression of developing patterns of conflict between the rich and poor, each group developing its spokespersons. On the one side were people such as Jean-Baptiste Say in France and David Ricardo and Thomas Robert Malthus in England who argued that the poor had only themselves to blame for their condition. On the other side were those such as Karl Marx, Friedrich Engels, Robert Owen, Henri Saint-Simon, and Charles Fourier who blamed the exploitation of labor for poverty. The debate is not unlike the ones still being argued over such issues as welfare and the role of the state in alleviating poverty. Malthus argued, for example, that

> it is not in the power of the rich to supply the poor with an occupation and with bread, and consequently, the poor, by the very nature of things have no right to demand these things from the rich.... No possible contributions of sacrifices of the rich, particularly in money, could for any time prevent the recurrence of distress among the lower members of society. (cited Beaud 1983:78)

It is a matter of morality, said Malthus, that those who are poor must not produce children until they can adequately provide for them. To those who violate this rule, there should be no pity.

> To the punishment, therefore of nature he should be left, to the punishment of want. He has erred in the face of a most clear and precise warning, and can have no just reason to complain of any person but himself when he feels the consequences of his error. All parish as-

sistance should be denied him; and he should be left to the uncertain support of private charity. He should be taught to know that the laws of nature, which are the laws of God, had doomed him and his family to suffer for disobeying their repeated admonitions.... It may appear to be hard that a mother and her children, who have been guilty of no particular crime themselves, should suffer for the ill conduct of the father; but this is one of the invariable laws of nature. (Malthus 1826:343)

One French industrialist could write matter-of-factly that "the fate of the workers is not that bad: their labor is not excessive since it does not go beyond thirteen hours.... The manufacturer whose profits are poor is the one to be pitied" (cited in Beaud 1983:101).

For others, such as Karl Marx and Friedrich Engels, society was being divided up into two hostile camps and classes—the bourgeoisie and the proletariat.

Masses of laborers, crowded into the factory, are organized like soldiers. As privates of the industrial army, they are placed under the command of a perfect hierarchy of officers and sergeants. Not only are they the slaves of the bourgeoisie class, and of the bourgeoisie State, they are daily and hourly enslaved by the machine, by the overlooker, and above all, by the individual bourgeoisie manufacturer himself. The more openly this despotism proclaims gain to be its end and aim, the more petty, the more hateful and the more embittering it is. (Marx and Engels 1848/1941:14)

The proletariat must, said Marx and Engels, embody the suffering, rise against it, and produce a classless society free from the exploitation of one class by another. It must free itself but only by transcending the inhumane conditions of present-day society. Marx had attempted in his writings to create a scientific theory of the fall of capitalism, in the same way that Adam Smith and David Ricardo had tried to create a scientific theory of the rise of capitalism. The results were not only a blueprint to be used by union organizers and revolutionaries but also the creation of two utopian ideologies—that of capitalism and that of socialism—which would do battle into the twentieth century.

These, then, are some of the characteristics of the laborer and the relationship between labor and capital as established in the nineteenth century. There were other features as well, such as the increased vulnerability of the laborer to hardship and the greater likelihood of impoverishment. To understand better how the laborer was constructed, let's turn to the contemporary world. In countries all over the world, the nineteenth-century processes through which the laborer was constructed are being repeated. We can see this most clearly in the growth of overseas assembly plants.

The Growth of Overseas Assembly Plants

In capitalism, profits and interest depend on the difference between the cost of producing a product and the price at which it is sold. If someone has a monopoly on a product, and if people need it, producers can charge as much as they need to to maintain or increase profits. But if other companies produce the same merchandise, it is likely that the price a company can charge will be determined by what others charge. Thus, Nike can charge one hundred dollars for its sneakers, but if its competitors are charging only forty dollars for the same product, Nike had better lower its price or face bankruptcy. Consequently, profit must come not from increasing the price that people pay but from controlling the cost of producing the product. Cost increase can be contained by controlling the cost of raw materials and machines—the means of production—or by controlling the price of labor.

The activity of work is common to all societies. In gathering and hunting societies, women and men spend a portion of their time gathering wild foods and hunting game; in pastoral societies people spend time herding and caring for animals; and in agricultural societies they work at tending fields, harvesting and storing crops, and so on. But work in the black box of capitalism takes a different form. In fact, some economists believe the key to understanding the way money creates more money is understanding the way labor figures in the production process. For them, profit comes directly from what they call the *surplus value of labor.*

As we noted earlier, to produce commodities for sale, labor must be purchased and combined with the means of production. For example, I might buy cloth and make shirts to sell. I may pay two dollars for the cloth and sell the shirt for ten, thereby making a profit of eight dollars. Where does that profit come from? One obvious place is the labor that went to convert the cloth into a shirt. In this case we might say the labor was worth eight dollars. But what if, instead of making the shirt myself, I paid someone else to do it, but paid him or her only two dollars, and still sold the shirt for ten. The value of the labor that went into making the shirt is still eight dollars, but the worker I hired received only two; I get to keep the other six dollars. It is this money that constitutes the *surplus value of labor.*

Obviously, then, one way for a company to maximize profits is to maximize the surplus value of labor and pay workers as little as possible. Another way to increase profits is to get the laborer to produce more in the same period of time. Thus, if I paid my shirtmakers an hourly or daily wage, I could double my profits by getting them to produce two shirts in the time that they used to produce one shirt. This I could do by getting them to work faster or by improving the technology or process of shirt-making to make it more efficient.

Companies that produce commodities such as textiles, electronic goods, and toys are labor intensive; that is, they require human labor more than improved technology to manufacture their products and are, consequently, always trying to minimize what they pay workers. Given the economic logic of capitalism this makes perfectly good sense: The more they save on labor costs and the less they charge for their product, the more they will attract consumers. Furthermore, the more they sell, the greater their profits and greater the return for investors and stock owners. Thus, the role of labor in the black box is critical to our understanding of the amount of profit the box can generate.

There are various ways that producers can keep labor costs down. For example, they can import labor from peripheral areas, particularly for low-paying jobs. In 2000, there were 15.7 million immigrant workers in the United States, some 12 percent of the nation's workforce. In fact, from 1990 to 2001, half of the new workers in the United States were immigrants. Most of these people worked as poultry plant workers, meatpackers, gardeners, hotel maids, seamstresses, restaurant workers, building demolition workers, and fruit and vegetable pickers (Greenhouse 2000). Corporations are also making use of the growing prison population; in the United States there are almost 2 million inmates, more than any other country in the world. Presently, thirty states have enacted laws allowing the use of convict labor by private enterprise who now employ more than 80,000 prisoners. Then there is slave labor. Kevin Bales (1999:8) estimates that there are 27 million slaves in the world today, largely in the form of bonded labor in India, Pakistan, Bangladesh, and Nepal. Bonded laborers give themselves into slavery as security for a loan or when they inherit a debt from a family member. Clearly, the greatest source of cheap labor exists in the periphery where, officially, more than 185.9 million people are unemployed (International Labor Organization 2003), and it is there that corporations often go to reduce their labor costs.

Corporations in core countries, such as the United States, made much use of foreign labor in the nineteenth century. However, as previously discussed, most of that labor moved to the source of employment, traveling largely from Europe and Asia to work in American mines, railroad yards, and factories. By 1900, 14 percent of the population of the United States was foreign born (see Haugerud, Stone, and Little 2000). Once jobs were filled, however, the immigrants or their descendants who filled them were not anxious to see more immigrants arrive and compete for their jobs. Consequently, they lobbied through unions, churches, and political parties for the government to pass restrictive immigration laws. When Chinese laborers were brought over to help build the transcontinental railroad, groups such as the Knights of Labor protested, even demanding that the Chinese get out of the laundry business. As a result, the U.S. Congress passed the Chinese Exclusion Act of 1882, and anti-Chinese agitation broke out on the West Coast, marking one more stage in the emergence of racism in the United States.

Although importing laborers from overseas worked for a time, corporations soon found that they could more easily tap into pools of cheap labor by relocating their manufacturing processes when possible to countries on the periphery of the world system whose governments were committed to economic development through industrialization. For example, to facilitate the establishment of assembly plants, governments in Indonesia, Malaysia, Guatemala, and Mexico, among others, created in their countries *free trade zones,* areas in which large corporations were permitted to deliver goods to be assembled—cut cloth for wearing apparel, electronic components, and so on—and for which they were not required to pay tariffs, provided that the items were not then sold in the country in which they were assembled. In exchange, the multinational corporations, such as Nike, agreed to hire local workers. The home countries, such as the United States, contributed by passing legislation that allows corporations to transfer the assembled goods back to the United States, paying an import tariff only on the labor cost of each product rather than on the total value of the product. Thus, the sneakers you wear were probably cut by machines in the United States, shipped to Indonesia or Vietnam to be assembled, and then shipped back to the United States to be distributed and sold there and elsewhere in the world. As an economic arrangement, almost everyone seems to benefit from the growth of assembly plants or *outsourcing,* as it is sometimes called.

- Nike and other companies are able to compete with other manufacturers by paying workers in Third World countries a fraction of what they would have to pay American workers.
- Workers in the Third World find employment.
- Consumers pay less for their clothes, electronic devices, toys, and so on.
- Investors get a higher return on their money.

It seems that the only ones who don't benefit are the American workers who lose their jobs (some half-million in the textile industry alone in the 1980s).

As a result, the growth in assembly plants was dramatic. In 1970 there were an estimated 1,000 women working in manufacturing in Malaysia, for example; by 1980, there were 80,000 concentrated in textiles, electronics, and food processing. In Mexico, the number of *maquiladoras,* as assembly plants are called, grew from virtually none in the 1960s to 1,279 employing 329,413 people in 1988, to more than 4,000 employing more than 1 million workers in 1999 (Hodder 1999). However, there are some problems. Critics have cited assembly plant workers' poor working conditions, their low pay, the actions of foreign governments in discouraging the formation of workers' unions, and the loose environmental regulations that have in some cases resulted in considerable environmental degradation around free trade zones. Furthermore, as corporations seek out new areas of cheap labor, they abandon old sites, such as Mexico, in favor of new sites, such as China or Vietnam. Consequently, after hitting a peak in 1999, the number of *maquiladora* workers in Mexico is on the decline.

In response to abuses, in 1995, American labor and children's rights groups called for a boycott of all garments assembled in Bangladesh to protest the estimated 25,000 to 30,000 children working in garment factories in Bangladesh. The United States is Bangladesh's biggest apparel customer, with nearly 50 percent of Bangladesh's $1.6 billion in garment exports arriving in the United States. In some assembly factories in El Salvador, where women earn $4.51 for the day, or 56 cents an hour, union organizers are often summarily dismissed, bathrooms are locked and can be used only with permission, and talking on the job is prohibited. In Guatemala, workers are required to work overtime at a moment's notice and are dismissed if they refuse. There have been reports of systematic violence against union organizers in Mexico, El Salvador, and Guatemala. And, as we shall see, assembly plants have far-reaching consequences on the societies and cultures of the cities and countries in which they are located.

The Creation of Free Labor

One defining feature of capitalism is the creation of a class of people who are willing to sell their labor. There must be a working class and, subsequently, a demand for jobs. A key question then is, *why do people, particularly the workers, play the game of capitalism?* For example, if the pay is poor and working conditions harsh, *why do people work in assembly plants?* Although the United States is and has been largely a wage economy in which the vast majority of people, in effect, sell their labor to companies, we sometimes forget, as mentioned earlier, that the existence of a so-called working class is a recent development historically in the United States, and particularly in countries such as Malaysia and Mexico where, until recently, most people earned their livings from the land or from what they themselves produced and sold. Thus, turning landed peasants and artisans into wage laborers required that they lose their land or sources of livelihood.

In Malaysia and Mexico, countries trying to industrialize and attract foreign manufacturers such as Nike, political developments in the nineteenth and early twentieth centuries led to the systematic dispossession of peasants from their land and to the increased importation of cheap products (e.g., textiles, iron implements) that put local artisans out of business. For example, up to the nineteenth century, Malaysia consisted of small states ruled over by sultans and so-called big men, who extracted tribute from peasants. Peasants held use-rights to land and could pass on to children whatever land they worked but no more than that. The center of life was the *kampung,* or village. However, British colonialists took over the land and converted its use to the production of cash crops, leaving the unlanded population to seek labor on large plantations or migrate to cities in search of jobs. There was still more than enough land in Malaysia for everyone to farm, but it was used instead to produce crops, such as palm oil, for export rather than to produce food for the local population.

In Mexico a similar history has left most of the population without land to produce food. In the mid-nineteenth century, the vast majority of the Mexican population lived in villages. The land was divided among the residents but owned not by individuals but by the whole village. People were given the right to use land but not the right to sell it. Then, in the mid-nineteenth century, legislation was passed in Mexico declaring communally held lands to be illegal, giving peasants legal rights to their own land, which they could then also sell or mortgage to repay debts. The result was that wealthy persons—largely Americans—bought up huge tracts of land. By 1910, the year of the beginning of the Mexican Revolution, more than 90 percent of the population was landless and forced to work on large agricultural estates or migrate to the cities in search of jobs. In the course of half a century, the vast majority of the Mexican population was transformed from an autonomous peasantry working their own land to a population of dependent wage laborers.

The process of land dispossession has continued to the present time (as will be discussed later) not only in Mexico and Malaysia but also in many other parts of the world, resulting in a large population of landless people with only their labor to sell. As a result, the governments of these countries are under great pressure to facilitate the growth of jobs for the population. It is into these situations that American, Japanese, German, and British corporations, among others, have come to build assembly plants.

Assembly factories, however, involve a paradox. In countries such as Malaysia and Mexico the men traditionally were the wage laborers, but women are sought by corporations, such as Nike, as employees. The women, for some reason, are willing to accept a wage level less than that needed for subsistence. Thus, we need to ask *why are there jobs that pay less than a living wage and why do certain categories of people seem relegated to them?*

The Segmentation of the Workforce

One consequence of the establishment of offshore assembly growth was the entrance into the labor market of a new working population of young, single women between the ages of sixteen and twenty-four. *Why do the assembly plants choose to employ young women, and why is it that women choose to work under sometimes unpleasant conditions?* The answer to this question requires us to understand how and why labor is segmented into different levels.

Take, for example, the case of Malaysia. Aihwa Ong (1987) spent two years studying assembly plants in Malaysia owned by Japanese and American corporations. One of the first questions she asked was, why did the plants prefer to hire young women? Plant managers that she interviewed gave a number of reasons. One Japanese manager told Ong (1990:396–397) that "females [are] better able to concentrate on routine work" and "young girls [are] preferable than older persons, that is because of eyesight." Another explained, "You cannot expect a man to do very fine work for eight hours [at a stretch]. Our work is designed for females...if we employ men, within one or two months they would have run away.... Girls [sic] below thirty are easier to train and easier to adapt to the job function."

The idea that women are somehow more suited biologically for assembly plant work is widespread in developing countries. For example, here is what a brochure designed to bring foreign investments into Malaysia says about its female workforce:

> Her hands are small and she works fast with extreme care. Who, therefore, could be better qualified by *nature and inheritance* to contribute to the efficiency of a bench assembly production line than the oriental girl? (Ong 1987:152 [emphasis added])

In Mexican *maquiladoras* the situation is much the same. María Patricia Fernández-Kelly (1983) was also interested in the effects of the assembly plants on women. To study these effects she found a job in a *maquiladora* to share the experiences of the workers and to meet the women and learn about their lives. She, too, found that companies preferred to hire young females because managers believed that women have higher skill levels; are more docile; and are more willing to comply to the monotonous, repetitive, and exhausting assignments. Men are described by managers as more restless or rebellious, less patient, more likely to unionize, and less tolerant of the working conditions. As one manager related to Fernández-Kelly (1983:181),

> We hire mostly women because they are more reliable than men, they have finer fingers, smaller muscles and unsurpassed manual dexterity. Also, women don't get tired of repeating the same operation nine hundred times a day.

Assembly plants in both Malaysia and Mexico also preferred single women because managers believed that older, married women had too many other obligations; were often unwilling to work night shifts; and may have accumulated enough wage increments to be paid more than a new, young, single woman would earn.

There is also a large population of unemployed women that assembly factories can choose from. In Malaysia and Mexico there are three applicants for every available position. Thus one *maquiladora* manager could announce to a conference organized by the American Chamber of Commerce that the 30 percent unemployment rate in Ciudad Juárez allows for high employee selectivity. Moreover, village elders in Malaysia and family heads in Mexico are eager to send otherwise non-wage-earning women to work in the assembly plants.

There is another reason, however, for the employment practices of assembly plants, one that tells us even more about the black box of capitalism: You don't have to pay women and children as much as you have to pay men. Nor do you have to pay foreign workers as much as domestic workers. By extension you do not have to pay people of color as much as you pay Whites. That is, the contemporary labor force in peripheral countries, such as Mexico and Malaysia, is already segmented through various forms of social discrimination, as was the labor force in nineteenth-century North America and Europe. Whether capitalism creates this type of discrimination, reinforces it, or simply takes advantage of it where it exists is arguable. Regardless, there is no question that, at least to some extent, social discrimination and prejudice—sexism, racism, discrimination against immigrants—is profitable. It is an important part of the black box. But why?

Young women, such as these uniformed workers at a Nike assembly plant in Indonesia, comprise the vast majority of workers at overseas assembly plants.

Let's return to basic economics. Modern industries can be loosely divided into two types. There are *primary industries* whose markets are well defined, whose profits are relatively certain, whose capital investment is high, and who are able to pay good wages and ensure decent working conditions. These industries include automobile manufacturing, communications, and energy industries, to name a few. They require a well-paid, well-trained, and relatively content workforce.

Then there are *secondary industries* that include the fast-food industry; agriculture; electronics; and, most notably, the clothing, garment, and/or textile industries. There is intense competition, uncertain or changing demand, a lower profit margin, and a greater dependence on unskilled labor in these industries. They are the least desirable for workers because to stay competitive companies must pay the lowest wages and yet maximize worker output. These are the industries most likely to expand operations to poorer countries. They are also the companies that are likely to hire the most vulnerable and the lowest-ranking members of a population. Traditionally, these people have been women, children, or members of subjugated minorities. Thus, when corporations locate assembly factories abroad, they are, in effect, expanding the secondary labor market.

Of course the hiring of women for low-paying, labor-intensive work has long been a feature of industrial capitalism. Women and children formed the bulk of the factory workforce at the beginnings of the industrial revolution in the late eighteenth and early nineteenth centuries. In 1851, 31 percent of the labor force in England consisted of women, 45 percent of whom were in manufacturing. In the English textile industry of 1840, more than 75 percent of the workforce consisted of women and children. The locating of assembly plants overseas is simply the latest version of utilizing a socially vulnerable workforce to secure low-paid labor. This expansion of the secondary labor market abroad, however, has had the following economic consequences for workers and corporations at home and abroad:

1. It has meant the transfer of jobs abroad and resulting unemployment at home.
2. It has widened the gap between primary and secondary labor in the wealthier countries.
3. From the perspective of workers in peripheral countries of the world system, it has meant the development of poorly paid, unstable jobs with little opportunity for promotion.

The process of targeting the most vulnerable segment of the population for low-wage jobs also affects the meaning that societies give to specific tasks. For example, the division between skilled and unskilled jobs is often not based on the nature of the work, as one would suppose; instead, it is based on who is doing the work. In other words, the work that women do in assembly factories is not necessarily less skilled than other work; it is considered unskilled because it is performed by women. Fernández-Kelly discovered this when she tried to learn the sewing techniques of women in Mexican garment *maquiladoras.* She could barely keep up with them; it required a skill level equal to or greater than many jobs that we call skilled. In Brazil, women are hired to tend grape vines to produce the large, unblemished grape that consumers in industrial countries desire. The work is skilled (e.g., involving the grafting of vines), but because the work is done by women, it is described as requiring "manual dexterity, delicacy, and nimbleness of fingers" (Collins 2000:102). Thus, work that women do is defined as "unskilled" because it is done by women, as work that Blacks or Irish did in the nineteenth century was defined as unskilled because it was done by Blacks or Irish.

From the standpoint of the corporation, however, the transfer of secondary jobs to underdeveloped countries and the ensuing expansion of a cheap labor reserve pool affords corporate employers the greatest degree of political and economic control over workers. They are able to employ the most socially vulnerable sector of the working class, the people least likely to organize, demand better wages, or press for better working conditions. As one Mexican *maquiladora* worker put it, men are unwilling to perform the monotonous labor; women are more shy and submissive and are more used to following orders. They are more easily intimidated and forced to obey. They are the easiest to discipline.

In sum, for corporations women represent a major source of inexpensive, transient labor; thus, women, although making up the vast majority of assembly plant workers throughout the world, occupy few skilled or managerial positions. And because they occupy the lowest positions, women can be hired and fired, depending on the overseas demand for such things as textiles, shoes, plastics, electrical appliances, and, increasingly, electronics.

In spite of the often poor pay and harsh working conditions that women working in assembly plants endure, some economists and public policymakers argue that such employment is necessary if women are ultimately to gain access to better positions and change their often subjugated positions in societies around the world. They argue that the money that women earn gives them control over resources that they would otherwise not have, that as families become dependent on the income that these women bring into their households, their positions in society will improve. Some also argue that the creation of this kind of work is a necessary stage of economic development and will eventually lead to better lives for all. We must remember, however, that if the labor market remains divided between primary and secondary industries, then someone must continue to do the low-paying work. Women may escape low-paying jobs, but only, as the Irish in the nineteenth century learned, if there is another group to take their places.

Control and Discipline

In nineteenth-century America, as young men and women sought work in the growing factory towns and cities, factory owners, as well as local citizens, faced a problem. These young people had been integrated into the social institutions of their hamlets and villages. As members of families and churches, they were expected to conform to certain standards of behavior; deviance from those standards could bring condemnation, punishment, and even social ostracism. But in the towns and cities to which they moved, migrant workers often were freed from such constraints, free to experiment with behaviors previously denied to them. Consequently, men often gained reputations as "rowdies," or "hoodlums," whereas women were labeled "immoral" or "loose." Thus, the creation of free labor created a problem: *How do you control the labor force?*

For example, in turn-of-the-twentieth-century New York City, thousands of young women found employment in factories and used their new-found freedom and the wages they earned for shopping, dating, dancing, or going on excursions to recreation areas, such as Coney Island. However, their behavior alarmed some people who saw it as immoral; consequently, groups of social reformers organized and proposed ways to "protect" working women from these "temptations." Some of their solutions to the problem resulted in the formation of social and religious clubs and associations for young women, organizations such as the Young Women's Christian Association (YWCA).

These organizations also served another function as well; they relieved the fears of the parents of these young workers who otherwise might have been reluctant to allow the women to migrate to cities and factory towns.

As in nineteenth-century America and Great Britain, employment in the new assembly plants of such countries as Malaysia and Mexico often requires young men and women to leave their homes and move to cities, freeing them from the traditional constraints imposed by family and church, and, thus, freeing them to spend their leisure time in nontraditional activities. Take, for example, the situation of the largely female workforce in the new assembly plants of Malaysia. Most of the women are young, generally ranging from sixteen to twenty years old. In their villages they would have lived at home, perhaps attended school, and been involved in various household chores under the direction of their mothers. Dating would have been rare and, when it occurred, would have been carefully supervised by parents. Marriages were often arranged by parents. Factory work, however, allows these same young women to earn wages, a portion of which they control. Although most workers contribute one-half or more of their earnings to their families, they are free to spend the rest on themselves. Some use it for typing or academic classes to prepare for civil service jobs, in effect attempting to control their own job prospects and "careers." Some become consumers, taking shopping trips to town or going to the movies, "making jolly with money," as they say. They exchange traditional *kampung* garb for tight T-shirts, jeans, and Avon makeup, trying to achieve what they call the "electric look."

Because working women are now expected to save money to contribute to their own wedding expenses—money that had been traditionally supplied by their families—they feel justified in choosing potential spouses. Sexual freedom may be increasing, as indicated by an increase in abortions, and women are beginning to cross social boundaries, having "illicit" relationships and marrying men of other ethnic groups (e.g., Chinese), something traditional family and church authorities would never have allowed.

One consequence of the growth of the number of working women in Malaysia is a stream of criticism about the loose morals of factory girls, especially from Islamic fundamentalists. The Malay media portrays factory women as pleasure seekers and spendthrifts engulfed in Western consumer culture. A story about prostitution might promote sensational headlines, such as "Factory Girls in Sex Racket."

All of this has resulted in a call for greater control of working women, in spite of the fact that similar behavior, such as dating and moviegoing, among upper-class college students has not received the same notice. Even the academic community and religious and state officials have claimed to recognize the problem of declining morals of young women and proposed measures to arrest the decline, such as counseling and recreational activities. There have also been public calls for control of working women's leisure time, despite the fact that they tend to work about three hours a day more than women engaged primarily in traditional household chores.

In some ways, the newfound freedom of factory workers is as welcome by businesspeople as it is by the young. Their new income—and their willingness to spend a portion of it on themselves—has turned young village men and women into consumers who buy many of the products they make. But the new freedoms create yet another problem. Capitalist enterprise requires a disciplined and reliable workforce; with old forms of discipline falling away new forms must be developed to replace them. The question is, how is that done?

Although family and church are largely absent from the lives of working young men and women, factory managers try to use these traditional institutions to control their workers. Malaysia is an Islamic country, and according to Islamic practice, parents are obligated to care for their children up to age fifteen, and traditional customs decree that children must also care for their parents. Thus children, particularly women, are obligated to return to their parents the care that their parents gave them. One of the major appeals made to young women by factory owners and managers is that they use their wages to pay back part of what they owe their parents.

Factory managers also seek to maintain discipline by building relations with people in the women's home villages, thus enlisting their help in controlling workers. For example, managers make donations to community organizations in the villages that supply workers. They also devise regulations to help parents monitor the activities of their daughters. When workers commute from their villages to the factories, the managers deliver workers to their homes by bus, or they allow parents to see overtime forms so they know how much time their daughters were spending at work and at other activities. These efforts enhance the prestige of managers in the eyes of village elders whose moral support could then be obtained for the social control of working daughters.

Corporations also use traditional family values to encourage workers to comply with company goals (Ong 1987:169). Thus, managers tell workers that they are part of "one big family." One factory had posters proclaiming the company philosophy:

- To create one big family
- To train workers
- To increase loyalty to company, country, and fellow workers

Managers portray themselves as parent figures to the larger community from which women workers come, and, although workers complain of too much control, parents rarely tell their daughters to quit.

Religion is also used as a means of discipline (Ong 1987:185). Because it is an Islamic country, the Malaysian government includes special departments and agencies that have jurisdiction over the application of religious law. For example, under the current interpretation of religious law, Muslims may be arrested for *khalwat,* "close proximity" between a man and a woman who are not immediate relatives or married to each other. Those caught in situations that simply suggest sexual intimacy, but not necessarily in the sex act, are fined or sentenced to jail for a few months. Muslims arrested for *zinah,* that is, illicit sexual intercourse, may be more severely punished. As a result of the increase in the number of young women working in assembly factories, there have been more raids by the government's Religious Department on the poor lodgings and cheap hotels used by the workers.

Then there is the factory discipline itself. We mentioned earlier that eighteenth- and nineteenth-century factories were modeled after prisons. Modern assembly plants have much the same character. In Malaysian assembly plants, workers are sometimes watched through glass partitions. In one factory, for example, three supervisors and twelve foremen controlled 530 operators. Discipline was verbally enforced as women workers were scolded by overvigilant foremen for wanting to go to the prayer room, the clinic, or the toilet. Some foremen would even question workers in a humiliating manner about their menstrual problems or nonwork activities. Others were reported to have forced women to run laps around the assembly plant as a form of punishment for reporting late to work or not meeting their production quotas.

As in prisons, clothing can be used to instill discipline. Malaysian workers are required to wear factory overalls that they complain are too tight and which they are not allowed to unbutton. They are also required to wear heavy rubber boots. These clothes are very different from the loose-fitting clothes and sandals Malaysians traditionally wear while working.

Assembly plants also bring with them a Western, factory-oriented sense of the relationship between work and time to which contemporary assembly workers must adapt. Traditionally, in Malaysia, for example, young girls carried out their household or farm tasks relatively free from modern time and work discipline; their activities were interspersed with social visits, usually free of female supervision and always free of male supervision. If there was anything to mark the passage of time, it was the cycle of daily Islamic prayer.

Female workers in the factories, however, are clocked in daily for eight consecutive hours with two fifteen-minute breaks and a half-hour lunch break. Every month their work schedules are changed. Women begin to divide their lives into "work time" and "leisure time." They were watched over by overzealous foremen, screened before they could leave their workbenches to go to the toilet, and fined if they were late for work (in spite of the fact that pay was based on piecework). This is in vivid contrast to the traditional work routine where there was no distinction between work and life and no conflict between labor and "passing the time of day."

People in Malaysia are aware of the shift from traditional social time to the capitalist clock time, and they have developed their own ways to critique it. Ong (1987:112) told the story of a married couple, Ahmad and Edah, driven, say their neighbors, by the acquisition of wealth to carefully spend their time on capital accumulation at the expense of social obligations. Their neighbors said their obsession with time was the result of a *toyal,* a spirit helper that they raised to filch money from neighbors. The *toyal,* they concluded, turned the tables on the couple by driving them even harder to use all their time to accumulate wealth.

Resistance and Rebellion

Capitalism requires a disciplined working class—people willing to work for wages that allow enterprises to make their necessary profit. But herein lies a problem: In general, people do not readily accept discipline and control and will seek a way to resist, either directly or indirectly.

Resistance to capitalist discipline can take direct forms, as in worker protests, formation of unions, and even revolution (subjects examined in later chapters). Resistance may also take the form of a moral critique, such as that of Colombian peasants who see capital accumulation represented in the baptism of money as the loss of a child's soul. Such indirect forms of resistance are not unique to the peoples of the periphery of the world system. For example, one of the stories that comes down to us from early industrial Europe is that of Rumpelstilskin. Folktales are more than simply stories; they are statements about people's beliefs. Often they are morality tales that dramatize the consequences of proper or improper behavior. Jane Schneider (1989), for example, suggested that the meaning of the Rumpelstilskin tale lies in the development of the linen industry in early modern Europe. In fact, in many ways, it offers a critique of capitalist production not unlike that of the Colombian peasants.

In one version of the Rumpelstilskin story, a father brags that his daughter is able to spin straw into gold. The king, hearing of this boast, offers to take the girl as his wife if she is able to spin the straw in his castle into gold. The girl, tries, fails, then enters into a pact with a strange dwarf, Rumpelstilskin, who promises to spin the straw into gold for her, but only if she promises to give him her firstborn child. The girl accepts, Rumpelstilskin spins the gold, and she marries the king and has a child. The dwarf comes to claim his fee but is distressed by her tears and grief and offers her a way out. If she can guess his name, he will free her from the contract.

We have forgotten much of what this tale meant to sixteenth- and seventeenth-century European peasants. For example, one of the main industries of the period was linen production. Linen was produced by spinning flax straw into linen thread that was woven into a fabric that was sold for gold coins. So straw, in effect, really was spun into gold. Moreover the spinning process was performed largely by young women. A woman's spinning skill was not only a source of money but it also was a quality men sought in wives—as the king sought in his future wife. Furthermore, the story contains a pact with a demon, and the price is the firstborn. Thus, as in the Colombian baptism of money, we find the symbolic statement that the generation of wealth comes only with social and personal sacrifice, often of children or their souls.

Malaysian assembly plant workers have also found a subtle, generally symbolic means of expressing their resistance to capitalist discipline. It takes the form of spirit possession. Although Malaysia is a Muslim country, Islam exists side by side with indigenous beliefs about magic and spirits. Thus, in the 1980s, assembly plant managers in Malaysia—especially American and Japanese managers—were unexpectedly confronted with an epidemic of spirit possessions in their factories (Ong 1987:204). Forty Malaysian operators were possessed in one large American electronics plant; three years later in another incident 120 operators were possessed. The factory was shut down for three days while a spirit-healer (*bomoh*) was called in to sacrifice a goat to the possessing spirit on the premises.

Another American microelectronics factory was closed down when fifteen women were possessed. According to factory personnel officers, possessed girls began to sob and scream hysterically. When it looked as though the possession would spread, the other workers were immediately ushered out. The women explained that the factory was "dirty" and consequently haunted by a *datuk*.

The Malay universe is still full of spirits moving between the human and nonhuman domain. Spirit possession seemed to express themes of filth, angry spirits, and fierce struggles. Particularly prominent in the possession episodes were spirits, such as *toyal*, who help their masters gain wealth out of thin air; and the *pontianak*, who threaten the lives of newborn infants.

Aihwa Ong suggested that the women were not reacting to anything as abstract as industrial capitalism but against a sense of violation, of a dislocation in human relations, in much the same way the Colombian peasants reacted to wage labor with the notion of the baptism of money and the sacrifice of children's souls.

Beliefs about the baptism of money in Colombia and spirit possession of factory workers in Malaysia are examples of the widespread critiques of capitalism that we find among people confronting capitalist production for the first time. Such beliefs are ways that people find to express their sense that capitalist production brings a modicum of economic betterment at high social and personal costs.

CONCLUSION

A major assumption of this book is that it is impossible to understand the modern world and its problems—population growth, hunger, poverty, environmental degradation, health, war, religious violence, and so on—without an understanding of the capitalist economy that, with its goal of accumulating more and more wealth, has in the past four to five centuries redefined and created new social and cultural forms and altered traditional cultural institutions to serve its own purposes. Capitalism has been characterized here as a black box whose purpose it is to convert money into more money, to take monetary investments and convert them into profits and interest. For most people, this process is as magical as is the behavior of baptized money among Colombian peasants. They place money in banks, stocks, or other investments and expect to get more money back without ever questioning the process through which this conversion occurs.

We began to examine how the black box performs its conversion by looking at the growth of overseas assembly plants and the creation, segmentation, and disciplining of the labor force necessary for the box to function at its greatest efficiency. Historically, free labor has been created by removing people from the land or destroying the small-scale industry that allowed them to support themselves. In different countries this was done in different ways, but the overall result has been the creation of populations whose sole means of support is in the sale of their labor. This is as true in industrialized countries as it is in developing or undeveloped countries. In fact, all of us who depend on wage employment—from nuclear physicists to garment workers—constitute the pool of "free" labor. This labor pool is further divided along a continuum comprising at one end relatively well-paid, desirable jobs in industries or enterprises that require a well-trained workforce, and at the other end relatively low-paying, undesirable jobs in industries that are highly competitive and dependent on the existence of a cheap labor supply. Industries and enterprises that depend on a cheap labor supply are able to take advantage of social divisions and discrimination that generally follow lines of gender, race, age, and country of origin to minimize labor costs and control the labor force.

In creating or taking advantage of the increasing supply of cheap labor, the capitalist economy must also develop ways to maintain workforce discipline, which it does through the factory system; the redefinition of time; and the use of traditional institutions, such as the family and the church. Yet in spite of the new forms of discipline, workers offer resistance in the indirect form of masked criticism—as in the baptism of money, spirit possession, or moral tales such as that of Rumpelstilskin—or in the direct forms of protest and the organization of unions.

The mobility, segmentation, and disciplining of the workforce is, of course, only one feature of modern capitalism, and an examination of labor is only the beginning of an understanding of how the black box is able to transform money into more money. It is necessary to examine other components. In order to do so, let us turn to other major questions: How did the entire system develop historically? How did the black box evolve to where it is today? Most specifically, *how and why did the capitalist evolve from the merchant trader?*

CHAPTER THREE

THE RISE OF THE MERCHANT, INDUSTRIALIST, AND CAPITAL CONTROLLER

From the fifteenth century on, European soldiers and sailors carried the flags of their rulers to the four corners of the globe, and European merchants established their storehouses from Vera Cruz to Nagasaki. Dominating the sea-lanes of the world, these merchants invaded existing networks of exchange and linked one to the other. In the service of "God and profit" they located sources of products desired in Europe and developed coercive systems for their delivery. In response, European craft shops, either singly or aggregated into manufactories, began to produce goods to provision the wide-ranging military and naval efforts and to furnish commodities to overseas suppliers in exchange for goods to be sold as commodities at home. The outcome was the creation of a commercial network of global scale.
—Eric Wolf, *Europe and the People without History*

When I think of Indonesia—a country on the Equator with 180 million people, a median age of 18, and a Moslem ban on alcohol—I feel I know what heaven looks like.
—Donald R. Keough, President of Coca-Cola

At no other time in human history has the world been a better place for capitalists. We live in a world full of investment opportunities—companies, banks, funds, bonds, securities, and even countries—into which we can put money and from which we can get more back. These moneymaking machines, such as the Nike Corporation, have a ready supply of cheap labor, capital, raw materials, and advanced technology to assist in making products that people all over the world clamor to buy. Moreover, governments compete for their presence, passing laws and making treaties to open markets, while maintaining infrastructures (roads, airports, power utilities, monetary systems, communication networks, etc.) that enable them to manufacture products or provide services cheaply and charge prices that remain competitive with other investments. Nation-states maintain armies to protect investments and see that markets remain open. Educational institutions devote themselves to producing knowledgeable, skilled, and disciplined workers, while researchers at colleges and universities develop new technologies to make even better and cheaper products. Our governments, educational institutions, and mass media encourage people to consume more and more commodities. Citizens arrange their economic and social lives to accommodate work in the investment machines and to gain access to the commodities they produce. In return the investment machines churn out profits that are reinvested to manufacture more of their particular products or that can be invested in other enterprises, producing yet more goods and services. Never before have people had so much opportunity to accumulate great wealth. Among the 400 richest Americans in 1999, 298 of them were worth a billion dollars or more, and the top 400 had a net worth of $1.2 trillion, about one-eighth of the total gross domestic product (GDP) of the United States (see Forbes 2000b).

But there are economic, environmental, and social consequences of doing business and making money. We live in a world in which the gap between the rich and poor is growing, a world that contains many wealthy and comfortable people and more than 1 billion hungry people, one-sixth of its population. Then there are the environmental consequences of doing business: Production uses up the earth's energy resources and produces damaged environments in return. There are health consequences as well, not only from damaged environments but also because those too poor to afford health care often do without it. Finally, there are the political consequences of governments' using their armed forces to maintain conditions that they believe are favorable for business and investors.

In the long view of human history these conditions are very recent ones. For most of human history human beings have lived in small, relatively isolated settlements that rarely exceeded 300 or 400 individuals. And until some 10,000 years ago virtually all of these people lived by gathering and hunting. Then in some areas of the world, instead of depending on the natural growth of plant foods and the natural growth and movements of animals, people began to plant and harvest crops and raise animals themselves. This was not necessarily an advance in human societies—in fact, in terms of labor, it required human beings to do the work that had been done largely by nature. The sole advantage of working harder was that the additional labor supported denser populations. Settlements grew in size until thousands rather than hundreds lived together in towns and cities. Occupational specialization developed, necessitating trade and communication between villages, towns, cities, and regions. Political complexity increased; chiefs became kings, and kings became emperors ruling over vast regions.

Then, approximately 400 or 500 years ago, patterns of travel and communication contributed to the globalization of trade dominated by "a small peninsula off the landmass of Asia," as Eric Wolf called Europe. The domination by one region over others was not new in the world. There had existed prior to this time civilizations whose influence had spread to influence those around them—the Mayan civilization in Central America, Greek civilization of the fourth millennium B.C., Rome of the first and second centuries A.D., and Islamic civilization of the eighth and ninth centuries. But there was an important difference. The building of these empires was largely a political process of conquest and military domination, whereas the expansion of Europe, although certainly involving its share of militarism, was largely accomplished by economic means, by the expansion and control of trade.

Now let's shift our focus to the development of the *capitalist*—the merchant, industrialist, and financier—the person who controls the capital, employs the laborers, and profits from the consumption of commodities. This will be a long-term, historical look at this development because if we are to understand the global distribution of power and money that exists today and the origins of the culture of capitalism, knowledge of its history is crucial.

Assume for a time the role of a businessperson, a global merchant, or merchant adventurer, as they used to be called[1], passing through the world of the past 600 years. We'll begin searching the globe for ways to make money in the year 1400 and end our search in the year 2000, taking stock of the changes in the organization and distribution of capital that have occurred in that time. Because we are looking at the world through the eyes of a merchant, there is much that we will miss—many political developments, religious wars, revolutions, natural catastrophes, and the like. Because we overlook these events does not mean they did not affect how business was conducted—in many cases they had profound effects. But our prime concern is with the events that most directly influenced the way in which business was conducted on a day-to-day basis and how the pursuit of profit by merchant adventurers influenced the lives of people all over the world. Our historical tour will concentrate on three areas:

1. An understanding of how capital came to be concentrated in so few hands and how the world came to be divided into rich and poor. There were certainly rich people and poor people in 1400, but today's vast global disparity between core and periphery did not exist then. *How did the distribution of wealth change, and how did one area of the world come to dominate the others economically?*

2. An understanding of the changes in business organizations and the organization of capital, that is, *who controlled the money?* In 1400, most business enterprises were small, generally family-organized institutions. Capital was controlled by these groups and state organizations. Today we live in an era of multinational corporations, many whose wealth exceeds that of most countries. We need to trace the evolution of the power of capital over our lives and the transformation of the merchant of 1400 into the industrialist of the eighteenth and nineteenth centuries then into the investor and capital controller of the late twentieth century. *How and why did these transformations in the organization of capital come about?*

3. The increase in the level of global economic integration. From your perspective as a merchant adventurer, you obviously want the fewest restraints possible on your ability to trade from one area of the world to another; the fewer restrictions, the greater the opportunity for profit. Such things as a global currency, agreement among nations on import and export regulations, ease of passage of money and goods from area to area, freedom to employ whom you want and to pay the lowest possible wage are all to your advantage; furthermore, you want few or no government restrictions regarding the consequences of your business activities. *How did the level of global*

---

[1]The name is taken from a sixteenth-century English trading company, The Merchant Adventurers, cloth wholesalers trading to Holland and Germany with bases of operation in Antwerp and Bergen-op-Zoom and later Hamburg. The company survived until 1809.

economic integration increase, and what were the consequences for the merchant adventurer, as well as others?

With these questions in mind, let's go back to the world of 1400 and start trading.

THE ERA OF THE GLOBAL TRADER

A Trader's Tour of the World in 1400

If, as global merchants in 1400, we were searching for ways to make money, the best opportunities would be in long-distance trade, buying goods in one area of the world and selling them in another (see Braudel 1982:68). If we could choose which among the great cities of the world—Cairo, Malacca, Samarkand, Venice—to begin trading, our choice would probably be Hangchow, China. China in 1400 had a population of 100 million and was the most technologically developed country in the world. Paper was invented in China probably as early as A.D. 700 and block printing as early as 1050. China of 1400 had a thriving iron industry; enormous amounts of coal were burned to fuel the iron furnaces, equal in northern China alone to 70 percent of what metalworkers in Great Britain used at the beginning of the eighteenth century. The explosive power of gunpowder was harnessed around A.D. 650 and by 1000 was used by Chinese armies for simple bombs and grenades.

The splendor and wealth of fifteenth- and sixteenth-century China is portrayed in this engraving of a mandarin's terrace and garden.

Cannons were in use by 1300, some mounted on the ships of the Chinese navy, and by the fourteenth century the Chinese were using a metaled-barreled gun that shot explosive pellets (Abu-Lughod 1989:322ff).

If you were to tour the Chinese countryside you would have been struck by the networks of canals and irrigation ditches that crisscrossed the landscape, maintained by wealthy landowners or the state. China was governed by a royal elite and administered largely by mandarins, people selected from the wealthy classes and who were exempt from paying taxes. State bureaucrats were also selected and promoted through civil service examinations open to all but those of the lowest rank of society (e.g., executioners, slaves, beggars, boat people, actors, laborers) (Hanson 1993:186). China produced some of the most desired trade goods in the world, particularly silk, spices, and porcelain.

The economic conditions in China also favored traders. There were guilds and associations of merchants, such as jewelers; gilders; antique dealers; dealers in honey, ginger, and boots; money changers; and doctors. China had its own currency system. In the Middle East and Europe governments issued money in the form of coins of precious metals whose value depended on their weight. In China there was not only copper coin but also paper money (cotton paper stamped with a government seal) to provide merchants with a convenient means of exchange. Paper money also allowed the state to control the flow of money in and out of the country. Precious metals, such as gold and silver, could not be used by foreigners in trade, so foreign traders were forced to exchange their gold or silver for paper money, which they then exchanged for gold and silver when they left. Because they had usually purchased Chinese commodities to sell elsewhere, they usually left with less gold and silver than when they arrived (Abu-Lughod 1989:334).

China was also politically stable. The rulers, members of the Ming Dynasty, had successfully rebelled against the Mongols in A.D. 1368. The Mongols, nomadic horsemen who roamed the vast steppes of Central Asia, conquered China in 1276 and set up their own dynasty, the Yuan. The Mongols, eager to establish trade with the rest of the world, had established relatively safe trade routes to the rest of Asia, the Middle East, and Europe. At least at first, the Ming appeared to want to maintain that trade, sending its impressive navy as emissaries to ports along the Indian Ocean.

The city of Hangchow was situated between the banks of the Che River leading to the sea and the shore of an enormous artificial lake. According to Ibn Battuta, an Arab trader who visited the city in the 1340s, the city extended more than six to seven square miles and was surrounded by walls with five gateways through which canals passed. Thirteen monumental gates at which its great thoroughfares terminated, provided entry to the city. Situated on the hills overlooking the city were the imperial palace and homes of the wealthy state bureaucrats and merchants; at the opposite end of the city were the houses of the poor—crowded, narrow-fronted, three- to five-story houses with workshops on the ground floors. The main thoroughfare, the Imperial Way, was three miles long and 180 feet wide, crowded with carriages drawn by men or tiny horses.

The city was a trader's paradise. Inside the city were ten markets as well as tea houses and restaurants where traders could meet and arrange their business. Outside the city were a fish market and wholesale markets. Ibn Battuta said it was "the largest city on the face of the earth." Sections of the city contained concentrations of merchants from all over the world. Jewish and Christian traders from Europe in one; Muslim traders in another, with bazaars and mosques, and muezzins calling Muslims to noon prayer. The bazaars of Chinese merchants and artisans were in yet another section. In brief, Hangchow would have been an ideal place to sell merchandise from Europe, the Middle East, or other parts of Asia and to purchase goods, such as spices and silks, that were in demand in other parts of the world.

Silk was particularly desired by foreign traders because its light weight and compactness made it easy to transport and because China had a virtual monopoly in the silk trade. Syrian traders had smuggled silk worms out of China in the thirteenth century, and in 1400 one could purchase silk in India and Italy; but, the quality of Chinese silk was superior. Because the production of silk was likely in the hands of Chinese merchants, you would have purchased it directly from them. You might also purchase Chinese porcelain, especially if you planned to travel by ship because porcelain could be used as ballast by ships returning to the Middle East or Europe (see Figure 3.1).

Your next task would be to arrange to transport your goods to where you planned to sell them. Let's assume you had orders from merchants in cities such as Venice, Cairo, and Bruges, where Chinese goods were in demand. Your first task is to get your goods to the Mediterranean. You could go overland through China, through central Asia to Northern India, or to ports on the Black Sea, then travel to European ports such as Venice and Naples. The trip overland through Asia to Europe would take you at least 275 days using pack trains—camels over the deserts, mules through the mountains, ox carts where roads ex-

FIGURE 3.1   Major Trade Routes in 1400

isted, human carriers, and boats. The overland route was popular in the thirteenth and four-teenth centuries, when the Mongols had, through their conquests, unified Central Asia and issued safe conduct passes to traders. In 1400, however, with the Empire fragmented, you may have risked raiding by nomadic bands of Mongol horsemen.

A safer route in 1400 would have been the sea route, down the East Coast of China, through the Strait of Malacca to Southern India, and then either through the Persian Gulf to Iran and overland, through Baghdad to the Mediterranean, or through the Red Sea to Cairo, and finally by ship to Italy.

Traveling through the Strait of Malacca and into Southeast Asia, you would have found powerful elites ruling states from their royal palaces, surrounded by armed retainers, kin, artisans, and specialists. Beyond this was a peasantry producing rice to support them-selves and the elites. These were the civilizations that built Angkor Thom and Angkor Wat in Cambodia. You would likely have been more at home, however, in the seaports that dotted the Strait of Malacca, which owed their existence to trade. Occasionally, these ports would merge with inland kingdoms such as Madjapahit in Java. The main city of the area in 1400 was Malacca, founded by pirates led in rebellion twenty years earlier by a prince from Madjapahit. The prince converted to Islam, attracting to Malacca wealthy Muslim merchants, and by 1400 Malacca was a city of 40,000 to 50,000 people with sixty-one na-tions represented in trade. The Portuguese Tomé Pires, writing a century later, said "Who-ever is lord of Malacca has his hands on the throat of Venice" (cited Wolf 1982:58). While in Malacca, you likely would have obtained additional trade goods to take West. Spices, particularly cinnamon (at one time in Egypt considered more valuable than gold), were highly valued because they were easy to transport and brought high profits in the Middle East and Europe.

From Malacca you probably would have traveled along the coast of Southeast Asia and on to India, whose wealth in 1400 rivaled that of China. Southeast India had a thriving textile industry. Farmers grew cotton and passed it on to spinners, who made thread for the weavers. There is some evidence that merchants provided cotton and thread to spinners and weavers and paid the artisans for what they produced. There was a sophisticated tech-nology: a vertical loom, block printing, and the spinning wheel, probably introduced from Turkey. But cotton and textiles were not the only items you might have obtained in India for trade; there were also dyes, tannins, spices, oil seed, narcotics, lumber, honey, and ivory (see Wolf 1982).

From India you might travel to East Africa, where from Bantu-speaking peoples you might have obtained slaves, ivory, leopard skins, gold from Zimbabwe, and rhinoceros horns (still believed in some parts of the world to be an aphrodisiac).

Leaving East Africa you would have journeyed up the coast through the Red Sea to Cairo or through the Persian Gulf, through Iraq to Baghdad, and on to Constantinople and the Eastern Mediterranean. You would have found the Islamic countries of the Middle East fa-vorable to business, with a sophisticated body of law regulating trade, including rules for the formation of trading partnerships and the extension of credit. One law allowed people to pay for merchandise at a later date at a higher price, a convenient way around the Islamic prohi-bition of lending money at interest. Bags of gold coin whose value was printed on the out-side, and whose contents were apparently never checked, served as money. There were bankers who changed money, took deposits, and issued promissory notes, another way of extending credit and making loans. Merchants kept their accounts by listing credits and debits. Thus, all the rudiments of a sophisticated economy—capital, credit, banking, money, and account keeping—were present in Islamic trade (Abu-Lughod 1989:216ff).

From Cairo you could join a caravan to go south through the Sahara to West Africa, where textile goods were in demand and where you might obtain slaves or gold. Virtually two-thirds of the gold circulating in Europe and the Middle East came from West Africa. Or you might travel a short way to Alexandria, still a major city. From there you would travel by ship on the Mediterranean to one of the city-states of Italy, such as Venice or Genoa. Italy was the center of European and Mediterranean trade. At European fairs Italian traders would set up a bench (*banco,* from which bank is derived) with their scales and coins, enabling traders to exchange currency from one area of the world for another. Italian bankers monopolized the international exchange of money and credit, and it was they who pioneered the *bill of exchange.* This was a document in which a buyer agreed to deliver payment to a seller at another time and place in the seller's home currency. In the absence of any widely recognized currency, the bill of exchange greatly facilitated foreign trade (Abu-Lughod 1989:93).

You might then join other merchants from Genoa, Pisa, and Milan who formed caravans to take goods, such as silks and spices, from the Orient or the Middle East; alum, wax, leather, and fur from Africa; dates, figs, and honey from Spain; and pepper, feathers, and brazilwood from the Middle East, over the Alps to the fairs and markets of Western and Northern Europe, a trip taking five weeks. Or you could send your goods by ship, through the Mediterranean and the North Sea to trading centers such as Bruges.

Once you reached Northern or Western Europe, you had already left the wealthiest part of the world. After the decline of the Roman Empire Western Europe was a backward area, exploited for its iron, lumber, and slaves. Urban areas had declined and artisan activity retreated to rural areas. Moreover, Europe had been devastated in the fourteenth century by bubonic plague: In the mid-fourteenth century Europe's population was about 80 million (Abu-Lughod 1989:94). By 1400 plague had reduced it by 45 percent, to 40 million to 50 million. The plague likely originated in Central Asia or China. It traveled the trade routes, striking Chinese cities as early as 1320 and first striking Europe in Caffa, on the Black Sea, in 1346. It arrived in Alexandria in 1347, probably from Italian ports on the Black Sea. At its height in Alexandria it killed 10,000 people a day, finally killing 200,000 of the city's half million people. It struck Italy in 1348, appeared in France and Britain the same year, and reached Germany and Scandinavia a year later.

Feudalism was still the main form of political and economic organization in Europe. Kings bestowed lands, or fiefs, to subjects in return for their loyalty and service. Lords "rented" land to peasants, generally for a share of the produce, which they used to pay tribute to the kings and to finance their own expenses.

Woolen textiles were the most important products of Northern and Western Europe in 1400. Flanders (Western Belgium and Northwest France), the textile center of Northern Europe, had virtually monopolized the purchase of raw wool from England, and woolen textiles from Flanders were in demand throughout Europe and in other parts of the world.

Let's assume you have sold the commodities you brought from China and realized a handsome profit. The question is *what to do with your capital and profits?* You might buy Flemish textiles in Bruges or, depending on the political circumstances, travel to England to buy textiles. You might buy land or finance other traders in return for a share of their profits. If, however, you decided to undergo another trade circuit, returning east would be your likely alternative. The Americas were probably unknown, and certainly unreachable. You might have traveled down the European coast to West Africa, where European textiles were in great demand and where you could obtain slaves and gold. But while the wind patterns of the Eastern Atlantic would have carried your ship to West Africa, they made it impossible, given the sailing technology, to return by sea, and you would be forced to return overland across Northern Africa. Your likely trade route, then, would have been back to Italy and east through the Mediterranean to India, the East Indies, and China.

What if you had been able to cross the sea to the Americas? What would you have found in 1400? No one left a written record of life in the New World just prior to the arrival of Europeans. Archaeologists, however, have created a record from what was left behind. You would have discovered elaborate trade routes extending from South America into North America and the remains of great civilizations in Central Mexico and the Yucatan Peninsula.

The Inca were just beginning their expansion, which would produce the Andean Empire confronted by Pizarro in 1532. Inca society in 1400 was dominated by the Inca dynasty, an aristocracy consisting of relatives of the ruling group, local rulers who submitted to Inca rule. Men of local rank headed endogamous patrilineal clans, or *ayllus,* groups who traced descent to a common male ancestor whose members were required to marry within their clan. These groups paid tribute to the Inca aristocracy by working on public projects or in military service. Women spent much of their time weaving cloth used to repay faithful subjects and imbued with extraordinary ritual and ceremonial value. The state expanded by colonizing new agricultural lands to grow maize. It maintained irrigation systems, roads, and a postal service in which runners carried information from one end of the empire to another. Groups that rebelled against Inca rule were usually relocated far from their homeland (Wolf 1982:62–63).

If you had traveled into the Brazilian rain forests you might have encountered peoples such as the Tupinambá, who lived on small garden plots while gathering and hunting in the forests. Sixteenth-century traveler Calvinist pastor Jean de Léry, concluded that the Tupinambá lived more comfortably than ordinary people in France (cited Maybury-Lewis 1997:13).

In Mexico in 1400 the Aztecs were twenty years from establishing their vast empire with its capital at Tenochtitlán. In the Caribbean there were complex chieftainships with linkages to the civilizations of Mesoamerica and the Andes. A merchant of 1400 would have been able to follow trade routes that spread from Mexico into the southeastern and northeastern United States, encountering descendants of those who archaeologists called the Mississippians. In this society goods and commodities were used to indicate status and rank. A trader would have encountered towns or ceremonial centers focused on great terraced, earthen platforms. The Mississippians relied on the cultivation of maize, beans, and squash, called "the three sisters" by the Iroquois. You might have met the Iroquois at the headwaters of the Ohio River, the Cherokee in the southern Appalachians, the Natchez on the lower Mississippi River, and the Pawnee and the Mandan on the Missouri River. On the surrounding prairies you would have encountered the peoples of the Northwest, the buffalo hunters of the plains (the horse, often associated with the Plains Indians, wouldn't arrive for another century) and the Inuit hunters of the Arctic and subarctic. These civilizations and cultures might, in later centuries, have provided a lucrative market for the sale and purchase of goods had not other events led to their devastation.

As we complete our global tour, the barriers to commerce are striking. For example, most political rulers were not yet committed to encouraging trade. Although states might value trade for the taxes, tolls, and rents they could extract from traders, merchants were still looked down on. Rulers generally viewed trade only as a way to gain profit from traders and merchants, and some states even attempted to control some trade themselves. In China, for example, trade in salt was monopolized by the government. Religious authorities in Europe, the Middle East, and China discouraged trade by extracting high taxes or forbidding loans at interest.

Geography was obviously a major barrier: Trade circuits might take years to complete. Roads were few and ships relatively small and at the mercy of winds and tides. Security was a problem: A merchants' goods were liable to be seized or stolen, or merchants might be forced to pay tribute to rulers along the way.

Economically, there were various restrictions. We were a long way in 1400 from anything resembling a consumer economy. Most of the world's population lived on a subsistence economy, that is, produced themselves whatever they needed to exist. In Europe, for example, where 90 percent of the population was rural, people might buy an iron plow, some pots, and textile products, but that was all. Consumers tended to be the urban dwellers, largely the clergy; aristocracy; and the small middle class consisting of artisans, merchants, and bureaucrats. Furthermore, if people wanted to buy more, there was virtually no currency with which to do it; even if all the gold and silver of Europe had been in circulation, it would have amounted to only about two dollars per person (Weatherford 1988:14).

Thus, overall the world of 1400 seemed little affected by trade. China and India were probably the richest countries in the world, and there is little doubt that royal rulers controlled most of the wealth, largely through the extraction of tribute from peasants, artisans, and traders. Much of this they redistributed in the form of gifts, feasts, and charity. Moreover, the people who worked the soil, as those who remained gathering and hunting at the fringes and outside the world system, had ready access to food. Though there is evidence of periodic famine in which thousands perished, it is unlikely that, as now, one-sixth of the world's population in 1400 was hungry. Thus, although a growing system of trade was beginning to link more of the world's people together, there had yet to develop the worldwide inequities that exist today. This, however, would rapidly begin to change over the next one hundred years.

The Economic Rise of Europe and Its Impact on Africa and the Americas

Two events dominate the story of the expansion of trade after 1400: the increased withdrawal of China from world trade networks and the voyage of Vasco da Gama around the southern tip of Africa. These events resulted in a shift in the balance of economic dominance from a country of 100 million occupying most of Asia to a country of 1 million occupying an area just slightly larger than the state of Maine.

The date and reason for China's withdrawal from its position of commercial dominance is something of a mystery and subject to considerable academic debate (see, e.g.,

Frank 1998; Landes 1998). The ruling dynasty moved the capital of China inland and allowed its powerful navy gradually to disintegrate. Regardless of the reasons for these actions, they resulted in a diminished role for China in global trade, and Portugal, with the most powerful navy in the world, was quick to fill the vacuum left by China in the East Indies. Portugal used its navy to dominate trade and supplemented trading activities with raiding (Abu-Lughod 1989:243).

Japan also took the opportunity after China's withdrawal to expand its trading activity in Southeast Asia. Japan, like England, was in the fifteenth century a feudal society divided into an upper nobility, the *daimyo,* or great lords; the *samurai,* vassals of the *daimyo;* and the *chonin,* or merchants, who were looked down on by the nobility. There was contact between Japan and Europe by the mid-sixteenth century, and Christian missionaries soon established themselves in Japan. But around 1500 Japan was involved in heavy trade with China, trading refined copper, sulfur, folding fans, painted scrolls, and, most important, swords. One trade expedition carried 10,000 swords to China and returned with strings of cash, raw silk, porcelains, paintings, medicines, and books. Thus in the fifteenth century, Japan was beginning economic expansion to areas vacated by China (Sanderson 1995:154).

Technological advances in boat building were partially responsible for Portugal's power. Around 1400 European boat builders combined the European square rigger with the lateen rig of the Arabs, the square rig giving ships speed when running and the lateen rig allowing the boat to sail closer to the wind. They also equipped their ships with cannons on the main deck and upper decks by cutting holes in the hull. The result was a speedy and maneuverable galleon, half warship and half merchantman (Wolf 1982:235).

Equally important for Portugal was location. Prior to the fifteenth century, Portugal was at the edge of the world system. The Mediterranean was controlled by the city-states of Italy and by Islamic powers. The Americas were seemingly out of reach, even if traders were aware of them. The west coast of Africa was inaccessible by boat unless one sailed south down the coast and returned overland. But once the route east to India and China was restricted, action shifted to the Atlantic, and as Africa and the Americas became readily accessible, Portugal was suddenly at the center of world trade.

It was the era of discovery and conquest, of the voyages of Columbus, of efforts to find alternative routes to China and the East Indies. Columbus believed he had discovered China or Ciangu (Japan), and as late as 1638 the fur trader Jean Nicolet, on meeting Winnebago Indians on the shores of Lake Michigan, wore a Chinese robe he brought to wear when meeting the Great Kahn of China (Wolf 1982:232).

Much is made in popular culture and history books of the spirit of adventure of early "explorers" such as Marco Polo, Vasco da Gama, and Christopher Columbus. But they were less explorers than merchant sailors. Their motivation was largely economic; they were seeking alternative ways to the riches of China and the East Indies. One might say that European economic domination, to the extent it was fueled by the wealth of the Americas, was due to the accidental discovery of two continents that happened to be in the way of their attempts to find alternative routes to China, Japan, and India.

If you were a global trader in the sixteenth century and if your starting point were Lisbon, Portugal, you had a choice of trade routes. You could go east to the Middle East, India, or Southeast Asia, all kept open to Portuguese traders by Portugal's navy. You could go south along the African coast, or follow Columbus's route to the New World. Or you could simply trade into the rest of Europe. All routes could prove profitable. In our reincarnation as a Portuguese trader, let's first go south to Africa.

Let's assume you have the capital to hire a ship to carry yourself and your goods to Africa. You would probably be carrying Mediterranean wine, iron weapons, perhaps horses, much in demand in Africa, and a consignment of textiles consisting perhaps of Egyptian linen and cotton. *What sort of commodities would you acquire in Africa for trade in Europe?*

Africans were already producing the same things as Europeans—iron and steel (possibly the best in the world at the time), elaborate textiles, and other goods. As a trader, you would have been interested in the textiles made in Africa, which were in demand in Europe. You would also have been anxious to trade in gold mined in West Africa, the source until that time of most of the gold in Europe and the Middle East. But your real interest would likely have been slaves.

The institution of slavery goes back well into antiquity. The ancient Greeks kept slaves, and slave labor was used throughout the Middle East and Europe in 1500. Moslems enslaved Christians, Christians enslaved Muslims, and Europeans enslaved Slavs and Greeks. Coal miners in Scotland were enslaved into the seventeenth and eighteenth centuries, and indentured servitude was widespread in Europe. However, there was about to be a huge surge in the demand for slave labor from the new colonies being established in the Americas.

The nature of the slave trade has long been a contentious issue among historians. Many believe the slave trade was forced on Africa, if not by direct military intervention then by economic extortion, Europeans offering guns and horses needed by rulers to maintain their authority in exchange for slaves. But there is increasing evidence that the slave trade was largely an African institution in which Europeans and others were only too happy to partake. Slavery in Africa was different from slavery in Europe, however, and different from what it was to become in the Americas.

Slaves were regarded traditionally in Africa as subordinate family members, as they were in Europe going back to Aristotle's time. Thus, slaves in Africa could be found doing any duties a subordinate family member might do. To understand the African institution of slavery it is also necessary to understand that among people in African states there was little notion of private property; for example, land was owned by "corporate kinship groups," networks of related individuals who together owned land in common. People were given the right to use land but not to own it. Slaves comprised the only form of private, revenue-producing property recognized in African law. Slaves could produce revenue because if you had the labor in the form of family members, wives, or slaves, you could claim the use of more land. African conceptions of property are reflected also in the fact that, whereas in Europe taxes were paid on land, in Africa taxes were paid on people, "by the head" (Thornton 1992).

The size of African states may have reflected the lack of concern with land as property. John Thornton (1992:106) estimated that only 30 percent of Atlantic Africa contained states larger than 50,000 square kilometers (roughly the size of New York state), and more than half the total area contained states of 500 to 1,000 square kilometers. Africans went to war generally not to acquire land, as in Europe, but to acquire slaves, with which more land could be worked.

Given these attitudes toward land and toward labor, there existed in Africa at the time of European arrival a large slave population and a thriving slave market. Slaves were a major form of investment; a wealthy African could not buy land but could acquire slaves and, as long as land was available, claim more land to use. Moreover, slaves, because they were property, could be inherited by individuals, whereas land, because it belonged to the corporate kin group, could not. Investing in slaves would have been the wealthy African's equivalent of a European investing in land, and if you were not using slaves, you could sell them (Thornton 1992:87). Thus European traders found ready sources of slaves, not because Africans were inveterate slave traders but because in Africa the legal basis for wealth revolved around the idea of transferring ownership of people (Thornton 1992:95).

Once you obtained the slaves, you might have obtained a special ship to transport them back to Europe or to one of the Atlantic Islands, where they were in demand as workers on the expanding sugar plantations. Sugar in the sixteenth century was still a luxury item, used by the wealthy to decorate food or as medicine. The primary areas of supply were around the Mediterranean—Egypt, Italy, Spain, and Greece. But with the opening of the Atlantic, sugar plantations were established first on the Canary Islands and the Azores and later in the Caribbean. Sugar production was a labor-intensive activity, and slaves from Africa supplied much of that labor. From 1451 to 1600 some 275,000 slaves were sent from West Africa to America and Europe. In the seventeenth and eighteenth centuries sugar would begin to play a major role in the world economy, but in the sixteenth century its possibilities were only beginning to be recognized.

Let's assume that after buying slaves in Africa and selling them in the new sugar plantations of the Azores, you resume your journey and go west to the Americas. The opening of the Americas brought into Portugal and Spain vast amounts of gold and silver plundered from the Inca and Aztec Empires and extracted from mines by slave and indentured labor. When Pizarro invaded Peru and seized Atahualpa in 1532, he demanded and received a ransom of a roomful of gold and killed the emperor anyway. When Cortes conquered the Aztec he demanded gold; after the Aztec's counterattack, Cortes's fleeing men carried so much loot that one-quarter drowned as they fell from a causeway into a lake, so burdened down were they by their cargo (Weatherford 1988:7).

At the time of the conquest of the Americas, there was approximately $200 million worth of gold and silver in Europe; by 1600 that had increased eight times. Some 180 to 200 tons of gold, with a contemporary value of $2.8 billion, flowed into Europe, much of it still visible in the robes, statuary, and sacred objects of European churches (Weatherford 1988:14).

Most of the silver came from San Luis Potosí. Cerro Rico ("rich hill" in Spanish), the mountain above Potosí in Bolivia, is the richest mountain ever discovered, virtually a mountain of silver. In 1545 slaves and indentured laborers recruited from the indigenous population began digging silver out of the mountain, forming it into bars and coins, and sending it to Spain. By 1603 there were 58,800 Indian workers in Potosí, 43,200 free day laborers, 10,500 contract laborers, and 5,100 labor draftees. By 1650, Potosí rivaled London and Paris in size, with a population of 160,000 (Wolf 1982:136).

The amount of currency in circulation worldwide increased enormously, enriching Europe but eroding the wealth of other areas, and helping Europe expand into an international market system. China reopened its trading links to Europe and took in so much silver that by the mid-eighteenth century its value had declined to one-fifth what it had been prior to the discovery of America. The gold from the Americas also had the effect of destroying the African gold trade (Weatherford 1988).

Gold and silver were not the only wealth extracted from the New World. Spain imported cochineal, a red dye made from insects (it took 70,000 dried insects to produce one pound of cochineal), indigo (blue dye), and cocoa. Portuguese traders established sugar plantations on the northeast coast of Brazil.

The cost of the European expansion of trade to the Americas, at least to the people of the Americas, was enormous. It resulted in the demographic collapse of the New World, what Eric Wolf called "the great dying" (1982:133).

There is broad disagreement about the population of the Americas at the time of the European conquest. Alfred E. Kroeber (1939), one of the founders of American anthropology, estimated that the total population of the Americas was about 8.4 million of which 900,000 were in North America. Harold Herbert Spinden, relying on archeological evidence, suggested there were 50 million to 75 million people in the Americas in A.D. 1200. Henry F. Dobyns (1983), working with archeological evidence, estimates of the carrying capacity of given environments, and historical documents, estimated 90 million to 112 million in the hemisphere and 12.5 million in the area north of Mexico. The disagreement reflected in these numbers is not unimportant, for it involves an important legal question: *Did the "discovery" of the New World permit Europeans to move on to unoccupied wilderness, or did they displace and destroy a settled indigenous population?* If the latter in the case, then European claims of legal ownership of the land based on the doctrine of *terra nullius*– land belonging to no one—would be legally invalid.

There is little doubt, we think, that the higher estimates are closer to the actual population of the Americas. In 1500, Europe, a fraction the size of the Americas, had a population of 45 million; France alone had a population of 20 million, and tiny Portugal 1 million. And this was after the bubonic plague epidemics. There seems little doubt that the environment and societies of the Americas were capable of supporting large populations. The peoples of the Americas built empires, palisaded settlements, temples, great pyramids, and irrigation complexes. There was certainly an adequate supply of foodstuffs to support a large population; most of our diet today comes from plants domesticated first in the New World, including corn, potatoes, sweet potatoes, tomatoes, squash, pumpkins, most varieties of beans, pepper (except black), amaranth, manioc, mustard, some types of rice, pecans, pineapples, bread fruit, passion fruit, melons, cranberries, blueberries, blackberries, coffee, vanilla, chocolate, and cocoa.

In 1496 Bartolomé Colón, Christopher's brother, authorized a headcount of adults of Española, the present day Haiti and Dominican Republic, then the most populous of the Caribbean Islands. The people of the island, the Tainos, created a culture that extended over most of the Caribbean. Colón arrived at a count of 1.1 million working adults; if we add children and the elderly, and consider that disease and murder had already diminished the population, there must have been at least 2 million and as many as 8 million on that island alone (Sale 1991:160–161). Thus, it is hardly unreasonable to suppose that the population of the Americas as a whole was upward of 50 million to 100 million people.

The scale of death after the arrival of the Europeans is difficult to conceive and rivals any estimate made for the demographic consequences of a nuclear holocaust today. When the

Spanish surveyed Española in 1508, 1510, 1514, and 1518, they found a population of under 100,000. The most detailed of the surveys, taken in 1514, listed only 22,000 adults, which anthropologists Sherburne Cook and Woodrow Borah estimated to represent a total population of 27,800 (Cook and Borah 1960). Thus, in slightly more than twenty years there was a decline from at least 2 million to 27,800 people. Bartolomé de Las Casas, the major chronicler of the effects of the Spanish invasion, said that by 1542 there were only 200 indigenous Tainos left, and within a decade they were extinct. Cook and Borah concluded that in Central America an estimated population of 25.3 million was reduced by 97 percent in a little more than a century. In all, it is estimated that 95 to 98 percent of the indigenous population of the Americas died as a consequence of European contact.

Many died in battles with the invaders; others were murdered by European occupiers desperate to maintain control over a threatening population; and still others died as a result of slavery and forced labor. But the vast majority died of diseases introduced by Europeans to which the indigenous peoples had no immunity.

The most deadly of the diseases was smallpox. It arrived sometime between 1520 and 1524 with a European soldier or sailor and quickly spread across the continent, ahead of the advancing Europeans. When Pizarro reached the Incas in 1532, his defeat of a divided empire was made possible by the death from smallpox of the ruler and the crown prince. When a Spanish expedition set out from Florida for the Pacific in 1535, they found evidence of the epidemic in West Texas. Dobyns (1983) assumed that virtually all the inhabitants of the hemisphere were exposed to smallpox during that one epidemic. *What would the mortality rate have been from this one pathogen alone?*

Dobyns (1983:13–14; see also Stiffarm and Lane 1992) estimated that in the epidemic of 1520–1524 virtually all indigenous peoples—certainly those in large population areas—would have been exposed to smallpox, and because there would have been no immunity, the death rate, judging by known death rates among other Native American populations, must have been at least 60 to 70 percent. Spanish reports of the time that half of the native population died, said Dobyns, most certainly were underestimates.

This, was not the only smallpox epidemic. Dobyns calculated that there were forty-one smallpox epidemics in North America from 1520 to 1899, seventeen measles epidemics from 1531 to 1892, ten major influenza epidemics from 1559 to 1918, and four plague epidemics from 1545 to 1707, to name a few. In all, he said, a serious epidemic invaded indigenous populations on average every four years and two and half months during the years 1520 to 1900.

Thus, the occupation of the New World by Europeans was not so much an act of conquest as it was an act of replacing a population ravaged by pathogens that Europeans carried with them. Depopulation was not the only consequence of the economic expansion of Europe into the Americas. The deaths of indigenous peoples proved a boon to the slave trade, as Europeans transported millions of Africans to the plantations and mines to replace the dying indigenous laborers. Much of the remaining native population gathered around mining communities and Spanish agricultural estates, providing a surplus labor supply, producing cheap crafts and agricultural products, and paying tribute and taxes to the colonizers (Wolf 1982:149). Their descendants today still suffer economic and social discrimination at the hands of descendants of European and indigenous unions.

In 1776, Adam Smith, in *The Wealth of Nations,* wrote, "The discovery of America, and that of a passage to the East Indies by the Cape of Good Hope, are the two greatest and most important events recorded in the history of mankind" (cited Crosby 1986:vii).

A decade later there was a debate among the savants of France over whether the discovery of the New World was a blessing or a curse. Abbé Guillaume Reynal, author of a four-volume study of trade between Europe and the East and West Indies, wrote a paper to answer this question. In it he listed the gains that Europe had received and discussed the costs to the peoples of Asia and the Americas. He concluded:

> Let us stop here, and consider ourselves as existing at the time when America and India were unknown. Let me suppose that I address myself to the most cruel of the Europeans in the following terms. There exist regions which will furnish you with rich metals, agreeable clothing, and delicious food. But read this history, and behold at what price the discovery is promised to you. Do you wish or not that it should be made? Is it to be imagined that there exists a being infernal enough to answer this question in the affirmative! Let it be remembered that there will not be a single instant in futurity when my question will not have the same force. (cited Sale 1991:366–367)

The Rise of the Trading Companies

The expansion of trade into the Americas marked an important development in the control of global trade and commerce: States began to take a much more direct interest in commerce within their borders. For example, states controlled much of the trade with the Americas. Each year two fleets of the Spanish Crown would leave from Cadiz or Seville carrying European goods, one landing at Vera Cruz and the other, with goods bound for Peru, landing at Cartagena or Portobelo in Panama. From there mules carried the goods into the Andes, returning with silver and American goods for shipment home. The two fleets converged in Havana before returning to Spain (Wolf 1982:149).

The seventeenth century marked the era of what economists call *mercantilism,* as European states did all they could to protect, encourage, and expand industry and trade, not for its own sake but to prevent wealth, largely in the form of gold and silver, from leaving their countries. States enacted protective legislation to keep out foreign goods and to prevent gold and silver from leaving, and they subsidized the growth of selected industries by ensuring the existence of a cheap labor supply. Also during the seventeenth century the so-called trading or joint stock company evolved, a joining of trade and armed force designed to ensure the continued extraction of wealth from areas around the world.

As a global merchant in 1700 your best chance of making profits would have been to join a trading company, by far the most sophisticated instrument of state-sponsored trade. The companies consisted of groups of traders, each of whom invested a certain amount of capital and were given charters by the state and presented with monopolistic trade privileges in a particular area of the world. Because other countries also gave monopolistic trading privileges to their companies, there was often armed conflict between them. For example, in 1600 the British crown issued a royal charter to the governor and the Company of Merchants of London trading with the East Indies, later known simply as the British East India Company. The company was formed to share in the East Indian spice trade but met with resistance from the Dutch, who in 1602 formed the Dutch East India Company to monopolize Asian trade.

The Dutch maintained political control over its posts in India with an army of 10,000 to 12,000 troops and a navy of forty to sixty ships. The company brought 10 million to 12 million florins worth of goods to Europe each year, producing a profit of 25 to 30 percent (Braudel 1982). In 1623 the Dutch authorities in what is now Ambon, Indonesia, executed ten Englishmen, ten Japanese, and one Portuguese, believing that the English planned to attack the Dutch garrison when their ships arrived. In India, however, the British East India Company defeated Portuguese troops and gained trading concessions from the Mughal Empire. The British East India Company gradually extended its trade into Southeast Asia. In 1757 it defeated Indian troops and took control of all of Bengal, looting the Bengal treasury of some £5 million. Eventually its control expanded to most of India, and it became the managing agency for the British colonization of India.

Other trading companies granted charters by the British state include the Virginia Company in 1606, the English Amazon Company in 1619, the Massachusetts Company in 1629, the Royal Adventurers into Africa in 1660, and the Hudson's Bay Company in 1670.

The Dutch were initially best able to exploit the new developments in trade, largely because of their large merchant fleet and the development of the *fluitschip,* a light and slender vessel that carried heavy cargoes. The availability of funds in financial centers such as Antwerp and Amsterdam, much of it originating in the gold and silver of the Americas, allowed builders to get the best woods and best artisans and employ foreign sailors. Gradually, however, England and its navy gained, and the English trading companies soon dominated world trade.

As a merchant adventurer in the first part of the eighteenth century you may have joined the Virginia Company and established a trading post, or "factory," in southern Appalachia, probably in a Cherokee village. The Cherokee were necessary to supply the commodities you would want to acquire for trade, items such as deerskins, ginseng and other herbs in demand in Europe as aphrodisiacs and cures for venereal disease, and war captives that you could sell as slaves. In exchange, you would supply the Cherokee with European goods such as guns, ammunition, iron utensils, and European clothing. Your normal business practice would be to advance these goods to the Cherokee, thus obligating them to repay you. But to succeed in making a profit, you would need the cooperation of the Cherokee. This is where the British government came in.

Prior to European contact the Cherokee lived in large towns in which land was owned communally, and subsistence activities consisted of hunting, fishing, gathering, and agriculture. The Cherokee population had been decimated by disease by the early eighteenth century, but they still retained most of their traditional culture. For example, Cherokee villages were relatively independent from each other, each having its own leaders and each relatively self-sufficient in food and production of necessities, such as clothing, weapons, and cooking utensils. The independence of village leaders, however, made it difficult for the British government and traders to deal with the Cherokee. If there were overall leaders who could make agreements binding on large groups, with whom government and merchants could deal, it would be far easier to make treaties, collect trade debts, and engineer political alliances (Dunaway 1996:31). Consequently, using their military power and the threat of withdrawing trade, the British government appointed chiefs who they recognized as having the power to make agreements binding on the entire Cherokee nation regardless of whether their autonomy was recognized by other Cherokee. The British government also encouraged conflict between indigenous groups, reasoning, as the South

Carolina governor reported in the 1730s, "…for in that consists our safety, being at War with one another prevents them from uniting against us" (Dunaway 1996:28).

Thus merchants, such as yourself, along with the Cherokee, became integrated into a global trade network in which slaves and deerskins were sent through Charleston, Virginia, to England, the northern colonies, and the West Indies. In return, Charleston received sugar and tobacco from the West Indies and rum from the northern colonies that was manufactured from molasses from the West Indies, which the northern colonies acquired in exchange for lumber and other provisions. In exchange for the deerskins sent to England, Charleston received goods manufactured in England, such as woolens, clothing, guns, and iron tools. The deerskins were converted in England into leather goods, which merchants in England traded for raw materials, luxury goods, and meat provisions from all over the world (Dunaway 1996:34).

For traders, these arrangements worked very well: By 1710 as many as 12,000 Indians had been exported as slaves and by 1730 some 255,000 deerskins were being shipped annually from British trading posts to England and other parts of the world (Dunaway 1996:32). Furthermore, with the help of the British military strength and diplomacy, traders were making a 500 to 600 percent profit on goods advanced to the Cherokee in exchange for deerskins, slaves, and herbs.

But what of the Cherokee? By becoming integrated into the global economy on terms dictated by British government officials and traders, the Cherokee economy was transformed from self-sufficient agricultural production to a "putting-out" system in which they were given the tools for production (e.g., guns) along with an advance of goods in exchange for their labor—an arrangement that destroyed traditional activities and stimulated debt peonage. To pay off debts accumulated to acquire European goods, communal Cherokee land was sold by chiefs appointed by the British: In little more than fifty years the British extinguished title to about 57 percent of the Cherokee traditional land (some 43.9 million acres).

In addition, the new economy brought profound changes in Cherokee social life. Trade was male oriented, men being responsible for acquiring the items—slaves and deer—desired by the British. This removed men from traditional agricultural activities as well as incapacitating them with rum (Dunaway 1996:37). By the mid-1700s, British observers noted that "women alone do all the laborious tasks of agriculture," freeing men to hunt or go to war.

Furthermore, traditional crafts deteriorated with the increased consumption of European goods, such as guns, axes, knives, beads, pottery, clothing, and cooking utensils. By the mid-1700s the British could report that "the Indians by reason of our supplying them so cheap with every sort of goods, have forgotten the chief part of their ancient mechanical skill, so as not to be able now, at least for some years, to live independent from us" (Dunaway 1996:38). In 1751, the Cherokee chief Skiagonota would observe that "the clothes we wear we cannot make ourselves. They are made for us. We use their ammunition with which to kill deer. We cannot make our guns. Every necessity of life we have from the white people" (cited Dunaway 1996:39).

THE ERA OF THE INDUSTRIALIST

By 1800, England had militarily, politically, and economically subdued her closest rivals of the early eighteenth century—France and Holland. British commerce thrived, fueled largely by the growth of industry, particularly textiles, and the related increase in the availability of cheap labor. And although Britain lost her American colonies—politically if not economically—she gained in many ways a wealthier prize—India.

But the big news was the industrial development of England. From 1730 to 1760 iron production increased 50 percent; the first iron bridge was built in 1779 and the first iron boat in 1787. In 1783 Watt produced the double-effect steam engine. From 1740 to 1770 consumption of cotton rose 117 percent, and by 1800 mechanized factories were producing textiles at an unprecedented rate.

Social scientists often pose the related questions, *what made England take off? and why was there an industrial revolution at all?* These are more than academic questions. As planners in so-called economically undeveloped countries attempt to improve peoples' lives through economic development, they often look to the history of Great Britain to discover the key ingredients to economic success. England became, to a great extent, the model for economic development, the epitome of progress, so it was believed, particularly in Great Britain.

The reasons for the industrial revolution in England and the emergence of the capitalist economy are varied, and although analysts disagree on which were the most important, there is general agreement on those that played some part. They include the following (see Wallerstein 1989:22–34).

1. An increase in demand for goods. This demand may have been foreign or domestic, supplemented by increased demands for largely military products from the state. The textile industry was revolutionary also in its organization of labor and its relationship to the foreign market, on which it depended for both raw materials (in the case of cotton) and markets. Historian Eric Hobsbawm argued that there was room for only one world supplier, and that ended up being England.

2. The increase in the supply of capital. An increase in trade resulted in greater profits and more money, and these profits supplied the capital for investment in new technologies and businesses.

3. A growth in population. Population increased dramatically in England and Europe in the eighteenth century. From 1550 to 1680 the population of Western Europe grew by 18 percent, and from 1680 to 1820 by 62 percent. From 1750 to 1850 England's population increased from 5.7 million to 16.5 million. Population increase was important because it increased the potential labor force and the number of potential consumers of commodities. But there is disagreement as to why population increased and the effects it had on industrialization.

Some account for the increase with lower mortality rates attributable to smallpox inoculation and an improved diet related to the introduction of new foodstuffs, such as the potato. Life expectancy at birth went from thirty-five to forty years (Guttmann 1988:130). Others attribute the rise in population to an increase in fertility. Indeed, families were larger in the eighteenth century. In England between 1680 and 1820 the gross reproduction rate (number of females born to each woman) went from two to nearly three and the average number of children per family from four to almost six. Later we examine the relationship of population growth to industrialization because it is key to understanding the rapid growth of population today.

4. An expansion of agriculture. There was an expansion of agricultural production in England in the eighteenth century that some attribute to enclosure laws. These laws drove squatters and peasants from common lands and forests from which they had drawn a livelihood. The rationale was to turn those lands over to the gentry to make them more productive, but this also had the effect of producing a larger landless and propertyless population, dependent on whatever wage labor they might find. Regardless, some argue that the increased agricultural yields allowed the maintenance of a larger urban workforce.

5. A unique English culture or spirit. Some, notably sociologist Max Weber (1958), attribute the rise of England to the development of an entrepreneurial spirit, such as the Protestant ethic, that motivated people to business success in the belief that it would reveal to them whether they were among God's elect.

6. State support for trade. Some claim that a more liberal state structure imposed fewer taxes and regulations on businesses, thus allowing them to thrive. The state did take action to support trade and industry. There was continued political and military support for extending Britain's economy overseas, along with domestic legislation to protect merchants from labor protest. A law of 1769 made the destruction of machines and the buildings that housed them a capital crime. Troops were sent to put down labor riots in Lancaster in 1779 and in Yorkshire in 1796, and a law passed in 1799 outlawed worker associations that sought wage increases, reduction in the working day, "or any other improvement in the conditions of employment or work" (Beaud 1983:67).

7. The ascendance of the merchant class. Stephen Sanderson (1995) attributed the development of capitalism to an increase in the power of the merchant class. There has always been, he suggested, competition between merchants and the ruling elites, and although elites needed merchants to supply desired goods and services, they nevertheless looked down on them. But gradually the economic power of the merchant class grew until, in the seventeenth and eighteenth centuries, the merchant emerged as the most powerful member of Western, capitalist society. Capitalism, said Sanderson (1995:175–176), "was born of a class struggle. However, it was not, as the Marxists would have it, a struggle between landlords and peasants. Rather, it was a struggle between the landlord class and the merchants that was fundamental in the rise of capitalism."

8. A revolution in consumption. Finally, some attribute the rapid economic growth in England to a revolution in the patterns of retailing and consumption. There was a growth in the number of stores and shops and the beginning of a marketing revolution, led by the pottery industry and the entrepreneurial genius of Josiah Wedgewood, who named his pottery styles after members of the Royal Family to appeal to the fashion consciousness of the rising middle class.

Regardless of the reasons for England's rise and the so-called industrial revolution, there is little doubt that in addition to the traditional means of accumulating wealth—mercantile trade, extracting the surplus from peasant labor, pillage, forced labor, slavery, and taxes—a new form of capital formation increased in importance. It involved purchasing and combining the means of production and labor power to produce commodities, the form of wealth formation called capitalism that we diagrammed earlier as follows: $M \rightarrow C \rightarrow \frac{mp}{lp} \rightarrow C' \rightarrow M$ [money is converted to commodities (capital goods) that are combined with the means of production and labor power to produce other commodities (consumer goods), that are then sold for a sum greater than the initial investment]. *How did this mode of production differ from what went before?*

Eric Wolf offered one of the more concise views. For capitalism to exist, he said, wealth or money must be able to purchase labor power. But as long as people have access to the means of production—land, raw materials, tools (e.g., weaving looms, mills)—there is no reason for them to sell their labor. They can still sell the product of their labor. For the capitalistic mode of production to exist, the tie between producers and the means of production must be cut; peasants must lose control of their land, artisans control of their tools. These people, once denied access to the means of production, must negotiate with those who control the means of production for permission to use the land and tools and receive a wage in return. Those who control the means of production also control the goods that are produced, and so those who labor to produce them must buy them back from those with the means of production. Thus the severing of persons from the means of production turns them not only into laborers but into consumers of the product of their labor as well. Here is how Wolf (1982:78–79) summarized it:

> Wealth in the hands of holders of wealth is not capital until it controls means of production, buys labor power, and puts it to work continuously expanding surpluses by intensifying production through an ever-rising curve of technological inputs. To this end capitalism must lay hold of production, must invade the productive process and ceaselessly alter the conditions of production themselves.... Only where wealth has laid hold of the conditions of production in ways specified can we speak of the existence or dominance of a capitalistic mode. There is no such thing as mercantile of merchant capitalism, therefore. There is only mercantile wealth. Capitalism, to be capitalism, must be capitalism-in-production.

Wolf (1982:100) added that the state is central in developing the capitalist mode of production because it must use its power to maintain and guarantee the ownership of the means of production by capitalists both at home and abroad and must support the organization and discipline of work. The state also has to provide the infrastructure, such as transportation, communication, judicial system, and education, required by capitalist production. Finally, the state must regulate conflicts between competing capitalists both at home and abroad, by diplomacy if possible, by war if necessary.

The major questions are *how did this industrially driven, capitalist mode of production evolve, and what consequences did it have in England, Europe, and the rest of the world?*

Textiles and the Rise of the Factory System

Assume once again your role as a textile merchant; let's examine the opportunities and problems confronting you as you conduct business. Typical textile merchants of the early eighteenth century purchased their wares from specialized weavers or part-time producers of cloth or from drapers, persons who organized the production of cloth but did not trade in it. The merchant then sold the cloth to a consumer or another merchant who sold it in other areas of Europe or elsewhere. The profit came from the difference between what the merchant paid the artisan or draper and what the customer paid. This is not a bad arrangement.

It does not require a large capital outlay for the merchant because the artisan has the tools and material he or she needs, and as long as there is a demand for the cloth, there is someone who will buy it.

But as a merchant you face a couple of problems. First, the people who make the cloth you buy may not produce the quantity or quality that you need, especially as an expanding population begins to require more textiles. Moreover, the artisan may have trouble acquiring raw materials, such as wool or cotton, further disrupting the supply. What can you do?

One thing to do is to increase control over what is produced by "putting out"—supplying the drapers or weavers with the raw materials to produce the cloth—or, if you have the capital, buy tools—looms, spinning wheels, and so on—and give them to people to make the cloth, paying them for what they produce. Cottage industry of this sort was widespread throughout Europe as merchants began to take advantage of the cheaper labor in rural areas, rather than purchasing products from artisans in towns and cities. In England of the mid-eighteenth century there was probably plenty of labor, especially in rural areas, supplied by people who had been put off their land by enclosure legislation or because of failure to pay taxes or repay loans. In the land market of the eighteenth century, there were far more sellers than buyers (Guttmann 1988).

Another problem English textile merchants faced in the mid-eighteenth century was that the textile business, especially in cotton, faced stiff competition from India, whose calico cloth was extremely popular in England. How do you meet this competition? The first thing England did was to ban the import of Indian cloth and develop its own cotton industry to satisfy domestic demand. This not only helped protect the British textile industry but it also virtually destroyed the Indian cotton industry, and before long India was buying British cotton textiles. The result was summed up in 1830 in testimony before the House of Commons by Charles Marjoribanks (cited Wallerstein 1989:150):

> We have excluded the manufactures of India from England by high prohibitive duties and given every encouragement to the introduction of our own manufactures to India. By our selfish (I use the word invidiously) policy we have beat down the native manufactures of Dacca and other places and inundated their country with our goods.

And in 1840, the chairman of Britain's East India and China association boasted

> that This Company has, in various ways, encouraged and assisted by our great manufacturing ingenuity and skill, succeeded in converting India from a manufacturing country into a country exporting raw materials. (cited Wallerstein 1989:150)

The next, and to some extent inevitable, stage in textile production was to bring together in one place—the factory—as many of the textiles production phases as possible: preparing the raw wool or cotton, spinning the cotton yarn and wool, weaving the cloth, and applying the finishing touches. This allowed the merchant or industrialist to control the quantity and quality of the product and control the use of materials and tools. The only drawback to the factory system is that it is capital intensive; the merchant was now responsible for financing the entire process, whereas the workers supplied only their labor. Most of the increase in cost was a consequence of increased mechanization.

Mechanization of the textile industry began with the invention by John Kay in 1733 of the flying shuttle, a device that allowed the weaver to strike the shuttle carrying the

Power loom weaving in a cotton textile factory in 1834. Note that virtually all the workers are women.

thread from one side of the loom to the other, rather than weaving it through by hand. This greatly speeded up the weaving process. However, when demand for textiles, particularly cotton, increased, the spinning of thread, still done on spinning wheels or spindles, could not keep up with weavers, and bottlenecks developed in production. To meet this need James Hargreaves introduced the spinning jenny in 1770. Later, Arkwright introduced the water frame, and in 1779 Crompton introduced his "mule" that allowed a single operator to work more than 1,000 spindles at once. In 1790 steam power was supplied. These technological developments increased textiles production enormously: The mechanical advantage of the earliest spinning jennies to hand spinning was twenty-four to one. The spinning wheel had become an antique in a decade (Landes 1969:85). The increase in the supply of yarn—twelve times as much cotton was consumed in 1800 than in 1770—required improvements in weaving, which then required more yarn, and so on.

The revolution in production, however, produced other problems. *Who was going to buy the increasing quantity of goods that were being produced, and from where was the raw material for production to come?*

The Age of Imperialism

The results of the industrial revolution in Europe were impressive. The period from 1800 to 1900 was perhaps one of the most dynamic in human history and, certainly until that time, the most favorable for accumulation of vast fortunes through trade and manufacture.

Developments in transportation, such as railroads and steamships, revolutionized the transport of raw materials and finished commodities. The combination of new sources of power in water and steam, a disarmed and plentiful labor force, and control of the production and markets of much of the rest of the world resulted in dramatic increases in the level of production and wealth. These advances were most dramatic in England and later in the United States, France, and Germany. In England, for example, spun cotton increased from 250 million pounds in 1830 to 1,101 million pounds in 1870. World steam power production went from 4 million horsepower in 1850 to 18.5 million horsepower twenty years later; coal production went from 15 million tons in 1800 to 132 million tons in 1860, and 701 million tons in 1900. The consumption of inanimate energy from coal, lignite, petroleum, natural gasoline, natural gas, and water power increased sixfold from 1860 to 1900; railway trackage went from 332 kilometers in 1831 to 300,000 kilometers in 1876. The Krupp ironworks in Germany employed 72 workers in 1848; there were 12,000 by 1873.

There was also a revolution in shipping as ocean freight costs fell, first with the advent of the narrow-beamed American clipper ship and later with the introduction of the steamship. A clipper ship could carry 1,000 tons of freight and make the journey from the south coast of China to London in 120 to 130 days; in 1865 a steamship from the Blue Funnel Line with a capacity of 3,000 tons made the journey in 77 days. The construction of the Suez Canal, completed in 1869 with the labor of 20,000 conscripted Egyptian *fellaheen,* or peasants, cut the travel time from England to eastern Asia in half—although it bankrupted the Egyptian treasury and put the country under Anglo-French receivership. These events initiated a military revolt that the British stepped in to put down, consequently cementing the British hold on Egypt and much of the Middle East. Politically, the United States emerged as a world power, and Japan was building its economy and would be ready to challenge Russia. The Ottoman Empire was on its way to disintegrating as France, England, and Russia sought to gain control over the remnants.

But it was not all good news for the capitalist economy. There was organized worker resistance to low wages and impoverished conditions, resistance and rebellion in the periphery, and the development of capitalist business cycles that led to worldwide economic depressions. Thus, although business thrived in much of the nineteenth century, it had also entered a world of great uncertainty. First, with the expansion of the scope of production, capital investments had increased enormously. It was no longer possible, as it had been in 1800 when a forty-spindle jenny cost six pounds, to invest in the factory production of textiles at fairly modest levels. Furthermore, there was increased competition, with factory production expanding dramatically in Holland, France, Germany, and the United States. There was the constant problem of overproduction, when supply outstripped demand and resulted in idle factories and unemployed workers. Unlike agricultural production—there seemed always to be a market for food—industrial production depends on the revolution in demand or, as Anne-Robert-Jacque Turgot put it, "a transformation of desires" (cited in Braudel 1982:183). Until the eighteenth century manufacturers launched their enterprises only when profit was guaranteed by subsidies, interest-free loans, and previously guaranteed monopolies. Now manufacturers simply had to hope people would buy their products.

The Great Global Depression of 1873 that lasted essentially until 1895 was the first great manifestation of the capitalist business crisis. The depression was not the first economic crisis: For thousands of years there had been economic declines because of famine, war, and disease. But the financial collapse of 1873 revealed the degree of global economic integration, and how economic events in one part of the globe could reverberate in others. The economic depression began when banks failed in Germany and Austria because of the collapse of real estate speculation. At the same time, the price of cast iron in England fell by 27 percent because of a drop in demand. The drop in iron prices increased British unemployment, while European investors, needing to cover their losses from real estate, withdrew their money from American banks. This led to bank collapses in the United States. In England from 1872 to 1875, exports fell by 25 percent, the number of bankruptcies increased, and rail prices fell by 60 percent. In France, the Lyon stock market crashed in 1882; bank failures and rising unemployment followed. Competition among railroads decreased profits and led to the collapse of railroad securities in the United States (Beaud 1983:119–120; see also Guttmann 1994).

The depression of 1873 revealed another big problem with capitalist expansion and perpetual growth: It can continue only as long as there is a ready supply of raw materials and an increasing demand for goods, along with ways to invest profits and capital. Given this situation, *if you were an American or European investor in 1873, where would you look for economic expansion?*

The obvious answer was to extend European and American power overseas, particularly into areas that remained relatively untouched by capitalist expansion—Africa, Asia, and the Pacific. Colonialism had become, in fact, a recognized solution to the need to expand markets, increase opportunities for investors, and ensure the supply of raw material. Cecil Rhodes, one of the great figures of England's colonization of Africa, recognized also the importance of overseas expansion for maintaining peace at home. In 1895 Rhodes said

> I was in the East End of London yesterday and attended a meeting of the unemployed. I listened to the wild speeches, which were just a cry for "bread," "bread," and on my way home I pondered over the scene and I became more than ever convinced of the importance of imperialism.... My cherished idea is a solution for the social problem, i.e., in order to save the 40,000,000 inhabitants of the United Kingdom from a bloody civil war, we colonial statesmen must acquire new lands for settling the surplus population, to provide new markets for the goods produced in the factories and mines. The Empire, as I have always said, is a bread and butter question. If you want to avoid civil war, you must become imperialists. (cited Beaud 1983:139–140)

P. Leroy-Beaulieu voiced the same sentiments in France when, to justify the conquest of foreign nations, he said

> It is neither natural nor just that the civilized people of the West should be indefinitely crowded together and stifled in the restricted spaces that were their first homes, that they should accumulate there the wonders of science, art, and civilization, that they should see, for lack of profitable jobs, the interest rate of capital fall further every day for them, and that they should leave perhaps half the world to small groups of ignorant men, who are powerless, who are truly retarded children dispersed over boundless territories, or else to decrepit populations without energy and without direction, truly old men incapable of any effort, of any organized and far-seeing action. (cited Beaud 1983: 140)

As a result of this cry for imperialist expansion, people all over the world were converted into producers of export crops as millions of subsistence farmers were forced to become wage laborers producing for the market and to purchase from European and American merchants and industrialists, rather than supply for themselves, their basic needs. Nineteenth-century British economist William Stanley Jevons (cited Kennedy 1993:9) summed up the situation when he boasted:

> The plains of North America and Russia are our cornfields; Chicago and Odessa our granaries; Canada and the Baltic are our timber forests; Australasia contains our sheep farms, and in Argentina and on the western prairies of North America are our herds of oxen; Peru sends her silver, and the gold of South Africa and Australia flows to London; the Hindus and the Chinese grow tea for us, and our coffee, sugar, and spice plantations are all in the Indies. Spain and France are our vineyards and the Mediterranean our fruit garden, and our cotton grounds, which for long have occupied the Southern United States are now being extended everywhere in the warm regions of the earth.

Wheat became the great export crop of Russia, Argentina, and the United States, much of it produced in the United States on lands taken from the Native Americans. Rice became the great export of Southeast Asia, spurred by Great Britain's seizure of lower Burma in 1855 and its increase in rice production from 1 million to 9 million acres. Argentina and Australia joined the United States as the major supplier of meat as cattle ranchers in Australia and the United States turned indigenous peoples into hired hands or hunted them to extermination, as did the ranchers in California into the late nineteenth century (see Meggitt 1962).

In 1871 a railroad promoter from the United States built a railroad in Costa Rica and experimented in banana production; out of this emerged in 1889 the United Fruit Company that within thirty-five years was producing 2 billion bunches of bananas. The company reduced its risk by expanding into different countries and different environments and by acquiring far more land than it could use at any one time as a reserve against the future.

The demand for rubber that followed the discovery of vulcanization in 1839 led to foreign investments in areas such as Brazil, where one major supplier increased production from 27 tons in 1827 to an average of 20,000 tons per year at the end of the nineteenth century. The laborers who collected the rubber were workers who had lost their jobs with the decline in the sugar industries and Indians, who were sometimes held captive or tortured or killed if they didn't collect their quota of rubber, or whose wives and children would be killed if they didn't return (Taussig 1987).

In the nineteenth century palm oil became a substitute for tallow for making soap and a lubricant for machinery, resulting in European military expansion into West Africa and the conquest of the kingdoms of Asante, Dahomey, Oyo, and Benin.

Vast territories were turned over to the production of stimulants and drugs, such as sugar, tea, coffee, tobacco, opium, and cocoa. In the Mexican state of Chiapas and in Guatemala, legislation abolished communal ownership of land. Land could now be privately owned and subject to purchase, sale, and pawning, allowing non-Indians to buy unregistered land and foreclose mortgages on Indian borrowers (Wolf 1982:337). These lands were then turned to coffee production and, later, cattle ranching. In Ceylon, common land was turned into royal land and sold to tea planters. In 1866 diamonds and gold were discovered in the Orange Free State of West Africa. By 1874, 10,000 Africans were working in the European-owned diamond mines and by 1884 almost 100,000 were working in the gold mines. By 1910, 255,000 were working the mines, and by 1940 there were 444,000.

Colonization was not restricted to overseas areas; it occurred also within the borders of core states. In 1887 the U.S. Congress passed the General Allotment Act (the "Dawes Act") to break up the collective ownership of land on Native American reservations by assigning each family its own parcel, then opening unallotted land to non–Native American homesteaders, corporations, and the federal government. As a consequence, from 1887 to 1934 some 100 million acres of land assigned by treaty to Native American groups was appropriated by private interests or the government (Jaimes 1992:126).

At first glance it may seem that the growth in development of export, goods such as coffee, cotton, sugar, and lumber, would be beneficial to the exporting country because it brings in revenue. In fact, it represents a type of exploitation called *unequal exchange*. A country that exports raw or unprocessed materials may gain currency for their sale, but they then lose it if they import processed goods. The reason is that processed goods— goods that require additional labor—are more costly. Thus, a country that exports lumber but does not have the capacity to process it must then re-import it in the form of finished lumber products, at a cost that is greater than the price it received for the raw product. The country that processes the materials gets the added revenue contributed by its laborers.

Then there is the story of tea and opium and trade in China. China, of course, was a huge prize, but the British and Western European nations had a problem with trade into China: Chinese products, notably tea, were in high demand, but there was little produced in England or the rest of Europe that the Chinese wanted or needed. However, there was a market in China for opium, virtually all of which was produced and controlled by the British East India Company. Opium was illegal in China, but the government seemed incapable of stopping the smuggling that was hugely profitable for British, American, and French merchants. When, in 1839, the Chinese government tried to enforce laws against opium sales by seizing opium held by British merchants in warehouses in Canton, the British government sent in troops and effectively forced the Chinese government to stop enforcing opium laws. An analogy today might be the Colombian government sending troops to the United States to force acceptance of Colombian cocaine shipments. Moreover, using its military superiority, the British demanded and received additional trading rights into China, opening a market not only for opium but for British textiles as well.

The British-led opium trade from India to China had three consequences. First, it reversed the flow of money between China and the rest of the world; during the first decade of the nineteenth century, China still took in a surplus of $26 million dollars; by the third decade $34 million dollars left China to pay for opium. Second, it is estimated that by the end of the nineteenth century one out of every ten Chinese had become an opium addict. Finally, cotton exports to India and China had increased from 6 percent of total British exports in 1815 to 22 percent in 1840, 31 percent in 1850, and more than 50 percent after 1873 (Wolf 1982:255ff).

Thus, as a merchant adventurer, your economic fortune has been assured by your government's control over foreign economies. Not only could you make more money investing in foreign enterprises but also the wealth you accumulated through trade and manufacturing gained you entry into a new elite, one with increasing power in the core countries. Power was no longer evidenced solely in the ownership of land but in the control of capital. In England, for example, the great families of high finance and international trade, businesspeople, manufacturers, shipowners, bankers, parliamentarians, jurists, families of the aristocracy and gentry, all crisscrossed by ties of marriage and kinship, became the new ruling class. This new elite depended for their economic power on business and industry to a great extent: In the eighteenth century landed inheritance accounted for 63.7 percent of national wealth in Great Britain; toward the end of the nineteenth century that figure had decreased to 23.3 percent. Meanwhile, during the same period, wealth linked to capitalist development increased from 20.8 percent to almost 50.0 percent.

In the United States a new capitalist elite emerged during and after the Civil War, as people such as J. P. Morgan, Jay Gould, Jim Fisk, Cornelius Vanderbilt, and John D. Rockefeller—most of whom made their fortunes in dealings with the U.S. government—emerged as a new bourgeoisie. More importantly, they were the driving force behind the emergence of a relatively new form of capital organization—the multinational corporation.

THE ERA OF THE CORPORATION, THE MULTILATERAL INSTITUTION, AND THE CAPITAL CONTROLLER

Although the imperialist activities of the core powers allowed their economies to grow, they also created international conflict on a scale never before imagined. In 1900, each of the great powers sought to carve out a sphere of domination in Asia, Africa, and South and Central America that, with the help of nationalism, racism, and xenophobia, turned economic competition into political and military conflict. These conflicts fed on myths of national or racial superiority—British, French, American, White, and so on—and the supposed civilizing mission of the West (Beaud 1983:144). At the Berlin Conference of 1885, great European powers met to carve up zones of influence and domination in Africa, laying the groundwork for levels of colonialization from which Africa still has not recovered.

Attempts to extend or defend these zones of economic influence triggered what was until then the bloodiest war ever fought—World War I. Eight million people were killed. Britain lost 32 percent of its national wealth, France 30 percent, Germany 20 percent, and the United States 9 percent. Germany was forced to pay $33 billion in reparations. Industrial production fell in all countries except the United States. Then the Russian Revolution cut off its huge markets for European and American products, while colonized countries demanded independence.

The United States emerged from World War I as the world's leading economic power: Its national income doubled and coal, oil, and steel production soared. However, workers' real wages and the power of labor unions declined; new forms of factory organization led to greater fatigue—there were 20,000 fatal industrial accidents per year in the 1920s; and the courts blocked the formation of new unions and the application of social laws, such as those prohibiting child labor. It was an era of the rise of a new, great economic power—the corporation.

The Rise of the Corporation

From your perspective as a merchant adventurer, the most important development of the early twentieth century was the merger frenzy in the United States that would be unrivaled until the 1990s. Companies such as Ford, General Motors, and Chrysler in automobiles, General Electric and Westinghouse in electric, Dupont in chemicals, and Standard Oil in petroleum dominated the market. In 1929, the 200 largest companies owned half of the country's nonbanking wealth. Since then, of course, corporations have become one of the

Painter Diego Rivera's depiction of the symbols of corporate wealth as John D. Rockefeller (rear left), J. P. Morgan (rear right), Henry Ford (to Morgan's left), and others read a ticker tape while dining.

dominant governance units in the world. By 1998 there were more than 53,000 transnational corporations (French 2000:5). From their foreign operations alone they generated almost $6 trillion in sales. The largest corporations exceed in size, power, and wealth most of the world's nation-states and, directly or indirectly, define policy agendas of states and international bodies (Korten 1995:54). As a merchant adventurer, you have now entered the corporate age. *What kind of institution is the corporation and how did it come to accumulate so much wealth and power?*

Technically, a corporation is a social invention of the state; the corporate charter, granted by the state, ideally permits private financial resources to be used for a public purpose. At another level, it allows one or more individuals to apply massive economic and political power to accumulate private wealth while protected from legal liability for the public consequences. As a merchant adventurer, clearly you want to create an institution in which you can increase and protect your own profits from market uncertainties (Korten 1995:53–54).

The corporate charter goes back to the sixteenth century, when any debts accumulated by an individual were inherited by his or her descendants. Consequently, someone could be jailed for the debts of a father, mother, brother, or sister. If you, in your role as merchant adventurer, invested in a trading voyage and the goods were lost at sea, you and your descendants were responsible for the losses incurred. The law, as written, inhibited risky investments. The corporate charter solved this problem because it represented a grant from the crown that limited an investor's liability for losses to the amount of the investment, a right not accorded to individual citizens.

The early trading companies, such as the East India Company and the Hudson's Bay Company, were such corporations, and some of the American colonies themselves were founded as corporations—groups of investors granted monopoly powers over territory and industries. Consequently, corporations gained enormous power and were able to influence trade policy. For example, in the eighteenth century the English parliament, composed of wealthy landowners, merchants, and manufacturers, passed laws requiring all goods sold in or from the colonies to go through England and be shipped on English ships with British crews. Furthermore, colonists were forbidden to produce their own caps, hats, and woolen or iron goods.

Suspicion of the power of corporations developed soon after their establishment. Even eighteenth-century philosopher and economist Adam Smith, in *Wealth of Nations,* condemned corporations. He claimed corporations operated to evade the laws of the market by artificially inflating prices and controlling trade. American colonists shared Smith's suspicion of corporations and limited corporate charters to a specific number of years. If the charter was not renewed, the corporation was dissolved. But gradually American courts began to remove restrictions on corporations' operation. The U.S. Civil War was a turning point: Corporations used their huge profits from the war, along with the subsequent political confusion and corruption, to buy legislation that gave them huge grants of land and money, much of which they used to build railroads. Abraham Lincoln (cited Korten 1995:58) saw what was happening and just before his death observed

> Corporations have been enthroned.... An era of corruption in high places will follow and the money power will endeavor to prolong its reign by working on the prejudices of the people...until wealth is aggregated in a few hands...and the Republic is destroyed.

Gradually, corporations gained control of state legislatures, such as those in Delaware and New Jersey, lobbying for (and buying) legislation that granted charters in perpetuity, limited the liabilities of corporate owners and managers, and gained the right of corporations to operate in any way not specifically prohibited by the law. For example, courts limited corporate liability for accidents to workers, an important development in the nineteenth century when fatal industrial accidents from 1888 to 1908 killed 700,000 workers, or roughly one hundred per day. Other favorable court rulings and legislation prohibited the state from setting minimum wage laws, limiting the number of hours a person could work, or setting minimum age requirements for workers.

A Supreme Court ruling in 1886 by a single judge, however, arguably set the stage for the full-scale development of the culture of capitalism. The Court ruled that corporations could use their economic power in a way they never before had. Relying on the Fourteenth Amendment, added to the Constitution in 1868 to protect the rights of freed slaves, the Court ruled that a private corporation is a *natural person* under the U.S. Constitution, and consequently has the same rights and protection extended to persons by the Bill of Rights, including the right of free speech (Hartmann 2002). Thus, corporations were given the same "rights" to influence the government in their own interest as were extended to individual citizens, paving the way for corporations to use their wealth to dominate public thought and discourse. The debates in the United States in the 1990s over campaign finance reform, in which corporate bodies can "donate" millions of dollars to political candidates, stem from this ruling, although rarely, if ever, is that mentioned. Thus, corporations, as "persons," were free to lobby legislatures, use the mass media, establish educational institutions such as the many business schools founded by corporate leaders in the early twentieth century, found charitable organizations to convince the public of their lofty intent, and in general construct an image that they believed would be in their best interests. All of this in the interest of "free speech."

Corporations used this power, of course, to create conditions in which they could make more money. But in a larger sense they used this power to define the ideology or ethos of the emerging culture of capitalism. This cultural and economic ideology is known as *neoclassical, neoliberal,* or *libertarian economics, market capitalism,* or *market liberalism* and is advocated in society primarily by three groups of spokespersons: economic rationalists, market liberals, and members of the corporate class. Their advocacy of these principles created what David Korten called *corporate libertarianism,* which places the rights and freedoms of corporations above the rights and freedoms of individuals—the corporation comes to exist as a separate entity with its own internal logic and rules. Some of the principles and assumptions of this ideology include the following.

1. Sustained *economic growth,* as measured by gross national product (GNP), is the path to human progress.
2. *Free markets,* unrestrained by government, generally result in the most efficient and socially optimal allocation of resources.
3. *Economic globalization,* achieved by removing barriers to the free flow of goods and money anywhere in the world, spurs competition, increases economic efficiency, creates jobs, lowers consumer prices, increases consumer choice, increases economic growth, and is generally beneficial to almost everyone.

4. *Privatization,* which moves functions and assets from governments to the private sector, improves efficiency.
5. The primary responsibility of government is to provide the infrastructure necessary to advance commerce and enforce the rule of law with respect to *property rights and contracts.*

Hidden in these principles, however, said Korten, are a number of questionable assumptions. First, there is the assumption that humans are motivated by self-interest, which is expressed primarily through the quest for financial gain (or, people are by nature motivated primarily by greed). Second, there is the assumption that the action that yields the greatest financial return to the individual or firm is the one that is most beneficial to society (or, the drive to acquire is the highest expression of what it means to be human). Third, is the assumption that competitive behavior is more rational for the individual and the firm than cooperative behavior; consequently, societies should be built around the competitive motive (or, the relentless pursuit of greed and acquisition leads to socially optimal outcomes). Finally, there is the assumption that human progress is best measured by increases in the value of what the members of society consume, and ever-higher levels of consumer spending advance the well-being of society by stimulating greater economic output (or, it is in the best interest of human societies to encourage, honor, and reward the preceding values).

Although corporate libertarianism has its detractors, from the standpoint of overall economic growth, few can argue with its success on a global scale. World economic output has increased from $6.7 trillion in 1950 to more than $41.6 trillion in 1998. Economic growth in *each decade* of the last half of the twentieth century was greater than the economic output in all of human history up to 1950. World trade has increased from total exports of $308 billion in 1950 to $5.4 trillion in 1998. In 1950 world exports of goods was only 5 percent of the world GNP; by 1998 this figure was 13 percent (French 2000:5)

There were still, however, some problems for the merchant adventurer in the early twentieth century. As corporations rose to power in the 1920s and 1930s, political and business leaders were aware that corporations, by themselves, could not ensure the smooth running of the global economy. The worldwide economic depression of the 1930s and the economic disruptions caused by World War II illustrated that. That every country had its own currency and that it could rapidly rise or fall in value relative to others created barriers to trade. Tariffs and import or export laws inhibited the free flow of goods and capital. More importantly, there was the problem of bringing the ideology of corporate libertarianism, and the culture of capitalism in general, to the periphery, especially given the challenge of socialism and the increasing demands of colonized countries for independence. The proposed solution to these problems was to emerge from a meeting in 1944 at a New Hampshire resort hotel.

Bretton Woods and the World Debt

In 1944 President Franklin D. Roosevelt gathered the government financial leaders of forty-four nations to a meeting at the Mt. Washington Hotel in Bretton Woods, New Hampshire. From your perspective as a merchant adventurer it was to be one of the most far-reaching events of the twentieth century. The meeting was called ostensibly to rebuild war-ravaged economies and to outline a global economic agenda for the last half of the twentieth century. Out of that meeting came the plan for the International Bank for Reconstruction and Development (the World Bank), the International Monetary Fund (IMF) to control currency exchange, and the framework for a worldwide trade organization that would lead to the establishment in 1948 of the General Agreement on Tariffs and Trade (GATT) to regulate trade between member countries. Although GATT was not as comprehensive an agreement as many traders would have liked, its scope was widely enlarged on January 1, 1995, with the establishment of the World Trade Organization (WTO). The functions of these agencies are summarized in Table 3.1.

The IMF constituted an agreement by the major nations to allow their currency to be exchanged for other currencies with a minimum of restriction, to inform representatives of the IMF of changes in monetary and financial policies, and to adjust these policies to accommodate to other member nations when possible. The IMF also has funds that it can lend to member nations if they face a debt crisis. For example, if a member country finds it is importing goods at a much higher rate than it is exporting them, and if it doesn't have the money to make up the difference, the IMF will arrange a short-term loan (Driscoll 1992:5).

The World Bank was created to finance the reconstruction of Europe after the devastation of World War II, but the only European country to receive a loan was Holland, then engaged in trying to put down a rebellion of its Southeast Asian colonies. The World Bank then began to focus its attention on the periphery, lending funds to countries to foster economic development, with, as we shall see, mixed results.

The GATT has served as a forum for participating countries to negotiate trade policy. The goal was to establish a multilateral agency with the power to regulate and promote free trade among nations. However, because legislators and government officials in many countries, particularly the United States, objected to the idea of an international trade agency with the power to dictate government trade policy, the creation of such an agency did not occur until the WTO was finally established on January 1, 1995. In essence, the agency can react to claims by member nations that other nations are using unfair trade policies in order to give businesses in their country an unfair advantage (see Low 1993:42). For example, in 1989 the European Union instituted a ban on the importation of beef injected with bovine growth hormones. These hormones are manufactured in the United States by Monsanto Corp. and are used to boost milk production in cows. The hormone was approved in 1993

TABLE 3.1   The Bretton Woods Institutions

INSTITUTION OR AGENCY	FUNCTION
International Monetary Fund (IMF)	To make funds available for countries to meet short-term financial needs and to stabilize currency exchanges between countries
International Bank for Reconstruction and Development (World Bank)	To make loans for various development projects
General Agreement on Tariffs and Trade (GATT)	To ensure the free trade of commodities among countries

by the U.S. Food and Drug Administration, but public interest groups maintain that, because it increases udder infections in cows, it requires greater use of antibiotics in cows, and that these antibiotics end up in the milk. Some scientists even link the use of the hormone to cancer development (see BGH Bulletin 2000). The United States, on behalf of Monsanto, claimed to the WTO that the ban amounted to an unfair barrier to U.S. beef exports. The WTO ruled in favor of the United States and allowed the U.S. government to impose a 100 percent tariff on $116.8 million worth of European imports, such as fruit juices, mustard, pork, truffles, and Roquefort cheese. Thus, the WTO can rule that a country's food, environmental, or work laws constitute an "unfair barrier to trade," and penalize a country that does not remove them (see French 2000).

The year 1994 marked the fiftieth anniversary of the Bretton Woods institutions, prompting a worldwide review of their successes and failures. Generally, the reviews were not favorable, leading, as we shall see in Chapter 13, to widespread protests and demonstrations against the World Bank, the IMF, and the WTO. Even the World Bank's own evaluations were highly critical of its performance. In spite of lending some quarter of a trillion dollars to peripheral countries, 1 billion people in the world are desperately poor; furthermore, the disparity of wealth in the world between the core and periphery has doubled in the past thirty years. The richest 20 percent of the world's people now consume 150 times more of the world's goods than the poorest 20 percent (United Nations 1993:11).

One of the most profound influences of the Bretton Woods meeting is the accumulation of the debt of peripheral countries; some consider this "debt crisis" the gravest one facing the world. The reasons for the debt crisis, and the possible impact it can have on everyone's lives, is complex but essential to understand. Overwhelming debt of peripheral countries is one of the major factors in many global problems that we will explore, including poverty, hunger, environmental devastation, the spread of disease, and political unrest.

Three things were particularly important in creating the debt crisis: the change during the last third of the twentieth century in the meaning of money; the amount of money lent by the World Bank and other lending institutions to peripheral countries; and the oil boom of the early 1970s and the pressure for financial institutions to invest that money.

Money, as noted earlier, constitutes the focal point of capitalism. It is through money that we assign value to objects, behaviors, and even people. The fact that one item can, in various quantities, represent virtually any item or service, from a soft drink to an entire forest, is one of the most remarkable features of our lives. But it is not without its problems. The facts that different countries have different currencies and that currencies can rise or fall in value relative to the goods they can purchase have always been barriers to unrestricted foreign trade and global economic integration. Furthermore, there have always been disputes concerning how to measure the value of money itself. Historically, money has been tied to a specific valuable metal, generally gold. Thus, money in any country could always be redeemed for a certain amount of gold, although the amount could vary according to the value of a specific country's currency.

Although the meeting at Bretton Woods would not lead to the establishment of a global currency, the countries did agree to exchange their currency for U.S. dollars at a fixed rate, and the United States guaranteed that it would exchange money for gold stored at Fort Knox at thirty-five dollars per ounce. But in the 1960s, during the Vietnam War and the increase in U.S. government spending on health, education, and welfare programs, the United States was creating dollars far in excess of its gold supply, while at the same time guaranteeing all the rest of the money in the world. As a result, in 1971 the United States declared it would no longer redeem dollars on demand for gold. This totally divorced the American dollar and, effectively, all the other currencies in the world, from anything of value other than the expectation that people would accept dollars for things of value. Money became simply unsecured credit.

Because countries no longer needed to have a certain amount of gold in order to print money, money became more plentiful. How this happened, and the impact it has had on all our lives requires some elaboration.

We generally assume that governments create money by printing it. And, in fact, when money was linked to gold, there was a limit on how much could be printed. However, with the lifting of these restrictions, most money is now created by banks and other lending institutions through debt. We generally assume also, that the money that banks lend is money that others have deposited. However, that is not the case; only a fraction of the money that banks lend needs to be in deposits. In effect, whenever a bank lends money, or whenever a product or service is purchased on credit, money has been created. In effect, then, there is virtually no limit on the amount of money that lending institutions can create; furthermore, the interest on the loan payments creates yet more money. Economists call this "debt money" (Rowbotham 1998:5), or "credit money" (Guttmann 1994).

Debt provides an important service to the culture of capitalism; it allows people to buy things with money they don't have—thereby fueling economic growth—and it requires people to work in order to pay off their debts. Furthermore, it stimulates greater need for economic growth to maintain interest rates—that is return on investments. It also means, however, that there is more money that has to be invested and lent, and a considerable amount of that went to peripheral countries. This proved to be a boon not only for individual borrowers but also for peripheral countries seeking to develop their economies. The problems were that the interest on most loans was adjustable (could go up or down depending on economic circumstances) and that debts began to accumulate beyond what countries could repay.

The second factor that led to the debt crisis was the operation of the World Bank. The Bank itself had a problem. European countries, whose economies it was to help rebuild, didn't need the help. With a lack of demand for their services, what could they do? How could the institution survive? The Bank's solution was to lend money to peripheral countries to develop their economies. The plan was to help them industrialize by funding things such as large-scale hydroelectric projects, roads, and industrial parks. Furthermore, the bigger the project, the more the Bank could lend; thus, in the 1950s and 1960s money suddenly poured into India, Mexico, Brazil, and Indonesia, the Bank's four largest borrowers. From 1950 to 1970, the Bank lent some $953 million. We should not overlook the fact that these loans also benefited wealthy core countries, who largely supplied the construction companies, engineers, equipment, and advisors needed to develop these projects.

But the success of the Bank in lending money created another problem—what economists call *net negative transfers;* borrowing nations collectively were soon paying more money into the Bank than the Bank was lending out. Put another way, the poor or peripheral nations were paying more money to the rich core nations than they were receiving from them. Aside from the consequences for poor countries, this would lead ultimately to the bank going out of business—its only purpose would be to collect the money it had already lent out. This is not a problem for regular banks because they can always recruit new customers, but the World Bank has a limited number of clients to whom it can lend money. Now what do you do? The Bank's solution was to lend still more. Robert McNamara, past chief of the Ford Motor Company and secretary of defense during the John F. Kennedy and Lyndon B. Johnson administrations, more than any one person, made the World Bank into what it is today. During his tenure from 1968 to 1981, the Bank increased lending from $953 million to $12.4 billion and increased staff from 1,574 to 5,201. The result was to leave many peripheral countries with staggering debt burdens. There were other problems as well.

The third source of the debt crisis was the oil boom of the early 1970s. Oil producers were making huge profits ("petrodollars"). The problem was that this money needed to be invested, particularly by the banks into which it went and from which depositors expected interest payments. But banks and other investment agents had problems finding investments. One of their solutions was to lend even more money to peripheral countries. The source of the debt crisis is illustrated in Figure 3.2.

Thus, by the late 1970s peripheral countries had borrowed huge sums of money and, with this infusion, were doing generally well. But then financial policies in the wealthy countries precipitated an economic collapse. With their own economies in recession because of the increase in oil prices in the 1970s, core governments reacted by raising interest rates. Countries such as Brazil, Mexico, and Indonesia that had borrowed large sums of money at adjustable, rather than fixed, interest rates suddenly found that they could no longer pay back what they owed. Many couldn't even pay back the interest on the loans. Furthermore, an economic recession in the core nations decreased the demand for whatever commodities peripheral countries had for sale, further undermining their economies.

This all sounds largely like an economic problem that would have little effect on people such as you or me, or on a peasant farmer in Mexico, craftsperson in Africa, or

FIGURE 3.2   The Source of the Global Debt Crisis

TABLE 3.2   **External Debt of Selected Countries, 1980, 1994, and 2001**

Country	TOTAL EXTERNAL DEBT (MILLIONS $)			EXTERNAL DEPT AS % OF GNP		
	1980	*1994*	*2001*	*1980*	*1994*	*2001*
Bangladesh	4,327	16,569	9,700	33.4	63.4	20.6
Brazil	72,920	151,104	237,600	31.8	31.8	46.6
China	4,504	100,536	164,100	2.2	19.3	13.6
Ecuador	5,997	14,955	14,500	53.8	96.6	69.0
Egypt	19,131	33,358	25,100	89.2	78.3	25.5
India	20,582	98,990	67,800	11.9	34.2	14.1
Indonesia	20,944	96,500	131,400	28.0	94.7	93.0
Mexico	57,278	128,302	172,900	30.5	35.2	27.7
Nigeria	8,921	33,485	30,900	10.1	102.5	72.3
Pakistan	9,930	29,579	25,500	42.4	56.6	43.5
Peru	9,386	22,623	28,100	47.6	46.2	51.8
Philippines	17,417	39,302	55,300	53.7	59.7	77.5
Russian Federation	4,447	94,232	146,700	—	25.4	47.3
Tanzania	2,616	7,441	1,300	—	229.5	14.0

Data from World Development Report 1996:220–221; World Development Report 1999/2000: http://www.worldbank.org/wdr/2000/; *World Development Indicators database,* August 2003.

small merchant in Indonesia. But, in fact, it has had an enormous impact, and it illustrates how global problems are tied closely to today's merchant adventurers. It is estimated that the amount of money owed by peripheral countries increased from $100 billion in 1971 to $600 billion by 1981 (Caufield 1996:134). And the problem hasn't improved: The total owed by countries in the periphery increased in 1998 to well over $2 trillion. Table 3.2 shows the increases in external debt for a few selected countries, along with the percentage of their yearly GNP (total of goods and services produced) that the debt represents. For example, the external debt of the Philippines went from $17 billion in 1980 to more than $55 billion in 2001. Indonesia's debt went from some $20 billion in 1980 to $131 billion in 2001, or some 93 percent of its GNP.

This debt has not only created problems for the debtor countries but it also has created a major problem for lending institutions and investors. There is an old joke that says that when an individual can't pay his or her bank debts, he or she is in trouble, but when a big borrower, such as a corporation or country, can't repay its debts, the bank is in trouble. This, in brief, was the dilemma posed by the global debt crisis for private lending institutions and the World Bank.

The World Bank and the IMF responded to the debt crisis by trying to reschedule the repayment of debts or extending short-term loans to debtor countries to help them meet the financial crises. However, to qualify for a rescheduling of a debt or loan payment a government had to agree to alter its fiscal policies to improve its balance-of-payments problems;

that is, it had to try to take in more money and spend less. But how do you do that? There are various ways, all creating, in one way or another, serious problems. For example, countries had to promise to manage tax collecting better; sell government property; increase revenues by increasing exports; reduce government spending on social programs, such as welfare, health, and education; promise to refrain from printing more money; and take steps to devalue their currency, thus making their goods cheaper for consumers in other countries but making them more expensive for their own citizens.

Although these measures are rarely popular with their citizens, governments rarely refuse IMF requests to implement them because not only might they not receive a short-term loan but agencies, such as the World Bank, and private capital controllers, such as banks and foundations, would also then refuse to make funds available. There is pressure on the World Bank and IMF to forgive or reduce debt, and forty-one of the poorest countries in the world have been targeted for debt relief of some sort (see Jubilee 2000). But for most countries, the interest alone on their debts dictates economic, environmental, and social policies that are devastating.

First, debt means that countries must do whatever they can to reduce government expenses and increase revenue or attract foreign investment. Reducing government expenses means cutting essential health, education, and social programs. In Zambia, between 1990 and 1993, the government spent thirty-four times as much on debt service as it did on education ($1.3 billion compared to $37 million). Since then, educational spending has decreased. The United Nations estimates that had severely indebted countries been relieved of their debts from 1997 to 2000, they could have saved the lives of 21 million children and provided basic education to 90 million girls and women (United Nations Development Program 1997). Yet recently, the IMF insisted that indebted countries impose user fees for health services and education. In countries where such fees have been imposed, visits to health clinics and attendance at schools, particularly for women, has declined dramatically.

Second, the effects on environmental resources are equally devastating. To increase revenues, countries must export goods and resources. Because most indebted countries, particularly those in sub-Saharan Africa, have little industrial capacity, they must export raw materials, such as minerals and lumber. This requires dismantling whatever environmental regulations may have existed. But because so many countries (including the wealthy countries of the world) are in debt, each must adopt the same export strategy. Thus, as each country tries to export more and more goods to raise revenue to pay debts they all have accumulated, the competition and glut of goods and resources drives down prices and reduces the revenue that can be raised, while at the same time gutting natural and human resources (see Rowbotham 1998:89).

Third, there is the question, *where did all the money that was lent to peripheral countries go?* Because "capital flight"—money leaving the periphery—increased dramatically during the period of rising debt, the prevailing view is that loans were siphoned off by the elites in the periphery and invested back in the core. For example, while the IMF and other financial institutions were lending billions to restore the Russian economy after the fall of communism, $140 billion (U.S.)—almost $2 billion per month—fled Russia during the first six years of market reforms. The World Bank estimates that between 1976 and 1984 capital flight from Latin America was equal to the area's whole external debt (Caufield 1996:132). Capital flight from Mexico alone from 1974 to 1982, invested in everything from condominiums to car dealerships, amounted to at least $35 billion. "The problem," joked one member of the U.S. Federal Reserve Board, "is not that Latin Americans don't have assets. They do. The problem is they are all in Miami" (Caufield 1996:133).

There is one additional thing that, as a merchant adventurer, you need to know: the relationship between the so-called debt crisis and the U.S. dollar. Of all the countries in the world, the United States, in 2003, had the greatest foreign debt of all, more than $2.3 trillion, or almost $5,000 for every man, woman, and child in the country. A good part of that debt comes from the fact the consumers in the United States are such free spenders, buying more from other countries than consumers in other countries buy from us. In fact, the amount of the debt, if the United States were a peripheral country, would be drawing warnings from the IMF. The fact that consumers in the United States can spend so much more than they have is a great advantage, but it also carries a grave risk.

The United States is able to accumulate so much debt simply because the U.S. dollar presently serves as a global currency; it is the money of choice, so to speak, of merchant adventurers all over the world. The best way to understand how this translates into an advantage is to imagine having a checking account in which none of the checks that you wrote were ever returned to your bank for redemption. Whoever you wrote a check to simply used that check to buy things from other people who were willing to accept that check. You could write as many checks as you wanted without ever worrying about having enough money in your checking account. That essentially is the situation the United States is in regarding the U.S. dollar. The United States and its citizens can accumulate foreign debt for whatever amount it wants. However, there is a problem; if the U.S. dollar were ever replaced as the global currency of choice by, say, the European euro or the Japanese yen, countries and persons holding dollars would want them redeemed, and that could cause a crisis. It is perhaps no coincidence that when President George W. Bush identified certain countries as comprising an "axis of evil," all had threatened to convert their dollars into euros.

The Power of Capital Controllers

One of the enduring tensions in the culture of capitalism is the separation between political power and economic power; in a democracy, people grant the government power to act on their behalf. However, in capitalism, there are, in addition to elected leaders, capital controllers, individuals or groups who control economic resources that everyone depends on but who are accountable to virtually no one, except perhaps a few investors or stockholders. Their goals often conflict with state goals. As a merchant, industrialist, or investor your goals are simple: You want to attain the highest possible profit on your investment, you want to be certain your right to private property is protected, and you want to keep your financial risks to a minimum. As Jeffrey A. Winters (1996:*x*) suggested, if capital controllers, who are unelected, unappointed, and unaccountable, were all to wear yellow suits and meet weekly in huge halls to decide where, when, and how much of their capital (money) to invest, there would be little mystery in their power. But, of course, they don't. Collectively they make private decisions on where, when, and how to distribute their investments. Furthermore, under this system of private property, capital controllers are free to do whatever they wish with their capital: they can invest it, they can sit on it, or they can destroy it. States are virtually helpless to insist that private capital be used for anything other than what capital controllers want to do with it.

The anonymity of investors and the hidden power they hold (or that is hidden from us) present problems for political leaders: Although the actions of capital controllers can greatly influence our lives, it is political leaders who we often hold responsible for the rise and fall of a country's financial fortunes. When unemployment increases, when prices rise, when taxes are raised or important services discontinued or decreased, we can fire our governmental representatives at the next election. However, we do not have the power to "fire" the board of General Motors or the investment counselors at Smith, Barney's or Chase Manhattan.

Though investors may not consciously coordinate their actions, their choices have enormous consequences for societies and state leaders. The reasons for this are obvious. States depend on revenue for their operation and maintenance. This revenue can come from various sources, including income taxes; corporate taxes; tariffs on imported goods; revenue from state-run enterprises (e.g., oil revenue); charges for state services (e.g., tolls); foreign aid; and credit, loans, or grants from abroad. In the case of peripheral countries, much of this money comes from international lending agencies. But money from international lending agencies represents only a small percentage of the money that flows into peripheral countries. Far more comes from capital controllers. As a final stop on our historical tour as merchant adventurers, let's assume the role of capital controller. *You have substantial sums of money to invest; what do you do with it?*

During the last half of the twentieth century there was enormous growth in the number of people with capital to invest. Many are the very wealthy, the elite 1 or 2 percent who control vast resources, such as the major corporations of the world. Others, as mentioned previously, are responsible for deciding where to invest public moneys from multilateral organizations or state agencies. In addition, there are the less wealthy who save in banks and have pension funds or insurance policies. Investment capital from these different sources and held by capital controllers represents enormous power. Furthermore, with modern methods of communication most of this money is now extremely mobile: Billions of dollars can be transferred from one place to another with the touch of a computer key. Capital was not always so mobile. For example, if you had money to invest fifty years ago in a textile plant, you might be constrained by import laws to build your factory in the country in which you wanted to sell your merchandise. In today's free trade environment, however, you can build your factory wherever you can get the cheapest labor. And if labor prices increase, you can simply move your factory production where labor is cheaper yet.

With an increase in free trade, standardized currencies, and economic globalization in general, capital can move freely all over the world. This can greatly increase the power of the capital controller, because if more regions or countries compete to attract capital investment, you, as a capital controller, are more able to demand conditions that guarantee profits and minimize risk. If you could build a textile factory in a country with strong labor unions or one with weak ones, which would you choose? If one country had strong environmental laws that required you to control toxic waste, whereas another had few such regulations, where would you build? If one country had a high minimum wage, whereas another had none, where would you likely realize the highest profit? These issues have become subsumed under the term *competitiveness;* that is, to be competitive in a global economy, a country must institute policies that allow it to compete successfully for mobile capital with other countries.

This fact determines social, economic, and political policy in countries and regions all over the world, and it affects your life as well. The mobility of capital means that social systems that produce profitable investment climates will attract the most investment capital. *What constitutes a favorable investment climate?* Investment climate refers to the constellation of policies within a given jurisdiction (city, state, region, country) that either advance or inhibit the key goals of investors (profit, property guarantees, and low risk). A bad climate might involve the risk of the expropriation of private property, political instability, high taxes, strong worker's unions, strong environmental regulations, and social laws regarding minimum wage and child labor. A favorable climate can be created by low tax rates, tax holidays and other special incentives, weak unions, little environmental regulation, and few social regulations. Furthermore, capital (money) will flow away from locations (e.g., countries) that do not create profitable investment climates. This capital, constantly flowing in and out of communities, regions, or countries, represents what Winters (1996:x) calls "power in motion."

The amount of power in motion is difficult to measure; the United Nations world investment report for 2002 shows that in 2001 the amount of direct foreign investment—money invested in such things as factories, equipment, and research facilities—reached $735 billion, up from $464 billion in 1997. On an average day the volume of money transacted around the world amounted to almost $2 billion. But the amount that flows into any given area can vary enormously; in 2001, for example, forty-nine of the poorest countries in the world received only 0.5 percent of the total.

The case of Indonesia offers a good example of what countries need to do to attract capital (Winters 1996). Indonesia fought for and gained independence from the Dutch in 1949. After a period of intense political competition President Sukarno, the victor in this competition, instituted a policy to free the country from foreign influence, carefully trying to balance power between the army and a strong Communist Party. Among his actions, he began nationalizing foreign firms. With their property at risk, and no longer guaranteed by the state, companies and investors began to pull their money out of the country. Consequently, the economy collapsed. Then in 1965 the military, under General Suharto, put down an alleged coup by the PKI, the Indonesian Communist Party. The subsequent blood bath led to the slaughter of hundreds of thousands of Indonesians believed to be sympathetic to or members of the Communist Party and removal of Sukarno from power.

With little money, the new ruler, President Suharto, faced the problem of rebuilding an economy in ruins. To solve the problem Suharto turned to economics professors at the University of Jakarta and assigned them the task of designing a policy to attract foreign investors. The first thing they did was to send signals through the press that they were changing economic policies and appointing people to government offices known to be friendly to foreign investors. Next, they applied for loans from multilateral institutions such as the World Bank and the IMF, hoping their approval would build the confidence of foreign investors in their country. Then, to assure capital controllers that their country was politically stable, the government suppressed all political dissent and limited the power of workers to mobilize unions. Finally, the government modified its tax structure to favor foreign investors. The result was that foreign capital began to flow into the country, and in the late 1960s and early 1970s the Indonesian economy began to thrive.

The story did not end there; what happened next illustrates how the power of capital controllers to create conditions favorable to investment is not absolute. Indonesia has large oil reserves, and when in the early 1970s oil revenue increased, Indonesia's need for foreign investment decreased. Because it had another source of money, the country became less friendly to foreign investors: Taxes increased, preference was shown to domestic industries, and bureaucratic procedures became more cumbersome for foreigners wanting to do business in Indonesia. As a result, foreign investments decreased dramatically. As long as oil revenues were stable, Indonesia had no problem. But in the early 1980s, oil prices plunged, and once again the Indonesian economy was close to ruin. Once again, in response to domestic political pressure from those who were suffering from economic decline, the government, still under the control of President Suharto, found itself instituting the measures outlined previously to attract capital investors once again.

Foreign investment did indeed return to Indonesia, particularly in the growth of assembly plants; consequently until late 1997, the economy was doing well. However, the collapse of the value of Asian currencies in late 1997 resulted in capital controllers once again pulling funds out of Indonesia, leaving its currency plummeting in value, unemployment spreading, and social unrest increasing (see Bello 1998). The IMF, seeking to restore financial stability, forced currency reevaluations and government cutbacks that made things even worse, forcing half the businesses in Indonesia into virtual bankruptcy, increasing unemployment tenfold, and sending real wages plummeting. Thus, from 1996 to 1997 economic growth rate went from some 8 percent a year to –14 percent and unemployment climbed from 4.7 percent to 34 percent (see Firdausy 2000).

Thus, virtually all countries today, core nations as well as those in the periphery, seek to create conditions to attract or keep capital investment, to create or keep jobs for the millions of people dependent on wage labor. To this end they work to maintain and promote the confidence of foreign banks and investors in the viability of their economy and the stability of their political regimes. But in an era in which capital may flow out of a country faster than it will flow in, the prospect of economic collapse is ever-present. What capital controllers give, they can just as quickly take away.

The major lesson of this analysis is that the economic goals of capital controllers—profit, a guarantee for private property, and little risk—can often conflict with larger societal goals, such as relative economic equality and security, environmental safety, equal access to medical care, and equal access to food. In other words, making the world safe for capital sometimes means making it unsafe for people. Many of the global problems that we examine in later chapters—population growth, poverty, hunger, environmental devastation, disease, ethnic conflict, and the oppression of indigenous peoples—all, in one way or another, find their origins in the drive of capital to profit, to keep the profit, and to minimize the risks of capital investment. Having said that, we must also recognize that no other large-scale economic system has been able to do as well for so many, and that many of the vast gains in areas such as food production, technology and science, and medicine are directly attributable to the same economic drives. The important thing is to understand the dynamics of the system so that we can understand what we may need to give up and what we are able to maintain if we ever hope to solve global problems.

CONCLUSION

We began this chapter with the goal of trying to understand three historical developments that have had a profound influence on today's world and in the development of the culture of capitalism—the increase in the division of world wealth, changes in the organization of capital, and the increase in the level of economic globalization. We found that the division of wealth has grown enormously, between both countries and areas of the world. In 2000 more than 1.2 billion people lived in absolute poverty, earning the equivalent of less than one dollar per day. The three top ultrarich people, including Microsoft's Bill Gates, own more than the gross national product of the forty-eight poorest nations combined. Furthermore, the gap is increasing. In the U.N. World Development Report of 1997, of the 173 countries in the study, 70 to 80 have lower per capita incomes than they did ten or thirty years ago. People in Africa consume 20 percent less than they did twenty-five years ago. The U.N. report pointed out that the 20 percent of the world's population living in the wealthiest countries consume 86 percent of the world's goods and services. The poorest 20 percent consume only 1.3 percent.

The organization of capital has changed dramatically. We began our journey with capital largely in the hands of individual merchants, family groups, or limited partnerships and ended with the era of capital controllers, such as transnational corporations, multilateral institutions, and investment firms. In 1400, it might take a global merchant a year's journey from one area of the world to another to complete an investment cycle of buying and selling goods; today a capital controller can transfer billions from one area of the world to another without ever leaving her or his computer.

Finally, we have seen global economic integration increase to the extent that global trade is easier today than trade between adjacent towns was in 1400, as trade treaties dissolve regional and country boundaries, freeing capital to migrate where it is most likely to accumulate. Furthermore, we have seen how global financial and multilateral institutions, such as corporate controllers, the World Bank, the International Monetary Fund, and the World Trade Organization, function to open international markets to corporations and force countries to dismantle environmental, social, and labor reforms.

Our analysis of how the culture capitalism functions is incomplete, however, until we understand the development and function of the nation-state, how it has functioned in the evolution of the culture, and how it mediates between the consumer, laborer, and capitalist.

CHAPTER FOUR

THE NATION-STATE IN THE CULTURE OF CAPITALISM

*Among the primary goals of the modern, post-Enlightenment state are
assimilation, homogenization, and conformity within a fairly narrow ethnic and
political range, as well as the creation of societal agreement about the kinds of
people there are and the kinds there ought to be. The ideal state is one in which
the illusion of a single nation-state is created and maintained and in which
resistance is managed so that profound social upheaval, separatist activity,
revolution, and coups d'état are unthinkable for most people most of the time.*
—Carole Nagengast, "Violence, Terror, and the Crisis of the State"

*Due to the unqualified and unstoppable spread of free trade rules, and above
all the free movement of capital and finances, the "economy" is progressively
exempt from political control;... Whatever has been left of politics is expected
to be dealt with, as in the good old days, by the state—but whatever
is concerned with the economic life the state is not allowed to
touch; any attempt in this direction would be met with prompt
and furious punitive action from the world markets.*
—Zygmunt Bauman, *Globalization: The Human Consequences*

Imagine an alien from another planet who lands on Earth after a nuclear holocaust has destroyed all life but has left undamaged terrestrial libraries and archives. After consulting the archives, suggested Eric Hobsbawm (1990), our observer would undoubtedly conclude that the last two centuries of human history are incomprehensible without an understanding of the term *nation* and the phenomenon of *nationalism.*

The nation-state, along with the consumer, laborer, and capitalist, are, we suggest, the essential elements of the culture of capitalism. It is the nation-state, as Eric Wolf (1982:100) suggested, that guarantees the ownership of private property and the means of production and provides support for disciplining the workforce. The state also has to provide and maintain the economic infrastructure—transportation, communication, judicial systems, education, and so on—required by capitalist production. The nation-state must regulate conflicts between competing capitalists at home and abroad, by diplomacy if possible, by war if necessary. The state plays an essential role in creating conditions that inhibit or promote consumption; controls legislation that may force people off the land to seek wage labor; legislates to regulate or deregulate corporations; controls the money supply; initiates economic, political, and social policies to attract capital; and controls the legitimate use of force. Without the nation-state to regulate commerce and trade within its own borders, there could be no effective global economic integration. But *how did the nation-state come to exist, and how does it succeed in binding together often disparate and conflicting groups?*

Virtually all people in the world consider themselves members of a nation-state. The notion of a person without a nation, said Ernest Gellner (1983:6), strains the imagination; a person must have a nationality as he or she must have a nose and two ears. We are Americans, Mexicans, Bolivians, Italians, Indonesians, Kenyans, or members of any of close to 200 states that currently exist. We generally consider our country, whichever it is, as imbued with tradition, a history that glorifies its founding and makes heroes of those thought to have been instrumental in its creation. Symbols of the nation—flags, buildings, monuments—take on the aura of sacred relics.

The attainment of "nationhood" had become by the middle of the twentieth century a sign of progress and modernity. To be less than a nation—a tribe, an ethnic group, a regional bloc—was a sign of backwardness. Yet fewer than one-third of the almost 200 states in the world are more than thirty years old; only a few go back to the nineteenth century; and virtually none go back in their present form beyond that. Before that time people identified themselves as members of kinship groups, villages, cities, or, perhaps, regions, but almost never as members of nations. For the most part, the agents of the state were resented, feared, or hated because of their demands for tribute, taxes, or army conscripts.

States existed, of course, and have existed for 5,000 to 7,000 years. But the idea of the nation-state, of a people sharing some bounded territory, united by a common culture or tradition, common language, or common race, is a product of nineteenth-century Europe. Most historians see the French Revolution of 1789 as marking the beginning of the era of the nation-state. Yet in spite of the historical newness of the idea, for many people nationality forms a critical part of their personal identity. Some of the questions we need to explore are as follows: *How did the nation-state come to have such importance in the world? Why did it develop as it did, and how do people come to identify themselves as members of such vague abstractions? Finally, why does the nation-state kill as often as it does?*

The question of killing is important, because today most killing and violence is either sanctioned by or carried out by the state. This should not surprise us: most definitions of the state, following Max Weber's (1947:124–135), revolve around its claim to a monopoly on the instruments of death and violence. "Stateness," as Elman Service (1975) put it, can be identified simply by locating "the power of force in addition to the power of authority." Killing by other than the state, as Morton Fried (1967) noted, will draw the punitive action of organized state force.

The use of force, however, is not the only characteristic anthropologists emphasize in identifying the state; social stratification—the division of societies into groups with differing access to wealth and other resources—is also paramount. Yet even here the state is seen as serving as an instrument of control to maintain the privileges of the ruling group, and this, too, generally requires a monopoly on the use of force (see Cohen and Service 1978; Lewellen 1992).

Thus, to complete our description of the key features of the culture of capitalism we need to examine the origin and history of the state and its successor, the nation-state.

THE ORIGIN AND HISTORY OF THE STATE

The Evolution of the State

States represent a form of social contract in which the public ostensibly has consented to assign to the state a monopoly on force and agreed that only it can constrain and coerce people (Nagengast 1994:116). Philosophers and political thinkers have long been fascinated by the question of why the state developed. Seventeenth-century philosopher Thomas Hobbes assumed the state existed to maintain order, that without the state life would be, in Hobbes's famous description, "nasty, brutish, and short." However, anthropologists have long recognized that some societies do very well without anything approaching state organization; in fact "tribes without rulers," as they were called, represented until 7,000 to 8,000 years ago the only form of political organization in the world. Government in these societies was relatively simple. There might be a chief or village leader, but their powers were limited. In gathering and hunting societies most decisions were probably made by consensus. Village or clan chiefs may have had more authority than others, but even they led more by example than by force. Power, the ability to control people, was generally diffused among many individuals or groups.

The state as a stratified society presided over by a ruling elite with the power to draw from and demand agricultural surpluses likely developed in the flood plains between the Tigris and Euphrates in what is now Iraq 4,000 to 5,000 years ago. The fortified cities of Uruk and Ur, forming the state of Sumeria, had populations of 40,000. States developed independently in Egypt, the Indus River Valley of India, the Yellow River Valley of China, and, later, Mesoamerica and Peru.

Anthropologists have long been concerned with the idea of the origin of the state (see Lewellen 1992). *Why didn't human aggregates remain organized into small units or into villages or towns of 500 to 2,000 persons? What made the development of densely settled cities necessary? Why, after hundreds of thousands of years, did ruling elites with control of armed force emerge to dominate the human landscape?*

One theory is that as the population increased and food production became more complex, a class of specialists emerged and created a stratified society. Who comprised this class or why they emerged is an open question. Karl Wittfogel (1957), in his "hydraulic theory" of state development, proposed that neolithic farmers in the area where states developed were dependent on flooding rivers, such as the Tigris, the Nile, and the Yellow Rivers, to water their fields and deposit new soil. But this happened only once each year, so to support an expanding population farmers began to build dikes, canals, and reservoirs to control water flow. As these irrigation systems became more complex, groups of specialists emerged to plan and direct these activities, and this group developed into an administrative elite that ruled over despotic, centralized states.

Others propose that an increase in population, especially where populations cannot easily disperse, requires more formal means of government and control and will lead to greater social stratification and inequality. These theories of state development emphasize the integrative function of the state and suggest that it evolved to maintain order and direct societal growth and development.

However, another framework emerges from the work of Marx and Engels. In this framework early societies were thought to be communistic, with resources shared equally among members and little or no notion of private property. However, technological development permitted production of a surplus of goods, which could be expropriated and used by some persons to elevate their control or power in society. Asserting control permitted this elite to form an entrepreneurial class. To maintain their wealth and authority, they created structures of force.

The major criticism of this framework from anthropologists is that there is little evidence of this kind of entrepreneurial activity in prehistoric societies; moreover, it is difficult to apply notions such as "communism" and "capitalism" to early societies. However, Morton Fried (1967) proposed that differential access to wealth and resources creates stratification, and once stratification emerges it creates internal conflict that will lead to either disintegration of the group or to the elite imposing their authority by force.

Yet another view proposes that external conflict is the motivation for state development: Once a group united under a strong central authority develops, it could easily conquer smaller, less centralized groups and take captives, land, or property. Following this line of reasoning, if smaller groups were to protect themselves from predator states they too had to organize, the result being the emergence of competing states with the more powerful ones conquering the weaker ones and enlarging their boundaries. Robert Carneiro (1978) reasoned that war has served to promote consolidation of isolated, politically autonomous villages into chiefdoms of united villages and into states. At first war pits village against village, resulting in chiefdoms; then it pits chiefdom against chiefdom, resulting in states; and then it pits state against state, creating yet larger political units.

It should be clear that these theories are not mutually exclusive; the emergence of states may be a result of any one or a combination of factors. Thus, other theorists, such as Marvin Harris (1971) and Kent Flannery (1972; 1973), propose that the evolution of the state required the interaction of various factors such as control of birth rates, nature of food resources, and the environment.

Regardless of why the state emerged as a human institution, it is clear that by 1400 the world was very much divided into states and empires ruled by groups of elites who maintained their positions through the use of force. But the states of prehistoric times—the city-states of ancient Greece, the Roman Empire, the Chinese dynasties—were very different from the modern nation-state. It is doubtful that subjects of the Ming Dynasty or Roman Empire identified themselves as members of a state, let alone a nation. It is unlikely that a British or French soldier of the sixteenth or seventeenth century felt he owed allegiance to his "nation"—to his king or queen, perhaps, but not to anything so abstract as a "country." The nation-state is a very recent historical development, one we need to understand to appreciate its role in the culture of capitalism.

The History and Function of the Nation-State

The state as it exists today is obviously very different from the state that evolved 7,000 years ago or the state as it existed in the years 1500 or 1800. We have gone from being states to being nations or nation-states. The differences are important. A state is a political

entity with identifiable components. If someone asked citizens of the United States to identify a constituent of the "state," they could point to federal buildings (e.g., the Congressional Office Building, the White House, federal courthouse) or name federal
bureaucracies (e.g., Congress, the Internal Revenue Service, the Department of Agriculture); they could list the things that the state requires of them—to pay taxes, register for
social security, obtain citizenship, vote. However, if someone asked them what constituted
the "nation," to what, other than the flag, could they point? Other than being "patriotic,"
what could they say is required of them by the "nation"? The American nation is a far more
abstract concept than the American state; a nation, as Benedict Anderson (1991:5–6) put it,
is "an imagined political community." Yet in the past 200 years, states have evolved to nations or nation-states. *But why did a new form of political entity develop, and what function
did it perform?*

The modern state, suggested Fernand Braudel (1982:515–516), has the following
tasks: to secure obedience and gain a monopoly on force with legitimate violence; to exert
control over economic life to ensure the orderly circulation of goods and to take for itself a
share of the national income to pay for its own expenditure, luxury, administration, or
wars; and to participate in spiritual or religious life and derive additional strength by using
religious values or establishing a state religion. We examine later the use of violence by the
state and the use of religious values. Let's first examine the state control of economic life.

The state has probably always been involved in its subjects' economic life in one
way or another. The ancient state existed partly to protect the privileges of the elites by ensuring production of resources, offering protection from other elites, and extracting surplus
wealth from a largely peasant population. Traders supplied wealth to the elite in the form
of taxes, tributes, and fees required to do business. The state also performed some functions for the trader—it might mint coins and produce paper money, establish standards for
weights and measures, protect the movement of merchants and goods, purchase goods, and
create and maintain marketplaces where merchants could sell their products. But the ancient states probably did little actively to encourage trade, and in many ways they may
have inhibited it. For example, they may have taxed the merchant to an extent that making
a profit became difficult. The elite may have limited the goods that merchants could trade
or limited the market for goods, for example by claiming exclusive rights to wear certain
kinds of clothes or furs, hunt certain animals, eat certain foods, and inhabit certain sites.

In sixteenth- and seventeenth-century Europe and Japan states began to take a truly
active role in promoting and protecting trade, recognizing that the state's wealth depended
on the success of its manufacturers and traders. They began to protect their manufacturers
and traders by imposing protective tariffs on goods from other states, using military force
to open markets in peripheral areas, and granting trading monopolies to firms within their
borders. States created and maintained ports, built roads and canals, and, later, subsidized
railroad construction.

The state was also involved in the consumption of goods, either by purchasing goods
or, again, using its military or bargaining power to open up foreign markets to its merchants. One of the most lucrative sources of manufacturers' profits was (and still is) the sale
to governments of weapons and other goods and services (food, clothing, and transportation) necessary to maintain the military and other government services. Although ostensibly the military existed in core countries to protect the state against foreign invaders, it was

far more often used to create and maintain colonies necessary for the success of domestic manufacture and trade and to maintain domestic order. Finally, the state organized and directed financial institutions, such as banks, that ensured the ready availability of capital.

The nation-state, said Immanuel Wallerstein (1989:170), became the major building block of the global economy. To be part of the interstate system required that political entities transform themselves into states that followed the rules of the interstate system. This system required for its operation an integrated division of labor, along with guarantees regarding the flow of money, goods, and persons. States were free to impose constraints on these flows but only within a set of rules enforced collectively by member states or, as it usually worked out, a few dominant states.

At the beginning of the nineteenth century, the new capitalist state faced two problems. The first was political. With the downfall of the doctrine of the divine right of kings and the absolute state, political leaders faced a crisis of political legitimacy. *On what basis could they claim control of the state apparatus that had become so critical for the emergence and success of the "national economy"? A second and related problem was economic: How could the state promote the economic integration of all those within its borders?* Although the English state could claim control over England, Scotland, and Wales and the French state over the regions of France (Bretagne, Picardie, Provence, Languedoc, etc.), the situation in the countryside did not reflect that control. At the beginning of the nineteenth century few residents of the British Isles would identify themselves as Britons; few residents of the state of France would identity themselves as French—at least 25 percent of them didn't even speak French. Germany and Italy, of course, didn't yet exist.

Thus, the degree of economic integration of regions was weak or nonexistent. Not only did people speak different languages but they also used different currencies, had different standards and measures, and were downright hostile to state officials. Wages and prices varied from area to area and standardized vocational training was virtually nonexistent. Furthermore, tastes in commodities differed; things manufactured or produced in one area might not appeal to people in other areas. Thus, local economies existed either side by side with or independent of the so-called national economy. While countries such as England, France, and the Netherlands were busy incorporating territories in South and North America, Asia, Africa, and the Middle East into their national economies, they hadn't yet fully incorporated members of their own states.

There was, however, a single solution to both the political and the economic problem: to turn states into nations—groups of people who shared a common culture, language, and heritage and somehow belonged together (or thought they did), worked together, and shopped together. This was not easy to accomplish because virtually all of the major European states in the eighteenth and nineteenth centuries were hodgepodges of languages, cultures, and religions. When Garibaldi united a group of provinces into what was to become Italy, less than 3 percent of the population spoke Italian as their native language. German became the language of Germany only because Joseph II arbitrarily decided it should be. Thus nations had to be created: Frenchmen, Italians, Germans, and Americans had to be manufactured by convincing them they had something in common, preferably loyalty and devotion to their respective states.

If members of a state would see themselves as sharing a common culture—a common heritage, language, and destiny—not only could state leaders claim to represent the "people," whoever they might be, but the people could be more easily integrated into the national economy. They would, ideally, accept the same wages, speak the same language, use the same currency, have similar skills, and similar economic expectations, and, even better, demand the same goods. The question is, *how do you go about constructing a nation?*

CONSTRUCTING THE NATION-STATE

It has been argued by some, especially ardent nationalists of various persuasions, that nation-states are expressions of preexisting cultural, linguistic, religious, ethnic, or historical features shared by people who make up or would make up a state. For many of the nineteenth-century German writers who were instrumental in creating the idea of the nation-state—Johann Gottfried von Herder, Johann Gottlieb Fichte, and Wilhelm Freiherr von Humboldt—nations were expressions of shared language, tradition, race, and state. Thus, today we see some of the citizens of Quebec claiming that their cultural heritage and language differentiates them from the rest of Canada and entitles them to nationhood; Kurds aspiring to their own state on the basis of cultural unity; Bosnian Serbs demanding their own state on the basis of their ethnic purity; and Sikhs demanding their own state based on their mode of worship.

However, the more generally held view, certainly among scholars, is that nation-states are constructed through invention and social engineering. Traditions, suggested Eric Hobsbawm, must be invented. People must be convinced that they share or must be forced to share certain features, such as language, religion, ethnic group membership, or a common historical heritage, regardless of whether they really do. As Hobsbawm and Ranger (1983:1) put it,

> "Invented tradition" is taken to mean a set of practices, normally governed by overtly or tacitly accepted rules and of a ritual or symbolic nature, which seek to inculcate certain values and norms of behavior by repetition, which automatically implies continuity with the past. In fact, were it possible, they normally attempt to establish continuity with a suitable historic past.

Creating the Other

An understanding of how the nation-state and, by extension, people's national identities are constructed is critical to understanding nationalism and ethnicity. Let's begin by examining some of the ways Great Britain and France, pioneers in nation building, went about the task. Linda Colley (1992) illustrated how this was done in Great Britain. Colley's book includes a painting by Sir David Wilkie, *Chelsea Pensioners Reading the Gazette of the Battle of Waterloo,* that caused a sensation when it was exhibited at the Royal Academy in 1822. The painting depicts a crowd celebrating the news of the British victory over Napoleon at Waterloo. The distinguishing feature of the painting is its clear identification of people from all over Britain. There are Welsh, Scottish, and Irish soldiers; women and children; rich and poor; even a Black military bandman. It is, Colley said, a celebration of pa-

Sir David Wilkie's painting Chelsea Pensioners Reading the Gazette of the Battle of Waterloo *represents the power of the nation-state to transcend boundaries of age, gender, class, ethnicity, and occupation.*

triotism that transcends boundaries of age, gender, class, ethnicity, and occupation. It is war, the painting suggests, that forged a nation by uniting this diverse group against a common enemy. Even the signs on the taverns celebrate past wars and victories. According to Colley, Wilkie recognized the importance of war in nation building, and that uniting diverse people and groups against outsiders is one of the most effective ways to create bonds among them (1992:366–367).

Outsiders, however, can be used in more symbolic ways to build national unity. For example, Colley suggested that the making of the British nation from its culturally and linguistically diverse populations would have been impossible without a shared religion, that British Protestantism allowed the English, Scots, and Welsh to overcome their cultural divergence to identify themselves as a nation. However, that would not have been so effective had their religion not also distinguished them from their arch rival, Catholic France.

Furthermore, the founding of a colonial empire created additional Others from whom members of the British nation could distinguish themselves. Britons thought the establishment of an empire proved Britain's providential destiny, that God had chosen them to rule over other peoples and to spread the Gospel. Contact with manifestly alien peoples fed Britons' belief about their superiority. They could favorably compare their treatment of women, their wealth, and their power. The building of a global empire corroborated not only Britain's blessings, but what Scottish socialist Keir Hardie called "the indomitable pluck and energy of the British people" (cited Colley 1992:369).

Thus, one of the most effective ways to construct a nation is to create some Other against whom members of the nation-state can distinguish themselves. That Other needn't be a country; it may be a category of persons constructed out of largely arbitrary criteria, such as racial characteristics or religion. Thus, a group may insist that only people of a particular skin color or religion or who speak a particular language can be members of their nation. War, religion, and the creation of colonies full of subjugated peoples provided for Britons a sense of their collective identity as a people, allowing them to overcome their own significant differences in language, culture, and economic status. Of course, people must find it in their own self-interest as well to proclaim their identity as members of a nation-state. As Colley pointed out, men and women became British patriots to obtain jobs in the state or to advertise their standing in the community. Some believed that British imperialism would benefit them economically or that a French victory would harm them. For some, being an active patriot served to provide them full citizenship and a voice in the running of the state.

Yet the creation of hated or feared Others through such means as war, religion, and empire building is probably not in itself sufficient to build loyalty and devotion to a nation. If it were, the nation-state would likely have emerged well before it did. Constructing a nation-state also requires a national, bureaucratic infrastructure that serves in various ways to unite people.

Language, Bureaucracy, and Education

Eugen Weber, in his book *Peasants into Frenchmen* (1976), provided a classic account of nation building; he documented how peoples in France were administratively molded into a nation by bringing the French language to the countryside, by increasing the ease of travel, by increasing access to national media, through military training, and, most importantly, through a national educational system. Weber (1976:486) compared the transformation of peasants into citizens of a French nation-state to the process of colonization and acculturation: Unassimilated masses had to be integrated into a dominant culture. The process, he suggested, was akin to colonization, except it took place within the borders of the country rather than overseas. *What kind of transformation of national identity did take place in France in the nineteenth century?*

At the beginning of the nineteenth century, even after the French Revolution, a significant portion of rural France still lived in worlds of their own. Few if any would have called themselves "French." The peasants of France were for the most part subsistence farmers, producing not for market or cash but for themselves and their families. People spent their lives in their villages. It is estimated that one-fourth of the residents of France did not speak French, including half the children who would reach adulthood in the last quarter of the nineteenth century. Arnold van Gennep would write as late as 1911 that "for peasants and workers, the mother tongue is patois, the foreign speech is French" (cited Weber 1976:73).

State officials saw linguistic diversity as a threat not to administrative unity but to ideological unity, a shared notion of the interests of the republic, a oneness. Linguistic and cultural diversity came to be seen as imperfection, something to be remedied (Weber 1976:9). As a result, in the 1880s, at the insistence of the government, the French language began to infiltrate the countryside, a process more or less complete by 1914, although even in 1906 English travelers in France had problems communicating in French.

With the homogenization of language came the homogenization of culture. Local customs began to be replaced, dress and food preferences became standardized. Although many aspects of local culture began to disappear, some were adopted as national symbols. The beret, worn only by Basques in 1920, became by 1930 a symbol of France; by 1932 some 23 million were manufactured, one for every French citizen.

Another sign of state integration and the decline of local traditions and values is the decay of popular feasts and rituals that celebrated the unity of local groups, and their replacement by private ceremonies and rituals along with a few national holidays. Communal celebrations, such as Christmas, New Year, and Twelfth Night, turned into family affairs. Where once they were public rituals, baptisms, first communions, and marriages became private ceremonies. Renewal ceremonies that glorified time (the season), work (harvest), or the community (through its patron saint) disappeared as the redistribution of goods, once done through ritual at these ceremonies, was now managed more efficiently (and more stringently) by the state (Weber 1976:398). The replacement of local holidays and festivals with national holidays also allowed these occasions to be turned into periods

Third graders in Palo Alto, California, pledge their allegiance to their nation-state.

of massive consumption and gift giving, similar to Valentine's Day, Easter, Mother's Day, and Christmas in the United States (Schmidt 1995).

National unity in France was also evidenced by the growth of patriotism. In the early nineteenth century draft evasion in the provinces was high; for most, the military was a foreign institution. There was great tax resistance. Even toward the end of the nineteenth century some French citizens had never heard of Napoleon; national authority was embodied in the tax collector and the recruiting sergeant. This is not to say, as Weber (1976:114) pointed out, that the French were unpatriotic, only that they had no uniform conception of patriotism. As he said, "patriotic feelings on the national level, far from instinctive, had to be learned."

Thus, in the nineteenth century, people living within the boundaries of the French state gradually learned to be French. *But how did this happen; how were peasants turned into French citizens?* As with Great Britain, war and the struggle against outsiders certainly played a role in the conversion. The war against Prussia in 1870–1871 was a significant unifying event for most residents of France. The expansion of a colonial empire helped create Others to whom the French could feel superior. But more significant, as Weber pointed out, there were far-reaching changes in the infrastructure and bureaucracy of France.

New roads were built, connecting people to others to whom they had never been connected; the growth of the railroads further increased mobility and contact between people of different regions. The railroads helped to homogenize tastes. Although we now associate the French with wine drinking, wine was not common in the countryside in the first half of the nineteenth century, becoming more available only with the railroads. The roads and railroads brought peasants into a national market; it allowed them to grow and sell crops they couldn't sell before and to stop growing those they could purchase more cheaply—bringing ruin to some local enterprises no longer protected by isolation. Fashions from the cities began to penetrate the countryside. And the roads and railroads set people on the move. If people migrated in the early part of the nineteenth century to find work, they almost always returned. This was no longer true by the end of the century.

As more people spoke French and became literate, they gained access to newspapers and journals, which in turn increased knowledge of national affairs and interests, demonstrating that events at the national level affected their lives. Military service increased identification with the state. Prior to the 1890s there was little sense of national identity in being a soldier; soldiers were either feared or thought to bring bad habits to their communities. Local men who joined the army were forced to conform when they returned to their villages lest their newly learned habits affect others. Many returned not even having learned to speak French. But the war with Prussia seemed to mark the beginning of a national identity in the rank and file of the military and among the peasants. The army began to become a school for the fatherland. Furthermore, for most recruits life in the army was better than life at home; the soldier ate better, dressed better, and was healthier than the average French citizen, and toward the end of the century more and more soldiers did not return to their villages after finishing their military obligations.

As important as all these agents of nation building were in France and other countries, perhaps none was as important as the school. Weber credited the school with being the ultimate source of acculturation that made the French people French.

At the beginning of the century educational conditions were abysmal in France, as in most countries; some teachers couldn't read, and some classes were conducted by nuns who could read only prayers. In 1864, a French school inspector commented that none of the children understood what they read, and when they could read they could not give an account of it. Furthermore, schooling in the countryside had little practical benefit; it could not improve the lives of students economically or socially. Although improving education in the countryside had been a goal of the state since the 1830s, great changes occurred only in the 1880s, when the state began to subsidize education and every hamlet with twenty children or more was required to have a school.

It was clear to state officials that education was necessary as a "guarantee of order and social stability" (Weber 1976:331). "To instruct the people," one said, "is to condition them to understand and appreciate the beneficence of the government" (Weber 1976:331). Clearly there was an explicit link in the minds of state officials between education, nation building, national identity, and economic expansion. Following is a passage from a first-year civics textbook that helped students in "appreciating their condition."

> Society (summary): (1) French society is ruled by just laws, because it is a democratic society. (2) All the French are equal in their rights: but there are inequalities between us that stem from nature or from wealth. (3) These inequalities cannot disappear. (4) Man works to become rich; if he lacked this hope, work would cease and France would decline. It is therefore necessary that each of us should be able to keep the money he has earned. (cited Weber 1976:331)

Schooling was to be the great agent of nationalism. As one teacher said in 1861, it would teach national and patriotic sentiments, explain the benefits of the state and why taxes and military service were necessary, and illustrate for students their true interest in the fatherland. In 1881, another wrote that future instructors must be taught that "their first duty is to make [their charges] love and understand the fatherland." By the 1890s officials considered the school "an instrument of unity," an "answer to dangerous centrifugal tendencies," and the "keystone of national defense" (Weber 1976:332–333).

The best instrument of indoctrination, said school officials, was history, which, when properly taught, "is the only means of maintaining patriotism in the generation we are bringing up." In 1897 candidates for the *baccalauret moderne* were asked to define the purpose of history in education; 80 percent replied essentially that it was to exalt patriotism (Weber 1976:333).

Before 1870 few schools had maps of France; by 1881 few classrooms, no matter how small, were without one. By the end of the century the educational system seemed to be accomplishing its task, as evidenced by boys in rural France who began to enact the exploits of historical heroes.

Ernest Gellner (1983:34) drew the connection between nation building, education, and economic integration even more tightly. According to Gellner, work in industrial society no longer means working with things, rather it involves working with meanings, exchanging communications with other people, or manipulating the controls of machines, controls that need to be understood. It is easy to understand the workings of a shovel or a plow; it is another thing to understand the complex process through which a button or control activates a machine. As a consequence, a modern capitalistic economy requires a mobile division of labor and precise communication between strangers. It requires universal literacy; a high level of numerical, technical, and general sophistication; mobility where members must be prepared to shift from area to area and from task to task; an ability to communicate with people they don't know in a context-dependent form of communication, in a common, standardized language. To attain the standard of literacy and technical competence needed to be employable, people must be trained, not by members of their own local group but by specialists. This training could be provided only by something like a "national" education system. Gellner (1983:34) went so far as to suggest that education became the ultimate instrument of state power, that the professor and the classroom came to replace the executioner and the guillotine as the enforcer of national sovereignty, and that a monopoly on legitimate education became more important than the monopoly on legitimate violence to build a common national identity and to provide the training necessary for the full integration of national economies.

Violence and Genocide

While creating a feared or hated Other, a national bureaucracy, and an educational system are essential in constructing the nation-state, violence remains one of the main tools of nation building. In fact there is a view, shared in anthropology by Pierre van den Berghe (1992), Leo Kuper (1990), Carole Nagengast (1994), and others, that the modern nation-state is essentially an agent of genocide and ethnocide (the suppression and destruction of minority cultures). Given the glorification of the nation-state as a vehicle of modernization, unity, and economic development, this seems a harsh accusation. Yet there exists ample evidence that one of the ways states have sought to create nations is to eliminate or terrorize into submission those within its borders who refuse to assimilate or who demand recognition of their status as a distinct ethnic or national group. In the United States the attempt first to kill all indigenous peoples, then forcibly to assimilate those who remained, followed by a policy of "benign neglect," is but one example of state hostility to cultural variation, as we shall see. The claim that states are agents of death and oppression against minority or even majority groups (e.g., South Africa) is often provided in daily news reports.

Between 1975 and 1979, in one of the worst cases of state killing in the twentieth century, the government of Cambodia, the Khmer Rouge, systematically killed as many as 2 million of its 7 million citizens. These killings were carried out in the name of a program to create a society without cities, money, families, markets, or commodity-money relations. Millions were disembowelled, had nails driven into the backs of their heads, or were beaten to death with hoes. This program involved destroying what the leaders saw as the enemy classes—imperialists (e.g., ethnic Vietnamese, ethnic Chinese, Muslim Chams), feudalists (the leaders of the old regime, Buddhist monks, intellectuals), and comprador capitalists (ethnic Chinese). The goal was as much nationalistic as it was socialistic—to return Cambodia and the Khmer race to its previous glory. They took over a country devastated by U.S. bombing during the Vietnam War and ended up by killing millions who they deemed didn't belong (Kuper 1990). But the killing of its citizens by the Khmer Rouge, while reaching an intensity matched by few states, was hardly an exception.

As Carole Nagengast (1994:119–120) wrote:

The numbers of people worldwide subjected to the violence of their own states are staggering. More than a quarter of a million Kurds and Turks in Turkey have been beaten or tortured by the military, police, and prison guards since 1980; tens of thousands of indigenous people in Peru and Guatemala, street children in Brazil and Guatemala, Palestinians in

Kuwait, Kurds in Iraq, and Muslim women and girls in Bosnia have been similarly treated. Mutilated bodies turn up somewhere everyday. Some 6,000 people in dozens of countries were legally shot, hung, electrocuted, gassed, or stoned to death by their respective states between 1985 and 1992 for political misdeeds: criticism of the state, membership in banned political parties or groups, or for adherence to the "wrong" religion; for moral deeds: adultery, prostitution, homosexuality, sodomy, or alcohol or drug use; for economic offenses: burglary, embezzling, and corruption; and for violent crimes: rape, assault, and murder.

R. J. Rummel (1994), in a series of books on state killing, documented the carnage committed by states against their own citizens: 61 million Russians from 1917 to 1987; 20 million Germans from 1933 to 1945; 35 million Chinese killed by the Chinese communist government from 1923 to 1949 and 10 million killed by the Chinese nationalists; almost 2 million Turks from 1909 to 1918; and almost 1.5 million Mexicans from 1900 to 1920. In total, Rummel (1994:9) said, almost 170 million men, women, and children from 1900 to 1987

> have been shot, beaten, tortured, knifed, burned, starved, frozen, crushed, or worked to death; buried alive, drowned, hung, bombed, or killed in any other of the myriad ways governments have inflicted death on unarmed, helpless citizens and foreigners. The dead could conceivably be nearly 360 million people. It is as though our species has been devastated by a modern Black Plague. And indeed it has, but a plague of Power not germs.

Rummel attributed state killing to power and its abuses, claiming it is largely totalitarian regimes that resort to democide, genocide, or ethnocide. Democracies also kill, as evidenced in the twentieth century by indiscriminate bombings of enemy civilians in war, the large-scale massacre of Filipinos during U.S. colonization of the Philippines at the turn of the century, deaths in British concentration camps during the Boer War in South Africa, civilian deaths in Germany as a result of the Allied blockade, the rape and murder of helpless Chinese in and around Peking in 1900, atrocities committed by Americans in Vietnam, the murder of helpless Algerians by the French during the Algerian War, and the deaths of German prisoners of war in French and U.S. prisoner of war camps after World War II. But Rummel said even these prove his point about power, for virtually all of these cases were committed in secret behind a trail of lies and deceit by agencies and power holders who were given the authority to operate autonomously and shielded from the press. Even attacks on German and Vietnamese cities were presented as attacks on military targets. He concluded that as we move from democratic through authoritarian and to totalitarian governments, the degree of state killing increases dramatically (Rummel 1994:17).

Pierre van den Berghe (1992:191) attributed state killing not to the misuse of authority but to nation building itself. Taking what he called a frankly anarchist position, he said

> the process euphemistically described as nation-building is, in fact, mostly nation-killing; ...the vast majority of so-called "nation-states" are nothing of the sort; and...modern nationalism is a blueprint for ethnocide at best, genocide at worst.

Van den Burghe said that the nation-state myth has been allowed to persist because international bodies, such as the United Nations, insist that internal killing is a state matter, a "gentlemen's agreement" between member states not to protest the butchering of their own citizens. Also, scholars perpetrate the myth with the use of nation-state designation. The result is to legitimize genocide in the interests of building nation-states that function to further economic and political integration.

Carole Nagengast (1994:122) proposed that state-sponsored violence serves to aid in the construction and maintenance of the nation-state. She examined not only state killing but also the institutionalization of torture, rape, and homosexual assault. The purpose of this state-sponsored violence is not to inflict pain but to create what Nagengast called "punishable categories of people," to create and maintain boundaries and legitimate or delegitimate specific groups. State violence against its own citizens, she suggested, is a way to create an Other, an ambiguous underclass that consists on the one hand of subhuman brutes and on the other hand of superhuman individuals capable of undermining the accepted order of society. Arrest and torture serve to stigmatize people and to mark them as people who no one wants to be. Arrest and torture become, in effect, a way of symbolically marking, disciplining, and stigmatizing those categories of people whose existence or demands threaten the idea, power, and legitimacy of the nation-state. Furthermore, because the torture and violence are committed only against "terrorists," "communists," or "separatists," it becomes legitimate. "We only beat bad people," said a Turkish prison official in 1984. "They are no good, they are worthless bums, they are subversives who think that communism will relieve them of the necessity of working." He revealed with apparent pride that he had "given orders that all prisoners should be struck with a truncheon below the waist on the rude parts, and warned not to come to prison again." "My aim," he said, "is to ensure discipline. That's not torture, for it is only the lazy, the idle, the vagabonds, the communists, the murderers who come to prison" (cited Nagengast 1994:121).

Terrorist acts are often depicted as being extralegal; that is, committed by persons outside state control. Yet there is considerable evidence that most terror is applied by states to integrate or control a reluctant citizenry. As Jeffery Sluka (2000:1) puts it:

> if terrorism means political intimidation by violence or its threat, and if we allow the definition to include violence by states and agents of states, then we find that the major form of terrorism in the world today is practiced by states and their agents and allies, and that quantitatively, anti-state terrorism pales into relative insignificance in comparison to it.

Death squads operate outside the law but with the tacit approval of the state. Thus their actions carry out state goals of eliminating dissidents without due process of law but are enough removed from official state agencies to allow the state "plausible denial." Rarely are members of death squads punished, and many are also members of official state agencies, such as the police, militia, or army.

Targets of death squads are often portrayed by the state as "terrorists" or subversives but tend to be anyone that challenges the status quo. These include people who organize unions, offer Bible classes, propose land reforms, or advocate tax increases on the rich. They include clergy, labor organizers, human rights activists, social workers, journalists, and so on. Victims include women, children, the elderly, and relatives of activists. More recently, particularly in Latin America, victims include street children.

Few countries are immune to the operation of state-sanctioned death squads. In the United States, for example, there were 4,743 recorded lynchings from 1882 to 1968. Of these people who were lynched 3,446 were Black. Not only were people never prosecuted for participating in a lynching, they requested often to have their pictures taken next to the victim, often turning the photograph into a postcard (Allen 2000).[1]

Core countries play a major role in supporting violent regimes in the periphery by either training officers or offering direct military aid. Virtually all this military support is used, not to defend against foreign invasion, but to suppress political dissent or unionization or to discipline a resistant citizenry. And the financial cost of maintaining militaries and supplying client states is high (see Table 4.1). Alexander George in his book *Western State Terrorism* concludes that

> The plain and painful truth is that on any reasonable definition of terrorism, taken literally, the United States and its friends are the major supporters, sponsors, and perpetrators of terrorist incidents in the world today...many, probably most, significant instances of terrorism are supported, if not organized, by the U.S., its partners, and their client states (George 1991:1–2)

THE FUTURE OF THE NATION-STATE

The nation-state as currently conceived is 200 to 300 years old. But what is its future? Some suggest that nation-states are no longer viable or necessary and will disintegrate into smaller, more culturally homogeneous units. Others (see, e.g., Smith 1995) suggest that the nation-state is still the most sensible solution to problems of social and economic order.

There are, however, three developments that seem to threaten the integrity of nation-states: transnationalism, an increase in the number of people living and working in countries other than the one in which they hold citizenship; the growing power and influence of transnational corporations; and the growth in the number, and possibly the influence, of nongovernmental organizations. Let's complete our examination of the nation-state by reviewing each of these developments.

Transnationalism and Migration

Lenin (1976) made the point that imperialism transported surplus capital from developed to undeveloped areas of the world and, as a consequence, destroyed local economies, replacing peasant farming and small-scale industry with wage labor. But the economies of underdeveloped areas are incapable of absorbing the labor it has created, and that labor is now spilling over into the core of the world capitalist economy. Currently some 2 percent of the world's population—more than 100 million people—live and work in countries of which they are not citizens.

Massive labor migration is not a new thing; in the last half of the nineteenth century and the first decades of the twentieth, as we saw in Chapter 2, millions of people migrated in search of land and wage labor. The migrations of the 1980s and 1990s, however, are dif-

---

[1]Many of these photographs are available on the Web. See for example: http://www.berea.edu/ENG/chesnutt/history.html.

TABLE 4.1   Military Expenditures and Arms Exports and Imports by Country, 1999

ARMS EXPENDITURES			ARMS EXPORTS			ARMS IMPORTS		
Rank	Country	$ in millions	Rank	Country	$ in millions	Rank	Country	$ in millions
1	United States	281,000	1	United States	33,000	1	Saudi Arabia	7,700
2	China	88,900	2	United Kingdom	5,200	2	Turkey	3,200
3	Japan	43,200	3	Russia	3,100	3	Japan	3,000
4	France	38,900	4	France	2,900	4	China–Taiwan	2,600
5	United Kingdom	36,500	5	Germany	1,900	5	United Kingdom	2,600
6	Russia	35,000	6	Sweden	675	6	Israel	2,400
7	Germany	32,600	7	Israel	600	7	South Korea	2,200
8	Italy	23,700	8	Australia	550	8	Greece	1,900
9	Saudi Arabia	21,200	9	Canada	550	9	United States	1,600
10	Taiwan	15,200	10	Ukraine	550	10	Germany	1,300
11	South Korea	11,600	11	Italy	380	11	Australia	1,100
12	India	11,300	12	China–Mainland	320	12	Switzerland	1,100
13	Turkey	9,950	13	Belarus	310	13	Canada	1,000
14	Brazil	9,920	14	Bulgaria	200	14	Pakistan	1,000
15	Israel	8,700	15	North Korea	140	15	Singapore	950
16	Canada	8,320	16	Netherlands	140	16	United Arab Emirates	950
17	Spain	7,560	17	Indonesia	100	17	Malaysia	925
18	Australia	7,060	18	Greece	90	18	France	800
19	Netherlands	7,030	19	Czech Republic	80	19	Netherlands	775
20	Iran	6,880	20	Spain	70	20	Spain	750
21	Poland	6,690	21	Turkey	70	21	Kuwait	725
22	Greece	6,060	22	Finland	50	22	Egypt	700
23	Sweden	5,330	23	Switzerland	50	23	India	700
24	Congo	5,150	24	Romania	40	24	Italy	700
25	Ukraine	5,110	25	Austria	30	25	China–Mainland	675
26	Burma	4,650	26	Belgium	30	26	New Zealand	575
27	Syria	4,450	27	Georgia	30	27	Algeria	550
28	Singapore	4,400	28	Libya	30	28	Norway	480
29	Argentina	4,300	29	Mexico	30	29	Russia	470
30	North Korea	4,260	30	Poland	30	30	Indonesia	450
31	Belgium	3,600	31	South Africa	30	31	Finland	400
32	Pakistan	3,520	32	Brazil	20	32	Angola	350
33	Switzerland	3,400	33	China–Taiwan	20	33	Belgium	350
34	Vietnam	NA	34	Eritrea	20	34	Cyprus	340
35	Norway	3,310	35	Japan	20	35	Thailand	330
36	Czech Republic	3,000	36	South Korea	20	36	Venezuela	310
37	Denmark	2,780	37	Moldova	20	37	Denmark	290
38	Mexico	2,700	38	Norway	20	38	Ethiopia	270
39	Kuwait	2,690	39	Serbia and Montenegro	20	39	Sweden	230
40	Colombia	2,670	40	Singapore	20	40	Czech Republic	220
41	Angola	2,460	41	Chile	10	41	Syria	210
42	Portugal	2,410	42	Croatia	10	42	Romania	200
43	Egypt	2,390	43	Denmark	10	43	Brazil	180
44	Romania	2,190	44	Hungary	10	44	Eritrea	170
45	United Arab Emirates	2,180	45	India	10	45	Kazakhstan	160
46	Croatia	2,090	46	Iran	10	46	Mexico	160
47	Thailand	2,040	47	Kazakhstan	10	47	Iran	150
48	Libya	NA	48	Pakistan	10	48	Morocco	130
49	Chile	1,990	49	Slovakia	10	49	Qatar	120
50	South Africa	1,960	50	Uzbekistan	10	50	Congo (Kinshasa)	110

From U.S. Department of State, *World Military Expenditures and Arms Transfers* (2003); http://www.state.gov/
t/vc/rls/rpt/wmeat/1999_2000/.

ferent in at least two respects. First, labor migrants are maintaining or attempting to maintain close ties with their home countries, and home countries are also attempting to
maintain those ties. Not only do Haitian migrants to the United States maintain close ties
with their families in Haiti, but the Haitian government refers to those people as Le Dix-
ième Département (Dizyém Depatman-an in Creole) of a country with nine geographical divisions or Depatman. It is as if Americans working abroad were referred to as a fifty-first
state. Second, migrants are no longer as welcome in host core countries as they were in the
nineteenth century, when there was an abundance of land and a shortage of labor. These
two differences have created a very different view of migrants in their home countries and
in the core countries in which they seek to work.

Linda Basch, Nina Glick Schiller, and Cristina Szanton Blanc (1994:7), in their book
Nations Unbound, labeled the process where people's lives are stretched across national
boundaries as transnationalism. They defined *transnationalism* as

> The process by which immigrants forge and sustain multi-stranded social relations that link
> together their societies of origin and settlement. We call these processes transnationalism to
> emphasize that many immigrants today build social fields that cross geographic, cultural,
> and political borders.

Transnationalism, they suggested, requires a reconceptualization of the nation-state;
whereas it was once thought of as people sharing a common territory, it now must include
citizens who are physically dispersed among other states but who remain socially, politically, culturally, and sometimes economically part of the nation-state of their ancestors
(Basch et al. 1994:8).

They believe transnational migrants are a product of global capitalism as the debt of
peripheral countries has created massive unemployment. The unemployed are vulnerable
in their own countries because they cannot find work and in the countries to which they migrate because they cannot compete on an equal basis and often are used as scapegoats. It is
because of this economic and political vulnerability that migrants construct a transnational
existence seeking work in core countries while at the same time maintaining ties with
family at home (Basch et al. 1994:27). Consequently, transmigrants are engaged in the
nation-building process of two or more nation-states, the state of their origin and the one to
which they have migrated in search of work.

Haitian migrants to the United States, for example, often send money and goods
home both to aid their family and to advance their social position for their expected return
home. One estimate is that in 1989, Haitian immigrants sent $99.5 million from New York
to Haiti (Basch et al. 1994:165). Many Haitians living in the United States build, buy, and
maintain homes in Haiti and send home furnishings both for their own home and for their
kin. Children are sent each year to visit or, in many cases, left in Haiti with kin because it
is easier and cheaper to raise them there.

One motivation for maintaining ties arises from loyalty, sentiment, and emotional
ties to Haiti. But there is also a sense of precariousness of rooting oneself in the United
States because of racism and discrimination, fear of unemployment, national chauvinism,
the high cost of living, and, for some, the continued undocumented status that leaves them
vulnerable to discovery and deportation. Marie Rose was born in Haiti but grew up in the
United States, was educated in Brooklyn and received a master's of nursing, and became

head of a nursing unit in a Brooklyn hospital. She continues to invest in her home in Haiti, where she spends two weekends each year. Her husband moved back to Haiti, taking with him the Mercedes Marie bought in the United States.

For the migrant's home country, migrants are valuable sources of foreign exchange. The home country's dilemma is how to take advantage of the money and goods that transnational migrants send home, while maintaining their identity and loyalty. For example, to promote transnationalism in the mid-1980s, Haitian leaders used Zionists as a model, Jews who were permanently part of U.S. political, social, and economic life but who were made to understand that they had a "homeland" in Israel. Father Jean Bertrand Aristide accelerated this process when he was elected president in 1991, going so far as to appoint to government posts Haitians who had become citizens of other countries. In his address to the United Nations, Aristide insisted his government had a right to intervene on behalf of Haitians living in other countries.

Viewed from the core, transnational migrants pose a different set of problems. The problem is that the often cheap labor supplied by the transnational migrant is desired, but the person who does the labor is not. The question is *how to keep the borders open to cheap transnational labor while at the same time maintaining the boundaries of the nation-state?* In the United States, for example, businesses want foreign labor, but the increase in the number of immigrants threatens some people's sense of their national identity; thus the increase in Spanish-speaking immigrants in the United States increased efforts to have Congress declare English the country's official language.

Michael Kearney (1991:58), examining the situation of the Mexican worker in the United States, suggested that immigration policy in core countries is largely directed to trying to separate the labor from the laborer: Foreign labor is desired, but the person in which it is embodied is not. Consequently, the immigration policies of host countries must somehow separate labor from the person who supplies it, must "disembody the labor from the migrant worker."

One way to do this is to pass punitive antimigrant legislation that allows migrants to work in the United States but prohibits access to services, such as education for their children, welfare, and medical assistance. Thus, American employers can obtain cheap labor, while the state can deny benefits accorded to citizen laborers. Another solution is to pass language laws that mark any non-English speaker as unqualified to be a member of the nation-state. Kearney pointed out also that even such things as border patrols function not so much to apprehend illegal migrants as to force them to accept low-paying jobs while not claiming benefits accorded to other laborers. He cited the example of migrant Mixtecs, who walk through the mountains in winter to find work and who because of their work ethic are desired by American employers. They don't understand why the *Migra* (border patrol) seek to apprehend them, forcing them to work harder and faster before they are apprehended, and forcing them to take whatever work at whatever wages they can. But, as Kearney (1991:61) pointed out, that is exactly the point of the *Migra;* it is not intended to stop migrants from coming into the United States to work; rather it functions to discipline them to work harder and accept low wages.

Thus, border areas become contested zones, manifestations of the dilemma of exploiting the laborer while denying the rights of the individual. Kearney noted that the border is as or more troubling to Mexico than it is to the United States. Given the economic situation in

Mexico in the 1990s, where income was dropping and unemployment was increasing, transmigration was highly valued. If Mexicans living and working in the United States were repatriated to Mexico, the increase in unemployment in Mexico would result in an impossible situation and possible social unrest. Furthermore, their return would mean the loss of Mexico's third or fourth most important source of foreign exchange (Kearney 1991:69).

The differences in wealth between the periphery and the core, the need of citizens of peripheral countries to find jobs wherever they are, and the desire in capitalist economies to seek the cheapest labor combine to create a dynamic that increases the number of transnational migrants working in core countries and threatens the boundaries between nation-states. Kearney suggested that boundary-maintaining activities, such as language laws and punitive antimigrant legislation, represent a sign of a threat to national boundaries. In the era of transnationalism, there is a dissolution of boundaries and a frantic attempt to deal with it by further defining, maintaining, and defending borders.

Will Corporations Rule the World?

Some see yet another entity as a threat to the power of the nation-state—the transnational corporation. In many ways this institution seems a natural development in a process of economic integration that began centuries ago. One of the major dynamics for the development of the nation-state, as previously mentioned, is the need to integrate national economies. The growth of business and the creation of the consumer required standardized weights, measures, and currencies; common wages and prices; and a homogeneous consumer population such that a product produced in a given country would be desired by everyone in that country. The state was the main agency enforcing integration, through regulatory agencies, enforced wage and labor standards, and, perhaps most importantly, through the development of state education and schools that would construct populations of Americans, French, English, Germans, Italians, and so on.

As states required economic integration within their borders, however, the modern global economy requires global, not only state, integration. The institution best equipped to perform the task of global integration, some argue, is the transnational corporation. David Korten (1995:12) suggested that these entities represent a shift of power away from governments, which are ideally responsible for the public good, toward a few corporations and financial institutions, in which are concentrated massive economic and political power and whose sole motive is the quest for short-term financial gain. The corporation, Korten argued, has evolved from an institution with limited power to one that some claim is the dominant governance institution of the world and that exceeds most governments in size and power (see Table 4.2). One consequence is that corporate interest, as opposed to human interests, defines the policy agendas of states and international agencies.

As we saw in Chapter 3, the corporate charter is a social invention that originally was supposed to promote the use of private financial resources for public purposes. It can be traced back to the sixteenth century. Since that time corporations have assumed enormous power and have advanced an ideology that Korten labeled *corporate libertarianism,* which places the rights and freedoms of corporations above the rights and freedoms of individuals. The question is, *how have corporations managed to convince governments of the worth of this ideology? Perhaps more importantly, how have they managed to convince the public that*

TABLE 4.2   The Top 100 Global Financial Entities, 1999/2000

RANK	COUNTRY/ CORPORATION	GNP/REVENUE $U.S. IN MILLIONS	RANK	COUNTRY/ CORPORATION	GNP/REVENUE $U.S. IN MILLIONS
1	UNITED STATES	8510.6750	47	Sumitomo	95.7010
2	JAPAN	3782.9460	48	VENEZUELA	95.0164
3	GERMANY	2141.6780	49	Nippon T & T	93.5910
4	FRANCE	1435.2030	50	Marubeni	91.8070
5	UNITED KINGDOM	1387.4400	51	ISRAEL	91.3171
6	ITALY	1169.2660	52	COLOMBIA	90.4063
7	CHINA	960.7851	53	INDONESIA	88.5515
8	BRAZIL	776.8286	54	AXA	87.6450
9	CANADA	598.8625	55	Intl. Business Machines	87.5480
10	SPAIN	554.8851	56	SINGAPORE	84.3786
11	MEXICO	424.5240	57	BP Amoco	83.5660
12	INDIA	420.3054	58	Citigroup	82.0050
13	NETHERLANDS	378.1987	59	EGYPT	81.5282
14	AUSTRALIA	363.9098	60	Volkswagen	80.0720
15	ARGENTINA	339.8068	61	Nippon Life Insurance	78.5150
16	KOREA	310.1118	62	IRELAND	78.3242
17	RUSSIA	283.8242	63	Siemens	75.3370
18	SWITZERLAND	262.6460	64	CHILE	74.3185
19	TAIWAN	258.8676	65	Allianz	74.1780
20	BELGIUM	251.3653	66	Hitachi	71.8580
21	SWEDEN	226.8869	67	MALAYSIA	67.4845
22	AUSTRIA	212.4617	68	Matsushita Electric Industrial	65.5550
23	TURKEY	196.9821	69	Nissho Iwai	65.3930
24	MYANMAR	189.7544	70	PHILIPPINES	64.5262
25	General Motors	176.5880	71	PAKISTAN	64.1293
26	DENMARK	174.1033	72	PERU	64.0548
27	Wal-Mart Stores	166.8090	73	U.S. Postal Service	62.7260
28	HONG KONG	166.4958	74	ING Group	62.4920
29	Exxon Mobil	163.8810	75	AT&T	62.3910
30	Ford Motor	162.5580	76	Philip Morris	61.7510
31	DaimlerChrysler	159.9860	77	Sony	60.0520
32	POLAND	148.9580	78	LIBYA	59.5000
33	NORWAY	145.8926	79	Deutsche Bank	58.5850
34	SAUDI ARABIA	125.8401	80	Boeing	57.9930
35	FINLAND	125.4124	81	Dai-ichi Mutual Life Insurance	55.1040
36	GREECE	120.7235	82	Honda Motor	54.7730
37	Mitsui	118.5550	83	Assicurazioni Generali	53.7230
38	IRAN	118.5098	84	Nissan Motor	53.6790
39	Mitsubishi	117.7760	85	CZECH REPUBLIC	53.2500
40	THAILAND	117.0386	86	NEW ZEALAND	52.7135
41	SOUTH AFRICA	116.3242	87	E. ON	52.2270
42	Toyota Motor	115.6710	88	Toshiba	51.6340
43	General Electric	111.6300	89	Bank of America Corp.	51.3920
44	Itochu	109.0690	90	Fiat	51.3310
45	PORTUGAL	107.7889	91	Nestlé	49.6940
46	Royal Dutch/Shell Group	105.3660	92	SBC Communications	49.4890

(continued)

TABLE 4.2   Continued

RANK	COUNTRY/ CORPORATION	GNP/REVENUE $US IN MILLIONS	RANK	COUNTRY/ CORPORATION	GNP/REVENUE $US IN MILLIONS
93	Credit Suisse	49.3620	97	Fujitsu	47.1950
94	Hewlett-Packard	48.2530	98	Metro	46.6630
95	HUNGARY	47.8293	99	ALGERIA	46.6016
96	UNITED ARAB EMIRATES	47.2339	100	Sumitomo Life Insurance	46.4450

Country GNP data from the World Economic Outlook 1999 Database (IMF) at http://www.imf.org/external/pubs/ft/weo/2000/02/data/index.htm; corporate income data from Forbes' Global 500 at http://www.fortune.com/fortune/global500/

its interests are identical to those of the corporation? Korten argued that corporations have advanced their interests by gaining control of various international and domestic agencies as well as social, political, and economic institutions (see Table 4.3).

The first group of agencies that function to advance corporate interests, according to Korten, are the Council on Foreign Relations, the Bilderberg (named for the Hotel de Bilderberg of Oosterbeek, Holland), and the Trilateral Commission. These are private forums created to bring together people from government, business, the media, and academia to discuss the creation of public policy and create a consensus that aligns our most powerful institutions with the economic globalization agenda. For example, it was the Council on Foreign Relations and its journal, *Foreign Affairs,* that in the late 1930s recommended to President Roosevelt that he create a network of worldwide financial institutions

TABLE 4.3   The Mechanisms of Corporate Control

AGENCY	METHOD OF CONTROL	WHOM IT CONTROLS
Trilateral Commission, Council on Foreign Relations, Bilderberg	Consensus building	Corporate, government, academic elites
World Bank	Financial control	National financial institutions
Public relations	Consensus building	Government leaders, voters, etc.
Advertising, media, and education	Consumers educational institutions, newspapers, TV, magazines, etc.	General population
World regulatory agencies	Political control	State agencies
Military force	State military organizations, private armies	Dissenters to corporate control and influence

to stabilize currencies and provide capital for the development of peripheral countries. This recommendation led to the conference in 1944 at Bretton Woods at which the World Bank and the International Monetary Fund were created. The Bilderberg began with informal meetings of North American and European leaders in 1954; participants have included virtually every major industrialist, financier, and government leader. The Trilateral Commission was formed in 1973 by David Rockefeller, chair of Chase Manhattan Bank, and Zbigniew Brzezinski, who was to be National Security Advisor during the Carter administration. They describe themselves as a group of 325 distinguished citizens. Members have included heads of all the major corporations as well as American presidents (Carter, Bush, Clinton) and many who hold influential government posts. These institutions and others have brought together government, academic, and corporate leaders to create policy that directs the actions of governments and influential world agencies, such as the World Bank, the International Monetary Fund, and the United Nations, toward full integration of the world's capitalist economy.

In addition to these "informal" discussion groups, corporate libertarianism is evident in the working of the World Bank, which functions partly to control the financial links between corporations and borrowers. Thus, the International Finance Corporation, one arm of the World Bank, functions to make government-guaranteed loans to private investors on projects deemed too risky for commercial banks.

Another way corporations sell their agenda is through lobbying groups and public relations efforts targeted to political leaders and the public. Until the 1970s this was done through straightforward lobbying groups, such as the Beer Institute and the National Coal Association. Today corporations try to mask their involvement by forming "citizen" groups, such as the National Wetlands Coalition (with its logo of a duck flying over a swamp), sponsored by oil and gas drilling companies and real estate developers fighting for reducing restrictions on the conversion of wetlands to drilling sites and shopping malls. Keep America Green, sponsored by the bottling industry, argues for antilitter campaigns rather than mandatory recycling legislation.

Protected by the free speech provision of the First Amendment, corporations marshal huge public relations efforts on behalf of their agendas. In the United States the 170,000 public relations employees whose job it is to manipulate news, public opinion, and public policy in the interests of their clients outnumber news reporters by 40,000. A study in 1990 discovered that almost 40 percent of the news content of a typical U.S. newspaper originates as public relations press releases, story memos, and suggestions. The *Columbia Journalism Review* reported that more than half the news stories in the *Wall Street Journal* are based solely on corporate press releases (cited Korten 1995:148). U.S. corporations spend almost half as much on advertising (approximately $120 per person) as the federal government spends on education ($207 per person). Korten (1995:146) suggested that the world outlined by George Orwell in *1984* has occurred, but it is the corporation rather than the state that is oppressing us: "We are ruled by an oppressive market, not an oppressive state."

Finally, in the 1980s and 1990s corporations gained formal control over international regulatory agencies. The assumption of this control began with the Bretton Woods initiative and culminated with the World Trade Organization. The WTO has the power to override rules and legislation passed by countries and local governments if its three-person panel, in private, decides that the rules "unfairly" inhibit free trade. Thus, the modern

The powers exercised by corporations through government, through private and public institutions, and through public relations specialists can often result in the voting public supporting actions that may not be in their best interest.

Reprinted with the permission of John Jonik.

transnational corporation can use public policy forums, international financial agencies, public relations organizations, the media, schools, and world regulatory agencies to convince government leaders and the public of courses of action that ensure profit making and reduce the risk of financial failure. Furthermore, to the extent that individual lives are influenced by corporate ideology, we may also be witnessing the increase of the authoritarian governance systems common to corporations.

It would seem that the only agency of control lacking in the corporation is armed force. Yet corporations have sometimes managed to co-opt the military of nation-states to serve their own ends or even, on occasion, to organize and equip their own private armies. Early in their development, corporations made use of armies, national guards, and sometimes even their own private military forces to end strikes or punish or repress urban and rural protests. Even today corporations often become closely involved in state repression.

In 1995 Shell Oil Corporation supplied arms to the Nigerian government as it sought to repress the Ogoni peoples, who were demanding that Shell cease polluting Ogoni lands. Shell earned worldwide condemnation for its involvement and possible acquiescence in the execution of Ogoni leader Ken Saro Wira. Oil companies such as Local 66 have lent direct or indirect support to the repressive regime in Myanmar (Burma), whereas other corporations appear to seek out relations with repressive regimes that ban labor organizing. We may be witnessing the birth of a new kind of war—"investor wars"—in which governments, to keep or attract foreign corporate investment, systematically repress and make war on minorities whose demands lend an impression of government instability that state leaders fear will scare away foreign investors.

In addition to marshalling private armies to protect their own interests, corporations are rapidly emerging to supply nation-states with privatized armed services. In his book, *Corporate Warriors: The Rise of the Privatized Military Industry,* Peter Singer (2003) describes the role of corporate military in Sierra Leone where a South African firm called Executive Outcomes was hired to battle a rebellion and in Bosnia where Military Professional Resources Inc. (MPRI) helped the Croats turn back the Serbs. The United States has turned to Brown and Root Services, a subsidiary of Halliburton, to feed troops and maintain weapons systems and vehicles in Kosovo and Iraq.

Yet, as powerful as corporations have become, it is difficult to see them operating without the nation-state. Some have argued that, in fact, the nation-state is, by and large, an extension of the corporation, creating conditions necessary for the maintenance of perpetual growth (see, e.g., Wallerstein 1997). Nation-states must adopt policies to promote "competitiveness," to promote the free movement of capital, and confine labor within national boundaries. Furthermore the nation-state must create and enforce rules that permit the various costs involved in doing business to be "externalized" and passed on to the general public, marginalized persons, or to future generations.

Corporations rarely, if ever, pay the full cost of production. And consumers never directly pay the real price of things. For example, a gallon of gasoline is currently selling in the United States for approximately $1.50 to $2.00. But the real cost, according to a report from the International Center for Technology Assessment (ICTA nd) is closer to from $10 to $15. How is it then, that oil companies can sell it for $2 and still make a huge profit?

First, the U.S. government provides domestic companies with tax breaks to enable them to compete with other producers, as well as to keep gasoline prices down. There is, for example, the percentage depletion allowance that amounts to almost $1 billion a year, foreign tax credits of some $1.11 billion to $3.4 billion, along with other tax subsidies that save oil companies some $9.1 billion to $17.8 billion. Second, there are program subsidies that support the extraction, production, and use of petroleum projects that total $38 billion to $114.6 billion each year. This includes the construction, maintenance and repair of roads and bridges, direct support of research and development, and government expenditures for pollution cleanup and regulation. Then there are protection subsidies, particularly the military protection for oil-rich regions. The U.S. Defense Department spending allocated to safeguarding the world's petroleum resources amounts to some $55 billion to $96.3 billion per year. The maintenance of the Strategic Petroleum Reserve costs $5.7 billion per year.

Then there are the environmental, health, and social costs that are not reflected in the price we pay at the pump. The International Center for Technology Assessment reports that these expenses total some $231.7 billion to $942.9 billion every year. The environmental costs of pollution caused directly by the internal combustion engine costs at least $39 billion per year, and some estimates place the cost at closer to $600 billion. Because researchers have directly linked automobile pollution to health problems, annual uncompensated health costs are estimated to run from $29.3 billion to $542.4 billion a year.

These are only samples of the hidden costs of gasoline; if we were to add to these the hidden costs of our dependence on the automobile, of course, these costs would skyrocket. Thus, without the nation-state to pass laws and regulations and to provide needed services for the maintenance of trade, the direct cost of virtually all the items that we buy, from candy bars (see Robbins 2000) to automobiles, would be many times higher than they are. And if we were to add up the hidden costs of all the items that define even a middle-class lifestyle in the culture of capitalism, we would be able to appreciate the role of the nation-state in making that lifestyle economically feasible. Of course, these hidden prices need to be paid at some point by someone; consequently, we must pay them in higher taxes or health costs, or others must pay them in lower wages or health or environmental risks; otherwise, the costs must be paid by future generations.

Nongovernmental Organizations

Another set of global organizations that some claim presents an alternative to the nation-state is the nongovernmental organization (NGO). These organizations—also called the nonprofit sector, independent sector, volunteer sector, civic society, grassroots organizations (GROs), transnational social movement organizations, and nonstate actors—generally represent any organization, group, or institution that fulfills a public function but is not a part of the government of the territories in which it works. Nongovernmental organizations may be large transnational organizations, such as Amnesty International or the Red Cross, or small, local-level groups, such as a neighborhood group organized to provide day care. Generally, it is the large international groups that some see as alternatives to nation-states.

There are various ways of conceptualizing the role of NGOs in relation to other political and economic bodies. Lester M. Salamon and Helmut K. Anheier (1996:129) suggested that NGOs represent a third sector in global governance, the other two being the state and the corporation (or "market"). Marc Nerfin (1986) suggested that politically we can conceptualize NGOs using the metaphor of the prince, the merchant, and the people, with governmental power and the maintenance of public order the job of the prince, economic power and the production of goods and services the job of the merchant, and NGOs representing the citizen, the power of the people. In this framework, NGOs developed from citizen demands for accountability from the prince and merchant, competing with them for power and influence, and demanding that neglected groups (e.g., the poor, children) be heard (see Korten 1990:95ff; Weiss and Gordenker 1996:19).

The NGO as we know it dates from the founding of the International Red Cross in Switzerland in 1865. Since that time there has been spectacular growth in the number of recognized NGOs, particularly in the 1980s and 1990s in the periphery. In 1909, for example, there were 176 international NGOs; by 1993 there were 28,900, and by 2000, well over 30,000. In Nepal the number of registered NGOs rose from 220 in 1990 to 1,210 in 1993; in Bolivia from 100 in 1980 to 530 in 1992; in Tunisia from 1,886 in 1988 to 5,186 in 1991.

Often NGOs in the periphery serve and employ thousands of people. In south Asia, for example, the Bangladesh Rural Advancement Committee (BRAC) delivers health, education, and credit services to almost 3 million people and employs 12,000. Some suggest (see, e.g., Edwards and Hulme 1995) that the development of NGOs may be as important in the last part of the twentieth century as the development of the nation-state was in the nineteenth.

Why have NGOs increased in importance? First, some suggest that the end of the Cold War made it easier for NGOs to operate without being drawn into the conflict between the West and the Communist Bloc. Second, revolutions in communication, particularly through the Internet, have helped create new global communities and bonds between like-minded people across state boundaries. Third, there are increased resources and a growing professionalism in NGOs. In 1994, 10 percent of public development aid ($8 billion) was channeled through NGOs, including 25 percent of U.S. assistance and 30 percent of projects funded by the International Bank for Reconstruction and Development. Nongovernmental organizations represent a major growth sector for people seeking employment. Fourth, there is the media's ability to inform more people about global problems. With this increased awareness, the public, particularly but not exclusively in core countries, demand that their governments take action. Finally, and perhaps most importantly, some people suggest that NGOs have developed as part of a larger, neoliberal economic and political agenda. Edwards and Hulme (1995:4), in *Non-Governmental Organizations,* maintained that the rise in importance of NGOs is neither an accident nor simply a response to local initiative or voluntary action. More importantly, they said, is the increasing support of NGOs from governments and official aid agencies acting in response to shifts in economic and political ideology.

Neoliberal economics assumes that markets and private initiative are the most efficient mechanisms for achieving economic growth and providing effective services. Governments, the theory assumes, should minimize their role in government because NGOs are more efficient in providing service. Thus, NGOs are seen by nation-states themselves as the preferred way of delivering educational, welfare, and health services (Edwards and Hulme 1995:4). As a consequence, there is a good deal of evidence to suggest that NGOs are growing because of increased amounts of public funding. In recent years NGOs not dependent on state aid are the exception rather than the rule; furthermore, most of the aid has gone primarily to finance welfare services and development. Thus, NGOs serve to replace, perhaps at a lower cost, the services in welfare, health, and education that peripheral countries are being forced to cut in exchange for World Bank loans, foreign investments, or loan restructuring.

There is plenty of evidence that the growth in size and number of NGOs is fed by increased governmental contributions along with greater contributions from multilateral developmental organizations, such as the World Bank. On the one hand, these conditions have created additional monies for NGOs and GROs to develop; on the other hand, they risk becoming so dependent on governments that they have been co-opted and their independence threatened.

Regardless of the reasons for their increase there is little doubt of the continuing global influence of NGOs. As Salamon and Anheier (1996:129) conclude

Fundamental historical forces—a widespread loss of confidence in the state, expanding communications, the emergence of a more vibrant commercial and professional middle class, and increased demands for a wide range of specialized services—have come together in recent years to expand the role of private, nonprofit organizations in virtually every part of the world. Such organizations enjoy distinctive advantages in delivering human services, responding to citizen pressure, and giving expression to citizen demands. As a consequence, the nonprofit sector has come into its own as a major social and economic force, with substantial and growing employment and a significant share of the responsibility for responding to public needs.

CONCLUSION

The state emerged some 7,000 to 8,000 years ago to politically integrate largely heterogeneous peoples and cultures. Military conquest was the main vehicle for its creation and maintenance. Two hundred to three hundred years ago, the nation-state developed to fulfill a new need, that of economic integration. Military conquest as a device was not entirely abandoned, but new strategies of integration, such as improved means of communication and transportation, national education systems, and the ideology of nationalism, became preferred means of attaining desired economic ends.

The nation-state helped create the type of people—laborers and consumers—required to maintain and protect the interests of the capitalist. It created and maintained an unprecedented division of labor and imposed a shared culture that enabled workers to communicate with precision, while thirsting for the commodities that labor produced and which served as the basis of the elite's wealth.

More importantly, terror and violence remained state instruments of integration, serving to eliminate those who refused to assimilate into the new ideal of the nation-state or to mark as undesirable Others against whom the majority could unite. As a consequence, millions have died as victims of their own governments.

The need to integrate regions and territories economically, however, is being replaced by the need for global integration, whereas variations in the availability and price of labor is leading to massive labor migrations that threaten state boundaries. In the absence of a world government, organizations, such as corporations and NGOs, have moved in to fulfill functions once thought the purview of the state, as other organizations have developed to protect the rights of individuals and indigenous groups—who, as we shall see, have suffered disproportionately in the drive to create the nation-state.

With this discussion of the nation-state, we conclude our outline of the culture of capitalism and the origins of and relations among consumer, laborer, capitalist, and nation-state. These relationships may seem complex, but they are written on virtually every commodity we possess. For example, sneakers were once for kids or tennis or basketball players. Consumers for this commodity have been cleverly created through massive advertising campaigns involving, among other things, endorsements from popular sports figures, which not only make the shoes fashionable but also allow Nike and other corporations to sell them for up to hundreds of dollars. To make the shoes Nike has, as they should do to please their investors, sought out cheap sources of labor. The labor for a pair of Nike sneakers costs less than one dollar per pair, and the total amount Nike spends on labor is about the same as that paid to major sports figures for endorsements. As a consequence,

Nike earns billions of dollars, returning much of it to banks and investors and using some to influence government legislation that would be favorable to its interests. To help generate this profit, nation-states support the entire operation by supporting and maintaining communication networks, financial institutions, and favorable labor legislation. Without the nation-state, businesses could not prosper, and consumers could not buy, at least not as cheaply as they do. Thus, countries, such as Vietnam and Indonesia, offer tax breaks to Nike and control and discipline their labor forces to ensure an inexpensive and docile workforce, many of whom use their wages to purchase Nike products.

Thus, although the historical, social, cultural, economic, political, and ideological factors that have helped create and maintain the culture of capitalism are in their totality complex, they can be identified in virtually every element of our culture, at least for those who care to look. Furthermore, as we shall see, these same factors contribute in one way or another to virtually every global issue that we discuss in the remainder of this book.

PART II

THE GLOBAL IMPACT OF THE CULTURE OF CAPITALISM: INTRODUCTION

Our thesis is that the idea of a self-adjusting market implied a stark utopia. Such an institution could not exist for any length of time without annihilating the human and natural substance of society; it would have physically destroyed man and transformed his surroundings into a wilderness. Inevitably, society took measures to protect itself, but whatever measures it took impaired the self-regulation of the market, disorganized industrial life, and thus endangered society in yet another way. It was this dilemma which forced the development of the market system into a definite groove and finally disrupted the social organization based upon it.

—Karl Polanyi, *The Great Transformation*

A problem faced by every society is how to distribute wealth; that is, *what are the principles established in a society that determine people's access to desired resources?* In the rare case where wealth is plentiful and people are few, there is, theoretically, no problem; everyone gets what he or she wants. But if resources are scarce, or if, for whatever reason, human wants are great, some way must be devised to determine who gets what. In traditional societies the most common ways of distributing goods were through sharing or gift giving, principles that we still recognize and use. If people had more than they needed, or others had less, resources were freely given. In the case of gift exchange or in systems of reciprocity people gave things to others or helped with some task in the expectation that at some time in the future the recipient of the gift would offer some return. It is quite possible, theoretically, to organize even large-scale societies using the principles of sharing and gift exchange as the major means to distribute resources (see Graeber 2001).

Tribute or taxes are other ways to distribute wealth. In this case goods or services—in the form of crops, animals, crafts, textiles, or money—are delivered or paid to a central authority (i.e., a chief, lord, king, or state) which, after keeping a portion for its own expenses, redistributes the rest. Taxes that we pay to the government, for example, are used to finance government functions and the remainder, ideally, is redistributed to fund such things as education, welfare, health programs, infrastructure (roads, water systems, waste removal, etc.), and the military.

Finally, there is the market. Marketplaces are thousands of years old. Traders, artisans, and farmers for centuries brought their goods to marketplaces and there traded them for other goods or sold them for money. Virtually every town and city in the world going back thousands of years had their marketplaces or systems of markets where people could go and purchase or trade for whatever they needed. Today, of course, virtually the entire world is a marketplace, and when we speak of "the market" we are referring to a principle of wealth distribution rather than a specific place, although the principle is the same; people produce things or supply services for other people in exchange for money.

Ideally people will supply only those goods and services for which there are demands and, generally, a balance will be established regarding what is demanded and what is supplied. In his classic work, *The Wealth of Nations* (1776), Adam Smith saw the workings of the market as an "invisible hand" by which a benevolent God administered a universe in which human happiness was maximized, an ideal system whereby each person, seeking personal ends, would contribute to the betterment of society as a whole. Thus, by seeking money and wealth, each person would work toward supplying what others needed or demanded. For Smith, the market represented a utopian vision in which wealth was perpetually created for the benefit of all.

For the market to work as Smith predicted, however, certain conditions had to be met, and three were particularly critical. First, to benefit from the market, individuals had to be able to exert demand, and to do that they had to have money. If a person had no money, no one was going to produce anything for her or him or provide him or her with any services. Second, competition between people supplying goods and services to the market is necessary; with competition, producers auctioned their goods and services to buyers who were able to choose the best and most efficient among them, thus continually forcing producers to provide the best and the least expensive goods and services. Third, there had to be a means of enforcing contracts, a means of upholding the rule of law, and a way to supply information to people about the products and services available; each of these was to be the function of the state.

There is no doubt that the market as a means of distributing goods and services is highly efficient. However, because the conditions that Smith outlined for the working of the market are rarely met, (e.g., not everyone has enough money), most societies divide goods and services between those that should be supplied only by the market (e.g., luxury goods and other nonessentials) and those goods or services that should be available to everyone regardless of their ability to pay. In the United States, for example, education is considered a service that is so essential to the workings of a democratic society that, at least to a point, it is available (indeed required) for everyone. Food, water, shelter, and health care are available, to some degree in most societies, to people outside the market.

Thus, an additional function of the state is to decide what is and what is not too important to be left to the operation of the market.

But in addition to the problem of deciding what should be left to the market and what should be provided outside the market, there is the problem of what economists call *market externalities*. These are specific consequences of the working of the market, some positive, but most negative, and include some of the hidden costs of gasoline that we examined in Chapter 4. For example, operating with no regulation, the market can have dire consequences on the environment as more and more people exploit natural resources to produce goods and services that people demand. The sickness and death that result from the inability of people to pay for food is a market externality as is the unequal distribution of wealth and its consequences. The following chapters are, in one way or another, about market externalities, but it might help to illustrate better what we mean by externalities by examining a couple of items of our culture and the effects that their production and operation have on the larger society.

A PRIMER ON MARKET EXTERNALITIES: POLANYI'S PARADOX

In his classic book on the industrial revolution, *The Great Transformation,* Karl Polanyi (1944) posed what might be called "Polanyi's paradox": *How is it possible to get the market to perform efficiently without, at the same time, "annihilating the human and natural substance of society"?*

The paradox is beautifully illustrated in an ingenious piece of work called *Stuff: The Secret Lives of Everyday Things* by John C. Ryan and Alan Thein Durning (1997). They describe what happens in the rest of the world to supply an average North American with the stuff of everyday life, such as a cup of coffee, a newspaper, a T-shirt, shoes, a car, a hamburger, French fries, and a glass of cola.

The coffee, for example, required about one hundred beans from a coffee tree grown, perhaps, on a small farm in Colombia; ranchers cleared the hillside to pasture cattle, and poor farmers used the less productive area to plant coffee and fruit trees. Prior to the 1980s, dense trees shaded the coffee plants and harbored numerous birds and other wildlife. However, in the 1980s these trees were cut down and the farmers planted high-yielding varieties of coffee, in the process increasing soil erosion and decimating the bird population. With the absence of birds and other insect eaters, pests increased, thus requiring the use of more pesticides by workers clothed in T-shirts and shorts who unavoidably inhaled residues of pesticides into their lungs. Because coffee is the second-most traded commodity in the world, prices are low, as are the less-than-a-dollar-a-day wages paid to the workers that relegate them to crowded shanty towns. After picking the beans for our cup of coffee, workers hand fed the beans into a diesel-powered crusher, and the pulp was dumped into the river. Dried by the sun, the remains of the beans (one pound of beans to two pounds of pulp) were shipped to New Orleans on a freighter made in Japan of Korean steel mined on the lands of indigenous peoples in western Australia and powered by Venezuelan oil.

Once in New Orleans the beans were roasted for thirteen minutes at 400 degrees in ovens fueled by natural gas from Texas. Packed in bags constructed of polyethylene, nylon, aluminum foil, and polyester, the coffee was shipped in an eighteen-wheeler getting six miles to a gallon to a local warehouse and then taken by a smaller truck to our local grocery. From there, we brought it home in a large, brown paper sack made in paper mills in Oregon. We traveled by car using about one-fifth of a gallon of gasoline. Once we arrived home, we measured out the beans in a plastic scoop molded in New Jersey. We spooned the beans into our Chinese-made grinder of aluminum, copper, and plastic parts. We poured the coffee beans into an unbleached paper filter and put the filter in our plastic and steel drip coffeemaker. The water came by pipe from our local reservoir via a water processing plant and was then heated to some 200 degrees, the electricity coming from our local gas, coal, oil, or nuclear powered utility. We drank from a cup made in Taiwan, added sugar from the cane fields that had once been sawgrass marshes south of Lake Okeechoobee, denuded of some 75 to 95 percent of its animal life largely by the growth of sugarcane fields.

That, of course, is only a partial story of our cup of coffee, but it should serve as an idea of the secret life or biography of a cup of coffee (see Igor Kopytoff 1988). For the coffee consumer, the main economic consideration is its market price, about ten dollars a pound, or two dollars a cup. The problem is that the market price doesn't include the cost of the market externalities, such as the damage to the environment caused by the coffee's production and distribution, the health and impoverished lives of the coffee workers, or the waste and decimation of water resources in the production process. These represent the externalized costs of coffee and are simply passed on to others or to future generations. The external costs of things are rarely calculated and, consequently, never directly paid. In fact, the economy could not function as it does if we had to pay the money costs of externalities (see Wallerstein 1997). Table II.1 provides some idea of how market factors—the things that go into the production, sale, distribution, and disposal of goods and services—translate into market externalities.

We can also understand Polanyi's paradox by examining an example of the market working as perfectly as it can—the case of Wal-Mart stores. The explicit goal of Wal-Mart is to sell things at the lowest cost. It even has a policy that a commodity that is unchanged from one year to the next be sold at a *lower* cost. This formula has worked extremely well, particularly for price-conscious shoppers. In 2004 there were almost 3,000 Wal-Mart stores in the United States with plans to add another 1,000 during the next five years. The company ranks number one in sales in the world ($245 billion in 2002). In the United States it is the largest grocer, toy seller, and furniture retailer. Wal-Mart is now the largest private employer in Mexico. Economists credit Wal-Mart for the nonexistent inflation in the United States and with about 12 percent of the economy's productivity gains in the second-half of the 1990s. And admirers credit Wal-Mart with making goods more readily available to the poor. Analysts say grocery prices, for example, drop an average of 10 to 15 percent in markets Wal-Mart has entered (see Fishman 2003).

Wal-Mart succeeds in lowering prices by pressuring its more than 21,000 worldwide suppliers to be efficient, to produce goods at lower costs, savings which it then passes on to consumers. In effect, Wal-Mart is acting as Adam Smith's "invisible hand." "Wal-Mart," said former labor secretary Robert B. Reich, "is the logical end point and the future

TABLE II.1   **Market Factors and Externalities**

MARKET FACTORS	POSSIBLE MARKET EXTERNALITY
Labor costs	Low wages, slavery, poverty, disease, hunger, alienation
Extraction of raw materials	Habitat devastation, pollution, military expansion
Transportation and distribution	Infrastructure creation and environmental consequences, pollution, and so on
Disposal costs	Pollution, disease, habitat destruction
Manufacturing and production costs	Environmental pollution, resource depletion
Advertisement and market expansion	Exploitation of children, conversion of relations of reciprocity into market relations, and so on
Maintaining market-friendly laws and regulations	Corruption, military expansion, distortion of the political process, and so on

of the economy in a society whose preeminent value is getting the best deal" (cited Lohr 2003).

But the sticker price of a Wal-Mart item is only part of the story, and this is where Polanyi's paradox comes in. In addition to the direct cost of an item (the sticker price), there is, as in the case of coffee, the externalized cost. In order to provide the lowest prices, Wal-Mart forces those companies that supply their goods to reduce production and labor costs. In the United States, this has resulted in the shutting down of hundreds of factories and the loss of thousands of jobs as companies shift operations to countries with cheaper labor costs. Carolina Mills, which supplies thread yarn and finishing materials to apparel makers, half of whom sell to Wal-Mart, has closed ten of seventeen factories and reduced its labor force from 2,600 employees to 1,200 because its customers couldn't compete with clothing imported into the United States by Wal-Mart. In some cases even companies that don't sell to Wal-Mart have had to reduce costs in order to compete. Hoover, for example, has been the leading name in vacuum cleaners in the United States for more than one hundred years. Recently, Hoover's sales declined 20 percent because cheaper models were being made in China for Wal-Mart. Hoover's parent company, Maytag, demanded that its workers in Ohio take cuts in insurance and other benefits; otherwise, the company will move its production facilities to *maquiladoras* in Ciudad Juarez, Mexico (Fishman 2003).

Wal-Mart imports 12 percent of all Chinese exports, and even in China, where wages are low, they insist on even more "efficiency." The Ching Hai Electric Works Company in Shajing, China, makes several million electric fans per year, selling them under many of the world's leading brands as well as two of their own. The workers were paid thirty-two dollars per month, about 40 percent below China's minimum monthly wage of fifty-six dollars per month. In the late 1990s, Wal-Mart demanded that the price of the fans be lowered, and they have since fallen from approximately seven dollars to four dollars per fan. But to do this, the manager of the plant fired half the workforce while continuing to produce the same number of fans. Consequently, the remaining workers must work for fourteen hours a day (Fishman 2003).

The loss of jobs, the low pay, the environmental damage done in areas where environmental laws don't exist or aren't enforced, and the health costs to underpaid and overworked laborers represent the cost of commodities that don't appear in the sticker price. And it is probably not inaccurate to say that *as the sticker price of items goes down, the externalized costs go up*. The buyer is not really saving money; he or she is simply passing the cost on to someone else. The situation was summed up well by Steve Dobbins, president of thread maker Carolina Mills: "We want clean air, clear water, good living conditions, the best health care in the world," he said, "yet we aren't willing to pay for anything manufactured under those restrictions" (cited Fishman 2003).

Thus, to produce goods at the cheapest cost, certainly an admirable economic goal, we must use up more environmental and social capital. But it doesn't stop there. As corporations such as Wal-Mart succeed, they are able to exert political influence that dwarfs that of ordinary citizens in a democracy. For example, in 2000, Wal-Mart ranked sixth in political donations by retail stores in the United States, giving a total of $738,182, 88 percent to the Republican Party and 11 percent to Democrats. In 2002, Wal-Mart ranked first, giving $1,690,123, 82 percent to Republicans and 18 percent to Democrats, whereas in the 2004 election cycle, Wal-Mart again ranked first, giving $1,049,850, 85 percent to Republicans and 15 percent to Democrats (Opensecrets.org nd). Political contributions clearly translate into political influence, replacing corporate legislative agendas—which include rules and laws that increase market externalities—for those of citizen voters. Although these agendas may on occasion overlap, they are clearly not the same.

Many of the problems we examine in the following chapters—poverty, hunger, disease, environmental destruction, ethnic conflict—represent, at least in part, market externalities, part of the cost of the goods and services that we crave. This fact is, or should be, relatively transparent. It certainly is no secret that Wal-Mart forces its suppliers to cut wages, reduce or eliminate health benefits, move operations to places without unions (Wal-Mart is notoriously antiunion), follow few environmental regulations, and supply little, if any, worker protection. It is no secret that the transport of goods from half-way around the world uses vast energy resources, or that local stores, if they are not put out of business by Wal-Mart, are forced to cut wages or lay off employees. *Why, then, are people not more concerned about market externalities?*

One of the tasks of the culture of capitalism, as we've mentioned, is to mask from its members (or to allow its members to mask from themselves) the negative consequences of the operation of the market. Corporations spend billions, for example, to distance themselves from the processes used to manufacture and distribute their products. They hide the "dirt" in the biographies of commodities through advertising and public relations efforts. They hide the effects of their production and distribution practices by controlling the information that is allowed to reach the public or through legislative or legal measures to discourage public criticism.

The language used often helps hide negative market externalities. We speak of "malnutrition" rather than "starvation," somehow implying that it is the fault of victim. Deadly riots, massacres, and genocides are blamed on "ancient hatreds," whereas the underlying economic factors are obscured or ignored. "Environmentalists" are labeled a "special interest group," rather than properly "concerned citizens." We develop ideologies that seek to explain global problems in ways that distance the problems from the operation of the market. One of the tasks of the following chapters is to examine some of the ways that we hide from ourselves, or ways that others hide from us, the consequences of our demand for perpetual economic growth. We begin, therefore, with one of the most common explanations for global problems—overpopulation.

CHAPTER FIVE

THE PROBLEM OF POPULATION GROWTH

*America and other rich nations have a clear choice today. They can continue
to ignore the population problem and their own massive contributions to it.
Then they will be trapped in a downward spiral that may well lead to the end
of civilization in a few decades. More frequent droughts, more damaged crops
and famines, more dying forests, more smog, more international conflicts,
more epidemics, more gridlock, more drugs, more crime, more sewage
swimming, and other extreme unpleasantness will mark our course. It is a
route already traveled by too many of our less fortunate fellow human beings.*
—Paul Ehrlich and Anne Ehrlich, *The Population Explosion*

*So why did the policies concerning population and family planning programs
change so drastically in the last [few] decade[s]? As in late eighteenth century
Britain, population has been growing rapidly. The expanding numbers of third
world people, who are no longer dutiful subjects toiling in their mines and
fields are not consumers either for an ever-expanding flow of manufactured
products, have become a burden for the industrial powers. They
are not only a burden, but also a threat, for, as in the time
of Malthus, a great revolution is taking place.*
—Steven Polgar, "Birth Planning"

Some modern research on the genetic structure of human populations suggests that we are
all descended from a relatively small number of individuals, and no more than a few families, who lived in Central Africa as recently as 100,000 to 200,000 years ago. By 15,000
years ago their progeny numbered 15 million (the present population of Mexico City). The
world population at the time of Christ had increased to about 250 million (a little less than
the present population of the United States) and on the eve of the industrial revolution had
tripled to about 700 million (about twice the size of the current population of Indonesia). In
the following two centuries the population increased at an annual growth rate of 6 per 1,000,
reaching 2.5 billion by 1950. In the following five decades it has more than doubled, at a
growth rate of 18 per 1,000, to reach more than 6 billion in 2000. In spite of signs that the
growth rate is slowing, barring some demographic catastrophe, the world population will

TABLE 5.1   Population, Annual Growth, Doubling Time, Projected Growth, 10,000 B.C. to A.D. 2050

YEAR	10,000 B.C.	0	1750	1950	2000	2025	2050
Population (millions)	16	252	771	2,330	6,100	7,810	9,039
Annual growth	0.008	0.037	0.064	1.845	1.400	1.000	—
Doubling time (years)	8,369	1,854	1,083	116	51	70	—

Data from United Nations. 1998. *Revision of the World Population Estimates and Projections.* http://www.popin. org/pop1998/; Population Reference Bureau. 2000. *2000 World Population Data Sheet.* http://www.prb.org/pubs/ wpds2000/.

reach 8 billion to 10 billion by the year 2030 (Livi-Bacci 1992:31–32). Growth in world population is summarized in Table 5.1.

Here are some interesting facts and projections about world population growth (see Table 5.2):

■ The rate of population increase, now approximately 1.4 percent per year, is expected to decline to a little less than 1 percent sometime between 2020 and 2025.

■ Because the rate of population increase applies to an increasing population, the actual increase will be 88 million to 97 million people per year presently before falling to 81 million per year in 2025.

■ By 2045–2050, fifty-six countries will experience a negative population growth, including all European countries, Japan, and China.

■ The population of the more-developed regions as a group is expected to reach a peak of 1,617 million in 2020, then it will start a gradual decline and by 2050 will be 2 percent smaller than in 1998. By contrast, the population of the less-developed regions will increase by 64 percent, from 4,719 million in 1998 to 7,754 million in 2050.

■ The fastest population growth will take place in Africa: Its population will more than double during the first half of the twenty-first century; and Africa's share in the world population growth will increase from the current 22 percent to 55 percent in 2045–2050.

■ AIDS will take a devastating toll with respect to mortality and population loss. In the twenty-nine African countries in which the impact of AIDS was studied, life expectancy at birth had decreased to forty-five years in 2000 whereas it would have been expected to have reached fifty-four years, in the absence of the AIDS epidemic, a loss of seven years.

The rate of population growth over the past century has prompted concern that the world is poised on the brink of disaster; that we are running out of enough food to sustain the growing population; and that population growth is responsible for poverty, environmental destruction, and social unrest. Moreover, so the argument goes, economic development in poor countries is impossible as long as populations continue to rise because any increase in economic output must be used to sustain the increased population instead of

TABLE 5.2   Population Information by Development Status

	POPULATION MID-2000 (MILLIONS)	BIRTHS PER 1,000 POPULATION	DEATHS PER 1,000 POPULATION	NATURAL INCREASE (ANNUAL, %)	DOUBLING TIME IN YEARS AT CURRENT RATE	PROJECTED POPULATION (MILLIONS), 2025	PROJECTED POPULATION (MILLIONS), 2050
World	6,067	22	9	1.4	51	7,810	9,039
More developed	1,184	11	10	0.1	809	1,236	1,232
Less developed	4,883	25	9	1.7	42	6,575	7,808
Less developed (excluding China)	3,619	29	9	1.9	36	5,144	6,439

Data from Population Reference Bureau. 2000. http://www.prb.org/pubs/wpds2000/wpds2000_Population2000-PopulationProjected.html.

being invested to create new jobs and wealth. These concerns have led to concerted efforts by international agencies and governments to control the rate of population growth, especially in peripheral countries where it is highest.

A number of people, however, seriously question whether population growth is a problem. Some economists argue that population growth is a positive factor in economic development; some environmentalists claim that environmental destruction is a result of rapid industrialization and capitalist consumption patterns, not population growth; and some religious authorities are opposed to any form of birth control.

In 1994 the United Nations sponsored a conference in Cairo to examine the problem of population growth and propose measures to control it. The Cairo conference debated several approaches to controlling fertility; these included promoting modern contraception, promoting economic development, improving survival rate of infants and children, improving women's status, educating men, and various combinations of these. Except for the religious objections to promoting decreased fertility, few people questioned that there was a population problem, that it was a problem primarily of the poor nations, and that the solution required women to limit their fertility. Yet few if any of the assumptions underlying the issue of population growth and control were seriously questioned or examined. Some of these assumptions are as follows.

- Population growth contributes to economic decline and stagnation in the periphery and thus is responsible for global poverty, hunger, environmental devastation, and political unrest.
- Population increase in the periphery historically resulted from decreased mortality (death) rates, especially of infants, attributable to medical advancements, better nutrition, and improved sanitation.
- Population stability before the rapid population growth beginning in the eighteenth century was solely the result of a high mortality rate balanced by a high fertility rate.
- Efforts to control population growth in the periphery are hampered by religious beliefs that promote large families and lack of education for women.

■ The only way to slow the birth rate is through birth control techniques and educational programs developed in Western countries.

These assumptions constitute part of the ideology of the culture of capitalism, which assumes that the problem of population growth is a problem of the periphery. This ideology drives not only public perception of the issue of population growth but also the policies of governments and international agencies such as the United Nations. Population growth, so the ideology goes, is a problem in Latin America, Africa, and Asia, and if the problem is to be solved, these countries are the ones that must do it. These assumptions are given legitimacy by "scientific" theories that purport to explain population growth. Furthermore, this ideology leads us to "blame the victim," to assume the people who suffer from the supposed evils of population growth—hunger, poverty, environmental devastation, and political unrest—are the ones who have caused the problem.

As we shall see, however, the situation is more complex than that. To understand better the demographic and ideological issues involved in the population debate, we need first to examine the major frameworks used to explain population growth, the Malthusian or neo-Malthusian position, and the framework provided by demographic transition theory. We will try to show how they are seriously flawed, ethnocentric, and self-serving for core nations. Then we examine some of the factors known to determine how many children are born and specifically examine what social scientists can contribute to the debate over population growth.

THE MALTHUSIANS VERSUS THE REVISIONISTS

Interest in the effects of increasing population date back at least as far as the Reverend Thomas Malthus's famous *Essay on the Principle of Population,* written in 1798, which outlines his well-known argument that whereas population "increases in a geometrical ratio," the resources for survival, especially food, "increase only in an arithmetical ratio" (see Livi-Bacci 1992:76). Without preventive checks to control fertility, such as "moral restraint" or "marriage postponement," argued Malthus, population will constantly increase, deplete resources, and bring into play "positive checks"—famine, disease, and war—that will return population to a balance with resources.

Malthus had some historical confirmation for his ideas. For example, he predicted that as population rose and the demand on resources increased, food prices (e.g., grain) would increase and result in increased mortality rates. Indeed, this seemed to have been the case in Europe in the seventeenth and eighteenth centuries. Likewise, he predicted that a decreased demand because of population decrease would result in lower prices, decreased mortality, and a subsequent rise in population, exactly as occurred in Europe after the plague epidemics of the fourteenth century.

Malthus predicted that disaster was imminent. What he failed to foresee was that in the face of increasing population, innovations in agricultural techniques would result in constantly increasing food production. Even though the world population today is at least six times what it was in 1800, there is still more than enough food produced worldwide to support the population.

In spite of his failed predictions, others have recently revived Malthus's message, arguing that, although Malthus may have been wrong in his early projections, no one could foresee the explosive growth of population in the past fifty years. Food production, they say, is now beginning to fall behind population growth, and even innovations that improve production are only stopgap measures. Neo-Malthusians may disagree on how close we are to disaster, but they unanimously agree that unless we take measures to reduce population growth, especially in the periphery, the whole planet faces ruin. The consequences of this population growth, they say, are now all around us in overcrowded cities, polluted environments, increased crime, and massive immigration. But their arguments have the most far-reaching implications in policies regarding economic development. It is impossible, according to neo-Malthusians, for poor countries to escape poverty when their populations grow at a rate greater than 2 percent per year because resources that could be used to increase living standards must instead go to maintaining the people added to the population. Thus, any economic innovations will provide only temporary relief because the gains are quickly offset by the increase in population. They conclude that the only way economic development can provide benefits is for these countries to lower their birth rates. The governments of most countries must agree because 127 countries, representing 94 percent of the world's population, express support for family planning.

Economist J. E. Meade (1967; see also Livi-Bacci 1992) provided a parable to illustrate what he saw as the folly of population growth. He tells of two imaginary countries, Sterilia and Fertilia. Sterilia is a coastal country with a democratic government and an ethnically mixed population. Fertilia, an inland country with a homogenous population, is ruled by upper-class landowners who have little contact with the outside world. Both countries were colonized; both received their independence at the same time and had similar demographic characteristics—high fertility (birth rate) and high mortality (death rate). Mortality, however, was sharply reduced in both countries by DDT spraying that eliminated malaria-bearing mosquitoes and penicillin that controlled disease.

Sterilia's government promoted economic development and to that end instituted a well-organized family planning program. The imperial elite of Fertilia, however, did little to control their growing population. Consequently, the surplus rural population flooded into the cites, and economic capital had to be used to support the growing number of poor, leaving little to invest in education, roads, communications, and health. People in Sterilia, however, began having smaller families and were able to save money, which became capital for economic investment. Their well-fed, healthy, efficient workers produced and sold products and goods that earned more money to be invested in education, creating a still more efficient and profitable workforce. Consequently, Sterilia surged ahead, with growing commerce, increasing literacy, and expanding health programs, whereas Fertilia became trapped in a spiral of increasing poverty. The moral of Meade's parable is clear: Those countries that institute successful programs of birth control will prosper; those that do not will suffer economic and social decline. *But is that really true?*

The Case of India and China

We do have a real-life Sterilia and Fertilia—China and India, countries that together represent 38 percent of the population of the periphery. India, the Fertilia of our parable, has since the early 1950s promoted family planning programs but with little success. When early attempts to convince couples to have fewer children failed, the government tried more coercive means, attempting to pass laws requiring sterilization after the third child (one province passed such a law but never enforced it). When that failed, the government attempted to convince women to use an intrauterine device, but this failed because of exaggerated rumors about the dangers of the devices. Oral contraceptives were never authorized for use in India. Consequently, the policy of population reduction has not been successful. Although the birth rate fell from 5.97 children per woman in 1950 to 3.3 in 2000, increases in life expectancy decreased the population growth rate over the same period from 2.0 percent to only 1.8 percent per year.

China, our real-life Sterilia, embarked on a concerted effort to control population growth in 1970, twenty years after India. In 1980 they developed a program to ensure that their population of 996 million would not exceed 1.2 billion by the year 2000. The government instituted policies to raise the age at marriage, increase birth intervals, and limit to two the number of children couples could have. Provincial leaders were assigned birth quotas and groups were formed to encourage the use of contraceptives, sterilization, and

This billboard in China promotes family planning and idealizes the single-child nuclear family. The fact that the child is female is a significant attempt to make acceptable a single female child in a society in which only males can continue the ancestral line.

abortion, which was widespread, free, and did not require the husband's consent. Later, a one-child policy was encouraged by providing incentives for those complying (higher wages, larger houses, priority for children's education, and free medical care) and penalties for those not complying (wage cuts, smaller houses, lower priorities for education and medical care).

In spite of public resistance and a population with a large number of women of reproductive age, China has succeeded where India failed. Population growth fell from 2.2 percent in 1970 to 1.4 percent in 1990 and to 0.877 in 2000. Whereas India's population in 2025 will be four times what it was in 1950, China's population will have increased by a factor of less than three. One would predict, therefore, that the rate of economic growth will be higher in China than in India.

But that hasn't happened. Both countries, as we noted in Chapter 1, have among the most thriving economies in the world (see United Nations 2003). India's growth rate was more than twice the world average in 2002 (4.5 percent) and nearly three times the world average in 2003 (6.1 percent). China's economy grew at 8 percent in 2002, 8.5 percent in 2003, and is projected to grow 8.5 percent for 2004 (United Nations 2004). Moreover, if we compare economic growth and standard of living as measured by the gross domestic product (GDP) of poor countries in general to population growth in those countries, there is no relationship. If we measure progress, as some have suggested, by an index of social freedom, India ranks well above China (see Livi-Bacci 1992:186–187). There are still significant differences between India and China: China has done notably better in improving the quality of life of the bulk of its population, ranking ahead of India in areas such as literacy, health care, life expectancy, and nutrition. But the reasons for these improvements are largely attributed to China's social policies and seem to have little to do with the rate of population growth.

Economists and demographers who have examined the connection between economic development and population growth in other countries have discovered little evidence that population growth inhibits economic development. In fact, historically, population growth correlates with economic prosperity, whereas population decline or stability is generally associated with economic stagnation or decline. For example, from 1820 to 1987, the population of the four leading Western nations (Great Britain, France, Germany, and the United States) grew by a factor of 5.5, whereas their combined GDP (in constant prices) increased by 93.0. In other words, while population increased five times, production increased seventeenfold. Demographer Massimi Livi-Bacci (1992:145), after reviewing studies that examine the relationship between demographic and economic growth, concluded that during the past two centuries population growth has not hindered economic development and quite possibly the reverse is true, with the countries that experienced the greatest population increase assuming the leading role in the global economy.

Does the real-life failure of the parable of Fertilia and Sterilia mean there is no connection between population growth and economic development? That's difficult to say, but it does suggest that the connection is obscured by factors that probably cancel each other out. It also means population growth has not been an insurmountable obstacle to economic development.

The question is, then, *why doesn't population growth inhibit economic growth?* There are several possible reasons. First, predictions of decline in resources accompanying population growth have not been borne out. Resources—foodstuffs, raw materials, energy, and so on—are neither more scarce nor more expensive, and the efficiency with which we use resources has clearly improved. For example, in 1850 production of $1,000 worth of goods or services required the equivalent of 4.6 tons of petroleum equivalent; in 1900 this figure had dropped to 2.4 tons and in 1978 to 1.5 tons, a tripling of the ratio between cost and profit.

Second, neo-Malthusians tend to see people as consumers only; they fail to take into account the fact that people also produce and that what they produce is often greater than what they consume. To some extent, they forget that human culture, unlike that of other animals, allows us to marshal additional energy sources.

To illustrate, economists at the United Nations developed a table based on the idea that people consume a certain amount of wealth and energy, that they also produce a certain amount, and that the amount produced and consumed varies by age. That is, at certain ages people consume more than they produce, whereas at others they produce more than they consume (see Table 5.3).

From birth to the age of twenty, and again beginning at age sixty-five, people consume more than they produce. Between the ages of twenty and sixty-five, people produce more than they consume; that is, they contribute more to the economy than they detract from it. This means that as life expectancy of a population increases, the excess of production over consumption will also increase; that is, there is an excess in consumption when life expectancy is twenty or thirty years, whereas at a life expectancy of forty years output exceeds consumption. The table also suggests that societies whose members have life expectancies of fifty years or more produce the greatest excess of production over consumption, and this corresponds to the so-called economic take-off of several countries, including England, Wales, Sweden, and Japan (Omran 1971:532).

Of course, the table represents only a rough approximation of the relationship between life expectancy and productivity; productivity also varies according to available technology and the division of labor in a given society. In some areas of the world, for example, children contribute to household work or income as early as six or eight years old

TABLE 5.3   Production and Consumption by Age

AGE	EXCESSES IN CONSUMPTION	AGE	EXCESSES IN OUTPUT
0–1	50	20–25	260
1–5	225	25–30	300
5–10	332	30–35	350
10–15	450	35–40	350
15–20	350	40–45	320
65–70	350	45–50	290
70–75	400	50–55	260
75–80	500	55–60	215
80+	650	60–65	85

See also A. Sauvy, *General Theory of Population,* New York: Basic Books, 1969.

and are fully functioning members of the workforce at thirteen. In those instances people are net economic contributors at earlier ages than in societies where members enter the workforce in their twenties.

The third reason why population increase may not lead to economic decline is because of economies of scale; that is, the benefits of resources multiply by their use. For example, a road's usefulness is clearly related to how heavily it is traveled. Because its function is to help trade, increase communication, and create a larger market, the more people use it the more benefits it creates. Or if education is thought to stimulate growth, it follows that once schools are created, the more people attend them the more benefits will accrue. Thus, increases in population may make existing resources, such as roads, schools, factories, and hospitals more economically profitable.

Fourth, because the consumption of commodities is what drives a capitalist economy, the more people there are, the greater, theoretically, is the demand for goods and services.

Finally, agricultural economist Ester Boserup (1965) suggested that human population growth can serve as a stimulus to agricultural and technological innovation. For example, in agricultural societies, as population increases people will farm more territory, farm the same territory more often, and use new technology, such as a plow or irrigation, thus producing more food to support the growing population. This may require more work, but it will feed more people.

In sum, there is little evidence to indicate that economic growth is slowed by population increases. This does not necessarily mean there is no relationship, only that the evidence linking economic growth with population is far too tenuous to account for the alarms that Malthusians and neo-Malthusians have raised. *But isn't is possible that human beings are simply using up the space and resources allotted to them?*

The Issue of Carrying Capacity

Even if we accept the idea that population has not yet inhibited economic growth, *can we say, as many neo-Malthusians do, that although we haven't felt the impact yet, the reduced doubling time of the population will soon result in the human population exceeding the carrying capacity of the Earth?* Biologists use the term *carrying capacity* to denote the maximum number of organisms a given environment will support. For example, we can examine the types of food that sustain wolves in a specific environment and, by calculating how much of that food is available, estimate the number of wolves the environment will support. This is the kind of assumption Malthusians makes about the human population: Given food and other resources on the planet, how many people can survive before those resources are depleted? For example, David Pimentel and his associates (1999) estimate that, because of declining fertile land, declining water resources for irrigation, and declining fertilizer usage, by the year 2100 the world will be able to support only a population of 2 billion people living at a standard half that of the United States in the 1990s.

However, the problem with applying the theory of carrying capacity to human beings is that our capacity for culture and symbolic thought enables us constantly to alter our diets and the way we exploit the environment for food. It is true, for example, that a given environment will support only so many people who live by gathering wild plants and hunting wild animals. But when a gathering and hunting people exceeded the population a given area could support and were restricted from migrating to another area, they could and did begin to plant and harvest their own plants and herd and breed their own animals. Later, when agricultural populations began to grow, they began to farm yet more land using techniques that allowed them to grow more food on the same land. Human beings are capable of constantly changing the rules of subsistence by altering their resource base. In fact, estimates of the Earth's carrying capacity vary widely, from 7.5 billion to 147.0 billion, depending on the technology employed to produce food (Livi-Bacci 1992:207; Cohen 1995). It is, consequently, difficult if not impossible to predict when our ability to provide for additional people will end, if ever. And that is one of the major arguments between Malthusians and Revisionists.

If we conclude that the alarms raised by neo-Malthusian arguments are unsubstantiated, it is fair to ask, *why do Malthusian alarms dominate the dialogue about the so-called problems of population growth?* More specifically, *why are their arguments so attractive to politicians and policy planners, and why do people so readily accept their assumptions?*

The Ideology of Malthusian Concerns

One of the important questions addressed by anthropologists concerns why people believe what they do about themselves and the world. That is, what social purpose or function does a particular belief serve? For example, if people believe that witches exist, and that they will punish people who harm others, the belief will serve to enforce proper social behavior. If people believe that gazing at someone with envy can harm that person, members of that society will be reluctant to flaunt their wealth, fearing it might attract an "evil eye." It is legitimate to examine the social function or purpose of any viewpoint, even those that are scientifically founded. Regardless of whether Malthusian assumptions are correct, it is legitimate to ask what social interests or purposes might be advanced by their acceptance (see Barnes 1974). Put another way, *do Malthusian arguments about population growth mask other concerns or social interests?*

For example, population growth was not, for Thomas Malthus, the major issue. What concerned him was the rising number of poor in England, why they should exist, and what should be done about them. Poverty, according to Malthus, was not a consequence of expanding industrialism, enclosure laws that evicted people from common lands, or the need of manufacturers for a source of inexpensive labor; it arose from the laws of nature, the discrepancy between the powers of reproduction and the ability to expand food production. People were poor because there were too many of them and because they kept having children in spite of their poverty. Providing relief to the poor, argued Malthus, would simply encourage them to have more children. Instead, they should be forced to delay marriage (Malthus was opposed to all forms of birth control). In 1834, encouraged to a large extent by Malthus's writings, the British government revised the so-called Poor Law, repealing various forms of relief that had been in place for centuries and leaving the destitute to decide whether their condition required their access to public shelters that were deliberately made into places of horror (Polgar 1975:86).

The Malthusian position assumes that if poverty exists it must be because of overpopulation, which is the fault of those people who, because of a lack of moral standards, refuse to change their reproductive behavior. There also may have been in the Malthusian position a fear that the army of the poor gathering in cities such as London would stimulate revolution, much as it did in France in 1787.

Malthus's ideas did not go unchallenged during the nineteenth century. Karl Marx, as we examined earlier, saw poverty not as a consequence of excess population but as a condition produced by the capitalist mode of production, which required a surplus of labor, an "industrial reserve army" condemned to compete for wages, with the losers doomed to unemployment and underemployment. It is their exclusion or partial exclusion from the economy and their dependence on wage labor, not their numbers, said Marx, that determined their impoverished condition.

Malthusian explanations for poverty and demographic theory were resurrected by neo-Malthusians after World War II. In his 1968 book *The Population Bomb,* biologist Paul Ehrlich, whose work is among the most influential in reviving Malthusian theory, described how he came to discover the significance of the population problem. It dawned on him, he said, "one stinking hot night in Delhi."

> As we crawled through the city [in a taxi], we entered a crowded slum area. The temperature was well over 100 degrees and the air was a haze of dust and smoke. The streets seemed alive with people. People eating, people washing, people sleeping. People visiting, people arguing and screaming. People thrust their hands through the taxi window, begging. People defecating and urinating. People clinging to buses. People herding animals. People, people, people, people. As we moved slowly through the mob, hand horn squawking, the

Whether a place is perceived as "overpopulated" or not often depends on its degree of opulence; although these crowded streets of Seoul, South Korea, are packed, few would see a "population problem." The poverty represented by this beggar's line in Varanasi, India, would more likely create concerns about "overpopulation."

dust, noise, heat, and cooking fires gave the scene a hellish aspect. Would we ever get to our hotel? All three of us were, frankly, frightened…since that night I've known the feel of overpopulation. (Ehrlich 1968:15)

As Indian sociologist Mahmood Mamdani (1972) pointed out, had Ehrlich been in Times Square in New York or Picadilly Circus in London he would have been in the midst of an even larger population, but those situations would not likely have led Ehrlich to fear overpopulation. Ehrlich was disturbed not by the number of people but by their poverty and the physical threat posed by a poor and potentially unruly populace.

In addition to those who blamed the poor for their poverty and targeted them for population reduction, Malthusian demographic and social theory also appealed to eugenicists, those who saw poverty as a consequence of faulty genes rather than national social or economic policy. Eugenic theory is rooted incorrectly in Charles Darwin's ideas about natural selection and "fitness." Eugenicists reason that Darwin's ideas can be applied to human populations, and that if people with defective genetic endowments had more offspring than those with superior genetic endowments, the quality of the human race (or German "race" or British "race") would decline. Consequently, for eugenicists it makes sense to promote policies that discourage or prevent people with defective genes from reproducing, while encouraging people with superior genes to have as many offspring as possible. Clearly, they reason, people are poor because they have a faulty heredity.

Eugenics has long been discredited by most scientists, although it sometimes appears in modified forms, as it has recently in the debate over the inheritance of intelligence and IQ (see Robbins 2001:210–215; Cohen 1998). But in the heyday of eugenics in the 1920s, groups such as the Committee to Study and Report on the Best Means of Cutting Off the Defective Germ-Plasm of the United States concluded that "Society must look upon the germ-plasm as belonging to society and not merely to the individual who carries it" (cited Polgar 1975:189).

Another advocate of Malthusian demography, Garrett Hardin would write:

How can we reduce reproduction?… But in the long run a purely voluntary system selects for its own failure: non-cooperators outbreed cooperators. So what restraints shall we employ? A policeman under every bed?… We need not titillate our minds with such horrors, for we already have at hand an acceptable technology—sterilization…. If parenthood is only a privilege, and if parents see themselves as trustees of the germ plasm and guardians of the rights of future generations, then there is hope for mankind. (cited Polgar 1975:190)

We will probably never know how many women in the world or in the United States were sterilized by those who felt they were ridding the population of "defective" genes. Allan Chase, in *The Legacy of Malthus* (1977), estimated that up to 1975 half of the 1 million sterilizations performed yearly in the United States were involuntary.

It should be apparent that it is difficult historically to separate advocates of birth control from racist and eugenic agendas. In the past, and perhaps today, programs to control or reduce population have often masked racist and sexist policies aimed at controlling the poor. Early concerns about population growth were directed at the poor in the core—the urban poor of England, Blacks and Native Americans in the United States, immigrants, and the rural poor. It was not until the 1950s that Western nations began to concern themselves with the fertility of people in the periphery. One question is, *why, in the 1950s and 1960s, did population growth in the periphery begin to concern Western governments?*

One reason may be the same as that for concern over poor populations in the core: It cost money to try to help them. Malthusians, such as Paul Ehrlich, embraced ideas such as those advocated by William and Paul Paddock, who in their 1967 book *Famine—1975* advocated using the military triage policy for food aid. The Paddocks recommended that the United States use its excess food production to halt starvation only in those countries that would submit to its power:

> During the coming Age of Food that nation which has the most food will be, if it uses that food as a source of power, the strongest nation. This will be, then, clearly an era which the United States can dominate—if the United States picks up the challenge. (Paddock and Paddock 1967:232)

Furthermore, advocates of population control share a concern for mass migration of the poor to their countries as well as for social unrest that could upset economic and political stability in the countries of the periphery. For example, a National Security Study memorandum produced in 1974 by the National Security Council at the request of U.S. Secretary of State Henry Kissinger (Africa 2000) concluded that population growth in the periphery is a threat to U.S. national security for four reasons: because larger nations will gain greater political power; because populous nations may deny the United States access to needed strategic materials; because a growing population will include a large number of young people who may be more likely to challenge global power structures; and because the growing population may threaten U.S. investors in those countries. The memorandum targets India, Brazil, Egypt, Nigeria, Indonesia, the Philippines, Bangladesh, Pakistan, Mexico, Thailand, Turkey, Ethiopia, and Colombia as the countries of greatest concern.[1]

Thus, as Steven Polgar (1972; 1975) suggested, U.S. foreign policy was driven less by a concern for overpopulation than by a concern that increasing population in the periphery hindered the possibility of raising the income level (and purchasing power) of people in the periphery and a concern that increased populations might represent a political and economic threat to the United States. Polgar said that population concerns in core countries stem not from a fear of overpopulation but from a change in the role of exploited countries. People in the periphery were needed at first for labor and later for markets. In fact, until the 1940s core countries not only were unconcerned with population growth in the periphery but they also complained it was too slow. Once the need for certain raw materials declined as synthetics were developed, and as the poverty of these people precluded their being turned into consumers, they ceased being useful, especially because they became potential revolutionaries, migrants, and criminals. "The subjects," as Polgar (1972:197) put it, "have become burdens."

Not everyone who believes there is a population problem or that poverty is a consequence of overpopulation is a racist or an imperialist. But people have been far too ready to

---

[1]The original memorandum is available online at *Africa 2000* at http://www.africa2000.com/INDX/nssm200.htm. A link can also be found at the Web site for this book at http://www.plattsburgh.edu/legacy/Population_Resources.htm.

accept the basic Malthusian assumptions without question. The consequence is that Malthusian explanations for poverty, environmental destruction, disease, and social unrest may mask other, more pertinent, reasons for these problems and divert our attention from them. But it is not only Malthusian assumptions that have dominated the public discussions about population.

DEMOGRAPHIC TRANSITION THEORY

The other framework that dominates discussions of the population problem is *the theory of demographic transition* (see Table 5.4). According to this theory, world population growth increased only very slowly from human beginnings to around 1750. This relatively steady state of population growth was maintained largely because high birth rates were offset by high death rates. Toward the end of the eighteenth century and the beginning of the nineteenth, mortality began to decline in developed countries because of advances in medicine and sanitation, whereas birth rates remained the same; consequently, population rose rapidly. Then, because of population pressures and the availability of contraception, birth rates declined to close to "replacement levels" and the rate of population growth stabilized, at least in the developed countries (see Coale 1974).

The population rise in the periphery came later, beginning in the mid-twentieth century, but was particularly explosive because mortality rates were reduced much more quickly than they had been in core countries, especially among children. Fertility rates in the periphery, according to demographic transition theory, are only now beginning to decline in response to population growth. This occurs when the increasing costs of education and child care in modernizing societies, along with the availability of modern forms of contraception, provide the incentives and means for people to reduce their family size.

The demographic transition model shares assumptions with neo-Malthusian theory: It, too, links lowered fertility with economic development. However, instead of arguing that economic development requires lower fertility, demographic transition theorists suggest that lowered fertility will result from economic development. The problem with this model is that it makes some decidedly ethnocentric assumptions.

First, it assumes that throughout history fertility rates have always been uniformly high. High fertility rates were necessary, reason demographic transition theorists, to balance the number of deaths that occurred because of the harsh living conditions of preindustrial peoples. Yet there was clearly an ethnocentric bias in this assumption; although demographic theorists recognized that fertility rates among preindustrial Europeans did

TABLE 5.4   Stages of Demographic Transition

	BIRTH RATE	MORTALITY RATE	POPULATION GROWTH
Stage 1	High	High	Stable
Stage 2	High	Low	Accelerated
Stage 3	Low	Low	Stable

vary depending on the age at which marriage occurred, as we'll see, they assumed that pre-industrial non-Europeans would not or could not control their fertility rates.

Second, the demographic transition model assumes that the only way of stabilizing population growth is to make available Western methods of birth control and contraception. As we shall see, the model significantly ignores variations in fertility that are based on various economic and social factors as well as the fact that preindustrial populations were significantly healthier than we give them credit for.

Third, it assumes that the resistance of people in poor countries to adopt Western standards of fertility is the result of irrational thinking, outmoded religious values, or traditional or fatalistic worldviews. Fertility control, in contrast, is consistently viewed as rational and modern (Caldwell 1982:119).

Finally, some claim that demographic transition theory has its own ideological bias, that its goal is to provide an alternative to Marx's idea of a surplus reserve of workers. As we noted earlier, Marx saw capitalism as creating a surplus population because competition for scarce jobs would allow merchants, manufacturers, and governments to keep wages as low as possible. If labor were scarce, however, employers would have to compete for laborers and wages would increase. If Marx were correct, one would have expected colonial governments to encourage population growth in the periphery, rather than restrict it. In fact, that is exactly what happened. In the early twentieth century, colonial governments in Africa worried about the low population and subsequent lack of laborers and did everything they could to increase the birth rate.

Demographic transition theorists blame high population growth in the periphery on the people themselves, arguing that capitalist expansion, rather than causing the problem of population growth, can cure it. In other words, demographic transition models see economic development as an answer to the problem; Marx viewed economic development as a cause (O'Brien 1994).

Demographic transition theorists generally ignore the fact that human populations have consistently adjusted fertility rates to local economic and social conditions. Moreover, if that is so, we can assume that high fertility in peripheral countries is not solely the result of a lack of ability to control births and that it is not, given the context of people's lives, irrational. That is, high fertility rates are not the result of ignorance, outmoded religious values, or lack of education but the result of social or economic factors that people, largely women, react to in order to adjust the size of their families. However, to understand how populations regulate their size without having access to modern means of birth control, we need to answer the question, *how have human societies historically controlled the size of their population?*

A Primer on the Determinants of Population Growth and Decline

At its simplest, worldwide population growth is a factor of only two things—births and deaths. If the rate of death is lower than the rate of birth, population increases. If deaths exceed births, population declines. In regional populations migration also contributes to population increases or declines, but for now let's focus on natural increases or decreases. The question is, *what economic, social, and cultural factors dictate birth and death rates?*

Fertility.   Birth rates are a factor of the number of children born in a given population; this is determined by biological and social factors including the frequency of births during a woman's fecund period and the portion of the fecund period—between puberty and menopause—used for reproduction.

Frequency of births—the interval between births—is determined by a number of factors, including the following.

- Period of infertility after birth: There is a period after birth when ovulation does not occur.
- Time between ovulation and conception: Although some women may conceive during the first ovulation after giving birth, others do not. The average is five to ten months.
- Average length of pregnancy (nine months).
- Fetal mortality: About one in five recognized pregnancies ends in miscarriage. (The actual percentage of interrupted pregnancies, including those that are unrecognized, may approach 80 percent.)
- Presence or absence of birth control techniques.

Of these factors, the length of time between births and the presence or absence of birth control techniques provide for most of the variation in birth rates. Length of time between births can be influenced by various cultural factors. For example, breast-feeding suppresses ovulation. In societies in which children are not weaned until the age of three, four, or five years, breast-feeding leads to greater intervals between births. Attitudes toward breast-feeding vary significantly: In some societies it is encouraged and expected; in others it is discouraged, perhaps because of concerns about body image or because it has sexual connotations.

Economic and consumption patterns may also influence breast-feeding. For example, breast-feeding in the periphery has markedly decreased in the past thirty to forty years because of increased advertising and sales of powdered infant formula. Thus, cultural or social factors that inhibit breast-feeding, especially in the absence of modern birth control methods, may result in shorter spacing between births and an increase in fertility and population growth.

Many societies practice a postpartum sexual taboo, a rule that women should not have sexual intercourse for a set period of time after the birth of a child. The period can vary from a few months to a few years, but regardless of the length, the taboo is likely to increase birth spacing.

Thus, even leaving aside the influence of modern birth control techniques, the spacing of births through so-called natural means may vary from eighteen to forty-five months (1.5 to 3.5 years).

A second major factor in fertility is the fecund period used for reproduction, or the number of years in which a woman can conceive. This, too, can vary considerably because of cultural, social, or economic factors. Biological fecundity is the period shortly after the onset of menses until the onset of menopause; this can range from eleven years of age to over fifty years of age, although the average is fifteen years of age to forty years of age. More importantly, however, is cultural fecundity, the age at which a woman becomes sexually active. This is determined in most societies by age at marriage, which varies, on the average, from fifteen to twenty-five years of age.

Combining the minimum and maximum period between births attributable to natural factors with the minimum and maximum age at marriage produces two very different population growth scenarios (see Livi-Bacci 1992:13). Assuming a fifteen-year reproductive period (fecundity lasting from age twenty-five to age forty) with a maximum interval between births produces a fertility rate of 4.3 children per woman:

$$\frac{\text{15-year reproductive period}}{\text{3.5-year birth internal}} = 4.3 \text{ children}$$

However, assuming a reproductive period of twenty-five years (fecundity lasting from age fifteen to age forty) and minimum birth spacing of 1.5 years produces a fertility rate of 16.7 children per woman:

$$\frac{\text{25-year reproductive period}}{\text{1.5-year birth internal}} = 16.7 \text{ children}$$

The latter condition is not likely to be realized because it does not account for the increased risk of death or pathological conditions resulting from childbearing that may lower fecundity; in fact, the highest fertility rates recorded range from eleven to twelve children per woman. The aforementioned projections provide, however, some idea of the possible range of differences in fertility rates based solely on cultural factors, such as age at marriage and age of weaning, independent of the availability and use of modern contraceptive techniques.

Anthropologists have also examined the extent to which other cultural practices, such as polygamy and monogamy, affect birth rates. For example, some predict that polygamy—the practice of a man having more than one wife—might lower birth rates because the frequency of intercourse with each wife would be lower than in a monogamous marriage. Studies, however, have been inconclusive. Frequency of sexual intercourse itself is another culturally determined variable that may affect fertility rates but which also has not been shown to influence fertility rates significantly (see Nag 1975).

Death.   A second major determinant of population growth is death, particularly the average life expectancy in a population. Most important is the percentage of the reproductive period realized in the life expectancy ranges. For example, in a population with a life expectancy of twenty years, the number of women who live through their full reproductive period is far less than in a population with a life expectancy of sixty years. In fact, demographers have calculated that with a life expectancy at birth of twenty years, only 29.2 percent of the potential reproductive period is lived, whereas with a life expectancy of eighty years, 98.2 percent of the potential fecund period is lived (Livi-Bacci 1992:19).

Most demographers have assumed that mortality rates in preindustrial societies were consistently high, but, as we shall see, that is probably mistaken. It seems we have consistently underestimated the general health levels of preindustrial societies.

The other major mortality factor in population growth is infant mortality, especially because this is where the greatest variation in life expectancy rates occur. It is also an area in which control on population growth can be exercised with the practice of infanticide and abortion. For example, one factor in death rates may be preference for male or female children, a preference that may be determined by economic needs. In societies that practice traditional agriculture there is evidence that boys and girls are equally valued as farm workers. In early industrial society, however, when wage labor began to be more prevalent, there was a preference for boys, a preference that gradually began to subside as women entered the factory workforce (Harris and Ross 1987a:156).

Migration.   Migration is another factor in population growth rates. Although migration may not appear to influence world population, it can influence regional patterns of population growth and decline (and, consequently, influence global population) (see Manning 1990). For example, migration can affect reproductive rates: A population in which many people migrate may feel reduced population pressure, which may result in earlier marriages and rising birth rates. If more men migrate, fewer women may marry, causing the birth rate to decline. Migration rates may in turn be affected by cultural factors: In agricultural areas that practice impartible inheritance, in which land is passed on undivided to an older or younger child, those who do not inherit are more likely to migrate out; in agricultural societies that practice partible inheritance, in which land is divided among some or all children, people are less likely to leave.

Other factors can influence the rate of population growth, such as the percentage of a population of childbearing age and factors relating to environmental constraints. But what is important, and sometimes ignored by demographic transition theorists, is that populations have in the past been able to maintain population stability without modern methods of birth control; dramatic increases in population growth have sometimes occurred because of economic or social factors, not because modern health or sanitation practices reduced death rates. Because this is critical for understanding some of biases in alarmist projections of population growth, let's examine a few historic cases of demographic transitions.

Some Examples of Demographic Change

To illustrate how the cultural and social factors previously outlined can influence rates of population growth independent of modern birth control methods, let's look briefly at three cases of demographic change: the case of prehistoric gathering and hunting societies, the story of French Canadian fertility, and demographic changes in Ireland in the late eighteenth and early nineteenth centuries. We will see, as Marvin Harris and Eric Ross (1987a) noted, that historic populations did adjust their fertility rates to fit local economic and environmental conditions.

The First Demographic Transition.   One of the assumptions of demographic transition theorists is that preagricultural peoples suffered from high mortality that was balanced by correspondingly high fertility to keep the population from dying out. Let's examine the first great demographic transition of 10,000 to 12,000 years ago, when human populations began to switch from gathering and hunting to agriculture.

We know from archeological evidence and research among gatherers and hunters that population growth rates before 10,000 B.C. were slow. However, chemical and anthropometric analysis of skeletal remains and ethnographic studies reveal that gatherers and hunters had fewer health problems than later agricultural and industrial peoples, and that the rate of infant mortality was comparable to or well below that of European rates up to the nineteenth century and below those of peripheral countries through the mid-twentieth century (Cohen 1994:281–282). Moreover, life expectancy was relatively high, around thirty years—higher than some nineteenth century Western countries and higher than that in many peripheral countries until recently. If infant mortality was lower than many have assumed and life expectancy was higher yet the rate of population growth was low, then there must have been other means of controlling population size.

Assuming life expectancy varied from twenty-five to thirty-five years and that a woman's reproductive period extended from ages fourteen to twenty-nine, with birth spacing of twenty-three months, we would expect six births per woman; if three of these children survived, there would be a 50 percent increase in population for each generation. Because we know this did not occur, there must have been some limit placed on population growth. War and conflict between groups, given what we know about conflict among gatherers and hunters, cannot account for that much population loss, and episodic disasters would not have occurred with the frequency required to check population at that level.

The only other way population growth could have been limited is through a check on fertility. Research among contemporary gatherers and hunters, such as the Ju/wasi of Namibia studied by Nancy Howell (1979) shows that they have on average 4.7 children, well below the average in the periphery of six to eight. Howell suggested that the leanness characteristic of these populations is associated with late menarche, irregular ovulation, long postpartum amenorrhea (suppression of ovulation), and early menopause. She also suggested that an active physical life stimulated the contraceptive hormone prolactine in gathering and hunting populations, as does exercise in contemporary female athletes. Probably of greater influence is prolonged breast-feeding, which would have suppressed ovulation and resulted in greater birth spacing. Moreover, it is likely that abortion and infanticide played a major role in keeping population growth levels at near zero (Polgar 1972; Cohen 1994).

Regardless of the reason, gatherers and hunters do have lower fertility rates than sedentary neighbors, and research shows that their fertility levels increase when they settle. In other words, gathering and hunting peoples were able to control fertility and adjust it to changing conditions.

The French Canadians.   People have not only been able to maintain low fertility levels when conditions required it but they have also been able to increase their rate of growth. French Canadians represent a classic case of demographic success. In the seventeenth century 15,000 people migrated from France to what is now Quebec; some of these moved on, and in 1680 the population was about 10,000 people. In one hundred years, from 1684 to 1784, the population grew from 12,000 to 132,000—an elevenfold increase representing an annual growth rate of 2.4 percent. Because only approximately one-third of the original settlers established families, it is estimated that the vast majority of the current 8 million French Canadians are descended from some 1,425 women.

The demographic success of French Canadians was due not to declining death rates but to high birth rates resulting from early marriages. Probably because of a higher proportion of males in the population, women married at ages fifteen to sixteen; moreover, unlike women in France, widows in Quebec had little trouble remarrying and consequently giving birth to more children. Thus, women in Quebec averaged only twenty-five months between pregnancies, compared to twenty-nine months in France. Finally, there was a lower mortality rate and a life expectancy five years greater in Quebec than in France, perhaps because low population density kept down the spread of disease. Of the Quebec pioneers who began families, each couple had 6.3 children, of whom 4.2 married; consequently, the population doubled in thirty years. The 4.2 children of each family in turn produced an average of thirty-four offspring. That is, each original couple had more than fifty children and grandchildren. Moreover, daughters of pioneers had even higher fertility rates than their mothers and grandmothers, those marrying between fifteen and nineteen years of age having an average of 11.4 offspring, compared to 10.1 for the original pioneers marrying between the ages of fifteen and nineteen (which contrasted with 9.5 in northwest France, where most of the pioneers came from). Table 5.5 compares the number of offspring of women in the area from which the pioneers migrated with that for pioneer women and their offspring.

The fertility rate of French Canadians in the eighteenth century is among the highest ever recorded. Finally, some people assume religion was a factor in the fertility of Quebec women; however, today, with Catholicism still the dominant religion in Quebec, as it was in the seventeenth and eighteenth centuries, the province has one of the lowest birth rates in the world.

The Case of Ireland.   The case of Ireland reveals some of the mechanisms through which people can raise their fertility levels in response to local economic conditions and demands of colonial powers. At the beginning of the eighteenth century, population growth in Ireland was relatively low. People married later, reducing the fecund period, and mortality was high, life expectancy generally being under thirty years. Then from 1780 to 1840 the population doubled, from 4 million to more than 8 million. There seems little doubt that the reason was that women began to marry earlier, between ages fifteen and twenty, and in some areas even younger (Connell 1965:425). The question is, *why were Irish women marrying earlier?*

Marriages in Ireland were arranged but only when the prospective bride and groom had access to land to farm. Before the late eighteenth century, marriage was at a relatively

TABLE 5.5   Fertility Rates of Women in Northwest France Compared to Pioneer Women in Quebec and Their Offspring

AGE AT MARRIAGE	NO. OF OFFSPRING, NW FRANCE	NO. OF OFFSPRING, PIONEER WOMEN, QUEBEC	NO. OF OFFSPRING, DAUGHTERS OF PIONEERS
15–19	9.5	10.1	11.4
20–24	7.6	8.1	9.5
25–29	5.6	5.7	6.3

See also Massimi Livi-Bacci, *A Concise History of World Population.* Cambridge: Blackwell, 1992.

late age—between twenty and twenty-five years for women—because there was not enough land to support early marriage. Two things happened that increased the availability of land and encouraged earlier marriages. Virtually all the farms in Ireland were owned by British landlords, who extracted rents from the tenants. Their profits rose when a new land-holding was created, so they had a vested interest in increasing the number of farms. In addition, population was rising in England in the late eighteenth century, increasing the demand for food, particularly corn. Landlords who increased their number of farms and the amount of land devoted to corn production, therefore, could realize greater profits. As a result, landlords subdivided farms into smaller and smaller plots, reclaimed swamps, and extended farming into mountainous areas.

Families were able to subsist on smaller plots of land than before because of the potato. Introduced to Ireland in the sixteenth century, the potato had become the staple subsistence crop of the Irish farmer. Potato cultivation is very productive: An acre of potatoes can feed a family of six, including their livestock. A barrel of 280 pounds of potatoes can feed a family of five for a week at a daily consumption rate of eight pounds per person. Estimates are that people ate about ten pounds a day, which, along with a liter of milk, would provide some 3,800 calories along with all necessary nutrients. This allowed landlords to divide land into smaller parcels, providing a greater number of farms.

Thus, from 1791 to 1831, the amount of agricultural land increased, whereas the size of individual farming plots became smaller. The result was an increase in the number of farming plots, which permitted people to marry earlier, resulting in a rate of population increase of greater than 1 percent per year.

In 1845, a potato fungus struck, destroying the harvest of 1846 entirely and leading to the great famine of 1846–1847. This and epidemics resulted in 1.1 million to 1.5 million deaths and an exodus from Ireland of 200,000 people per year. The average age at marriage increased from twenty-three to twenty-four in 1831–1841 to twenty-seven to twenty-eight by 1900, and one-fifth of the population never married. As a result, the population of Ireland decreased from 8.2 million in 1841 to 4.5 million in 1901.

In sum, the cases of the gatherers and hunters, Quebec pioneers, and Irish peasants reveal that, contrary to the assumptions of demographic transition theory, populations historically adjusted their fertility rates when they needed to adapt to local social and economic conditions, and they did so without the benefits of modern contraception. This raises the question, *why are populations in the periphery not, for the most part, lowering their fertility rates in the face of increasing population and supposedly declining economic resources?*

POPULATION GROWTH IN THE PERIPHERY

Traditional demographic transition theory, and most public policy and government analysts, suggest that the rapid rise in population in the poor nations is because of lowered mortality, itself a result of the importation of Western medical technology and public health measures. There is no question that life expectancy has increased remarkably in the periphery since 1950 and that a reduction in child mortality is the biggest factor in mortality decline.

Population growth in the periphery, however, began "exploding" well before the introduction of Western medicine and public health measures. Egyptian population grew in the nineteenth century from 2.5 million to 9.0 million, whereas the Mexican population grew from 5.8 million to 16.5 million. Cuba's population rose from 550,000 in 1800 to 5.8 million in 1953 (Wolf 1969:281). Furthermore, we saw how in Ireland the population increased not because of improvements in health but as a consequence of the economic demands of English landlords. The question is, *how and why did the economic expansion of the world capitalist economy change reproductive behaviors?*

The case of Java in the nineteenth century offers some clues. In 1830 the Dutch introduced into Indonesia the "Culture System" of colonial exploitation, requiring peasants to devote one-fifth of their land to Dutch-owned export crops (e.g., sugar, indigo, tea, tobacco) or to work sixty-six days on government-owned plantations or estates. In addition, as the Dutch demanded more land to produce export crops, thus taking land once used to grow subsistence crops, the remaining subsistence land had to be worked more intensively or subsistence production had to be extended to less productive land.

The introduction of the Culture System correlated closely with a rapid population increase in Java. In 1830 there were about 7 million people on Java; in 1840, 8.7 million; in 1850, 9.6 million; in 1860 12.7 million; in 1870, 16.2 million; in 1880, 19.5 million; in 1890, 23.6 million; and in 1900, 28.4 million—an average annual increase of approximately 2 percent for seventy years. It was during the era of the Culture System that people in Java began talking about the Dutch growing in wealth and the Javanese in number (Geertz 1963:70). Suggestions that these population increases can be attributed to better public health and sanitation facilities introduced by Europeans make little sense given the life expectancies of nineteenth century European urban dwellers; life expectancy in Amsterdam in 1800 was twenty-five years and for men in Manchester in the mid-nineteenth century was twenty-four years (Cohen 1989:202). Benjamin White (1973:224) suggested that the demand by Dutch colonialists for labor on Dutch estates or state projects removed men from subsistence agriculture, creating a labor shortage in the subsistence sector of the economy. Furthermore, subsistence production on less productive land required more work. Because the extended family unit both worked together to earn a living and controlled population growth, it was natural for them to react to the labor shortage by increasing family size.

Even when men began to be compensated for their labor with wages, according to White, it made sense to have more children. When the income of a production unit, in this case the family, depends on the wages brought in by each member, it makes good sense to maximize the size of the production unit. And this, apparently, is what the Javanese did. Moreover, the areas of Java that were most influenced by Dutch colonial policies were the areas with the greatest population increases (White 1973).

Other anthropologists, such as Carol R. Ember (1983), suggest that in general fertility increases with the intensification of agricultural activities (as occurred in Java and elsewhere). Ember pointed to evidence that women reduce birth spacing as agricultural activities intensify, partly to compensate for the increased domestic work for women when men increase their agricultural labors.

Thus, it should be no surprise that populations grew under colonialism. As long as the production of commodities for export was essential to economic growth in the core, and as long as profits exceeded the costs of maintaining the colonies, policies that led to increases in the labor force served colonial aims (Polgar 1972:207). If there was any concern about population on the part of colonial rulers, it was too low. One Frenchman complained in 1911 that Equatorial Africa lacked labor for its development (Cordell 1994:137). Women in Africa, like women in Java, responded to colonial economic pressures by increasing their fertility rates. For example, in villages in the Sudan, after the British established cotton growing in the 1920s to produce raw materials for its textile mills and increased the need for workers either to grow cotton or to replace those removed from subsistence agriculture, women began to wean their children earlier so they could become pregnant again (O'Brien 1994).

Wealth Flows Theory

It is clear, then, that people, particularly women, can and do adjust fertility in response to local economic and social conditions, and they do so without the assistance of Western methods of contraception. Yet fertility rates, while dropping in some countries, remain high in most. The question is, *why does the demand for children in developing countries remain high?* Among the reasons generally given are the following:

- The cost of raising children in rural areas is low, and in terms of cost children may represent a net gain economically.
- For security in old age. Surveys in Indonesia, the Koreas, Thailand, Turkey, and the Philippines reveal that 80 to 90 percent of parents expect economic assistance from children in their old age.
- Cultural factors encourage people to see children as an affirmation of family values, a guarantee of family continuity, and the expression of religious principles.

Family form has much to do with family reproductive strategies. The many children in the extended Nigerian family pictured on the left are expected to contribute to its wealth, whereas the small number of dependents of the typical Western nuclear family, as this one above in Boston, are expected to be a drain on family resources.

Demographer John Caldwell (1982), beginning with the idea that people in some so-cieties resist attempts to limit fertility because of the economic benefits of children, formu-lated the *wealth flows theory* to explain the reproductive decisions made by families. There are, according to Caldwell, only two types of reproductive strategies that families can adopt: One occurs where there is no economic gain to restricting fertility; the other occurs when there is an economic gain. Furthermore, where it is beneficial to have children, people will maxi-mize family size; where it is not economically beneficial, people will minimize family size. In other words, when children contribute wealth to the family, when wealth flows from children to parents, parents will maximize the number of children they produce; when wealth flows from parents to children, parents will minimize family size. Caldwell defined "wealth" in broad terms to include not only money or wages but also economic security, labor assistance, prestige, the expansion of social and political networks, and so on.

The Yoruba of Nigeria, for example, desire large families because they increase the size of the security system in times of need, increase the number of cooperating individuals in less serious situations, and expand the range of economic and political contacts of family members. They also increase the number of political allies and the number of rela-tives who attend family ceremonies, both of which enhance prestige and status. For both urban and traditional Yoruba, family numbers are taken as signs of political strength and affluence. Moreover, a large family provides a springboard for success in the modern econ-omy by supplying funds for education or personal connections to aid in finding jobs (Cald-well 1982:136). Children perform services not only by producing goods but by providing services that adults regard as children's work—carrying water; collecting fuel, messages, and goods; sweeping; looking after siblings; and caring for animals. Adult children help with labor and gift giving and assist in making family contributions to community ceremo-nies, funerals, and birth ceremonies. Adult children also care for aging parents and contrib-ute to farms and businesses in such a way that aged parents can still participate. Finally, parents can invest in training or education of children to maximize later returns. When sur-veyed, 80 percent of Yoruba said that children are better than wealth, and even that chil-dren are wealth. Only 6 percent said that children consume wealth.

In core countries, however, children clearly consume wealth. For example, the U.S. Department of Agriculture estimates that in the United States a middle-income family will spend for each child $160,140 over seventeen years for food, housing, and other basic ne-cessities. Lower-income families raising a child can expect to spend $117,390, and upper-income families will likely pay $233,850 per child (USDA 1999). As a result of his re-search, Caldwell (1982:140) concluded:

> The key issue here, and, I will argue, the fundamental issue in demographic transition, is the direction and magnitude of intergenerational wealth flows or the net balance of the two flows—one from parents to children and the other from children to parents—over the period from when people become parents until they die.

Furthermore, said Caldwell, for intergenerational wealth flow to change there must be a fundamental change in family structure; programs that simply emphasize family plan-ning or increase the availability of contraception will not provide incentives to reduce fer-tility. Given these conclusions, the questions are, *what kinds of changes are required in family structure to reduce fertility, and if in some circumstances fertility decline is desir-*

able, under what economic and social circumstances will families be motivated to have fewer children?

The Social Implications of Wealth Flows Theory

Wealth flows theory highlights an area of research that demographers have tended to neglect—the relationship between family structure and fertility. Anthropologists have been traditionally concerned with kinship and family relations because in small-scale and preindustrial societies kinship more than any other factor tends to define a person's relationship to everyone else. In small villages and towns, for example, it is not unusual for everyone to be related in some way to everyone else and for everyone to know exactly what those relations are. In fact, in many societies, in the absence of kin a person is viewed with suspicion and hostility. Many anthropologists who have lived and done fieldwork in such communities have had the experience of being assigned some fictional kinship designation—the sister, brother, daughter, or son of someone in the community.

One of the major distinctions that anthropologists make about different types of families is the distinction between the so-called *nuclear family* and the so-called *extended family.* The nuclear family consists of a father, mother, and children. This is the standard family unit in most Western countries and (although not the most common) in the United States. In other societies, extended families consisting of mothers and/or fathers and brothers, sisters, parents, grandparents, and others are the norm. Extended family structure can also vary considerably depending, for example, on whether a person is considered to be more strongly tied to his or her father and his kin (*patrilineal descent*), his or her mother and her kin (*matrilineal descent*), or equally to both (*bilateral descent*).

Whether a society emphasizes nuclear family ties or extended family ties can obviously have great significance on patterns of family relations. In nuclear families, for example, parents or siblings are clearly responsible for the care of children; in extended families, children may be cared for by parents, siblings, members of the mother's or father's family, grandparents, and so on. In nuclear families resources (income, possessions, etc.) are shared among mother, father, and children; in extended families resources may be shared and distributed among a far greater number of individuals.

Furthermore, emotional ties may vary considerably. In a patrilineal extended family a man may have closer ties to his brother than to his wife, or a woman closer ties to a brother or sister than to her husband. In nuclear families the main tie is between husband and wife, and their main obligation is to their children. The question is, *what implications do population control programs have for family structure and relations?*

If wealth flow is the main determinant of fertility in a society, then fertility behavior will change only if there is a shift from extended family structures, in which wealth almost always flows from children to parents, to nuclear family structures, in which wealth almost always flows from parents to children. In Nigeria, for example, government efforts at reducing fertility have met with almost no success, even among modernized urban families. This is because the extended family, even in the cities, remains the norm. In the few instances of so-called demographic innovators—those who have changed their fertility behavior—there has been a marked change in attitudes toward family and children to the emotional and economic patterns that resemble those found in nuclear families. These people have withdrawn emotionally from ancestors and extended family relatives and become more involved with their children and their children's future. They give more emotion and wealth to their children than they expect to get back. Caldwell (1982:149) speculated that those couples who have adopted the Western form of family, and consequently Western notions of family size, have probably done so not because of population control and family programs but because of the long-standing attempt by missionaries, colonial administrators, and educational authorities to persuade people to abandon their traditional family structure and adopt a Western family ideal.

To the extent that such efforts are successful and that population control and family planning programs contribute to these efforts, we will see a loss of extended families along with the patterns of emotional, economic, and social ties that characterize them, and the adoption of emotional, economic, and social characteristics of the Western family. In other words, fertility change requires a nucleation of obligations, expenditures, and emotions in which conjugal family ties take precedence over all external relationships and that foster the belief that what parents owe their children is more important than what children owe their parents. The Western nuclear family is also marked by a greater emphasis on the rights of individuals to act independently of the family by, for example, choosing a spouse on the basis of mutual attraction, choosing a residence independent from one's parents, choosing a career, and making decisions together with a spouse about family size.

The Question of Gender and Power

In its report, *The State of the World's Population, 2000,* the United Nations Population Fund (UNPF 2000:2) concludes that the status of women is one of the prime determinants of fertility and population growth. They conclude that if

> women had the power to make decisions about sexual activity and its consequences, they could avoid many of the 80 million unwanted pregnancies each year, 20 million unsafe abortions, some 500,000 maternal deaths (including 78,000 as a result of unsafe abortion), and many times that number of infections and injuries. They could also avoid many of the 333 million new sexually transmitted infections contracted each year.

Anthropologists suggest also that relations between husbands and wives may be as important as the influences of extended and nuclear family structure in influencing fertility. In situations where there is high unemployment, where women have limited access to economic resources and must depend on men and children for economic contributions or economic security, fertility will be high. This is clearly revealed in the research of W. Penn Handwerker (1989) in Barbados.

In the 1950s, according to Handwerker, the West Indian family was characterized by weak conjugal bonds, a relative absence of stable nuclear units, weak bonds between fathers and children, and strong bonds between mothers and children. Family interactions among men, women, and children tended to take place in visiting relationships, consensual cohabitation, and legal marriage, which tended to occur late if at all. Consequently, 80 percent of births occurred outside of marriage.

Historically, marriage patterns were a function of sugar production and the demand for sugar on the world market. The British freed their Barbados slaves in 1833, but the freed slaves were still dependent on wage labor in the sugarcane fields. Furthermore, to replace slaves who left, the British encouraged the migration of thousands of indentured laborers from India and the East Indies. As a result, the population of Barbados increased in the nineteenth century from 60,000 to 200,000. Because the sugar growers controlled the economy, and because there was a more than adequate workforce competing for available jobs, wages were low. To get a job, a laborer often needed the patronage of someone connected to the sugar growers. As a result, living conditions for the bulk of the Black laborers were among the worst in the British West Indies. Infant mortality, for example, was 25 percent in the early 1900s and remained as high as 15 percent into the 1950s.

Handwerker claimed that the scarcity of jobs created severe competition among the poor for available work, such that men and women could optimize their resources only by exploiting each others' weaknesses. Because only men were employed on the sugar plantations, they earned most of the money, money they used to gain sexual conquests, rum, and unquestioned authority. Meanwhile, women exploited men's desire for sex, their absence from the home, and their distance from children to attach the children emotionally to themselves and distance them from their fathers.

This does not mean women didn't have jobs—60 percent worked from age fifteen to age fifty-five. Their work was low-paying manufacturing work, or they worked as seamstresses, domestics, and petty traders. Wages were so low that one women commented, "You are lucky if a daughter can earn enough to help herself, let alone help you" (Handwerker 1989:77). To survive, a woman needed to supplement her income with that of a man.

These patterns of male–female relations resulted in a family pattern in which women attracted men as cohabitants, boyfriends, and, later, husbands in a unit in which men sought to dominate and control women. Men continued to meet their social obligations by working long hours, often at several jobs, providing an adequate material base for their wives and children; they exercised absolute authority in the home and spent free time with either men or other women. Women, needing men for economic support, submitted reluctantly, often complaining that their husbands or coresidents simply wanted a slave and expressing a desire to be treated as equals. Yet because of the pattern of outmigration of men, and the resulting greater number of women, men were able and expected to have extramarital affairs.

The result was a family in which men had minimal emotional attachments to their wives and children, whereas women worked to maintain close ties to their children. Women used sex to cement the tie to men, and children, according to Handwerker's informants, were by-products of the exchange. Moreover, older children were expected to help support their mothers and even to protect them from their fathers or stepfathers. As Handwerker (1989:88) said:

> Women could optimize or improve their resource control only by unrestricted childbearing. Getting pregnant and bearing children tended to be viewed as both a woman's duty and as her goal, and mothers generally took the view that their children owed them support for bringing the children into the world.

Even the belief system worked to enhance high fertility. Women believed that abstention from sex was unhealthy and that a woman who failed to bear all the children she was capable of bearing would suffer from high blood pressure and other diseases. "You have children until you can have no more," as one woman in her fifties put it. Thus, patterns of economic exploitation created a family form in which women, acting according to the logic of their social and economic conditions, maximized the number of children they would have.

Beginning in the 1960s, however, family structure slowly began to change in response to changing economic conditions. The colonial sugar economy declined to the point that sugar represented only about 6 percent of domestic output and 10 percent of employment. Manufacturing and tourism grew, and with it the importance of education for access to jobs. Connections to people of influence mattered less. More importantly, women gained access to jobs unavailable to them before.

As a consequence, the Barbadian family of the 1980s was very different from the family of the 1960s and earlier. Women expect their husbands to be companions, and there have been equivalent expectations on the part of husbands. Although women still suffer from job discrimination, education provides them with access to better paying jobs as technical specialists, secretaries, receptionists, business executives, university employees, and lawyers. From 1950 to 1980 the percentage of women working in manufacturing increased from less than 15 percent to more than 50 percent. The competition for resources between men and women lessened, and the exploitative pattern of relations decreased. Marriages came to resemble more the so-called companionate marriages that emerged in England in the nineteenth century (Stone 1976); men began to enjoy their families, and their lives began to center more on their wives and children.

This did not occur without conflict, however. Because the stronger emotional ties within the nuclear family required weakening to some extent ties outside the family, especially between sons and mothers, relations between wives and mothers-in-law became strained as they competed for the affections of husbands. Regardless, the family of the 1980s came to resemble the idealized Western nuclear family. Women viewed children as a cost rather than as a future resource, and young Barbadian women explicitly denied owing anything to their parents.

With the change in family patterns there has been a dramatic decrease in fertility, from a birth rate of about 5.0 per woman in the 1950s to a low of about 2.0 in the 1980s. Handwerker (1989:210) concluded that changes in patterns of family relations, not large-scale population control programs of the sort advocated by the Cairo Population Conference, will determine fertility. It is not knowledge of contraceptive techniques or a population problem per se that inhibits women from having smaller families but an issue of power relations. Family planning programs, said Handwerker

> should not be expected to bring about fertility transition because they can neither create the jobs, nor provide the education necessary for many jobs that would permit women to achieve meaningful control over their own lives. The "right" to have a small family is not a real option for women who are dependent for basic material well-being on their children.

Problems and Prospects

Does all of the foregoing mean there is no population problem or that there should be a more concerted attempt to change family patterns in the periphery to a nuclear family type, to encourage reduced fertility, and to promote greater gender equality?

Whether there is a population problem remains a moot question at best and clearly depends at least as much on the economic and social pressure put on the earth's resources by an existing population than on the total number of people. There is little doubt, for example, that if more than 2 billion people in India and China were to choose to live as the slightly more than 1 billion in the core, we could pass well over the limits of our planet's sustainability. There is no evidence, however, that population increases in the periphery inhibit economic development, or that population increases are the major cause of poverty and environmental devastation. Poverty clearly is related to colonialism and the expansion of the capitalist world economy, and, as we shall see, population growth in the periphery is at best a minor factor in global pollution. This does not mean population regulation is universally undesirable, but it does mean fertility decisions are best made by women and men together based on local economic and social conditions, not by central planners whose ulterior motives may not be in the best interest of the people involved. It is foolhardy at best to expect a woman to have fewer children if they are her major source of economic security. And it is foolish to force families to reduce their size if the family's economic well-being depends on the size of the family production unit and its ability to supply labor or bring in additional wages.

Yet it is clear that smaller families can confer benefits. Research suggests, for example, that educational opportunities for children, particularly women, decline in larger families. Thus, if education is a condition for economic independence, limiting fertility is likely to be desirable (Birdsall 1994). Research also reveals that it is desirable to space births at least two years apart to limit the risk of infant death (Lloyd 1994:183). Thus, in some situations, controlling the number and spacing of births is clearly beneficial.

Can we assume, then, that promoting the adoption of a Western-style nuclear family is desirable because it promotes greater equality of women? Possibly, although, as we shall see in Chapter 11, many researchers associate the nuclear family with the exploitation of women. Furthermore, extended families offer protection and security, so much so that in poor areas of the United States people "create" extended families through fictive or invented kinship ties to others and form reciprocal supportive relationships (see Stack 1974). Moreover, it is quite possible to have extended family relations in which women exercise as much power and authority as men, if not more.

In addition, few researchers have considered the negative features of nuclear family arrangements. Setting aside the obvious issues of broken families and concern and care for children and the elderly, we may be in danger of exporting the consumption patterns of Western families in addition to the social patterns. Nuclear family structure may tend to maximize consumption in various ways. For example, we noted in Chapter 1 how in the late 1940s and 1950s the American economy grew as a result of a home-building boom and a boom in the consumption of all those items that go with home ownership—furniture, appliances, automobiles, and so on. *Will the nucleation of the extended family in peripheral countries result in similar patterns of consumption? Will that create an economic boom as in the United States? Will it result in increased environmental pollution and waste?*

Nuclear family structure, especially to the extent that it requires a reversal of wealth flow from children to parents, to parents to children, has created, again since the 1950s, a whole new class of consumers—twelve to twenty year olds, with their own supply of wealth and their own consumer desires (and culture). *Will that create new markets and economic growth, or will it bring with it the same social problems that the so-called youth culture creates in our own society?* Obviously, it is difficult to predict, yet there has been virtually no discussion of the implications of changes in family structure that are required if we continue to promote fertility decline.

CONCLUSION

Western scientific and popular discussions of population growth have been dominated by two frameworks. The Malthusian perspective predicts that population growth threatens the world with starvation, poverty, environmental destruction, and social unrest. Demographic transition theory, while sharing the Malthusian concern over population growth, predicts that, as in the wealthy countries, population in poor countries will eventually stabilize if they adopt Western programs of economic development designed to bring them into the modern world. From an anthropological perspective, both views are faulty, both in their assumptions about the connections between population growth and economic development and in their ethnocentric assumptions about the reasons for population rise and decline in premodern societies. Furthermore, the Malthusian position has a clear class and perhaps ethnic bias in its tendency to blame the victims of poverty and environmental decline for their economic, social, and ecological state, ignoring the effects of the historical expansion of capitalism. The ethnocentrism of demographic transition theory is evident in its assumptions that modernization will result in lowered fertility because, somehow, modernity encourages rationality in choices about family size. However, as we have seen, there is nothing irrational about large families in societies where the family is a major source of economic support and security, and where the wealth received from children throughout one's life far exceeds the wealth that flows to children.

We examined the relationship between fertility and family structure, describing John Caldwell's intergenerational wealth flows theory, and demonstrated that lowering fertility requires a change in family structure from an extended family pattern to a nuclear family pattern. We also noted that unless women also gain access to economic resources, it remains in their interest to maximize fertility. Yet, if fertility decline is a major priority for international agencies and countries, and if, as anthropological research indicates, such a decline requires the adoption of the Western nuclear family along with its values, attitudes, and consumption patterns, we need to examine the consequences of such a change. In particular we need to consider whether the social and economic effects of such a change are worth whatever might be gained by slowing population growth.

CHAPTER SIX

HUNGER, POVERTY, AND ECONOMIC DEVELOPMENT

The persistence of widespread hunger is one of the most appalling features of the modern world. The fact that so many people continue to die each year from famines, and that many millions more go on perishing from persistent deprivation on a regular basis, is a calamity to which the world has, somewhat incredibly, got coolly accustomed.... Indeed, the subject often generates either cynicism ("not a lot can be done about it") or complacent irresponsibility ("don't blame me—it is not a problem for which I am answerable").
—Jean Drèze and Amartya Sen, *Hunger and Public Action*

Poverty is the main reason why babies are not vaccinated, why clean water and sanitation are not provided, why curative drugs and other treatments are unavailable and why mothers die in childbirth. It is the underlying cause of reduced life expectancy, handicaps, disability and starvation. Poverty is a major contributor to mental illness, stress, suicide, family disintegration and substance abuse. Every year in the developing world 12.2 million children under 5 years die, most of them from causes which could be prevented for just a few US cents per child. They die largely because of world indifference, but most of all they die because they are poor.
—World Health Organization, *World Health Report* (1995)

At the end of World War II public officials and scientists from all over the world predicted that with advances in modern technology it would be possible by the end of the century to end poverty, famine, and endemic hunger in the world. Freed from colonial domination and assisted by new global institutions such as the United Nations and the World Bank, the impoverished countries of Africa, Asia, and Latin America, people assumed, would follow paths to economic development blazed by the core countries.

Today these optimistic projections have been replaced by hopelessness and resignation as 1.2 billion people are estimated to still live on less than one dollar per day, and almost 3 billion on less than two dollars per day. Estimates of the number of people with insufficient food range from 800 million to well over a billion, virtually one-sixth of the world's population. Children are particularly vulnerable; food aid organizations estimate that 250,000 children per week, almost 1,500 per hour, die from inadequate diets and the diseases that thrive on malnourished bodies. And hunger is not only a problem of the poor countries of the world. Estimates of the number of Americans living in hunger rose from 20 million in 1985 to 31 million Americans who presently live in households that are food insecure (hungry or at risk of hunger).

Common misunderstandings about world hunger should be quickly dispelled. First, world hunger is not the result of insufficient food production. There is enough food in the world to feed 120 percent of the world's population on a vegetarian diet, although probably not enough to feed the world on the diet of the core countries. Even in countries where people are starving, there is either more than enough food for everyone or the capacity to produce it.

Second, famine is not the most common reason for hunger. Although famines, such as those in recent years in Ethiopia, Sudan, Somalia, and Chad, receive the most press coverage, endemic hunger—daily insufficiencies in food—is far more common.

Third, famine itself is rarely caused by food insufficiency. When hundreds of thousands starved to death in Bangladesh in 1974, it was not because of lack of food. In fact, there was more food than there had been in the years leading up to the disaster and more food than was produced in the years following. The starvation resulted from massive unemployment brought on by flooded farmland and high food prices brought on by a fear of food shortages. People starved to death because they couldn't afford to buy food and had no land to grow their own.

Finally, hunger is not caused by overpopulation. Although growing populations may require more food, there is no evidence that the food could not be produced and delivered if people had the means to pay for it. This does not mean population and food availability play no role in world hunger but that the relationship is far more complex than it appears.

The question, then, is *why do people continue to starve to death in the midst of plenty?* More importantly, *is it still possible to believe that poverty and hunger can be eliminated? If so, how?*

To answer these questions we need to know about the nature and history of food production and to understand the reasons why people are hungry. There is a prevailing view that hunger is inevitable, but that need not be the case. We examine some possible solutions to world hunger, and how specific countries, some rich and some poor, have tried to ensure that people have adequate food.

THE EVOLUTION OF FOOD PRODUCTION: FROM THE NEOLITHIC TO THE NEOCALORIC

Until recently in world history virtually everyone lived on farms, grew their own food, and used whatever surplus they produced to pay tribute or taxes, to sell at local markets, and to keep for seed for the following year. Since the beginning of the industrial revolution people have left the land in increasing numbers, converging on cities and living on wages. As late as 1880, half of the U.S. population was engaged in agriculture; this figure decreased to 38 percent by 1900, and 18 percent by 1940. Today, less than 2 percent of Americans feed the other 98 percent, as well as millions of others around the world who purchase the products of American agriculture (Schusky 1989:101). This shift of the population from farming to other sources of livelihood is intensifying all over the world. *Why do people leave the land on which they produce their own food to seek wage employment, which requires that they buy food from others?*

To answer this question we need to understand the history of agriculture, why food production has changed, and how economic and agricultural policies have resulted in increased poverty and hunger.

From Gathering and Hunting to the Neolithic

For most of their existence human beings produced food by gathering wild plants—nuts, roots, berries, grains—and hunting large and small game. Generally, these people enjoyed a high quality of life. They devoted only about twenty hours per week to work, and archeological studies and research among contemporary gathering and hunting societies indicate that food was relatively plentiful and nutritious. Life span and health standards seem to have been better than those of later agriculturists. Consequently, a major question for anthropologists has been why human populations that lived by gathering and hunting began to plant and cultivate crops. Before 1960 anthropologists assumed that domesticating plants and animals provided more nourishment and food security than gathering and hunting. But when the research in the 1960s of Richard Lee and James Woodburn (see Lee and DeVore 1969) revealed that the food supply of gatherers and hunters was relatively secure and that the investment of energy in food production was small, speculation turned to the effects of population increase on food production. Mark Cohen (1977) suggested that increases in population densities may have required people to forage over larger areas in search of food, eventually making it more efficient to domesticate and cultivate their own rather than travel large distances in search of game and wild plants. Even then the shift from gathering and hunting to domestication of plants and animals must have been very gradual, emerging first on a large scale in Mesopotamia about 10,000 years ago during the Neolithic era. From that point until 5,000 years ago settlements domesticated such plants as wheat, barley, rye, millet, rice, and maize and began to domesticate animals such as sheep, goats, pigs, camels, and cattle. Traditionally, animals have served as a farmer's food reservoir, fed with surplus grains in good times and killed and eaten when grain became scarce. Some, such as sheep, goats, cattle, and camels, eat grasses that human beings cannot eat, thus converting cellulose to protein for human consumption in the form of meat and dairy products.

Slash and burn or *swidden agriculture* is the simplest way of cultivating crops; although it is highly efficient when practiced correctly, it requires considerable knowledge of local habitats. In swidden agriculture a plot of land is cleared by cutting down the vegetation, spreading it over the area to be used for planting, and then burned. Seeds are planted and the plants cultivated and then harvested. After one to three years of use, the plot is more or less abandoned and a new area cut, burned, and planted. If there is sufficient land, the original plot lies fallow for ten years or more until bushes and trees reestablish themselves; then it is used again. Of the four major factors in agricultural production—land, water, labor, and energy—swidden agriculture is land intensive only. It uses only natural rainfall and solar energy and requires about twenty-five hours per week of labor. Tools consist of only an ax or machete and a hoe or digging stick.

Swidden agriculture is still practiced in much of the periphery, but only recently have researchers begun to appreciate its efficiency and sophistication. Burning vegetation, for example, once thought only to add nutrients in the form of ash to the soil, also kills pests, insects, and weeds. When practiced correctly, it is environmentally sound because it recreates the natural habitat. Swidden agriculturists must choose a site with the proper vegetation and desirable drainage and soil qualities. They must cut and spread the brush properly and evenly to maximize the burn and the heat. Cuttings that dry slowly must be cut earlier than those that dry quickly. Unlike in monoculture—the growing of a single crop—swidden plots are planted with a variety of foodstuffs as well as medicinal plants and other vegetable products. Swidden agriculturists must know when to abandon a plot so that grasses do not invade and prevent regeneration of brush and forest. Furthermore, abandoned plots are rarely truly abandoned, being used to grow tree crops or attract animals that are hunted for food.

Just as there is debate as to why gatherers and hunters began to practice agriculture, there is some question as to why swidden agriculturists began to practice the more labor-intensive *irrigation* or *plow agriculture*. These techniques do not necessarily produce a greater yield relative to the labor energy used; however, they do allow use of more land more often by reducing or eliminating the fallow period. Land that in swidden agriculture would lie fallow is put into production. Irrigation agriculture also allows continual production on available land, sometimes allowing harvest of two or three crops in a year. Moreover, it permits the use of land that without irrigation could not be used for agriculture. Ester Boserup (1965) suggested that increasing population density required more frequent use of land, eliminating the possibility of allowing land to lie fallow to regain its fertility. Thus, plow and irrigation agriculture, while requiring greater amounts of work, does produce more food.

The productivity comes at a cost, however. Of the four agricultural essentials—land, water, labor, and energy—irrigation requires more water, more labor, and more energy than swidden agriculture. In addition, irrigation generally requires a more complex social and political structure, with a highly centralized bureaucracy to direct the construction, maintenance, and oversight of the required canals, dikes, and, in some cases, dams. Furthermore, irrigation can be environmentally destructive, leading to salinization (excess salt buildup) of the soil and silting. For example, it is estimated that 50 percent of the irrigated land in Iraq and 30 percent in Egypt is waterlogged or salinized (Schusky 1989:72). Irrigated sites may also be used to dump sewage and often harbor disease-carrying parasites and insects, resulting in an increase in such diseases as cholera, typhoid, schistosomiasis, and malaria. Irrigated areas also serve as a haven for weeds. Finally, the shift to plow or irrigation agriculture changed the division of labor between men and women (Boserup 1970). Generally, in swidden agriculture men clear the land and women burn the cuttings and care for the crops. In some areas today, such as sub-Saharan Africa, women do the majority of the agricultural labor. However, in plow or irrigation agriculture, women tend to do less of the labor. Women's labor shifts to domestic chores, and often the total amount of women's labor increases as their agricultural labor decreases (Ember 1983).

If we surveyed the world of 2,000 years ago, when virtually all of the food crops now in use were domesticated and in use somewhere, we would find centers of irrigation agriculture in China, Mesopotamia, Egypt, and India, with later developments coming in the

Andes and Mesoamerica. Plow agriculture was practiced extensively in areas of the Middle East and Europe. But where agriculture was necessary, swidden agriculture, when population levels and state demands for tribute permitted, must have been by far the most common. Moreover, until the twentieth century there was little change or improvement in agricultural techniques.

Capitalism and Agriculture

The next great revolution in food production was a consequence of the growing importance of world trade in the sixteenth through eighteenth centuries and the gradual increase in the number of people living in cities and not engaged in food production. The expansion of trade and growth of the nonfarming population had at least four profound consequences for agricultural production.

First, food became a commodity that, like any other commodity, such as silk, swords, or household furniture, could be produced, bought, and sold for profit. Second, the growth of trade and the number of people engaged in nonagricultural production created competition for labor between agricultural and industrial sectors of the economy. Third, the growth of the nonagricultural workforce created greater vulnerability on the part of those who depended on others for food. The availability of food no longer depended solely on a farmer's ability to produce it but also on people's wages, food prices, and an infrastructure required for the delivery, storage, and marketing of food products. Finally, the increasing role of food as a capitalist commodity resulted in the increased intervention of the state in food production. For example, food prices needed to be regulated; if they were too high not only might people starve but industrial wages also would need to increase; if they were too low, agricultural producers might not bring their food to market. Import quotas or tariffs needed to be set to maximize food availability on the one hand and protect domestic food producers on the other. New lands needed to be colonized, not only to produce enough food but also to keep food production profitable. The state might also regulate agricultural wages or, as in the United States, not regulate them. (Although the United States has had a minimum wage for industrial workers since 1937, there is still no minimum wage for farm workers.)

As it turned out, the most important change in food production inspired by the transformation of food into a capitalist commodity was the continual reduction of the amount of human energy and labor involved directly in food production and the increase of the amount in nonhuman energy in the form of new technologies, such as tractors, reapers, and water delivery systems. The results of this trend continue to define the nature of agricultural production in most of the world.

Reducing labor demands in agriculture and increasing technology accomplishes a whole range of things that contribute to trade and profit in both the agricultural and industrial sectors. First, substituting technology for human labor and reducing the number of people involved in agriculture makes agriculture more profitable. Labor costs are reduced and agricultural wealth is concentrated in fewer hands. Increasing technology also creates a need for greater capital investments. As a result, those people with access to capital, that is the more affluent, are able to profit, forcing the less affluent to give up their farms. This further concentrates agricultural wealth. The increase in the need for capital also creates opportunities for investors (banks, multilateral organizations, commodity traders) to enter the agricultural sector, influence its operation by supplying and/or withholding capital, and profiting from it.

Second, reducing the number of people in agriculture and concentrating agricultural wealth to ensure profits of those who remain helps keep food prices and, consequently, industrial wages relatively low. This creates a danger of food monopolies and the potential for a rise in prices. For example, cereal production in the United States is controlled by only a few companies, and the prices of processed cereals such, as corn flakes and oats, are exorbitant. Yet as long as consumers are able to pay, the government is content not to intervene. As it is, food cost as a percentage of the cost of living in the United States is among the lowest in the world.

Third, reducing agricultural labor frees labor to work in industry and creates competition for industrial jobs, which helps keep wages low. That is, the more people who are dependent for their livelihood on jobs, the lower the wages industry needs to pay.

Finally, to keep labor costs down and increase the amount of technology required for the maintenance of food production, the state must subsidize the agricultural sector. In the United States, for example, the government has financed irrigation and land reclamation projects, conducted agricultural research, and subsidized farm prices and/or energy costs. The U.S. government also subsidized agriculture by investing billions of dollars in food aid, buying surplus farm products and using them for foreign aid (although this aid often created a dependence on U.S. farm products while forcing local producers out of business).

In sum, the results for the capitalist economy of the reduction of agricultural labor and the subsequent increase in technology are

- A capital-intensive agricultural system dependent on the use of subsidized energy
- The exploitation of domestic farm labor and of foreign land and labor to keep food prices low and agricultural and industrial profits high
- A large labor pool from which industry can draw workers, whose wages are kept down by competition for scarce jobs and the availability of cheap food

It is important to note that until the 1950s the technological intensification of agriculture did not substantially increase yield. That is, though an American corn farmer needed only one hundred hours of labor to produce one hectare (2.41 acres) of corn, the amount of corn produced was no greater than that produced by a Mexican swidden farmer, working ten times as many hours using only a machete and hoe. In other words, although mechanization made the American farm more economical by reducing labor energy and costs, it did not produce more food per hectare (Schusky 1989:115). One question we need to ask is, *what happens when we export the American agricultural system to developing countries?*

The Neocaloric and the Green Revolution

The culmination of the development of capitalist agriculture, a system that is technologically intensive and substitutes nonhuman energy for human energy, was dubbed the *neocaloric revolution* by Ernest Schusky. For Schusky, the major characteristic of the neocaloric revolution has been the vast increase in nonhuman energy devoted to food production in the form of fertilizers, pesticides, herbicides, and machinery.

David and Marcia Pimentel (1979) provided a unique perspective on the neocaloric. Their idea was to measure the number of kilocalories[1] produced per crop per hectare of land and compare it to the amount of both human and nonhuman energy expended in kilocalories to produce the crop. Their work dramatized both the efficiency of traditional forms of agriculture and the energy use required of modern capitalist agriculture.

For example, to produce a crop of corn a traditional Mexican swidden farmer clears land with an ax and machete to prepare it for burning and uses a hoe to plant and weed. Pimentel and Pimentel (1979:63) figured that crop care takes 143 days and the worker exerts about 4,120 kilocalories per day. Thus, labor for one hectare amounts to 589,160 kilocalories. Energy expended for ax, hoe, and seed is estimated at 53,178 kilocalories, for a total of 642,338 kilocalories. The corn crop produced yields about 6 million kilocalories, for an input–output ratio of one to eleven; that is, for every kilocalorie expended, eleven are produced, a ratio that is about average for peasant farmers. Nonhuman energy used is minimal, consisting only in the fossil fuel (wood, coal, or oil) used in producing the hoe, ax, and machete.

Now let's examine plow agriculture with the use of an ox. One hour of ox time is equal to four hours of human time, so labor input for one hectare drops to 197,245 kilocalories from 589,160 kilocalories. But the ox requires 495,000 kilocalories to maintain. Moreover, the steel plow requires more energy in its manufacture, so fossil fuel energy used rises to 41,400, with energy for seeds remaining at 36,608, for a total of 573,008. However, the corn yield drops significantly, to half, so the input–output ratio drops to 1 to 4.3. The reason for the drop is likely the lowering of soil fertility. If leaves, compost, or manure is added to the soil, yields might increase, but so would the energy required to gather and spread the fertilizer.

Finally, if we consider a corn farmer in the United States in 1980, we find that, using modern farming machinery, herbicides, insecticides, fertilizers, transport, and irrigation, the farmer produces about 7,000 kilograms of corn per hectare, almost seven times that produced by the Mexican swidden farmer, but at a cost of almost 25 million kilocalories. Consequently, the input–output ratio is 1 to 3.5, far below the ratios of most "primitive" swidden farmers. In fact, in the United States the ratio of kilocalories used in crop production to kilocalories produced declined from 3.7 to 1 in 1945 to 2.8 to 1 in 1970. The question is, *why has modern agriculture become so energy intensive?*

The intensification of the use of technology in agriculture is largely the result of what has been called the *green revolution.* The green revolution began with research conducted in Mexico by American scientists in the 1940s and 1950s sponsored by the Rockefeller Foundation. Their goal was to develop higher-yielding hybrid strains of corn and wheat suitable for Mexican agriculture. Soon the research produced dramatic results all

---

[1]A calorie or gram-calorie is the amount of heat needed to raise one gram of water one degree Celsius to fifteen degrees Celsius. The kilocalorie (kcal) or kilogram-calorie is 1,000 gram-calories or the amount of heat needed to raise one kilogram of water one degree Celsius to fifteen degrees Celsius. It can also be conceptualized as follows: One horsepower of energy is the same as 641 kilocalories; one gallon contains 31,000 kilocalories; if used in a mechanical engine that works at 20 percent efficiency, one gallon of gasoline is equal to 6,200 kilocalories of work, or one horse working at capacity for a ten-hour day, or a person working eight hours per day, five days per week, for 2.5 weeks.

over the world as farmers began using specially produced strains of crops, such as wheat, corn, and rice, called *high-yielding varieties* (HYVs). The productivity of the new seeds lay largely in their increased capacity for using fertilizer and water. Whereas increased use of fertilizer and water did not increase the yields of old varieties (in fact, it might harm them), it vastly increased the yields of the new varieties. Consequently, more and more farmers around the world adopted them. Use of these new varieties was encouraged by the petrochemical industry and fertilizer production plants, which sought to expand their markets. Thus, research efforts to develop HYV plants were expanded in India, the Philippines, and Taiwan, encouraged by the U.S. Agency for International Development (USAID) and the Rockefeller Foundation.

But the green revolution soon ran into some problems. First, the new plants required greater inputs of fertilizer and water. Because of the added energy costs, farmers often skimped on fertilizer and water use, resulting in yields similar to those prior to the adoption of the new crops. Consequently, farmers returned to their previous crops and methods. Second, the OPEC oil embargo in 1973 raised oil prices, and because fertilizers, irrigation, and other tools of the green revolution were dependent on oil, costs rose even higher. Some people began to refer to HYV as *energy-intensive varieties* (EIVs).

The expense was increased further by the amount of water needed for fertilizers. Early adaptations of the new technology tended to be in areas rich in water sources; in fact, most of the early research on HYV was done in areas where irrigation was available. When the techniques were applied to areas without water resources, the results were not nearly as dramatic. It also became apparent that the energy required for irrigation was as great in some cases as the energy required for fertilizer.

In addition, the green revolution requires much greater use of chemical pesticides. If farmers plant only a single crop or single variety of a crop, it is more susceptible to the rapid spread of disease, which, because of the added expense, could create catastrophic financial losses. Consequently, pesticide use to control disease becomes crucial. Furthermore, because the crop is subject to threats from insect and animal pests at all stages of production—in the fields, in storage, in transportation, and in processing—pesticide costs rise even further.

Finally, the new fertilizers and irrigation favor the growth of weeds; therefore, herbicides must be applied, further increasing energy expenditure.

One result of the change from subsistence farming, in which the major investment was land, to a form of agriculture that is highly land, water, and energy intensive is, as Ernest Schusky (1989:133) noted, to put the small farmer at a major disadvantage because of the difficulty in raising the capital to finance the modern technological complex. The result in the United States and elsewhere is the concentration of agricultural wealth in fewer hands and a constant reduction in the number of small family farms (see Table 6.1.)

It is in livestock production, however, that the neocaloric revolution really comes into focus. One innovation of the past hundred years in beef production was feeding grain to cattle. By 1975 the United States produced about 1,300 kilograms of grain for every person in the country. But 1,200 kilograms of that was fed to livestock. Dairy cows are relatively productive compared to beef cattle; it takes about 190 kilograms of protein to produce sixty kilograms of milk or about thirty-six kilocalories of fossil energy to produce one kilocalorie of milk protein. Beef get about 40 percent of their protein from grazing and 60 percent from grain. If we calculate the energy that goes into grain production and the oper-

TABLE 6.1   Changes in Number of U.S. Farms by Size, 1950–1992

SIZE OF FARM (ACRES)	1992	1969	1950	%CHANGE
1–59	1,310,000	1,944,224	4,606,497	−172%
260–499	255,000	419,421	478,170	−47%
500–999	186,000	215,659	182,297	+.08%
1,000+	173,000	150,946	121,473	+58%
Total	1,925,000	2,730,250	5,388,437	−166%

Adapted from Eric Ross, *Beyond the Myths of Culture: Essays in Cultural Materialism.* New York, Academic Press, 1980; and 1992 USDA Census of Agriculture.

ation of feedlots, the productive ratio is as low as one kilocalorie produced for every seventy-eight kilocalories expended.

If we factor in processing, packaging, and delivery of food, the energy expenditure is even higher. David Pimentel estimated that the American grain farmer, using modern machinery, fertilizer, and pesticides, uses eight calories of energy for every one calorie produced. Transportation, storage, and processing consume another eight fossil calories to produce one calorie (see Schusky 1989:102).

As Schusky said, in a world short on energy such production makes no sense, but in a world of cheap energy, particularly oil, especially if it is subsidized by the nation-state, it is highly profitable. The real problem comes when agricultural production that substitutes fossil fuel energy for human energy is exported to developing countries. To begin with, there is simply not enough fossil energy to maintain this type of production for any length of time. One research project estimated that if the rest of the world used energy at the rate it is used in the United States, the world's petroleum resources would be exhausted on the food supply alone in the next ten to twelve years (Schusky 1989:119).

Furthermore, in countries with large rural populations the substitution of energy-intensive agriculture for labor-intensive agriculture will throw thousands off the land or out of work, resulting in more people fleeing to the cities in search of employment. And because modern agriculture is capital intensive, the only farmers who can afford to remain will be those who are relatively wealthy, consequently leading to increasing income gaps in rural as well as urban areas. Where the green revolution has been successful, small-farm owners have been driven off the land to become day laborers or have fled to cities in search of jobs, as commercial investors bought up agricultural land. Or more wealthy farmers have bought their neighbors' farms because only they had the capital to invest in fertilizers and irrigation.

Then there is the potential for *green revolution II,* the application of genetic engineering to agricultural production. Genetically engineered crops are controversial, largely because of claims that they have not been rigorously tested and because we do not know yet what affects the crops may have on the environment or on the people who eat them. Clearly, claims by agribusiness concerns, such as Monsanto Corporation, that such crops will help us feed the hungry are, as we shall see, disingenuous at best. Furthermore, in some cases, genetically engineered crops simply try to correct the damage done by capitalist agriculture. For example, there is the much touted "golden rice," a genetically engineered variety with vitamin A that is a cure for blindness that afflicts some 300,000 people a year. Yet, as Vandana Shiva (2000) notes, nature ordinarily provides abundant and diverse sources of vitamin A; rice that is not polished provides vitamin A, as do herbs, such as bathua, amaranth, and mustard leaves, which would grow in wheat fields if they were not sprayed with herbicides.

This is not to say there have not been some successes in modernizing agriculture without creating greater social and economic inequality and depriving people of access to food. Murray Leaf (1984) described how one Indian village succeeded in increasing access to water, using chemical fertilizers, and increasing production while maintaining landholdings and building farm cooperatives and credit unions. In fact, some countries, including South Korea, Taiwan, and Cuba, have had notable successes in improving agriculture, alleviating poverty in the countryside, and promoting prosperity. But overall it is clear that we have developed a system of food production that is capital intensive, favors large, state-subsidized agribusiness, minimizes the use of labor, and subsequently makes more people dependent on wage labor with which to obtain food. In the culture of capitalism, access to food is determined almost entirely by the ability to pay, not by the need to eat.

THE POLITICS OF HUNGER

The obvious consequence of the reduction of labor needed for food production and the concentration of food production in fewer hands is that the world's population is more dependent on wage labor for access to food. Consequently, people are more vulnerable to hunger if opportunities for employment decrease, if wages fall, or if food prices rise; they can starve even in the midst of food availability. This is not to say that lack of food is *never* a factor in hunger, but it is rare for people to have economic resources and not be able to acquire food.

The role of food in a capitalist economy has other important consequences. For example, food production is not determined necessarily by the global *need* for food, it is determined by the *market* for food, that is how many people have the means to pay for it. That is why world food production is rarely at its maximum and why it is difficult to estimate how much food could be produced if the market demand existed. The problem is that not only are there not enough people with sufficient income to pay for all the food that could be produced but also so-called overproduction would result in lower prices and decreased profitability. For that reason, in many countries food production is discouraged. Furthermore, land that could be used to grow food crops is generally dedicated to nonfood crops (e.g., tobacco, cotton, sisal) or marginally nutritious crops (e.g., sugar, coffee, tea) for which there is a market. Finally, the kind of food that is produced is determined by the demands of those who have the money to pay for it. For example, meat is notoriously inefficient as a food source, but as long as people in wealthy countries demand it, it will be produced in spite of the fact that the grain, land, and water required to produce it would feed far more people if devoted to vegetable crops. Thus, people in Mexico go hungry because land is devoted to the production of beef, which few Mexicans can afford, but which brings high prices in the United States.

In sum, we need to understand the economic, political, and social relations that connect people to food. Economist Amartya Sen (1990:374) suggested that people command food through entitlements, that is their socially defined rights to food resources. Entitlement might consist of the inheritance or purchase of land on which to grow food, employment to obtain wages with which to buy food, sociopolitical rights such as the religious or moral obligation of some to see that others have food, or state-run welfare or social security programs that guarantee adequate food to all. Not all of these kinds of entitlements exist in all societies, but some exist in all. From this perspective, hunger is a failure of entitlement. The failure of entitlement may come from land dispossession, unemployment, high food prices, or lack or collapse of state-run food security programs, but the results are that people may starve to death in the midst of a food surplus.

Viewing hunger as a failure of entitlements also corrects ideological biases in the culture of capitalism, the tendency to overemphasize fast growth and production, the neglect of the problem of distribution, and hostility to government intervention in food distribution. Thus, rather than seeing hunger or famine as a failure of production (which it

An image that emerged from the famine in Somalia in 1992.

seems not to be), we can focus on a failure of distribution (see Vaughn 1987:158). Furthermore, we are able to appreciate the range of possible solutions to hunger. The goal is simply to establish, reestablish, or protect entitlements, the legitimate claim to food. Seeing hunger as a failure of entitlement also focuses on the kinds of public actions that are possible. For example, access to education and health care are seen in most core countries as basic entitlements that should be supplied by the state, not by a person's ability to pay. And most core countries see basic nutrition as a state-guaranteed entitlement, in spite of recent attempts in countries such as the United States to cut back on such entitlements. Thus, by speaking of entitlements, we can focus on the importance of public action in dealing with world hunger.

To understand the range of solutions to hunger, we also need to distinguish between the more publicized instances of famine, generally caused by war, government miscalculations, civil conflict, or climatic disruptions; *food poverty,* in which a particular household cannot obtain sufficient food to meet the dietary requirements of its members; and *food deprivation,* in which individuals within the household do not get adequate dietary intake (Sen 1990:374).

To illustrate, let's take a look at two situations of hunger, first the more publicized instance of famine and then the less widely publicized endemic hunger.

The Anatomy of Famine

Famines have long been a part of history. Administrators in India as early as the fourth century B.C. wrote of measures to avert famines, and the people of India have been subject to massive famines throughout its history. China has also suffered major famines. The latest occurred in 1958–1961, when 15 million to 30 million people starved to death.

Many historic famines were caused by crop failures, climatic disruptions, and war. Archaeologists have speculated that widespread climatic changes reduced the yields of Mayan agriculturists and resulted in the destruction of Mayan civilization. Yet it is clear that even historically famines resulted from entitlement failures rather than insufficient food (Newman 1990). Even during the Irish potato famine of 1846–1847, when one-eighth of the population starved to death, shiploads of food, often protected from starving Irish by armed guards, sailed down the Shannon River, bound for English ports and consumers who could pay for it.

We can better appreciate the dynamics of famine and the importance of entitlements by examining a famine crisis in the African country of Malawi in 1949. It was by no means the most serious famine in Africa in the past fifty years, but Megan Vaughn (1987), in her analysis of it, provides answers to the key questions, *who starves and why?*

The famine began with a drought. The lack of rain was first noticed after Christmas 1948 and drew serious attention when in January, normally the wettest month of the year, there was no rain at all; it remained dry until some rain fell in March. In some areas the first and second plantings of maize, the main food crop, failed completely, and wild pigs, baboons, and hippos devastated the remaining crops. Old people who remembered the last famine in 1922 said there were signs of a major crisis, and within a few months it was apparent that people were starving. The British colonial government began to organize relief efforts, sending agricultural representatives into the countryside to organize the planting of root crops, replanting of crops that failed, and opening food distribution camps. By the time the rains came in October, there were reports of real malnutrition and of hundreds of children and adults starving to death. Many died, ironically, at the beginning of 1950 as the maize crop was being harvested, many from eating the crop before it ripened (Vaughn 1987:48).

According to Vaughn, women suffered most from the famine. The question is, *what happened to women's food entitlements that resulted in their being the most severely affected?* To answer this question we need to know a little about food production, the role of kinship in Malawi life, and the changing role of women in African economies.

Malawi at the time was under British control; agriculture was divided between cash crop agriculture—tobacco was the most important crop—and subsistence agriculture, the growing of such crops as maize, sorghum, and a few root vegetables. In addition, many people worked at wage labor, either in the formal employment sector, for European or Indian farmers or merchants, or the government, or in the informal employment sector, working on farms owned or worked by Africans. Cash could also be earned through migrant labor, almost exclusively a male domain, although women could earn money making and selling beer or liquor.

The predominant form of kinship structure was matrilineal, that is people traced relations in the female line. The most important kin tie was between brother and sister, and the basic social unit was a group of sisters headed by a brother. Under this system rights to land were passed through women, men gaining rights to land only through marriage. Traditionally, women would work their land with their husbands, who lived with their wives and children. In this system a woman's entitlement to food could come from various sources: her control of land and the food grown on it, sharing of food with matrilineal kin, wages she might earn selling beer or liquor or working occasionally for African farmers, or wages her husband or children might earn. In addition, during the famine the government established an emergency food distribution system from which women could theoretically obtain food. *What happened to those entitlements when the crops failed?*

Changes in the agricultural economy and the introduction of wage labor under European colonial rule had already undermined women's entitlements (Boserup 1970). The British colonial government was under pressure, as it was in other parts of Africa, to produce revenue to pay the cost of maintaining the colonies. Consequently, they introduced cash crops, such as coffee, tea, cotton, and tobacco. The latter proved to be the most profitable in Malawi and was the major cash crop when the famine struck. But cash cropping was generally a male prerogative and provided wages for African men only when they worked for Europeans or Indians. Cash cropping by Europeans and Indians also took land that might have been used for food crops, contributing to a growing land shortage for Africans. Thus, in addition to providing new ways for men to gain economic power, European practices led to the decrease of women's power in the agricultural sector. This combination of changes in access to land, decreasing amounts of land available for Africans, and the growing importance of wage labor for men made women more dependent on men for their food entitlements when the famine struck.

When the famine became evident to the British authorities, they took measures that further reduced women's entitlements. First, partly to conserve grain and partly because of a fear of social disorder, they forbade the making and sale of beer, removing a major source of income for women. Next, they assumed the family unit consisted of a husband, wife, and children, presided over by the husband, and, consequently, refused to distribute food relief to married women, assuming they would obtain food from their husbands. However, many husbands were traveling to seek work elsewhere to buy food, and they might or might not send food or money home. Next, the government food distributions gave preference to those, mostly urban people who were employed in the formal economy by Europeans, Indians, or the government, neglecting those in the rural economy such as part-time women laborers. Furthermore, Europeans and Indians, who had ample food supplies during the famine, often shared with their workers who, again, were mostly men. Many of these men, of course, were conscientious husbands, fathers, brothers, and uncles and shared the food they received. But some did not, either keeping it for themselves or selling it at high prices on the black market.

To make matters worse, as the famine wore on social units began to fragment. This is a common feature of famines. Raymond Firth (1959) reported that during the early phases of a famine on the island of Tikopia, families recognized extended kin ties in the sharing of food, but as the famine wore on food was shared only within individual households. In Malawi the situation was even worse; at the beginning of the famine there seems to have been sharing within the main matrilineal kin group, but as it wore on the sharing unit became smaller and smaller until people ate secretly. Because one of a woman's entitlements consisted of food received from relatives, this would have further reduced the amount of food she received. Finally, divorce rates apparently increased significantly, particularly in families where the husband was a migrant laborer, further isolating women and reducing their food entitlements.

In sum, then, the most vulnerable portion of the population was women without male support but for whom the colonial authorities took no responsibility, married women whose husbands had abandoned them, and wives of long-term migrants who did not remit money (Vaughn 1987:147). In addition, of course, the children of these women suffered and died disproportionately.

The lesson of the Malawi famine is that starvation can be very selectively experienced within a population because of the distribution of food entitlements. Given the amount of food already available in the areas most affected by the famine and the food available through relief efforts, it is unlikely that anyone had to starve. But many did.

The Anatomy of Endemic Hunger

Although famine as a cause of hunger has decreased, endemic hunger caused by poverty has increased. One problem with endemic hunger is that it goes largely unnoticed, particularly by the press who prefer to cover the more spectacular instances of famine and by governments whose economic and social policies might be held responsible for the hunger. Yet endemic hunger is a far more serious problem. India, for example, which has done an excellent job of famine prevention, has done poorly in solving the problem of endemic hunger. Consequently, every eight years, more Indians die as a result of hunger than Chinese died in the famine of 1958–1961. Yet the deaths in India do not receive nearly the public attention that is given to famine. One of the questions we need to ask is, *how and why is endemic hunger ignored, unrecognized, and sometimes denied by state agencies, as well as by the hungry themselves?*

Governments often refuse to recognize hunger because it marks an admission of failure to provide adequately for its citizens. And hunger sometimes goes unrecognized because it is assumed to be a medical problem, rather than a problem of food entitlements. Doing anthropological fieldwork in Mali, Katherine A. Dettwyler (1994:71–73) encountered a little girl with swelling of the face, hands, feet, and abdomen, classic symptoms of *kwashiorkor,* a disease that results from a diet that is sufficient in calories but deficient in protein. The girl's mother said she had *funu bana,* "swelling sickness," and asked Dettwyler for medicine for her daughter, failing to recognize that what her daughter needed was extra meat or milk. When Dettwyler suggested just that, the mother responded by saying the little girl wasn't hungry and that she needed medicine. For the mother it continued to be a medical problem not a food problem.

The denial of hunger prevents the development of programs to alleviate it. More insidiously, when hunger goes unrecognized or unacknowledged, problems that are a consequence of hunger, such as poor work performance, poor academic achievement, and stunted growth, are attributed to other factors, such as lack of motivation or cultural background.

To illustrate how social, economic, and cultural factors converge to produce hunger in the midst of plenty, as well as the complexity of identifying hunger and even admitting it exists, let's examine the problem of starvation in Brazil. Brazil is not a poor country, in fact it is among the top ten to fifteen economies in the world. During the period of great optimism following World War II, Brazil was one of the first of the so-called underdeveloped countries to embark on a concerted policy of economic and industrial development. A large number of Brazilians have become very wealthy, yet 40 percent of its population lives in poverty, and it has one of the highest rates of infant mortality in Latin America, with some regions having an infant mortality rate as high as those in impoverished countries of Africa. Exploring why this happened will help us understand the dynamics of world hunger.

Brazil set out to develop economically by imitating the pattern followed by core countries such as England, France, and the United States. The strategy was to build industry, export cash crops, and create jobs, with the idea that the wealth created would "trickle down" to others in society. However, to date that hasn't happened. Instead, peasants once able to secure a reasonable subsistence through simple agriculture are deprived of land, through either expropriation of land or privatization of communal land, and forced to work as wage laborers on the surviving farms or to flee to cities to seek work, often ending up in the shantytowns that surround the cities. Their wages are insufficient to buy food, and structural adjustment policies imposed by international lending institutions have forced the reduction of social support programs. One thing stands out: The vast majority of the population becomes dependent on others for food, food they must buy and which must be affordable. Unfortunately, in many cases, they do not have the means to buy food, or prices keep it out of reach. The problem of hunger and poverty is particularly severe in northeastern Brazil.

Sugar has dominated the economy of northeastern Brazil for more than 400 years. Fueled by a growing European demand for sugar, Portuguese colonists established plantations in the sixteenth century and imported slaves to grow and process sugarcane. The colonialization of Brazil and the nature of the economic relations created by sugar production created a pattern of class relations that remained largely intact through the mid-twentieth century. A plantation-owning elite ruled over a large peasant population that cut sugarcane for wages, using unused land to grow their own food crops. A few others worked for wages in the sugar mills and refineries. However, as the sugar industry expanded and as technological improvements were made in the 1950s and 1960s because of government policies to expand production for export, many peasants were evicted from the land, fleeing to the cities in search of jobs. Poverty was widespread, and even people with jobs did not earn enough to meet family expenses. For example, in northeastern Brazil in 1989, the legal minimum monthly income was forty dollars, whereas food expenses alone for a family of four were four times that amount.

To make matters worse, in the mid-1980s Brazil and other countries could not keep up their payments to the World Bank and other Western financial institutions from which they had borrowed to industrialize and, consequently, threatened to default on their loans. To help these countries avoid default, the World Bank allowed them to renegotiate their loans. These countries had to agree to change their economies by, among other things, reducing government spending on such things as public education, welfare, housing, and health, entitlement cutbacks that resulted in still greater hardships for the poorest portion of the population.

In 1982 Nancy Scheper-Hughes returned to a shantytown, Alto do Cruzeiro, located in the city of Bom Jesus da Mata, where she had worked as a Peace Corps volunteer in 1965. The shantytown consisted of 5,000 rural workers, one-third of whom lived in straw huts. The vast majority of residents had no electricity, and water was collected by the women twice a day from a single spigot located in the center of the community. Most men and boys worked as sugarcane cutters during the harvest season. A few men and some women worked in the local slaughterhouse. Other than this part-time work, there was little employment. Many women found jobs as domestics among the middle- and upper-class families or sold what they could in the market. Many women and children worked in the cane fields as unregistered workers at less than minimum pay.

The economics of hunger in the shantytowns is simple—there is not enough money to buy food. Because of the economic situation in Brazil, Scheper-Hughes reported that groceries cost twice in 1987–1988 what they cost in 1982. Furthermore, a basic subsistence costs one and a half times minimum wage. Many of the residents do not make minimum wage and are unemployed from February to September when there is no cane to cut. Furthermore, fresh vegetables that some used to grow or that were available from relatives in the countryside are no longer available because so many have been forced off the land by the sugarcane growers. In the 1960s brown beans cooked with slices of native squash, pumpkin, and onions were a staple; now the beans are cooked with only a little salt and flavoring. Dried beef was once available but is now prohibitively expensive and has been replaced by salted fish caught in the polluted river that passes through town. Even dried beans have become prohibitively expensive and dried cornmeal has taken its place.

With jobs scarce, available wages inadequate, land unavailable to grow food, and government assistance inadequate or nonexistent, residents of the shantytown scramble as best they can to acquire food. In fact, according to Scheper-Hughes, slow starvation is a primary motivating force in the social life of the shantytowns. People eat every day, but the diet is so meager that they are left hungry. Women beg while their children wait for food, and children's growth is stunted by hunger and malnutrition. Children of one and two years of age cannot sit unaided and cannot or do not speak. Breastbones and ribs protrude from taut skin, flesh hangs in folds from arms, legs, and buttocks, and sunken eyes stare vacantly. The plight of the worker and his or her family is, according to Scheper-Hughes (1992:146), "the slow starvation of a population trapped...in a veritable concentration camp for more than thirty million people."

Perhaps the most tragic result of hunger is the death of infants. Approximately 1 million children younger than five years of age die each year in Brazil. Northeastern Brazil, which accounts for 25 percent of child deaths, has an infant mortality rate of 116 of every 1,000 live births, one of the highest in the world. And not all deaths are reported. In northeastern Brazil Scheper-Hughes estimates that two-thirds of infants who die do so without a medical diagnosis.

Scheper-Hughes found that reliable statistics on infant mortality in the shantytowns were difficult to acquire. She finally obtained statistics for selected years in the 1970s, all of which indicated an infant mortality rate of 36 to 41 percent. From information she collected by combing public records, Scheper-Hughes found the following infant mortality rates for Bom Jesus da Mata: 49.3 percent in 1965; 40.9 percent in 1977; 17.4 percent in 1985; and 21.1 percent in 1987.

Although the infant mortality rate in northeastern Brazil has generally declined, the decline, said Scheper-Hughes (1992:280), is misleading. Instead of a decline in infant mortality there is a "modernization of child mortality," characterized by containing child death to the poorest families and by a change in the major reported causes of child death from the "old killers," diseases now controlled by immunization, to "new killers," especially infant malnutrition and dehydration caused by diarrhea.

News reports and government studies about poverty in Brazil do mention the problem of infant mortality, but they generally attribute it to malnutrition and disease. But Scheper-Hughes's study revealed a more basic problem: People, especially infants and children, are not only malnourished, a term that implies simply a poor diet; in fact they are starving to death. Yet even medical authorities rarely mention starvation. When Scheper-Hughes examined medical records of children and infants who died, she found that in 34.8 percent of cases the cause of death was cessation of heart beat and respiration; in 22.2 percent it was listed as dehydration. Only 3.4 percent were attributed to malnutrition and only 1.7 percent to diarrhea. One wonders, wrote Scheper-Hughes (1992:303),

> Amid the sea of froth and brine that carried away the infants and babies of the Alto do Cruzeiro, what kind of professional prudery it was that "failed to see" what every mother of the Alto do Cruzeiro knew without ever being told. "They die," said one woman going to the heart of the matter, "because their bodies turn to water."

One way to mask the evidence of starvation is to turn it into a medical problem; the medicalization of hunger is exactly what Scheper-Hughes discovered in Brazil. People interpret the symptoms of starvation, even in children, as conditions that require medical treatment rather than food.

One of the things anthropology teaches about the human capacity for culture is that people place experiences in systems of meaning that allow them to make sense of their

A homeless mother and child trying to survive on the streets of a Brazilian city.

experiences. Illness and disease are no exception; different people define differently what constitutes illness as opposed to something that is not illness. Moreover, people will define what constitutes a medical problem (e.g., infant diarrhea) as opposed to, say, a social problem (e.g., hunger). In northeastern Brazil hunger, a social problem, has been redefined as a medical problem. How and why this has been done reveals much about how human beings construct their own world of experience and how people construct systems of meaning that best enhance their social or political interests.

One of the major traditional illness syndromes in Brazil, and indeed in much of Latin America, is *nervos,* assumed to be a wasting sickness that leaves the victim weak, shaky, dizzy, tired, depressed, and disoriented. When people are suffering from these symptoms, they say they are sick with *nervos.* People believe *nervos* is the result of an innately weak and nervous body. In years past when people thought they suffered an attack of *nervos,* they drew on their traditional store of herbal medicines and the practical knowledge of elderly women in the household. Today they seek medical help from one of the local clinics; now *nervos,* a traditional disease category, is thought to be treatable by modern medicine.

But there was another more insidious change in how people defined their physical condition: Symptoms associated with hunger began to be talked about as *nervos.* That is, hunger and *nervos* became synonymous. This was not always the case. Starvation and famine have long been a feature of life in northeastern Brazil; people frequently complained of *fome* (hunger) and its terrifying end, *delirio de fome,* the madness that signaled the end of life from starvation. But hunger is rarely mentioned today. If a person is weak, tired, or dizzy, he or she will not complain of hunger and seek food but instead complain of *nervos* and seek medicine to cure it. In other words, people who may be suffering from hunger and who twenty years ago would have defined themselves as suffering from *fome* now define themselves as suffering from *nervos,* an illness separate from hunger that simply happens or is the result of innate weakness. Moreover, if weakness, fatigue, dizziness, and other symptoms that may be related to slow starvation simply happen, then no one is at fault and social causes of the problem can be ignored.

Nancy Scheper-Hughes (1992:174) said a hungry body represents a potent critique of the nation-state in which it exists, but a sick body implicates no one and conveys no blame, guilt, or responsibility. Sickness simply happens. The sick person and the sick social system are let off the hook. A population suffering from starvation, however, represents a threat to the state that requires economic and social solutions—social programs, jobs, or land redistribution. *Nervos,* a sickness, is a personal and "psychological" problem that requires only medical intervention and faults no one, except perhaps the person suffering from it. Sickness requires little state action, other than supplying the occasional prescription of tranquilizers, vitamins, or sleeping pills. Instead of the responsible use of state power to relieve starvation and hunger, there is a misuse of medical knowledge to deny that there is a social problem at all.

Scheper-Hughes (1992:207) related the story of a young single mother who brought her nine-month-old child to the clinic, explaining that the baby suffered from *nervoso infantil.* She complained that the small, listless, and anemic child was irritable and fussy and disturbed the sleep of family members, especially the grandmother, who was the family's economic mainstay. Herbal teas did not work, and the grandmother threatened to throw them out if the child did not sleep. The doctor refused to give her sleeping pills for the child and instead wrote a prescription for vitamins. The doctor failed to acknowledge the mother's real distress, as well as the child's state of malnutrition, and the vitamins served virtually no purpose other than to redefine the infant's condition from starvation to sickness or malnutrition.

On other occasions children will be brought to doctors with severe diarrhea, a classic symptom of starvation. Simple rehydration therapy, feeding the child special fluids, will usually cure the diarrhea for a time. But the child is still returned to an environment where, with lack of food, the problem is likely to recur until after being "saved" perhaps a dozen times the child finally dies of hunger.

The question, said Scheper-Hughes, *is how do people come to see themselves as primarily nervous, and only secondarily hungry? How do they come to see themselves as weak, rather than exploited? How does overwork and exploitation come to be redefined as a sickness for which the appropriate cure is a tonic, vitamin A, a sugar injection? Why do chronically hungry people "eat" medicines and go without food?*

One reason is that since hungry people truly suffer from headaches, tremors, weakness, irritability, and other symptoms of nervous hunger, and they look to doctors, healers, political leaders, and pharmacologists to "cure" them. They look for strong-acting medicines, so they line up at clinics and drugstores until they get them. One cannot, said Scheper-Hughes, underestimate the attractiveness of drugs to people who cannot read warning labels and who have a long tradition of "magical medicines."

Furthermore, she said, health is a political symbol subject to manipulation. Slogans such as "health for all by the year 2000," or "community health," filter down to poor, exploited communities where they serve as a cover for neglect and violence. There is power and domination to be obtained by defining a population as sick or nervous and in need of the power of politicians and doctors:

> The medicalization of hunger and childhood malnutrition in the clinics, pharmacies, and political chambers of Bom Jesus da Mata represents a macabre performance of distorted institutional and political relations. Gradually the people of Bom Jesus da Mata have come to believe that they desperately need what is readily given to them, and they have forgotten that what they need most is what is cleverly denied. (Scheper-Hughes 1992: 169–170)

Conspiracy by medical workers is not necessary to effect this transformation. Doctors and clinic workers themselves accept the magical efficacy of cures; either that or they are demoralized to the extent that they prescribe drugs as the only solution they have to ills they are ill-prepared to solve but called on to treat. As one doctor (cited Scheper-Hughes 1992:204) said:

> They come in with headaches, no appetite, tiredness, and they hurt all over. They present a whole body in pain or in crisis, with an ailment that attacks them everywhere! That's impossible! How am I to treat that? I'm a surgeon, not a magician! They say they are weak, that they are nervous. They say their head pounds, their heart is racing in their chest, their legs are shaking. It's a litany of complaints from head to toe. Yes, they all have worms, they all have amoebas, they all have parasites. But parasites can't explain everything. How am I supposed to make a diagnosis?

SOLUTIONS TO POVERTY AND HUNGER

What solutions are there to the problem of world hunger and the poverty that ultimately causes it? Is it best to focus on economic development or, as some call it, growth-mediated security systems, assuming so-called market mechanisms will improve people's lives? Or are famine and endemic hunger best addressed by public support systems in the form of state-financed food and nutrition programs, state-financed employment, or cash distribution programs? The answer to these questions are not easy. Some argue, for example, that state-run programs take money needed for economic development and divert it to programs that may in the short run alleviate poverty and hunger but in the long run will simply aggravate the problem by undercutting the growth of private enterprise. This is the position generally taken by multilateral organizations, such as the World Bank and IMF, which insist on limitations or cutbacks in state spending as conditions for loans or structural adjustment programs to assist countries in debt. Others respond that state-run antipoverty programs represent an investment in the human capital necessary for economic development, that a population that is hungry, undernourished, and subject to disease is less productive. To answer these questions we first examine the role of economic development in reducing poverty and hunger, then examine the role of foreign aid, and, finally, examine the potential of what are called "microcredit" programs.

Economic Development

The concept of "economic development" is generally traced to U.S. president Harry S. Truman's inaugural address before Congress in 1949 in which he referred to the conditions in "poorer" nations and described them as "underdeveloped areas." At that point multilaterial institutions, such as the World Bank and the IMF, were mobilized to further development goals, often recommending massive economic and social changes and a total reorganization of societies deemed to be "undeveloped." For example, the 1949 World Bank report sent back from Colombia (and similar to that of hundreds to be issued in subsequent years) advised that

> piecemeal and sporadic efforts are apt to make little impression on the general picture. Only through a generalized attack throughout the whole economy on education, health, housing, food, and productivity can the vicious circle of poverty, ignorance, ill health, and low productivity be decisively broken (IBRD 1950: *xv*)

Proponents of economic development point to successes in raising life expectancy rates worldwide, lowering infant mortality rates, and raising literacy rates. They can point to the development of successful national economies in South Korea, Malaysia, and Brazil, among others.

Critics, however, paint a different picture. They argue that the goal of economic development to raise the living standards of people in the periphery, fifty years after its inception, has largely failed. A higher percentage of the world's population, they say, is hungrier today than in 1950. Studies by the very institutions at the forefront of development, such as the World Bank and IMF, conclude that the goals of development have not been met. Although poverty rates have declined somewhat in East Asia (from 26.6 percent in 1987 to 15.32 percent in 1999) and the Middle East (from 4.3 percent to 1.95 percent), elsewhere they have remained the same or increased. The poverty rate in Latin America and the Caribbean remains at 15.57 percent, at 39.99 percent in South Asia, and at 46.30 percent in sub-Saharan Africa (Chen and Ravallion 2000). In Eastern Europe the number living in poverty has climbed from 0.24 percent (1.07 million) in 1987 to 5.14 percent (24 million) in 1999. Furthermore, the absolute number living in poverty in the periphery increased over the same period from 1.1 billion to almost 1.2 billion. If the number of people living on less than two dollars a day is added, those living in poverty number 2.8 billion people.[2]

---

[2] The figures of one dollar and two dollars a day used by the World Bank, the United Nations, and other international agencies to measure poverty may also be misleading. In the United States, for example, poverty is measured not by an arbitrary dollar amount but by the costs of necessities, such as food, clothing, shelter, and education. In 1996 in the United States, that amounted to eleven dollars a day per person. The poverty standard used by the United Nations Development Program (UNDP) reports a lower poverty rate in Mexico than the United States, and a lower rate for Jamaica than Canada (see, e.g., Chossudovsky nd).

Furthermore, the projects that were to promote "development" have notably decreased people's quality of life. Hundreds of millions of people have been displaced from their communities and homes or thrown off their land by World Bank hydroelectric and agricultural mega-projects. Instead of lifting the standard of living of peripheral countries, there has been a doubling of the degree of economic inequality between rich and poor countries in the past forty years. As one study concludes

> there is no region in the world that the [World] Bank or [International Monetary] Fund can point to as having succeeded through adopting the policies that they promote—or, in many cases, impose—in borrowing countries (Weisbrot et al. 2000:3)

The question then is, *why, up to this point, has the economic development initiative largely failed?*

There are three features of the economic development program that we need to examine. The first is the tendency to define the goals of development and an acceptable standard of living in the very limited terms of income and gross national product (GNP). Income and the level of production has become the measure of the worth of a society.

Second, economic development embodies an ideology that assumes that the culture and way of life of the core is universally desirable and should be exported (or imposed, if necessary) on the rest of the people of the world. As Wolfgang Sachs (1999:5) notes, "development meant nothing less than projecting the American model of society on the rest of the world."

Third, the concept of development greatly increased the power of core governments over the emerging nation-states of the periphery. If development was to be the goal, then "undeveloped" or "underdeveloped" countries must look to the expertise of the core for financial aid, technological aid, and political help. Furthermore, by embracing development as a goal, leaders of peripheral states gain military assistance and support that permit many of them to assume dictatorial powers over the rest of the population.

In his book, *Seeing Like a State: How Human Schemes to Improve the Human Condition Have Failed* (1998), James C. Scott examines a series of failed development projects. Among these, says Scott, are the design and building of cities such as Brasilia, the Soviet collectivization of agriculture, the Russian revolution itself, and compulsory villagization in Tanzania. All were characterized, he says, by the same basic features previously mentioned of economic development programs.

First, all these projects engaged in a form of economic reductionism; social reality was reduced to almost solely economic elements, ignoring institutions and behaviors essential to the maintenance of societies and environments. Reductionism of this sort is attractive to nation-states because it makes populations and environments more "legible," and, consequently, amenable to state manipulation and control. The guiding parable for understanding this reductive tendency is, for Scott, that of the "scientifically" managed forest.

Scientific forestry emerged in Prussia and Saxony in the last half of the eighteenth century. It viewed the forest almost solely as a source of revenue for the timber that might be annually extracted. Missing in this view was the foliage that might have been feed to animals, game that might be hunted by farmers, or social interactions for which the forest served as a backdrop. Consequently, the first scientifically planted forests were set only with "productive" trees; anything that was thought to interfere with timber production was eliminated. Underbrush was cut, flora and fauna eliminated, and so on. The result in the first generation of trees was impressive; however, forestry officials soon found that the new forest was living off of the capital of rich soil created by the disordered forest, and by the second and third generations, not only had timber production declined dramatically but also the soil itself lost the capacity to produce. Thus, without all of the "worthless" elements of the forest, the forest itself collapsed.

The language of capitalism, says Scott, constantly betrays its tendency to reduce the world to only those items that are economically productive. Nature, for example, becomes "natural resources," identifying only those things that are commodifiable. Plants that are valued become "crops"; those that compete with them are stigmatized as "weeds." Insects that ingest crops are called "pests." Valuable trees are "timber," whereas species that compete with them are "trash" trees or "underbrush." Valued animals are "game," or "livestock," whereas competitors are "predators," or "varmints" (Scott 1998:13). In the language of economic development the focus is on GNP, income, employment rates, kilowatts of electricity produced, miles of roads, labor units, productive acreage, and so on. Absent in this language are items that are not easily measured or that are noneconomic (e.g., quality of social relations, environmental aesthetics, etc.).

The second ingredient in failed projects, says Scott, is what he refers to as "high modern ideology." This ideology is characterized by a supreme (or, as Scott refers to it, a "muscle-bound") version of self-confidence in scientific and technical progress in satisfying human needs, mastering the environment, and designing the social order to realize these objectives. This ideology emerged as a by-product of unprecedented progress in the core and was attributed to science and technology. High modern ideology does not correspond to political ideologies and can be found equally on the left and the right. Generally, however, it entails using state power to bring about huge, utopian changes to people's lives.

The idea of economic development is a product of high modern ideology. It represents an uncritical acceptance of the idea of scientific and technological progress, and an unrestrained faith in the wisdom of core economic, scientific, and technological principles. The green revolution and the attempt to widely apply the technology of genetic engineering discussed earlier are but two other products of high modern ideology.

Scott is careful not to reject outright the application of high modern ideology. In some cases it can and has led to significant improvements in peoples' lives. Thus, economic reductionism and high modern ideology are not, in themselves, sufficient to contribute to a failed project. For failure to occur there is a third ingredient—an authoritarian state. When high modern ideology and the nation-state's tendency to reduce the world to legible, manipulative units is combined with an authoritarian state willing and able to use the full weight of its coercive power to bring these high modernist designs into being, along with a civil society that is unable to resist its manipulations, the stage is set for a development disaster. As Scott says

> the legibility of a society provides the capacity for large-scale engineering, high-modernist ideology provides the desire, the authoritarian state provides the determination to act on that desire, and an incapacitated civil society provides the leveled social terrain on which to build. (1998:5)

To illustrate how the goals of economic development and modernization can lead to disruption, Scott describes the *ujamaa* village campaign in Tanzania from 1973 to 1976. It represented a massive attempt to permanently settle most of the country's population in villages planned, partly or wholly, by officials of the central government (Scott 1998:221).

Clearly, the village scheme emerged from a desire of the Tanzanian state to make its population more legible and manipulable. At the beginning of the development scheme, there were some 11 million to 12 million rural Tanzanians living in scattered settlements, growing crops and herding animals, using techniques developed over generations. As the natural forest contained elements to sustain it, so these settlements sustained themselves with local knowledge and practice built up over the years. From the viewpoint of the state, however, these populations were economically unproductive, disordered, and, somehow, primitive. The project, which succeeded in moving more than 13 million people into 7,684 villages (Scott 1998:245), was to transform the citizenry into producers of exportable crops, strung out along paved roads, where state services could be easily delivered and where the population could be easily monitored. Furthermore, the success of the villagization program could be easily tracked by counting the number of people moved, the number of villages built, and so on.

Clearly, the project was driven by a high modern ideology imported from the West that assumed that "modern" settlement patterns, agricultural techniques, and modes of communication were clearly superior to those practiced by the indigenous population. In fact, notes Scott (1998:241), these premises were holdovers from the colonial era. Project designers and supporters assumed that African cultivators and pastoralists were backward, unscientific, and inefficient. They assumed that only through the supervision or, if necessary, coercion by specialists in scientific agriculture could they contribute to a modern Tanzania.

Finally, as with most development schemes, there had to be an authoritarian state to impose the program and to suppress resistance to it. From the beginning, Tanzanians were skeptical about villagization. Whereas they had knowledge of the areas in which they lived, the new, selected sites were chosen without consideration of water or fuel resources and they feared that being in villages would result in overcrowding for people and domestic animals. To meet this resistance the state moved its machinery into place to force compliance. It was, said officials, for the people's own good. "We cannot tolerate," said Tanzanian president Julius Nyerere, "seeing our people live a 'life of death'" (cited Scott 1998: 230). All of this was in keeping with World Bank reports, such as one in 1964 that said

> How to overcome the destructive conservatism of the people and generate the drastic agrarian reform which must be effected if the country is to survive is one of the most difficult problems political leaders of Tanzania have to face. (cited Scott 1998:241)

Given the situation, violence was inevitable. The police and militia were given authority to move people, first threatening that they would not be eligible for famine relief if they did not move, later forcing them to tear down and load houses and belongings onto trucks. In some cases houses were burned or run over with trucks. When people realized that resistance was futile, they saved what they could move and fled the new villages at the first opportunity (Scott: 1998:235–236).

As might be expected, the results of villagization were disastrous. Huge imports of food were necessary from 1973 to 1975 because of the immediate decline of agricultural production, the cost of which would have bought a cow for every Tanzanian family. Some 60 percent of the new villages were built on semiarid land that required long walks to reach farm plots. Peasants were moved from fertile farmlands to poor lands or land on which the soil was unsuitable for the crops the government demanded farmers grow. Villages were located at a distance from crops, which left the crops open to theft and pests. The concentration of people and livestock resulted in cholera and livestock epidemics, while herding cattle in concentrated areas devastated both rangeland and livelihoods (Scott 1998:247). Instead of achieving legitimacy, the villagization campaign created an alienated and uncooperative peasantry for which Tanzania would pay a huge financial and political price.

Of course, the scheme was not totally Tanzanian. It resembled hundreds of colonial schemes, built on the supposed promise of modern science and technology, as well as projects still supported by the World Bank, the U.S. Agency for International Development (USAID), and other development agencies. That it was a disaster should come, in retrospect, as no surprise, in spite of the conviction of virtually everyone involved that it would vastly improve the life of the subjects. More disturbing yet is that the Tanzanian government, at the urging of the World Bank and the U.S. government, continues to relocate indigenous peoples with similar negative results (see, e.g., Fratkin 1997a; 1997b).

Based on his examination of failed projects, Scott (1998:348) concludes that the major fault is that the project planners thought that they were smarter than they really were and that they regarded the subjects of their plans as far more stupid and incompetent than they really were. By trying to impose a vision of modernization and progress built largely on economic criteria and a vision of life that emerged in the West, high modern ideologues fostered the social and cultural equivalent of unsustainable, impoverished, monocropped, "scientifically managed" forests, environments devoid of the social stuff that enable people in communities to form cooperative units and work together to achieve common goals.

Yet the same ingredients for failure—economic reductionism, high modern ideology, and an authoritarian state combined with a suppressed civil society—are evident (and yet unexamined) in countless development efforts. Another of these involves the case of U.S. foreign aid to Russia.

Foreign Aid: The Case of Russia

The ideologues of high modern ideology received a wonderful opportunity with the breakup of the Soviet Union in 1989. Through an infusion of aid and expertise from core countries and international financial agencies, the ex-Communist economy was to be transformed into a market economy modeled after those in the West. By the end of 1992 the major industrial countries, along with international financial institutions, contributed some $129 billion in debt relief, loans, and export credits to the former Communist Bloc countries (Wedel 1998a:18). The IMF alone contributed another $22.6 billion bailout to Russia in July 1998.

The plan to transform Russia and the former Soviet Bloc countries from centralized socialist economies to market economies resembled many of the development schemes of the past fifty years that advocated "a generalized attack throughout the whole economy" (IBRD 1950, xvi). Economists, such as Jeffery Sachs of Harvard's International Institute of International Development (HIID) were advocating "shock therapy" for Eastern Europe and Russia—an immediate rather than gradual shift to a market economy. "You can't leap a chasm in two jumps" (IBRD 1950, xvi), was one of Sachs' favorite metaphors. And, as in most other grand development schemes, it was the "people" of Russia and Eastern Europe who would benefit. But, so far, that is not the way it has turned out.

In 1998 an estimated one out of every five people in the transition countries of Europe and Central Asia survived on less than $2.15 per day. A decade ago fewer than one out of twenty-five lived in such absolute poverty. The decline in Russian economic output rivaled that of the 1930s global depression. Unemployment soared, the Russian currency lost most of its value, male life expectancy fell by five years between 1989 and 1994, largely due to a 100 percent increase in mortality in males between the ages of forty-nine and fifty-nine. Suicides of young males increased by 50 percent between 1989 and 1997. Prostitution and drug use rose rapidly, and economic inequality in Russia, which in 1989 had been among the lowest, now is among the highest in the world. Even the population is collapsing as women have fewer children and as the death rate from disease, including HIV/AIDS, increases. If trends continue, Russia's population will be 134 million by 2015, down from 150 million in 1991 (see, e.g., Klugman and Braithwaite 1998).

Why, in spite of billions of dollars of foreign aid and the influsion of expertise from the West, have these conditions developed? There are probably no simple answers. Among the factors contributing to Russia's collapse are the economic crisis of 1997 triggered in Asia, the decline in the price of oil (one of Russia's major exports) through the 1990s, and wars fought by Russia in Afghanistan and Chechnya. Massive capital flight certainly didn't help. One estimate is that as much as $140 billion (U.S.)—almost $2 billion per month—fled Russia during the first six years of market reforms, as much as left Brazil, Venezuela, Mexico, and Peru during the economically turbulent 1980s. Another factor, however, was aid efforts directed largely by the United States that funneled millions of taxpayer dollars to individuals in Russia for privatization efforts that enriched a few people but did little for and may have helped impoverish the bulk of the Russian population.

The case of foreign aid to Russia is described by anthropologist Janine R. Wedel, and involves three major players: the U.S government, HIID, and a group of Russian businessmen and government officials Wedel refers to as the "Clan" (1998b:122). The affair, which Wedel in one article dubbed "The Harvard Boys Do Russia (1998b)" provides a cautionary tale of the dangers and difficulty of distributing foreign aid.

As in most failed projects, foreign aid to Russia first involved a form of economic reductionism. The element to be transformed was the state ownership and control of production characteristic of Soviet socialism. Aid was to be used to privatize these institutions in the belief that this particular reform would result in the restructuring of Russia's economy and society. Much of the money was supplied by the USAID and was to encourage privatization. Privatization had the added benefit of being easily quantified; officials could count the number of businesses, farms, or services that had been transferred to private hands or the number of people employed by privately run enterprises. Missing from this view, of course, were the social, political, and legal structures necessary for a society built around the private ownership of property. Missing also was the recognition of the extent to which "private" businesses and services in the capitalist core are subsidized by the state (see Chapter 4).

The second ingredient in the story is a high modern ideology. This was supplied, in this case, by Western economic experts who were paid by core governments and agencies to "advise" their counterparts in Russia and the former Soviet Bloc on the proper steps to take to transform the socialist economy into a market economy.

The third ingredient was an ability by those involved in loan schemes to bypass democratic institutions and rely for reforms on the authority of the Russian state. In this case, this involved a few Russian government officials who, because of their ties to Western economic institutions, were able to work around elected officials.

The story begins with Western governments searching for "Russian reformers" to work with to transform the Russian economy. They focused on a group of men from St. Petersburg, the "Chubais Clan" after its leader, Anatoly Chubais. The United States needed a nongovernmental group to work with the reformers and selected HIID, members of which had already been serving as advisors to Eastern European governments. HIID was given some $40.4 million from USAID between 1992 and 1997 to help facilitate privatization and ended up controlling an additional $300 million in USAID funds that were supposed to be used for privatization, legal reform, and the establishment of other Western-style financial institutions (Wedel 1999:6).

Chubais, who spoke English, had Western contacts, and was conversant with aid donor vernacular of "markets," "reform," and "civil society," served as a useful intermediary both for American advisors and for the Russian government of Boris Yeltsin. Chubais was appointed head of Russia's first privatization agency, served as head of Yeltsin's reelection campaign, and became Russia's first deputy prime minister and minister of finance. Access to USAID money also catapulted other members of the Clan into influential government positions. One of Chubais's functions as head of Russia's first privatization agency was to prevent corruption in the transfer of state property to private hands. Instead, the program instituted by Chubais (a "voucher" scheme that was viewed from the beginning with suspicion by most Russians) allowed a few people to accumulate vast amounts of state property. Furthermore, to implement many of the reforms supported by U.S. agencies, Chubais was forced to bypass the Russian parliament, the Duma, and implement programs by presidential decree. In effect, Chubais, largely with the support of American aid officials, circumvented Russia's democratically elected representatives. This had the effect of greatly weakening support for reforms among the very people—elected officials—who, in the end, would have been responsible for sustaining them (Wedel 1999:7–8).

The privatization program led by Chubais shaped the new distribution of wealth in Russia as well as its citizens' perception of democracy and capitalism. The Russian public began to associate terms such as *market economy, economic reform,* and *the West* with dubious activities that benefited a few at the expense of everyone else who suffered a devastating decline from the standard of living under socialism (Wedel 1998a:132–133).

In addition, the Clan leveraged its support from USAID and HIID to solicit funds from other international donor agencies. One of the agencies set up by the Clan and HIID was the Russian Privatization Center, a supposedly private organization to provide funds and loans for privatization efforts and to establish democratic institutions and nongovern-mental organizations (NGOs). The head of the agency estimated that some $4 billion in Western funds were managed by the center.

Unfortunately, the Clan seemed less interested in market reform than in establishing political power. Furthermore, they were not well regarded by Russians who considered them little more than a communist-styled group that created and shared profits (Wedel 1999:11). As a result, by supporting one specific political faction, U.S. assistance under-mined its objectives and generated skepticism by most Russians of capitalism, reform, and privatization. Chubais, because of his association with failed economic reform, was con-sidered the most "hated" man in Russia (Wedel 1998a:133). By the end of the 1990s, Rus-sian economists actually advised against more loans, claiming that most of the money went for speculation on financial markets, had no effect on the economy, and simply were left for the Russian people to repay.

The situation was also ripe for corruption. Thus, members of the Clan and of HIID were in the position of recommending aid policies while being, at the same time, recipients of aid money, as well as overseeing aid contracts. The situation made it easy for Clan mem-bers and supporters to, as Wedel put it, "work both sides of the table." It perhaps is not sur-prising that in September 2000, the U.S. government filed a $40 million civil complaint against Harvard University, and two members of HIID and their wives, charging that they used their positions and insider information for personal business interests and investments while doing research in Russia for USAID.

To what extent the case of foreign aid to Russia is typical of other aid initiatives is difficult to say, although many critics of foreign aid would claim it is the norm. More im-portantly, perhaps, the case of Russia illustrates how a group of advisers with limited goals, a high modern ideology, and considerable power can contribute to the disruption of an entire society. The same arrogant assumptions of "expert knowledge," the ignoring of the social underpinnings of society, and a lack of trust or outright denigration of the ability of the people to which the aid is directed led to the failure of foreign aid to Russia to effect any benefits for the larger population while greatly enriching a few.

Targeting Vulnerable Populations:
The Grameen Bank and Microcredit

As we saw in the case of the 1949 famine in Malawi, women are particularly vulnerable to hunger and poverty. Globally, more than 60 percent of those living in poverty are women as are two out of every three poor adults in the United States. Therefore, one possible way of alleviating hunger and poverty is to focus on women.

One oft-cited example of programs to aid women is the Grameen Bank in Bang-ladesh. The simple premise of the Grameen Bank is that small loans ($100 or less) mostly to poor women who, with no collateral, are unable to borrow from regular banks will enable them to establish small retail businesses (e.g., vegetable vendor, fruit seller, tea stall owner, lime seller, egg seller) or small manufacturing businesses (e.g., incense maker, plas-tic flower maker, wire bag maker, mat weaver, toy maker) whose income will enable them to pay back the loan with interest.

Bangladesh is one of the poorest countries in the world. Unemployment is high, and women in Bangladesh suffer systematic discrimination revealed by, among other things, the 0.940 to 1 ratio of females to males in the population. Descent in Bangladesh is patrilineal and residence is patrilocal, that is women are expected to live with or near their husband's family after marriage. Most Bangladesh families also observe *purdah,* a system based on the belief that women must be isolated to protect them and ensure that they observe socially accepted standards of modesty and morality. *Purdah* effectively limits a woman's physical mobility to the area around her homestead and her social contacts to immediate family members. Consequently, girls learn to accept dependence on male family members and, later, husbands. Education for women is often considered irrelevant.

The Grameen Bank was founded by Mohammad Yunus, an economics professor at Chittagong University in Bangladesh. Yunus reasoned that women are more likely to invest earnings in their children. Thus, funds lent to women are more likely to promote a qualitative change in the living conditions of more members of the household. As of 2000, the Grameen Bank lent more than $2 billion to more than 2 million villagers, most of them women.

The Grameen Bank is unique also because it combines its lending activities with a regimented social program. Money is lent, not to individuals, but to groups of five to six

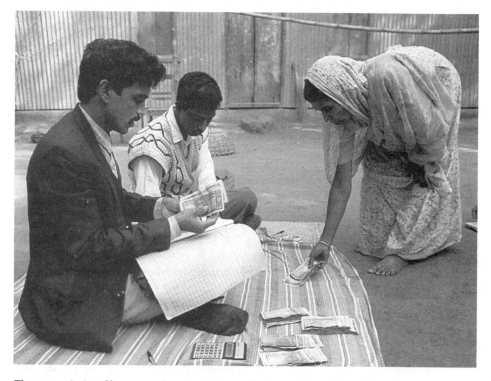

The vast majority of borrowers from the Grameen Bank are women. Here a borrower makes one of her regular loan payments.

persons who, as a group, meet regularly with bank staff. They are required to observe the bank's four major principles—discipline, unity, courage, and hard work. They must also pledge to shun child marriage, keep families small, build and use pit latrines, and plant as many seedlings as possible during planting seasons. At meetings they are required to salute, recite their obligations, do physical drills, and sit in rows of five to mark their group affiliation. Furthermore, they are responsible, as a group, for the repayment of loans; that is, if one person in the group defaults, others in the group are responsible for the payment.

The question we need to ask is, *does extending financial credit to poor women serve to empower them economically, socially, or politically?* Some research suggests that women borrowers work more, have higher incomes, and eat better (Wahid 1994). Other ethnographic research (Schuler and Hashemi 1994) suggests that bank membership not only empowers women economically but also significantly increases contraceptive use and fertility control. One study revealed that more than 50 percent of Grameen members escaped poverty over a ten-year period, as opposed to only 5 percent in a control group (Gibbons and Sukor 1994).

However, although the Grameen Bank, and microcredit institutions themselves have been widely praised by development agencies and emulated worldwide, recent research by anthropologist Aminur Rahman (1999) suggests that the highly patriarchal structure of Bangladesh society undermines many of the goals of the bank. In the villages in which he worked, Rahman found that loans to women are often considered a household resource and that the patriarchal norms of the society allow men to claim control over them (Rahman 1999:151). He found also that 71 percent of the women who asked for permission to join the bank were persuaded by husbands or other male relatives to do so. Furthermore, he found that loans were generally used by persons other than the female borrower. Of general loans, 61.4 percent were used by husbands, 17.5 percent by sons, 5.26 percent by the borrower, 6.1 percent jointly, and 9.6 percent by others (Rahman 1999:110). Rahman concluded that in the study community it is the men who use the loans and supply the installment payments to the women.

Rahman also questioned whether the loans were economically viable. He found that only 33 percent of installment payments came from the investment, 10 percent were paid by using the principal from the loan, and 57 percent were paid from other sources—relatives, peers, moneylenders, and others.

The loans may also negatively affect relations between women and other family members. Whereas 18 percent or 120 women borrowers interviewed by Rahman (1999:123) reported a decrease of verbal and physical assault because of involvement with the bank, 57 percent reported an increase of verbal assault, and 13 percent reported an increase in verbal and physical assault.

Rahman (1999:148) concluded that women are targeted for microcredit largely because they are vulnerable, submissive, shy, passive, immobile, and easy to discipline. It is only because of their vulnerable societal positions that women regularly attend the weekly meetings of borrowers and honor the rigid schedule for repayment of loans. For example, if a woman fails to make installment payments on time, according to one of Rahman's informants, she is verbally humiliated by peers and male bank workers. If a woman is publicly humiliated, it gives males in the household a bad reputation. Peers may take the defaulter and lock her in the bank building. To do this to a man would mean almost nothing in the village; but, for a woman it will bring *durnam* ("bad reputation") to her household, lineage, and village (Rahman 1999:75).

Whether the problems reported by Rahman in Bangladesh is an anomaly in micro-credit because of the society's highly patriarchal social structure or whether other micro-credit programs have similar problems is difficult to say. However, as Rahman (1999:150–151) puts it,

> loans alone (which are also debt-liability), without viable opportunities for women to transform the power relations and create their own spaces in the prevailing power structure, make equitable development and empowerment of women unattainable in the society.

CONCLUSION

It is apparent that hunger is not caused by a lack of food, but rather by some people's lack of ability to purchase food. It is apparent, also, that the poverty that causes hunger is a consequence of global economic forces, such as the financial debt that peripheral countries accumulated in the 1970s. Other instances of hunger and famine are generally a consequence of political unrest. Even in relatively wealthy countries, such as Brazil, the growing gap between rich and poor that has seemingly resulted from growing integration into the world economy results in thousands dying of starvation.

We have seen, furthermore, that economic policies of the wealthy countries are not designed to help the poor countries but to further the interests of corporate and political agendas. Economic development programs, as we have seen, have, by and large, done very little to help their intended beneficiaries, and, in many cases, have created enormous suffering and economic and environmental devastation.

Finally, we examined the role of women in development and examined programs and initiatives, such as the Grameen Bank, that, by improving the position and power of women, have attempted to reduce poverty and the threat of hunger. We have also seen, however, that their potential for success is severely compromised by societies in which women are oppressed.

CHAPTER SEVEN

ENVIRONMENT AND CONSUMPTION

If the life-supporting ecosystems of the planet are to survive
for future generations, the consumer society will have to
dramatically curtail its use of resources—partly by shifting to
high-quality, low-input durable goods and partly by seeking fulfillment
through leisure, human relationships, and other nonmaterial avenues.
—Alan Durning, *How Much Is Enough?*

A man is rich in proportion to the things he can afford to let alone.
—Henry David Thoreau, *Walden*

The first sweetened cup of hot tea to be drunk by an English
worker was a significant historical event, because it prefigured the
transformation of an entire society, a total remaking of its economic and social
basis. We must struggle to understand fully the consequences of that and
kindred events, for upon them was erected an entirely different conception of
the relationship between producers and consumers, of the meaning of work, of
the definition of self, of the nature of things.
—Sidney Mintz, *Sweetness and Power*

All animals alter their environments as a condition of their existence. Human beings, in addition, alter their environments as a condition of their cultures, that is by the way they choose to obtain food, produce tools and products, and construct and arrange shelters. But culture, an essential part of human adaptation, can also threaten human existence when short-term goals lead to long-term consequences that are harmful to human life. Swidden agriculture alters the environment but not as much as irrigation agriculture and certainly not as much as modern agriculture with its use of chemical fertilizers, pesticides, and herbicides. Domesticated animals alter environments, but keeping a few cattle for farm work or cows for dairy products does far less damage than maintaining herds of thousands to supply a meat-centered diet.

The degree to which environments are altered and damaged is determined in part by population and in part by the technology in use. Obviously, the more people in a given area, the more potential there is for environmental disruption. Tractors and bulldozers alter the environment more than hoes or plows. But the greatest factor in environmental alteration—in the use of raw materials, the use of nonhuman energy, and the production of waste—is consumption. Because of our level of consumption, the average American child will do twice the environmental damage of a Swedish child, three times that of an Italian child, thirteen times that of a Brazilian child, thirty-five times that of an Indian child, and 280 times that of a Chadian or Haitian child (Kennedy 1993:32).

The United States alone uses 25 percent of the world's energy and accounts for 25 percent of the world's carbon emissions that are responsible for global warming (see Table 7.1). The United States and Canada have by far the highest per capita rates of energy usage and carbon emissions of any countries on earth. They are also the countries most resisting the implementation of the Kyoto Accord, an international agreement negotiated in 1992 to reduce global carbon emissions to 1990 levels.

Mathis Wackernagel and William Rees (1996) estimate that four to six hectares of land are required to maintain the consumption level of the average person from a high-consumption country. The problem is that in 1990, worldwide there were only 1.7 hectares of ecologically productive land for each person. They conclude that the deficit is made up in core countries by drawing down the natural resources of their own countries and expropriating the resources, through trade, of peripheral countries. In other words, someone has to pay for our consumption levels, and it will either be our children or inhabitants of the periphery of the world system.

Our consumption of goods obviously is a function of our culture. Only by producing and selling things and services does capitalism in its present form work, and the more that is produced and the more that is purchased the more we have progress and prosperity. The single most important measure of economic growth is, after all, the gross national product (GNP), the sum total of goods and services produced by a given society in a given year. It is a measure of the success of a consumer society, obviously, to consume.

The production, processing, and consumption of commodities, however, require the extraction and use of natural resources (wood, ore, fossil fuels, and water) and require the creation of factories and factory complexes, which create toxic by-products, whereas the use of commodities themselves (e.g., automobiles) creates pollutants and waste. Yet of the three factors to which environmentalists often point as responsible for environmental pollution—population, technology, and consumption—consumption seems to get the least attention. One reason, no doubt, is that it may be the most difficult to change; our consumption patterns are so much a part of our lives that to change them would require a massive cultural overhaul, not to mention severe economic dislocation. A drop in demand for products, as economists note, brings on economic recession or even depression, along with massive unemployment.

The maintenance of perpetual growth and the cycle of production and consumption essential in the culture of capitalism does not bode well for the environment. At the beginning of Chapter 1 we mentioned that the consumer revolution of the late nineteenth and early twentieth centuries was caused in large part by a crisis in production; new technologies had resulted in production of more goods, but there were not enough people or money to buy them. Because production is such an essential part of the culture of capitalism, society quickly adapted to this crisis by convincing people to buy things, by altering basic

TABLE 7.1 Energy Use and Carbon Emissions of Selected Countries, 1998–1999

COUNTRY	POPULATION (IN MILLIONS)	TOTAL ENERGY CONSUMPTION (IN QUADRILLION BTU*)	% OF WORLD CONSUMPTION	PER CAPITA CONSUMPTION (MILLION BTU)	TOTAL CARBON EMISSIONS (MILLION METRIC TONS)	% WORLD TOTAL EMISSIONS	PER CAPITA EMISSIONS (METRIC TONS)	PERSONS PER AUTO
United States	274.5	96.1	25	350.7	1,552	25	5.5	1.3
China	1,200	33.9	8.9	27.0	740.4	12.1	0.6	125
Russia	146	26.0	6.9	177.3	405.0	6.6	2.8	6.5
Japan	126.1	21.3	5.6	168.4	288.5	4.7	2.3	1.8
Germany	82.8	13.8	3.6	168.6	227.5	3.7	2.8	1.9
India	1,000	12.5	3.3	12.9	252.6	4.1	0.3	142.9
Canada	31.3	11.9	3.1	391.0	138.5	2.3	4.6	1.8
France	59	10.0	2.6	170.0	106.6	1.7	1.8	1.9
United Kingdom	59.1	9.8	2.6	165.3	147.4	2.4	2.5	2.4
Italy	57.6	8.0	2.1	139.0	120.0	2.0	2.1	1.7
Brazil	171.9	8.1	2.1	50.0	84.5	1.4	0.5	12.7
Mexico	100.3	5.9	1.6	59.1	95.0	1.5	1.0	7
Indonesia	216.1	3.6	1.0	17.7	67.8	1.1	0.3	45.5
Nigeria	113.8	1.0	0.3	9.0	27.1	0.4	0.3	38.5
Bangladesh	125	0.4	0.1	3.3	6.4	0.1	0.05	1,000
Guatemala	12.3	0.1	0.03	10.6	1.9	0.03	0.2	52.6
Congo	2.83	0.02	0.006	8.27	1.1	0.018	0.39	50

*BTU = British thermal unit. It is the amount of heat that increases the temperature of a pound of liquid water one degree.
Data from U.S. Energy Information Agency (EIA) (2000), http://www.eia.doe.gov/emeu/cabs/contents.html.

institutions, and even by generating a new ideology of pleasure. The economic crisis of the late nineteenth century was solved but at considerable expense to the environment in the additional waste that was created and resources that were consumed. At that time the world's population was about 1.6 billion, and those caught up in the consumer frenzy were a fraction of that total.

The global economy today faces the same problem it faced one hundred years ago, except that the world population has almost quadrupled. Consequently, it is even more important to understand how the interaction between capital, labor, and consumption in the culture of capitalism creates an overproduction of commodities and how this relates to environmental pollution. To illustrate, let's take a quick look at the present state of the global automobile industry.

In capitalism competition between companies for world markets requires that they constantly develop new and improved ways to produce things and lower costs. In some industries, such as textiles, as we saw in Chapter 2, competition requires seeking cheaper sources of labor; in others, such as the automobile industry, it means creating new technologies that replace people with machines to lower labor costs. Twenty years ago the production of one automobile took hundreds of hours of human labor. Today a Lexus LS 400 requires only 18.4 hours of human labor, Ford Motor Company produces several cars with 20.0 hours of human labor, and General Motors lags behind at about 24.8 hours per car (Greider 1997:110–112).

In addition to reducing the number of jobs available to people, advanced productive technology creates the potential for producing ever more cars, regardless of whether there are people who want to buy them. In 1995 the automobile industry produced more than 50 million automobiles, but there was a market for only 40 million. What can companies do? Obviously they can begin to close plants or cut back on production, which some do. In the 1980s some 180,000 American autoworkers lost their jobs because of cutbacks and factory shutdowns. But the producers, of course, hope the problem of selling this surplus is someone else's problem, so they continue to produce cars.

From the perspective of the automobile companies and their workers, the preferred solution to overproduction is to create a greater demand for automobiles. This is difficult in core countries, where the market is already saturated with cars. In the United States, for example, there is one car for every 1.3 persons. However, there are places in the world where there are few cars. In China, for example, there is only one car for every 125 people, in India only one in 142.9, and in Bangladesh only one in 1,000 (see Table 7.1). Imagine the environmental impact if the consumption rate of automobiles in China alone, with a population of well over a billion people, even began to approach the consumption rate in the United States.

But that is exactly the goal of automotive manufacturers and the nation-states that operate to help them build and sell their products. Not only would automobile makers in the core like to enter the Chinese market, the Chinese themselves plan to build an automobile industry as large as that in the United States, to produce cars for their own market and to compete in other markets as well. If China—or India, Indonesia, Brazil, or most of the rest of the periphery—even approached the consumption rate of automobiles common in the core, the increased environmental pollution would be staggering. There would be not only massive increases in hydrocarbon pollution but also vastly increased demands for raw materials, especially oil. And the overproduction dilemma is not unique to automobiles: The steel, aircraft, chemical, computer, consumer electronics, drug, and tire industries, among others, face the same dilemma.

The environmental problem could be alleviated if consumers simply said "enough is enough" and stopped consuming as much as they do. Indeed, there have been a number of social movements to convince people to consume less. But, as previously noted, any reduction of consumption would likely cause severe economic disruption. Furthermore, few are aware of how large a reduction would have to be to effect a change. A study by Friends of the Earth Netherlands asked what the consumption levels of the average Dutch person would have to be in the year 2010 if consumption levels over the world were equal and if resource consumption was sustainable. They found that consumption levels would have to be reduced dramatically. For example, to reduce global warming by the year 2010, people in the Netherlands would have to reduce carbon dioxide emission by two-thirds; to accomplish that a Dutch person would have to limit the use of carbon-based fuel to one liter per day, thus limiting travel to 15.5 miles per day by car, 31 miles per day by bus, 40 miles per day by train, or 6.2 miles per day by plane. A trip from Amsterdam to Rio de Janeiro could be made only once every twenty years (see Korten 1995:34).

Thus, significantly reducing our consumption patterns is no easy task. Consumption is as much a part of our culture as horse raiding and buffalo hunting were part of Plains Indian culture; it is a central element. Consequently, there is no way to appreciate the problem of environmental destruction without understanding how people are turned into consumers, how luxuries are turned into necessities. That is, *why do people choose to consume what they do, how they do, and when they do?*

Take sugar, for example. In 1997, each American consumed in his or her soft drinks, tea, coffee, cocoa, pastries, breads, and other foods sixty-six pounds of sugar (USDA 2000). In addition, Americans consume almost 200 grams, or fifty-three teaspoonfuls, of caloric sweeteners each day (Gardner and Halweil 2000:31). Why? Liking the taste might be one answer. In fact, a predilection for sweets may be part of our biological makeup. But that doesn't explain why we consume it in the form of sugarcane and beet sugar and in the quantities we do. Then there is meat. Modern livestock production is one of the most environmentally damaging and wasteful forms of food production the world has known. Yet Americans eat more meat per capita than all but a few other peoples. Some environmentalists argue that we can change our destructive consumption patterns if we desire. But *is our pattern of consumption only a matter of taste and of choice, or is it so deeply embedded in our culture as to be virtually impervious to change?*

To begin to answer this question, we shall examine the history of sugar and beef, commodities that figure largely in our lives but involve environmental degradation. The combination of sugar and beef is appropriate for a number of reasons:

1. The production and processing of both degrade the environment; furthermore, the history of sugar production parallels that of a number of other things we consume, including coffee, tea, cocoa, and tobacco, that collectively have significant environmental effects.
2. Neither is terribly good for us, at least not in the quantities and form in which we consume them.

3. Both have histories that closely tie them to the growth and emergence of the capital-ist world economy. They are powerful symbols of the rise and economic expansion of capitalism; indeed, they are a result and a reason for it.

4. With the rise of the fast-food industry, beef and sugar, fat and sucrose have become the foundations of the American diet, accounting for more than one-half of the caloric intake of North Americans and Europeans (Gardner and Halweil 2000:15). Indeed, they are foundation foods of the culture of capitalism symbolized in the hamburger and Coke, a hot dog and soda, and the fat and sucrose dessert—ice cream.

THE CASE OF SUGAR

The history of sugar reveals how private economic interests, along with economic policies of the nation-state and changes in the structure of society combined to convert a commod-ity from a luxury good believed to have health benefits into a necessity with overall harm-ful health consequences. In the process, it vastly increased the exploitation of labor—first in the form of slavery, then in migrant labor—converted millions of acres of forest into sugar production—in the process expelling millions from their land—and changed the di-etary habits of most of the world. It illustrates how our consumption patterns are deter-mined in capitalism and why we engage in behavior that may be environmentally unsound and personally harmful. The story of sugar is an excellent case study of how the nation-state mediated interaction of the capitalist, the laborer, and the consumer produces some of our global problems.

Sugar Origins and Production

Sugarcane, until recently the major source of sugar, was first domesticated in New Guinea, then grown in India and the Middle East. The processing of sugarcane into sugar is com-plex and environmentally damaging. There are various kinds of sugar plants, most of which grow quickly after regenerating from cuttings left in the fields after harvests or from the controlled planting of cuttings. The stalk matures in nine to eighteen months and must be cut when the juice in the stalk contains the most sucrose. The juice must be extracted quickly before it rots or ferments; it is squeezed from the cane by chopping, pressing, or pounding, then heated to evaporate the liquid, leaving crystals from which centrifugal ma-chines extract most of the molasses. The molasses may be used as a sweetener or, more im-portantly, processed into rum. The raw sugar that remains after the molasses is extracted can be consumed as is, turned into a liquid syrup, or processed further to obtain the granu-lar white sugar that most Americans and Europeans favor.

Sugar production alters the environment in a number of ways. Forests must be cleared to plant sugar; wood or fossil fuel must be burned in the evaporation process; waste water is produced in extracting sucrose from the sugarcane; and more fuel is burned in the refining process. When Spain sought to expand sugar production into the Atlantic islands in the sixteenth century, it colonized the Canary Islands, then inhabited by the Guanche. The Spaniards transformed the Canarian ecosystem, clearing the forests and hillsides to make way for cane fields and to obtain fuel for the fires of the *ingenio,* or sugar house.

Within a few decades wood was so scarce that the government tried, in vain, to protect the forests from the lumberjacks (Crosby 1986:96). The Guanche were also gone within a century. When sugar production expanded in the seventeenth century, the sugar refineries of Antwerp caused so much pollution that the city banned the use of coal. Contemporary sugar production in Hawaii not only has destroyed forests but also waste products from processing have severely damaged marine environments. "Big sugar," as the sugar industry is called in Florida, is largely responsible for the pollution, degradation, and virtual destruction of the Everglades.

Sugar, therefore, like virtually all commodities, comes to us at a heavy environmental cost. Yet people did not always crave sugar. For that to happen, a luxury had to be converted into a necessity, a taste had to be created.

Uses of Sugar

By A.D. 1000, when sugar was grown in Europe and the Middle East, it was a highly valued trade item and a luxury. Sugar was used largely as a spice and a medicine and was available only to the wealthy. In Arabian medical works from the tenth and fourteenth centuries, for example, sugar was an ingredient in virtually every medicine. So useful was sugar as a medicine that one way of expressing desperation or helplessness was the saying "like an apothecary without sugar" (Mintz 1985:101). According to one source, "nice, white sugar" from the Atlantic islands cleaned the blood and strengthened the chest, lungs, and throat; when used as a powder it was good for the eyes, and when smoked it was good for the common cold. Mixed with cinnamon, pomegranate, and quince juice, it was good for a cough and fever (Mintz 1985:103).

Sugar was also used for decoration, mixed with almonds (marzipan) and molded into all kinds of shapes, the decorations becoming central to celebrations and feasts. And it was used as a spice in cooking and, of course, as a sweetener. It was also used as a preservative. We still use sugar to preserve ham, and it is often added to bread to increase its shelf life. But through the seventeenth century, even with its diverse uses, it was an expensive luxury item reserved for the upper classes.

The Development of the Sugar Complex

As a luxury item, sugar brought considerable profits for those who traded in it. In fact, it was the value of sugar as a trade item in the fifteenth and sixteenth centuries that led Spain and Portugal to extend sugarcane production, first to the Atlantic Islands, then to the Caribbean islands, and finally to Brazil, from which, beginning in 1526, raw sugar was shipped to Lisbon for refining.

Modern economists like to talk about the spin-off effects of certain commodities, that is the extent to which their production results in the development of subsidiary industries. For example, production of automobiles requires road construction, oil and petroleum production, service stations, auto parts stores, and the like. Sugar production also produced subsidiary economic activities; these included slavery, the provisioning of the sugar producers, shipping, refining, storage, and wholesale and retail trade.

The increased demand for sugar in the eighteenth and nineteenth centuries represented a boon for West Indies sugar plantations and created a demand for more laborers, including slaves and children.

The slave trade was a major factor in the expansion of the sugar industries. Slaves from Europe and the Middle East were first used on the Spanish and Portuguese plantations of the Canary Islands and Madeira, but by the end of the fifteenth century slaves from West Africa were working the fields. The growing demand for and production of sugar created the plantation economy in the New World and was largely responsible for the expansion of the Atlantic slave trade in the sixteenth, seventeenth, and eighteenth centuries. From 1701 to 1810 almost 1 million slaves were brought to Barbados and Jamaica to work the sugar plantations.

Money was to be made also from the shipment of raw sugar to European refineries, more yet from the wholesale and retail sale of sugar, and probably more yet from the sale by European merchants of necessary provisions to the plantation owners. Investors in Europe, especially England, put money into the sugar industry in the development of plantations, the sale of provisions to the colonial plantations, in shipping, or in the slave trade. Attorneys, grocers, drapers, and tailors invested small amounts to form partnerships to finance slave-buying expeditions to Africa and the subsequent resale of slaves to buyers from the sugar plantations of the New World. Thus, it was during the sixteenth and seventeenth centuries that sugar became the focus of an industry, a sugar complex that combined the sugar plantations, the slave trade, long-distance shipping, wholesale and retail trade, and investment finance.

The Expansion of Sugar Consumption

It was not until the late seventeenth century that sugar production and sales really began to influence sugar consumption in Europe. Sugar consumption increased fourfold in England and Wales from 1700 to 1740 and doubled in the next thirty-five years. From 1663 to 1775 consumption increased twentyfold. Sugar consumption rose more rapidly than that of bread, meat, and dairy products in the eighteenth century. Although the per capita annual consumption in 1809 of eighteen pounds of sugar per person does not compare to our present consumption of almost seventy pounds, it was more than sufficient to generate large profits.

Why did people in England begin to consume sugar in greater and greater quantities? First, increased sugar production led to reduced prices, making it accessible to more people, although its use was still largely confined to the upper and emerging middle classes of English society. One reason prices remained as high as they did was the imposition of high import tariffs on sugar produced in other countries. Planters in the British West Indies and people who invested in their enterprises were a powerful force in English politics. To protect their profits, they lobbied and received protection from foreign competitors. They were also powerful enough to prevent British abolitionists from winning legislation to end the slave trade, at least until the beginning of the nineteenth century.

Second, the benefits of sugar were widely touted by various authorities, notably popular physicians. Dr. Frederick Slare found sugar a venerable cure-all. He recommended that women include at their breakfast bread, butter, milk, and sugar. Coffee, tea, and chocolate were similarly "endowed with uncommon virtues," he said, adding that his message would please the West Indian merchant and the grocer who became wealthy on the production of sugar. Slare also prescribed sugar as a dentifrice, a lotion, a substitute for tobacco in the form of snuff, and for babies. Sidney Mintz (1985:107–108) said of Slare that although his enthusiasm for sugar is suspect, it is more than a curiosity because it relates to so many aspects of what was then still a relatively new commodity; furthermore, by stressing sugar's value as a medicine, food, and preservative, he was drawing additional attention to it.

Slare's enthusiasm for sugar was not an oddity; others shared his enthusiasm. No contemporary advertising executive could improve on the description of sugar by John Oldmixin, a contemporary of Slare:

> One of the most pleasant and useful Things in the World, for besides the advantage of it in Trade, Physicians, and Apothecaries cannot be without it, there being nearly three Hundred Medicines made up with sugar; almost all Confectionery Wares receive their Sweetness and Preservation from it, most Fruits would be pernicious without it; the finest pastries could not be made nor the rich Cordials that are in the Ladies' Closets, nor their Conserves; neither could the Dairy furnish us with such a variety of Dishes, as it does, but by their Assistance of this noble Juice. (cited Mintz 1985:108)

A third reason that sugar consumption increased in the eighteenth century was its use as a sweetener for three other substances, all bitter and all technically drugs (stimulants)—

tea, coffee, and cocoa. All of these were used in their places of origin without sugar, in spite of their bitterness. All three initially were drinks for the wealthy; by the time they were used by others, they were generally served hot and sweetened.

Fourth, sugar's reputation as a luxury good inspired the middle classes to use it to emulate the wealthy—sugar was a sign of status. The powerful used sugar for conspicuous consumption, as a symbol of hospitality and the like. When sugar was a luxury the poor could hardly emulate these uses, but as the price declined and as its use expanded, sugar became available to the poor to use in much the same way as their social betters.

Finally, sugar consumption increased because the government increased its purchase of sugar and sugar products. After the capture of Jamaica and its sugar plantations from the French in 1655, the British navy began to give its sailors rum rations, set in 1731 at half a pint per day and later increased to a pint per day for adult sailors. The government also purchased sugar to distribute to poorhouse residents.

Thus, sugar production and consumption increased, as did the amount of land devoted to its production and the number of sugar mills and refineries, distilleries producing rum, and slaves employed in the whole process. Most importantly, the profits generated by the sugar trade increased dramatically.

The Mass Consumption of Sugar

By 1800, British sugar consumption had increased 2,500 percent since 1650 and 245,000 tons of sugar reached European consumers annually from the world market. By 1830 production had risen to 572,000 tons per year, an increase of more than 233 percent. By 1860, when beet sugar production was also rising, world production of sucrose increased another 233 percent to 1.373 million tons. Six million tons were produced by 1890, another 500 percent increase (Mintz 1985:73).

Two acts by the British government helped spur this massive increase in sugar production and consumption. First, the government removed tariffs on the imports of foreign sugar. This made foreign sugar more accessible to British consumers and forced domestic producers to lower their prices, making it affordable to virtually all levels of British society. Second, England abolished slavery during the years 1834–1838 (it had abolished the slave trade in 1807). This had the effect of forcing technological improvements, but it also spurred the creation of a labor pattern that exists to the present. The freed slaves were without land and tools and were dependent on whatever labor they could get. As Mintz (1985:176) noted, although freed from the discipline of slavery they were reduced to laborers by the discipline of hunger. The surplus supply of labor was increased when the British Foreign Office went to the aid of the planters in the West Indies by helping them import contracted laborers from India, China, and elsewhere. The freed slaves, unable to secure a livelihood independent of the sugar industry or to use collective bargaining, settled into obscurity until they reentered British consciousness as migrants to England more than a century later.

The lower price of sugar increased its use in tea and stimulated a dramatic rise in the production of preserves and chocolate. More importantly, it must have been apparent to sugar producers and sellers that there was a fortune to be made by increasing the availability of sugar to the working mass of England. Certainly, there were those who worked hard to expand its availability.

Sidney Mintz's history of sugar reveals how much social, political, and economic power had to do with increased sugar consumption. Planters, slavers, shippers, bankers, refiners, grocers, and government officials, all profiting in one way or another from increased sugar consumption, exercised power to support the rights and prerogatives of planters, the maintenance of slavery, the availability of sugar and its products (molasses, rum, preserves) and products associated with it (tea, coffee, cocoa), and to supply it to the people at large at prices they could afford. Thus, the consumption of sugar was hardly only a matter of taste—it had to do with investments, taxes, the dispensation of sugar through government agencies, and a desire to emulate the rich, among other things. It also had to do with convenience and the changes in household structure, labor, and diet that accompanied the industrial revolution.

Rural workers in England in the eighteenth and nineteenth centuries typically had diets that consisted of oatmeal, porridge, milk, homemade bread, and vegetable broth. Although it was simple, the diet was relatively nutritious. In the industrial cities, however, it could be costly. Fresh food in general would have been more costly in the city, and food preparation, especially if it needed cooking, required fuel, which cost yet more money. Furthermore, urban women were, as noted earlier, also working in the factories twelve to fourteen hours per day, reducing the time they could spend on food preparation.

As a result, the diet of the urban working class and poor was transformed to one dominated by tea, sugar, store-bought white bread, and jam. Hot tea replaced vegetable broth. Jams (50 to 65 percent sugar) were cheaper than butter to put on bread, were easily stored, and could be left open on shelves for children to be spread on bread in the absence of adults. In other words, the cultural and social constraints of time and cost created in the urban, industrial setting combined with the convenience of sugar and the prodding of those who profited from its sale to shape the diet of the British working class. It was an ideal arrangement, for, as E. P. Thompson (1967) noted, after providing profits to plantation and refinery investors, sugar provided the bodily fuel for the working people of Britain. Sugar is also what Sidney Mintz referred to as a "drug food," a category that includes coffee, tea, cocoa, alcohol, and tobacco—foods that deaden hunger pangs and stimulate effort without providing nutrition and do so cheaply. That is one reason why they have been transformed from upper-class luxuries to working-class necessities.

Modern Sugar

Sidney Mintz (1985:180–181) suggested that the consumption of goods such as sugar is the result of profound changes in the lives of working people, changes that made new forms of foods and of eating seem "natural," as new work schedules, new sorts of labor, and new conditions of life became "natural." This does not mean that we lack a choice in what we consume, but that our choice is made within various constraints. We may have a choice between a McDonald's hamburger and a Colonel Sanders chicken leg during a half-hour lunch break. The time available acts to limit our choice, removing, for example, the option of a home-cooked vegetarian lunch.

Sugar has become, as it did for the nineteenth-century British laborer, a mainstay of the fast-food diet in the United States, the perfect complement to fat. Both fat and sugar are made more attractive by the clever use of language. The fat side of our diet is advertised with words like "juicy," "succulent," "hot," "luscious," "savory," and "finger-licking good." The sugar side is advertised as "crisp," "fresh," "invigorating," "wholesome," "refreshing," and "vibrant." And the sugar in soft drinks serves as the perfect complement to hamburgers and hot dogs because it possesses what nutritionists call "go-away" qualities—removing the fat coating and the beef aftertaste from the mouth.

Thus, sugar fits our budgets, our work schedules, and our psychological needs while at the same time generating monetary profits and growth. As Mintz (1985:186) put it, sugar

> [s]erved to make a busy life seem less so; in the pause that refreshes, it eased, or seemed to ease, the changes back and forth from work to rest; it provided swifter sensations of fullness or satisfaction than complex carbohydrates did; it combines easily with many other foods, in some of which it was also used (tea and biscuit, coffee and bun, chocolate and jam-smeared bread).... No wonder the rich and powerful liked it so much, and no wonder the poor learned to love it.

THE STORY OF BEEF

The story of beef is very much like that of sugar, except that livestock breeding has been indicted for even greater environmental damage than sugar production, largely because of the vast amount of land needed to raise cattle. As an agricultural crop, sugar is quite efficient; although it has little nutritional value, it is possible to get about 8 million calories from one acre of sugarcane; to get 8 million calories of beef requires 135 acres. In addition, much of the beef we eat is grain-fed to produce the marbling of fat that makes it choice grade and brings the highest prices; as mentioned earlier, 80 percent of the grain produced in the United States is fed to livestock. In addition, two-thirds of U.S. grain exports go to feed livestock in other countries. Thus, to the amount of land needed for rangeland, we must add the farmland devoted to animal feed; moreover, as we saw in Chapter 6, this grain production requires tons of chemical fertilizer, pesticides, and herbicides, all of which negatively alter the environment.

Cattle raising consumes a lot of water. Half the water consumed in the United States is used to grow grain to feed cattle; the amount of water used to produce ten pounds of steak equals the household consumption of a family for an entire year. Fifteen times more water is needed to produce a pound of beef protein than an equivalent amount of plant protein. There are also environmental problems associated with beef waste products; a feedlot steer produces forty-seven pounds of manure per day (Ensminger 1991:187), not to mention the methane gases that contribute to the destruction of the ozone layer. Even more pollution is produced by the slaughter, refrigeration, transport, and cooking of beef.

Cattle raising has also been criticized for its role in the destruction of tropical forests. Hundreds of thousands of acres of tropical forests in Brazil, Guatemala, Costa Rica, and Honduras, to name only a few countries, have been leveled to create pasture for cattle. Because most of the forest is cleared by burning, the extension of cattle pasture also creates carbon dioxide and contributes significantly to global warming. In addition, with increasing amounts of fossil fuel needed to produce grain, it now takes a gallon of gasoline to produce a pound of grain-fed beef.

Much of the rangeland of the United States has been devastated by livestock herding to the point that it has become desert. Currently 2 million to 3 million cattle graze on 306 million acres of public land. According to the General Accounting Office (GAO) more plant species are being threatened by cattle grazing than by any other single factor, and populations of pronghorn, antelope, and elk have virtually disappeared from western rangelands. Much of this is a consequence of government policy. For example, the Bureau of Land Management, responsible for allotting land for livestock use, in one district in Oregon allots about 252 million pounds of herbage to livestock and 8 millions pounds to wildlife. To protect livestock, the government also participates in the killing of thousands of coyotes and other so-called predator animals each year, as well as animals such as bison and deer that may carry disease. It is not surprising that the Bureau of Land Management reported that almost 95 million acres of rangelands are in "unsatisfactory condition," a condition attributed by researchers to overgrazing (Rifkin 1992:211).

The same problems are occurring in areas of Africa that have a long tradition of cattle raising. When cattle populations were managed by traditional means and for traditional consumption, there was little environmental damage. When attempts were made to introduce Western livestock raising practices and technologies to increase the number of cattle and develop a larger beef export industry, pasture was turned to desert and wild animals disappeared, largely because of overgrazing by cattle (Rifkin 1992:216).

In addition, beef is terribly inefficient as a source of food. By the time a feedlot steer in the United States is ready for slaughter, it has consumed 2,700 pounds of grain and weighs approximately 1,050 pounds; 157 million metric tons of cereal and vegetable protein are used to produce 28 metric tons of animal protein. Finally, beef in the quantities that Americans consume it is unhealthy, being linked to cardiovascular disease, colon cancer, breast cancer, and osteoporosis.

Americans are among the highest meat consumers in the world and the highest consumers of beef. More than 6.7 billion hamburgers are sold each year at fast-food restaurants alone. Furthermore, we are exporting our taste for beef to other parts of the world. The Japanese, who in the past consumed only one-tenth the amount of meat consumed by Americans, are increasing their consumption of beef. McDonald's sells more hamburgers in Tokyo than it does in New York City.

Marvin Harris (1986) suggested that animal foods play a special role in the nutritional physiology of our species. He pointed out that studies of gathering and hunting societies reveal that 35 percent of the diet comes from meat, more than even Americans eat, and that this dietary pattern has existed for hundreds of thousands years. Many cultures have a special term for "meat hunger." The Ju/wasi of Botswana, for example, say "hunger is grabbing me," not simply because they haven't eaten but because they haven't eaten meat. Harris pointed out that it is also an especially efficient protein source and that when people can afford it, they eat more meat.

Historically, few societies, however, have made meat the center of their diet. If we look around the world, we find that most diets center on some complex carbohydrate—rice, wheat, manioc, yams, taro—or something made from these—bread, pasta, tortillas, and so on. To these are added some spice, vegetables, meat, or fish, the combination giving each culture's food its distinctive flavor. But meat and fish are generally at the edge, not the center, of the meal (Mintz 1985). Moreover, regardless of whether we simply like meat, *why do American preferences run to beef?* Anthropologists Marvin Harris and Eric Ross (1987b) have some interesting answers that may help us understand why, in spite of the environmental damage our beef consumption causes, we continue to eat it in such quantities. The answers involve understanding the relationships among Spanish cattle, British colonialism, the American government, the American bison, indigenous peoples, the automobile, the hamburger, and the fast-food restaurant.

The Ascendancy of Beef

The story of the American preference for beef begins with the Spanish colonization of the New World. The Spanish, as noted earlier, introduced the so-called cattle complex to the New World, where it became established in Argentina, areas of Central America, particularly northern Mexico, and Texas. By the 1540s, cattle were so numerous around Mexico City that the Spaniards had to train Native Americans to handle them. Fortunes were made in cattle in the sixteenth century on meat and leather.

In Argentina, the number of feral cattle increased so rapidly on the pampas that by the seventeenth century meat was eaten three times a day, and animals were killed for their hides and the meat left to rot. One seventeenth-century traveler wrote of Argentina,

> All the wealth of these inhabitants consists in their animals, which multiply so prodigiously that the plains are covered with them...in such numbers that were it not for the dogs that devoured the calves...they would devastate the country. (cited Rifkin 1992:49)

In colonial America, however, pigs, not beef, were the meat of choice. Eric Ross (1980) pointed out that the preference for beef or pork is related in part to environmental factors. Pigs tend to be raised in forested areas and can be maintained in areas of relatively dense populations because they eat the same food as human beings. In densely populated West Germany in 1960, the ratio of cattle to hogs was 0.06 to 1, whereas in sparsely populated Argentina, with its large tracts of rangeland, it was 11.2 to 1.0. Another reason pork was preferred in America was that the preservation process—smoking, salting, and pickling—improved the flavor of the meat, whereas for beef it did not. In fact, pork was the meat of choice in the United States until the 1960s, when beef overtook it. Although meat consumption in the United States has declined since the 1970s, beef is still preferred (see Table 7.2).

The Emergence of the American Beef Industry

On the eve of the industrial revolution, England was the beef-eating capital of the world, with 100,000 head of cattle slaughtered annually in London. But in the nineteenth century, with its population increasing and more people migrating to the factory towns and cities, England began to look toward its colonies and ex-colonies for food, especially meat. Eric Ross (1980) suggested that the motivation was not simply to get food but to keep meat

TABLE 7.2   U.S. per Capita Meat Consumption, 1900–1998 (in pounds)

YEAR	BEEF	PORK	YEAR	BEEF	PORK	YEAR	BEEF	PORK
1998	64.9	49.1	1977	125.9	61.6	1950	63.4	69.2
1997	63.8	45.6	1975	120.1	54.8	1940	54.9	73.5
1996	65.0	49.9	1970	113.7	66.4	1920	59.1	63.5
1993	61.5	48.9	1960	85.1	64.9	1900	67.1	71.9
1990	64.0	46.4						

See also Ross 1980:191; U.S. Bureau of Census, 1990, 1993, 1994; USDA/NASS Agricultural Statistics, 2000, http://www.usda.gov/nass/pubs/agr00/acro00.htm

prices low in order to keep wages low and allow industry in Great Britain to remain competitive with industries in other countries. As we saw earlier, the British increased cattle production in Ireland by increasing the amount of land devoted to pasture, pushing people onto smaller plots of land and increasing dependence on the potato. When the potato blight hit Ireland in 1846–1847 and millions starved, the export of Irish grain and livestock intensified. In fact, because of the massive outmigrations caused by the famine, English landlords were able to intensify cattle production even more; from 1846 to 1874 the number of Irish cattle exported to England climbed from 202,000 to 558,000, and more than 50 percent of the total landmass of Ireland was devoted to cattle raising.

England next turned to Argentina, where the development of the refrigerated steamer permitted the shipment of fresh beef to England. In the 1870s English, Scottish, and Irish colonists already owned 45 percent of the sheep and 20 percent of the cattle herds in Argentina, and English demand and English capital helped develop the Argentine beef business. One of the greatest nineteenth-century fortunes made in England, that of the Vesteys, was made by dominating the Argentine meat market.

Who was eating all this meat? It was not the working class, whose breakfast consisted of little more than bread, butter or jam, and tea with sugar and whose dinner might include a meat by-product, such as Liebig's extract (made from hides and other residue), or inferior cuts. The gentry, however, apparently consumed vast quantities. Beef, in fact, had been for some time the choice of the British well-to-do. For example, in 1735 a group of men formed the Sublime Society of Beef Steaks, most renowned for the invention of the sandwich by one of its members. The society consisted largely of members of the British elite but also included painters, merchants, and theatrical managers. It existed until 1866. Twice a year the group would meet for dinner, at which, according to the society's charter, "beef steaks shall be the only meat for dinner" (Lincoln 1989:85).

Here is one description, dating from 1887, of a typical breakfast table of the British nobility (Harris and Ross 1987b:35–36):

In a country house, which contains, probably, a sprinkling of good and bad appetites and digestions, breakfasts should consist of a variety to suit all tastes, viz.: fish, poultry, or game, if in season; sausages, and one meat of some sort, such as mutton cutlets, or fillets of beef; omelets, and eggs served in a variety of ways; bread of both kinds, white and brown, and fancy bread of as many kinds as can conveniently be served; two or three kinds of jam, orange marmalade, and fruits when in season; and on the side table, cold meats such as ham, tongue, cold game, game pie, galantines, and in winter a round of spiced beef.

The army and navy consumed enormous amounts of meat, each sailor and soldier getting by regulation three-fourths of a pound of meat daily; in fact, the diet of the military was vastly superior to that of the bulk of the population. Between 1813 and 1835 the British War Office contracted for 69.6 million pounds of Irish salted beef and 77.9 million pounds of Irish salt pork; as Harris and Ross (1987a:37–38) noted, Irishmen were able to eat the meat of their own country only by joining the army of the country that had colonized theirs. Furthermore, the British military, by distributing rum and meat to their men, helped to subsidize both the sugar and meat industries.

Laying largely untapped in the latter half of the nineteenth century, by either the British or the Americans, were the American Great Plains and the vast herds of Texas longhorns. The longhorn was the remnant of the Spanish herds that ran wild. It was uniquely adapted to the extremes of heat and cold of the prairies; it could eat almost anything, including leaves and prickly pear, and by the 1830s and 1840s cowboys began to round up the strays and herd them to New Orleans. In the 1830s there were 100,000 head of cattle roaming Texas; by 1860 there were more than 3.5 million.

But cattle traders faced three problems in trying to make a profit from longhorn cattle. The first problem was shipping cattle to areas in the Midwest from where they could be distributed. They could be driven overland, but that was too costly. The second problem was the availability of rangeland; in the 1860s the plains were occupied by indigenous peoples and their major food source, the buffalo. Finally, there was the quality of the beef; longhorn beef was too lean and tough for British tastes. The solutions to these problems would define the American taste for beef and a good part of the history of the American West.

The problem of transporting cattle to the Midwest and East was solved by a young entrepreneur, Joseph McCoy, who convinced the Union Pacific Railway to construct a siding and cattle pen at its remote depot in Abilene, Kansas, and agreed to pay him a commission on every animal he delivered for shipment. The animals would be driven from Texas to Abilene on the Chisholm trail. McCoy first needed and got the governor of Kansas to lift a quarantine on Texas cattle that had been imposed because of the spread of Texas fever; then he persuaded the Illinois legislature to allow his shipment of cattle into their state. On September 5, 1867, McCoy shipped twenty railway cars of cattle east from Abilene. By 1871 he was shipping 700,000 cattle annually. Through the 1870s the Chisholm Trail was traveled by herd after herd headed for the slaughterhouses, tables, and leatherworks of the East.

But as the demand for meat, leather, and tallow grew, more land was needed for cattle; the plains, once considered the Great American Desert, were being promoted as a land of a "fairy-tale" grass that required no rain and could support millions of head of cattle (Rifkin 1992:73). Only two things stood in the way of its use—buffalo and Native Americans.

Cattlemen, eastern bankers, the railroads, and the U.S. Army believed the solution to both problems could be effected by the extermination of the buffalo, and they joined in a systematic campaign to that end. In a period of about a decade, from 1870 to 1880, in one of the world's greatest ecological disasters, buffalo hunters ended 15,000 years of continuous existence on the plains of the American bison, reducing herds of millions to virtual extinction. Stationed in Kansas, Colonel Richard Henry Dodge wrote that in 1871 buffalo around the post were virtually limitless; by the fall of 1873 "there was now myriads of car-casses. The air was foul with a sickening stench, and the vast plain, which only a short twelve months before teemed with animal life, was a dead, solitary, putrid desert" (cited Rifkin 1992:74).

Buffalo hunters were getting one to three dollars a hide, and heroes such as William F. Cody (Buffalo Bill) were entertaining European royalty on buffalo hunts, while railroad passengers, armed with rifles provided by the conductors, shot the animals from the moving trains. Not everyone approved of the slaughter, and some newspaper editorials condemned it but to no avail. Even the bones were ground up for fertilizer and sold for eight dollars a ton. The "white harvest," as it was called, even engaged indigenous groups, who would bring the bones in wagons for sale at the railroad depots; meat met sugar as "fresher bones" were made into char and used in the refining process to remove the brown-ish coloration of sugar. In a speech to the Texas legislature in 1877, General Phillip Sheri-dan said of the buffalo hunters,

> These men have done…more to settle the vexed Indian question than the entire regular army has done in the last thirty years. They are destroying the Indians' commissary; and it is a well-known fact that an army losing its base of supplies is placed at a great disadvan-tage. Send them powder and lead if you will; but for the sake of lasting peace let them kill, skin, and sell until the buffalo is exterminated. Then your prairies can be covered with speckled cattle and the festive cowboy who follows the hunter as a second forerunner of an advanced civilization. (cited Wallace and Hoebel 1952:66)

With the buffalo went the Indians of the plains. With their major food and source of ritual and spiritual power removed, they were soon vanquished and confined to reserva-tions, while land granted to them in earlier treaties was taken away.

In one of the great ironies of history, cattlemen made fortunes selling beef to the U.S. government for distribution to Native Americans forced onto reservations and hungry be-cause of the buffalo slaughter. Furthermore, cattlemen grazed their animals on what re-mained of Native American land, paying them in beef or cash only a fraction of what the grazing rights were worth.

The final problem in the story of England and the Texas longhorn involved the toughness or leanness of plains cattle. The British liked their beef generously marbled with fat. This problem was solved by a historic bargain; western cattle would be transported to the midwestern farmbelt and fed corn until their meat was speckled with fat, then shipped by rail and steamer to English ports (Rifkin 1992:58–59). The integration of the plains and the prairie, rangeland and farmland, was so complete that to this day the price of corn is closely linked to the demand for and price of cattle.

As a consequence of the merger of cattle and corn in the 1870s, British banks were pouring millions into the American West. They formed the Anglo-American Cattle Com-pany Ltd. with £70,000 of capital; then the Colorado Mortgage and Investment Company of London, buying 10,000 acres of rangeland north of Denver; then the Prairie Cattle Com-pany Ltd. and the Texas Land and Cattle Company, Ltd. The Scottish-American Company invested £220,000 in land in Wyoming and the Dakotas. Cattlemen associations were formed that controlled millions of acres and often became spokespersons for foreign cattle barons. In all, the British invested some $45 million in western real estate, and by the 1880s America was responsible for 90 percent of beef imported to England (Harris and Ross 1987b:38). By the mid-1880s, 43,136 tons of fresh beef were being shipped yearly to Great Britain (Rifkin 1992:95).

The takeover of the West by the British so alarmed some Americans that in the 1884 presidential election both parties included planks that would limit "alien holdings" in the United States. The Republican campaign slogan of 1884, "America for Americans," was directed not at poor Latin Americans or Asian migrants or European minorities, as it would be later, but at the British elite. But the British invasion of the American cattle industry had one other long-lasting effect: It defined for the next one hundred years the American taste in beef.

In response to both British tastes and midwestern farm interests, the U.S. Department of Agriculture (USDA) developed a system of grading beef that awarded the highest grade—prime—to the beef with the most fat content, choice grade to the next fattiest, select grade to the next, and so on. Thus, the state participated in creating a system that inspired cattle raisers to feed cattle grain and add fat because it brought the best price, while at the same time communicating to the consumer that, because it was most expensive, the most marbled cuts of beef must be the best.

The federal inspection and grading standards also aided another important sector of the beef industry: the meatpackers. Beef packers wanted to centralize their operations, to bring live animals to one area to be butchered, but most states had laws that required inspection of live animals twenty-four hours before slaughter. Butchers were opposed to the centralized slaughter of beef because, since most animals were slaughtered and butchered locally, centralizing the operation would put many of them out of business. The beef packing industry lobbied successfully to convince Congress to pass a federal meat inspection system that, unlike state inspection systems, would not affect out-of-state centralized operations (Harris and Ross 1987b:202).

Aided by the government, the meatpacking business proceeded to dominate the production and distribution of beef. Refrigeration technology and the new federal inspection standards allowed individuals, such as George H. Hammond in 1871, Gustavus Swift in 1877, and Philip and Simeon Armour in 1882, to slaughter beef in one area of the country—Chicago—and ship it fresh to any other area of the country. Their growth and domination of the meatpacking industry resulted in the concentration of production in five companies that by World War I handled two-thirds of all meatpacking in the United States. By 1935 Armour and Swift controlled 61 percent of meat sales in the United States.

One of the great technological innovations in meatpacking was the assembly (or, as Jeremy Rifkin [1992] called it, "disassembly") line. Henry Ford is generally credited with developing assembly line technology in the construction of his Model T Ford in 1913. However, even Ford said that he got his idea from watching cattle hung on conveyor belts passing from worker to worker, each assigned a specific series of cuts until the entire animal was dismembered. The working conditions in the meatpacking industry were then, and remain, among the worst of any industry in the country. At the turn of the century they prompted Upton Sinclair to produce his quasi-fictional account *The Jungle* (1906), whose descriptions of the slaughterhouses promoted such public outrage that the government acted to regulate the meatpacking industry.

The state has also heavily subsidized our taste in beef by allowing cattlemen to graze cattle on public lands at a fraction of market costs for grazing on private land, thus making beef more affordable and encouraging its consumption. As early as the 1880s, cattlemen were fencing millions of acres of public land, to which they had no title, with the newly invented barbed wire. In fact, at that time most of the cattle companies grazing their cattle on public land were British. After objections to the practice were raised, the government passed the Desert Land Act of 1887, which awarded land to anyone who improved it. The Union Cattle Company of Cheyenne dug a thirty-five-mile-long ditch, called it an irrigation canal, and claimed 33,000 acres of public land (Skaggs 1976:62).

In 1934 Congress passed the Taylor Grazing Act, which transferred millions of acres of public land to ranchers if they took responsibility for improving it. In 1990, some 30,000 cattle ranchers in eleven western states grazed their cattle on 300 million acres of public land, an area equal to the fourteen East Coast states stretching from Maine to Florida (Rifkin 1992:105–106). These permit holders pay a third to a quarter less than they would pay on private lands.

The victory of beef, however, was not yet complete. To appreciate the story of American beef consumption, we need to understand the role of the American government in creating the legal definition of a hamburger and the infrastructure that encouraged the spread of the automobile.

Modern Beef

Legend has it that the hamburger was invented by accident when an Ohio restaurant owner ran out of pork sausages at the Ohio Fair in 1892 and substituted ground beef on his buns. The hamburger was the rage of the St. Louis World's Fair of 1904, and by 1921 White Castle had opened its hamburger chain in Kansas City. But the hamburger still needed an assist, and it got it from the automobile and the government.

Henry Ford's Model T began the American romance with the automobile, and the number of Americans with cars grew enormously in the twentieth century. There are now as many automobiles as there are licensed drivers in the United States. But it was the surge in highway construction after World War II (a $350 billion project to construct a network of 41,000 miles of superhighways) that made the automobile boom possible. This led to the growth of the suburbs and the fast-food restaurants that were to make beef, and particularly the hamburger, king.

Pork, as mentioned earlier, had always competed with beef for priority in American meat tastes. Whereas beef was more popular in the Northeast and the West, pork was the meat of choice in the South; however, in the Mid-Atlantic states and the Midwest they were relatively evenly matched. But by the 1960s beef clearly became the meat of choice for most Americans.

One advantage of beef was its suitability for the outdoor grill, which became more popular as people moved to the suburbs. Suburban cooks soon discovered that pork patties crumbled and fell through the grill, whereas beef patties held together better. In addition, because the USDA does not inspect pork for trichinosis because the procedure would be too expensive, it recommended cooking pork until it was gray, but that makes pork very tough. Barbecued spare ribs are one pork alternative, but they are messy, have less meat, and can't be put on a bun. In 1946 the USDA issued a statute that defined the hamburger:

Hamburger. "Hamburger" shall consist of chopped fresh and/or frozen beef with or without the addition of beef fat as such and/or seasonings, shall not contain more than 30 percent fat, and shall not contain added water, phosphates, binders, or extenders. Beef cheek (trimmed Beef cheeks) may be used in the preparation of hamburgers only in accordance with the conditions prescribed in paragraph (a) of this section. (Harris 1987:125)

Marvin Harris (1987:125–126) noted that we can eat ground pork and ground beef, but we can't combine them, at least if we are to call it a hamburger. Even when lean, grass-fed beef is used for hamburger and fat must be added to bind it, the fat must come from beef scraps, not from vegetables or a different animal. This definition of the hamburger protects not only the beef industry but also the corn farmer, whose income is linked to cattle production. Moreover, it helps the fast-food industry because the definition of hamburger allows it to use inexpensive scraps of fat from slaughtered beef to make, in fact, 30 percent of its hamburger. Thus, an international beef patty was created that overcame what Harris called the "pig's natural superiority as a converter of grain to flesh."

The fast-food restaurant, made possible by the popularity of the automobile, put the final touch on the ascendancy of beef. Ray Kroc, the founder of McDonald's, tapped into the new temporal and work routines of American labor. With more women working outside the home, time and efficiency were wed to each other as prepared foods, snacks, and the frozen hamburger patty became more popular. In many ways, the fast-food restaurant

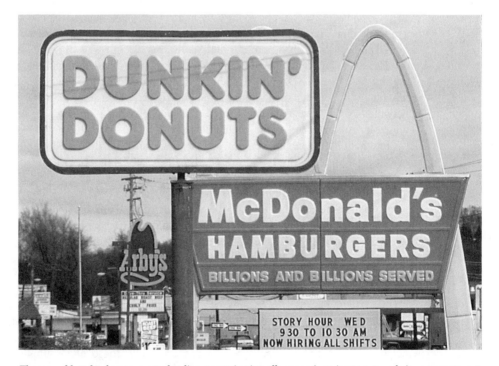

The row of fast-food restaurants that line streets in virtually every American town and city represents not only the union of sugar and fat but also the fast-paced lives required in a consumer-oriented society.

and the beef patty on a bun were to the American working woman of the 1970s and 1980s what sugar, hot tea, and preserves were to the English female factory worker of the latter half of the nineteenth century. They both offered ease of preparation and convenience at a time when increasing numbers of women worked outside the home.

As with sugar, therefore, our "taste" for beef goes well beyond our supposed individual food preferences. It is a consequence of a culture in which food as a commodity takes a form defined by economic, political, and social relationships. We can, as many have done, refuse beef. But to do so requires a real effort, as those who try to follow a strictly vegetarian diet can attest.

In addition, as with much of what Americans do, the matter of beef does not stop in the United States. The United States produces about 9 percent of the world's beef but consumes 28 percent of it. In 2001, U.S. ranchers produced 26.2 billion pounds of beef, while Americans consumed 63.2 pounds per capita. The consumption of beef in core countries is having more of an impact on countries in the periphery, and this is likely to worsen as other countries, such as Japan and China, begin to emulate American and European dietary patterns. Let's look at one example, in Costa Rica, of peripheral countries converting their forests into grazing land for cattle to profit from the core's demand for beef.

The Internationalization of the Hamburger

In the 1960s, with the help of the World Bank, governments in South and Central America began to convert tropical forest into pasture to raise beef for the international market. The case of Costa Rica, analyzed by Mark Endelmann (1987), is illustrative. The United States began to purchase beef from Central America in the 1950s, largely because prices were about 40 percent lower than in the United States.

The state plays a role in the production and importation of foreign beef. Foreign beef suppliers must meet USDA certification of their herds and packing facilities and are subject to import quotas that are more informal than formal because the quotas themselves are in violation of WTO regulations. Therefore, countries from whom we import beef must "voluntarily" restrict sales to the United States.

International financial agencies, such as the World Bank, also play roles in promoting cattle production by financing and requiring the establishment of a cattle infrastructure. For example, international lending institutions required Costa Rica's Central Bank to add a cattle technical extension division and the Banco Nacional de Costa Rica to add animal husbandry and veterinary sections to the branches of the bank located in cattle ranching areas. The loans themselves were used for such things as road building in cattle-raising regions and livestock improvement. In fact, the International Development Bank devoted 21 percent of its loans in the 1960s to the cattle sector of the economy. Furthermore, the U.S. Agency for International Development (USAID) helped develop roads and livestock-related extension and research agencies for Costa Rican cattle farmers.

A powerful livestock lobby developed in Costa Rica. The "chambers of cattlemen" is a national federation that placed spokespersons in the legislative assembly, banks, ministries, and major political parties. This lobby convinced the government to increase exports, which had the effect of drastically reducing beef available for local consumption. Only inferior beef that would be rejected by USDA inspectors was made available for domestic consumption.

The increase in cattle production also had environmental consequences for Costa Rica. From 1950 to 1973 the area of pasture in Costa Rica doubled from 622,402 hectares to 1,558,053 hectares. Because brushland is also used, it may be that as much as 89.9 percent of the country's productive land is used for livestock. It has also resulted in widespread destruction of the forests. In 1950, 72 percent of Costa Rica consisted of rain forest; by 1973 only 49 percent of the country was forested, and by 1978 this had decreased to only 34 percent (Endelmann 1987:554).

The expansion of cattle raising often occurred at the expense of peasant subsistence agriculture as cattleman evicted or forced peasants off their land or bought the land. Because cattle raising uses far less labor than agriculture, the peasants were forced into the cities, where unemployment was already high. And because cattle raising is profitable only on a large scale, the expansion led to further concentrations of wealth.

Yet if countries such as Costa Rica can escape the poverty discussed in Chapter 6, *is it fair to expect them to reduce their cattle production because of concerns in core countries about rain forest destruction? Might there be ways for countries, such as Costa Rica and Mexico, to raise beef, reduce environmental destruction, and assist the poor?* Let's examine one example of how anthropologists, working with agricultural specialists, can supply some answers.

Environmentally Sustainable Cattle Raising

Is it possible to develop ways of producing cattle that are not environmentally destructive? This is a question that some anthropologists are examining. Ronald Nigh, for example, has developed a project in Mexico in which indigenous methods of agriculture and stock raising are being applied not only to raise crops but also to regenerate rain forests destroyed by stock breeding.

Mexico, along with most Central American countries, has lost vast amounts of its rain forests. At the beginning of the twentieth century Mexico had 13 million hectares (31 million acres) of rain forest. Today, only 2.4 million hectares remain. Of the total destroyed, 5.5 million hectares were converted to pasture, and more than half of that is in an advanced stage of degradation and erosion. Furthermore, whereas 60 percent of Mexico's productive land is devoted to pasture or forage for animals, more than 50 percent of its population never consumes animal products.

Nigh (1995) maintains that the destruction of the rain forest by cattle grazing is largely the result of the importation of what he called the *factory model* of agricultural production. The factory model is designed to produce a single product (corn, soy, beef, pork, etc.) in as short a time as possible. It tends to be technology intensive and environmentally damaging. Furthermore, it tends to convert whole regions to a single type of agricultural production—cattle in one area, corn in another, wheat in another, and so on. In Central America the factory model of cattle raising has required clearing large tracts of land with fire and herbicides and reseeding with grasses that are not well suited to the environment. The result is degradation of the land by uncontrolled grazing and its eventual abandonment and return to secondary vegetation.

Nigh suggested that it is far more productive and far less damaging to the environment to look at agriculture as an ecological, rather than a manufacturing process and to adopt what S. R. Gleissman (1988; see also Posey et al. 1984) referred to as an *agroecological approach.* One foundation of this approach is to combine indigenous practices that have produced food yet preserved the environment with contemporary agricultural research. The major difference between a factory approach and an agroecological approach is that the latter creates a polyculture—the production of multiple crops and animals—rather than a monoculture—the growth or production of a single crop or animal. Indigenous methods of production in the rain forest create a system that enhances regeneration of land, flora, and fauna.

For example, there are sites of secondary vegetation in the Mexican rain forest left by Mayan farmers who practice swidden agriculture. The farmers clear a site, use it to grow corn for five to eight years, and then move on. These sites may soon look like the land abandoned by cattle ranchers, but Mayan farmers do not abandon the sites. They continue to work the garden, perhaps planting fruit trees, and use the site to attract mammals and birds to hunt. In fact, the area is designed to attract an animal crop and the Maya refer to it as "garden hunting" (Nigh 1995). Because, unlike the factory model, no herbicides are used to clear the land, plant and animal life can regenerate. Thus, traditional agriculture creates an environment that mixes fields, forests, and brushlands.

The idea is to create productive modules, each a mosaic of productive spaces. The agroecological model, drawing as it does on indigenous systems developed over centuries, creates an ecologically sustainable system of production modeled after natural systems, rather than a system that displaces natural ones.

Rather than demonizing cattle, Nigh said, it is possible to design an agricultural system modeled after indigenous systems in which cattle are integrated into an agroecological model, one in which diversity rather than uniformity is emphasized. For example, one area would be used for annual crops, such as corn, squash, root crops, spices, and legumes. Secondary areas, including those previously degraded by overgrazing, can be used for fruit trees, forage, and so on. Other secondary areas, using specially selected animal breeds and grasses, can be devoted to intensive grazing. In his project, for example, they selected a breed developed in New Zealand that is small but a high milk producer. Intensive grazing frees up tropical rain forest land that should never have been converted to pasture to begin with. Nigh maintains that by using only organic fertilizers and controlled grazing, it is possible to recover aquatic areas (ponds, rivers, and lakes) and take advantage of water resources such as fish, mollusks, turtles, and birds.

EXPORTING POLLUTION

We can now see how economic, political, and social factors contribute to our patterns of consumption. The same analysis can be applied to many other commodities that we consume in great numbers, which have a detrimental effect on the environment. Some examples are large houses, electronic devices, and appliances. Furthermore, there are the host of environmental problems caused by industrial pollution, the use, storage, and disposal of nuclear energy, the mountains of garbage that are accumulating as packaging becomes as much of a problem as the commodities they enclose. But there is a paradox here: Although the consumption patterns of core countries are the primary cause of environmental pollution, resource depletion and destruction, and the production of toxic substances, the core countries suffer far less from environmental problems than peripheral countries. The United States, for example, while having its share of environmental problems, enjoys relatively cleaner air, cleaner water, and more open spaces than peripheral countries whose people consume and produce a fraction of what Americans do. *How do we explain the spread of environmental destruction to the periphery?*

On December 12, 1991, Lawrence Summers, then chief economist of the World Bank, later undersecretary of treasury in the Clinton administration, and now president of Harvard University, sent a memorandum to some of his colleagues, intending only, the World Bank later said, to provoke discussion. The memo, in brief, argued that it made perfectly good economic sense for the United States to export its pollution and toxic waste to poor countries. The memo then appeared in *The Economist,* the prestigious British publication, under the headline, "Let Them Eat Pollution."

Summers argued that the World Bank should encourage the movement of "dirty industries" from core countries to less developed countries. He based his argument on three things: First, from an economic point of view, the cost of illness associated with pollution measured in working days lost is cheapest in the country with the lowest wages; second, underdeveloped countries are "underpolluted," and, consequently, the initial increases in pollution will have a relatively low cost; and finally, because people in less developed countries have a lower life expectancy, pollutants that cause diseases of the more elderly, such as prostate cancer, are less of a concern. In sum, Summers argued that a clean environment is worth more to the inhabitants of rich countries than to those of poor countries; therefore, the cost of pollution is less in poor countries than in rich countries; consequently, it makes perfect economic sense to export "dirty" industries to the less developed countries (Foster 1993).

The reaction to the memo from most environmentalists was scathing. José Lutzenberger, Brazil's secretary of the environment, issued a response in which he said, among other things,

> [i]t was almost a pleasant surprise to me to read reports in our papers and then receive [a] copy of your memorandum supporting the export of pollution to Third World countries and the arguments you present for justifying it. Your reasoning is perfectly logical but totally insane. (cited Rich 1994:246–248)

Yet, John Bellamy Foster (1993:12) said, there was little in the memo that has not been stated in other terms many times, largely by economists and public policy analysts. The memo was a perfect expression of the view of the environment and of people that emerges logically from the culture of capitalism. From an anthropological perspective, the memo is illustrative of our culture's cosmology, its view of the person and the environment. The premises of Summers's argument include

1. The lives of people in the Third World, judged by "foregone earnings" from illness and death, are worth less—hundreds of times less—than those of individuals in

advanced capitalist countries where wages are hundreds of times higher. Therefore, it makes sense to deposit toxic wastes in less developed countries.

2. Third World environments are underpolluted compared to places such as Los Angeles and Mexico City (where children had to be kept home from school for a month in 1989 because of air pollution).

3. A clean environment, in effect, is a luxury good pursued by rich countries because of the aesthetic and health standards in those countries. Thus, the worldwide costs of pollution could decrease if waste was transferred to poor countries where a clean environment is "worth" less, rather than polluting environments of the rich where a clean environment is "worth" more.

Essentially, the memo expresses a perspective in which a monetary value can be put on both human life, based on wage prospects, and the environment, based on the value people place on a clean environment. It reveals the tendency of the culture of capitalism to commodify virtually everything, including human life and the environment. As Foster (1993:12) said, Summers's memo is not an aberration; in his role as chief economist for the World Bank, Summers's job was to help create conditions for the accumulation of profit and to ensure economic growth. The welfare of the world's population, the health of the environment, "nor even the fate of individual capitalists themselves—can be allowed to stand in the way of this single-minded goal."

According to *The Economist,* governments constantly make decisions regarding health, education, working conditions, housing, and the environment that are based on differential valuations of certain people over others. For example, in the 1980s the U.S. Office of Management and Budget (OMB) sponsored a number of studies that concluded that the value of a human life was between $500,000 and $2 million, then used those figures to argue that some forms of pollution control were cost effective and others were not. Other economists have argued that the value of a human life should be based on earning power, thus a woman is worth less than a man, a Black's life worth less than a White's.

As shocking as that may sound, that is exactly how we, for the most part, operate. For example, three out of four off-site commercial hazardous landfills in southern states were located primarily in African American communities, although African Americans represent only 20 percent of the population. One of the best-hidden, environmental secrets in the United States, documented in Valerie Kuletz's (1998) book *The Tainted Desert: Environmental and Social Ruin in the American West,* is the nuclear landscape that has been created by weapons testing, uranium mining, and waste repositories. The Southwest nuclear landscape includes all five major American deserts and parts of the states of Nevada, New Mexico, California, Arizona, Utah, Colorado, and Texas. It is a place of thousands of open-pit uranium mines and the site of more than 900 above- and belowground nuclear explosions. It is the site of the largest nuclear material repository, and, not incidentally, the home of the majority of surviving, land-based, Native Americans (Kuletz 1998:10). The largest nuclear disaster in U.S. history occurred with the collapse of the tailings dam in Rio Puerco in 1979 that sent 94 million gallons of contaminated water into the river. It took a week for signs to be posted indicating that the water was dangerous and made the livestock that drank from the river uneatable and unsalable. The United Nuclear Corporation, owner of the mine that produced the tailings, offered some $525,000 in compensation, and the incident was never reported in the national press. One epidemiological study suggested that Navajo children were five times more likely to get bone cancer and fifteen times more likely to get ovarian and testicular cancer than the general population. Yet funding for follow-up studies were never authorized (Kuletz 1998:26). The core countries already ship 20 million tons of waste annually to the periphery. In 1987 dioxin-laden industrial waste was shipped from Philadelphia to Guinea and Haiti; in 1988, 4,000 tons of PCB-contaminated chemical waste from Italy was found leaking from drums in Nigeria.

Economists, such as Summers, argue that it is more important to build an economic infrastructure for future generations than to protect against global warming. They compare the cost of rain forest destruction with the economic cost of conserving it, without recognizing that rain forest destruction is irrevocable. They argue that rather than halting economic development because of global warming, countries will be able to use their newly developed riches to build retaining walls to hold back the rising sea; furthermore they argue that money spent to halt carbon dioxide output could be better spent dealing with population growth (Foster 1993:16).

Foster concluded that capitalism will never sacrifice economic growth and capital accumulation for environmental reform. Its internal logic will always be "let them eat pollution." Opposition will develop, as we shall see in later chapters, and some changes will be made, as have been made in the United States during the past thirty years, but environmental concerns will never be allowed to threaten the system itself. This is clearly evident if we turn again to the latest developments in the American automobile industry.

The latest development in American tastes for automobiles is the preference for so-called sport utility vehicles (SUVs). In 2000 they constituted one of every two family vehicles sold (65 million in all). These vehicles emit 57 percent more carbon dioxide than standard automobiles, are the fastest-growing source of global warming gases in the United States, and use 50 to 100 percent more gasoline than ordinary passenger automobiles (Bradsher 1997). Because they were used primarily on farms and construction sites, they were classified in the 1970s as light trucks, and pollution emission standards and minimum mileage requirements that applied to other vehicles did not and do not apply to them. These vehicles are highly profitable; not only do the profit margins exceed those for other vehicles but also the American automobile industry is protected by high import tariffs on light trucks made overseas (because of a trade war with Germany in 1964) that do not apply to other foreign-made automobiles. For this reason, automobile manufacturers and workers' unions have lobbied heavily to prevent Congress from extending pollution and gasoline consumption standards to SUVs. As Foster concluded (1993:19):

> Where radical change is called for little is accomplished within the system and the underlying crisis intensifies over time. Today this is particularly evident in the ecological realm. For the nature of the global environmental crisis is such that the fate of the entire planet and social and ecological issues of enormous complexity are involved, all traceable to the forms of production now prevalent. It is impossible to prevent the world's environmental crisis from getting progressively worse unless root problems of production, distribution, technology, and growth are dealt with on a global scale. And the more that such questions are

raised, the more it becomes evident that capitalism is unsustainable—ecologically, economically, politically, and morally—and must be superseded.

CONCLUSION

We began this chapter by asking why people choose to consume what they do, how they do, and when they do. We concluded that our tastes are largely culturally constructed and that they tend to serve the process of capital accumulation. There is no "natural" reason why we engage in consumption patterns that do harm to the environment. Furthermore, we suggested that of all the contributing factors to environmental pollution, the most difficult to "fix" is our consumption behavior because it serves as the foundation of our culture.

To illustrate we examined how the American taste for sugar and fat was historically constructed largely to serve the interests of sugar and beef producers. We examined how anthropological research is trying to help peripheral countries in their effort to meet Western demands for products, such as beef, without destroying their environmental resources.

We also examined how core countries are attempting to maintain their culture by exporting by-products—pollution and resource depletion—and how from some perspectives that seems to make perfect sense.

Most importantly, we examined the historical and cultural dynamic that drives the consumption of specific commodities and our attitudes about the environmental damage that results, and concluded that it is not an aberration but an intrinsic part of our way of life.

CHAPTER EIGHT

DISEASE

Cities…were microbe heavens, or, as British microbiologist John Cairns put it, "graveyards of mankind." The most devastating scourges of the past attained horrific proportions only when the microbes reached urban centers, where population density instantaneously magnified any minor contagion that might have originated in the provinces. Any microbes successfully exploited the new urban ecologies to create altogether novel disease threats.
—Laurie Garrett, *The Coming Plague*

A thorough understanding of the AIDS pandemic demands a commitment to the concerns of history and political economy: HIV…has run along the fault lines of economic structures long in the making.
—Paul Farmer, *AIDS and Accusation*

In the halcyon days after World War II, when the advance of science and economic prosperity inspired government leaders and leading academics to predict a coming era of worldwide peace and prosperity, medical professionals were predicting the end of infectious disease. Universal health was set as a realistic and achievable goal. The U.S. Surgeon General in 1967 said it was time to close the door on infectious disease. There was some reason for this optimism. As a result of a worldwide vaccination campaign, smallpox had been completely eliminated, the last case in the world being diagnosed in 1979. Malaria, one of the world's major killers, had been reduced worldwide and even eliminated in some areas by controlling the vector—the mosquito—that spread the disease and through the development and massive distribution of curative drugs. Tuberculosis, the major killer of the nineteenth century, was disappearing. The U.S. Surgeon General declared that measles would be eliminated by 1982 with an aggressive immunization campaign. Jonas Salk developed a vaccine for poliomyelitis, the scourge of childhood, and the development of antibiotics promised to rid us of every infirmary from pneumonia to bad breath. Then, in the space of a decade, everything changed.

AIDS was one of the shocks that changed universal optimism to what Marc Lappé (1994) called "therapeutic nihilism," an attitude common today among hospital personnel that nothing will work to cure patients. But there were other reasons for the change: the emergence of antibiotic-resistant strains of disease; the reemergence of malaria, cholera, and tuberculosis in even deadlier forms; the emergence of other new diseases, particularly Lyme disease, dengue-2, severe acute respiratory syndrome (SARS), and hemorrhagic fevers such as ebola that result in massive internal bleeding and have mortality rates of up to 90 percent. Measles, supposed to have been eradicated from the United States in 1982, was ten times more prevalent in 1993 than 1983. These developments and others have required medical researchers in biology, epidemiology, and anthropology, among others, to reexamine the relationship between human beings and the microbial world, particularly those pathogens that cause disease. It is clear that we underestimated the ingenuity of microbes to adapt to our adaptations to them and failed to appreciate how our patterns of social, political, and economic relations affect the emergence and transmission of disease.

Each age, it seems, has its signature disease. Bubonic plague in the fourteenth and fifteenth centuries emerged as a result of the opening of trade routes to Asia, and was carried by merchants and warriors from the middle of what was then the world system west to Europe and east to China. Syphilis spread in the sixteenth and seventeenth centuries through increased sexual contact of people in towns and cities. Tuberculosis was the disease of the nineteenth century, spread through the air in the densely packed cities and slums of Europe, the United States, and the periphery.

As we shall see, AIDS is very much the signature disease of the latter quarter of the twentieth and the beginning of the twenty-first century, serving as a marker for the increasing disparities in wealth between core and periphery and the accompanying disparity in susceptibility to disease. More than 98 percent of deaths from communicable disease (16.3 million a year) occur in the periphery. Worldwide 32 percent of all deaths are caused by infectious disease, but in the periphery infectious disease is responsible for 42 percent of all deaths, compared to 1.2 percent in industrial countries (Platt 1996:11). Table 8.1 summarizes the major diseases afflicting the world today, the number of people affected, annual mortality, and whether the disease is on the rise, declining, or stable.

The fact that each historical epoch has its characteristic illness reveals clearly that how we live—the social and cultural patterns at any point in time and space—largely define the kinds and frequencies of diseases to which human beings are susceptible. The questions we need to ask are, *what do we do that exposes us to disease? What do we do that exposes others to disease? How do we create the conditions for unique interactions between pathogens, their environments, and their hosts? Furthermore, what features of human societies make pathogens more or less lethal?*

Many of the things we discussed in previous chapters are relevant. For example, increases in population density clearly relate to the emergence and frequency of disease, as does the division of the world into rich and poor. The crowding into cities of rural workers and peasants as agricultural land becomes concentrated in the hands of a few influences disease susceptibility. Public policy that makes economic growth a priority and neglects health programs encourages the spread of disease, as do International Monetary Fund structural adjustment programs in peripheral countries that demand the cutting of health, sanitation, and education programs. The alteration of the environment has enormous consequences for the spread and emergence of disease.

As food is available to those who can pay for it, so too, medical cures are available largely to those with the money to buy them. In a capitalist medical system, as in a capital-

TABLE 8.1   Characteristics of Major Infectious Diseases, 2002 Estimates by Death Counts*

DISEASE	DEATHS (IN MILLIONS)	% OF TOTAL DEATHS (ALL CAUSES)	TREND	VECTOR	SYMPTOMS
Acute respiratory infections	3,845	6.7	Stable	Bacterium and virus, airborne	Cold, sore throat, influenza, pneumonia and bronchitis
AIDS	2,821	4.9	Up	Virus, HIV types 1 and 2, sexual contact, shared hypodermic needles	Autoimmune dysfunction progresses from asymptomatic to lethal; any organ system can be targeted; initially, fever, weight loss, diarrhea, fatigue, cough, skin lesions; opportunistic infections such as cancer and tuberculosis
Diarrheal diseases	1,767	3.1	Down	Bacterium and virus, water and food-borne	Frequent liquid stools, sometimes bloody
Tuberculosis	1,605	2.8	Stable	Bacterium, airborne	Severe coughing, sometimes with blood chest pain, exhaustion, weight loss, and night sweats
Malaria	1,222	2.1	Up	Protozoan, mosquito-borne	Fever, headache, nausea, vomiting, diarrhea, malaise, enlarged spleen; liver renal, and respiratory failure; shock; pulmonary and cerebral edema
Measles	760	1.3	Down	Virus, airborne	Rash and fever, encephalitis in rare cases
Meningitis	173	.03	Stable	Bacterium and virus, airborne	Inflammation of meninges of brain and spinal cord
Hepatitis B	103	.02	Stable	Virus, sexual contact	Anorexia, abdominal pain, sometimes rash, jaundice, cirrhosis of liver (chronic infection)
Leishmaniasis	51	.01	Stable	Protozoan, sandfly	Skin lesions, inflammation and crusting skin ulcers, tissue destruction in nose and mouth
Schistosomiasis	15	.001	Stable	Protozoan, snail-borne	Cirrhosis of liver and anemia

Data from World Health Organization. 2003. *World Health Report.* http://www.who.int/whr/2003/en/annex2-en.pdf.
*Data collected from WHO member organizations.

ist food system, market demand, not need, determines what and how much is produced. Of the 1,233 new medicines patented between 1975 and 1997, only thirteen—1 percent— were for tropical diseases. One American drug company stumbled on a drug for sleeping sickness, currently infecting some 300,000 people a year, largely in sub-Saharan Africa.

The drug company that now owns the patent for the drug, however, has decided not to market it because of the poor profit potential. It did donate the patent to the World Health Organization (WHO), but WHO lacks the financial resources to develop it (see Tardieu 1999). Malaria infects an estimated 500,000 and kills from 1 million to 3 million people a year, mostly in poor countries, yet drug companies invest little to find cures because there is little profit in addressing the needs of the poor. "The poor have no consumer power, so the market has failed them," said Dr. James Orbinski, international president of Doctors Without Borders/ Médecins Sans Frontières; "I'm tired of the logic that says, 'He who can't pay, dies'" (cited McNeil 2000). Thus, although drug companies invest some $27 billion a year in research, most of that is for drugs to grow hair, relieve impotence, fight cholesterol, control depression and anxiety, and relieve arthritis and high blood pressure, all problems of the wealthiest 10 or 20 percent of the world's population. Those priorities make good economic sense in the short term but, given the rapidity of the spread of disease, endanger everyone.

Infectious disease, of course, is not the only health problem we face. Environmental pollutants, often a direct outgrowth of industrialization, cause sickness. For example, asthma, often aggravated by industrial pollutants, is on the rise. Millions of people face malnutrition and starvation, conditions that further expose them to disease. Commercially promoted products, such as alcoholic beverages and tobacco, endanger health. Of the estimated 1.1 billion smokers in the world today, 800 million are in the periphery (World Health Organization, *The Tobacco Epidemic,* 1995). The WHO estimates that 4 million people die annually from tobacco; this figure, they say, will increase to 10 million by 2030, and 70 percent of these deaths will be in developing countries. As cigarette sales continue to fall in the core in response to antismoking campaigns and state legislation, cigarette companies, with the support of core governments, have intensified their efforts to sell their products to people in other countries, particularly to women and the young. For example, the United States has used free trade arguments to pressure other nations—Thailand, Taiwan, and South Korea—with economic sanctions to open their markets to American cigarettes. In such cases it is easy to see a direct connection between the capitalist world system and the onset of disease. However, the relation that exists between the culture of capitalism and infectious pathogens is often more subtle and hidden.

A PRIMER ON HOW TO DIE OF AN INFECTIOUS DISEASE

Human beings swim in a sea of microbes; we eat them, breathe them, and absorb them through skin openings and membranes. Most do us no harm, and many are useful. Millions of bacteria live in our intestinal system to aid digestion, and in nature they serve as catalysts for decomposition of material that can then be reused by plants and animals. Many we never meet because they exist in distant parts of the world. Some microbes, however, do harm us. Harmful or pathogenic microbes include bacteria, viruses, and parasites that invade our bodies and cause illness and, in some cases, death. The question we need to ask is, *what determines the relationships that we have with the infectious pathogens whose world we share?*

To answer this question let's ask what is required for a pathogen to kill us; that is, *what does it take for us to die of an infectious disease?* At least four things have to happen.

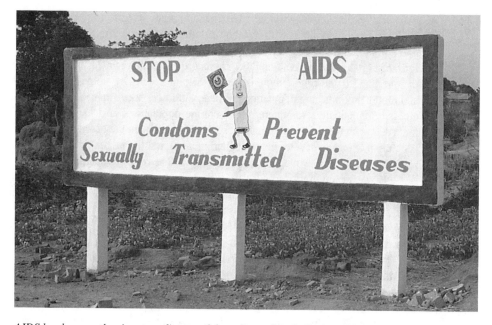

AIDS has become the signature disease of the culture of capitalism, striking particularly hard in the poor countries of the periphery, such as Gambia where this sign advises condom use.

First, we must come into contact with the pathogen or a vector—such as a mosquito, tick, flea, or snail—that carries it. Second, the pathogen must be virulent, that is, have the capacity to kill us. Third, if we come into contact with a deadly pathogen, it must evade our body's immune system. Finally, the pathogen must be able to circumvent whatever measures our society has developed to prevent it from doing harm. As we shall see, human actions are critical in each step.

What actions of human beings increase their likelihood of coming into contact with an infectious pathogen? Various behaviors may serve to expose an organism to an infectious agent. For example, carnivorous animals create an opportunity for pathogens to spread when the animals eat the flesh of other animals; animals that congregate create opportunities for the spread of pathogens by physical contact. Because human behavior is dictated largely by our culture, cultural patterns that characterize human populations play a major role in creating or inhibiting opportunities for pathogens to spread. Actions that change the environment or change the size, density, and distribution of human settlement patterns increase or decrease the likelihood of our meeting an infectious parasite or influence the size of the parasite population. The emergence of Lyme disease is a good example of many of these factors.

Lyme disease was first reported in 1975, when two women, in Old Lyme and Haddam, Connecticut, reported to a Yale physician that their children had strange symptoms, including aching bones, malaise, and neurological symptoms such as poor memory and concentration. Study revealed that the disease, now spread throughout much of the United States, is carried by four varieties of ticks. The question is, *why did it quite suddenly become a major health problem?* The reason apparently has to do with human alterations of the environment along with human settlement and recreational patterns.

In the seventeenth and eighteenth centuries much of the New England forest was cleared for farming. As farming declined the forests grew back, but with a very different ecology than the one that existed originally: Gone were certain species of animals, such as wolves, bears, and mountain lions, and populations of deer and mice, once controlled by these predators, increased dramatically. Also increasing were the populations of ticks associated with deer and mice and, with the ticks, the *Borrelia* organism, a pathogen they carried in their salivary gland. As human beings built settlements (suburbs) along the forests and ventured into them for recreational activities, they were exposed to the tick. The result was Lyme disease.

However, coming into contact with a pathogen is not sufficient, in itself, to kill us. The pathogen itself must be virulent enough to disrupt critical bodily functions or reproduce so extensively in the body that the damages it causes will result in death. *What makes a pathogen lethal?* There is obviously a big difference between "catching" a cold, and "catching" HIV. We seem to take for granted that some diseases are more severe than others, but the reality is far more complex. A pathogen that is harmless to one host may be lethal in another. There is a herpes virus, for example, that has evolved to survive, spread, and do no harm in one type of monkey but is 100 percent lethal when it infects another type (Garrett 1994:573).

Generally, it is not in the best interest of a parasite, bacteria, or virus to seriously harm its host; it is far better to allow the host to survive, to provide an environment for the pathogen to reproduce and spread. Furthermore, it is a distinct advantage to the pathogen if the host remains mobile to help the pathogen spread to new hosts. The rhinoviruses that cause the common cold, for example, reproduce in the cells that line the nasal passages; they are shed by sneezing or by a runny nose. If a person with a cold wipes the nose with a finger and then touches the finger of another person, the exposed person may inhale the contaminated air or touch the finger to his or her mouth. However the pathogen is spread, it requires the host to move, so killing or disabling the host is counterproductive.

Thus, most microbes that we come into contact with and even those that infect us do us little or no harm. However, there are certain exceptions to the rule that microbes should not harm their host. First, the newer the disease, the more deadly it is likely to be because microbe and host will not have had sufficient time to adapt to each other. Anything that human beings do that exposes them to diseases to which they haven't been previously exposed increases the likelihood that the disease can kill them. The destruction of the peoples of North, South, and Central America in the sixteenth and seventeenth centuries, as we saw in Chapter 3, is a case in point. Having never been exposed to such diseases as smallpox, measles, influenza, and even, in some cases, a common cold, millions died. Something as simple as increased travel can bring people into contact with a disease that is far more lethal for them than for the people who share their environment with the pathogen. Intestinal illnesses that are the bane of travelers are but one example; the traveler can be devastated by a pathogen that people native to the area harbor in their bodies with little or no effect. HIV-2 is carried in the bodies of African green monkeys with apparently little effect, but when it "crossed over" to human beings the result was fatal.

A second exception to the rule that pathogens should do no harm is when the disease is carried and spread by a vector. When a disease is spread from human to human by another species, such as the mosquito, flea, or tick, and does not depend on human beings for its existence, reproduction, or transmission, the pathogen is under no selective pressure to spare human beings and can be as virulent as it likes. In fact, extensive multiplication in the human host might be beneficial to the microbe because it increases the likelihood of the vector picking it up and continuing the microbe's reproductive cycle. It might be even better for the host to be disabled if, for example, the host would be less able to protect itself from the vector. As we might expect, pathogens are generally very kind to vectors, generally causing them no harm whatsoever (Lappé 1994:25). What this means is that anything that human beings do to increase their exposure to vector-borne pathogens will increase their likelihood of contracting a deadly disease.

A third exception to the "do no harm" rule is when a pathogen is spread by contaminated water or another external medium. For example, diarrheal diseases tend to be more virulent if they are spread by water systems and do not require person-to-person contact. The reason, suggested biologist Paul Ewald (1993:88), is that diseases that are spread by contaminated water lose nothing by incapacitating their host, but they gain a great deal by reproducing extensively in the host. Their large numbers make it more likely that they can contaminate water supplies through the washing of sheets or clothing or through bodily wastes. Thus, human activities that create contaminated water supplies are likely to create more virulent forms of diarrheal diseases.

Finally, the fact that diseases are spread by vectors or external mediums suggests that the virulence of a disease is affected also by the ease of transmission: The easier a disease is to transmit, the more virulent it is likely to be, or, conversely, the more difficult a pathogen is to transmit, the less virulent it will be. If a disease is difficult to transmit, the microbe that can lurk in the body without harming it (thus allowing the host to survive until an opportunity arises to jump to another host) has a decided advantage over a microbe that quickly kills or disables its host. Thus, chronic diseases, such as tuberculosis, can lie dormant for years without doing damage to the host, waiting for an opportunity first to infect the host and then to spread to another. However, reasoned Ewald, if the disease is easy to transmit, then it is under no selective pressure to spare the host. Diseases such as ebola, for example, reproduce so rapidly in the body, and infect virtually every organ, that anyone who comes into contact with any of the victim's bodily fluids is likely to contract the disease.

The notion that diseases that are difficult to transmit are likely to be less lethal has important implications. For example, sexually transmitted diseases in generally monogamous populations should be less virulent, according to Ewald, because the pathogens have to wait longer to be transmitted from host to host. If sexual activity increases, however, it is to the pathogen's advantage to increase rapidly in the body to take advantage of the increased likelihood of transmission. This seems to fit with some developments with HIV, the virus that causes AIDS. In populations in which transmission was more difficult because people had fewer sex partners or were more likely to use condoms, the disease evolved into a less virulent form (Garrett 1994:587).

Even if Ewald's hypothesis that diseases that are easier to transmit are more lethal does not apply universally, its implications are striking. It means, as Ewald (1993:93) suggested, that we should be able to make a pathogen less lethal by increasing the price it pays for transmission; in other words, by making the pathogen more difficult to transmit, we should be able to force it to evolve toward a less lethal form. Thus, by cleaning up water supplies, protecting ourselves from mosquitoes, and reducing the likelihood of the spread of sexually transmitted diseases, we are working not only to prevent the disease but also to make it less deadly when it does occur.

Having examined how human actions bring us into contact with a pathogen and help determine how lethal it is, let's move on to the next step toward our death. Let's assume we have come into contact with a pathogen that is highly virulent to human beings. *Is there anything that can save us?* Fortunately, the human body has evolved a highly sophisticated immune system that generally prevents microbes from harming us. When a microbe infects the body, specific cells of the immune system, T cells, attach themselves to the invader, signaling other cells, macrophages, to envelop and destroy it. Once destroyed, other cells of the immune system call off the attack, lest the system overreact and destroy its own cells.

It is an ingenious system and, under stable conditions, one that will hold in check most microscopic invaders. However, if an immune system is weakened, for example by hunger, it is less able to fight off disease. Furthermore, in unstable conditions, when the opportunity exists for rapid changes in the number and type of microbes, the microbes have a decided advantage. Microbes are extremely adept at evolving ways to escape the body's immune system. The reason is that viruses and bacteria mutate and reproduce at a much faster rate than larger organisms, such as human beings. Consequently, if a microbe evolves that can somehow get around the immune system, that particular variety of microbe will have a distinct adaptive advantage, and more of its offspring will survive. Ultimately, this will lead to the emergence of a microbe for which our bodies have no defense.

Simple arithmetic demonstrates how quickly microbes can adapt to changed or threatening environments. Let's assume that a variety of an organism—let's call it X—emerges with a characteristic that gives it only a 1 percent reproductive advantage over another variety—Y—of the same organism. That means that 101 of the X variety will survive in each generation to only 100 of Y. Arithmetically, this means that X will become the dominant form of the organism in only thirty generations. In human terms thirty generations is a long time—700 to 800 years. But for microorganisms thirty generations is a very short time—for bacteria that reproduce every twenty to thirty minutes, thirty generations can elapse in a day, at the end of which two bacteria have produced 1 billion.

Because of this ability to adapt so quickly, some microbes have developed the ability to evade the immune system. The bacterium that causes dengue hemorrhagic fever has evolved to use the immune system to spread from the blood systems to the vital organs. The virus that causes influenza changes so rapidly that infection by one strain does not confer any immunity to subsequent strains. The AIDS viruses evolved to attack and destroy the body's immune system, not only allowing the virus to survive and spread but also creating the opportunity for other diseases, such as tuberculosis, to take root and thrive. In fact, one of the major threats of the HIV is that the rapid change in its genetic structure, about 1 percent per year in some varieties, will allow it to evolve resistance to whatever defenses the body or medical researchers may develop.

Assuming, then, that we have met a lethal pathogen and that the body's immune system is unable to destroy it, what next? As far as we know, human beings have always sought to cure whatever illness afflicted them. Ritual and ceremonial cures are known in societies throughout the world, as are the use of plants and other natural resources. However, there is little question that one of the major success stories of the culture of capitalism is the development of measures to protect people from and cure them of infectious disease. The discoveries of the causes of infectious disease and then the development, manufacture, and distribution of vaccines and antibiotics has, in general, extended the human life span in societies throughout the world. Worldwide, life expectancy at birth was forty-eight years in 1955; fifty-nine years in 1975; and sixty-five years in 1995 (World Health Organization 1997).

Unfortunately, just as microbes can quickly adapt and evade the natural defenses of our immune system, they can also quickly evolve to render modern drugs useless. When antibiotics are overused or used incorrectly or prescribed for viral infections against which they are useless, new varieties that are resistant to existing antibiotics may evolve. Some researchers claim that half of the 150 million antibiotic prescriptions written by American doctors each year are misprescribed or misused in this way. Patients take a portion of the prescribed dosage and, once they feel better, neglect to take the rest. This results in killing the bacteria most susceptible to the antibiotic but may leave unaffected those that are more resistant. Those resistant bacteria then gradually become the dominant strain of the microbe; even if 99.9 percent of the original strain is destroyed, the survivor is likely to be a superstrain on which existing antibiotics have no effect (Platt 1996:54).

Furthermore, half of the antibiotics used in the United States are used for livestock, aquaculture, and other biological industries. Monocultural farming is a major source of the problem. When only one kind of animal or one kind of crop is grown, a disease outbreak can decimate a business. A commercial chicken farm, for example, may have 100,000 chickens; an aquaculture facility may have thousands of salmon. To protect themselves, growers use antibiotics to fend off disease, creating an opportunity for evolution of drug-resistant strains of pathogens, some of which may be capable of infecting people. Anne E. Platt (1996:52) summed up the problem when she wrote:

> Today, almost all disease-causing bacteria are on the pathway to complete drug resistance. More than a half century after the discovery of antibiotics, humanity is at risk of losing these valuable weapons and reverting to the pre-antibiotic era.

One of the greatest risks we face may come from drug-resistant tuberculosis that is finding its way from poor countries to the rich. The most dangerous source for this disease is the former countries of the Soviet Union. Because of the economic collapse, prison doctors treating tuberculosis were unable to give a full course of drug treatments to patients. The partial treatment triggered the rise of a new dominant strain of the disease that was causing 10,000 new drug-resistant cases a year, each 250 times more expensive to treat than the old strain of the disease. And tuberculosis spreads quickly. More than a dozen passengers on a flight from Paris to New York were infected by a lone Ukrainian infected with the drug-resistant strain (York 1999). Some estimate that, if it is not properly treated, 1 billion people will be newly infected—and 35 million will die—in the next two decades.

Thus, we get some idea of how human actions can influence the relationship between infectious pathogens and human bodies, and what it takes in a general sense for us to die of an infectious disease. Next let's examine how this translates to the relationship between disease and culture, and more specifically, how people's behavior in the culture of capitalism contributes to the creation and transmission of infectious disease.

THE RELATIONSHIPS BETWEEN CULTURE AND DISEASE

As we have seen, our world is filled with organisms that can cause us harm. Whether we come into contact with them, how deadly they are for us, and whether we can help the body fight them off or reach a mutually beneficial arrangement is greatly influenced by the kinds of lives we lead or, more specifically, the cultures and patterns of social relations that we construct, maintain, and reproduce. Let's examine this a little further and identify some of the specific cultural adaptations of human beings that either encourage or inhibit disease. One of the questions we want to consider is, *how has the emergence of consumer capitalism influenced the spread of disease?* Put another way, *how does the behavior appropriate to our culture expose people to the risk of disease or create opportunities for the creation and spread of infectious pathogens?* To illustrate the relationship between culture and disease, between our behavioral choices and how they affect our relationships with the world of microbes, let's examine what happened to disease during another great cultural transformation in human history, the shift from gathering and hunting to agriculture.

Gathering and Hunting to Early Agriculture

Early gathering and hunting societies were likely afflicted by a range of diseases far different from our own. Small, geographically scattered human populations did not afford infectious diseases the same opportunity for infection and transmission as do large, densely populated modern societies. Most pathogens in early human societies must have depended for their survival on nonhuman hosts. When they infected human beings it was when people got in the way of the reproductive cycle of the nonhuman host, not because the microbe depended on human beings for their survival.

Contact with wild animals likely exposed early human societies to such diseases as rabies, anthrax, salmonellosis, botulism, and tetanus (Cohen 1989:33). Worm parasites that infested animals' bodies would have been encountered by hunters. Malaria and yellow fever were transmitted by mosquitoes and other diseases by ticks. As Mark Cohen noted in *Health and the Rise of Civilization* (1989), these diseases strike rarely, cannot spread directly from person to person, and do not claim many victims. But because human beings would not have built up an immunity to these diseases and because the offending microbes would not have depended on human transmission, the diseases were often fatal.

There were also categories of disease that could be transmitted from person to person; these would have had to live in hosts for a long time to have the opportunity to spread and must have been transmitted fairly easily by touch, breathing, sneezing, or coughing and in food or other shared items. Yaws was probably one such disease, as may have been the herpes virus and a variety of intestinal illness (Cohen 1989:37). Because diseases tend to evolve toward less virulent forms the longer they coexist with a population, diseases that we recognize today as mild may have been more serious in earlier human populations.

However, it was during the transition of human societies from gatherers and hunters to sedentary agriculturists that began some 10,000 years ago that whole new relationships developed between culture and disease. By remaining sedentary people probably came into contact with fewer pathogens, and by remaining in one place people likely developed greater immunities to localized bacteria, viruses, and parasitic infection. Sedentariness also makes it easier to care for the sick. But, as Cohen pointed out, sedentariness also has some major disadvantages. First, sedentary societies are more likely to engage in long-distance trade, which may increase contact between groups and, as a consequence, spread disease from one group to another. Second, sedentary populations create more favorable conditions for pathogens to spread; permanent shelters attract vermin—insects and rodents—that may carry disease, while the buildup of garbage and human waste may serve in sedentary societies to harbor and spread microbes, especially if water sources are infected with human waste.

Third, alteration of the landscape through horticulture, animal husbandry, and agriculture exposed people to new disease. Malaria-bearing mosquitoes would have thrived in the ponds and bodies of stagnant water created by human environmental intervention. Ponds and irrigation ditches would have provided opportunities for expansion of the snail that carries schistosomiasis.

Fourth, improvements in cooking technology, particularly pottery, may have helped cook food more thoroughly and destroyed disease-carrying microbes, but porous pots may have encouraged the growth of some bacteria. Storage of food for extended periods increased the possibility of bacteria buildup and fungal contamination and attracted disease-carrying vermin.

Finally, regular contact with domesticated animals exposed human populations to additional infections. Living in close contact with animals gives parasites, such as tapeworms, opportunities to involve human hosts in their life cycles as they pass between humans and domestic animals. There is evidence that most human respiratory disease arose after animals were domesticated, and a whole range of disease now or once common in human beings—measles, smallpox, influenza, and diphtheria—are thought to have had their origins in domestic animals (Cohen 1989).

"Graveyards of Mankind"

Much as agriculture changed the relationship between microbes and humans, the voluntary or involuntary decisions of people to move to cities shifted the balance in favor of infectious disease. Simply put, the more people per square mile, the more easily an infectious agent could pass from one person to another. For example, as early as 2,000 to 4,000 years ago writers told of infestations of lice, bedbugs, and ticks that they associated with dense housing conditions and the onset of disease. The chances of a citizen of ancient Rome living to the age of thirty years was one in three, whereas 70 percent of rural residents survived until thirty (Garrett 1994:236). In 430 B.C. an epidemic of an unknown disease in Athens killed half the population.

Although cities have existed at least 6,000 to 7,000 years, they began increasing dramatically in size during the expansion of the capitalist world system, Cities became the hubs of financial activities and were themselves one of the main reasons for the growth of trade, city residents relying on food from rural agricultural areas and trade items from distant places. Cities also grew as a consequence of the commercialization or capitalization of agriculture because more people were pushed off the land and forced to seek sustenance in the cities of the core and then the periphery.

Five diseases in particular seem to have benefited from the expansion of urban environments—bubonic plague, leprosy (Hansen's disease), cholera, tuberculosis, and syphilis. Bubonic plague, as we saw in Chapter 3, was spread in the fourteenth century by traders and invaders from central Asia west into Europe and east into China and periodically reemerged, with disastrous demographic, economic, and social consequences. Cities tried to protect themselves by banning travelers from entering and by finding scapegoats on which to blame the disease. Tens of thousands of Jews and alleged devil worshippers were slaughtered for this reason, the city of Strasbourg alone killing 16,000 of its Jewish residents. The Brotherhood of Flagellants, a society of Christian men, beat themselves with leather straps embedded with iron spikes to drive out the sins they believed responsible for the disease (Garrett 1994:238). In 1665 the plague hit London, killing as many as 3,000 people per day.

Leprosy is a particularly good example of an apparent adaptation of a parasite. The disease swept over Europe in 1200, aided by the growing density of cities, disdain for bathing, wool clothing, and sharing of bedding with others to stay warm. The disease is caused by a bacterium passed by human contact that attacks the nerves of the extremities, causing them to go numb. Because there is no feeling in the fingers, toes, and other extremities, injuries go unnoticed by the victim, leading to the characteristic disfigurement and stigmatization of victims. By 1980, most of the world's 5 billion people had antibodies to the bacterium, indicating they had been harmlessly exposed to the disease (Garrett 1994:239).

Cholera struck the world's cities in four devastating pandemics between 1830 and 1896, spreading through contaminated water and sewage systems. In St. Louis in 1849, 10 percent of the population perished; in the city of Mecca some 15,000 residents and Muslim pilgrims died, and another 30,000 died in 1865; in London 53,000 died in 1847. Because the disease seemed to affect the most impoverished segments of the population, those in power assumed it was a result of lower-class "immorality." It was not until 1849 that London physician John Snow demonstrated that the disease was transmitted via water supplies. Snow removed the handle of a pump that was the sole water supply for a cholera-ridden neighborhood, and the local epidemic ended. Yet it was years before authorities were convinced that the disease was transmitted through the water supply and took measures to protect it.

Tuberculosis was the most deadly disease of the nineteenth century. Like others, the bacterium responsible for the disease, *Mycobacterium tuberculosis,* was ancient, dating back to at least 5000 B.C. Tuberculosis is a slow-growing disease, causing illness only after months or years of infection and then ultimately killing the host; however, only about 10 percent of those infected actually develop the disease. It is transmitted through microscopic droplets exhaled by victims, making people who inhabit densely populated, closed spaces—the kind typical of urban slums—particularly susceptible.

The effect of population density on the incidence of tuberculosis is evident in its history in the United States. In 1830, Boston had a crude death rate from tuberculosis of 21 per 1,000, half that of London, which had a far larger population. By 1850, when Boston's population had grown, the death rate was 38 per 1,000. In Massachusetts in general tuberculosis rates increased by 40 percent from 1834 to 1853. Then, toward the end of the nineteenth century, for unknown reasons, tuberculosis rates began to decline. In 1900, tuberculosis killed about 200 of every 100,000 Americans; by 1940, before the advent of antibiotic therapy, the rate was 60 per 100,000.

A number of hypotheses have been offered in the ensuing debate over why tuberculosis death rates declined. Some claim that better nutrition enabled people to withstand infection better. Rene Dubos, whose 1952 book *The White Plague* pioneered the study of the connection between human behavior and disease, claimed that the elimination of the deplorable working conditions of men, women, and children during the industrial revolution along with improved housing resulted in the decline.

Laurie Garrett (1994:244) suggested that a clue to the decline in tuberculosis can be found in the experience of South Africa. Even with the increased availability of antibiotics and an understanding of the transmission of the disease, death rates for tuberculosis rose 88 percent from 1938 to 1945. Cape Town saw a rise of 100 percent, Durban 172 percent, and Johannesburg 140 percent. Urban rates of infection were as high as 7 percent of the total population, whereas in rural areas, despite poverty and hunger, the rates were less than 1.4 percent. Virtually all cases struck the Black and Asian or "colored" population.

Housing, according to Garrett (1994:245), seemed the most likely culprit responsible for the outbreak. During that period South Africa had its own industrial revolution and, as in Europe in the eighteenth and nineteenth centuries, required inexpensive labor. Blacks and coloreds, by far the major source of cheap labor, were required by law to live in areas designated by the government and to carry identity cards that stipulated where they could and could not go. The government subsidized housing for the White population, but government-sponsored housing projects for Blacks actually declined during this period of expansion by 471 percent, resulting in abysmal living conditions. The South African medical authorities blamed the outbreak on an imagined genetic susceptibility of Blacks, thus blaming the victim for an affliction caused by the expansion of the capitalist economy.

Cities also seemed to provide ideal conditions for the emergence of sexually transmitted diseases such as syphilis. The density of population, anonymity of urban life, and influx of single people, especially men, in search of work, promoted greater sexual activity, experimentation, and prostitution.

There is some debate over the origins of syphilis (see Baker and Armelagos 1988). It is carried by a bacterium transmitted in sexual intercourse or at birth from an infected woman to her child. It was first reported in Europe in 1495 among French soldiers (explaining its early designation as the "French disease") fighting against Naples and within two years had spread throughout the world, apparently existing in a deadlier form than it does today. Because the outbreak of the disease coincided with the return of Columbus's sailors from the New World, many scholars believe its origin lay in the Americas, from which it was spread by European conquerors to the rest of the world. Others argue that the rate at which the disease killed indigenous people of the New World suggested a lack of any immunity that would likely have been conferred if the disease were native to that area of the world. Still others (see Hudson 1965) suggest that syphilis is caused by the same bacterium that causes yaws, a common but easily cured childhood skin disease with a worldwide distribution, and that local sanitary conditions determined whether the disease manifested itself as yaws or syphilis. Regardless of its origins, it spread throughout European cities from the sixteenth through the twentieth centuries.

The pace of urbanization from the fifteenth to the nineteenth centuries that created conditions for diseases such as plague, leprosy, cholera, tuberculosis, and syphilis to spread has dramatically increased in the twentieth century, especially in the periphery. In 1950 there were only two megacities—urban areas with 10 million or more people—New York and London. By 1980 there were ten: Buenos Aires, Rio de Janeiro, São Paulo, Mexico City, Los Angeles, New York, Beijing, Shanghai, Tokyo, and London. Currently, 45 percent of the world's people live in cities of 2,000 or more (Population Reference Bureau 2000). Many of these urban dwellers will be new migrants from rural areas flocking to cities, as they have for centuries, in search of jobs, often after being forced off their land by the continuing concentration of agricultural production and wealth in a few hands and by government policies that function to create cheap labor to fuel economic growth. These densely packed populations will continue, as they have for centuries, to be prime breeding grounds for the creation and dissemination of disease.

When New York and London were reaching megacity status, they were doing so in countries that were the richest in the world. That wealth allowed them to adjust to their growth by building sanitation services, public health networks, and medical services to accommodate not only growing numbers of people but also the special problems created by increasing population density. The new megacities, with the exception of some in East Asia, for the most part lack that luxury. Not only have they grown at unprecedented rates but also they are in countries on the brink of economic ruin. The international debt of countries such as Brazil, Egypt, Mexico, and India prevents them from building facilities to accommodate the growing urban populations. Residents live in hastily constructed shantytowns and slums that rival any of those in eighteenth- and nineteenth-century Europe and America for the extent of poverty and disease. Even the richer cities cannot keep up with the growth; in Tokyo in 1985 less than 40 percent of dwellings were connected to proper sewage, and tons of untreated human waste was dumped into the ocean. Hong Kong, another of the more wealthy cities, was dumping 1 million tons of untreated waste each day into the China Sea. In the poor cities, of course, the situation is far worse. In 1980, 88 percent of Manila's population lived in squatter settlements with houses built of scrap wood, cardboard, tin, or bamboo. Nairobi's slums, where 40 percent of the population lived, were deliberately left off official maps of the city (Garrett 1994:251).

A United Nations report reveals that the average child growing up in one of the urban slums of the periphery is forty times more likely to die before her or his fifth birthday of a preventable infectious disease than a rural child in the same country. No country is immune; the extent of neglect of inner-city children in the United States was underscored in 1993 when the World Health Organization announced that the United States had fallen behind Albania, Mexico, and China in childhood vaccination rates, largely because of the collapse of health services to inner-city poor (Garrett 1994:512).

Human demographic patterns, largely a consequence of labor movement and commerce, therefore, continue to generate environments that not only harbor pathogens and provide ample opportunity for their spread but also help opportunistic pathogens expand their base of operations. A case in point is cysticercosis, a disease produced by tapeworms found in undercooked pork and other animal flesh, which in some forms can infect the brain. Epidemiologists observed that in Mexico City people were being infected not from eating undercooked pork—those infected could not afford to eat meat—but from the water of the Tula River, highly polluted and the city's primary water source. Tens of thousands of people living in shantytowns downriver from the city's sewage system were being infected. Once a parasite adapts to a new environment, it may easily spread. By 1980 this pathogen had found its way to Los Angeles, carried back by travelers to Mexico, immigrants, or visitors to the United States.

Diseases of Environmental Change

Urban centers emerged as a natural outgrowth of the expansion of commerce, increased industrialization, and the need for financial hubs to serve as links between commercial and industrial centers. However, the environmental and social changes of the past fifty years that have influenced the spread of disease have been more methodical and controlled. We carefully plan and build massive hydroelectric projects that result in the flooding of millions of acres, in the process creating new environments for waterborne infectious parasites. We methodically destroy millions of acres of rain forests, in the process creating new habitats to be exploited by disease vectors. We plan and build roads that bring people into areas where they have never been, thus exposing them to new pathogens. We expand habitats, consequently changing the delicate ecological balances and promoting evolution of microbes that once infected only nonhuman species to infect human beings. We knowingly dump raw sewage into our oceans and waterways, not only spreading disease worldwide but also creating a massive evolutionary medium for new pathogens to develop. In modern warfare we devastate environments in ways that past armies were incapable of doing, in the process creating opportunity for pathogens to thrive.

For example, in 1985 the Daima Dam was built on the Senegal River by the Mauritanian, Senegalese, and Malian governments. The dam made possible the irrigation of 10,000 hectares of desert soil, converting it into fields of sugarcane, potatoes, mint, and rice. As a result of agricultural expansion, a few members of a local tribe became millionaires (Platt 1996:45). But with the dam came infectious disease. Sanitation in the area is poor, and the irrigation canals, from which people drink, bathe, and wash their clothes, have become infected with strains of diarrheal bacteria. The dam also halted the flow of saltwater that once penetrated up to 200 kilometers inland. The saltwater had kept the snail population in check, but the dam created ideal conditions for an epidemic of snail-borne schistosomiasis. The first cases were detected in 1988, and by 1990, 60 percent of the population exhibited symptoms. In one village that had profited from growing mint, 91 percent of the people were infected.

Schistosomiasis is an ancient disease. Egyptian mummies have evidence of infection and the disease was common in China around 200 B.C. during a time of expanding rice cultivation. Today, it ranks second only to malaria among diseases in tropical regions. It infects farmers and fishers who wade in shallow water infected with the snails that carry the disease. It is transmitted when people defecate the larvae of the parasite, which then travels through water supplies and infects other snails and people (Platt 1996:47).

In some areas the disease is so prevalent that it goes unrecognized. Katherine A. Dettwyler (1994:46) was doing anthropological work on disease in Mali and taking urine samples; she received one from a young boy that appeared to be full of blood. The urine contained over 500 *Schistosoma* eggs per milliliter, the highest count measurable with the technique she used. When she gave him a look of consternation, he asked, "What's the matter?" "Does your urine always look like this?" she asked. "Yes," he replied, "Isn't it supposed to? Doesn't everyone's?" She later learned that in some communities the first appearance of red urine in boys was believed to be equivalent to the onset of menstruation in girls and was thought to indicate sexual maturity. In some communities celebratory rites of passage were held when boys reached this milestone.

When Brazil completed its highway through the Amazon, a new disease, *oropouche*, began to strike residents of Belém; it affected 11,000 people. It seems that when settlers cleared the forest for cacao planting, they disturbed the habitat of a midge that harbored the virus that caused the disease. Discarded cacao shells provided a new breeding ground for the insect, and the explosion of their population in association with human settlements created the opportunity for disease spread.

One reason forest, especially rain forest, destruction unleashes disease is because of the variety of species that exist in forests. A single hectare of rain forest contains more insect species than the entire New England area or all of Great Britain. When human beings destroy that habitat, it brings them into contact with insects and pathogens that are then searching for new habitats and new hosts.

Dengue is an example of how new, more deadly diseases can emerge as a consequence of environmental damage and population movement. Dengue is a virus, a cousin of the yellow fever microbe and generally spread by the female *Aedes aegypti* mosquito. In any one of its four forms dengue was not life threatening, and it had virtually disappeared by 1950 after worldwide campaigns to eradicate the carrier mosquito. But in 1953 a new variant, dengue-2, struck in Manila in the Philippines. Dengue-2, or dengue hemorrhagic fever, was far worse than any of the other forms of the disease, causing internal hemorrhaging, shock, and soaring fevers. In 1958 it hit Bangkok, Thailand, infecting 2,297 people, mostly children, and killing 240; within five years 10,367 people were infected and 694 had died.

Researchers discovered two clues to the origins of the disease: First, it was carried by *A. aegypti*; second, all of the victims had at some time been exposed to one of the milder forms of dengue. Whereas the earlier disease did no damage, the immune systems of those afflicted had created antibodies to the disease. The researchers discovered that dengue-2 had developed a remarkable method to use those antibodies to its own advantage. As mentioned earlier, when a foreign body enters the human bloodstream, antibodies attach themselves to it, largely to identify it for other parts of the immune system that will then attack and destroy it. Antibodies attached themselves to the dengue-2 virus, signaling the macrophage cells to envelop the invading microbe and destroy it. But the dengue-2 virus had developed the ability to take over the immune system's primary killer cells, not only allowing it to evade the immune system's response but also giving it access to every organ of the body, producing fevers as high as 107 degrees Fahrenheit, convulsions, shock, and death.

Dengue-2 spread through East and South Asia with ever-expanding populations of *A. aegypti* and *Aedes albopictus,* better known as the tiger mosquito, probably named for its aggressive behavior. The disease spread to the Americas, likely in ships carrying the mosquitoes. When mosquito abatement programs were cut in various countries to reduce government expenses, an opportunity was created for the disease to spread. Dengue-2 made its appearance in 1981 in Havana, Cuba, where an epidemic that raged for six months caused 340,000 illnesses and 158 deaths.

The Cuban epidemic sent shockwaves through the U.S. public health community because in 1980 two residents of Laredo, Texas, had developed dengue hemorrhagic fever. In 1982 an epidemic in New Delhi, India, sickened 20 percent of the population, and by 1990 the disease would be endemic in Latin America. To make matters worse, a shipment of used tires from Japan to Houston, Texas, for retreading contained tiger mosquitoes, creating the likelihood of this aggressive mosquito invading urban environments and outcompeting the less aggressive mosquito. Unlike *A. aegypti,* which feeds only on humans, the tiger mosquito feeds on virtually any animal, raising the possibility that it can harbor and transmit viruses from other animals.

The question is, *what led to the creation of dengue hemorrhagic fever?* Tom Monath of the Centers for Disease Control and Prevention in Atlanta, Georgia, examined historical and laboratory evidence and concluded that World War II was responsible (see Garrett 1994:257). He surmised that the massive bombings, the population movements and dislocations, and wartime disruptions of mosquito abatement programs resulted in a surge in the population of *A. aegypti*. Then rapid troop movements brought into the Philippines people who, perhaps without knowing it, had been infected by one of the existing dengue varieties. American troops who arrived may already have been to dengue-infested areas, such as Burma, Thailand, Indonesia, the Pacific Islands, and China. Thus, all four varieties of dengue, each adapted to its specific environment, were brought together in one place and rapidly passed between people and mosquitoes, creating the cycle necessary for the ultimate mutation of one variety into dengue-2. The expansion of commercial travel and possibly the Korean and Vietnam Wars created further opportunities for cross-fertilization and spread of the disease to the slums of Latin America.

By 1981, when dengue-2 hit Havana, it had become an annual feature of the urban Philippines. There, when the mosquitoes emerged in full force after every rainy season, dengue-2 arrived like clockwork, infecting tens of thousands of children and killing 15 percent of those infected. Nonexistent before World War II, by 1980 dengue-2 was one of the major childhood killers in Asia.

The kinds of connections operative in the creation of dengue hemorrhagic fever, between microbes, disease vectors such as mosquitoes, and the movement and activities of human beings, can be enormously complex. New outbreaks of cholera in the 1990s involved not only microbes, vectors, and human beings but also such diverse events as global warming, the spread of oceanic algae, breakdown of sanitation, and the eating habits of the people of Peru. Dengue-2 also provides an example of the interconnectedness of people in the creation and transmission of disease.

Much of the pollution that human beings pour into the oceans—raw sewage, fertilizers, pesticides, and other chemical waste—serves as nutrients for algae blooms, thus increasing their size and frequency. Researchers discovered in the 1970s that cholera vibrio, which they labeled El Tor, could live inside algae, taking a form that allowed it to lie in a dormant state for weeks, months, and perhaps years. It was further discovered that El Tor is immune to a whole range of antibiotics.

El Tor is common in South Asia, particularly off the coast of Bangladesh. It is believed to have been picked up in algae by a Chinese freighter, which then dumped the cholera-carrying algae off the coast of Lima, Peru. The vibrio then infected shellfish in the area. The shellfish was used in making *ceviche*, mixed raw fish and shellfish in lime juice, a national delicacy of Peru. The ocean waters carried the algae up and down the South American coast, and by the end of 1991 cholera had struck at least 336,554 people, killing 3,538. By 1993 at least 900,000 people were reported infected, and 8,000 died. Tests showed that the cholera recovered from patients was identical to that in the algae.

In 1992 a whole new strain of cholera emerged off the coast of India. Dubbed Bengal cholera, it was unaffected by the antigens developed by the immune systems of people afflicted with either classical cholera or El Tor, thus leaving everyone open to reinfection.

Scientists trying to determine the cause of the outbreaks and the reason for the emergence of new strains of cholera hypothesized that algae blooms have exploded in size and frequency, fed by nutrients from fertilizer, garbage, and fecal waste incubated in the hotter waters resulting from global warming. The expanded algae blooms become giant floating gene pools in which bacteria, viruses, algae, and terrestrial microbes from human waste and runoff float around, possibly mutating rapidly because of the increased ultraviolet radiation caused by the damage from industrial pollutants to the atmosphere. The algae spread rapidly to different parts of the world, bringing new and more deadly variants of disease (Garrett 1994:563–567).

Anne E. Platt, in *Infecting Ourselves* (1996), outlines many of the social, political, and economic activities that result in higher risks for infectious disease (see Table 8.2).

AIDS AND THE CULTURE OF CAPITALISM

We mentioned earlier that AIDS is very much the signature disease of our age. By this we mean the conditions for its development and spread were essentially created by our patterns of beliefs, attitudes, and behaviors. AIDS burst on the world in 1981, when physicians in San Francisco and New York began to encounter symptoms in young men that either had been seen previously in older men or were so rare most physicians had never seen them. They turned out to be opportunistic infections, such as rare forms of pneumonia, cancer, and other diseases that attacked bodies whose immune systems had been destroyed. The new disease was first called gay-related immunodeficiency disease (GRID) because of its early diagnosis among gay men, but when it was acknowledged to occur in heterosexual populations the name was changed in 1982 to acquired autoimmune-deficiency syndrome (AIDS). In 1983 the disease appeared in Zaire, and some European researchers thought they had unearthed cases in European hospitals as early as 1967, and possibly 1959.

The early 1980s was a turbulent time for AIDS. Researchers were competing to be the first to isolate and identify the virus. Researchers in Europe and Africa could not publish their articles in the leading medical journals because the peer review panels did not believe the disease was transmitted heterosexually and claimed the researchers had missed some other mode of transmission. The Reagan administration, which had made millions of dollars available for research in Legionnaires' disease, was reluctant to release funds for AIDS research, education, and services. Leaders of the religious right in the United States opposed using federal funds for a disease they claimed was God's judgment against immorality and corruption. Pat Robertson, a Baptist minister, founder of the Christian Broadcasting Network, and presidential candidate in 1988, claimed scientists were "frankly lying" when they said AIDS could be spread heterosexually and that condoms would prevent infection. In the meantime, AIDS continued to spread among heterosexuals, gay men, intravenous drug users, and hemophiliacs given HIV-infected transfusions (Garrett 1994:469).

As of 2003, an estimated 2.8 million people have died from AIDS since the epidemic began and the Joint United Nations Program on HIV/AIDS (UNAIDS) and the World Health Organization (WHO) estimate that there are presently 34 million to 46 million people worldwide infected with HIV/AIDS (see Table 8.3). Sub-Saharan Africa has the highest rate with 25 million to 28 million infected, or 7.5 to 8.5 percent of the population, whereas Eastern Europe and South and Southeast Asia have the fastest rate of growth. In North America there are 790,000 to 1.2 million cases of HIV. This total is heavily skewed toward the poorest segments of the population with the incidence of AIDS being 6.5 times greater for Blacks and 4.0 times greater for Hispanics than for Whites.

We now think we know the origin of AIDS, that it likely crossed over from nonhuman primates in central and west Africa sometime after World War II, infecting only a few

TABLE 8.2 Causes of Infectious Disease Emergence and Representative Disease Examples

CAUSE OF EMERGENCE	INFECTIOUS DISEASE
Changing environmental conditions	
Deforestation	Malaria, hemorrhagic fever, rabies, Lyme disease
Agriculture and irrigation	Argentine hemorrhagic fever, Japanese encephalitis, Bolivian hemorrhagic fever, schistosomiasis, influenza (pandemic)
Dam building, road building	Schistosomiasis, malaria, Rift Valley fever
Poor sanitation and hygiene	Diarrheal diseases, malaria, schistosomiasis, lymphatic filariasis, river blindness, dengue, yellow fever, cholera, Guinea worm disease, Japanese encephalitis, salmonella, hemolytic uremic syndrome, cryptosporidiosis, giardiasis
Climate change	Hanta virus, plague, malaria, schistosomiasis, other vector-borne disease
Demographic changes	
Urbanization	Yellow fever, malaria, dengue, acute respiratory illness, plague, cholera
Increased trade, travel, migration	Cholera, yellow fever, influenza, dengue, dengue hemorrhagic fever, pneumonia, HIV/AIDS, influenza
Deteriorating social conditions	
Breakdown in public health services	Measles, diphtheria, pertussis, tuberculosis, cholera, influenza, HIV/AIDS, other sexually transmitted diseases
War and civil disorder	Malaria, cholera, diphtheria, waterborne diseases
Increased sexual activity	Hepatitis B and C, HIV/AIDS, other sexually transmitted diseases
Intravenous drug use	HIV/AIDS
Overuse of antibiotics	Antibiotic-resistant malaria, tuberculosis, staphylococci, pneumococci, enterococci, gonorrhea, others
Other	
Air-conditioning systems	Legionnaires' disease
Ultra-absorbent tampons	Toxic shock syndrome
Unknown	Streptococcus Group A, ebola

From Anne E. Platt. *Infecting Ourselves: How Environmental and Social Disruption Trigger Disease.* Washington, DC: Worldwatch Institute, 1996. Reprinted by permission.

TABLE 8.3   Regional HIV/AIDS Statistics and Features, End of 2003

REGION	START OF EPIDEMIC	ADULTS AND CHILDREN INFECTED WITH HIV/AIDS	ADULT AND CHILD DEATHS FROM AIDS	NEWLY INFECTED CHILDREN AND ADULTS	ADULT PREVALENCE RATE (%)	MAIN MODE OF TRANSMISSION*
Sub-Saharan Africa	late 1970s, early 1980s	25–28 million	2.2–2.4 million	3–3.4 million	7.5–8.5	Hetero
North Africa and Middle East	late 1980s	470,000–730,000	35,000–50,000	43,000–67,000	0.2–0.4	Hetero, IDU
North America	late 1970s, early 1980s	790,000–1.2 million	12,000–18,000	36,000–54,000	0.5–0.7	MSM, IDU, hetero
Western Europe	late 1970s, early 1980s	520,000–680,000	2,600–3,400	30,000–40,000	0.3	MSM, IDU, hetero
Eastern Europe and Central Asia	early 1990s	1.2–1.8 million	23,000–37,000	180,000–280,000	0.5–0.9	IDU
Caribbean	late 1970s, early 1980s	350,000–590,000	30,000–50,000	1.9–3.1 million	1.9–3.1	Hetero, MSM
Latin America	late 1970s, early 1980s	1.3–1.9 million	49,000–70,000	120,000–180,000	0.5–0.7	MSM, IDU, hetero
East Asia and Pacific	late 1980s	700,000–1.3 million	32,000–58,000	610,000–1.1 million	0.1	IDU, hetero
South and Southeast Asia	late 1980s	4.6–8.2 million	330,000–590,000	610,000–1.1 million	0.4–0.8	Hetero, IDU
Australia and New Zealand	late 1970s, early 1980s	12,000–18,000	<100	700–1,000	0.1	MSM
TOTAL		**34–46 million**	**2.3–3.5 million**	**4.2–5.8 million**	**0.9–1.3**	

Data from UNAIDS 2003. *AIDS Epidemic Update, 2003.* http://www.unaids.org/en/Resources/Publications/
Corporate+publications/aids+epidemic+update+-+december+2003.asp.
*IDU = intravenous drug users, MSM = males who have sex with males, hetero = heterosexual transmission

people until the late 1970s, when it made its breakthrough worldwide. But there are many questions we need to explore to understand the effects of human culture on the disease. For example, *what features of global culture influenced the spread of the disease? What features of our culture determined the people most at risk for AIDS? How did our culture influence the way people choose to react to the epidemic and those affected by it?*

How Did the Disease Spread?

AIDS reveals the extent to which we are interconnected in global space. We live in a world, as geographer Peter Gould (1993:66–69) noted, in which New York is closer to San Fran-

Advertisements for sex tours, such as this one for Thailand, attract tourists from Europe, North America, and other parts of Asia and create fertile breeding grounds for the AIDS virus and other sexually transmitted diseases.

cisco than it is to towns 200 miles away; in which Los Angeles is closer to Miami and Houston than it is to towns in Nevada; in which Kinshasa, Zaire, is closer to Paris than to villages in the center of the country. Gould meant by this that people located at the hubs of the capitalist world system, those cities connected by rapid air travel, are more likely to come into contact with each other than they are with people located spatially much closer to them. Viewed another way, patterns of contact are characterized by what Gould called "hierarchical diffusion" rather than "spatially contiguous diffusion." In the hierarchical diffusion that characterizes AIDS, or "AIDS space," as Gould called it, the disease jumps from travel hub to travel hub.

This is not the first time global space has been redefined by revolutions in trade and travel. In the earlier eras of sea travel seaports became economic hubs as well as the major points of distribution for disease. Today, with rapid air travel, economic centers such as Tokyo, New York, Paris, Jakarta, San Francisco, London, São Paulo, Bombay, Johannesburg, and Moscow form the geographic center of the world system and, as a consequence, the epicenters of the spread of AIDS.

With the exception of infected blood supplies, AIDS has to be carried from place to place by people and transmitted directly. There is no vector involved in AIDS as in plague, malaria, or dengue. But human travel provides an effective means of transmission. Therefore, to understand the spread of AIDS, we need to ask why in the culture of capitalism do people travel? Generally, they travel for one of four reasons: tourism, business, labor migration, and war, all of which have had a major role in the spread and distribution of AIDS.

Tourism is essentially a product of industrial capitalism of the nineteenth century. Although the wealthy of Europe had their country estates and cottages for centuries, travel and tourism were relatively new phenomena for the emerging middle class (Hobsbawm 1975:203). Made possible by the development of steamboats and railways, the tourist industry grew throughout the nineteenth and early twentieth centuries. For the British middle class, holiday travel became a serious enterprise in the 1860s and 1870s; this transformed the British coastlines with promenades and piers. In Europe mountain resorts, such as Biarritz, were becoming fashionable. Tours through Europe became popular, creating an industry and a form of travel that was probably unique. For the poor, day trips dominated; American resorts such as Coney Island in New York became popular for new immigrants to the United States. In the twentieth century tourism evolved into a major industry, and few people, certainly in the core, have not at one time or another been tourists. Tourism is one of the world's largest industries with tremendous annual growth rates. The industry's gains grew to $439 billion in 1998 (Pera and McLaren 1999).

Tourism has always been associated with disease, as any traveler can tell you who has sampled food and water laden with bacteria to which his or her system had no resistance. It is likely that such perils have confronted travelers for centuries. But in the age of AIDS it is not only the traveler who is at risk but also the people in the host country.

We have no figures on the number of people who have contracted AIDS as a consequence of tourist travel, but researchers suggest that it has had a major impact on at least two countries hardest hit by the epidemic, Haiti and Thailand. One reason for their susceptibility is that both were targeted for "sex tours."

Anthropologist and physician Paul Farmer (1992) suggested that the history of HIV/AIDS in Haiti is linked to its history as a tourist destination. In the 1970s, Haiti, the poorest country in the Western Hemisphere, became a major tourist attraction with the closing of Cuba in 1959 to American tourists. Tourist visits to Haiti increased to 100,000 per year by 1970 and 143,538 by 1979. (Later, the tourist industry was a casualty of the Haitian AIDS epidemic: Tourist visits dropped to 75,000 in the winter of 1981–1982 and under 10,000 the following winter.)

Tourism in Haiti brought with it an increase in institutionalized prostitution. Poverty and 60 to 80 percent unemployment rates made prostitution for males and females one of the only economic alternatives available. The country, particularly the Carrefour area of the capital city Port-au-Prince, gained a reputation for cheap sex. Travel guides published for homosexual men recommended Haiti to tourists.

Whether AIDS was brought to Haiti by American tourists, as some researchers suggest, or in some other fashion is a matter of debate, but it is clear that tourism accelerated the spread of the disease among Haitians and, probably, among tourists. By the late 1980s the rate of HIV in hotel workers catering to tourists was 12 percent, and Haiti had one of the highest rates of infection in the world. But even when Haitian workers became aware of AIDS, they seemed to treat it as just an "occupational hazard" (Farmer 1992:145).

In Thailand, also, tourism played a major role in the spread of AIDS. HIV/AIDS was relatively late in arriving in Asia, with the first recorded death in 1984, a gay man who had spent time in the United States. By 1987 the rate climbed in months from 15 percent to 43 percent among intravenous drugs users. The group hit hardest by AIDS was the commercial sex workers. Among Chiang Mai prostitutes the rate of infection went from 0.04 percent in 1989 to 70 percent twenty months later (Garrett 1994:489).

Thailand had for years an active trade in both drugs and prostitution, trades that accelerated when Thailand became a major rest and recreation zone for American military personnel during the Vietnam War. Both drugs and prostitution were, and continue to be, major sources of foreign exchange for Thailand's economy. By 1990, Thailand was attracting 5.3 million tourists a year, with a high proportion of single men from Malaysia, Japan, and Taiwan and with special "sex tours" arriving in Bangkok from Japan, the Middle East, and Europe, particularly Germany. As a consequence of the growth in the sex industry, there are

500,000 to 800,000 prostitutes representing some 10 percent of the female population between the ages of fifteen and twenty-four. In some areas of Bangkok in the early 1990s there was an AIDS infection rate of 90 percent.

Probably because of the economic importance of the sex industry, particularly for attracting tourists, government authorities in Thailand were slow to respond to the threatened epidemic. As cases began to increase in 1987, the government decided not to launch an anti-AIDS campaign for fear of "inciting panic." By 1989, 0.5 percent of all pregnant women were HIV-seropositive, with some northern provinces reporting rates of 3 percent. In 1991 the government reevaluated its policy and noted again that they did not want to create panic. A Bangkok newspaper reported that HIV/AIDS was spread only by anal sex and intravenous drug use, when in fact there were forty times more heterosexual cases than homosexual cases reported. The World Health Organization estimated that, by 1992, 450,000 people in Thailand were infected.

Another form of travel that characterizes the capitalist culture is labor migration. At least since the increase in slave trade in the seventeenth and eighteenth centuries, the world economy has required massive shifts of laborers from one area to another. Although it is difficult to determine exactly the extent of the worldwide transmission of AIDS by migrating workers, there is considerable evidence that this type of travel was a major cause of AIDS transmission in Africa. Male workers travel from rural areas to urban areas in search of work, sometimes visiting prostitutes, whose infection rate in some areas approaches 90 percent, and sometimes bringing the disease back to their rural villages.

Commercial and business travel were also instrumental in the spread of AIDS. The routes of infection in Africa travel along well-traveled truck and commercial transportation routes. The north–south alignment of AIDS starts at Djibouti at the mouth of the Red Sea, the port city and railway terminal for the city of Addis Ababa, the capital of Ethiopia, to which goods, and AIDS, flow. In 1991 some 50 to 60 percent of prostitutes and 1 percent of the general population were reported infected with HIV. In the Sudan 80 percent of the "bar girls" were seropositive for HIV-1. From Uganda to Mozambique, samples of truck drivers indicate that 30 to 80 percent are infected. Estimates are that Tanzania has 1.4 million infected people of a total population of 18 million, Zimbabwe has 1.5 million, and Kenya 1.6 million. The highway between Malawi and Durban, South Africa, is known as the "Highway of Death," truckers having an infection rate of 90 percent (Gould 1993:75).

Patterns of AIDS distribution seem to follow commercial routes in North America as well. Paul Farmer (1992:149) noted that the incidence of AIDS in the Caribbean correlates with the degree to which a country is economically integrated into the "West Atlantic system." Excluding Puerto Rico because it is not an independent country, the countries with the highest rates of AIDS—the Dominican Republic, the Bahamas, Trinidad/Tobago, Mexico, and Haiti—are also the countries most dependent on trade with the United States and most linked to the American economy. The country with the highest rates of AIDS—Haiti—was most dependent on U.S. exports.

Finally, the movement of soldiers and refugees precipitated by conflict played a role in the spread of AIDS. Researchers speculating about the origins of AIDS and the factors that may have contributed to its breakout in central and East Africa have concluded that something dramatic must have happened around 1975 to cause the emergence of the epidemic.

The period of 1970 to 1975 was characterized by guerrilla warfare, civil war, tribal conflicts, mass refugee migrations, and striking dictatorial atrocities. Laurie Garrett suggested that such social upheaval may have affected the course of AIDS both directly and indirectly. For example, most African conflict was characterized by rival forces trying to cripple each other economically, politically, socially, spiritually, and militarily. In such conflicts, civilian casualties are high. In any number of military campaigns of the past two to three decades in central Africa, rape was used (as it was in Bosnia) systematically to terrorize and dominate the enemy. Some armies have tested up to 50 percent HIV–positive. Other human activities resulting from social disruption, including increased multiple-partner sexual activity, famine and malnutrition that further stressed immune systems, large-scale migrations and concentrations of people in refugee camps, increased prostitution, and destruction of health care services, could have further spread the disease (Garrett 1994:367–368).

Who Gets Infected with AIDS?

Rene Dubos (1968) wrote in the 1950s and 1960s of the special vulnerability of the poor to infections; malnutrition, substandard housing, dense population, and lack of access to health care all promote the spread of infectious disease. Paul Farmer in *Infections and Inequality* (1999) documents the link between economic inequality and susceptibility to infectious disease. Certainly poverty played a role in the spread of tuberculosis, cholera, and syphilis. But AIDS has affected not only the economically marginalized but also those who are socially and politically marginalized—homosexuals, women, and children.

   Public and governmental responses to the AIDS epidemic, especially in the United States, was greatly influenced by the mistaken assumption that it was a disease of homosexual men, in spite of the fact that there was clear evidence of heterosexual transmission in the United States, Europe, and particularly Africa, where it was almost exclusively transmitted by heterosexual relations. We may never know to what extent the association of the disease with a socially marginalized portion of American society delayed research and education efforts, but it is clear that it didn't help.

   It is also clear that the poor, globally and in the United States, have been the most frequent victims of the disease. Africa, the poorest area of the world, has by far the highest incidence of AIDS, whereas Eastern Europe, economically devastated with the collapse of socialist economies and cutbacks in health services, has the highest rate of growth in HIV/AIDS. Poor countries in other areas of the world are the others most affected. For a particularly apt illustration of a poor and socially marginalized country that suffers disproportionately with AIDS, let's return to Haiti.

   Haiti itself is very much a creation of the capitalist world system. In the sixteenth and seventeenth centuries the indigenous population (the Taino) were exterminated and the country resettled with African slaves ruled by a European elite. Haiti passed from Spain to France in 1697 and was renamed Saint-Dominique. In 1804 a slave revolt led by Toussaint L'Ouverture succeeded in defeating the French, establishing the country of Haiti, the first, as Paul Farmer referred to it, of the Third World countries.

   The new country found itself in a world hostile to the idea of self-governing Blacks, a nightmare to every country in which slavery endured, particularly the United States. Every effort was made to undermine Black rule in Haiti. The French demanded that Haiti compen-

Women, particularly in Africa, comprise the majority of AIDS victims.

sate planters for the loss of land, and periodically in the nineteenth century European gun-
boats would appear in Haitian ports demanding compensation. By 1900, 80 percent of
national revenue was going to pay off international debts, and by the late 1920s Haiti was
being advertised in *Financial America* as a place where "easily directed" Haitian labor
could be had for twenty cents per day, as opposed to three dollars per day in Panama.

American domination has continued throughout the twentieth century, as Haiti has
lived with a series of despotic rulers supported by the United States. This history left Haiti
in 1983 with an annual per capita income of $315 overall and $100 in the countryside. The
agricultural situation was so bad that Haiti was a net importer of food, even sugar. Even
when Haiti had promise as a recreational playground for other North Americans, the tourist industry collapsed because of Haiti's reputation as the originator of AIDS. There were
few avenues out of poverty in Haiti. The 60 percent unemployment rate combined with the
country's dependence on the United States set the stage for what Farmer (1992:189–190)
called the "West Atlantic pandemic."

AIDS is not only a marker of poverty, it is becoming a marker of gender and age as
well. We saw in our discussion of famine and hunger that women and children are particularly at risk. In the instance of AIDS, women worldwide represent the majority of all reported
cases. The fact that women, who were at the fringe of the epidemic in the mid-1980s, have
frequently become victims reflects the role of women in global capitalist culture. Women
seem to become infected at younger ages; in many countries 60 percent of new AIDS infections are among women between the ages of fifteen and twenty-four; in surveys of several

African and Asian countries, women younger than twenty-five account for 30 percent of new AIDS cases, compared to 15 percent for men younger than twenty-five.

Women contract the disease largely through heterosexual intercourse; many of these are among women who are monogamous but have male partners who are not. This is in part because of the sexual subordination of women in many countries where men initiate sexual relations and women, especially wives, have little say. The attitudes toward women and sex in many countries inhibits conversation about sexual matters and virtually prohibits AIDS educational campaigns directed toward women. Furthermore, education is hampered by the higher illiteracy rates among women in many countries. Even in countries with well-developed campaigns to educate women about the risk of AIDS, men still often resist condom use because of decreased sensitivity, ignorance about how to use them, or fear that their use will cause sterility.

Women also contract the disease through prostitution, itself a reflection of the limited options available to women, especially in poor countries. As Laurie Garrett (1994:368) said about AIDS and prostitution in Uganda,

> [a]s a business, prostitution was second only to the black market. For most women there were only two choices in life: have babies and grow food without assistance from men, livestock, or machinery, or exchange sex for money at black-market rates.

Finally, the more women are infected with AIDS, the more likely children will be infected. Children are at risk of acquiring the disease at birth. AIDS can be transmitted by infected hypodermic needles; yet, many countries that depend on intravenous drugs are too poor to afford new needles. In some African countries needles are reused. Intravenous transmission of AIDS to children is not solely a problem of the periphery. In Russia, the collapse of communism and the social and economic chaos that followed virtually destroyed the country's health care system. Syringes were unavailable, and medical personnel, especially in rural areas, were forced to use the same syringes again and again, up to 400 times in some cases. In 1988 AIDS emerged in Elistya, capital of the Kalmyk Republic on the Caspian Sea. A baby had been infected by its mother. The baby was treated by staff who used the same syringes to draw blood samples and administer drugs to all the babies in the hospital's nursery for three months; HIV was unknowingly injected into all the babies on the ward and some of their mothers (Garrett 1994:501).

Socially marginalized members of the capitalist world system face another danger: Once infected with HIV, they are the ones least likely to receive treatment or to receive information to enable them to take measures to avoid the onset of AIDS. As AIDS researcher Renée Sabatier (cited Garrett 1994:475) noted in reference to AIDS education campaigns,

> I think there is a very real danger that we're going to end up as a [world] society divided between those who were able to inform themselves first and those who were informed late. Those who have access to information and health care, and those who don't. Those who are able to change, and those who aren't. I think there is a real danger of half of us turning into AIDS voyeurs, standing around watching others die.

The announcement in the summer of 1996 of a new drug treatment that restores the body's immune system and holds the AIDS virus at bay is a further development in the ghettoization of AIDS. Although the announcement was greeted with great enthusiasm, and the use of the drug has cut mortality rates in the United States by 75 percent, the treatment costs at least $10,000 to 20,000 per year and is, therefore, beyond the reach of the world's poor. When South Africa moved to make generic versions of HIV/AIDS drugs, or proposed importing the drugs from countries with the lowest prices, actions that could have helped cut the costs 50 to 90 percent, the United States raised objections and drug companies sued, although, under heavy public pressure, withdrew the threats. Drugs, however, remain largely unavailable to the poor. Of the 1 million people in Malawi who are HIV positive, only 30 are on the new drug therapy (Finkel 2000).

Who Gets Blamed?

We saw the phenomenon of blaming the victim when we examined population growth, poverty, hunger, and environmental degradation. Problems generated by core exploitation of the periphery are blamed on the periphery itself. However, nowhere is the phenomenon of blaming the victim more clearly illustrated than in the case of HIV/AIDS, and nowhere was that more clear than in the case of Haiti. When the AIDS epidemic was identified in the early 1980s, Haitians with AIDS were a "wild card": they didn't fit the categories of homosexuals, hemophiliacs, and heroin users. So they were added as a whole category, thus completing the early four-H club (homosexuals, hemophiliacs, heroin users, and Haitians). But this was clearly racist: There was no reason, based on some thirty-four cases, to place all Haitians in a risk group. This would be analogous to claiming that all San Franciscans or all New Yorkers were at special risk to contract and spread the disease. Risk designation was akin to being labeled a carrier. Then, in a leap that surprised few Haitians, AIDS was said to have originated in Haiti.

Bruce Chabner of the National Cancer Institute was quoted in 1982 as saying, "Homosexuals in New York take vacations in Haiti, and we suspect that this may be an epidemic Haitian virus that was brought back to the homosexual population in the United States" (cited Farmer 1992: 201). This epidemic of blame led to widespread discrimination against Haitians in job hiring and a rapid decline in the Haitian tourist industry.

The Haitian government was angry with the Centers for Disease Control (CDC) because, even when it became evident that the rate of infection was higher in other Caribbean Islands and most U.S. cities, the CDC refused to abandoned the designation of Haitians as a high-risk group. In 1985 the CDC finally removed the designation but without comment, refusing to admit it made an error. Then in 1990, the FDA ruled that Haitians could not donate blood. It was an absurd ruling; as one Boston newspaper editorial pointed out, if the FDA was consistent it would have banned donations from all San Franciscans, New Yorkers, Bostonians, and emigrants from other Caribbean Islands, some of whom had rates of AIDS/HIV as much as ten times greater than Haiti's (see Farmer 1992; 220).

Why was Haiti singled out? Largely, according to Paul Farmer, because the U.S. folk model of Haitians included images of superstitious natives, Blacks, immigrants, and the like that symbolized the stigma associated with AIDS. The model was driven to some extent by the media. The *New York Times* wrote that "Haitian voodooists may be unsuspectingly infected with AIDS by ingestion, inhalation, or dermal contact with contaminated ritual substances, as well as by sexual activity" (cited Farmer 1992:3). This view was furthered by the medical community. Jeffrey Viera, senior author of the paper that put Haitians at risk, blamed the media for stigmatizing Haitians, but he himself made reference to voodoo rituals, the drinking of menstrual blood, and the like. An article in the *Journal of the American Medical Association* entitled "Night of the Living Dead" considered these voodoo origin theories, asking whether necromantic zombies transmit HIV/AIDS (Farmer 1992:3). Blaming Haiti for AIDS was a classic case of blaming the victim.

The view from the periphery concerning the origins of AIDS was quite different than the view from the core. As researchers focused on Africa as the origin of the disease, African officials became sensitive to what they saw as a Western campaign to blame their countries for the epidemic. One result was official government denials that there was any AIDS in African countries, even after the epidemic had clearly become established. One African health minister was fired after admitting to international health agencies that AIDS was present in his country. Not surprisingly, conspiracy theories abounded. One theory was that the American CIA had introduced the disease; another, popular also in core countries, was that AIDS was the result of American germ warfare experiments gone awry.

Haitians saw AIDS as a disease visited on them by resentful Americans. As one Haitian school teacher (cited Farmer 1992:232) put it, "The Americans have always resented Haiti, ever since 1804. Being strong, they can punish us, humiliate us. The AIDS thing was a perfect tool."

Haitian teenagers in the United States, when asked if they thought the United States did what they did on purpose, almost universally said yes. Others said that AIDS was created in U.S. laboratories.

Paul Farmer (1992:58), in *AIDS and Accusation,* concluded that questions asked by Haitians and Americans such as

> Is AIDS a product of North American imperialism? Can one person send an AIDS death to another through sorcery? Are Haitians a special AIDS risk group? Are "boat people" disease-ridden and a risk to the health of U.S. citizens?…underscore several of the West Atlantic pandemic's central dynamics—blame, search for accountability, accusation, and racism—that have shaped both responses to AIDS and the epidemiology of a new virus.

CONCLUSION

The disease factors that we examined in this chapter have practical consequences. For example, knowledge of the effects of culturally defined human behavior can help us predict as well as treat disease. Might more careful application of this principle have made a difference? Could we have anticipated the emergence of AIDS, as many medical anthropologists once posited? Would we have let multidrug-resistant tuberculosis get out of hand? Would we have allowed so many antibiotic-resistant strains of disease to develop or relied so much on antibiotics? Would drug-resistant malaria be out of control? Would new diseases such as Lyme disease spread so quickly?

Even if we were to predict, as some scientists did, the dangers of overuse of antibiotics and other things, could we really have done something about it? Even knowing the dangers of AIDS, the U.S. government moved slowly in releasing research funds. Even when it was known that anal sex was responsible for AIDS, many in the homosexual community refused to heed advice for safe sex, believing AIDS was simply a tactic to discredit their lifestyles.

We continue to create "disease sinks," populations of poor and marginalized people among whom infectious pathogens thrive and who may serve as breeding grounds for new diseases. If there was some omnipotent microbe responsible for the survival and spread of all infectious pathogens, it could hardly improve on the actions of human beings in the culture of capitalism whose cumulative behavioral choices relegate some of their numbers to these sinks.

The lesson is that although we must be aware of how our behavior puts us in danger of contracting disease, we must also be aware of the factors that promote adoption or rejection of therapeutic regimes necessary to lower our risk of becoming ill, cure us, or inhibit the creation of new and more deadly strains of disease. If biologist Paul Ewald is correct and diseases become more lethal the more easily they are spread, then given the increase in travel, the increase in the number of poor, the cutback of medical and public health services for structural adjustment programs, the ecological destruction of habitats such as rain forests, and the emergence of drug-resistant strains of new and old killers, we are truly on the verge of a pandemic on a scale of that which struck the peoples of North and South America in the sixteenth and seventeenth centuries.

What can be done? That is difficult to say, but it seems that political, religious, and social associations that can marshal forces against largely imaginary social, political, and religious enemies certainly could rally populations to cope with the pathogens that threaten to overwhelm us.

■ ■ ■ ■ ■

CHAPTER NINE

INDIGENOUS GROUPS
AND ETHNIC CONFLICT

*At the present time indigenous societies that believe it is immoral not to share
with one's kin or with those less fortunate than oneself are...considered
backward, for this surely hampers capital accumulation and therefore
"progress" as the modern world defines it.*
—David Maybury-Lewis, *Indigenous Peoples, Ethnic Groups, and the State*

*Official statements frequently justify the extension of government control over
tribal populations as an effort to bring them peace, health, happiness, and
other benefits of civilization.... But, undoubtedly, the extension of government
control was directly related to protecting the economic interests of
nonindigenous peoples moving into formerly exclusive tribal areas.*
—John Bodley, *Victims of Progress*

There is a museum exhibit in Jakarta, Indonesia, of a Javanese wedding; the guests are arranged around the bride and groom, each dressed to represent a different Indonesian ethnic group, of which there are hundreds. The exhibit is reminiscent of an early nineteenth-century painting we mentioned earlier by the British painter Sir David Wilkie, *Chelsea Pensioners Reading the Gazette of the Battle of Waterloo,* in which all the various groups that made up the British nation-state and empire—Welsh, Scottish, Irish, Black, and so on—are depicted together reading of Wellington's victory over Napoleon. Indonesia is one of the most culturally diverse countries in the world. It is also one of the most officially tolerant toward ethnic diversity. Ethnic tolerance is incorporated into education programs and "hate speech" is a crime. But it is a tolerance with definite limits. Java is the dominant island in Indonesia, and the museum exhibit suggests, said Anna Lowenhaupt Tsing (1993:24), that minority groups are "invited" into the nation, but only as long as they bow to Javanese standards.

One of the casualties of the expansion of the culture of capitalism is cultural diversity. As noted in Chapter 4, one of the functions of the nation-state is to integrate, peacefully if possible, violently if necessary, the diverse peoples within its borders into a common culture.

At best, minority cultures are integrated into the larger culture in superficial ways—dress, art, dance, music, and food are maintained and represented as the culture itself. At worst, however, policies of the nation-state may lead to ethnocide, the destruction of culture, or, in more extreme instances, genocide, the destruction of a people.

The dilemma of minority groups in the modern nation-state is particularly evident in Indonesia because it officially recognizes and celebrates diversity, but this does not stop the nation-state from systematically destroying the culture of indigenous peoples. Anna Lowenhaupt Tsing, in her book *In the Realm of the Diamond Queen* (1993), described the fate of the Meratus Dyak, who subsist on swidden agriculture and gathering and hunting, and, although relatively isolated in the Meratus mountains, frequently trade with other groups. Their culture requires that they frequently move to establish new garden plots. Individuals also travel to maintain political contact with other Meratus groups, travel being a source of prestige.

According to Tsing (1993:41), however, the Indonesian government sees the Meratus as uncivilized, stuck in a timeless, archaic condition outside modern history. Furthermore, the government attributes their condition to their mobility and travel across the forest landscape. From the state's perspective, Meratus mobility constitutes "seminomadism" and labels them as runaways from state discipline and a threat to national security. For the Meratus, however, mobility is a sign of personal autonomy.

Although Indonesia officially recognizes and celebrates cultural diversity, the dominant culture is still Javanese, represented here in the wedding of the son of Indonesian ex-President Suharto (on the far left), Hutomo "Tommy" Mandala Putra (third from left) and his bride, Ardhia "Tata" Pramesti Rigita Cahyani (fourth from left).

In Indonesia, there are more than 1.5 million members of what the government calls "isolated populations." Most, like the Meratus, live in small, scattered mountain settlements. To transform these societies into forms acceptable to the Indonesian government, they established the Management of Isolated Populations, a program that operates, to quote one official document, to guide "the direction of their social, economic, cultural and religious arrangements in accord with the norms that operate for the Indonesian people" (Tsing 1993:92). To meet the goals of the project the government devised various strategies that amount largely to attempts to discipline these populations and bring them under government control. One strategy is resettlement. The government builds clustered housing and moves isolated populations to them. The state justifies this housing by saying it is more modern, but in fact it makes everyone visible, keeps them in one place, enables government control, and in some cases creates settlements designed specifically for military security. The Meratus quickly caught on to the government's game and built their villages with clustered housing so they would "look good if the government comes to visit" (Tsing 1993:93).

The government also initiated nutrition programs to reorganize the eating habits of isolated populations. The Meratus were given a demonstration in which locally unavailable meats and vegetables were prepared "the right way." The Meratus were considered unordered in their eating habits; as one village head explained: "[Indonesians] drink in the morning," referring to the typical morning diet of coffee or tea and a pastry, "and then have two meals during the day. We [Meratus] sometimes eat five times a day and sometimes once a day. It's not ordered" (cited Tsing 1993:93). But eating habits are dictated by work schedules, and in farming or hunting communities one can eat at very different times. For government planners even the way food is prepared is supposed to follow national standards; one government official complained that the Meratus butchered a chicken but cooked it without sour spices or chili peppers. To please government authorities the Meratus leaders now see to it that the chickens are cooked "properly when authorities visit."

The government also exercised control over isolated populations by introducing family planning programs. Once again, there was a distinct difference in how the government saw the program and how the Meratus viewed it. The program was essentially an attempt by the nation-state to discipline the population into following state-mandated views of family form and reproductive practices. In the early 1980s the state began a program to encourage women to use IUDs or take birth control pills. To advance the program the government encouraged a local male leader, Pa'an Tinito, to enroll women in the program. He signed up women, but it became apparent that they had little idea of what the program was about and expressed shock when Tinito explained to the men the purpose of contraception. The men were shocked; how could the government possibly want them to limit the size of their population? Weren't communities already too small and weak? The program was ridiculous and there must be some mistake. Pa'an Tinito responded that the government only wanted a list of women; nothing was said about limiting reproduction. When the supply of oral contraceptives arrived some months later, Pa'an Tinito brought them back to his house and hung them in the rafters, where they stayed (Tsing 1993:109).

In developing relocation, nutrition, and family planning programs, the nation-state was, in effect, imposing standards of social structure and family authority. There should be a fixed and stable "village" consisting of individual families, each with a family "head," generally a man. For the government, to get to women one must go through men. But this is not the way the Meratus were organized, nor was it the way the Meratus saw the situation. Their view of the world differed significantly from that of the nation-state in which they are subjects. The dilemma faced by the Meratus, as well as other indigenous and ethnic groups, is whether one can be simultaneously outside and inside the nation-state. As Tsing (1993:26) put it,

> Marginals stand outside the state by tying themselves to it; they constitute the state locally by fleeing from it. As culturally "different" subjects they can never be citizens; as culturally different "subjects," they can never escape citizenship.

However, whereas nation-states have systematically destroyed the culture of indigenous peoples, there has been, at the same time, growing divisions among ethnic groups. This problem is most severe in instances where, for one reason or another, one ethnic group enjoys an economic advantage over another. In some instances, as we'll see, the result is genocidal violence.

In this chapter we examine the dilemma of cultural and ethnic divisions in the nation-state. We need to ask, *why were indigenous cultures destroyed and what is likely to be the fate of the indigenous cultures that remain in the world? And what is the cause of ethnic conflict and attempted genocides?*

THE FATE OF INDIGENOUS PEOPLES

Who are indigenous or tribal peoples? They certainly include the aboriginal peoples of Australia, the Native Americans of North, South, and Central America, and the peoples of most of the African continent. At the second general assembly of the World Council of Indigenous Peoples, indigenous peoples were defined as follows (Bodley 1990:153):

> Indigenous people shall be people living in countries which have populations composed of different ethnic or racial groups who are descendants of the earliest populations which survive in the area, and who do not, as a group, control the national government of the countries within which they live.

The difficulty with this definition, said David Maybury-Lewis (1997:7), is that it assumes that should indigenous people gain control of the government they would no longer be indigenous; however, it is clear they are native to the countries they inhabit and that they claim they were there first and have rights of prior occupancy to their lands. They also have been conquered by peoples racially, ethnically, or culturally different from themselves; they generally maintain their own language and, most importantly, "are marginal to or dominated by the states that claim jurisdiction over them." That is, indigenous peoples are defined largely by their relationship to the state. Maybury-Lewis (1997:55) concluded that

> Many people are stigmatized as "tribal"…because they reject the authority of the state and do not wish to adopt the culture of the mainstream population that the state represents. They are in fact stigmatized as being "tribal" because they insist on being marginal.

Maybury-Lewis estimated that approximately 5 percent of the world's population fit this description of indigenous peoples; these are the descendants of peoples who have been marginalized in the global capitalist economy.

One of the problems faced by indigenous peoples, as we saw with the Meratus, is that their cultures often conflict with the culture of capitalism. Consequently, the first question we need to explore is, *how is the culture of indigenous peoples incompatible with the culture of capitalism?*

Some Characteristics of Indigenous Peoples

The cultures of indigenous peoples are vulnerable to destruction from capitalist expansion partly because their way of life differs so significantly from that in the culture of capitalism. Although there are significant differences among these cultures, they do tend to share certain characteristics. For example, they tend to be mobile; they may be nomads who threaten state integrity by traversing international boundaries or shifting agriculturists who require large tracts of land or whose frequent movements make them difficult to control.

A second characteristic of small-scale indigenous societies, and one that is quickly undermined by capitalist culture, is their communal ownership of valuable resources, particularly land. Communality creates all kinds of problems in the culture of capitalism. For example, communally held land is not readily sold or purchased, requiring group consensus. Financial institutions cannot use communally held land as collateral for individuals' debts because it cannot be repossessed. Furthermore, contrary to some writers' view (see Hardin 1968; Hardin and Baden 1977), communally held lands tend to be more subject to conservation measures and less subject to exploitation for short-term financial gain. Finally, communal resources and discoveries that are not legally incorporated cannot be protected from capitalist exploitation. For example, the Urueu-Wau-Wau peoples of the Amazon developed from plant extracts an anticoagulant that Merck Pharmaceuticals "discovered" and is attempting to develop, yet no benefits accrue to the Urueu-Wau-Wau, who are threatened with extinction. Thus, as Darrell Posey (1996:7) noted, traditional and communal knowledge that would be recognized as property if held by an individual or a legally designated "natural person," such as a corporation, is deemed in the culture of capitalism to be free for the taking.

A third characteristic of small-scale indigenous groups that is incompatible with capitalist culture is kinship-based social structure. In small-scale societies most relationships are defined by a person's kin links with others, and the primary social unit tends to be the extended family. The large network of relations that each person can call on for help promotes the sharing of resources and reduces the need to consume and to work to make money. The small, socially isolated nature of family units such as the nuclear family make them more susceptible to state control and discipline. As we shall see, one of the first features of indigenous societies to come under attack is the pattern of kinship relations. This does not mean kinship cannot be used as a basis for control and accumulation of capital; early business enterprises were family based, as noted in Chapter 3, and small family businesses still thrive. Yet, perhaps because of the need for a mobile and socially unattached labor force, extended family units do not do well in the culture of capitalism.

Fourth, most small-scale indigenous societies tend to be relatively egalitarian. As John Bodley (1990:4) noted, equality in social relations reduces the incentive and need to consume because people have far less need to use material possessions to mark their status. Furthermore, nation-states require a political hierarchy to govern effectively. Without a recognized local leader with the power to make decisions, who, for example, will collect the taxes? Who will enforce government directives? Who will ensure that the laws of the nation-state are enforced? As we shall see, one of the first things that nation-states do to control indigenous peoples is to impose a new pattern of authority.

Finally, and perhaps most importantly, indigenous peoples tend to control resources or occupy land desired by members of the capitalist nation-state or the nation-state itself. Thus, as John Bodley (1990:4) wrote,

> The struggle between tribes and states has been over conflicting systems of resources management and internal social organization. Tribes represent small-scale, classless societies, with decentralized, communal, long-term resource management strategies, whereas states are class-based societies, with centralized management systems that extract resources for the short-term profit of special interest groups. Understandably, then, the political conquest of tribal areas often brings rapid environmental deterioration and may impoverish tribal peoples.

The Process of Ethnocide

In *Victims of Progress,* Bodley described the various ways nation-states acted to transfer the rights of resources from indigenous peoples to settlers wishing to exploit the resources for themselves. The process occurs in stages, generally beginning with the establishment of a frontier situation and advancing through military intervention, the extension of government control, and the gradual destruction of indigenous culture through land takeovers, cultural modification, and economic development. Bodley's analysis provides insight into why indigenous peoples have disappeared and gives ample evidence that their "integration" into the modern world was neither voluntary nor beneficial to them.

The Frontier Situation.   Often the destruction of an indigenous culture begins with the establishment of a frontier, an area perceived to be abundant in natural resources that can be easily exploited but seems not to be controlled by a nation-state. Prior ownership rights and interests of indigenous peoples are considered irrelevant by both the nation-state and by invading settlers. For example, in 1909 the London magazine *Truth* published the account of a young American engineer, Walter Hardenburg, describing the brutality of the managers of a British- and Peruvian-owned rubber company in the Putumayo River region separating Peru and Colombia (see Taussig 1987). The article, which described the enslavement, torture, and killing of Indian rubber gatherers, caused a sensation and led the British government to send Roger Casement, then a consular representative in Rio de Janeiro, Brazil, to investigate the charges. Casement had already written a report describing the horrors inflicted by rubber traders on native workers in the Congo, horrors depicted in Joseph Conrad's fictional account, *Heart of Darkness.*

In his report to Sir Edward Grey, head of the British Foreign Service, Casement described again and again the horrors inflicted on the indigenous peoples of the Putumayo region, accounts that he collected from Black workers recruited by the rubber companies from Barbados, who themselves, under threat of death, had inflicted the horrors. For example, he wrote to Grey of the fate of Indians who did not fill the quota of rubber allotted to them (cited Taussig 1987:35):

> The Indian is so humble, that as soon as he sees that the needle of the scale does not mark the ten kilos, he himself stretches out his hands and throws himself on the ground to receive the punishment. Then the chief [of the rubber station] or a subordinate advances, bends down, takes the Indian by his hair, strikes him, raises his head, drops it face downwards on the ground, and, after the face is beaten and kicked and covered with blood, the Indian is scourged. This is when they are treated best, for often they cut them to pieces with machetes.

Casement said that 90 percent of the Indians he saw carried scars from floggings. He described other ways the company managers disciplined and controlled their Indian workers, including deliberately starving them, burning alive those who tried to run away, killing children, and inflicting virtually every form of torture imaginable. Casement's report became the centerpiece of a British House of Commons Select Committee called to investigate the charges against British-owned rubber companies operating in the Putumayo region. Yet virtually nothing was done to change the situation, partly because the British could not assert political control over the region; in fact, one of the most brutal of the company managers later became a head of state.

The kinds of frontier situations described by Hardenburg and Casement almost a century ago, common in most areas of the periphery, still exist today. For example, consider what is happening to the Yanomami Indians of Brazil. Yanomami is the name given the Indians who live along the border between Brazil and Venezuela; in 1980 there were 10,000 Yanomami. They were protected somewhat by their isolation until the 1970s, when the Brazilian military government built a road that passed through Yanomami territory. The highway was never finished, but the traffic it brought to Yanomami country carried with it disease, starvation, and death. The highway brought gold miners, who forced some Yanomami out of their villages and massacred others; federal police were unable or unwilling to expel the miners, and the governor of the area refused to take judicial action against the murderers. Even the Brazilian Indian Service (FUNAI) was literally under attack by uniformed gunmen hired by the miners.

In 1986 the military enlarged a small airstrip that had been used by FUNAI and missionaries, ostensibly to protect the borders against drug trafficking and subversion, but resulting in intensification of the gold rush into Yanomami territory. As a result, by 1988 at least one-fourth of the Yanomami had died and the majority of survivors were sick and starving. When the situation caused an international outcry, the president of Brazil declared that it was impossible to expel the miners from the territory and even proposed demarcating three reserves in the area, not for the Yanomami group but for the miners (Maybury-Lewis 1997:27). Alcida Ramos (1995:312) in a recent book on the situation among one Yanomami group, the Sanumá, concluded

> I didn't expect to be around, only ten years after my immersion into an autonomous and healthy culture such as I found among the Sanumá, to see one of the worst examples of cultural devastation in the recent history of Brazilian Indigenism.

Military Intervention.   Military force was another means of destroying indigenous populations. Clearly, the superiority of European weaponry made the difference in their confrontation with indigenous cultures, although not without some notable losses and defeats at the hands of less well-armed peoples. In 1860, when the Maori of New Zealand resisted the work of a survey team subdividing a large block of their land, the governor declared martial law and sent in the military to subdue them. The Maori managed to fight for twelve years against a force that at one time numbered 22,000 soldiers, costing the colony 500 people and 1.3 million pounds (Bodley 1990:50).

It was military intervention, of course, that finally subdued the Native Americans on the American Plains in the period from about 1850 to 1880. When Plains nations resisted takeover by Euro-Americans of their land and resources, the U.S. government sent in the military to control them, succeeding, as noted in Chapter 7, only after they destroyed the buffalo herds on which the Native Americans nations depended.

The Extension of Government Control.   Once indigenous nations were militarily subdued, the next step in the process of cultural transformation was the extension of government control. When the nation-state is able to extend its authority, the indigenous society ceases being an autonomous "nation" and becomes incorporated into the state. In most cases rulers of the nation-state justified control as bringing to indigenous peoples the benefits of civilization. As John Bodley (1990:58) noted, however, it was directly related to protecting the economic interests of nonindigenous peoples moving into indigenous territory.

Various techniques were used to establish political control. One was simply direct rule, in which a person from the dominant group was appointed, after the military had subdued a population, to administer the subjugated group. The French did this in Africa, appointing French commissioners or heads. More common, and probably more effective, was the technique pioneered by the British in Africa, called *indirect rule*. This involved maintaining and strengthening the role of traditional leaders or creating them when they did not exist and governing through them (Bodley 1990:71).

The base camp program used by Australia to extend governmental control in Papua New Guinea proved to be particularly effective. The territory of Papua New Guinea was relatively isolated; even into the 1940s there were indigenous groups that had never been in direct contact with outside areas. To extend their control the Australian government would send an armed patrol with trade goods to establish a base camp in an area already under government influence. While the patrol was in camp, they offered highly prized trade goods, such as salt, steel tools, and cloth, to visitors to establish contact with surrounding villagers. Then they would move out to the villages and ask permission to build a rest house to allow longer visits by the patrol. Although these requests were not always welcome, the villagers were generally convinced by native interpreters. Then more distant villagers would come for trade goods, and the officer would agree to give the goods, but only if the villagers would build a road for the office. When new villagers were visited, gifts would be distributed and perhaps a government-sponsored feast would be given. Peace agreements were drawn up and native police were strategically placed, after which village chiefs were appointed to act as intermediaries between the village and the government. Then annual visits by patrols were made. The Australian government considered the efforts at pacification successful when labor recruiters seeking workers for coastal plantations were allowed to operate freely in a village. In areas where resistance was more determined and where villagers might desert their homes when patrols were in the area, the patrols might kidnap old people left behind in the village until communications were established with resisters.

This process of peaceful penetration began in the 1920s and has continued uninterrupted, except during World War II, to the present. In 1950, for example, 168,350 square kilometers were not yet fully controlled. By 1970 only 1,735 square kilometers remained uncontrolled (Bodley 1990:66).

Land Policies.   The policies of nation-states toward land ownership are some of the more delicate issues in the process of incorporating indigenous peoples or the resources they control into the nation-state. International law, and most governments, generally recognize that aboriginal inhabitants possess rights to the lands they use. For example, in 1787 the U.S. government declared in the Ordinance for the Government of the Northwest Territory (Fey and McNickle 1970:56),

> [t]he utmost good faith shall always be observed towards the Indians; their lands and property shall never be taken from them without their consent; and in their property rights and liberty, they never shall be invaded or disturbed, unless in just and lawful wars authorized by congress.

However, that policy was honored only as long as the Native Americans had a viable political presence and only as long as there was land that Euro-Americans did not want. Most early treaties recognized Native American rights to land and designated large areas in the West as Native American land. However, as European migration increased and as Native American land became desired, the government pressed to renegotiate old treaties, generally finding someone to negotiate with who would sign such treaties. However, even treaties could not protect Native American land from the U.S. Congress, as we saw in Chapter 3; in 1887 Congress passed the Native American Allotment Act (Dawes Act), which led to the appropriation of almost 100 million acres of Native American land (Jaimes 1992:126).

Cultural Modification Policies.   After destroying the autonomy of indigenous peoples and gaining control of their lands and resources, the next step for the nation-state is to modify the culture. Any native custom considered immoral, offensive, or threatening was abolished. Indigenous kinship systems and social organization were particularly threatening to colonists. At various times such things as the payment of bride price, infant betrothal, polygamy, levirate (a man marrying his brother's widow), secret societies, and traditional kinship duties and obligations in general were attacked or banned. The extended family was particularly criticized by economic development agents even into the 1960s as a "drag on economic development and a serious obstacle to economic progress" (cited Bodley 1990:96).

Unfortunately, in retrospect anthropologists played an important role, unwittingly or not, in the efforts to modify indigenous cultures and incorporate them into the nation-state. Even Margaret Mead (1961:19–20), one of the great spokespersons for tolerance and understanding of indigenous peoples, was convinced that tribal peoples she worked with wanted to "modernize": "We do not conceive of people being forcibly changed by other human beings. We conceive of them as seeing a light and following it freely."

Development theorists (Goulet 1971:25–26) suggested that "traditional people must be shocked into the realization that they are living in abnormal, inhuman conditions as psychological preparation for modernization."

Indigenous students, carefully dressed in required Western-style clothing, attend class at the Carlisle Indian School. In this class, photographed in 1900, they are debating the resolution "that the Negroes of the South should not be denied the right of citizenship." The American government did not grant full citizenship to indigenous people until 1924.

Ward Goodenough (1963:219), one of the most respected figures in anthropology, noted in his book *Cooperation in Change,* that

> The problem that faces development agents…is to find ways of stimulating in others a desire for change in such a way that the desire is theirs independent of further prompting from outside. Restated, the problem is one of creating in another a sufficient dissatisfaction with his present condition of self so that he wants to change it. This calls for some kind of experience that leads him to reappraise his self-image and reevaluate his self-esteem.

Education for Progress.   One of the most effective ways indigenous cultures have been modified, as we noted in Chapter 4, is through formal education. As the French, British, German, and American governments used it to integrate those within their borders, so they used it to integrate colonial peoples. As John Bodley (1990:103) said,

> In many countries schooling has been the prime coercive instrument of cultural modification and has proved to be a highly effective means of destroying self-esteem, fostering new needs, creating dissatisfactions, and generally disrupting traditional cultures.

Formal education often conflicted with indigenous teachings and served to undermine them. The schools established by the French in its African colonies taught two subjects, the French language and "morale," meaning ideals of "good habits" such as order, politeness, respect, and obedience. In Italian East Africa, boys were taught to farm and make crafts, whereas girls were taught to cook native foods. Textbooks (see Bodley 1990:104) contained such passages as

> I am happy to be subject to the Italian government and I love Italy with the affection of a son.

or

> Help me, oh God, to become a good Italian.

Often the first efforts at education were controlled by missionaries. It was a useful partnership for both the church and the nation-state. The missionaries educated indigenous children in the ways of the nation-state while at the same time converting them to whatever religious faith they represented. Thus, French Jesuit missionaries opened schools along the St. Lawrence River in 1611 with a government edict to "educate the Indians in the French manner" (cited Noriega 1992:371).

In the United States missionaries and church groups played a major role in indigenous education and were paid by the government to develop educational programs. One of the earliest models for missionary schools was the Methodist Episcopal Society, established in 1839 in Leavenworth, Kansas. The school was modeled on a rigid, military-style regimen. Native American students worked a 400-acre farm to raise money to pay for their educations; because there were no labor costs, the school succeeded and became a model for hundreds more missionary-run manual labor schools. Soon separate schools were opened for girls. These schools remained missionary-controlled until the end of the nineteenth century.

By the end of the 1860s attendance at these schools was mandatory on many Native American reservations. However, it soon became apparent to government observers that day schools on the reservations left students too close to their family and culture. Consequently, the government initiated a program of Indian boarding schools to isolate Native American students from the "contaminating" influences of their own society. In its final form the boarding school drew heavily from the penal procedures used to break the wills of indigenous resistance leaders and owed much to the efforts of Richard H. Pratt. Pratt was an army captain who believed he could turn Native Americans into Whites; he convinced the government to allow him to run an educational program at the prison at St. Augustine, Florida, where captured Cheyenne leaders were held. He founded his first Indian boarding school in Carlisle, Pennsylvania; the school combined the manual labor model perfected by the missionaries with the penal model Pratt perfected in St. Augustine. Carlisle then served as the model for a national network of Indian boarding schools.

Native American children in boarding schools were isolated, given short haircuts, dressed in military-style uniforms, forced to maintain silence during meals, and forbidden to speak in their own language. Family visits were restricted and children were not allowed to return home, even during vacations. It was not unusual for a child who began at the school at the age of six not to see his or her home or family until the age of seventeen or eighteen. The boarding school program created individuals who, stripped of their own culture and language, did not fit into their culture of origin but were not accepted by the larger society.

People resisted. The Hopi, for example, hid their children from roving Mormon missionaries who wanted to gather the children and send them to the Intermountain School in Utah. Eventually the local Indian agent called in troops who assisted in the roundup, but not until they were bombarded with rocks from the tops of the mesas and forced to retreat temporarily. Although the boarding schools were gradually phased out, as late as 1973 of the 52,000 Native American children over whom the Bureau of Indian Affairs had control, 35,000 were in boarding schools. As Jorge Noriega (1992:381) noted,

> [t]he whole procedure conforms to one of the criteria—the forced transfer of children from a targeted racial, ethnic, national or religious group to be reared and absorbed by a physi-cally dominating group—specified as a Crime Against Humanity under the United Nations 1948 Convention on Punishment and Prevention of the Crime of Genocide.

Economic Development.   The next step in the destruction of indigenous cultures was in-tegrating them into the national economy. This was sometimes achieved through violence, as in slavery and forced labor, and was sometimes far more subtle, coming under the rubric of "economic development." As Bodley (1990:114) pointed out, "development" is a highly ethnocentric term denoting growth, inevitability, and progress; "transformation" is a far more appropriate term in this context.

Initially, the most common way of incorporating indigenous people into the capital-ist economy was through forced labor. Settlers and colonial governments found that many people didn't want or need to work for wages—their consumption needs were modest and they met their basic needs by growing their own crops or sharing products among kinsper-sons or other groups. In French West Africa, conscript labor forces were required to spend three years working on highways, railroads, and irrigation projects. In some forced labor situations the death rate ranged up to 60 percent per year (Bodley 1990:116). Forced labor, common throughout colonized areas, was not internationally outlawed until 1957.

Another technique for forcing indigenous peoples into the capitalist economy was through taxation; forcing people to pay taxes (head taxes, poll taxes, etc.) in cash forced them to labor on White plantations, work in mines, or raise cash crops to pay the taxes. These measures were staunchly defended as necessary to "civilize the savages." U.S. legal authority Alpheus Snow (cited Bodley 1990:118) wrote in 1921 that "natives simply lack the acquisitive drive characteristic of civilized man, and doing virtually anything that will correct this mental deficiency is permissible and even a moral duty of the state."

Economic change was also fostered through technological development. A good ex-ample is the Zande Development Scheme. The Azande were a large population of hunters and shifting cultivators living in scattered homesteads in the southwest corner of Sudan. The British assumed administrative control in 1905 and proceeded to outlaw features of Azande culture that they found threatening, such as shield making, warrior societies, and even iron smelting. In 1911 the entire population was relocated along roads built by conscripted Azande labor and prevented from locating their farm plots in favored places in the forests or along streams. A head tax was introduced in the 1920s to force people to seek wage labor, and importation of British trade goods was encouraged. But the isolation of the area, the self-sufficiency of the population, and the lack of any resource in demand in the rest of the world inhibited the economic integration of the Azande into nation-state. Then in the 1930s, the government decided on an "economic development" program to introduce cotton as a cash crop. The agricultural development expert appointed to study the feasibility of the project called for a conversion of the Azande into

> [h]appy, prosperous, literate communities…participating in the benefits of civilization through the cultivation of cotton and the establishment of factories to produce exportable products on the spot. (cited Bodley 1990:123)

In 1944 the government justified the project, saying, "We have a moral obligation to redeem its [the southern Sudan's] inhabitants from ignorance, superstition, poverty, malnutrition, etc." (cited Bodley 1990:123). By 1946 the project was under way with the building of a small complex that included facilities for spinning, weaving, and soap making and employing some 1,500 Azande workers under European supervision. Every man in the district was required to work at least one month per year at $0.85 to $1.30 per month. Furthermore, to facilitate development 50,000 Azande families, some 170,000 people, were removed from their roadside homes, where they had been forcibly resettled thirty years earlier, and relocated into geometrically arranged settlements and on to arbitrarily selected sites, without consideration of individual desires to be near kin.

The key to the project was the cotton growing, but the Azande had no desire to plant cotton; frustrated officials said the Azande had no "realization of what money could do for them." One solution was to force anyone who refused to grow cotton to do a month's labor on the roads as punishment. Yet, as remarkable as it seems, said Bodley (1990:124–125), the planners really did seem to have been driven by the best of intentions, "to bring progress, prosperity, and the reasonable decencies and amenities of human existence to the Azande." According to one district commissioner, "The object throughout has been to interfere as little as possible with the people's own way of life." In 1965, twenty years after the project began, one Sudanese journalist

> [r]eported enthusiastically that the standard of living in Zandeland was higher: consumption of sugar had doubled in just nine years; there were no naked people left; Azande women were dressed in the fashionable northern Sudanese style; and everyone had bicycles and lived in clean houses equipped with beds and mattresses...best of all, there were now swarms of children everywhere! (cited Bodley 1990:125)

By the 1980s, the decline of the cotton market and a civil war in Sudan had left the Azande economy in virtual ruin.

These kinds of projects, of course, are common today. Governments in the periphery turn to areas occupied by the few remaining indigenous cultures in order to raise cash to pay off the debts they accumulated in the 1970s and 1980s. The results, as we shall see, continue to be devastating.

THE GUARANÍ: THE ECONOMICS OF ETHNOCIDE

It is difficult for any member of the culture of capitalism to take an unbiased view of indigenous peoples, that is not to view such groups as backward, undeveloped, economically depressed, and in need of civilizing. This, of course, is the way indigenous peoples have been portrayed for centuries. Theodore Roosevelt (cited Maybury-Lewis 1997:4), famous for his campaign to conserve nature, said, "The settler and pioneer have at bottom had justice on their side; this great continent could not have been kept as nothing but a game preserve for squalid savages."

In the nineteenth century, "scientific" theories of evolution and racial superiority allowed people to rationalize the enslavement, confinement, or destruction of indigenous peoples. As late as the 1940s, British anthropologist Lord Fitzroy Raglan (cited Bodley

1990:11), who was to become president of the Royal Anthropological Institute, said that tribal beliefs in magic were a chief cause of folly and unhappiness. Existing tribes were plague spots: "We should bring to them our justice, our education, and our science. Few will deny that these are better than anything which savages have got." Although many of these attitudes have changed, indigenous peoples still tend to be seen as needy dependents or victims, largely incapable of helping themselves. We tend to see their destruction as a consequence of their weakness, rather than of patterns of behavior and exploitation built into the culture of capitalism.

It may help to change that view if instead of seeing indigenous peoples as needy dependents living largely outmoded ways of life we consider the resemblance between indigenous societies and a modern, socially responsible corporation that carefully manages its resources, provides well for its workers, and plans for the long term rather than the short term. Looking at indigenous societies in this way may help us better appreciate why they don't survive. The fact is that environmentally and socially responsible corporations do not fare well in the capitalist world; they fail not because of any inherent weakness but because they become targets for takeovers by individuals or groups who, after taking the corporation over, quickly sell off the carefully managed resources solely to make a quick profit, leaving the corporation in ruin and its workers unemployed.

Take the fate of the Pacific Lumber Company. The family-owned company was known as one of the most environmentally and economically sound companies in the United States. It pioneered the practice of sustainable logging on its large holdings of redwoods and was generous to its employees, even overfunding its pension plan to ensure that it could meet its commitments. Furthermore, to ensure the security of its employees, it had a no-layoff policy. Unfortunately, the very features that made the company a model of environmental and social responsibility also made it a prime target for corporate raiders. After they took control of the company in the late 1980s they doubled the cutting rate on company lands, drained $55 million of the $93 million pension plan, and invested the remaining $38 million in a life insurance company that ultimately failed (Korten 1995:210). And the fate of Pacific Lumber is not unique.

Indigenous peoples possess all the characteristics that make them prime targets for takeovers. Like responsible corporations, they have managed their resources so well that those same resources (e.g., lumber, animals, farmlands) become targets for those who have used up theirs or who wish to make a quick profit. The indigenous peoples themselves become expendable or resources to be exploited. To illustrate let's look at the case of the Guaraní as described by Richard Reed (1997).

History and Background

Most of the 15,000 Guaraní are settled in the rain forests of eastern Paraguay; they live in 114 communities ranging from three to four houses to more than one hundred families. They are a minority population in a country in which most citizens are *mestizo* or *criollos,* descendants of Europeans who married Guaraní.

When Europeans arrived, more than 1 million Guaraní and related groups lived in the area stretching from the Andes to the Atlantic Ocean. The Guaraní welcomed the first conquistadors, joining them in carving out trade routes to the Andes. The earliest reports of travelers indicate that the Guaraní system of production and standard of living were successful. In 1541 the region's first governor, Cabeza de Vaca (cited Reed 1997:8), noted that the Guaraní

> [a]re the richest people of all the land and province both for agriculture and stock raising. They rear plenty of fowl and geese and other birds, and have an abundance of game, such as boar, deer, and dantes (anta), partridge, quail and pheasants; and they have great fisheries in the river. They grow plenty of maize, potatoes, cassava, peanuts and many other fruits; and from the trees they collect a great deal of honey.

In addition to their economic success, the Guaraní were a relatively egalitarian society in which a person's place in society was determined by kinship. Leadership was usually determined by age, although political leaders had little or no power of coercion over others.

The Guaraní engaged European markets soon after contact, managing to combine their traditional subsistence activities of swidden agriculture and hunting and gathering with the collection of commercial products from the forests, such as yerba mate, a naturally growing tea, animal skins, and honey. Anthropologists call this combination of productive activities *agroforestry,* the active management of forest resources for long-term production.

To understand agroforestry as practiced by the Guaraní, we need to understand a little about the nature of tropical rain forests. They are the most diverse biosystems on Earth, containing half the recorded species in the world, although only about 15 percent of these species have even been discovered. They are also among the most fragile ecosystems. A rain forest is a layered system, the top layer, or canopy, provided by large trees protecting the layers underneath it, with each species of plant or animal in lower layers dependent on the other's, and all surviving on a very thin layer of soil.

Guaraní agroforestry focuses on three activities: horticulture, hunting and gathering, and commercial tree cropping. The agriculture is called *shifting* or *swidden* agriculture, in which small areas of the forests are cut and burned, the ash providing a thin layer of nutrients for the soil. These areas are planted until spreading weeds and decreased yields force the farmer to move to a new plot. The old plot is not abandoned but planted with banana trees and manioc, crops that need little care and that produce for up to four years. In this way land is gradually recycled back into tropical forest. Furthermore, these plots provide forage for deer, peccary, and other animals, which the Guaraní trap or shoot.

Fishing provides another source of protein. Usually the Guaraní fish with poison. They crush the bark of the timbo tree and wash it through the water, leaving a thin seal on top of the water. They wait for the water to be depleted of oxygen, and the stunned fish float to the surface. The Guaraní also fish with hook and lines. Other food sources are honey, fruit, the hearts of palm trees, and roots gathered from the forest floor.

Finally, to earn cash, the Guaraní collect yerba mate leaves, animal skins, oils, and food. In these activities the Guaraní use the forest extensively but not intensively. For example, they will cut leaves from all yerba trees but take only the mature leaves from each tree every three years, thus promoting the plants' survival. In addition, because the Guaraní harvest from a number of ecological niches and because their consumption needs are modest, they never overexploit a commodity to earn cash.

The Guaraní, therefore, use the forest to supplement their other subsistence activities, integrating this resource into their production system. It is a production system that is modeled after that of the rain forest itself; by incorporating trees the system preserves or recreates the forest canopy necessary for the survival of plants and animals below it. Crops grow in the shade of the trees. The surviving diversity of crops and animals ensures the recycling of nutrients necessary for their maintenance. In fact, as Richard Reed (1997:15) noted, "agroforestry often increases ecological diversity."

Agroforestry differs markedly from the typical exploitive forest activities in the culture of capitalism, such as intensive agriculture, lumbering, and cattle raising, activities modeled after factory production. First, indigenous production systems are diverse, allowing forest residents to exploit various niches in the forest without overexploiting any one niche. Second, unlike intensive agriculture, lumbering, or cattle raising, the Guaraní production system depends on the resources of plants and animals themselves rather than on the nutrients of the forest soils. Thus, by moderate use of the soils, water, canopy, and fauna of the forest the Guaraní ensure that the whole system continues to flourish. Third, Guaraní production techniques lend themselves to a pattern of social relations in which individual autonomy is respected and in which activities do not lend themselves to a division of labor that lends itself to status hierarchy. The basic work unit is the family, with both men and women involved in productive labor—farming, gathering food, and collecting commercial products—and reproductive labor—child care, food preparation, and the construction and maintenance of shelters.

Fourth, unlike the activities of the culture of capitalism, the Guaraní mode of production is neither technologically nor labor intensive. The Guaraní spend about 18 percent of their time in productive activities; one-third of that is devoted to horticulture, slightly less to forest subsistence activities, and about 40 percent to commercial activities. Another 27 percent of their time is devoted to household labor. In all, about half their daylight time is spent working; the rest is devoted to leisure and socializing. Reed said that the Guaraní workday is approximately half that of a typical European worker.

Finally, unlike capitalist production, which is tightly integrated into the global system, Guaraní production allows them a great deal of autonomy from the larger society. When prices for their products are too low, the Guaraní stop selling; if prices on store goods are too high, the Guaraní stop buying. Thus, they do not have to rely on commercial markets; their stability is in their gardens, not their labor.

This autonomy can be attributed in part to the Guaraní's modest consumption needs. Food accounts for about 40 percent of the average family's monthly market basket—about two kilograms of rice, pasta, and flour; one kilogram of meat, a half liter of cooking oil, and a little salt. Cloth and clothing is the next most important purchase, perhaps a new shirt or pants (but not both) each year. Another one-fifth of the budget is spent on tools, such as machetes and axes, and an occasional luxury, such as tobacco, alcohol, or a tape recorder. Thus, as Reed (1997:75) noted, the Guaraní engage the global economic system without becoming dependent on it.

Contemporary Development and Guaraní Communities

Guaraní culture and their system of adaptation are, however, being threatened. Since the 1970s the rate of forest destruction in Paraguay has increased dramatically as forests are cleared to make way for monocultural agriculture and cattle ranching. As a result, Guaraní house lots stand exposed on open landscapes and families are being forced to settle on the fringes of mestizo towns. Reed made the point that it is not market contact or interethnic relations that are destroying the Guaraní; they have participated in the market and interacted with mestizo townspeople for centuries. Rather, it is a new kind of economic development spawned by the needs of the global economy.

After decades of little economic growth, in the 1970s the Paraguayan economy began to grow at the rate of 10 percent per year. This growth was fueled by enormous expansion of agricultural production, particularly cotton, soy, and wheat. Most of this growth came at the expense of huge tracts of rain forest felled to make way for the new cultivation. As Reed said, since 1970 every effort has been made to convert the land of eastern Paraguay into fields for commodity production. A number of things contributed to rain forest destruction.

First, roads built into the forests for military defense against Brazil contributed to the influx of settlers into the rain forest. Second, large-scale, energy-intensive agriculture displaced small farmers, who flooded to the cities in search of work. This created pressures on these populations to find work or land; but rather than redistribute the vast tracts of cleared land held by wealthy cattle ranchers to peasants, the government chose to entice poor peasants into the forests with land distribution programs. Between 1963 and 1973, 42,000 families had been given land; between 1973 and 1976, 48,000 families were given a total of 4 million hectares of land.

A third factor was international finance. The oil boom of the 1970s, along with changes in currency, allowed core institutions to go on a lending spree as people sought ways to reinvest their profits. Like most other peripheral countries, Paraguay borrowed heavily in the 1970s to build roads, hydroelectric projects, and other things they believed necessary to build an industrial economy. The money that came into the country from the World Bank and other financial institutions needed to be reinvested by Paraguayan financiers, and some invested in farms and cattle ranches in the forests. Finally, to repay the loans, the country needed to raise funds, which it did by expanding agricultural growth in export crops, putting further demands on the rain forest.

The process of environmental destruction soon followed. For example, the Guaraní group Reed worked with (the Itanaramí) suffered their first major incursion in 1972, when the government cut a road into their forest. It was built partly to control the border with Brazil, but it also allowed logging in what had been impenetrable forests. Loggers brought in bulldozers to cut roads directly to the hardwood trees. Lumber mills were positioned along the roads, and the cut lumber was trucked to the capital city, where it was shipped to the United States, Argentina, and Japan. As Reed (1997:85) said, the forests that had provided the Guaraní with shelter and subsistence were cut down so that consumers in the United States, Europe, and Japan could enjoy furniture and parquet floors.

The roads also brought into the Guaraní forest impoverished Paraguayan families in search of land that they illegally cut to create fields in the forests, fields that will bear crops only for a short time before losing their fragile fertility. To complicate matters, Brazilian peasants, many displaced by large-scale agricultural projects in their own country, crossed the border seeking land on which to survive. The area even became home to a Mennonite community seeking to escape the pressures and problems of the larger world.

On the heels of these colonists came agribusiness concerns clearing more forest on which to raise soy and cotton. Within months of their arrival, thousands of hectares of forest were cut down and replaced by fields of cash crops. The road that had brought in the military, loggers, and peasant colonists was now used to haul out produce for foreign markets and for cattle drives to deliver meat to consumers across South and North America.

Thus, in the same way that corporate raiders seize responsible corporations to turn a quick profit, often destroying them in the process, people seeking a profit from the lands of the Guaraní quickly destroyed the forest. The logging companies cut the trees that provided the canopy for the forests as well as the trunks on which vines such as orchids and philodendron climbed. Without the protective cover of the large trees, the enormous diversity of life that thrived beneath the canopy, was no longer viable. Faunal populations declined immediately because their habitat was being destroyed and because they were being hunted to extinction by the new settlers. With the flora and fauna decimated, all that remained was a fragile layer of topsoil, which the harsh sunlight and rains quickly reduced to its clay base.

The rate of forest destruction was enormous. From 1970 to 1976, Paraguayan forests were reduced from 6.8 million to 4.2 million hectares. Half of the remaining forest was cut by 1984, and each year thereafter another 150,000 to 200,000 hectares has fallen to axes and bulldozers. At this rate, the Paraguayan forests will be gone by the year 2025.

More to the point for this discussion, with the rain forest went the way of life of the Guaraní. When Reed first began working with the Itanaramí in 1981 they were isolated in the forest, living largely as they had for centuries. By 1995 they were on a small island of forest in an "ocean of agricultural fields."

The Guaraní had no legal title to the land they have inhabited for centuries, such title being claimed by the nation-state; those who bought the land from the government assume they have both a legal and moral right to remove any people occupying the land. Even when Guaraní were allowed to retain their houseplots, their traditional system of agroforestry was impossible because their forest was being destroyed and they were forced to seek new and smaller plots. Furthermore, the settlers destroyed their hunting stock, so the Guaraní quickly came to depend for meat on the occasional steer slaughtered by ranchers in the towns, for which the Guaraní had to pay cash. But the ranchers destroyed the stands of yerba mate, a source of cash for the Guaraní, that they had cultivated for centuries.

Gradually, with their traditional production system destroyed, the Guaraní were forced to enter the market economy as cotton or tobacco growers or as wage laborers on the lands they had sustained for centuries. Those who entered the agricultural sector found that the new system of farming was capital intensive and required inputs of fertilizers, herbicides, and insecticides. Families went into debt becoming dependent on mestizo merchants and lenders. Those who chose to work found that wages were often too low to support a family, forcing several or all family members to work. Furthermore, labor required people to travel outside their communities so that even those families who managed to gain access to land on which to garden had little time for it. Because wage labor demands the strongest workers, it is often the youngest and strongest who must leave their communities.

There are other effects. Illness and disease became more prevalent. Suicide, virtually unknown previously in Guaraní communities, increased from a total of six in 1989 to three suicides per month in the first half of 1995. The leadership system collapsed, as religious leaders who earned their authority through their ability to mediate disputes found themselves helpless to mediate the new problems that arose between Guaraní and mestizo or government bureaucrats. Today the government appoints community leaders to make it easier for them to control and negotiate with Guaraní communities. These new leaders derive their power from assistance programs that funnel resources to the Guaraní, but which many leaders use to reward friends and relatives and punish nonkin and enemies.

In sum, the debt assumed by the Paraguayan government to foster economic expansion and the resulting expansion of capital-intensive farming and cattle ranching in the 1980s disrupted Guaraní society more than had four centuries of contact; as a result its members are dispersing and assimilating into the larger society. It would be easy to condemn the Paraguayan government and other governments whose indigenous peoples are being destroyed. Yet the nation-states are only doing what capital controllers are supposed to do: They are choosing modes of production and ways of life that will bring the greatest immediate monetary return and the most rapid economic growth.

DISADVANTAGED MAJORITIES
AND THEIR REVENGE

Although indigenous minorities are often endangered by the expansion of the culture of capitalism, it is common also for market expansion to disadvantage indigenous majorities, sometimes with deadly impact.

Consider the fact that in the past two to three decades, the software industry has produced the largest group of billionaires and multibillionaires in American history. Just imagine, suggests Amy Chua (2003:19), that all of these billionaires and multibillionaires were ethnic Chinese. Imagine that ethnic Chinese, while being only 2 percent of the U.S. population, controlled most of the largest corporations in America—Time Warner, General Electric, Chase Manhattan, Exxon, Mobil, United Airlines, and Microsoft—along with most banks, plus Rockefeller Center and two-thirds of the best real estate in the country. Then consider that the two-thirds of the country who thought of themselves as "White" were dirt poor, owned no land, and, as a group, had experienced no upward mobility as far back as anyone could remember. If you can imagine this, says Chua,

> you will have approximated the core social dynamic that characterizes much of the non-Western world…[where] free markets have led to the rapid accumulation of massive, often shocking wealth by members of an "outsider" or "non-indigenous" ethnic minority. (2003:19)

In her book, *World on Fire* (2003), Yale law professor Amy Chua examines situations in which the disadvantaged comprise the majority of the population, whereas a small minority controls most of the wealth. When there is a market-dominant minority, Chua suggests, capitalism and democracy are a volatile combination.

Markets, says Chua, often concentrate spectacular wealth in the hands of market-dominant minorities, whereas, at the same time, democracy increases the power of the impoverished majority. This is the situation, she says, in countries all over the world: the Chinese in Southeast Asia, Whites in South Africa, Lebanese in West Africa, Igbo in Nigeria, Indians in East Africa, Croats in the former Yugoslavia, and Jews in postcommunist Russia. In situations such as this, opportunistic, vote-seeking politicians pit the frustrated "indigenous" majority against the wealthy and resented minority. The resulting violence may take the form of a backlash against the market by targeting the wealth of the minority, it may take the form of a backlash against democracy by forces favorable to the market-dominant minority, or it may take the form of genocidal violence directed against the market-dominant minority itself (Chua 2003:10). Thus, since 1989, Chua (2003:123) says, the world has seen the proliferation of ethnic conflict, the rise of militant Islam, the intensification of group hated and nationalism, expulsions, massacres, confiscations, calls for renationalization, and two genocides of magnitudes unprecedented since the Nazi holocaust.

Chua begins her book by relating the story of her aunt who lived in the Philippines. She was murdered, her throat slit by her chauffeur. Chua was shocked, as were other members of the family, by the brutality of the crime; her aunt was single, and fifty-eight years old, and four-feet-eleven-inches tall; her attacker was six-foot-two. There was little doubt who did it and why; the police report detailed the confessions of the maids who knew and assisted with the murder, and jewelry and other valuables were found missing. At the funeral, Chua asked one of her uncles how the criminal investigation was going, and her uncle replied that the killer had not been found; his wife added that the police had essentially closed the case. Later Chua saw the police report; under the entry "motive for murder," instead of "robbery," there was only one word—"revenge."

Chua's aunt was relatively wealthy, part of the market-dominant ethnic Chinese minority. In the Philippines, millions of Filipinos work for Chinese; virtually no Chinese work for Filipinos. Global markets intensify the Chinese dominance of industry and commerce. If investors want to do business in the Philippines, they deal almost exclusively with Chinese. Although there are a few aristocratic families of Spanish descent, all Philippine billionaires are of Chinese descent. But Filipinos do all the menial jobs, and all peasants are Filipino as are all domestic servants and urban squatters. In Manila there is a twelve-block-wide mountain of fermenting garbage known as the "Promised Land." Surrounding the dump are makeshift shantytowns housing some 100,000 people who eke out livings by scavenging through rotting food and dead animal carcasses. In July of 2000, accumulated methane gas exploded, collapsing the mountain of garbage and killing more than one hundred people. When Chua asked her uncle about it, he responded with annoyance, "Why does everyone want to talk about that? It's the worst thing for investment" (Chua 2003:4).

All over Southeast Asia, ethnic Chinese comprise a market-dominant minority. In Burma, some 69 percent of indigenous Burmans cannot compete economically with the 5 percent Chinese minority. In Vietnam in the 1950s, the 1 percent Chinese minority controlled 90 percent of the non-European private economy. In Indonesia, with the help of the IMF and World Bank, and a corrupt indigenous leadership led by the Suharto family that accumulated a personal fortune estimated to be $16 billion, the Chinese, making up 3 percent of the population, owned 70 percent of the private economy. Although most of the Chinese are hard-working members of the middle class with no political connections, the resentments of the indigenous majority erupted in 1998, and rioters looted, burned, and raped their way through the Chinese neighborhood. "It was like Christmas," one woman said after hearing her neighbors trade stories about the various appliances they had carried out from burning Chinese stores. "Less festive were the hundreds of charred corpses lying in the rubble that had been commercial Jakarta" (Chua 2003:153). One result of the riot was that some $40 billion to $100 billion of mostly Chinese controlled capital fled the country. But most Chinese could not leave what was for most the only home they ever knew. Instead, women purchased stainless steel "antirape corsets" developed by a Chinese entrepreneur.

In Russia, the forced privatization plan, described in Chapter 6, resulted in a situation where only a handful of people managed to monopolize the country's wealth. The wealthiest comprised a group of seven oligarchs, all but one of whom was Jewish. Yet of the some 147 million people in Russia, Jews make up only 1 percent of the population. One result of this concentration of wealth has been growing anti-Semitism, making victims of the thousands of poor or middle-class Jews. Thus, a financial collapse in 1998 in Russia saw a spate of synagogue bombings, the beating of two rabbis, neo-Nazi marches on Moscow, and desecration of Jewish synagogues. In 2002, a new political party was formed calling for a better deal for ethnic Russians and blaming Jews for stealing the country's wealth (Chua 2003:94).

Leveling Crowds

Chua, of course, is not the first to connect poverty with violence, or to suggest that capitalism and democracy can be an explosive mixture. Eric Hobsbawm (1964) showed how the best predictor of the occurrence of riots in revolutionary France was the price of food. In the *Federalist Papers,* founders of the U.S. republic, including Alexander Hamilton, James Madison, and John Jay, questioned whether republics are doomed to failure because the "principle of liberty" that allows the free expression of hostility becomes impossible to check. Madison seems to take it as a feature of human nature when he said that

> So strong is this propensity of mankind to fall into mutual animosities…the most common and durable source of factions has been the various and unequal distribution of property." (cited Beard 1959:13)

Stanley J. Tambiah (1996) examined instances of riots and ethnic violence in South Asia. These riots, in which a dominant ethnic group attacks an ethnic minority—Sinhalese attacking Tamils in Sri Lanka, Hindus rioting against Sikhs in India, Sindhis attacking Muhajirs in Pakistan—follow the same sort of pattern outlined by Amy Chua: A majority group, feeling either disenfranchised or oppressed, attacks minority members who have achieved economic success. In 1983 in Colombo, the capital of Sri Lanka, crowds attacked Tamil residences and businesses. Existing tensions, which exploded into a Tamil insurgency and civil war, were high after Tamil insurgents killed thirteen soldiers. During the funeral, crowds broke away and began attacking Tamils, burning Tamil businesses, factories, and banks. Tambiah notes that much of the ensuing violence was purposive; rioters came equipped with weapons, such as metal rods and knives, and carried gasoline. They carried voter lists and the addresses of Tamil property owners supplied by government officials, and the rioters arrived in Tamil areas on government-owned trucks and buses (Tambiah 1996:96). Tambiah notes, also, that the riots may have been encouraged by what he calls "riot captains," such as Sinhalese businesspeople and shop owners who sought to eliminate Tamil competitors, or smugglers, crime figures or politicians who used the riots to eliminate rivals. The official death toll was 400, but Tambiah says it was closer to 2,000 or 3,000. It was the worst case of communal violence in Sri Lanka's history, and some 150,000 Tamils fled the country as a result.

In 1984, after the assassination of Indian prime minister Indira Gandhi by her Sikh bodyguards; Hindus rioted against Sikhs in Delhi. The riots lasted for days and seemed to increase each day in an orgy of arson, rape, and murder. Trains were stopped before getting into Delhi so that Sikhs could be attacked. Hundreds were burned either semiconscious or dead. From 2,500 to 4,000 people were killed and crowds destroyed Sikh houses, stores, and religious and educational institutions. Like the Tamils in Sri Lanka, Sikhs were perceived as economically advantaged. And like the riots in Colombo, prominent members of society directed the action. Members of the leading political party and local leaders actually identified Sikh houses, shops, businesses, religious sites, and schools for the mob to attack (Tambiah 1996:113).

Tambiah notes that the rioters in every case he examined represented a cross-section of society—teachers, store owners, government workers, and so on. Although the riots began as a result of some inflammatory incident, they were soon organized and purposive in their action, and not simply the action of a disorganized mob. They were sometimes flamed by the media and led by politicians or prominent members of the society. And almost always they involved an ethnic group that perceived itself as economically disadvantaged relative to the group being attacked. He concludes that

> certain kinds of rioting crowds in pursuit of collective entitlements are essentially "levelers," destroying property and life in a public cause that absolves them of individual crime and guilt. The leveling down of an ethnic group as an over-privileged enemy, an acquisitive other, an obstacle to one's own group's prosperity, is an orgiastic, short-lived action. If the ethnic group that is victimized still has in its possession the specialized knowledge, the material and symbolic capital, the networks that provide access to resources, it can usually pretty quickly recoup and regain its former position thus inviting another act of leveling and conspicuous, methodical destruction of its property. (Tambiah 1996:279).

The riots and violence contained, says Tambiah, an element of performance, routinized and ritualized acts that gain public acceptance and that confer on the actors a degree of prestige and legitimacy. There is, he says, a sense of "popular culture" in the violence as it entails public expression of collective values and motivations (Tambiah 1996:223).

Conflict, in this sense, he continues, does not represent episodic violence but becomes an everyday and permanent state of affairs; the violence of state security officers, on the one hand, and armed rebels or opponents, on the other, becomes what Tambiah (1996:223) calls "a patterned mode of conducting politics by other means."

Genocide as an Externality of the Market

Tambiah emphasizes that economic dislocation of one sort or another always preceded the riots. In Sri Lanka, for example, it was the Sinhalese who suffered most when the ruling party, under pressure from the IMF and World Bank, changed from a state-regulated, welfare, and protectionist policy to a capitalist, market-oriented, free trade policy. This suggests that ethnic violence is not, as Chua suggests, solely an incompatibility between democracy and the market but is also a problem of a group's reaction to sudden economic deprivation brought about by market reforms.

There is tyranny in the market, particularly in its neoliberal version. To the extent that all goods and necessities are available only through the market, each person's life must be directed to the acquisition of money. When large-scale sharing or redistributive mechanisms for obtaining goods are removed, life is possible only through the acquisition of money. Those who refuse to pursue money, or those who, for whatever reason, are excluded from access to it, end up, at best, in abject poverty with no access to life's necessities. Market capitalism in its present form leaves little room for any alternative.

Relations between ethnic groups in countries experiencing interethnic violence in the past two decades were often peaceful prior to some economic upheaval in which peoples' access to money, or the worth of money itself, was removed. One of the most prominent examples is Yugoslavia, the site of one of the two worst incidents of genocidal slaughter in the past decade. It is a case that dramatically reveals how we mask unpleasant market externalities.

"Ethnic Cleansing" in Yugoslavia.   Yugoslavia was formed after World War I by combining six republics—Serbia, Croatia, Bosnia-Herzegovina, Montenegro, Slovenia, and Macedonia. The country evolved a socialist economy modeled, to some degree, after that of the Soviet Union. But in 1991, after the breakup of the Soviet Union, Yugoslavia as a nation-state began to dissolve. Slovenia, the wealthiest of the republics, was the first to secede. Croatia declared its independence at the same time, but because it had a large Serbian minority and a lucrative coastline, the Yugoslav National Army refused to let it go, and a seven-month war followed leaving 10,000 dead. That put Bosnia-Herzegovina, which was 43 percent Muslim, 35 percent orthodox Serb, and 18 percent Roman Catholic, in a bind. If Bosnia-Herzegovina remained in the republic, Serbs, the largest group in a unified Yugoslavia, would get the plumb jobs, and Muslims and Croats would be marginalized. Consequently, Bosnia-Herzegovina, with instructions from Western diplomats, held a referendum for independence and 99.4 percent of the Bosnian-Herzegovinians voted to secede, although Serbs, who wanted to secede and make Bosnia part of a "Greater Serbia," boycotted the election. In response, the Yugoslav army teamed with local Bosnian Serb forces to create a new Bosnian Serb army of some 80,000 soldiers. Bosnian Muslims and Croats could not respond militarily because the United Nations imposed an arms embargo on the entire country. Thus, the stage was set for a genocide.

With their military superiority, Bosnian Serbs began to round up Muslim and Croat intellectuals, musicians, and professionals and beat and execute them. The Serbs also used their military superiority to prohibit non-Serbs from holding jobs, meeting in cafeterias, hunting or fishing, gathering in groups of more than three people, selling real estate, or exchanging homes. Sometimes Muslims and Croats were told that they had only twenty-four hours to pack their bags. But that was only the beginning. Serb gunmen knew that their violent deportation and killing campaign of Bosnian Muslims and other non-Serbs would not be enough to ensure the lasting achievement of ethnic purity and so began the campaign of "ethnic cleansing." They forced fathers to castrate their sons or molest their daughters, initiated a campaign to rape and impregnate young women (Power 2002:231), and engaged in mass killings. The result of the "ethnic cleansing" campaign by Bosnian Serbs was some 200,000 mostly Bosnian Muslims killed, 2 million people displaced, and the division of a multiethnic European republic into three ethnically pure statelets.

Although the violence continued in Yugoslavia until 1997, the conflict in Bosnia-Herzegovina ended in 1995 when the Croatian army overpowered the Serbs and peace accords were signed at a meeting called in Dayton, Ohio, by U.S. President Bill Clinton.

In many ways the genocidal violence in Yugoslavia fits the pattern outlined by Amy Chua whereby an ethnic majority attacks a market-dominant minority. Yugoslavia was characterized by significant economic differences between Slovenia and Croatia in the north (per capita income of $6,737 in 1997) and Serbia, Bosnia-Herzegovina, Macedonia, and Montenegro in the south (per capita income of $1,403 in 1997). The Serbs, although poorer, represented a majority of the population. In addition, the war and the killings were instigated by democratically elected demagogues—Franjo Tudjman in Croatia, and Slobodan Milosevic in Serbia—who campaigned on platforms of Croatian and Serbian nationalism. Thus, Chua concludes, opportunistic politicians were able to seize on economic inequalities to gain power. What is missing from Chua's account of the ethnic violence in Yugoslavia, however, and what was missing from virtually all of the media accounts, was the prior economic devastation of Yugoslavia wrought by global financial institutions.

Almost universally, explanations of the genocide were proposed that distanced it from its economic roots. Former U.S. ambassador to Yugoslavia Robert Zimmermann said that the plight of the Balkans is the outcome of an "aggressive nationalism." Others attributed the violence to a clash of political personalities—"Tudjman and Milosevic are tearing Bosnia-Herzegovina to pieces." Others spoke of "ancient hatreds." What almost no one mentioned was the devastating impact on the people of the neoliberal reforms imposed on the country by international financial institutions. The social and political impact of economic restructuring in Yugoslavia, writes economist Michel Chossudovsky (1996),

> has been carefully erased from our social consciousness and collective understanding of "what actually happened." Cultural, ethnic and religious divisions are highlighted, presented dogmatically as the sole cause of the crisis when in reality they are the consequence of a much deeper process of economic and political fracturing.

Neoliberal reforms—privatization, monetary revaluation, bank reform, and so on—were initiated in Yugoslavia in 1980. The result was a reduction in economic growth to 2.8 percent during the years 1980–1987, and to –10.6 percent by 1990. By 1989, 248 firms were steered into bankruptcy and some 89,400 workers laid off. New IMF and World Bank reforms and structural adjustments were adopted in 1990 by which time the GDP was –7.5 percent, declining another 15 percent in 1991. After these reforms were adopted, another 889 enterprises with a workforce of 525,000 workers (out of a total workforce of 2.7 million) were forced into bankruptcy. The largest concentration of layoffs was in Serbia and Bosnia-Herzegovina, Macedonia, and Kosovo. Of the remaining 7,531 enterprises, the World Bank classified another 2,435 employing some 1.3 million workers as "loss making," adding those workers to the 600,000 already laid off. The shedding of surplus workers continued right through the civil war (Chossudovsky 1996).

In retrospect, says Chossudovsky, it is worth recalling that prior to the beginning of economic reforms, since the end of World War II, and up until 1980, the growth of the GDP in Yugoslavia averaged 6.1 percent a year. There was free medical care with one doctor per 550 people, the literacy rate was 91 percent, life expectancy was seventy-two years, and ethnic groups lived in relative harmony with each other.

In sum, gross economic inequalities among ethnic groups are, indeed, the source of collective violence. But the evidence suggests that ethnic differences and economic inequalities, in themselves, are not enough to ferment violence. After all, Christian and Muslim Serbs had lived peacefully together for centuries, as had other ethnic groups who later found themselves battling each other. The problem emerges when economic differences that may exist between groups are exaggerated out of proportion by the expansion of neoliberal policies. Instructive in this regard is the most notorious genocide of the 1990s, the slaughter of some 800,000 Tutsis in Rwanda by majority Hutus.

Genocide in Rwanda.   Perhaps there is no better case than Rwanda of state killing in which colonial history and global economic integration combined to produce genocide. It is also a case where the causes of the killing were carefully obscured by Western governmental and journalistic sources, and blamed instead on the victims and "ancient tribal hatreds."

A country the size of Belgium, with a population of 7 million people (overpopulated according to most reports, but Belgium supports more than 10 million people), Rwanda experienced in 1994 one of the worst genocides of the twentieth century. Some 800,000 people, mostly but not exclusively Tutsis, were slaughtered by the Hutu-run state. Contrary to media and many government reports, the genocide was the result of Rwanda's political and economic position in the capitalist world system. It involved such global factors as its colonial history, the price of coffee, World Bank and International Monetary Fund policies, the global interests of Western nations, particularly France, the interests of international aid agencies, and Western attitudes toward Africa (Shalom 1996).

Archeological evidence suggests that the area that is now Rwanda was first inhabited by Twa-speaking hunters and gatherers, who dominated the area until around A.D. 1000. Hutu speakers then began to settle in the area, setting up farms and a clan-based system of monarchies that dominated the Twa. Around the sixteenth century, new immigrants from the Horn of Africa, the cattle-raising Tutsi, arrived and set up their own monarchy in Rwanda, establishing a system in which the Hutu were tied economically as "clients" to Tutsi "patrons." In reality, it was rarely possible based on physical characteristics to tell who was Hutu and who was Tutsi. Tutsi became a term applied to lineages that controlled wealth in the form of cattle, whereas Hutu were those without wealth and who were not tied to powerful people. The political system was not unlike that which existed in many other parts of Africa and which still exists today in some countries. The Hutu maintained their own chiefs, intermarriage was not uncommon, and many Hutu could attain power and influence virtually equal to that of Tutsi chiefs. In fact, a poor Tutsi could slide into becoming a Hutu and a wealthy Hutu lineage could become Tutsi (Maybury-Lewis 1997:101). When the Germans assumed control of the area after the Berlin Conference of 1884, they applied their racist ideology and assumed that the generally taller, lighter-skinned Tutsis were the more "natural" rulers, whereas the Hutus were destined to serve them. Consequently, the Germans increased Tutsi influence.

After the defeat of Germany in World War I, Belgium took over colonial control of Rwanda and further intensified the split between Tutsi and Hutu by institutionalizing racist doctrines. They replaced all Hutu chiefs with Tutsis and issued identity cards that noted ethnic identity, making the division between Hutu and Tutsi far more rigid than it had been before colonial control. They also gave the Tutsi elite the responsibility to collect taxes and administer the justice system. The Tutsi chiefs used this new power granted them by Belgian rule to gain Hutu land. However, excluding the wealth and status of Tutsi chiefs, the average financial situation of Hutus and Tutsis was about the same.

Both groups were subject to the harsh colonial rule of Belgium in which forced labor was common, taxes were increased, and the beating of peasants by Belgian colonists became standard practice. Furthermore, the colonial rulers transformed the economy, requiring peasants to shift their activities from subsistence or food crops to export crops, such as coffee. Coffee production had the effect of extending the amount of arable land because it required volcanic soil that was not productive for other, particularly food, crops. As we shall see, this had far-reaching consequences and would contribute to the conditions that precipitated the genocide.

In the 1950s the Tutsis began to campaign for independence from their colonial rulers. Because Belgians believed the Hutu would be easier to control, they shifted their support to them and began to replace Tutsi chiefs with Hutu. In 1959, when clashes between Hutu and Tutsi broke out, the Belgians allowed Hutus to burn down Tutsis houses. Belgium then allowed the Hutu elite to engineer a coup, and independence was granted to Rwanda on July 1, 1962. It is unclear how many Tutsis were killed in the actions preceding independence, but estimates vary from 10,000 to 100,000. In addition, 120,000 to 500,000 Tutsis fled the country to neighboring countries such as Burundi and Zaire, from which Tutsi guerrillas engineered raids into Rwanda. Within Rwanda, the Hutu rulers established ethnic quotas limiting Tutsi access to education and government employment.

In 1973 a military coup d'état brought to power Juvenal Habyarimana, who promised to establish "national unity." To this end he installed one-party political rule of the National Revolutionary Movement for Development (MRND) and made Rwanda a one-party state. Although the government or party was clearly totalitarian in nature, foreign powers appreciated the fact that Habyarimana "ran a tight ship," even requiring all Rwandans to participate in collective labor on Saturday. In fact, Habyarimana achieved many needed reforms: The civil service was modernized, clean water was made available to virtually everyone, per capita income rose, and money flowed in from Western donors. However, some projects, often imposed by multilateral organizations, were fiascoes and probably contributed to Hutu–Tutsi enmity. For example, in 1974 the World Bank financed a project to establish cattle ranches over an area of 51,000 hectares. The bank hired a Belgian anthropologist, René Lemarchand, to appraise the project; he warned that the Hutu were using the project to establish a system of patronage and spoils that served to reduce the size of Tutsi herds and grazing areas and to increase Tutsi economic and political dependence on the Hutu, and that the project was aggravating Hutu–Tutsi conflicts. Lemarchand's warnings were ignored (Rich 1994:93).

Soon, whatever progress Rwanda was making to climb out of the pit of its colonial past was undermined by the collapse of the value of its export commodities—tin and, more importantly, coffee. Until 1989, when coffee prices collapsed, coffee was, after oil, the second most traded commodity in the world. In 1989, negotiations over the extension of the International Coffee Agreement, a multinational attempt to regulate the price paid to coffee producers, collapsed when the United States, under pressure from large trading companies, withdrew, preferring to let market forces determine coffee prices. This resulted in coffee producers glutting the market with coffee and forcing coffee prices to their lowest level since the 1930s. Although this did little to affect coffee buyers and sellers in wealthy countries, it was devastating to the producing countries, such as Rwanda, and to the small-farm owners who produced the coffee.

If you are a coffee consumer, especially one who likes the new, premium, fresh-roasted varieties, you will pay between eight and ten dollars per pound. Of that, fifty to seventy cents represents the world market price, of which thirty to fifty cents goes to the farmer who produced the coffee. The remainder goes to midlevel buyers, exporters, importers, and the processing plants that sell and market the coffee. For Rwanda, the consequences of the collapse of coffee prices meant a 50 percent drop in export earnings between 1989 and 1991. Furthermore, because the soil in which coffee was grown is useless for most other crops (except coca, the source of cocaine), farmers could not shift production to other crops.

The sudden drop in income for small-farm owners resulted in widespread famine because farmers no longer had income with which to purchase food. The consequence for the Rwandan state elite was just as devastating; the money required to maintain the position of the rulers had come from coffee, tin, and foreign aid. With the first two gone, foreign aid became even more critical, so the Rwandan elite needed more than ever to maintain state power in order to maintain access to that aid.

Maintaining access to aid, however, particularly from multilateral organizations, required agreeing to financial reforms imposed by those organizations. In September 1990, the IMF imposed a structural adjustment program on Rwanda that devalued the Rwandan franc and further impoverished the already devastated Rwandan farmers and workers. The prices of fuel and consumer necessities were increased, and the austerity program imposed by the IMF led to a collapse in the education and health system. Severe child "malnutrition" increased dramatically, and malaria cases increased 21 percent largely because of the unavailability of antimalarial drugs in the health centers. In 1992, the IMF imposed another devaluation, further raising the prices of essentials to Rwandans. Peasants uprooted 300,000 coffee trees in an attempt to grow food crops, partly to raise money, but the market for local food crops was undermined by cheap food imports and food aid from the wealthy countries.

While the economy was collapsing, the Rwandan Patriotic Front (RPF), a group of Tutsi refugees from Uganda, invaded the country to overthrow the Habyarimana regime. Thus, the state was confronted with crises from two directions: economic collapse precipitated by the fall in coffee prices and military attacks from Tutsis who had been forced out of the country by ethnic rivalries fueled by colonial rulers. Fortunately, the Habyarimana regime was able to parley the invasion by the RPF into more foreign aid. The French, anxious to maintain their influence in Africa, began providing weapons and support to the Rwandan government, and the army grew from 5,000 to 40,000 from October 1990 to mid-1992. A French military officer took command of a counterinsurgency operation. Habyari-

Hutus being trained by the French military. Formed into special brigades, units such as this were largely responsible for the deaths of hundreds of thousands Tutsis and politically moderate Hutus.

mana used the actions by the RPF to arrest 10,000 political opponents and permitted the massacre of some 350 Tutsis in the countryside.

In spite of increased state oppression and the French-supported buildup of the armed forces, in January 50,000 Rwandans marched in a prodemocracy demonstration in Kigali, the country's capital. Hutu extremists in Habyarimana's government argued to crush the opposition on a massive scale, but instead, he introduced democratic reform and allowed the political opposition to assume government posts, including that of prime minister. However, he also authorized the establishment of death squads within the military—the *Interahamwe,* ("those who attack together") and the *Impuzamugambi* ("those with a single purpose")—who were trained, armed, and indoctrinated in racial hatred toward Tutsis. These were the groups that would control most of the killing that was to follow.

By this time, the coming crisis was becoming evident; human rights groups were warning about the existence of the death squads, and members of Habyarimana's inner circle set up a new radio station—a potent source of power in a country that is 60 percent illiterate—using it to denounce attempts to forge a peace agreement between the government and the RPF and inciting racial hatred. Acts of violence against Tutsis increased after the president of neighboring Burundi was killed in an attempted coup by Tutsi army officers. Hutus were incited to kill Tutsis, and the RPF responded by killing Hutus: Some 50,000 peasants were reported killed, slightly more Tutsis than Hutus.

As Habyarimana continued to negotiate with the opposition under international pressure to reach a settlement, his plane (a gift from President Mitterrand of France) was shot down, killing him and everyone on board. Within an hour of Habyarimana's death, roadblocks were put up throughout Kigali as militia and death squads proceeded to kill moderate Hutus, including the prime minister, whose names were on prepared lists. Then the death squads went after every Tutsi they could find, inciting virtually everyone in the civil service to join in the killing. The Hutu extremists set up an interim government committed to genocide. Yet, even when it was clear to most people that the genocide was orchestrated by an authoritarian state, journalists as well as U.N. Secretary-General Boutros Boutros-Ghali would characterize the slaughter as "Hutus killing Tutsis and Tutsis killing Hutus." Building on Western stereotypes of savage Africans, Mayor Ed Koch of New York City, characterized the genocide as "tribal warfare involving those without the veneer of Western civilization."

As long as the killing could be characterized as interethnic violence, the core states, whose actions had created the situation for the killings and whose economic policies precipitated the violence, could distance themselves from the conflict. U.S. and European leaders, in fact, went to great lengths *not* to use the word *genocide,* for to call it genocide may have required military intervention as agreed on in the United Nations Genocide Convention of 1948. It wasn't until months later, after some 800,000 Tutsis had been killed, that government leaders in the West began to acknowledge the genocide.

The slaughter did not end until the RPF finally defeated the government's armies and took control of the country. But the dying didn't stop. The fleeing Hutu elite used radio broadcasts to incite fear in the Hutu populace that to remain in the country meant certain retaliation from Tutsi survivors and the victorious RPF. Consequently, millions of Hutus fled the country, gathering in refugee camps in neighboring countries and becoming a country in exile for the Hutu extremists who fled with them, using their control over the fleeing army to maintain control of the Hutus in refugee camps. The press and media coverage of the refugees also served as a fund-raising bonanza for foreign aid organizations, although some 80,000 Hutus died in cholera epidemics in the camps. It was not until 1996 that Hutu refugees began to return to Rwanda and to the government of reconciliation established by the RPF.

In sum, the Rwandan disaster was hardly a simple matter of tribal warfare or ancient hatreds. It was the case of an ex-colonial, core-supported state threatened with core-initiated economic collapse and internal and external dissension resorting to genocide to remove the opposition that included, in this case, both Tutsis and moderate Hutus.

CONCLUSION

We observed at the beginning of the chapter that one of the casualties of the expansion of the culture of capitalism is cultural diversity. There are a number of reasons, including profound cultural incompatibilities, between indigenous peoples and the culture of capitalism and the need of the nation-state to ensure political authority and control over economic resources desired by corporations or the nation-state itself. We also observed that the very features that make indigenous peoples excellent custodians of the environment make them susceptible, as are responsible corporations, to takeover and destruction. According to John Bodley (1990:138–139), a careful examination of the conditions of indigenous peoples before and after their incorporation into the world market economy,

> [l]eads to the conclusion that their standard of living is lowered, not raised, by economic progress—and often to a dramatic decline. This is perhaps the most outstanding and inescapable fact to emerge from the years of research that anthropologists have devoted to the study of culture change and modernization.

Furthermore, we concluded that conflict between groups within nation-states, often characterized as ethnic violence, has more to do with the economic consequences of the expansion of consumer capitalism and the actions of the nation-state. The protagonists in these conflicts are not as much Sinhalese and Tamils, Hutu and Tutsi, Serbs and Croats, as they are those who have ready access to the market and those who don't. As multilateral institutions change the rules of the market to accommodate the need for capital accumulation, lives are disrupted and conditions created that fuel hatred and violence. In some cases disadvantaged groups direct their resentment at those who may have little to do with their oppression. But in other cases, as we see in Part Three, the protest takes the form of one sort of rebellion or another.

PART III

RESISTANCE AND REBELLION: INTRODUCTION

*People resist exploitation. They resist it as actively as they can,
as passively as they must.*

—Immanuel Wallerstein, "Antisystemic Movements"

One of the consequences of the expansion of the culture of capitalism is the redefinition of space. People are free to move around the globe as never before; in the interests of "free trade," countries have dissolved spatial barriers; with modern travel and communication technology, there is no place in the world that can't be accessed almost instantaneously. Capital, of course, is particularly mobile, as billions of dollars speed around the globe daily, moving in and out of countries at will. But not everyone can move, and herein lie a number of problems. First, by dissolving spatial barriers and creating global citizens, the market removes ties and obligations to specific localities and communities. In his autobiography, Albert J. Dunlap (1996:199–200), or "chainsaw Al," as he was known in corporate circles, said, "The company belongs to people who invest in it—not to its employees, suppliers, nor the locality in which it is situated."

Dunlap made a name for himself as a CEO by drastically reducing the labor force of corporations he headed: As CEO of Scott paper, he dismissed 11,200 people, or 20 percent of the workforce. At Sunbeam, he fired half of its 12,000 employees. These cost-cutting moves delighted investors as stock prices rose but devastated the lives and communities of laid-off employees. But by identifying investors as those to whom the corporate managers owed their allegiance, Dunlap acknowledged that capital was more important than people or communities and highlighted the disconnection of markets from local places and obligations, not only from employees but also from the younger and weaker, the unborn generations, and the need to contribute to daily life and the continuity of the community.

"Shedding the responsibility for the consequences," writes Zygmunt Bauman (1998:9), "is the most coveted and cherished gain which the new mobility brings to free-floating, locally unbound capital."

A second problem with the new "globalized space" is that it creates two kinds of citizens: those who are free to move about in this new space, and those who are unable to move; that is, while compressing space and allowing mobility for some, the market condemns others to remain local. Zygmunt Bauman (1998:92–93) calls these new categories of people "tourists" and "vagabonds." Tourists, he says, move "at their heart's desire." Like capital, they can abandon a site when new opportunities or experiences beckon elsewhere. Vagabonds, such as labor migrants, however, know they can't stay in one place too long, regardless of how much they want to; they also know that wherever they want to go, they will be unwelcome. Tourists move because they find the world "irresistibly attractive," whereas vagabonds move because they find the world within their reach unbearably inhospitable. The vagabond, forced to move, is relegated to society's margins.

The material symbols of the division include the invisible barriers that separate rich from poor—tourist from vagabond—in urban centers all over the world. They exist in tourist areas where the rich arrive and leave at will, whereas those who work on the margins—the maids, servants, waiters, taxi drivers, and store clerks—or those unfortunate enough not to work at all, are rooted in place. They exist in the annulment of entry visas for shoppers, and the reinforcement of immigration controls and identity checks for everyone else.

For the inhabitants of the world of global businesspeople, consumers, culture managers, or academics, state borders are dismantled as they are for the world's commodities, capital, and finances. But for the inhabitants of the other world, says Bauman (1998:89),

> the walls built of immigration controls, of residence laws and of "clean streets" and "zero tolerance" policies grow taller; the moats separating them from the sites of their desires and of dreamed-of redemption grow deeper, while all bridges, at the first attempt to cross them, prove to be drawbridges.

This division of the world between those who can participate as consumer/laborer/capitalist and those who cannot, between tourist and vagabond, creates a problem for everyone. The problem for the rich is what to do with all those superfluous people. There are various solutions. One is to imprison them. In the United States 2 percent of the population is under the control of the penal law system. In 1979 there were 230 prisoners per 100,000 people; in 1997 there were 649 per 100,000. In some areas, such as the Anacostia area where most of Washington's poorest residents live, half the male residents aged sixteen to thirty-five are currently awaiting trial, in prison, or on probation. And in all wealthy countries, the prison population is growing. The rich try to keep the rest of these people at a distance with gated communities or strict immigration laws. The rich use discipline with identity checks or keep the poorer population imprisoned, as it were, in far away ghettos and shantytowns, allowing them out only when needed to labor in one or another of the assembly plants constructed by capital free to move where it can enjoy the greatest return.

For the vagabonds, the choices are yet more stark. With the spread of a culture in which a person's only option is to be a consumer/laborer/capitalist, no space remains to be anything else. The expansion of markets systematically destroyed an untold number of indigenous ways of living by convincing the members who practiced them that they were "backward," or, more frequently, simply leaving them no choice. We seem to be doing the same with other "civilizations." After the 2003 invasion of Iraq by the United States, a U.S. sergeant in Iraq, the cradle of civilization itself, remarked, "We're not trying to offload Texas here. We want them to do it their way." Asked, then, what his mission was, he thought for a moment and added, "We're just trying to get them to evolve, to open their eyes. That's the mission" (Cohen 2003).

Finally, there is a third problem that emerges with the new notion of space; the invasion by those free to move into the space of those rooted in place. The invaders may be real people, as when, in "gentrification," developers evict the poor to build expensive housing for the wealthy, or the invasion may be of capital only, as corporate-run factory farms take over land occupied by peasant farmers. Regardless, another characteristic of a globalized world is an increase in "contested space," areas claimed, either literally or symbolically, by different individuals or groups.

The freedom of capital from local obligations, the divide between tourists and vagabonds, and the competition for space increases the potential for conflict and increases the resistance of those abandoned by capital, those rooted in place, and those whose space has been appropriated. Peasants, for example, who lost their land try to resist their dependence on sporadic wage labor; others resist colonial domination and the margins into which they have been pushed by colonizers; laborers resist exploitation; others resist the destruction of their environment; and still others seek to defend a threatened culture through religion or religious violence. Crime and drug use, as Phillipe Bourgois (1995) suggests in his study of drug use on the upper-east side of New York City, and as Paul Willis (1981) documents in his study of English working-class kids, can be seen as a form of symbolic resistance to the marginalization and displacement of the poor.

Most protest is local: That is, it is directed at a specific group for a specific purpose. Peasants revolt against landlords; workers against employers, environmentalists against specific government policies or corporate practices. A problem, however, is that, although the protest is local, the roots of the conflicts are global and there are no global mechanisms for resolving these disputes. There is no universally recognized world court and no legal entity called "the market." One consequence is the increasing appeal to violence to settle disputes, often in the form of "terrorism." The use of violence to resolve disputes is hardly a new phenomenon as centuries of warfare attest. But even most wars were fought between legal entities called states, and there could be agreements regarding what was permissible and what was not. Perhaps this is why civil wars were so bloody; there was no recognized limit on the violence and destruction that one side could inflict on the other. And, of course, there is no Geneva Convention of terrorism.

The labeling of violent protest as "terrorism" itself creates some problems. Ever since the attacks on the World Trade Center and the Pentagon on September 11, 2001, government and media are quick to label virtually any form of violent resistance "terrorism." By doing so, however, they obscure significant differences between acts of political violence and hide the economic and global roots of the problems. Therefore, before we examine different forms of protest, it will be useful to first examine what exactly "terrorism" means, and how, as a label for violent protest, it obscures more than it reveals.

A PRIMER ON TERRORISM

On March 10, 1982, then-U.S. president Ronald Reagan (1982) issued a proclamation declaring that date Afghanistan Day. "The tragedy of Afghanistan," Reagan said, "continues as the valiant and courageous Afghan freedom fighters persevere in standing up against the brutal power of the Soviet invasion and occupation." Among the "freedom fighters" supported by the United States was Abdullah Azzam, cofounder of the Makab al Khidmat lil Mujahidin al Arab (MAK) which ultimately housed, trained, and financed the anti-Soviet Afghan Jihad in 1984. Azzam was also the founder of al Qaeda al-Sulbah (The Solid Base) and the mentor of Osama bin Laden (see Gunaratna 2003; Cooley 2002; Coll, 2004).

The United States supplied money and weapons to the *mujahideen,* as the Muslim fighters were called, through the Pakistani Secret Service and they were instrumental in driving the Soviet Union (which had invaded Afghanistan in 1979) from the country. The United States supplied the means for many of those same Muslim fighters to travel to Bosnia in 1992 to aid the Bosnian Muslims who were being victimized by Bosnian Serbs.

Mahmood Mamdani (2004) suggests, in fact, that contemporary terrorism in general is a consequence of policy decisions by the United States, as well as other core nations, to support "proxy wars" in which extra-state groups are supplied with financial support, weapons, and intelligence in order to undermine states viewed as hostile to Western interests. Thus, not only did the United States and other Western nations support the mujahideen in Afghanistan against the Russians, they also supported the Contras in Nicaragua against the socialist government of the country, Renamo in Mozambique, and Unita in Angola against Marxist-Leninist states. The result has been, Mamdani suggests, the creation of privatized, stateless resistance forces composed of uprooted individuals with few ties to countries or families.

The fact that groups and individuals, who would later be labeled "terrorist," and be instrumental in the devastation of September 11, 2001, were supported and nurtured by the United States raises a number of significant questions. First, and most relevant is, *what is terrorism and how does it differ from other forms of collective violence?* Is one person's terrorist another person's freedom fighter? A second question is, *what has changed? How do the attacks on the World Trade Center and Pentagon differ, if at all, from the thousands of other violent acts committed around the world by small groups against both state and civilian targets? Is al Qaeda, for example, different from those thousands of groups going back for centuries that used violence to try to attain political goals?* And, finally, *what does it mean to conduct a "war" on terrorism?*

The declaration of a war on terrorism by the United States, Britain, and their allies was largely a consequence of the attacks of September 11. Whatever its rhetorical advantages, the term *war on terrorism,* intentionally or not, contains some assumptions that significantly obscure the nature of contemporary political violence.

Edmund Burke first used the term *terror* in the late eighteenth century in reference to the French Revolution and to violence calculated to induce widespread fear and achieve political goals. It gained its current meaning after the bombing of the U.S. Marine barracks in Beirut in 1983, and was associated in both U.S. and Israeli political discourse with anti-state forms of violence that were so criminal that any method of enforcement and retaliation was viewed as acceptable and above criticism (see Falk 2003). With the help of the media, notes Richard Falk (2003:xviii–xix), nation-states have won the battle of definitions, exempting their own violence against civilians from being labeled "terrorism," and being referred to instead as "use of force," "retaliation," "self-defense," and "security measures." But, as we mentioned, calling virtually all nonstate political violence terrorism, obscures the roots and the nature of the violence.

First, it is necessary to appreciate that what we have labeled terrorism is a technique, not an ideology and not a state (see Steele 2003). Violent protest goes back thousands of years, and is unlikely to stop, particularly given the billions of people in the world who have been marginalized in the global economy. As the United States did in Afghanistan, it is often supported by nation-states as a tool of international diplomacy. The United States, for one, has supported nonstate violence repeatedly during the past fifty years as part of its contest with the Soviet Union.

Second, as a technique, terrorism has its own strategy (see Merari 1993; Pape 2003). Terrorism is a form of asymmetrical warfare characterized by situations in which one side in the conflict has overwhelming military dominance over the other. Because the weaker side has no chance to militarily defeat the other, it seeks to use violence for political gains. In some ways, as a U.S. Army lieutenant colonel put it concerning insurgent attacks in Baghdad in 2003, "terrorism is Grand Theater" (Danner 2003). Recent targets—the World Trade Center, the Pentagon, the Oklahoma Federal Building—are selected for their symbolic significance and are intended to reveal the vulnerabilities of the nation-state, demonstrate that the nation-state is incapable of protecting its citizens, draw attention to the grievances of the attackers, and claim for the attackers the legitimacy of the use of violence. If, instead of bombing the Oklahoma Federal Building in 1995, Timothy McVeigh had machine-gunned the victims as they emerged from work, it would hardly have had the same effect (see Juergensmeyer 2000:123).

Third, there is no specific ideology common to the use of political violence. It has been used in the name of both right-wing and left-wing ideologies, and associated with religious beliefs, ethnic grievances, environmental issues, animal rights, and issues such as abortion (see Merari 1993).

Fourth, most political violence is local, directed at specific nation-states or their agents and is afforded a certain legitimacy by international and national laws. The Geneva Convention, for example, recognizes the rights of citizens to resist foreign occupation, and the right of citizens to bear arms and to violently resist a tyrannical state is embedded in the Second Amendment of the U.S. Constitution (Ahmad 2003).

However, political violence of the twenty-first century does seem to have changed. It has, in effect been "globalized." Global terror networks, such as al Qaeda, seek to destroy the whole foundation of the emerging global compact. "Megaterrorism," as Richard Falk refers to it (2003:39), differs from earlier forms of political violence by its magnitude, scope, and ideology, seeking to transform the world order, and not simply to challenge the power of a single nation-state. Al Qaeda, for example, has its origins in the global conflict that existed between the United States and the Soviet Union. It claims as part of its goal the defeat of the United States and the unification of Muslims all over the world. It is global in its reach, its cellular structure resembling the structure of international drug cartels. With active members from virtually every part of the world, al Qaeda represents what John Gray (2003:76) calls "a global multinational." Al Qaeda's organization, as those of various so-called terrorist groups, is also intertwined with global crime, particularly the trade in illegal drugs and international credit card fraud from which it draws a significant portion of its income (see Gray 2003:91).

Nevertheless, there is a sense in which al Qaeda and other so-called terrorist groups resemble traditional resistance movements. The target, generally, is a specific nation-state, particularly the United States. Since 1968 the United States has headed the list of countries whose property and citizens were most frequently the target of political violence. In the 1990s, 40 percent of all acts labeled "terrorism" were against U.S. citizens and facilities (see Juergensmeyer 2000:178–179).

Different reasons are given for hatred of America: Support of what are seen as corrupt or secular governments, the spread of American culture, globalization, and the expanded power of corporations are some of the reasons given.

According to Amy Chua (2003:231), the attacks on the United States were an expression of "demagogue-fueled" mass resentment of a global, market-dominant minority. This expression, she says

> varies enormously in intensity, ranging from benign grumbling by French bureaucrats about bad films and bad food to strategic alliances between Russia and China to terrorism. Like the ethnic cleansing of Tutsi in Rwanda, the suicidal mass murder of three thousand innocents on American soil was the ultimate expression of group hatred. The attack on America was an act of revenge directly analogous to the bloody confiscations of white land in Zimbabwe, or the anti-Chinese riots and looting in Indonesia—fueled by the same feelings of envy, grievance, inferiority, powerlessness, and humiliation.

Al Qaeda also resembles the secret societies that go back hundreds of years and that emerge as a consequence of oppression and exploitation (Hobsbawm 1959). Peter and Jane Schneider (2002), for example, draw a parallel between the mafia and al Qaeda. The mafia arose in Italy in the nineteenth century as a consequence of market reforms—enclosure of common lands and abolishment of feudal arrangements that forced thousands of peasants off their land, many of whom comprised the mass nineteenth-century migration to other countries, such as the United States. Some of the displaced took to banditry, attacking and kidnapping landowners, while those same landowners employed others as a bulwark against bandits. The mafia emerged from these arrangements, gaining power as protectors of the rich and influential. The mafia was generally tolerated by various Italian governments until the fascists took over Italy in the 1930s, but the mafia reemerged after World War II.

Similar to groups such as al Qaeda or the Nicaraguan Contras, the mafia was used by the nation-state, first in countering peasant protest—sometimes murdering peasant leaders with impunity—and then by the ruling Christian Democratic Party in their battle with the Communist Party of Italy, then the largest Communist Party in Europe. The government allowed mafiosi to penetrate Italy's land reform administration and urban produce markets, and it looked the other way as the mafia began to control the world heroin trade in the 1970s. Through its support of the Christian Democrats (and threats to withhold Marshall Fund money if the Communists won) the United States indirectly supported these arrangements between the Italian ruling party and the mafia.

But in the 1980s, a group of mafiosi from the Italian town of Corleone, dissatisfied about being left out of real estate, construction, and drug deals, launched an offensive in which they kidnapped wealthy persons and those allied with competing mafiosi groups. In the 1990s they began attacking public figures. By means of savage bombings they killed two of the most important antimafiosi prosecutors in Italy and also set off bombs at artistic monuments.

The Schneiders (2002) relate how the outbreak of violence led to a government crackdown. To attack the mafia, the Italian government traced the movement of funds and turned some 200 mafiosi (out of some 5,000) into "justice collaborators." The government also challenged political figures or government employees who had collaborated with the mafia (identifying them as "pieces of the state") and demanded their removal. The result was first a significant weakening of mafia control and its gradual destruction. However, the Schneiders note that conditions that supported mafia activity—poverty and unemployment—threaten to revive it. "Viva la mafia" graffiti has reappeared in poor neighborhoods.

The Schneiders compare the emergence of the mafia, its relationship to the state, and the measures taken to eliminate it with the emergence of al Qaeda and the war on terrorism. In Italy the action against the mafia was referred to as a "struggle," rejecting the notion of "war," and emphasized international intelligence gathering, police action, and prosecution in international tribunals.

By using the metaphor of war, the United States and its allies justify the use of the instruments of war—armed aggression against states, torture and interrogation, assassinations, bombings, and so on—the kinds of actions likely to elicit violent responses and create the kind of "failed" states in which global terrorism thrives. In addition, with no government to admit defeat, no territory to occupy, there is no reliable way to have confidence that the threat giving rise to the war has ended and no way to validate the disappearance of the threat (Falk 2003:8).

In the next three chapters we examine various forms of protest and resistance against market externalities. Many of these would, using the now-common rhetoric, be labeled terrorism. However, by labeling them as such, we would seriously misunderstand the conditions from which these protests arise, and, consequently, misjudge the steps necessary to address them.

▄ ▄ ▄ ▄ ▄ ▄

CHAPTER TEN

PEASANT PROTEST, REBELLION, AND RESISTANCE

The bourgeoisie cannot exist without constantly revolutionizing
the instruments of production, and thereby the relations of production,
and with them the whole relations of society.
—Karl Marx and Frederick Engels, *Manifesto of the Communist Party*

The cruelties of property and privilege are always more ferocious
than the revenges of poverty and oppression.
—C. L. R. James, *The Black Jacobins*

On January 1, 1994, the Zapatista Army of Liberation (EZLN) announced its existence by briefly occupying highland towns in the state of Chiapas in Mexico. In its declaration of war against the government, the Zapatistas claimed to represent the indigenous people of Mexico. It is unlikely that the Zapatistas, a group of poorly armed peasant farmers, had any hope of fighting and winning a revolution against a Mexican military equipped with modern weapons supplied largely by the United States, but they did threaten a guerrilla war in one of the most inaccessible areas of the country.

In this chapter we focus on peasant protest. Small-scale agriculturists have been among the groups most affected by the expansion of capitalism. As agriculture becomes more mechanized and landholdings concentrated in the hands of a few, more peasants have been driven off the land and forced to seek wage labor on the larger farms or in urban areas. Many resist this change in their living conditions. The question is, *how are we to understand the actions of peasant farmers who wish to resist or take up arms against a heavily armed and obviously superior opponent? Can they hope to win?*

History, of course, is full of successful and unsuccessful peasant revolutions. Eric Wolf (1969) examined successful peasant-inspired revolutions in Mexico, Russia, China, Algeria, and Vietnam. China, Russia, and England were the scene of thousands of peasant uprisings from the twelfth century onward. Yet in the vast majority of such rebellions, the rebels gain little. And we rarely see the more subtle forms of everyday resistance that serves to protect peasant interests and prevent excessive exploitation. For example, in many societies, peasants could protest simply by moving to a new landholding or abandoning farming.

301

Peasant societies have long been a major focus of anthropological study. It was societies of small-scale agriculturists that generally preceded the emergence of industrialization around the world, and peasant societies today are still being modified by globalization of the capitalist economy. Billions still try to survive by growing their own food, and the balance of their lives is often precarious. We can get an idea of how peasant farms work by looking at a typical medieval German farm. A forty-acre farm in northeast Germany in 1400 produced 10,200 pounds of grain crops. Of this 3,400 pounds was set aside for seed and 2,800 pounds went to feed working livestock. This is referred to as the replacement fund, the output needed to continue the cycle of agricultural production. Of the remaining 4,000 pounds, 2,700 pounds was paid to the lord who held domain over the land. This constituted the fund of rent. Thus of the 10,200 pounds produced, only 1,300 pounds of grain remained to sustain the farmer's family. With an average-sized family that amounted to only 1,600 calories per day (Wolf 1967:9). Consequently, the family needed to seek other food sources, perhaps a garden or livestock kept for food. In addition, some of what is produced often goes into what Eric Wolf called a ceremonial fund, produce that is shared, generally at ritual occasions, with others in the community. The ceremonial fund may be used to give dinners or feasts or to contribute to community-wide celebrations.

Although there is wide variation in the structure of peasant societies, the division of produce on medieval German farms into replacement funds, ceremonial funds, and funds of rent gives us a good idea of what is required of the produce of the farm. It also demonstrates the centrality of land to peasant life; obviously, what is produced depends largely on the amount and quality of land available for production. For this reason virtually all peasant protest focuses in some way on the struggle over land. How the protest is conducted, the form of protest, and whether it involves collective and/or violent action depends on a number of factors.

Let's examine three twentieth-century cases of peasant protest, all focusing on land and changes in the peasants' relationship to it. In a case of contemporary peasant protest in Malaysia we examine nonviolent resistance and the ways poor peasants try to deal with the impact on their lives of the green revolution. We examine a case of violent rebellion in Kenya inspired largely by British colonial policies during the first half of the twentieth century. Finally, in a case of peasant protest in Chiapas, we can appreciate how the globalization of the world economy can affect the lives of peasant farmers and precipitate a revolution. In all three cases the protest was clearly related to global factors: The protest of Malaysian peasants was a consequence of the spread of high-technology agriculture, the Mau Mau revolt in Kenya a result of British imperialist expansion of the late nineteenth century, and the protest in Chiapas a direct consequence of the globalization of the modern economy.

MALAYSIA AND THE WEAPONS OF THE WEAK

In his study of the plight of poor Malaysian peasants, James Scott (1985) made the point that we have for too long focused on violent forms of protest and have neglected to study everyday resistance to oppression or simply excessive demands. *How do the relatively powerless resist oppression of the relatively powerful?* Because open revolt and resistance can be foolhardy, people find more subtle ways of resistance. We can see this in our everyday behavior. Anthropologists who have studied the culture of grade school and college class-rooms have noted the different ways that students resist classroom discipline. For example, students may slump in the chairs designed to force their bodies into positions of upright compliance, refuse to participate, talk to other students, or read or sleep in class as forms of resistance to what they perceive as attempts at cultural domination (Alpert 1991).

Subtle and nonconfrontational forms of protest are common in situations where those with little power want to register their resistance to what is forced on them. In the context of peasant society, Scott (1985:29) referred to these kinds of actions as the "weapons of the weak." This resistance stops short of any kind of collective defiance; it is more likely to consist of such things as foot dragging, dissimulation, false compliance, pilfering, feigned ignorance, slander, arson, sabotage, and so forth. These actions, similar to those of the slouching, nonattentive student, require no planning or collective effort and avoid direct conflict with authority. But, said Scott, it is important to understand these *weapons of the weak* if we are to understand peasant resistance and begin to understand under what conditions these forms of resistance give way to violent rebellion.

Malaysian Peasants and the Green Revolution

Malaysia of the 1990s was, until the Asian economic collapse of 1997–1998, an excellent case of a country doing well economically. Its revenues from tropical hardwoods, oil, tin, rubber, and palm oil led to an annual economic growth rate of 3.9 percent from 1960 to 1976 and a per capita income twice as high as any other Southeast Asian country. But as in most Asian countries, the income is highly maldistributed, with agricultural incomes declining and many peasants finding their livelihoods threatened. Ironically, one of the reasons for the growing inequality of income involves agricultural changes wrought by the green revolution. In 1966 Malaysia, with the help of the World Bank, began the Mudra irrigation project on the Kedah Plain. It involved building two large dams that increased irrigation, permitting peasants to plant and harvest twice each year rather than once. Double-cropping of rice was extended to 260,000 acres. By 1974 the project was declared an unqualified success by the World Bank; it more than doubled production, reduced unemployment, and raised the rate of return on investments from 10 to 18 percent. There is little doubt that collectively the Malay peasantry is better off than before, and little doubt that if one wishes to be a rice farmer in Southeast Asia, the Kedah Plain is the place to be.

Scott said the changes in villages since the new prosperity are striking: There are new shops, roads, motorcycles, and mosques, and corrugated tin and plank siding has replaced attap roofs and siding. Peasants with the smallest plots can grow enough rice to feed their families. Infant mortality and malnutrition were cut by half. With securer incomes, fewer peasants lost their land, and ownership stabilized. Thus, there was much good news following the green revolution in Malaysia.

But there is bad news as well, largely in the growing inequities in land access and income. The rich in the village (most still poor by greater Malaysia's standards) were getting richer and the poor poorer. *What does it mean to be poor and held in little regard by others in a peasant village?* One of the poorest villagers in Sedaka was Razak. His home was so decrepit that he avoided asking people inside. His children were poorly fed, and one died while Scott resided in the village. Others in the village avoided and ridiculed Razak, and

Scott was regaled with the stories of Razak's unabashed begging, his fraudulent dealings (e.g., selling a pile of wood to two people), and his seeming lack of concern with village gossip about him.

The plight of poor villagers, such as Razak, was worsening because the traditional ties of dependence between rich and poor were being eroded by the green revolution. In the past, land-owning peasants could not farm all their land, so they rented it to land-poor tenants who worked the land for a rent. Although the rents may have been exploitative, they were negotiated after a harvest; after a bad harvest the rents could be negotiated downward, and after a good harvest rents would be higher.

In addition, traditionally the landowners needed the labor of the poorer farmers for plowing, transplanting the young rice plants, gathering the rice, and thrashing rice grains from the stalks. Although the wages were low, land-poor villagers could count on the income to supplement whatever they could grow themselves.

Finally, the land-rich and the land-poor farmers were bound together by gift giving and ceremonial exchange, with the rich expected to give gifts and charity to the poor. There were traditionally three forms of ritual giving in Sedaka: the Islamic *zakat,* alms that are given voluntarily; sharing of wealth by the rich with the poor, to cleanse the poor of envy, hatred, and resentment; and *derma* gifts and ritual feasts. Gift giving was a reciprocal arrangement: The recipient was obliged to return the gift at some later date. Because the poor were not expected to return charity, they repaid the rich with loyalty and an obligation to help with the labor of planting and harvesting.

In the past, then, the well-to-do villagers had justified their superior positions by claiming they benefited the poor; they rented land to them, paid them for their labor, and distributed gifts and gave feasts for the whole village. In effect, they legitimized their superior position by citing their services to the poor and claimed in return the poor's gratitude, respect, and deference. These traditional arrangements of dependency were disrupted by the agricultural changes that occurred in Sedaka, which operated virtually to make poor peasants superfluous.

First, the introduction of double-cropping and increased yield made the land more valuable. One effect of this was to change the conditions of land rental and tenancy. Because land was more valuable people from outside the community offered to rent it at higher prices than local land-poor peasants could pay. Moreover, because the land was more profitable, many richer peasants chose to farm it themselves, rather than renting it, or give it to family members. To make matters worse, rent began to be paid in advance, not after the harvest, and there was no longer rent adjustment in the event of a poor harvest. As a result, the poor peasants of Sedaka found their access to land much reduced after the introduction of double-cropping.

Second, with the increase in the value of land, rich farmers were able to take advantage of new technologies, specifically mechanical harvesters and broadcast sowing. The harvesters, which could bring in the rice harvest quicker and with little or no increase in cost compared with human labor, greatly reduced the number of jobs available to poor farmers and their family members.

Third, in addition to the loss of land and labor, the poor found that traditional gift giving and charity of the richer members of the community declined. The motivation for gift giving was likely always the need of the rich to cement the obligations of the poor so the rich could call on them for labor when it was needed. With mechanical harvesters available to do most of the work, farmers were no longer dependent on local labor.

Thus, in the course of a few years, the poor peasants of Sedaka saw their opportunities for land, jobs, and charity dramatically decreased. The social and economic ties that bound different levels of the community to each other began to unravel, and bonds of exploitation that tied the poor to the rich were freed, but, as Scott (1985:77) noted, "this is the freedom of the unemployed, the redundant."

The wealthier farmers, of course, were simply playing the economic game as it is played throughout the world. They took advantage of the increased value of land by raising rents, saving money and time with the use of mechanical harvesters, and redistributing less of their profit to others in the form of charity, gift giving, and ritual feasting. The problem is that their new behavior violated the old norms of the society, in which they were expected to rent land at prices people could afford; hire the poor to plant, harvest, and thresh the rice; and give charity, gifts, and feasts. These norms were once the basis of their authority. One of the accusations of the poor that rich must defend against is that they are failing to live up to their traditional obligations (Scott 1985:184).

In sum, advances in agricultural production wrought by the double-cropping of rice, made possible by the green revolution and the World Bank, increased the gap between rich and poor and, more importantly, weakened the social and economic ties between the various economic classes of the village. One solution available to poor peasants was flight; they could simply leave the village and migrate to another village or, more likely, to the urban centers to search for jobs. But for those unable to flee, there were few choices.

The question is, *what could the poor do to alleviate their condition? Was it possible to gain back what was lost?*

Fighting Back

The first question we might ask is, *what is resistance?* Scott (1985:290) defined it as

> any act(s) by member(s) of a subordinate class that is or are intended to either mitigate or deny claims (for example, rents, taxes, prestige) made on that class by superordinate classes (for example, landlords, large farmers, the state) or to advance its own claims (for example, work, land, charity, respect) vis-à-vis those superordinate classes.

Traditionally, peasants have found various ways to express their sense of being exploited or to resist directly what they see as excessive demands placed on them by landlords, the state, or others. As Scott (1985:300) pointed out, much of the folk culture of peasant societies legitimates resistance. Peasant folklore, for example, is full of stories of evasiveness and cunning, represented in Malaysia by the figure of *Sang Kancil,* a mouse deer figure—a small, weak being who survives and triumphs over more powerful figures using only wits and cunning. In the United States there is the figure of Br'er Rabbit. The myth and folklore of virtually every peasant society has a Robin Hood figure, a local hero who defends the peasant from the elite or represents the peasant who is willing and able to fight back. As Eric Hobsbawm (1959) pointed out, the bandit is almost always someone who is wrongly accused and convicted of a crime who then attempts to shield the peasants from their oppressors. In these ways peasant culture underwrites and legitimizes resistance.

As James Scott (1985:301) pointed out, however, the goals of peasant resistance are generally modest.

> The goal of most resistance is not necessarily to overthrow a system of oppression or domination, but, rather, to survive. The usual goal of peasants, as Hobsbawm has so aptly put it, is "working the system to their minimum disadvantage."

One of the ways the poor of Sedaka worked the system to their "minimum disadvantage" was through gossip, or character assault. But the gossip was of a particular sort, essentially an accusation against the rich that they were not living up to the rules of behavior the rich themselves had previously used to justify and legitimate their social position. It attempted to emphasize the apparent hypocrisy of the rich, much as American civil rights advocates of the 1950s and 1960s highlighted the ethical contradictions of racial segregation in a supposedly free society or as Solidarity members in Poland of the 1970s used the existence of worker repression in a supposedly worker state.

Poor peasants in Sedaka used Islamic law and traditional relations between rich and poor to put pressure on the rich to live up to their obligations to those less fortunate. For example, in Sedaka Haj Broom was notorious as a miser who, some people say, acquired his land and wealth through shady business dealings. For the poor of Sedaka, his name was synonymous with greed and arrogance, and the low esteem in which he was privately (never publicly) held served as a warning to other wealthy farmers of behaviors to avoid. Put another way, gossip represented an appeal by the poor to previously held norms of tenancy, generosity, charity, employment, and feasts taken for granted before double-cropping (Scott 1985:282). Gossip chipped away at the reputations of wealthy farmers much as theft chips away at their wealth. Gossip is also a relatively safe vehicle of protest because its author is generally unknown. The rich responded to these attacks by blaming the poor for their own plight, often using Razak as their example of the poor. Gossip, said Scott (1985:22–23), functions like propaganda and embodies whole stories. The mention of Razak's name by the rich conjured up visions of grasping and dishonest poor; the mention of Haj Broom by the poor incited visions of the "greedy, penny-pinching rich." The former represented to the rich where the poor were heading, as the latter represented to the poor the increasing violation of village standards by the rich.

In addition to gossip and an appeal to tradition, there were other ways the poor of Sedaka resisted their condition, such as theft. Although not as common as it once was when rustlers stole water buffalo, theft was relatively common. Stolen items included water bottles left out to be filled by the government water truck, bicycles, motorcycles, fruit from trees, and, fairly commonly, sacks of rice left out in the fields. Most of the theft was believed to be done by the local poor, and the victims were almost without exception the wealthier members of the community.

There is some evidence that the poor viewed such theft, especially of rice, as a substitute for the charity that was less forthcoming than in the past. And although the losses were not great for wealthier farmers, the gain by the poor was, for them, substantial. The wealthy farmers reacted to theft with a combination of fear and anger, yet no rice theft has ever been reported to the local police. And people didn't report a theft from a neighbor even if they knew the identity of the thief, for fear of having their own rice stolen in retaliation. Another act of resistance was the killing of livestock of the rich by the poor, especially when the livestock posed a nuisance, for example, when chickens pecked open a rice sack and ate the rice.

Sabotage was a weapon of the poor used in Sedaka, specifically against the mechanical harvesters that were taking their jobs. Combine parts were smashed, sand and dirt were put in gas tanks, and trees were felled to block their progress. The owners of the combines, generally Chinese businessmen from urban areas, occasionally posted watchmen to guard the harvesters when they were left in the fields, but in one incident a watchman was forced to climb down while protesters set the harvester afire.

Most of the protest in Sedaka was the acts of individuals, but there was some collective action, mostly by the women of the village. Women in Sedaka worked in crews that were hired by farmers to plant and transplant rice seedlings, something the combines could not do. Although the women would not openly tell a farmer that they would not be available to transplant if he used a combine to harvest, they could "let it be known," as they said, that they were upset at the loss of work. If they did "strike," they would not call it that; they would simply tell the offending farmer they had other work that had to be completed before they could get to his fields. In this way, the women avoided any open confrontation that might result in their loss of jobs while putting pressure on farmers to abandon the mechanical combines. The farmers retaliated by threatening to bring in outside laborers to transplant, and some in fact did so, and the threatened boycott collapsed. Farmers in other villages faced similar strikes that created a worker shortage, and women from Sedaka would go there to transplant fields. This "strike breaking" behavior undermined the larger effort, but made a point to the women's immediate bosses.

The people of Sedaka, thus, attempted to register their protest to the changes that affected their lives. *Were their protests effective?* To some extent they were. Some farmers hired people rather than use machines, even though they might have gotten their crops in quicker with the harvester; other farmers continued to lease their land to the poor when they could probably have gotten more money by renting it to outsiders or by farming it themselves. And some farmers still gave ritual feasts, thus honoring the traditional norms of the village rather than seeking to maximize their monetary gains.

Obstacles to Resistance

Although their income was declining in the face of agricultural change, there was little the peasants of Sedaka could do other than make use of the weapons of the weak. There were obstacles to more open resistance, not the least of which was a fear of losing what little was left. The rich were still powerful enough that gossip about them had to be done behind their backs. Moreover, the rich still had enough control over labor to maintain a viable threat. Thus, when the women "let it be known" that they wouldn't harvest unless wages were raised, the richer farmers, in turn, "let it be known" that they would bring in outsiders.

Furthermore, the change wrought by the green revolution was relatively slow. Changes in land tenure and technique did not hit all the poor and did not hit at once. For example, landlords began to collect rents before rather than after the harvest only gradually, the complete change taking several seasons. Had it been done by one landlord to many tenants, there might have been open protest. The loss of tenancies to landlords who wanted to rent to outsiders, to farm themselves, or to give to children happened gradually, as did the raising of rents. The only thing that happened quickly was the use of combines to harvest, but that was an ambiguous change and many middle-class peasants took advantage of the speed, as did even a few of the poor. Even they were torn between getting the crops in fast and the loss of some wage labor for themselves or their children.

Moreover, the changes did not involve more exploitation of the poor, it meant cutting off relations with them. Thus wages weren't reduced, they were done away with altogether; the poor were removed from the productive process rather than being directly exploited. In fact, it removed points of conflict: There was no longer a need to haggle over the end of harvest rent or over wages for harvesting or transplanting. And once the struggle in the realm of production is severed, so is the conflict in the realm of ritual. As Scott (1985:243) suggested, if the rich had increased their profits by demanding more from their tenants, rather than simply dismissing them, the protest would have been far more dramatic. The sites where class conflict had historically occurred had been bulldozed. The plight of the Malaysian peasants, Scott (1985:243) said, is analogous to that of the recently fired American factory worker who remarked, "The only thing worse than being exploited is not being exploited."

Finally, in addition to normal constraints against openly protesting or resisting, such as the fear of losing work, tenancy, and charity, there is the routine repression of arrest and persecution. Although the situation in Malaysia is not nearly as bad as in neighboring Indonesia, where killings, arrests, and repression from paramilitary units are more routine, there is in Malaysia still the real threat of arrests and persecution initiated by local political leaders.

Protest and Change

One of the great strengths of the modern capitalist economy is its adaptability, its ability to seek out sources of capital accumulation, that is, ways to make profit. However, although this may strengthen national economies and provide better lives for some, it can also disrupt the lives of others. We see this in the United States as thousands of people are thrown out of work by factory closings as corporations take advantage of cheaper labor in other countries. Whereas this provides jobs for others and lower-priced goods for American consumers, it creates hardship for those whose jobs have been replaced. We see the same thing happening to the poor villagers of Sedaka. Capitalist agriculture may grow more rice and make greater profits for some landowners and farmers, but it also undermines the economic base of others. Whether their lives or the lives of their children will be improved as a result is, of course, another question. It is the disruptions of the short term that the poor are attempting to resist. Thus, from the perspective of the poor, although they might have been exploited under the traditional system of land tenancy, labor, and charity, now they have been cut adrift into uncertainty.

The precapitalist norms of the village emphasized relations between rich and poor that involved what might be called a "politics of reputation." The rich employed the poor, rented their land to them, gave them charity and gifts; in return the poor supplied their labor and their respect. It was a system in which the rich benefited more than the poor, and which they had a major hand in constructing. But this is the very system the rich have had to violate to take advantage of new opportunities. Put another way, it is the capitalization of agriculture that has revolutionized life in Sedaka; the poor, rather than being revolutionary in their resistance, find themselves trying to resist a revolutionary social and economic order. Again, as Scott (1985:346) said,

> It has been capitalism that has historically transformed societies and broken apart existing relations of production. Even a casual glance at the record will show that capitalist development continually requires the violation of the previous "social contract" which in most cases it had earlier helped to create and sustain.... The history of capitalism could, in fact, be written along just such lines. The enclosures, the introduction of agricultural machinery, the invention of the factory system, the use of steam power, the development of the assembly line, and today the computer revolution and robotics have all had massive material and social consequences that undermined previous understandings about work, equity, security, obligation, and rights.

In the case of Sedaka, we see peasant farmers trying not to change a system but rather to defend and maintain a social order that, although exploitative, nevertheless looked better than what the green revolution ushered in. Whether they were correct is another matter. It may be that as they lose access to land and labor, they will find something better. But the point is that their efforts at resistance were largely conservative, an attempt to preserve or return to previous forms of dependence. They accused the rich not of making excessive profits but of violating the very behaviors that the rich previously used to exploit the poor.

KIKUYU AND THE MAU MAU REBELLION

The everyday resistance of Malaysian peasants to their worsening economic situation was largely individual resistance, and it was generally nonviolent. But peasant protest sometimes involves collective action and sometimes results in violent conflict. We need to ask, *at what point does resistance take on a more collective form, and what are the conditions that result in peasant protest turning violent? Furthermore, what is the reaction to protest?* The case of the Kikuyu in Kenya is instructive.

From 1952 to 1956 the British struggled to repress a rebellion by mostly Kikuyu peasant farmers. By the end of the revolt the British had taken the lives of more than 11,000 rebels and had forcibly detained nearly 100,000 people, while 200 Europeans and some 2,000 Africans loyal to the British were killed by the rebels. The Mau Mau rebellion was only one of hundreds that took place as Europeans attempted to assert colonial control over peoples of Africa, Asia, and the Americas, but it serves as a good example of the conditions under which a group is willing and able to go from passive resistance to active and even violent resistance. The Mau Mau rebellion also reveals the psychology of oppressors as they struggle to understand why they are objects of protest. Finally, it is important because it has been considered the first great African liberation movement and, according to Robert Edgerton (1989), was probably the most serious crisis of Britain's African colonies.

The British in East Africa

Toward the end of the nineteenth century most of East Africa became an economic battleground between Germany and England, each attempting to control the resources of the area. To avoid conflict, the two countries met in Berlin in 1884 to carve up much of East Africa among themselves. Kenya was to be included among Great Britain's "sphere of influence." Their efforts to control the economic life of East Africa were, of course, often resisted by Africans, sometimes violently. But British military actions, often ruthless, soon subdued most resistance (Edgerton 1989:4). Kenyans not only had to deal with the British invasion but they also were decimated by plagues of locusts, prolonged drought, cattle disease, and an epidemic of smallpox. Contemporary estimates of the number of Kenyan deaths during that period range from 50 to 95 percent of the population. When white settlers, at the encouragement of the British, arrived in 1902 to claim land, much of the territory seemed to them to be empty.

The Kikuyu, the largest cultural group in Kenya, reacted to the invasion by attacking settlers, prompting further British military expeditions and more Kikuyu deaths. In their rage, in early September 1902 the Kikuyu seized a white settler, pegged him to the ground, and wedged his mouth open with a stick; then an entire village urinated into his mouth until he drowned (Edgerton 1989:5). They cut off his genitals, disemboweled him, and defecated on his body. The British reacted by surrounding the village at night and massacring everyone, including old men and women, sparing only the children who had hidden in the forest.

The Kikuyu in many ways had the most to lose from the British occupation. They subsisted on a combination of horticulture and raising livestock on communally owned land, and they were governed by a council of elders soon to be replaced by the British with appointed chiefs. Consequently, the Kikuyu continued fighting the British, using spears and poisoned arrows. Their courage greatly impressed British officers, but by 1904 the resistance had ended. Other groups in Kenya, such as the Luo, Kamba, and Nandi, fought the British but with no more success than the Kikuyu. The cattle-herding Maasi, considered the most imposing warriors in Africa, fought alongside the British against the Kikuyu.

British officials made little effort to hide their intent to seize African land, confine the Africans to reserves, and use them as cheap labor. There was some protest registered in England to British actions and intents in East Africa. Sir William Harcourt (cited Edgerton 1989:3), a past professor of international law, exclaimed that "Every act of force you commit against a native within a sphere of influence is an unlawful assault; every acre of land you take is robbery; every native you kill is murder."

Settlement continued, however, and advertisements appeared in British newspapers at home and in British colonies describing the economic virtues of Kenyan settlements. Many of the settlers were South African, others came directly from Britain, traveling by ship to Mombassa, then taking the newly built Uganda Railroad to Nairobi, where they went by oxcart with their belongings to the farmland they had claimed. Many of the settlers were offspring of wealthy British lords sent to Kenya to make their fortunes, some receiving title to more than 100,000 acres. Even people of limited means, such as the father of British writer and aviatrix Beryl Markham, were able to save enough by working for the wealthy to buy a 1,000-acre farm. The often elaborate lifestyles of the White elite, especially in a part of the highlands called "Happy Valley," consisted of well-publicized drinking and drug parties, polo matches, and sexual escapades. A standard joke in Britain at the time was, "Are you married or are you from Kenya?" (cited Edgerton 1989:17).

To succeed, however, settlers both rich and poor needed African labor, and the Africans were not anxious to work for wages, and those who did hardly displayed the work ethic and discipline for which the settlers had hoped. The Kikuyu soon learned the value of money and would walk 300 miles to Mombassa to work, but the settlers were not willing to pay the wages available in Mombassa.

To solve the problem of getting the Africans to work for settlers the government introduced a hut and poll tax that forced Africans to work for wages to pay the taxes; at the same time, they prohibited them from growing cash crops, such as coffee, sisal, and maize. Each African was also forced to carry a pass *(kipande)* that bore the name, tribal affiliation, fingerprints, work history, and, later, photograph of the person. The *kipande* had to be worn around the neck in a metal container (Edgerton 1989:15). Any White could virtually ruin an African's prospect for employment by writing such descriptions as "lazy" or "arrogant" on a pass.

To administer their colonial holdings the British developed a system that became known as indirect rule. They assumed, wrongly, that every African group must have a ruling chief, so they appointed someone from each group to the position of paramount chief who served as an intermediary between colonial administrators and the group. The Kikuyu, for example, had no paramount chief. The major ruling body among the Kikuyu was the *ciama,* or council of elderly and respected people, who dealt with all aspects of life from settling disputes to circumcision (required for both boys and girls), marriage, and other rituals. They had the power to levy fines on wrongdoers and force them to pay compensation to victims, usually the sacrifice of a goat that would be eaten by the members of the council. The British practice of appointing paramount chiefs had the effect of creating a ruling elite with special access to the wealth and privilege that the colonial government had the power to bestow. Thus, the power of the chiefs originated in and depended on the armed might of the British. They used this authority to extort money from whomever they could, whenever they could, appropriating livestock, demanding land, and ordering women to have sex with them. If anyone protested the chief's behavior, he or she was killed. A chief could cane a person who did not remove his hat and bow to him or arrest someone who coughed while he was speaking at a meeting.

The British also selected and trained Africans to staff, under White officers, the police and their African army. These people also became part of an African elite generally loyal to the British.

The Mau Mau rebellion began in 1952, led largely by peasant agriculturists evicted from lands that they had worked, along with a disenfranchised urban group and others restricted to reserves that were soon unable to hold the growing African population. Probably the biggest role was played by peasants who had lived in the White Highlands, an area of fertile agricultural land on which British settlers were given farms.

The White Highlands

To take advantage of their domination of Kenya the British seized land held by Kikuyu in some of the most fertile areas of the country, such as the White Highlands, and distributed it to British settlers. The settlers were required to pay the sum of three rupees (approximately one dollar) per acre to the Kikuyu owners. Because the settlers required laborers to work the land for them and because the peasants required income to pay the newly imposed taxes, the people from whom the land was forcibly purchased were urged to remain in the Highlands and work for the new settlers. In exchange for three to five months of labor per year, each family was given six to seven acres (much of which had been theirs) on which to grow their own crops and graze their cattle and sheep (Kanogo 1987). They were also given a small wage, rarely exceeding fourteen shillings (about fourteen American cents at the time) per month. By way of comparison, the poll tax was twenty shillings and a cheap shirt cost four shillings.

At first the Kikuyu who remained in the White Highlands working for the settlers adapted quickly to their situation. The squatters, as they were called, were free to raise crops, cattle, and sheep and to support family members, many of whom did not work for the settlers. If a settler tried to limit the amount of land a squatter worked or to evict relatives who were not workers, the squatter was free to move to the land of another settler. The labor demands were relatively meager and could be met by a man's wife, children, or relatives. Moreover, the squatters could favorably compare their lives with those of other Africans working on farms for wages only.

More important for the Kikuyu, their livestock herds—cattle, goats, and sheep—thrived. Cattle and goats were particularly important for the Kikuyu. They represented wealth and were used in all kinds of ceremonial and economic exchanges. They served as brideswealth, presentations made by a groom's family to the bride's family at marriage. They were important in ritual observances and constituted a financial reserve that could be sold for cash to pay taxes or school fees or purchase consumer goods.

The squatter arrangement worked also for many of the European settlers. Although many were wealthy, a large number had little capital to pay workers but could acquire land cheaply enough to exchange for the labor they needed. In addition, many settlers allowed Africans to work land in exchange for cash or a portion of the produce, thus securing crops that they themselves might be having trouble growing. Thus, within twenty years of the British takeover of the White Highlands many Kikuyu had been converted from land-owning peasants to squatters working the same land in exchange for their labor and, occasionally, a portion of their produce. The squatters were able to sell their surplus produce and build up sizable herds of cattle and sheep.

But the settlers were not content with this arrangement; they wanted to limit squatter cultivation and livestock raising to what the squatters needed for subsistence. In effect, the settlers wanted to reduce the Kikuyu to dependent laborers by removing the peasant option. Thus, the period from 1920 to 1950 was marked by repeated attempts by the settlers to reduce the amount of land and livestock available to Kikuyu squatters. For example, by 1920 the settlers had convinced the colonial government to pass legislation requiring squatters to work for Europeans 180 days per year and allowing settlers to call on the labor of women and children during times of peak labor demand. In 1930 the government, at the settlers' urging, initiated what the Kikuyu called *kifagio,* or "sweeping away," when squatter stock was reduced from an average of several hundred head for each laborer to about five per family with no corresponding increase in wages. The losses in wealth to the squatters were considerable; some squatters had accumulated as many as 1,000 goats.

In 1937 the colonial government passed legislation that, in effect, gave the settlers the authority to reduce or eliminate squatter livestock and regulate the number of working days required of each squatter. The settlers reacted to this new authority by increasing the number of working days to 240 and then 270 per year. They passed regulations regarding the livestock squatters were legally able to keep; these regulations eliminated all cattle and goats, allowing each family to keep only fifteen to twenty sheep. The settlers enacted these regulations without increasing wages (which remained at about fourteen shillings per month) and against the advice of the colonial government (Kanogo 1987:63).

In addition to reducing the land and livestock held by squatters, there were other forms of squatter oppression. A settler might graze his animals on the African's fields or simply destroy the crop, or might evict the squatter before he could harvest his crop, the settler keeping the crop for himself. Thus, as the squatters struggled to remain economically viable and relatively independent, the settlers did all they could to turn them into dependent wage laborers.

The Kikuyu resisted the constant modifications of their relationship to the land and livestock and, consequently, each other in ways peasants had always resisted oppression. They failed to show up for work, settled illegally on unused land, tried to organize strikes, killed or maimed settlers' livestock, or fled to the forests, reserves, or cities. But the campaign to drive the Kikuyu off the land was highly successful. By 1948, 3,000 Europeans owned more arable land in the highlands than was available to the more than 1 million Kikuyu on their reserves.

The Roots of the Rebellion

Organized political resistance to British colonization of Kenya began in 1922, when a Kikuyu named Harry Thuku organized the Young Kikuyu Association to protest the poll tax and *kipande* identity containers and preached that the British had stolen Kikuyu land. He was quickly arrested, and a crowd that included the future first president of Kenya, Jomo Kenyatta, surrounded the jail. When a woman named Mary Nyanjira raised her dress over her head and insulted the manhood of the guards facing the crowd, they fired, killing her and 25 to 250 people, depending on whose accounts you believe. It was reported that Europeans dining on a verandah opposite the jail also fired into the fleeing crowd. Thuku was never put on trial, but he was exiled for nine years.

In 1925 the Kikuyu Central Association (KCA) was formed, and Jomo Kenyatta became its general secretary. Kenyatta was sent by the KCA to England to be educated because they saw him as a future leader. He traveled to Russia, became a skilled orator in English, married an English woman (in spite of a pledge to the KCA that he would never marry a European), studied anthropology under noted anthropologist Bronislaw Malinowski, and wrote a competent, if idealized, ethnography of the Kikuyu, *Facing Mount Kenya* (1962). He is pictured on the cover holding a spear.

Realizing that a successful movement would need to involve more than only the Kikuyu, Kenyatta organized the Kenyan African Union (KAU). To assure the loyalty of members and to establish a sense of solidarity and purpose, he used a traditional Kikuyu device, an oath. Oaths among the Kikuyu were common and used to prove one's innocence in legal cases, to pledge loyalty before going to war, to show devotion during religious services, or to prove they had not impregnated a particular woman. The Kikuyu believed the violation of an oath, like lying after swearing on a Bible, could kill you; the KAU oath (cited Edgerton 1989:48) stated simply:

> If you ever argue when you are called
> If you ever disobey your leader,
> If called upon in the night and you fail to come
> May this oath kill you

Seemingly typical of colonial regimes, the British either did not recognize or refused to admit that their African subjects wanted to drive them out. Even on the eve of the Mau Mau revolt in 1952 the retiring British Governor of Kenya, Sir Phillip Mitchell, announced that all was well in Kenya.

But all was not well. First, the peasant squatters were continually being squeezed by the settlers. The colonial government had tried to help by opening a resettlement area called Olegurone for Kikuyu who were evicted from the highlands and who had settled on Maasi land, sometimes marrying with Maasi. But the government insisted that the land was owned by the government and could only be used, not owned, by the Kikuyu. Furthermore, the government dictated inheritance patterns of anyone on the land, allowing a man to pass along his right as tenant only to the eldest son of the eldest wife, instead of dividing the land among children as Kikuyu had done traditionally. They also set strict rules over what could be planted, where it could be planted, and how it was to be farmed. When most Kikuyu refused to accept British directives on the control of land and agricultural activities, they were evicted and sent back to the reserves.

But the reserves were another flashpoint for revolt. Ignored and virtually never entered by settlers, the reserves had become overpopulated, and the resultant overplanting had eroded most of the land. Hunger was widespread, which the British should have realized because they rejected 90 percent of Kikuyu recruits for the British army at the start of World War II because of malnutrition. When the government introduced modern agricultural methods to the reserves, they never bothered to consult with the Kikuyu. One of the colonial government's pet projects was terracing the land to prevent erosion. This project required the chiefs to round up laborers, mainly women, to do the work. Not only did the Kikuyu not understand the need for terracing but also many assumed the work was being done to prepare it for British settlers.

As a result of the situation on the reserves, thousands of landless Africans fled to the cities in search of jobs. Few found them, and the cities became home to thousands of unemployed people. In Nairobi, the fortunate few who found shelter were living fourteen to a room, four to a bed; the less fortunate slept under buses, cars, or wherever they could find shelter. In Nairobi many Kikuyu organized themselves into gangs that roamed the streets, robbing non-Kikuyu Africans and Asians. The most powerful Kikuyu gang, called the Forty Group because most of its members were circumcised and initiated in 1940, controlled prostitution. But they also had decided that all Europeans had to be driven out of Kenya, and some took a secret oath to obey orders and kill if asked. One prominent gang leader was Fred Kubai, who would play a major role in the development of Mau Mau and later claim it was his brainchild (Edgerton 1989:35).

In addition to the poverty and the loss of land, the Kikuyu were split between those who benefited from and those who suffered under colonial rule. In fact, in many ways the coming rebellion resembled a Kikuyu civil war, with the rebels directing much of their rage against those who remained loyal to the British and continued to profit from the patronage they received.

Finally, another reason for protest was the color bar and racism. The British, especially the settlers, considered Africans to be one step removed from savagery, saved only by the thin veneer of civilization brought to them by the British. Settlers considered Africans to have the intelligence of twelve-year-olds, claimed they did not feel pain as Europeans did, and believed they could even will themselves to die. Although beating and killing of Africans by Whites was not uncommon, it was not until 1959, after the rebellion, that a White was convicted of killing an African, and even that conviction shocked and outraged the White community.

The Rebellion

The Africans resisted these conditions as best they could. For example, women refused to work on new agricultural projects imposed by the colonial government; the labor unions in the cities called strikes; and more and more people began to take the Mau Mau oath. The oath had become more demanding over the years and was accompanied by an elaborate ceremony. Fred Kubai was in charge of administering the oath and executing anyone who violated it (cited Edgerton 1989:52–53):

> If you ever disagree with your nation or sell it, may you die of this oath.
>
> If a member of this Society ever calls on you in the night and you refuse to open your hut to him, may you die of this oath.
>
> If you ever sell a Kikuyu woman to a foreigner, may you die of this oath.
>
> If you ever leave a member of this Society in trouble, may you die of this oath.
>
> If you ever report a member of this Society to the government, may you die of this oath.

The ceremony was patterned after the Kikuyu male initiation ceremony; it involved slaughtering a male goat of one solid color if possible and collecting its blood in a gourd bowl and cutting out its chest. Those who took the oath were cut seven times and their blood mixed with that of the goat. (This cutting was later stopped because the scars were conclusive evidence to colonial authorities that a person had taken the oath.) The initiate was asked, "What are you?" After answering "I am Kikuyu," a cross standing for Kikuyu and Mumbi, the mythical parents of the Kikuyu people, was made on the initiate's forehead with the blood. Then the initiate ate the goat's meat, which was dipped into the blood seven times; taken into a hut; and lectured about the oath and the "movement" (Edgerton 1989: 53).

Later, when the violence was about to begin, the rituals became more elaborate and the oath included promises to kill Whites and steal their guns and valuables and to kill anyone opposed to the movement. The British found out about the oath and reacted with horror. The secretary of state (cited Edgerton 1989:61), on hearing it, said,

> The Mau Mau oath is the most bestial, filthy, nauseating incantation which perverted minds can ever have brewed. I am not unduly squeamish, but when I first read it I was so revolted that it got between me and my appetite…I can recall no instance when I have felt the forces of evil to be so near and so strong.

The British government knew of Mau Mau but thought it was a religious movement. But, as we shall see, the oath obsessed Kenyan Whites, and they believed, or wanted to believe, that it was responsible for the entire rebellion.

As the rebellion was about to occur, as thousands of Kikuyu were fleeing the reserves for the Kenyan forests that were to become the rebel base, and as hundreds of thousands of Kikuyu were taking the Mau Mau oath, Jomo Kenyatta was kept ignorant about the Mau Mau plans. The militants in the KAU, which included most of the Mau Mau leaders, did not trust Kenyatta; they knew he was opposed to violence and that the British had sworn to arrest him if he did not publicly denounce Mau Mau. Yet Whites in Kenya never doubted that Kenyatta was the "evil genius" behind Mau Mau, its "puppet master," as writer Elspeth Huxley called him (cited Edgerton 1989:55).

Members of the movement did not call it Mau Mau, and there is no agreement on where the term originated. They called themselves "the movement," "the African government," or other native names, but the term "Land and Freedom Army" became the most common and survived the end of the rebellion. The British probably maintained the term Mau Mau because it conjured up images of a secret society and hid the fact that it was a rational political organization fighting for land and freedom. The British government and the police did everything they could to make sure Mau Mau was depicted to the world media as a group of criminals leading an irrational attack against the forces of law and order.

But the rebellion had been carefully planned. The central planning committee consisted of twelve members. Another group of thirty members directed the taking of oaths and shielded the central committee from the police. The committee was in charge of recruiting government employees who could provide information on British plans, setting up networks for food and provisions for the rebels in the forests, and acquiring weapons. This proved particularly difficult. The British had long banned Africans from owning guns, and those owned by Whites were locked in "gun safes" when not in use. One method of obtaining guns was to attack police officers, steal their weapons, and dismember and hide their bodies. This worked so well that the British thought that the disappeared police officers had simply gone home, until they discovered the dismembered foot and boot of one victim. Later the rebels secured arms by raiding police stations and army posts of the government's African soldiers. Rarely did they attack the well-armed British soldiers sent in to quell the rebellion.

Kikuyu women were to play a major role in the revolt. Women had already organized district committees to fight for land and become active in political processes. Although Kikuyu women traditionally never administered oaths, before and during the rebellion women became oath givers (Presley 1992:129). It was largely women who organized and ran the networks that supplied the rebels in the forests with food, medicine, guns, ammunition, and information. And whereas only about 5 percent of the rebel forces in the forest were women, many took active roles in military actions.

"State of Emergency"

Isolated attacks against Whites and Africans loyal to the British began in September 1952, but the act that precipitated the British declaration of a "state of emergency" was the assassination in October 1952 of Senior Chief Waruhiu when he left the native court where he presided. The sixty-two-year-old chief was with two friends in his Hudson sedan when it was stopped by three men wearing police uniforms; one approached and asked if Senior

Chief Waruhiu was in the car; when the chief identified himself, the man shot him in the mouth and three times in the body, leaving the two friends and the driver unharmed. One of the first government acts after the emergency was declared was to arrest Jomo Kenyatta, certain he was the mastermind and believing his arrest would end the rebellion.

The leaders of the movement targeted Kikuyu such as Chief Waruhiu who had cooperated with and, in some cases, benefited greatly from collaboration with the British. They also targeted settlers, causing outrage when they killed Roger Ruck, his wife Esme, a doctor, and their six-year-old son Michael. Kenyan and international newspapers gave great attention to the details of the killings, and Kenyans were particularly horrified when the man who confessed turned out to be one of Ruck's Kikuyu servants who had cared for Michael. International press reports about rebel attacks on settlers and Kikuyu loyal to the government appeared under headlines about "helpless" or "heroic" Whites being slaughtered by "fanatical," "bestial," "degraded," or "satanic" "gangsters" or "terrorists." Unreported were the stories of Kikuyu captives who were stripped of their clothing and possessions and machine-gunned to death as White officers looked on (Edgerton 1989:80).

By 1953 there were 30,000 young men and women assembled in the forest, with the active army consisting of 3,000 men. There was little coordination to Mau Mau operations; rebel actions consisted largely of hit-and-run attacks, often on symbolic targets such as the Royal Sagana Lodge where Queen Elizabeth had stayed the previous year on her visit to Kenya. The rebels did not have sufficient weapons to mount a concerted attack on well-armed British positions. Few of the leaders had any education; perhaps as a caricature of British titles, they gave themselves such names as General China, General Russia, and General Hitler. Dedan Kimathi, the leader of the rebels in the forest whose capture virtually ended the rebellion, called himself Field Marshall Sir Dedan Kimathi, later adding the title prime minister. Most of the rebels were young men and women who joined the rebellion in the forest with the enthusiastic belief that they would drive the British out of Kenya and receive land on which to farm.

By the end of 1953, 3,064 of the Mau Mau had been killed and 1,000 captured; almost 100,000 Mau Mau supporters had been arrested and 64,000 brought to trial. Nevertheless, the fight did not go well for the British army. They were ill prepared for forest warfare; they made noise, shot at phantoms, feared attacks from elephants and rhinoceros, and fared poorly in the high altitude of the mountain forests. Soon the British soldiers sent to fight were patrolling the periphery of the forest while African soldiers recruited after the emergency was declared for the "Home Guard" fought in the forest.

Mau Mau activity spread to neighboring Uganda and Tanganyika, and Mau Mau agitating in Nairobi was widespread. Theft of money and guns increased, and Kikuyu gangs forbade Africans in the cities to engage in such European practices as smoking European tobacco, drinking European beer, wearing hats, and riding city buses. They set up courts and were essentially running the city.

To end resistance in Nairobi, the British surrounded the city and went through it section by section, rounding up Kikuyu and others and sending them to detention camps or reserves. When 3,000 women and 6,000 children were rounded up to be sent back to the reserve on trains, the women threw the food given them at railway staff and out windows while singing Mau Mau songs. Thereafter, the British put screens on the train windows to "protect the railway staff."

Finally, British power wore down the rebels. They had destroyed the urban base and cut off most communication with the reserves by building a fifty-mile-long ditch between the forests and the reserve with sympathetic Kikuyu. The ditch was ten feet deep and sixteen feet wide in places, filled with barbed wire and sharpened bamboo stakes. It was dug by forced Kikuyu labor—women, children, and the elderly working from 6 A.M. to 6 P.M. under orders of loyalist chiefs. The British bombed the forests, often with nineteen-pound bombs from small Pipers and Cessnas; before the emergency was over they had dropped 50,000 tons of bombs on the forests and fired 2 million rounds of ammunition on strafing runs. Finally, the British relocated 1 million Kikuyu from their scattered homesteads into villages surrounded with barbed wire, where thousands died from hunger and disease. Dedan Kimathi's capture in October 1956 marked the end of the organized resistance.

The Mau Mau rebellion shook the British, but more interesting was the reaction to Mau Mau violence. There is no question that the rebels committed atrocities, especially against Africans loyal to the British. But if the atrocities committed by the rebels were awful, those committed by the settlers and the African police were far worse. Prisoners were routinely tortured and suspects killed with impunity. Settlers advocated killing all Kikuyu and even using an atomic bomb. Trials were rigged. When Kenyatta was tried on the charge of being the Mau Mau leader, the British judge, carefully selected by the governor of the colony, guaranteed a conviction in exchange for a payment of £20,000 on which he could retire to England. He received it. When the sole witness against Kenyatta admitted afterward that he had been bribed with the promise of an English university education, he was promptly arrested for perjury. Settlers openly "hunted" Kikuyu, others bragging that they had killed hundreds. Edgerton provided a particularly graphic account concerning two Kikuyu boys who were stopped by settlers reacting to a report of Mau Mau activity in the area. Unable to tell the settlers what they wanted to know, the boys were tied by the ankles to back of a Land Rover and dragged until their faces had been torn off. The men left them in the road and returned home, laughing, to drink brandy. Police came upon one group of Kikuyu and killed them all, later discovering they were loyalist Kikuyu who had huddled together for protection against the rebels. But the most gruesome charges were to come later because of atrocities committed against Kikuyu held in detention camps.

The Oath and the Detention Camps

One of the questions we asked at the beginning of this discussion was how those against whom protest is directed react. Obviously, the British and the settlers reacted brutally. Edgerton (1989:242) compared their reaction to that of the terrible vengeance wrought by White slaveholders in response to slave revolts. White Kenyans, he said, always feared a violent uprising but masked their fear with assurances that Africans were loyal, docile, and cowardly. When this illusion was shattered, they felt betrayed and tried to regain their pride, as well as their wealth and privilege, by reacting with torture, massacre, and mutilation, all to try to demonstrate the futility of protest.

So difficult was it for the British government and the settlers to understand the revolt that they attributed it almost entirely to the Mau Mau oath. They could understand no other reason why loyal retainers might be compelled to take up violence, why "decent, trusted servants" could turn into what they assumed were inhuman monsters. So fearful were they of the oath that of the first 1,015 Mau Mau who were hanged during the state of emergency, 222 were found guilty of no crime except administering oaths (Edgerton 1989:174). Thus, ignoring their expropriation of Kikuyu land, their racism, and the legislation that required Africans to carry identification cards, ignoring the conditions on the reserve, the poverty and destitution in the cities, and the destruction of Kikuyu livestock, they assumed that if they could wipe out the effects of the oath they could once more convert the savages into loyal workers and retainers. A thirty-one-year-old settler who was born in Kenya expressed the following sentiment (cited Edgerton 1989:241):

> I was raised with Africans, you know. Kyukes mostly. I thought I knew what they were like but when the Mau Mau terrorism began I realized I didn't know them at all. They weren't like us. They weren't even like animals—animals are understandable. They're natural. The Mau Mau were…what's the word? Perverted, I guess. It was the oath you see. Once they took it, life didn't mean anything to them. If we couldn't drive the [Mau Mau] poison out of them by getting them to confess, all we could do was kill them.

Statements such as this echo the European witch trials of the fifteenth through seventeenth centuries, when it was believed that only by getting a witch to confess could she or he be cured.

Following the advice of British psychiatrists in Kenya, the British assumed the way to resolve African protest was to reeducate Kikuyu, and the place to do so was the detention

Suspected Mau Mau rebels detained by the British army in 1953. By the end of the rebellion, the British had arrested almost 100,000 Kikuyu.

camps. By 1959, 80,000 suspected Mau Mau, Mau Mau sympathizers, or simply oath takers were imprisoned and subjected to everything from Christian schooling to beatings, mutilation, and torture. Although the horrendous conditions in the camps—starvation rations, electric shocks, torture, castration, rape, and so forth—were reported, little was done until eleven men were killed in a savage attack by prison guards resulting from a plan initiated by a senior superintendent of prisons.

Because the British believed the oath prevented Mau Mau from working for Europeans, the superintendent reasoned that if he could force Mau Mau leaders to work, their violation of the oath would release them from its hold. In 1959 he had an officer in charge of one camp at Hola march 85 men into the fields surrounded by 111 African guards to force them to work. Despite their willingness to work, the prisoners were attacked again and again by the guards until eleven were beaten to death. The officer in charged later claimed they died from drinking polluted water, not knowing that an autopsy was in progress and that the results would be made public. The outcry, especially in England, over indisputable proof of the conditions in the detention camps caused a political scandal that not only led to canceling the emergency and releasing all detainees but also set in motion a process that would lead to Kenyan independence four years later. What the deaths of more than 11,000 Mau Mau rebels could not accomplish was accomplished by the deaths of the eleven detainees.

Independence

At the time of the Mau Mau rebellion colonial rule was being threatened elsewhere in Africa. The French were involved in a long and costly rebellion in Algeria, Ghana had achieved independence in 1960, and Belgium was leaving the Congo. White settlers in Kenya still thought independence and Black rule was at least a decade or two off. But in Great Britain, the government, weakened by economic decline and in no condition to defend the colonies, developed a plan to turn Kenya into a parliamentary democracy and give Africans full participation in the government. Kenyatta was released from detention and soon became the head of the Kenyan African National Union (KANU). The British permitted elections and suffrage, and in a ceremony on December 12, 1963, with Jomo Kenyatta and Prince Phillip representing the royal family standing side by side, the British flag was lowered and the new Kenyan flag raised.

Whites began to leave. Those who remained did so largely because they couldn't sell their land. But Kenyatta did everything he could to allay their fears, proclaiming a doctrine of "forgive and forget" for both Africans and Whites and trying to steer a course through the fear of civil war among Africans of different ethnic groups, such as the one that had erupted in the Congo. We must remember that the European agreements that had carved up Africa into states paid little attention to cultural and ethnic boundaries, and ethnic groups had little opportunity or need to form political alliances or accommodations under repressive colonial rule. Thus, Kenyatta had to mold diverse ethnic groups—Luo, Kikuyu, Lao, Kanga, Maasi—into one government modeled after European states. Think of a country, such as Canada, which has been trying for hundreds of years with mixed success to accommodate only two linguistic groups—English and French—and you get an idea of the problems of African states with far greater cultural and linguistic divisions.

Kenyatta granted political office to one person who had tried to kill him while in prison and appointed judges who had been responsible for his detention. But he also largely ignored the sacrifices of the Mau Mau rebels and the allegiance of loyalists to the British. For example, Ian Henderson, a Kikuyu-speaking police officer who had interrogated and tortured General China in 1954 after his capture, was retained as an officer in the Kenya police. General China was denied a commission in the Kenyan army, being forced instead to enlist as a private and to endure basic training under the command of British officers who had been retained to train the army. In fact, those Africans who fought with the British against the Mau Mau fared far better than those who had fought against the British. Mau Mau veterans claimed they deserved free land and recognition for their sacrifices and even formed a political party to advance their demands, but to little effect. For this Kenyatta was severely criticized. He was also attacked for the wealth that he, his family, and his backers accumulated, earning them the nickname "The Royal Family."

Bitter stories surfaced, such as that of Wanjohi Mung'au, who was imprisoned for ten years by the colonial government. After his release he attempted to organize Mau Mau veterans into cooperatives to force Europeans off their land; he was imprisoned by Kenyatta's government for another seven years. Solomon Memia (cited Edgerton 1989:234), a Mau Mau veteran living in the Nairobi slums said,

> I regret to state that those of us who fought for freedom were never given a chance to participate in the present government. The majority of ex-freedom fighters are among those who live here in these shanties, because they have nowhere else to go. We weren't given jobs because it was alleged we were uneducated. The young who were in school during the freedom struggle are the ones who have the say in our government, and they are not concerned with our affairs.

Yet Kenya ultimately thrived; many Whites stayed, and many American Whites joined them. Tourism boomed, and the economy did relatively well. But most Kenyans remain poor, and, with the population now five times what it was when the British arrived, land is scarce.

By 1988, a vast gap had opened between the African elite and the bulk of the Kenyan population. Here is Edgerton's (1989:231) summary:

> The Kenya elite live luxuriously in the same neighborhoods that were once reserved for whites. They drive expensive cars, vacation in Europe, and send their children to private schools, and have their needs taken care of by servants. Their life-style resembles those of the wealthy whites who used to live in the same large houses, except that they hire more guards, have embedded more broken glass on top of the walls that surround their estates, and spend more money on electronic security systems. There are many more desperately poor people in Nairobi today than ever before, and they often burglarize and sometimes kill the wealthy "Black Europeans" (or "Benzi," as they are often called after the Mercedes-Benz cars they often drive). There are even more poor people in rural areas, many of whom remain landless. Only about 25 percent of Kenya's land is arable, and the fertile land that was once plentiful enough for six million people must now support four times that number. But the vast "white highlands" that were once a symbol of injustice and dispossession, are now almost entirely in African hands. Wealthy Africans are the new targets of discontent.

THE REBELLION IN CHIAPAS

We saw in the cases of Malaysia and Kenya how global economic developments—the green revolution in the case of Malaysia and nineteenth-century British imperial expansion in the case of Kenya—created conditions that spurred peasant protest. In the case of the Zapatistas, the revolt is clearly related to globalization of the economy. Not coincidentally, January 1, 1994, the day the Zapatistas declared their revolt, was also the day that marked Mexico's entrance into the North American Free Trade Alliance (NAFTA), a free trade treaty between Mexico, the United States, and Canada that would gradually phase out protective tariffs in all three countries. That the events were not unrelated in the eyes of the Zapatistas was made clear by the masked Zapatista leader, Sub-Commandant Marcos, when he said, "NAFTA was the death certificate of the indigenous peoples of Mexico."

The Zapatista army was named for Emiliano Zapata, one of the heroes of the Mexican Revolution of 1910. Zapata led the army of the state of Morelos against the sugar plantation owners in an attempt to gain land for landless peasants. Prior to 1860 most indigenous land in Mexico was owned collectively by village communities, but legislation passed under the leadership of Mexico's first president, Benito Juarez, gave individuals title to village land. The legislation was intended to free village residents from the domain of their community and give them control of their own property. But the right to own also included the right to sell, and over the course of the next fifty years 2 million acres of communally held land was absorbed into large haciendas or landholdings. In many cases it was

On the left is Emiliano Zapata, Mexican revolutionary leader, from whom the present-day Zapatistas took their name. On the right is the leader of the present Zapatista rebellion in Chiapas, Sub-Commandante Marcos, and one of his officers.

pawned to meet living expenses and the expenses of sponsoring religious feasts, from which people gained respect and prestige (Wolf 1969:17).

The succeeding government of Porfiro Díaz, which ruled Mexico from 1876 to 1910, sold huge tracts of state land, mostly to American corporations to attract foreign capital. The result of these changes in land ownership was that by 1910, the year the Mexican Revolution began, the vast majority of the Mexican population was landless. For example, in 1910, in the northern state of Chihuahua, where rebel leader Pancho Villa operated with his revolutionary army, seventeen persons owned two-fifths of the state whereas 95.5 percent of family heads owned no land at all (Wolf 1969:33).

The Mexican Revolution of 1910 was fought to regain the land that was lost, and the government installed by the victorious rebel armies lost little time in writing into the Constitution of 1917 a law (Article 27) that provided for the redistribution of land held by the state and private owners to landless peasants. The major provision for redistribution required at least twenty people to present a petition to the government for contiguous land-holdings *(eijidos)* that they would receive collectively, with the stipulations that they work the land and that they could not sell or mortgage it. Thus, the Constitution of 1917 reestablished, in part, the collective ownership of land that the government had done away with in the mid-nineteenth century.

Part of the paradox of the Zapatista rebellion of 1994 was that it occurred in a country whose constitution included a provision for land redistribution. To understand this apparent contradiction, it is necessary to know a little more about Chiapas, the Mayan Indian population, the globalization of the world's economy, and the Mexican government's altering in 1992 of Article 27 of the Constitution.

Poverty and Inequality in Chiapas

Chiapas is the southernmost state in Mexico, bordering Guatemala to the south and the Pacific Ocean to the west. It is the poorest state in Mexico, with the highest malnutrition and illiteracy rates; 28 percent of the population consists of Mayan Indians. The Mayans are the second-largest indigenous group in the Western Hemisphere, second in number only to the Quechua-speaking descendants of the Inca.

Chiapas is a highly stratified society, with a few wealthy landowners at the top; a small middle tier consisting of merchants, small-scale farmers, coffee growers, government bureaucrats, and political leaders; and a large poor population of small-scale landholders, wage laborers, artisans, and unemployed. In 1994 almost 20 percent of the population had no income and another 40 percent had an income less than the minimum wage.

The societies of Chiapas were always stratified to some degree. Mayan society had its elite, and when the Spanish conquered Mexico they maintained a two-tier society that remains in place today, with themselves and later their Ladino descendants on top and the indigenous people on the bottom. This division is particularly evident in the tropical forests of Chiapas, the area from which the Zapatistas have drawn most of their active support.

While Zapata and Pancho Villa were fighting at the beginning of the twentieth century for land for peasants in the north, ranchers in Chiapas created private armies, the *mapaches* ("raccoons," so-called because of their habit of raiding fresh corn from Indian corn fields), to suppress any movement for land reform on the part of the Indians of Chiapas.

These ranchers controlled huge landholdings and terrorized the local population, hanging virtually the entire male population (500 people) in one local church during the Mexican Revolution to demonstrate their power. *Mapache* officers received landholdings in exchange for their services. In 1916 the federal army moved into Chiapas to initiate land reform, but those officers and soldiers who did not take land themselves were driven back by the *mapaches,* whose acts are still celebrated by Chiapas ranchers. In 1916, 8,000 private landholders owned 3 million hectares (7.4 million acres), virtually all of the good land in the state; by 1993 the number of private landholders was reduced to 6,000, whereas the Indian population had grown ten times to 2 million (Nigh 1994:9).

As in the case of Malaysia and Kenya, the Zapatista protest concerned relationships within local communities and the divisions of power and wealth. There is in Chiapas a clear economic and political hierarchy, even in Mayan communities, with those at the top supporting the government and the ruling political party, the Partido Revolucionario Institucional (PRI), and those at the bottom supporting, or at least sympathizing with, the Zapatistas. Villages, towns, and cities in Chiapas are generally governed by political bosses *(caciques)* whose authority comes from their position in the ruling party. The *caciques* generally control such sources of wealth as soft drink and beer distributorships and trucking and communication services. These divisions within Mayan communities were clearly evident after the Zapatista began their rebellion and the army moved in to occupy the area. Representatives of human rights organizations reported seeing homes flying white flags, signaling the occupants' support for the army, whereas many homes without flags were empty. In addition, some Mayans formed local vigilante groups, which, along with the private armies of the ranchers, the *guardias blancas* ("white guards"), attacked and harassed Zapatista supporters and sympathizers. Thus, as with Malaysian villages and Kikuyu settlements and reserves, there was a clear division between the well-to-do and the poor and, as in the case of the Mau Mau rebellion, community members who sympathized with the rebels and those loyal to the government. The question is, *how did this inequality develop?*

The Zapatista base is largely in eastern Chiapas, in the foothills of the central highlands and the Lancandon rain forest that borders Guatemala. Until the 1950s the rain forest was largely unoccupied. The Chol and Cholti Maya who inhabited the area in the sixteenth and seventeenth centuries were either killed by military and missionary expeditions or relocated to work on Spanish haciendas (Nations 1994:31). In the 1950s the government encouraged settlement in the rain forest by Tzeltal and Tzotzil Mayans from the overpopulated central highlands. There the Mayan colonists competed with loggers and ranchers for land. A pattern developed whereby loggers would build roads into the rain forests, take whatever timber they wanted, and be followed by Mayans practicing slash and burn agriculture. However, because of poor planning and limited support from the government, along with the lack of relevant agricultural skills by the new settlers, the soil was soon denuded, and Mayan settlers found it necessary to move to other areas of the forest where the same cycle was repeated (Earle 1994:28).

Furthermore, the government never issued clear land titles to the Mayan farmers, paving the way for cattle ranchers to graze their stock on the cleared forest. As a result of this pattern, two-thirds of the Selva Lancandona has been cleared, leaving only the Montes Azules Biosphere Reserve with its original vegetation. In addition, the area's population increased from 6,000 in 1960 to more than 300,000 in 1994. Although some of the Mayans in the rain forest have received title to land (and the leaders of their communities quickly declared their loyalty to the government), the vast majority have not and have continually been harassed by the *guardias blancas* to move off the land.

Another category of Zapatista supporters are Protestant converts who were evicted from their villages in the 1970s and 1980s. They were expelled ostensibly because they undermined the traditional religious practices of the largely Catholic population, but most were forced to move because they challenged the traditional political system of local bosses, refused to pay taxes to support traditional religious ceremonies, and refused to consume liquor or beer, an important source of income for town officials (Gossen 1994:19).

In addition to the Mayans who moved into the area in the 1950s and 1960s and the religious and political refugees, there are others that the government encouraged to settle in the rain forests to serve as buffers against the Mayans from Guatemala, who were streaming across the border to escape the Guatemalan army fighting their own peasant revolt.

Economic inequality was aggravated by the economic boom of the 1960s and 1970s in Mexico. During that time Mexico borrowed heavily from world financial organizations to invest in energy. Much of the investment went for oil exploration and drilling and hydroelectric projects in Chiapas. Although Chiapas supplies fully 50 percent of Mexico's electricity, almost 35 percent of Chiapas homes have no electricity. The jobs and wealth that came into Chiapas in the 1960s and 1970s were not equally distributed, and one consequence was increased village conflict. Furthermore, as some members of the population were earning large sums working on government projects, others were losing their land to cattle and dairy ranchers and to the flooding created by the hydroelectric dams. June Nash (1994), who did fieldwork in a Chiapas village in the 1960s, reported that some poor peasants assumed that the rich had accummulated their wealth through the use of witchcraft, whereas others believed the wealth was given to the rich by cave dwellers in exchange for their souls. She also reports that interpersonal conflict that took the form of witchcraft accusations or expressions of envy—the evil eye—were settled by homicide.

The rebels, therefore, likely consisted of representatives of different Mayan groups, some religious and political victims of more prosperous Maya, along with some Ladinos. The question is, *why did they join in or support the revolt?*

The Rebellion and the Global Economy

One of the major reasons for the plight of poor Chiapas peasants is the decline in support for small-scale agriculture in Mexico. The debate over whether Mexico needed peasant agriculture at all increased in 1982 when the debt crisis (Mexico had a $96 million foreign debt) forced Mexico to adopt an austerity budget in exchange for a restructuring of the debt. One of the measures adopted that affected Chiapas peasants was the removal of the subsidy for fertilizer (Collier 1994:16). Cooperatives were formed, and the Indians began to agitate for political and economic reform. They were met by brutal repression from the *guardias blancas*. Next, believing the world coffee market had stabilized, Mexico ended coffee price supports for farmers. Coffee production was the major cash crop of Chiapas peasants. As soon as Mexico cut its price support, the world market price for coffee plunged, further damaging the livelihood of peasants in the Chiapas lowlands and throwing many into bankruptcy (Nations 1994:33).

Then, in the clearest sign of the government's withdrawal of support for small-scale agriculture, they modified Article 27 of the Mexican Constitution so that if landholders agreed, *ejido* land could be sold. In addition, the government let it be known that there was no more land to redistribute. This ended the land redistribution program, leaving Chiapas peasants without land or without title to land on which they were squatting.

Finally, NAFTA was negotiated and approved. Free trade in itself might not have damaged the economic prospects of Chiapas's peasants. They might have done well with their agricultural, forest, and handicraft products, but it was clear there was little or no support from the government. Furthermore, with NAFTA signed and dreams of an increase in American beef imports, ranchers in Chiapas began talking openly of expanding their cattle production, which clearly would have required taking over additional peasant land. This meant increased confrontations with the *guardias blancas*. In fact, many peasants had reportedly begun arming themselves before the revolt to protect themselves from the ranchers' private armies.

As James D. Nations (1994:33) put it, it is little wonder, therefore, that some Chiapas farmers began to feel they were victims of a conspiracy, with no market for their crops and no land to grow them on anyway:

> It is not difficult to imagine a Tzeltal or Tojolbal farmer sizing up his choices: he can move to San Cristobal de las Casas and sell popsicles from a pushcart, he can work for a cattleman punching cows, or he can rebel against a situation that seems to have him trapped. That hundreds of farmers chose to rebel should come as no surprise.

The Revolt and the Reaction of the Mexican Government

James Scott (1985) pointed out that poor farmers in Malaysia were protesting not so much their traditional position in their villages but rather the worsening of that position as a consequence of technological change. The Kikuyu in Kenya were not protesting the initial seizing of land by the British; they had adapted quite well as squatters. Their protest was against the constant worsening of their economic position as British settlers tried to increase their economic domination. The rebellion occurred only after the settlers destroyed African livestock and evicted people en masse from their farms. Likewise, the peasants in Chiapas had adapted to voluntarily or involuntarily leaving their villages in search of land in the rain forests of the Chiapas lowlands. Resistance occurred only after a whole series of changes by the Mexican government, culminating in the altering of Article 27 and NAFTA, as it tried to adapt to changes in the global economy.

The Chiapas rebellion reveals another feature of resistance that we saw in Sedaka as well as in Kenya: the attempt of those resisting oppression to use the past ideals and rhetoric of their oppressors against them. In Chiapas, the Zapatistas used the rhetoric and principles that gave the Mexican government and the ruling political party, the PRI, its original legitimacy, much as the peasants in Malaysia fight the rich with the ideology the rich once used to justify their legitimacy in the traditional social order. The Zapatistas made it clear that the government betrayed the very principles that gave it legitimacy in the beginning, even going so far as to negate the very laws and rationale that the Mexican Revolution was fought for and reinstituting the land alienation that created the conditions for the Mexican revolution to begin with.

Two aspects of the government's reaction are worth noting. First, they seem to have been relatively restrained in their reaction, in part, no doubt, because of the skilled handling of the media and the Internet by the Zapatistas, whose supporters maintained a Web site www.ezln.org to report the Zapatistas's version of events. With the story making international headlines and the Zapatistas compared with Mexican heroes of the revolution, the government could not move to crush the rebellion militarily. Certainly, given the effectiveness of the Guatemalan genocide against its Mayan population, the Mexican army, at least as well equipped as the Guatemalan military, could have, and may yet still, do the same. The Zapatistas also made skilled use of the Internet to distribute its communiqués and report moves of the Mexican military and the *guardias blancas.* The second interesting feature of the revolt is the reaction of the world's financial community. One of the fears created by the Zapatista rebellion is that it would undermine investor confidence in the Mexican government and investors would either pull their money out of Mexico, causing a further collapse of the Mexican economy, or dissuade them from putting money into the Mexican economy. These concerns were clearly voiced by an advisor to the Chase Bank; Riordan Roett, in an internal memo, advised that if the Mexican government was to retain investor confidence it must "eliminate the Zapatistas" (Silverstein and Cockburn 1995). Whether by coincidence or not, within three weeks of the memo's circulation, the Mexican military moved offensively against the Zapatistas.

James Nations (1994) suggested that there are some real problems for the Mexican government, problems that any government faces if confronted by peasant resistance. First, if the government does react with financial aid, it may become simply more political patronage and reach only those loyal to the PRI. Second, if the media—which has served to limit the violence of the government response and prevent it from mounting a genocidal campaign as in Guatemala—loses interest, massive repression may result. Some 50,000 Guatemalan refugees still in Chiapas may become targets of violence. Third, the factions have been arming themselves. Arms sales have increased and groups are forming to defend traditional rights and powers, reminiscent of the death squads formed by eastern Chiapas ranchers. This factional conflict exploded on December 22, 1997, with the massacre of forty-five unarmed Indian sympathizers of the Zapatistas, including four pregnant women and eighteen children. The killers were apparently pro-government gunman armed with AK-47 combat rifles distributed by a local PRI official (Preston 1998). Finally, the government must find some way to provide additional income and employment, but to do so by increasing the land under cultivation would mean taking land from cattlemen or from the Mayan farmers in the rain forest.

Whether or not the Mexican government can remedy the situation remains to be seen. The response up until now has been a virtual military occupation of the area, although the election in 2000 of a new Mexican government and the promise of new negotiations may lead to some agreement. The root causes of the Zapatista revolt—the global expansion of capitalist agriculture, the expansion of trading agreements, and the general marginal role of small-scale agriculturists—will likely remain, however, leading to the question of the future role of peasants in the world economy.

The Future of Peasants

The central dilemma of peasants in the expanding capitalist world, according to Duncan Earle (1994:27), is whether small-scale agriculture has any place in the modern world. Michael Kearney (1996:3) concludes that "peasants are mostly gone and that global conditions do not favor the perpetuation of those who remain." The option is the American system, where 2 percent of the population supplies food for the other 98 percent. Duncan made the point that peasant farmers do and can make profits; that it is a far more sustainable form of production; and that it does not degrade the rain forest, especially if it is based on coffee production that substitutes coffee plants for bushes under the rain forest canopy. But even coffee production is changing to a factory-type model, in which it is grown in vast open fields devoid of tree cover.

Another development is the demand in core countries for what are termed *nontraditional commodities (NTCs),* items that have not been produced traditionally in peripheral countries but for which there is a demand in core countries. Thus, in Gambia, people produce flowers, a range of Asian vegetables, and eggplants to sell to European and Asian buyers. But even with these commodities, the market is highly concentrated in a few hands, and wages are low (about eleven cents a day in 1994); however, large producers do contract out to small-scale farmers (Little and Dolan 2000).

Overall, however, the Mexican government and other governments around the world have taken actions that indicate that their answer is no, there is no place for peasants, and that the major question is whether it is best for peasants to move into the cities already burdened with millions living in squatter settlements or to have them in the countryside as laborers.

CONCLUSION

These three examples of peasant protest and rebellion reveal some of the factors that produce discontent in peasant populations. Peasant protest, however, will likely disappear as the need and opportunity for small-scale farmers disappears. It would take a major overhaul of the world economy to reverse the concentration of agricultural wealth that exists today. However, there remain other sources of discontent, much of it coming from those people or their descendants who were the peasant farmers of past generations.

CHAPTER ELEVEN

ANTISYSTEMIC PROTEST

*The paranoid scapegoating process at a time of social change, when
people are experiencing a sense of compulsion to live up to old moral
obligations even when they are ignoring them in day-to-day behavior,
is a common human event. It accompanies many social movements
and is apt to flare up when law and order lapse.*
—Anthony F. C. Wallace, *St. Clair*

*That man over there says that women need to be helped into carriages, and
lifted over ditches, and have to have the best place everywhere. Nobody helps
me into carriages, or over mudpuddles, or gives me any best place! And ain't
I a woman? Look at me! Look at my arm! I have ploughed and planted and
gathered into barns, and no man could head me! And ain't I a woman? I could
work as much and eat as much as a man—when I could get it—and bear the
lash as well! And ain't I a woman? I have born thirteen children, and seen
most of them sold into slavery, and when I cried out with my mother's grief,
none but Jesus heard me! And ain't I a woman?... If the first woman God
every made was strong enough to turn the world upside down all alone, these
women together ought to be able to turn it back, and get it right side up again.*
—Sojourner Truth (cited Silverblatt), "Women in States"

The rebellions of peasants in Malaysia, Kenya, and Mexico resemble the peasant rebellions of centuries ago against landlords, nobles, élites, or whoever controlled their land and whose demands became excessive or who threatened peasant survival. The major difference between the revolts we examined and those of centuries ago are that the conditions that today's peasants protest clearly are a consequence of the globalization of the capitalist economy and the resulting social and economic transformations. But what of other forms of protest, such as workers' organizations and strikes, national liberation, civil rights, feminist, militia, environmental, and fundamentalist religious movements? Is there any relationship among the diverse groups of people involved in these protests, and is there a way to conceptualize them as a whole? That is, can we place these movements in any sort of global perspective?

329

There is a school of thought in anthropology, sociology, history, geography, and political science that attributes these protests to the expansion of the capitalist world system. For that reason they term these *antisystemic protests* (Amin et al. 1990).

Capitalism requires constant change—new modes of production, new organizations of labor, the expansion of markets, new technology, and the like. It requires a society of perpetual growth. On the one hand this allows a capitalist economy enormous adaptability and flexibility. It allows business to take advantage of new technologies, to create new products and jobs, to pursue new markets, to experiment with new forms of financing, to abandon unprofitable products, forms of labor, or markets. On the other hand, this flexibility often has far-reaching effects on patterns of social and political relations.

The invention and development of the automobile revolutionized American society; it created millions of jobs and new industries and provided salaries for people to buy homes, appliances, and more automobiles. But the revolution wrought by the new technology also created pollution, dependence on petroleum, and industries that, in search of profit, open and close plants, first creating jobs and prosperity and then leaving unemployment and depression. Other innovations, such as the computer, revolutionized the workplace, possibly improved efficiency, created new modes of communication, and made vast stores of information available at a finger's touch. But the computer also made thousands of management jobs obsolete, just as agricultural changes made millions of peasants obsolete. While marveling over a technological innovation, we often neglect to consider those whose livelihoods are endangered. In our fascination with the benefits of the automobile, we rarely remember those whose livings depended on horse-drawn transportation.

One can argue, as many have, that in the long run these innovations will benefit everyone. We can, as some economists do, demonstrate that in the long run business fluctuations eventually balance out. But the ups and downs of the economist's growth chart are experienced by people as alternative phases of prosperity and crisis (Guttmann 1994:14). The economy may seek equilibrium in the long run, but people do not live in the long run; having a job and an income is an everyday concern.

In this chapter we examine the protests of those who claim that the culture of capitalism has had a detrimental effect on their lives or the lives of others. These protests can be seen as emerging from what world system theorists identify as the two world revolutions, in 1848 and 1968. We will look at labor protest associated with the revolution of 1848, feminist protest whose origins can also be said to lie in 1848, and environmental protest that, while originating in the nineteenth century, took on new meaning as a result of the revolution of 1968.

PROTEST AS ANTISYSTEMIC: THE TWO WORLD REVOLUTIONS

The first world revolution, suggested Immanual Wallerstein (1990), occurred in 1848, when workers, peasants, and others staged rebellions in eleven European countries. The series of revolts that began in France were all put down within a few months, but they succeeded in setting an agenda for protest that ultimately led to most of the reforms called for by protesters. The second world revolution occurred in 1968, when workers, students,

Citizens and workers in Paris, France, barricade the streets in the revolution of 1848.

peasants, and others in the United States, France, Italy, Czechoslovakia, Japan, and Mexico participated in popular uprisings. These movements also failed to gain the immediate objectives of the protesters, but they, too, set the agenda for reforms—civil rights, gay rights, women's rights, indigenous rights, environmental reform, among others—that have defined the goals of social movements since.

The Revolution of 1848

The revolution of 1848 began in France when on February 24 workers declared a new republic based on universal suffrage; within a month it had spread to southwest Germany, Bavaria, Berlin, and most of Italy. Within weeks the governments of most of continental Europe had been overthrown; the revolution even incited a rebellion in Brazil, as it would another revolution a year later in Colombia (Hobsbawm 1975:10). Within a year and a half, however, the revolution was defeated and, except in France, previous regimes restored to power. But although workers failed to gain their immediate objectives, the revolution of 1848 defined two sets of social movements: worker movements protesting the oppression of laborers originating in industrial revolution; and movements of national liberation motivated by a desire of peripheral countries to gain freedom from imperialism and colonial oppression. Both types of movements were modeled after the French Revolution of 1789 and its call for "liberty, equality, and fraternity." The year 1848 did not, of course, mark the beginning of such movements; organized worker protests against the abuses of industrialization go back at least to the seventeenth century in Europe, and the movements for national liberation include the American Revolution and the successful revolt against the French by Haitian slaves in 1802. But by 1848 the general guidelines and issues involved in the protests were clearly formulated.

Worker Movements.   The revolution of 1848 marked the first time a proletariat-based political group tried to achieve political power. Although they failed, said Wallerstein (1990), the revolution began an intense debate among labor rights advocates over the best way of improving the situation of the growing number of industrial workers. One option was to organize unions and gain the right to strike. The problem was that the nation-states of Europe and the Americas outlawed worker unions and made strikes a criminal offense. Another option was to fight for the right to vote and form political parties to represent workers' rights. If suffrage—the right to vote—was extended to more of the electorate, and the workers comprised a majority of the population, then they could simply assume power through the ballot box. Others argued that the governing elite would never let itself be voted out of power and that violent revolution was the only solution. The result was that two competing strategies emerged in Europe and the United States to improve the conditions of workers, one led by social democratic parties seeking political power through the vote, the other by Communist organizations advocating revolution.

By 1945 unions and labor-led political parties arose in the United States, England, France, and much of Western Europe, resulting in a vast improvement in the conditions of the working class. Most core countries recognized the rights of workers to strike and bargain collectively; developed programs of social insurance (e.g., social security programs, unemployment programs, workers' compensation programs, health programs, education programs); and extended the vote to the poor, ethnic minorities, and women. From the mid-nineteenth to the mid-twentieth century the number of people in poverty in the United States and Western Europe decreased dramatically. By 1949 most American and Western European workers enjoyed a level of prosperity that few would have dreamed of in 1848.

At the same time, workers in revolutionary states, including Russia and most of eastern Europe, achieved their goals under communist regimes, and although they were not as prosperous as their Western counterparts, they probably enjoyed greater guarantees of basic needs (e.g., jobs, food, shelter). Thus, within a century workers enjoyed benefits fought for in the revolution of 1848.

Nationalist Antisystemic Movements.   As working-class movements in Europe and the United States were struggling to improve their lives, national liberation movements were occurring on the periphery. Whereas the social democratic and communist movements in the core were led by the industrial proletariat, the nationalist movements in the periphery were initiated by the middle class and intelligentsia reaching out to other anticapitalist segments of their populations. Thus, virtually all the countries of Latin America gained their independence in the nineteenth century. The countries of Asia and Africa under European colonial rule gained their independence after World War II. By 1968, with the exception of the continuing struggle in Vietnam and continued colonial domination in a few African states, colonial powers had been forced to abandon politically their nineteenth- and early twentieth-century empires and ostensibly hand over power to indigenous elites.

The enormous world economic growth that followed World War II created an illusion. In the West, people thought they had found the solutions to the problems of economic depression and unemployment and that their world had entered a period of perpetual prosperity and growth; world hunger would be erased, infectious diseases would be eradicated, and class conflict would be a thing of the past. In the communist countries people believed they had discovered the economic formula for economic security; Russian Premier Nikita Khrushchev would boast that by 1980 the U.S.S.R. would have overtaken and surpassed the United States in providing for its citizens. In the Third World the leaders of national liberation movements, such as the one we examined in Kenya, felt that their mixtures of socialism and capitalism would enable them to develop economically and begin to achieve the prosperity of the West. In sum, as Samir Amin et al. (1990:96) suggested, in the period after 1945 in a majority of countries the ostensible objectives of the antisystemic movements of the nineteenth century had come to pass as workers' or other popular movements gained control of major nation-states (Wallerstein 1990:33).

Each of the movements that emerged out of the revolution of 1848, according to Wallerstein, can take credit for one fundamental reform. The social democrats of the West claimed to have transformed the core states into welfare states with social insurance and an increase in real wages, a compromise Wallerstein called "Fordism." Conservative forces acceded to these reforms because they subdued protest without endangering capital accumulation; furthermore, they made good economic sense. However, conservative forces still sought to whittle away at the welfare state and the reforms embedded in them. In the communist countries, the socialization of the means of production was the great reform, along with social insurance and welfare, but at a lower level than in the West, albeit with a higher degree of security and employment. The great achievement of the national liberation movements was not an increase in wages or social security or the socialization of the means of production, but the increased participation of indigenous people in government and the creation of an indigenous elite, such as we saw in Kenya, Mexico, and Malaysia.

Yet 1968 would see the beginning of another world revolution, this time against states that were controlled by or contained representation of the very groups that had initiated the revolution of 1848. The labor-oriented Democratic Party was in power in the United States, the labor party ruled in Britain, socialists controlled France and Italy, and Eastern European countries, at least in theory, were ruled by the workers through national communist parties. The question is *why, when so many of the objectives of the first world revolution were realized, did another revolution occur?*

The Revolution of 1968

The revolution of 1968 was marked in the United States by student protests over Vietnam, demonstrations at the Democratic National Convention in Chicago, and campus demonstrations that led to the killing of students at Jackson State and Kent State Universities by

Demonstrators outside the Democratic National Convention in Chicago in 1968 are attacked by police.

state militia. In France workers and students barricaded the streets of Paris; similar demonstrations occurred in Japan, Mexico, and elsewhere.

From a world system perspective, 1968 was as much a turning point as 1848. The "old" movements had attained state power or at least a voice in the state, so that the popular uprisings in 1968—in the United States, France, Italy, Czechoslovakia, Japan, and Mexico—were not so much uprisings against the existing world system as they were protests against the "old" antisystemic movements in power in the world system. The 1968 revolution was triggered by the conviction that the old movements had not fulfilled their objectives, that they had become "part of the problem." However, the 1968 revolution also represented a protest by groups who felt they were not sharing in the system (Wallerstein 1990:27).

In the United States people protested against the government's attempt to suppress brutally the nationalistic objectives of the Vietnamese peoples; in Russia and Eastern Europe people learned about the brutalities of Stalin and witnessed the repression of freedom movements in Hungary and Czechoslovakia; in the periphery the dream of economic development turned into a nightmare of poverty, government repression, and corruption.

These developments combined to leave those who had failed to gain relief with no place to turn. Thus, in the midst of a continuing and unpopular war in Vietnam and a growing "counterculture" protesting consumerism and the growing gap in wealth between the core and the periphery, the dissidents could turn to neither the social democrats nor the communists to express their discontent. Instead, new social movements were created that focused on "identity issues," such as civil rights, women's rights, gay and lesbian rights, indigenous people's rights, and handicapped rights (Wallerstein 1990:41). For a time, there was a sense of mutual solidarity among these movements expressed in the idea of a "rainbow coalition."

Whereas in the West the theme was the forgotten people—minorities, women, and gays—in the East the struggle was directed against the bureaucrats of the communist states, a protest that would culminate in what some claim was the world revolution of 1989 that toppled the communist regimes of Eastern Europe (Wagar 1991:102). In the periphery it was not that social and economic reforms failed to help half the people or that reforms created as many privileged people as they removed. Rather, it was that those in power promoted, or at least acquiesced in adopting, economic reforms and practices that resulted in continuing (often worsening) economic conditions, neocolonial subordination, and the emergence of a new elite.

Thus, in 1968 the antisystemic movements born in 1848 faced the new antisystemic movements born in 1968. Yet, as Immanual Wallerstein (1990:45) suggested,

> [w]hen all is said and done, all these movements (as movements) emerged out of a rejection of the injustices of the existing world-system, the capitalist world-economy. Each in its own way was seeking to fulfill the slogan of the French revolution: more liberty, more equality, more fraternity.

A range of antisystemic movements emerged out of the two world revolutions. Our assumption is that each of these we examine in this chapter represents protest against various features of the culture of capitalism. This is not to suggest that all the movements conceptualized their protest in that way; often they did not. Members of the militia movements in the United States, for example, do not focus on capitalism in their protests; their targets include the United Nations, Jews, Blacks, the World Trade Organization, and other agencies or groups that they blame for their economic distress. Yet on closer analysis, it is clearly the globalization of trade, the loss of manufacturing jobs to overseas assembly plants, the decline of small-scale farmers and ranchers that caused them economic harm (see Beeman 1997; Junas 1995).

THE PROTESTS OF LABOR: COAL MINERS IN NINETEENTH-CENTURY PENNSYLVANIA

In *St. Clair,* Anthony F. C. Wallace (1987) offered an intimate glimpse of life in the nineteenth-century Pennsylvania coal town of St. Clair and the conditions that led to labor protest, and the efforts of mine owners and operators to suppress it. For various reasons, coal mining was not economically viable in much of Pennsylvania, yet mine operators persisted in their efforts to make profits, scrimping on safety and workers' wages and then blaming the workers for their lack of success. As we shall see, the workers responded with a labor protest that was met with systematic repression.

The Coal Industry and the Worker's Life

In the 1820s and 1830s investors from Philadelphia and New York turned their attention to the coal fields of Pennsylvania, investing heavily in land they thought would yield high profits in coal. The landowners generally did not run the mining operations themselves but rented or leased the land to coal mine operators. The operators expected to make a profit because of the need for coal to provide warmth in homes and fuel for the furnaces of what they hoped would be a thriving U.S. iron industry. Labor for the mines came from new immigrants from England, Germany, Ireland, and Wales.

Coal mining in the anthracite region of southeastern Pennsylvania entailed digging shafts underground to locate the veins of coal, building tracks or hoists in the shafts to haul coal and transport men and equipment to and from the surface, and constructing pumps to drain the water shafts. Aboveground was a series of conveyer devices called breakers that broke the large pieces of coal into desired sizes and loaded the coal onto railroad cars or canal barges for shipment to its destination.

Each mine in southeastern Pennsylvania, where St. Clair is located, employed 200 to 300 persons. Work organization, as it is in most industries, was hierarchical and divided between those who worked belowground in the mines and those who worked aboveground. The lowest-level workers in the mines were boys eight to twelve years of age who worked the ventilation doors that controlled air flow in the mine as men, mules, and equipment passed back and forth. Next were the teenage boys who drove the mules that pulled the carts filled with coal. Next in the underground hierarchy were the miners' helpers, and next were the contract miners, who were paid according to the amount of coal they loaded. Toward the top of the worker's hierarchy were the craftsmen—masons, carpenters, blacksmiths, and pumpmen—who worked underground. In charge of this group were the mine boss and the fire boss, whose main duty was to inspect the mine each morning to ensure that it was safe from methane gas produced by the coal, rock falls, and flooding. Aboveground the bottom of the hierarchy consisted of the slatepickers, who picked debris out of the coal before it was loaded for shipment and who might be as young as four years of age, and other unskilled workers doing a variety of loading chores. Higher up in the aboveground hierarchy were the highly skilled workers, such as engineers, machinists, carpenters, and teamsters.

The workforce in the mine was also divided by ethnic group; the top jobs were held by migrants from areas with a coal mining tradition—England, Wales, and Germany; at the bottom were migrants from Ireland, who had little or no mining experience. The place of the Irish at the bottom of the hierarchy was also a consequence of their reputation for rowdiness, drunkenness, and unsafe conduct in the mines.

Mining grew significantly in the St. Clair area from the 1840s through the 1870s, in spite of the fact that few people were making any money and many were losing a great deal. The costs to operators of mining a ton of coal seemed to vary from $1.56 to $3.16. These figures did not include township taxes, canal or railroad shipping costs, commissions to sales agents, or depreciation on property or interest on loans. Railroad shipping costs var- ied, climbing or falling from an average of about $1.60 per ton. In sum, the actual cost of mining a ton of coal must have been at least $3.16 to $4.16, although, given the absence of accounting procedures, it is unlikely mine operators knew their full production costs. How- ever, depending on the competition, the time of year, the supply, and other factors, the price of coal to customers averaged only about $2.75 per ton. Moreover, there were frequent in- terruptions to mining operations caused by accidents, breakdowns, overproduction, and flooding.

Wallace suggested that one reason people continued to mine despite losing money was the inadequacy of their accounting procedures: By the time they realized that they were losing money, it was too late to do anything about it. Wallace (1987:25) estimated that 95 percent of all collieries failed from 1820 to 1875, and the median survival time of a company was less than one year.

Why was coal mining unprofitable in St. Clair and the surrounding area? Apparently there were two reasons: the geology of the area and the frequent work stoppages caused by accidents.

Veins of coal are stratified deposits of decomposed organic materials transformed underground by pressure and heat into masses of carbon-rich materials. Movements of the Earth's crust sometimes brings these veins to the surface, so that they form vertical or di- agonal deposits. The size and directions of these deposits determine how easy or difficult they are to mine. Those veins brought to the surface are obviously the easiest to mine, and these deposits were the first to be exploited. Other deposits can be reached only by dig- ging underground. For these the ease of mining depends on the size of the vein and the depth to which one has to dig to reach it. The problem in the St. Clair area was that the nature of the coal deposits required a lot of digging to reach veins that were often small or of poor quality.

Apparently, coal mine operators could have avoided their losses if they had taken se- riously the reports of geologists who concluded that mining in the area would not be prof- itable. But the landowners and the mine operators chose to ignore those reports, believing instead those who attacked the scientists' findings and claimed that the investments that had already been made could prove profitable.

The second reason the mines failed to make money—the frequency of work stop- pages because of accidents—was related to the first; given the small profit margin to be made mining coal in the anthracite district, mine operators had to save money on opera- tions, and one way they did that was by scrimping on safety. Coal mining is dangerous. In addition to cave-ins, flooding caused by pump failures, and the risks of working around the conveyor belts of the breakers, there was the constant danger of explosions. Coal produces methane gas, and when the amount of methane reaches a 5 to 12 percent mixture with oxygen any flame or spark will ignite it. Because miners of the period carried open-flame lamps attached to their helmets, the possibility of explosion was very great. One way to prevent the critical buildup of methane was to construct ventilation systems that ensured constant air flow through the shafts. Such systems were costly, however, and because the profit margins were so small, most mine operators invested a minimum in such systems. Moreover, there were no state or federal safety standards that the mine operators had to fol- low. The costs of neglecting safety were high to both miners and mine operators: Miners lost lives and limbs in accidents and explosions, and operators lost money in the destruction of equipment.

The mine owners failed to recognize or admit that the geology of the coal fields made it uneconomical to mine: They blamed their economic failure not on the geology or their business practices, but on the federal government for not putting a high enough tariff on British iron being imported into the country. Coal mining profits were closely tied to the rise and fall of the American iron industry; if the iron industry did not expand, the coal industry could not grow. But British iron was cheaper, and perhaps better, than American iron. If British iron was made more expensive by high import tariffs, both the American iron industry and the coal industry would expand and profit.

Accidents and work stoppages, however, could not be blamed on the British or the government. Mine operators and owners, instead of recognizing their own culpability, blamed careless workers. When Wallace reviewed accident reports for the period, he found that in almost every case the accident was blamed on miner negligence. This not only absolved the mine owner of blame for the economic losses but it also relieved the mine operator of any financial liability for the accident.

The accident and death rates as a result of inadequate ventilation and lack of emergency tunnels to allow miners to escape from explosions or cave-ins were appalling. It is difficult to get reliable figures on injuries and deaths in the mines from 1850 to 1880. After examining fatality rates from 1870 to 1884, Wallace estimated that fatality rates varied from 2.3 to 6.8 percent of the workforce per year—and this was after the passage of a mine safety law in 1869 in Pennsylvania. We do know that the numbers killed in Pennsylvania mines were far higher than in Great Britain; there was one fatality for every 33,433 tons mined in Pennsylvania as opposed to one fatality per 103,000 tons in Great Britain.

Before the passage of the mine safety law in 1869 no one kept consistent records, but by using reports in the *Miner's Journal,* the major publication for the mining industry, Wallace concluded that each year 6 percent of people employed in mining, including those who worked aboveground, were killed, another 6 percent were crippled for life, and yet another 6 percent were seriously injured. Thus, a mining employee had less than an even chance of surviving for twelve years, and he could expect to be killed or crippled for life in six (Wallace 1987:253). Because mine operators continued to see the accidents as caused by careless miners and because the courts absolved them of any responsibility for death or accidents, there was little need for them to change their practices.

Given the difficulty of making a profit in coal mining, mine operators not only cut costs on safety but also minimized the pay of miners. It was a buyer's market for labor. The transformation of agriculture in Europe, as we saw in Chapter 2, created millions of landless peasants, whereas the fluctuations in demand for such products as textiles, iron, and coal resulted in great economic insecurity for those dependent on jobs for their livelihood.

Mine managers made $1.95 per day, foreman $1.25 per day, blacksmiths $1.08 per day, and miners $1.16 per day if they worked twenty-four days in the four-week pay period (or about $28 per month). Contract miners were a different category and were paid by the wagonload or by the yard if they were cutting tunnels. But out of this the contract miner had to pay his helpers and other expenses, such as lamps and wicks. Helpers generally earned $0.85 to $0.95 per day, which meant the contract miner had to earn about $50 per month simply to earn as much as he paid his helper.

The income was above subsistence level for the time, but that assumed no work stoppages, no illness, and no layoffs—all three of which were likely at some point. This was compensated for, in some respects, by the fact that most households had more than one wage earner; a household with one worker might make $150 to $200 per year. Some households took in boarders and some women worked as seamstresses, cooks, and maids.

Food was cheap; corn was fifty cents per bushel, eggs eleven cents per dozen, flour five dollars per barrel, butter eighteen cents per pound, bacon seven cents per pound, beef eight cents per pound. Housing was also cheap. Thus, a laborer with a wife and two children who earned on the average twenty dollars per month could subsist and even save a little; families with more than two children would have required income from other family members, but children could be put to work by the time they were eight or nine. The problem was that work was often not steady—strikes, floods, and accidents often closed down the mines or disabled the miners.

Furthermore, working in the mines took a devastating toll on the miner's health. Coal mining produced not only methane gas but also tiny particles of coal dust that worked their way into the lungs. The rates of disability and death as a result of "miner's asthma," or black lung disease, were extremely high. As one mine inspector (cited Wallace 1987:257) of the time wrote,

> [a]fter six years' labor in a badly ventilated mine—that is a mine where a man with a good constitution may from habit be able to work everyday for several years—the lungs begin to change to a bluish color. After twelve years they are densely black, not a vestige of natural color remaining, and are little better than carbon itself. The miner dies at thirty-five of coal miner's consumption.

Worker Resistance and Protest

How could the laborers protect their interests, and formally or informally protest the dangers they faced in the mines and the economic insecurity brought about by low wages, layoffs, and work stoppages?

Miners protested their low wages and dangerous work conditions in various ways; there were spontaneous work stoppages, acts of sabotage against the mines, demonstrations and marches, and probably work slowdowns. Many of these acts were met with force from the police or state militia. The first regional strike occurred in 1858, when lower coal prices resulted in wage cuts. Miners closed down the mines and marched through the streets banging drums and waving flags. The sheriff called out the militia, and men were arrested on riot charges.

The first effective strike occurred in 1868, when the Pennsylvania legislature passed a law making eight hours a legal workday, although it also meant a cut in wages. Miners began a strike, demanding that the eight-hour day be instituted with no cut in wages, resulting, in effect, in a 20 percent pay raise. The dispute was settled after the miners closed down the mines, with workers obtaining a 10 percent wage increase.

Although unions were illegal, the miners formed the Workingmen's Benevolent Association of St. Clair in 1868, the forerunner of the United Mine Workers of America. Although the mine owners and operators refused to recognize the association as the bargaining agent for mine workers, it was effective in lobbying for safety legislation and improved living conditions, as well as in organizing strikes.

Also central to Irish protest against discrimination, both on the job and off, were the Molly Maguires. The term *Molly Maguires* originated in the south of Ireland and was applied to groups of peasants who organized to retaliate against landlords, magistrates, and others guilty of injustices to poor, Irish families. The name was suggested by the practice of young men who disguised themselves by blackening their faces with burnt cork and dressing in women's clothing. In these disguises they beat or killed gamekeepers, servers of eviction notices, cottage wrecking crews, or others responsible for oppressing Irish families. It was Benjamin Bannan, in his *Miner's Journal,* who began to articulate the idea of Irish Catholics and the Molly Maguires in the role of conspirators, calling it a secret Roman Catholic organization that aims to control the political process and the Democratic Party.

To what extent the Molly Maguires were a formal secret society or an imagined conspiracy is a moot question. There is no question, however, that Irish Catholics organized to protect themselves and to retaliate, sometimes with violence, against discrimination or what they perceived as injustice. Organizations, such as the Molly Maguires, are not uncommon in social situations in which there is little effective public order or among groups that view the state authorities as hostile to them. These groups become institutionalized systems of law outside the official law, a parallel government outside the official government. Eric Hobsbawm (1959:6) referred to such groups as *mafia,* seeing them as a form of organized rebellion again hostile groups or public authorities.

The main importance of the Molly Maguires in the struggle between Irish mine workers and the mine owners and operators was that they became the focus of the owners' and operators' attempts to destroy the miners association and to link it, as well as other worker organizations, with an international conspiracy. In many ways, the Molly Maguires represented to the mine owners what the Mau Mau oath represented to the British in Kenya. It also represented attempts by nation-states or capitalist enterprises to associate social protest with activities defined as illegal and to label such protest as criminal or terrorist activity.

Whether there was a secret society operating in the coal fields of Pennsylvania, or whether the name Molly Maguires was applied to any group seeking retributive justice is unclear. It was clear that there were individuals who did not hesitate to use violence on those who they felt inflicted injustice on the Irish or whose injustice went unpunished by the courts. Furthermore, labor violence was real enough: There were attacks on strike breakers, sabotage at the mines, and physical attacks on mine operators or their agents, and the workers' association often used the language of violence. In addition, many believed that the parent organization of the Molly Maguires was the Ancient Order of Hibernians, an Irish Catholic benevolent association modeled after fraternal organizations, such as the Knights of Columbus, from which Irish were excluded.

In September 1875 there was an epidemic of murders and attempted murders; the victims had been guilty of attacks on Irish or of firing or blacklisting Irish workers. As Wallace (1987:374) said, those who were called Molly Maguires acted on "the demand for retributive justice in an atmosphere of ethnic discrimination by the authorities and bitter resentment by those who felt that they had systematically been denied their rights."

The punishments dealt out by the Molly Maguires were carefully weighted according to the crime. Capital offenses included killing an Irishman and being acquitted by the court, trying to kill an Irishman and not being arrested, and depriving an Irishman of his livelihood. Verbally threatening an Irishman called for a severe beating. The victims were always selected because they were the ones who committed the injury and were never attacked as random targets; women and children were never targeted, even if they were witnesses (Wallace 1987:359). Defense funds were established for Mollies, as Irishmen believed, with some justification, that they were being discriminated against and could not expect justice from the courts or police.

Thus, workers had various means to protest their treatment by mine owners and operators, other miners, and state or local authorities. They ranged from informal and spontaneous acts, to formal labor organizing, to organized violence, much of which originated in ethnic discrimination, as it did in labor protest. But labor and ethnic discrimination were tied together by the mine owners and operators in their attempts to destroy the workers' organizations.

Destroying Worker Resistance

Mine owners and operators were vehemently opposed to any legislation that either increased safety in the mines or recognized workers' rights to collective bargaining. Additional safety measures, they argued, would make the mines uneconomical, and collective bargaining would give the workers too great a say in mine operation. The Pennsylvania legislature did pass safety legislation in 1869, but only five months later a mine explosion at Avondale, Pennsylvania, killed 108 people, most of whom were asphyxiated by gases while waiting to be rescued because there was no escape tunnel.

The owners also tried to destroy the Ancient Order of Hibernians, claiming it was simply a front for the Molly Maguires. But the ultimate goal of the mine operators was to destroy the union and other miner organizations. The leader of the attack was John Gowen, an ex–coal operator and attorney for the Philadelphia and Reading Coal and Iron Company, which by 1885 came to dominate the anthracite coal district.

Gowen's strategy was to portray the Workingmen's Benevolent Association and the Ancient Order of Hibernians as extensions of the Molly Maguires, in effect scapegoating worker organizations for real or imagined offenses of the Molly Maguires. First he hired the Pinkerton Detective Agency to infiltrate the Workingmen's Benevolent Association to uncover connections between it and the Ancient Order of Hiberbians and the Molly Maguires. The operative could find no evidence of any connection between the union and any secret organization.

Gowen then hired another agent to infiltrate the Ancient Order of Hibernians. The agent reported only that many people were leaving the organization because of the attempt to connect it to the Molly Maguires. In fact, the smear campaign against the order was so effective that some Irish clergy had condemned it, even threatening to excommunicate any Catholic who remained a member.

Gowen finally got his chance to destroy the order in a case of attempted murder of a Welshman, M. "Bully Bill" Thomas. Thomas, a prizefighter, was involved in a melee between the Welsh and Irish fire companies, both of which arrived to put out the same fire; shots were fired, a man was killed, and a young Irishman named Daniel Dougherty was charged with murder. Dougherty was acquitted, and this time the avengers were Welshmen, not Irish. Bully Bill Thomas and others made an attempt on Dougherty's life, and local members of the Ancient Order of Hibernians planned a retaliation. Thomas was attacked and shot but survived; based on his complaint and evidence from the Pinkerton agent, arrests were made. Gowen put the Ancient Order of Hibernians and the Workingmen's Benevolent Association on trial, painting them in such sinister terms that being a member was tantamount to having a bad reputation. A succession of trials resulted in the hanging of twenty men convicted of conspiracy to murder. The trial, in effect, succeeded in scapegoating the miners and their organizations for the economic failure of the coal fields.

In fact, according to Wallace (1987), there was little or no connection between the Workingmen's Benevolent Association and the Ancient Order of Hibernians, although there is little doubt that the Molly Maguires served as a mechanism for Irish Catholics to achieve retributive justice in a hostile world. More interesting, the reaction of Gowen and others is reminiscent of the reaction of the British to the Mau Mau, refusing to recognize any real oppression and blaming instead oath taking and secret ritual. The end result was to discredit an already broken union and fix the blame for the problems of the coal trade on forces outside the trade, such as the absence of protective tariffs on British iron and the workers themselves.

Wallace's story of St. Clair also provides some insights into the origin of labor conflict, a story being repeated today in industries all over the world. In St. Clair we found a marginally profitable industry trying to squeeze a profit by lowering wages and scrimping on safety measures, creating conditions ripe for labor protest. Today we find marginally profitable, highly competitive industries, such as textiles, electronics, and toys, cutting labor costs by moving into countries whose lack of labor legislation mirrors the labor situation in Pennsylvania in the nineteenth century. Workers in these countries face the same problems of low wages and unsafe working conditions that workers in the Pennsylvania coal fields of the nineteenth century faced. These conditions have led to attempts to organize, attempts generally met with legal repression or violence by industry owners or managers and the state.

Each year the International Confederation of Free Trade Unions (ICFTU) issues an annual report on labor violence and repression. In the 133 countries and territories covered by the 2003 annual survey, the ICFTU has listed a total of 213 deaths or disappearances of trade unionists, with 2,000 trade unionists arrested, some 1,000 injured, and 30,000 fired during 2002. In South Korea, a strike in five Catholic hospitals led to an armed intervention by the antiriot police, the sacking of 20 trade unionists, the "disciplining" of a further 573, and 7 of the 93 who stood trial were sent to prison. In Colombia, there were 184 murders of trade unionists, 27 attempted assassinations, 189 death threats against Colombian union officials and members, 9 "disappearances," 139 arbitrary arrests, and 27 abductions. Eighty trade unionists were forced to flee the country into exile. Long-term imprisonment, beatings, internment in psychiatric hospitals or labor camps, and harassment of families are systematically used in China to stamp out any free trade unions. Even in the United States at least one in every ten workers trying to form a union in 2002 was fired. In Denver, managers at a Wal-Mart store, the ICFTU report states, advised all their employees that any trade union activity would be monitored and encouraged workers to spy on their colleagues. Workers showing trade union sympathies were subjected to interrogation and verbal harassment (ICFTU 2003).

GLOBAL FEMINIST RESISTANCE

In September 1995, representatives from nongovernmental organizations all over the world gathered in Beijing, China, at the Fourth World Conference on Women to develop what conference participants called "strategic sisterhood," an international organization to unite the causes of women in the periphery with those in the core. The model for present-day protests about the rights of women can be traced to the world revolution of 1848. In that year 400 participants gathered in Seneca Falls, New York, to plan their strategy to fight for the abolition of slavery. At the meeting Elizabeth Cady Stanton, one of the leading social activists of the nineteenth century, introduced a resolution that women be given the right to vote. Such an idea was radical even in that setting, and it passed only after Frederick Douglass, the most prominent African American of the nineteenth century, supported the resolution. The resolution was greeted with contempt by most Americans: One newspaper called it an insurrection, another accused the women of being Amazons. And although Black men were given the right to vote in 1869, women, with the exception of those in a few western states such as Wyoming, Colorado, Idaho, and Utah, were not allowed to vote until 1920. Although it took more than seventy years, the right for women to vote was one of the changes that emerged out of the revolutionary mood of 1848.

Although the modern feminist movement has helped raise the status of women, at least in the West, women remain among the most economically, politically, and socially marginalized members of global society. As Martha Ward noted in *A World Full of Women* (1996:221), the major occupations of women worldwide are "street-selling, factory assembly lines, piecework, cash-cropping and commercial agriculture, prostitution or sex work, and service in domestic settings, like maids who change the sheets on hotel beds."

At the same time that women produce 75 to 90 percent of food crops in the world, they are responsible for the running of households. According to the United Nations, in no country in the world do men come anywhere close to women in the amount of time spent doing housework. Furthermore, despite the efforts of feminist movements, women in the core still suffer disproportionately, leading to what sociologists refer to as the "feminization of poverty," where two out of every three poor adults are women. The informal slogan of the Decade of Women became "Women do two-thirds of the world's work, receive 10 percent of the world's income and own 1 percent of the means of production" (cited Ward 1996:224).

These conditions have incited feminist protest in virtually every country of the world. In India, dowry—the money and gifts a bride brought with her to her husband's household—became an object of protest in the 1970s when a young woman was killed by her in-laws because her parents could not meet the in-laws' increasing demands for dowry. Apparently, this was not uncommon; there were other reports of in-laws dowsing daughters-in-law with kerosene and setting them on fire. These were often classed by authorities as suicide and passed off as family affairs of no concern to the state (Kumar 1995). In Bangladesh, women organized to gain access to employment and fair wages and to revise inheritance laws that favored men (Jahan 1995). In the Philippines, women organized to gain labor rights after the imposition in 1972 of martial law by President Ferdinand Marcos, a movement that contributed to the election of Corazon Aquino as the first woman president of the Philippines. In South Africa, women have organized to protest sexual abuse, economic inequality, and the exclusion of women from public policy decision making (Kemp et al. 1995). In Kenya, women's groups have proliferated to support the entry of women into business, community projects, and revolving loan programs (Oduol and Kabira 1995).

The women's movements that proliferated in the 1970s have had significant effects in some areas. In Peru, for example, it would have been unusual twenty years ago to see, as one can now, a woman conducting the national symphony orchestra, working in politics, or running a business. Twenty years ago Peruvian women's lives centered on their family and the home (Blondet 1995).

In spite of some gains, however, the economic position of women in global society remains, as a whole, marginal to that of men. For example, women represent about 60 percent of the billion or so people earning one dollar or less per day. We need to ask, *what are the factors that contribute to the inferior position of women in the world, and what are some of the strategies that can be employed to improve their position?*

Gender Relations in the Culture of Capitalism

Eleanor Leacock, who has studied the role of women in capitalism around the world, concluded that some women hold some measure of influence and power (1986:107). But the degree of power varies with the gender system of their culture; the status of the race, religious group, or class to which they belong; the political system under which they live; and their personal attributes and life histories. Leacock agreed with Karl Marx and Friedrich Engels that capitalism is patriarchal and paternalistic, that the mode of production that creates a hierarchy of labor and a family structure that relegates women to domestic work inevitably leads to the oppression of women. The question is, *what evidence is there that the marginalization of women and the protest that it inspires, particularly in the periphery, is a consequence of the expansion of the culture of capitalism?*

Four developments that accompanied the expansion of the culture of capitalism helped define its system of gender relations: the loss of control by women over valuable and productive resources; the transformation of extended families into male-dominated nuclear families; the expansion of industry into the periphery; and the imposition on peripheral countries by multilateral institutions of structural adjustment programs. Let's examine each of these developments.

In the eighteenth and nineteenth centuries capitalist expansion altered two sets of social relations in societies into which it spread. First, capitalism resulted in the loss of control by most members of societies of the means of production, making them dependent for survival on the sale of their labor. Second, capitalism undermined large, extended family groups, isolating people into individual or nuclear families, each a separate economic unit ruled over by male household heads. In these developments, said Leacock (1983:268), lie the origins of the modern suppression of women. For example women among the Cherokee and Iroquois in North America were equals or near equals of men. Women generally controlled the production of food crops and played a major role in public decision making; among the Iroquois, women chose the political leaders and could decide themselves to terminate a marriage. Colonists initiated changes by negotiating or trading only with men and by introducing a European model economy to replace horticulture and hunting. This undermined the authority of extended kin groups, in which women played a major role, thus creating a society based on male-dominated agriculture. Among the Montagnais-Nasksapi of Labrador, cooking, cleaning, and housework did not become institutionalized as women's work until women became dependent on fur-trapping husbands and individual households of husbands, wives, and children replaced family lodges. In this way, said Leacock (1986:117), women's productive activities and decision-making authority shifted from the larger kin groups and the fields to the household domain, whereas their social status was redefined as subservient to and dependent on male household heads.

Missionaries further undermined women's authority, especially in societies where women had important ritual responsibilities, by refusing to deal with women and by the missionaries using their power to undermine traditional family arrangements. The missionaries believed the patriarchal nuclear family was ordained by God and taught that a woman's role was to provide loving care for husband and children. As a result, women's unpaid household labor became, for all practical purposes, a gift to plantation or mine owners, manufacturers, or traders who realized their profit from the work of husbands and sons (Leacock 1983:271).

In her survey of Africa, Ester Boserup (1970:277) noted much the same process: The economic and social policies of British, German, Dutch, Portuguese, and French colonizers undercut the traditional role of women as farmers, merchants, and participants in the political process of families by undermining the power of extended families or clans, taking away women's rights to land, and relegating women to the household or low-paying wage labor. We saw the consequences of this in Chapter 6 in the case of the famine in Malawi.

Karen Sacks (1979) summarized these changes in Africa by contrasting the roles of "sisters" with the roles of "wives." "Sisterhood," Sacks argued, is shorthand for a relationship in which women have access to valuable resources (land, livestock, and money) based on their membership in the extended kin group of brothers and sisters. Sisterhood connotes autonomy, adulthood, and the possibilities of gender equality. Wife or "wifehood," however, connotes a relationship of dependency. According to Sacks, the development of nation-states in the culture of capitalism undermined women's status by dismantling the larger, family-based institutions on which "sister" relations rested, turning women into dependent wives.

The works of such writers as Leacock, Boserup, and Sacks raise an interesting issue (see Silverblatt 1988). Modernization theorists who argue about the benefits, and sometimes the inevitability, of modernization generally point to the decline of the extended family and the emergence of the nuclear family as the basic unit of society as a major example of progress. Most feminist theorists propose that the nuclear family is partly responsible for the inferior position of women. Because we propose that this change has little to do with "modernization" and more to do with the emergence and expansion of the culture of capitalism, we need to ask why was the extended family not compatible with other elements of capitalist culture?

We examined in Chapter 1 the reason the nuclear family promoted consumption by requiring each small unit to purchase and consume commodities that in extended family units could easily be shared. In Chapter 9, we examined why communal property held by extended families is problematic to the economic and legal relations in capitalism. But there are other reasons why small nuclear family units are preferred in the culture of capitalism. For example, the extended family, as a political entity, conflicts with the needs of the nation-state to educate and control its citizens. Members of large extended families are more difficult to control than are members of small, isolated, nuclear families. In addition, the demands for a flexible and mobile labor supply make the extended family impractical. It is far better for capitalism to reduce people's social and emotional ties to others, to make it easier for them to relocate to where labor is needed. *If we assume that it is the preferred family unit in the culture of capitalism, how does the nuclear family lend itself to the relegation of women to an inferior position?*

First, the emergence of the nuclear family tended to release men from the ties to the extended family and make them more autonomous, giving them greater control over resources and over the members of their households. In societies where women retain close ties to their families, such control is rarely present. Furthermore, recognition of the male as head of the household conveys to male household heads control of those resources.

Second, the nuclear family and the patrilocality of the workforce serves to separate adult women from their peers, therefore reducing the potential for the social support of other women and for building class consciousness among women. The classic example, of course, is the nuclear family with a mother who does not work outside the home (Tétreault 1994:10). In some cases, as in Japan and China, the young bride is brought into the patriarchal home and virtually isolated from outside society.

A third feature of the nuclear family that supports the subservient position of women is the prevalent form of marriage. The nuclear family is traditionally composed of a larger, older, better-educated, richer, more sexually experienced, and generally legally favored man who is married to a smaller, younger, less well educated, propertyless, inexperienced, and socially less well protected woman. Although this form of marriage is not restricted to the culture of capitalism, its historic prevalence in European cultures and its spread through economic colonization and missionary activity to the periphery certainly helped sustain or create households of dominant men and subservient women (Tétreault 1994:9–10).

In addition to removing from women access to the means of production and making the male-dominated nuclear family the main social unit of society, the expansion of industrial production from the core to the periphery served to marginalize women economically. The growth of assembly plants in countries such as Mexico, Haiti, Guatemala, and Indonesia beginning in the 1960s and 1970s depended on a disproportionately female workforce in low-paying jobs. Although some have argued that such work expanded women's economic options, the fact remains that, as global capital spread, women worked harder, either in and from their homes or in assembly plants. Yet the work is economically marginal, temporary, or low paying. Globally, two-thirds of all part-time workers and 60 percent of all temporary workers are women. Furthermore, while working for pennies an hour, women remained responsible for all or most of the household labor necessary to sustain their families (Eisenstein 1997).

The global economic trends of the 1990s have further undermined women as nation-states, at the urgings of such groups as the International Monetary Fund and the World Bank, terminate social services intended to alleviate the conditions of people living in poverty, a disproportionate number of whom are women and children (Basu 1995:6). Thus, the withdrawal or reduction by the state of its support of workplace legislation, social service programs, job programs, health programs, and education programs disproportionately affects the position of women in society (Eisenstein 1997).

In sum, feminist protest arises from conditions that relegate women to the private or domestic sphere, that offer only low-paying jobs, and that undermine public policies geared to protect women and children from the widespread poverty that exists in the periphery. The question is, *what are some of the ways people can resist the marginalization and subjugation of women globally?*

Strategies of Protest

Clearly, to the extent that the inferior status of women is linked to the nature of the economy, family, and the nation-state, it becomes difficult, if not impossible, to change. For this reason some have suggested that the revolutionary overthrow of capitalist nation-states is the only solution to female oppression. Historically, this may help explain the prominent role of women in revolutionary programs. We saw in Chapter 10 the prominent role played by women in the protests of peasants in Malaysia, the Mau Mau revolt in Kenya, and the revolt in Chiapas. Women were given prominent places, at least initially, in the communist revolutions in Russia, China, and Cuba. Yet it is arguable how much these revolutions improved the status of women.

One of the first acts of the Chinese government after its victory in 1949 was to establish the All-China Women's Federation to further the status of women. The communist government banned the Chinese custom of foot binding of women, built a system of universal health care, and dramatically improved women's health. Yet today some of the worst cases of female labor exploitation are found in China. In an incident reminiscent of the notorious 1911 Triangle Shirtwaist Factory fire in New York City that killed 145 garment workers and prompted new labor legislation, a fire in November 1993 killed eighty-four female workers in a toy factory in Shenzhen in south China. They were prevented from escaping by doors and windows barred to prevent stealing. Furthermore, the Chinese government repeatedly cracks down on the formation of independent labor unions whose work, although not specifically aimed at improving the condition of women, would greatly benefit women laborers.

After the socialist revolution of 1959 in Cuba, Fidel Castro's government moved to integrate women better into the public spheres of government and labor. In 1960 the government formed the Federation of Cuban Women (FMC) to consolidate existing women's institutions in support of the revolution and integrate women into the workforce. Whereas only 13.7 percent of the potential female workforce was active in 1953, by 1990 45 percent of working-age women were employed. Yet in spite of such apparent gains, "motherhood" remains at the heart of the official view of women in Cuba; child care and domestic duties remain at the core of the female role, and Cuban women continue to bear the brunt of domestic labor—housework and child care (Lutjens 1994).

Although the goals of socialist revolutions to improve the status of women clearly did not live up to their promise, clearly the fall of communism in Eastern Europe has worsened the condition of women. Seventy-three percent of Russia's unemployed are women, half of whom have college educations. The overwhelming number of peddlers on the streets of Moscow are old women and young mothers. Without the protection of the socialist nation-state, the traditional view of women as housewives has reemerged. Gennady Melikyan, Russia's labor minister, made this clear when he said, "Why should we employ

Women in New Delhi marching to protest high food prices in 1973.

women when men are unemployed? It's better that men work and women take care of children and do the housework"(Eisenstein 1997).

In Western countries women's movements have focused on affirmative action, reproductive rights, and greater access of women to education. At the Fourth World Conference on Women in Beijing, there was a strong movement to encourage women in the periphery to adopt the strategies employed by feminists in the core. Yet many women and women's groups in the periphery are wary of Western forms of feminist protest. Many women's groups in the periphery or the ex-communist countries of Eastern Europe see attempts to export Western feminism as a new form of colonialism or imperialism. In Muslim countries, in particular, many women reject what they see as the "man-hating" feminism of Western women's movements.

Anthropologists, such as Aihwa Ong (1997), have warned against the tendency of Western feminists to impose their value system of individual autonomy on women's movements in peripheral countries. Ong noted that male leaders in Asian countries, such as China, Indonesia, and Malaysia, have argued that women's rights are not simply about individual rights but about culture, community, and the nation-state. These leaders counter accusations that men are exploiting female labor in assembly plants by arguing for the community's right to develop economically and for the obligation of all members of the community or nation to contribute to that development in any way they can; they argue that the right to develop is also a "human right." Asian leaders claim that the family, state, or nation is the primary unit of advancement, not the individual. The question, said Ong, is *how can women's movements in the periphery counter these arguments that in their cultural context are so persuasive?*

Insufficient attention has been given to cultural and religious differences between core and peripheral countries regarding the role of women and the place of political protest (Ong 1997). Feminists must be sensitive to "othering," wherein Westerners gain their sense of being liberated by defining others, particularly women from the periphery, as being backward and oppressed. For example, when delegates at the conference from Catholic and Muslim countries argued for a strategy that recognized a "separate but equal" status for women, they were accused of being traditional and marginalized by Western representatives.

Ong (1997) suggested that it would be more fruitful for women's movements in the core to be more receptive to an exchange of ideas and to consider the idea that strategies for improving the status of women must recognize cultural differences and the nature of power relations in different societies. We must, said Ong, "analyze the ways women and men in different societies struggle over cultural meanings that structure their lives."

To illustrate, Ong related the story of the Sisters in Islam, a group of Western-educated feminists who are trying to change gender relations in Malaysia, not by employing Western feminist methods but within the context of their own culture through the reinterpretation of Islamic texts. Islam, particularly Islamic fundamentalism, has been targeted by Western feminists and human rights advocates as being particularly oppressive toward females. Islam permits polygyny, restricts the inheritance rights of females to half that of males, restricts the movements of women, and, in extreme cases, denies women education or any position outside the home.

Sisters in Islam, instead of condemning Islamic belief, argue that women should be afforded the same access to religious education as men, and with this education they should enter into debate with the almost exclusively male Muslim clerics about the meaning of sacred texts such as the Qur'an and their interpretation of the role of women in society. Using newspaper columns to reach the public, the Sisters in Islam argue that the interpretation of the sacred texts must put Qur'anic recommendations in historical context. For example, male clerics justify Islam's approval of polygyny by claiming the Qur'an justified polygyny because the male sex drive made them "adulterous by nature." The Sisters in Islam counter this interpretation by pointing out that the Qur'an does not give men a blanket right to more than one wife; the sanctioning of polygyny in the Qur'an must be understood in the historical context in which the death of men through wars left women and children without male support. Allah thus sanctioned polygyny, they argue, not because of any intrinsic difference in the sex drive of men and women, but because it helped alleviate the problem of war orphans and widows, by allowing widows to remarry men who already had a wife or wives.

The Sisters in Islam also argue against the stringent dress codes that male clerics say are demanded by the Qur'an. Citing verses of the sacred texts, the Sisters in Islam argue that "[c]oercion is contrary to the spirit of the Qur'an which states that there is no compulsion in [Islamic] religion" (cited Ong 1997) and that it is wrong to try to enforce faith through authority. The proper way to protect women, they say, is through decent and respectful treatment. Coercive dress policy, "in fact, runs counter to Islam's emancipatory emphasis upon reason [and] freedom as the basis of human morality" (cited Ong 1997).

Groups such as the Sisters in Islam have produced results. One Malaysian official (cited Ong 1997:89) who is now chair of the U.N. Commission for Human Rights noted:

> Malaysia used to be a male-dominated society.... In the old days, there was no talk of women's rights, but through the gradual process of politicization, women...are able to assert themselves. Compared with ten years ago, there is much more publicity, consciousness, and more sensitivity on questions of women's rights.

Malaysia is still a male-dominated society, but by entering into a dialogue with Muslim clerics on their own terms, the Sisters in Islam have produced what Ong called a kind of "feminist communitarianism" that combines the liberal right to question authority, certainly recognized in the Qur'an, with the cultural norms of their own community. These kinds of movements, said Ong, should not be dismissed by Western feminists; rather, the idea of women's rights makes sense only in the context of specific cultural communities.

ECOLOGICAL RESISTANCE MOVEMENTS

There is little question, as we have seen, that the culture of capitalism is environmentally destructive and that the need for perpetual economic growth requires perpetual environmental exploitation. But, as in changes in other areas of life, such as agriculture, technology, and family structure, not everyone suffers equally. It is true that everyone may be affected by global warming and the increase in acid rain, but not everyone is affected by the flooding of farmland or hunting territories, disposal of waste products, or pollution of water supplies. These problems are disproportionally borne by people who inhabit the margins and periphery of the culture of capitalism. It is peasants, gatherers and hunters, and the poor in general who lose their livelihoods when huge hydroelectric projects dam rivers and flood land, when demand for lumber destroys the forests, when nuclear and other waste is disposed of in or near poor communities or shipped to peripheral countries. Furthermore, some people benefit far more than others from the economic activities that affect the environment and, for that reason, are far less likely to object or protest. But at some point environmental damage does and will affect everyone.

Earth First!

Most contemporary ecological resistance movements, as Bron Taylor (1995) called them, originated in the 1960s, although concerns about environmental alterations go back to the nineteenth century. Many of these movements seek, as do most peasant, labor, and feminist movements, somehow to limit the detrimental effects of capitalist economic expansion. Others seek to revolutionize the culture they see as responsible for environmental devastation. Activists in these movements attribute environmental destruction to an ideology associated with capitalism that human beings must dominate and "tame" nature; they argue furthermore that this belief emerges directly out of the domination of human beings by other human beings. Consequently, as long as human beings seek domination of others, so will they seek domination over nature and, eventually, destroy the planet. One of these ecological resistance movements is Earth First!

Earth First! originated in the early 1980s, often with humorous protests, such as un-furling a plastic "crack" down the face of the Glen Canyon Dam, symbolically freeing the Colorado River. Protests became more confrontational when members blockaded logging roads, conducted "tree-sits," or resorted to "ecotage" or "monkeywrenching," by vandaliz-ing equipment or driving metal, ceramic, or quartz stakes into trees to make their harvest dangerous and, hence, unprofitable. Earth First! clearly promotes an ideology that at-tributes to the nonhuman world an animate force, expressed in the slogan "I am the rain forest, recently emerged into consciousness, defending myself." Some events held for Earth First! members have mythic significance, such as biologist Aldo Leopold's story of watching the "green fire" die in the eyes of a wolf he had just shot, or in Paul Watson's de-scription of the intelligence he saw in the eyes of a harpooned whale he was trying to save, an "intelligence...that spoke wordlessly of compassion...that communicated [that he knew] what we had tried to do"(cited Taylor 1995:15).

Earth First! closely identifies with the social protests of indigenous peoples. One of their first symbolic acts was to create a memorial to Apache chief Victorio, whose armed resistance to the European conquest marked for them the effort to preserve the environ-ment (Taylor 1995:18). They have supported and identified with the struggles of indige-nous people in the Amazon to protect the forests and stop destructive oil exploitation. They raised funds for the Ecuadorian Huaorani to clear three- to four-meter-wide corridors through the rain forest and plant palm trees to demarcate territory allotted them by the gov-ernment and prevent "accidental" colonization of their land. They organized boycotts against lumber from the Sarawak Rainforest to support the resistance of the Penan and Iban tribes. They allied themselves with the Kalinga and the Bontoc peoples of the Philip-pines to prevent the construction of a dam that would have inundated their villages and burial grounds. In North America they have allied themselves with indigenous groups such as the Apache Survival Coalition and the Coalition for Nitassian comprising Innu and Cree Indians and others, who hope to stop Hydro Quebec's hydroelectric dam projects that would flood thousands of acres of Innu and Cree hunting grounds.

The ties between ecological resistance movements and indigenous protest reveal the extent to which antisystemic protest are intertwined, often bringing together peasants, in-digenous peoples, women, and others in a common cause. One of the more interesting pro-test movements that contains strands of different types of protest is Chipko, the attempt to save the forests of India. It is particularly interesting because it emerged out of a peasant protest over the conversion of common lands to state control and private exploitation, and it resulted in the questioning of one of the central arguments over environmental destruc-tion, the idea of "the tragedy of the commons."

Chipko and the Tragedy of the Commons

In his often cited 1968 article, "Tragedy of the Commons," Garrett Hardin implied that land held in common is more likely to be abused and exploited than land held privately. Hardin based his argument on the premise that what each person gains individually by exploiting the commons for his or her own ends is far greater than what they individually lose. For example, if a pasture is held in common by a community, each person, said Hardin, has more to gain by adding one more sheep to his or her herd than what they lose individually by their exploitation of the pasture. People are motivated, therefore, to exploit the commons as much as possible, and if each person follows his or her own individual interests by adding more sheep, the commons will soon be destroyed. If each person, however, controlled his or her individual plot, people would be less motivated to damage it because what they gain is clearly offset by what they lose. A contemporary example might ask what each of us has to gain by purchasing an automobile, as opposed to what we lose from the pollution our individual car adds to the environment. Because we gain a lot by having a car, but individually increase pollution only slightly, we are motivated, as is everyone else, to buy cars.

Hardin's argument is logically ingenious but empirically flawed. Anthropologists, particularly, have argued that communally held land, especially in the periphery, tends to be better preserved and regulated than privately owned resources (see McCay and Fortmann 1996; Fratkin 1997a:240–242). A good example is that of the forests in northern India and the Chipko movement.

Chipko (literally "to hug") originated in nineteenth-century peasant protests over the destruction of the forests of northern India that were once described by British colonial officials as "inexhaustible." The peasants in the area lived largely on small-scale agriculture, livestock herding, and gathering and hunting in the surrounding forests. The society was organized into castes, that is hereditary occupational groups into which each person married.

Agricultural land in most villages was owned by the people who worked it, with a portion of what they produced serving as their share of village revenue payable in tribute or taxes to area rulers or British colonial authorities. The surrounding forests were managed collectively. The forests were a necessary feature of economic life as a place for grazing animals, for medicinal herbs, and for food. Moreover, the forests held spiritual significance as a place of deities and shrines. There were particularly magnificent species of trees, and although there was no formal management, protection of the forests was secured by the ritual significance of areas and by rules that abusers of the forests would suffer boycott or exclusion from the forest (Guha 1990:33–34).

The isolation of the area left it largely untouched until 1878, when the colonial government passed regulations closing segments of the forest to peasant use and designating some areas for lease to private developers. The government was particularly interested in certain trees suitable for the construction of railway sleeper cars for the expanding the Indian railway. British colonial regulations fixed the amount of building timber the peasantry could use, restricted grazing rights to certain types of forests within a five-mile radius of the villages, and even specified where dry grass could be gathered. The government also banned burning of the forest floors that peasants had used to grow and gather wild grass.

Peasants protested their exclusion from portions of the forests; they ignored the regulations, continuing to graze their animals and cut wood for their own use. They also burned the underbrush in the forests where new saplings had been planted by lumber interests for later harvesting. But the most violent form of protest was incendiarism, the deliberate setting of fires in the forests. In 1919–1920 there were 13,457 breaches of the fire laws in one area of northern India.

Restrictions on peasant use of the forests, exploitation of lumber, and peasant protest continued after India gained its independence from Great Britain in 1947 because the new Indian government, faced with the need to raise revenue, continued the forestry policies of the British colonial government. The results were continuing forest destruction, alienation of the peasants from the forests they had protected for centuries, and continuing protest. In 1962 a new road was built into the forest with funding from the World Bank, further increasing forest exploitation. Satellite photographs reveal that of the 34,042 square kilometers of land declared as forests in the area, only 6.6 percent has good tree cover, another 22.5 percent has medium tree cover, and another 13.8 percent has poor tree cover. More than half the land classified as forest has no tree cover at all (Guha 1990:146).

Two events triggered the emergence of an organized environmental protest movement. First, floods in the foothills in 1970 resulted in the loss of life and property; the population recognized that losses were greater in villages that lay below land on which forests had been destroyed. The second thing that triggered Chipko was the awarding of rights to a cricket bat manufacturer to cut trees after a peasant cooperative had been denied rights to cut trees in the same forest to make farm implements. It was then that organizers thought of wrapping themselves around (hugging) trees to prevent their being cut. Women gained prominence in the movement because of an attempt by the government to deceive one village by calling the men of the village to a meeting, while they sent in laborers to cut the forest; however, the women of the village, alerted by a young girl, placed themselves between the laborers and the trees and forced the laborers to leave. In another area, 5,000 trees were marked for cutting, and villagers camped out in the forests until men hired by a private company were forced to withdraw.

Chipko has become only one of many such protests against forest destruction in the Himalayan foothills, but it is by far the most publicized and soon gained broad international appeal as both an environmental and a women's movement. Often forgotten, however, are the peasant roots of the protest: It began as a struggle for subsistence before it emerged as a movement for environmental preservation.

Ramachandra Guha, in *The Unquiet Woods* (1990), noted some other interesting lessons in Chipko that relate to social protest in general and peasant protest in particular. Chipko reveals how, as in the cases of Kenya and Mexico, policies of "economic development," or "modernization" formulated at the top levels of states, corporations, and international financial institutions are often experienced by lower levels—such as peasants, women, and laborers—as exploitation. In the strategies of economic development, indigenous peoples, landless peasants, and women are expected to bear the brunt of industrialization; such problems as disease, social unrest, food scarcity, and land hunger testify to the impact of this process (Guha 1990:195). Moreover, while the negative social and economic consequences on the poor in the periphery of programs of economic development are well documented, often ignored is the impact on the environment and the social protest that is likely to ensue. Guha (1990:195–196) concluded,

[f]rom an ecological perspective, therefore, peasant movements like Chipko are not merely a defense of the little community and its values, but also an affirmation of a way of life more harmoniously adjusted with natural processes. At one level they are defensive, seeking to escape the tentacles of the commercial economy and the centralizing state; at yet another level they are assertive, actively challenging the ruling-class vision of a homogenizing urban-industrial culture.... Far from being the dying wail of a class about to drop down the trapdoor of history, the call of Chipko represents one of the most innovative responses to the ecological and cultural crisis of modern society. It is a message we may neglect at our own peril.

CONCLUSION

We suggested in this chapter that rebellion and protest that seems endemic to the culture of capitalism is largely antisystemic, consisting of responses of groups who at some time were socially or economically marginalized or who have suffered disproportionately in the expansion of capitalism into the periphery. However, it is important to note that in only a few cases is protest directed explicitly at the culture of capitalism itself. Rather, protesters select as objects of their protest groups or individuals who they hold individually responsible. We saw in the case of the protests of poor Malaysian peasants that the object of their ire was peasants who were richer than themselves, rather than the green revolution or the institutions, such as the World Bank, that ultimately were responsible for their distress. Likewise, laborers in the coal mines of Pennsylvania blamed mine operators, many of whom made virtually no profit from their efforts, rather than the system that drove them and the mine operators to try to accumulate capital in a failing industry. In other words, rarely do social protest movements specifically attack the system that is the source of their distress, instead they focus on real or symbolic figures who, for them, embody their oppression.

■ ■ ■ ■ ■

CHAPTER TWELVE

RELIGION AND ANTISYSTEMIC PROTEST

Religious distress is at the same time the expression of real distress and the protest against real distress. Religion is the sigh of the oppressed creature, the heart of a heartless world, just as it is the spirit of spiritless conditions.
—Karl Marx, *Critique of Hegel's "Philosophy of Right"*

[I]f one's goal is not harmony but the empowerment that comes with using violence, it is in one's interest to be in a state of war. In such cases war is not only the context for violence, but also the excuse for it. War provides a reason to be violent. This is true even if the worldly issues at heart in the dispute do not seem to warrant such a ferocious position.
—Mark Juergensmeyer, *Terror in the Mind of God*

The rebellions and movements that we examined in Chapters 10 and 11 each sought, in their own way, to reform what participants saw as the excesses of capitalism. Few of these movements, however, offered a radical cultural alternative; that is, although they decried the constant economic and social change, the uneven distribution of wealth, the exploitation and marginalization of selected groups, or the environmental damage fostered by the culture of capitalism, none actively sought to replace it with another. Peasants seek land, not the overthrow of the society that displaces them; laborers seek higher wages and better working conditions within the culture of capitalism from which, in their other roles as consumers and capitalists, they benefit; women and minorities seek improved status within the existing society; indigenous groups struggle to be left alone; and environmental protesters, with the exception of those who offer a largely undefined spiritual alternative, seek only greater environmental safeguards.

Communism was often depicted as a major challenger to capitalism, yet communism and its authors—Lenin, Stalin, and Mao—never rejected the larger nineteenth-century culture of industrial capitalism. They sought largely to modify the nation-state to give workers greater influence and to obtain a more equitable distribution of wealth within a system of production, distribution, and consumption that differed little, if at all, from that of capitalism. They simply wanted to replace private capitalism with state capitalism. Even Marx and Engels did not call for overthrow of the industrial order; their solution was to seize the nation-state and raise the power of labor above or at least equal to the power of capital (the power of people over the power of money). The views of Marx and Engels (as were those of many early nineteenth-century industrialists) were utopian; they called for the end of private property, recognition of the equality of women, dismantling of the patriarchal nuclear family, and discarding of organized religion. But the only groups to attempt to follow that or a similar agenda were the small utopian or intentional communities that proliferated in the first half of the nineteenth century, such as New Harmony, the Oneida Community, and Amana, and later, following the political unrest of 1968, Twin Oaks and the many small communal groups that thrived in late 1960s and early 1970s, a few of which survive today (Erasmus 1972; Kanter 1972; Oved 1988).

Although the peasant, labor, feminist, indigenous, and environmental protests and rebellions did not seek to change the basic tenets of the culture of capitalism, there were and are movements to overthrow and replace it. Most of these are religious in character; through some spiritual agency these groups seek either the removal or destruction of what they believe is an immoral culture, a withdrawal from it, or the forceful or voluntary adoption of a new way of life.

Religion has always had a revolutionary element; most religions began as a rebellion against one or another established order. Christianity began as a Jewish protest against behaviors and beliefs that the protesters felt were violations of God's word. The gospels of the New Testament are clearly revolutionary in intent, as we shall see when we examine the emergence of liberation theology, whereas the Old Testament documents the struggles of people against what they believe is illegitimate authority.

Yet the fact that religion is often the source of antisystemic protest should not obscure the role of religion in legitimizing some of the basic premises of the culture of capitalism. Certainly, there was a good deal of cooperation between the church and the state in the early expansion of the world system. Missionaries accompanied the conquerors and explorers and helped pacify populations, convert them to one or another brand of Christianity, and transform them into willing laborers for the global economy. Missionaries served as a vanguard of capitalism by introducing their converts to Western concepts of time, space, and the person embedded in the culture of capitalism. As Jean Comaroff (1985:27) observed,

> [t]he mission was an essential medium of, and forerunner to, colonial articulation; it was the significant agent of ideological innovation, a first instance in the confrontation between the local system and the global forces of international capitalism. The coherent cultural scheme of the mission—its concepts of civilization, person, property, work, and time—was made up of categories which anticipated and laid the ground for the process of proletarianization.

In his classic work, *The Protestant Ethic and the Spirit of Capitalism,* Max Weber (1958) suggested that the Protestant Reformation provided an ideological basis for capitalism as well as a motivation for making a profit by equating material success with personal salvation and a sign of God's blessing. Historians have seen in religion of the nineteenth century a replacement for the moral restraints that had been provided by family and community but destroyed by the explosive growth of cities and the mobility of labor. Anthony F. C. Wallace (1987), for example, pointed out how Irish immigrants in Pennsylvania confronted in the local Catholic Church a replacement for behavioral restraints that had been provided by extended families in Ireland, a moral restraint very much welcomed by mine owners, businesspeople, and others. Paul E. Johnson (1978) traced the religious revival in the United States in the 1830s and 1840s to the need for religion to replace the moral guidelines and social constraints that had been provided in small rural communities by the family but absent in the newly industrialized cities of the Northeast. As we saw in Chapter 1, most religious leaders in the early twentieth century had little difficulty accommodating to the shift from an ideology of self-denial to one of self-fulfillment and indulgence. Nevertheless, although religion has served to buttress the assumptions of the culture of capitalism, it has served in some forms also to resist them.

The goal of this chapter is to ask the questions, *to what extent have religious movements been expressions of antisystemic sentiments? That is, how have religious movements served as a means of protest against the expansion, both in the core and in the periphery, of the culture of capitalism? And why does religious protest sometimes manifest itself in spectacular violence?* To answer these questions we first examine some religious movements in the periphery, and then turn our attention to the large-scale protests that have emerged from the world's major religions.

INDIGENOUS RELIGIOUS MOVEMENTS AS PROTEST

Central in anthropology to the idea of religious change is Anthony F. C. Wallace's concept of revitalization movement. Wallace (1966:30) suggested that religious beliefs and practices start from situations of social and cultural stress as a "conscious, organized effort by members of a society to construct a more satisfying culture." All religion, he said, originates in a revitalization process. The origins of all the major religions lay in reactions to social and/or cultural systems that the founders found unsatisfying; anthropologists, historians, and sociologists have documented hundreds of instances of religious movements around the world that originated in protest over people's conditions and have used the idea of revitalization to conceptualize everything from Melanesian cargo cults to the militia movements in the United States (Beeman 1997).

As useful, however, as the concept of revitalization has been in furthering our understanding of religious change and protest, it has a basic weakness. As applied to religious movements of the past 200 years, it has failed to consider the fact that virtually all such movements have been reactions to a single phenomenon—the development and expansion of industrial or consumer capitalism. Generally, revitalization movements, such as the cargo cults of Melanesia and New Guinea; the Ghost Dance among the Native Americans of the American Plains; and large-scale religious movements that have emerged from Islam, Christianity, Judaism, and others, have been as much antisystemic protest as they have been revitalization. That is, the attempt to construct a more "satisfying culture," as Wallace put it, has generally been a protest to the negative affects of capitalist expansion. For this reason, it may be more fruitful to view these movements as expressions of antisystemic protest rather than solely attempts at revitalization.

To illustrate, let's examine three religious movements of peoples in the periphery, the Ghost Dance, the cargo cults, and the Zionism movement in South Africa. Each was an expression of protest against economic and social conditions emerging from capitalist expansion but with important differences: They varied in the degree to which they used the trappings of core religions as opposed to indigenous belief and ritual. Furthermore, they varied in the extent to which they expressed overt hostility to the nation-state and, consequently, the extent to which they prompted oppressive and violent retaliation.

The Ghost Dance

In 1889 a missionary-educated Paiute Indian named Wovoka had a vision (Mooney 1965). He had been taken up to heaven where, he said, he met God; he also met Indians who had died and who were in heaven living their traditional life. God, he said, instructed him to return to Earth and tell people that they must live in peace with Whites and with each other. He was also given instructions for a ritual dance that, if performed for five days and five nights, would reunite people on Earth with friends and relatives in the other world. Converts carried Wovoka's message from Nevada to indigenous groups throughout the United States and Canada, where it was often embellished in various ways. In some versions Whites and Native Americans would live in harmony; in others the world would be destroyed and only indigenous people brought back to life. In other versions the buffalo would return, and people would live as they had before the invasion of European peoples.

The message of the Ghost Dance, as it became known, was carried by representatives sent by rail by indigenous groups to meet with Wovoka and spread to groups throughout the American Plains and beyond to peoples seeking a revival of a way of life disrupted by capitalist expansion. The message of the Ghost Dance was particularly attractive to groups such as the Lakota who had been systematically deprived through treaty and deceit of most of their land and confined to reservations where they were dependent on government provisions that were often not delivered. However, the Ghost Dance, which held the promise to the Lakota of a revival of their traditional culture, ended in one of the great military tragedies in American history.

Alarmed that the Ghost Dance might presage an open rebellion by the Lakota, an Indian agent assigned to one of the Lakota reservations called in the military. Frightened that they might be attacked, some of the Lakota fled; they were pursued by the Seventh Cavalry, George Armstrong Custer's old command that had been defeated by a combined force of Lakota and Cheyenne in 1876. The army caught up to the Lakota at a place called Wounded Knee and, with cannon and rifles, surrounded them. A surrender was arranged. As soldiers rummaged through Lakota shelters searching for guns, a shot was fired. The army responded by pouring cannon and rifle shot into the encampment, killing hundreds of men, women, and children, some of whom had sought shelter from the barrage hundreds of yards away.

In many ways, the Ghost Dance is a prototype of a form of religious resistance that parallels the "weapons of the weak" discussed in Chapter 10. They are religious movements that serve, if only symbolically, to protest economic, social, or political oppression. When they result in violence, it is almost always violence initiated by the nation-state or their representatives, either against whole groups, as in the massacre at Wounded Knee, or against leaders of the movements who the agents of the nation-state fear are leading or are capable of leading a general revolt. It was probably not a coincidence that days before Wounded Knee, the Lakota spiritual leader Sitting Bull was assassinated by Lakota police as they tried to arrest him.

The Cargo Cults

Among the most dramatic of the indigenous religious protests were the cargo cults of Melanesia and New Guinea. These movements arose in the late nineteenth century and early twentieth century as core nations sought to exploit the resources in the Pacific Islands. Cargo cults generally began when a prophet announced the imminence of a cataclysm that would destroy the world, at which point the ancestors, God, or some other liberating power would appear and deliver the cargo—commodities possessed by Europeans—and bring a reign of eternal bliss. People prepared themselves to receive the cargo by building storehouses, jetties, and plane runways, sometimes abandoning their gardens, destroying their livestock, eating all their food, or throwing away their money. Cargo cults represent a paradoxical response to capitalist expansion. On the one hand, they evidence themselves in a passionate desire to possess the commodities thought to be in abundance in the dominant culture; on the other hand, they tend to reject the power and influence of the Westerners who bring the cargo.

The story of European exploitation and the effects on indigenous peoples of the Pacific closely followed the patterns we examined in Chapter 9. Cargo cults were a response to the excesses of colonial exploitation and were documented by Peter Worsley (1968) in his classic analysis, *The Trumpets Shall Sound*. Capitalist expansion came to Fiji in the eighteenth century, for example, as Europeans sought sandalwood to supply the Chinese market with material for joss sticks and incense for religious services. By 1813 the supply of trees on Fiji was exhausted.

By the 1860s there was a large influx of European settlers to Fiji, which resulted in a vastly increased alienation of land from Fijians as well as increased lawlessness in the European community, which local governments were unable to control. There was also an increase in the need for native laborers to supply the growing coconut plantations. Colonial powers countered the reluctance of indigenous peoples to work on the plantations by introducing tax laws, forcing them to work to earn cash when they could have easily subsisted on their own produce. Treatment of native laborers, as in other areas, was harsh. In New Guinea colonial governments sanctioned various forms of punishment, such as flogging or hanging by the wrists, for laborers whose efforts did not satisfy labor supervisors. Equally harsh were the economic dislocations, ill understood by indigenous peoples, that were part of the global economy. Prices for coconuts, oil, and other cash crops rose and fell with the vagaries of the market, creating either new demands for labor or widespread unemployment.

Missionary activity was also a major factor in the development of the cargo cults. Missionaries played a major part in the colonial process in the South Pacific, comprising 15 percent of the European population in most areas. The missionaries divided up territories among themselves, often leading natives to question why rivalries existed between the different denominations. Religion was one area of European life that the natives did not reject. In fact, religion was thought by those participating in the cargo cults to be the source of the magical power that created the goods. Native peoples had no knowledge of the material reality of European society and the production process that created commodities, and the Europeans they knew apparently did not work for the goods they possessed; with their missionary education the natives concluded that secret magical power was the key to European wealth, power they wished to obtain (Worsley 1968).

It was in response to these conditions that the cargo cults flourished. A good example was the "Vailala madness" first reported in New Guinea in 1919. The most obvious manifestation of the Vailala madness was the trancelike state or possession into which adherents fell. The movement occurred in an environment of colonial exploitation; oil had been discovered and plantations were being built. Most followers had been indentured laborers, often in conditions of severe discipline and illness. In June 1910, for example, in the Lakekamu gold fields, 225 of 1,100 workers died of dysentery and other causes.

The originator of Vailala madness was said to be an old man named Evara, who fell into a trance when he disappeared for four days. He said that a sorcerer had "ripped up his belly." He prophesied the coming of a steamer carrying spirits of dead ancestors who would bring the cargo with them. Rifles were among the expected goods. Cargo would be contained in crates, each identified according to the village to which it would be delivered. The spirits, said Evara, revealed that all the flour, rice, tobacco, and other trade belonged to Papuans, not Whites, and that the Whites would be driven away (Worsley 1968:81).

The hostility to Whites in Papua New Guinea was not surprising. One plantation manager used his whip to silence the lamentations of some "boys" mourning for a dead friend; another said "I want the nigger to work for me so I can make my pile and leave this so-and-so country" (cited Worsley 1968:82). Although the movement evidenced hostility to Whites, people believed also that the ancestors would be White. Some Whites were actually followed around by natives who believed the Whites were their deceased relatives.

Ceremony and ritual accompanied the movement. People had visions of heaven in which food was abundant and people wore long, flowing robes. Many claimed to receive messages from Jesus Christ or God. Villagers set up tables and decorated them with flowers in beer bottles, bowls of rice, betel, and coconut husks; relatives of the dead who were thought to be returning sat around these tables feasting, while other villagers sat silently, their backs to the tables, awaiting the arrival of the cargo. Temples were built that resembled mission churches, and a flagpole was erected that was thought to be the medium through which people could communicate with the dead ancestors. There was a strict moral code that encouraged the giving of feasts for the ancestors, abandoning adultery and theft, and observing the Sabbath. There was also the idea that all native paraphernalia should be destroyed and gardens should be abandoned.

The movement lasted twelve years before it ceased spreading; by the time it ended, in the 1930s, people claimed the prophesies had been fulfilled; that they had seen the steamers, that messages had been received from flagpoles, and that tracks of the dead were seen on beaches. Furthermore, the cargo had been delivered as more and more people gained access to the European commodities they desired.

Zionism in South Africa

Both the Ghost Dance and cargo cult movements were influenced to some extent by missionary activity. This should not be surprising. The message of the Bible, particularly the

New Testament, must have contained a very appealing message to participants in the movements: The equality of all under God, the favored divine status of the weak, the common stewardship over God's earthly domain are all messages designed to appeal to an oppressed people. Furthermore, if indigenous religious movements derived, at least in part, from missionary teachings, participants in the movement might expect them to be sanctioned by political authorities. Missionary activity was tolerated by European and American colonizers, indeed, it was welcomed, but only to the extent that it contributed to the maintenance of a disciplined and submissive population. Thus, the degree of the protest and resistance contained in indigenous religious movements had to be carefully measured against the likelihood of government retaliation.

One of the most repressive nation-states to emerge out of the culture of capitalism was the apartheid government of South Africa, whose military power made open rebellion by Africans virtually impossible. In that setting religious protest was often the only way to express resistance. Let's examine one such movement, the Full Witness Apostolic Church in Zion described by Jean Comaroff (1985) in her work on the Tshidi of South Africa, *Body of Power, Spirit of Resistance.*

The Tshidi are representative of many of the peoples of South Africa who lived primarily by a combination of agriculture and herding. The takeover of South Africa by the British resulted in African people being confined to theoretically self-governing protectorates or homelands. Agricultural and livestock production declined not only because of such factors as cattle disease and drought but also because agricultural labor was being drained by the demand for labor in the diamond mines, gold fields, factories, and White farms.

The result for people such as the Tshidi was the underdevelopment of their rural base and the emergence of a system in which they were dependent on the sale of their labor for their survival. By 1970 more than half the women were employed outside the home for extended periods and more than three-quarters of the men were working away from home for at least nine months each year. Labor on the farms was left to the remaining women and children, who were prevented by South African law from accompanying their husbands and fathers to industrial centers. Furthermore, the passage of Blacks between the town and countryside was carefully regulated by the apartheid government; movement outside the homelands required a pass, strict curfews were imposed, and the African population was carefully watched by uniformed police and bureaucrats. Thus, the Tshidi came to realize their state of oppression in the brutal mine compounds and in the degrading rituals of apartheid.

Suppression of African resistance has long been a feature of the South African landscape. Only in the past few years has the degree of violence—assassinations, kidnapping, and torture—used by the South African government to suppress dissent become public. Consequently, resistance needed to be more subtle. People could not directly challenge the mechanisms of political, social, and economic domination of the apartheid South African government; instead, they contested the logic of the system on which it is based and of which they are a part. Resistance was to be symbolic.

To appreciate this kind of resistance we might think back to the means of resistance used by Malaysian peasants, the weapons of the weak, as James Scott (1985) called them. Or we might consider symbols of resistance and independence used by American youth—

the clothing, music, and other activities used to contest the discipline imposed by schools, parents, and the larger community. The Tshidi used as their vehicle a religious movement imported from the core, the Full Witness Apostolic Church in Zion. Comaroff sees the Zionist movement as a means by which Tshidi members protested their marginality to and the effects of the capitalist world system. The protest is expressed in dress, in ritual, and in ideology.

The Christian Catholic Apostolic Church of Zion (CCACZ) was founded in 1847 by a Scotsman, Alexander Dowie, who came to North America in 1888. In 1899 he built his Zion City on 6,500 acres on Lake Michigan, forty-two miles north of Chicago. Within a year the "city" boasted a population of several thousand, a bank, brickyard, stores, small factories, schools, and a printing press.

Zion City was to be a haven from the sinful environment represented by the city of Chicago. The majority of its members were clerics, self-employed artisans, struggling small-scale businesspeople—mostly poor and working class. This was a population marginal to nineteenth-century capitalism who rejected much of the emerging capitalist culture, which they found alienating (Comaroff 1985:179). Zionists conceptualized the alienation they felt as an uncoupling of man and God; they expressed it in metaphors of sickness and health, which replaced the established doctrines of damnation and salvation. Through the metaphor of healing, Zionists sought to cast out disease and the influence of Satan by reintegrating body, soul, and spirit. As Zionism was exported to the periphery, it seemed to draw together everything that the experience of colonialization and wage labor had driven away, offering the possibility of rebuilding a holistic community from which the culture of capitalism could be resisted.

The first representative of the CCACZ to South Africa arrived in Johannesburg in 1904, largely at the invitation of a Dutch Reformed missionary. Zionism was introduced to the Tshidi by returning migrant laborers or lone itinerant prophets searching for a local following. At that time most Tshidi had converted to Methodism, the dominant colonial religion in the area. Although Black and White churches were carefully separated, by the 1970s the CCACZ had made considerable inroads. According to Comaroff (1985), 4,750 people were still members of the orthodox churches, but at least 3,750 had converted to Zionism, whereas another 1,000 were members of other independent churches.

The Full Witness Apostolic Church in Zion was founded in 1956 by Bishop N, a Zulu contract worker in the Johannesburg mines. The church itself is a 240-square-foot mud brick structure. Followers dress distinctively in white robes, green tunics, and white head scarves with red, black, and white yarn cords that are never removed.

Typical Sunday services begin with a meal; when all have eaten the bishop's senior wife signals the start of hymn singing, clapping, and drumming. Church members dance and the men sink to their knees facing east, the direction of the rising sun. The spirit seizes several women and people begin to testify. The testimony contains themes of oppression, often contrasting the outside world (wage labor, the city, strangers) with the inside world (home, the congregation). Central to the act of testifying is the idea of healing (Comaroff 1985:210).

The Full Witness Apostolic Church in Zion represents what anthropologists refer to as a "cult of affliction," a community of sufferers, a solitary band of "wounded healers," whose bodies reflect their oppressed social state. Indeed, many converts, Comaroff noted,

The white robes worn by members of the Zionist Church in South Africa contrast sharply with the drab khaki, black, or tight-fitting uniforms required of workers.

come to the church with real organic distress. The ritual of testimony involves a healing process that dramatizes the difference between the corruption of the outside world and the healing spirit of the congregation.

The Zionist church also serves to ritually cleanse the commodities that Tshidi must purchase, at the same time rejecting the culture in which they originate. Members bring all their purchased commodities, such as foodstuffs, shoes, and blankets, and place them on a table located in the center of the church; during the service they are sprinkled with holy water. Thus, the cargo of the rejected system is not itself repudiated; rather it is reformed and cleansed through a ritual act. As Comaroff (1985:218–219) said, "as alienated products are given a new social and spiritual identity, the experience of alienation is reversed."

In the same way that Zionists rework commodities through ritual, they also rework the body in dress. Members of the church clothe themselves in a combination of Protestant and indigenous garb to re-create an order that rejects the one prevailing in their lives. Their white robes, flowing hair, and colored tunics contrast sharply with the drab, often thread-bare clothing worn by the majority of rural Tshidi, clearly communicating their "otherness," dress that combines the biblical appearance of the world of the Christian mission with hints of a precolonial Tshidi past. These clothes also contrast in color and form with the drab khaki or black, tight-fitting uniforms of the military, mine, mission, or domestic service.

Comaroff noted that dissenting movements in the periphery seem to adopt these "side alleys" of Western culture, such as faith healing and occultism. But despite often diverse origins, these symbolic orders share an opposition to the culture of capitalism and seek to subvert the structures of colonial societies. The Zionist Church, like other small-scale religious movements, serves as a refuge and emblem for those who are marginalized by the expansion of capitalist culture. As Comaroff (1985:254) said,

> Zionism is part of a second global culture; a culture lying in the shadow of the first, whose distinct but similar symbolic orders are the imaginative constructions of the resistant periphery of the world system.

THE GLOBAL CHALLENGE OF ANTISYSTEMIC RELIGIOUS PROTEST

Religious movements such as the Zionist protest, of which there are probably thousands in the world, cannot hope to challenge the domination of global capitalism. Instead, they offer a respite from the hopelessness and alienation felt by those at the economic periphery of capitalist culture. The rituals, services, and gatherings represent periods of withdrawal from the system during which members can collectively regain their integrity and identity. They are not unlike the various utopian or alternative communities that flourished after the revolutions of 1848 and 1968, which sought to create alternative worlds within tightly bound, sometimes physically isolated, communities that gain public attention only when their members commit an illegal or seemingly irrational act.

Far more prominent are the large-scale religious protests represented by "fundamentalist movements" that have gained public attention in the past three decades. Rather than small-scale, isolated instances of religious protest, these movements are offshoots of the world's major religions, contain millions of participants, and have serious designs on the control of the nation-state. The cultures represented by these movements remain the only legitimate challengers to the global domination of capitalist culture.

In many ways these movements are difficult to characterize. They are called fundamentalist movements by the media, government analysts, and many religious scholars, but the designation has been criticized by some as containing derogatory connotations. Mark Juergensmeyer (1993; 1996) suggested calling them "nationalist religious movements." However, that implies that the movements are primarily political in nature, whereas they seem to be protesting a much greater range of cultural features. For that reason, perhaps antisystemic is a more accurate phrase, although we will retain the term *fundamentalism*, largely because of its widespread use.

To explore the extent to which large-scale religious protests represent antisystemic movements, we will examine the rise of Islamic fundamentalism in the Middle East and the role of Protestant fundamentalism in the United States. Each fundamentalism arose out of discontents with specific features of the industrial revolution and modern life, and each claims to provide a formula for transforming modern culture and society. Although each of the movements is rooted in a particular cultural tradition, and often in local conditions, they share some features in common.

1. Contrary to impressions left by the mass media that these are recent movements, most had their origins in the nineteenth century, as a reaction to the secularization of

religion in modern life or as a reaction to the expansion of the world economy and/or domination by colonial powers.

2. Each is historically oriented and interprets contemporary global events (the debt crisis, war and ethnic strife, disease) as divine portents that validate their central doctrines. Furthermore, each attributes what it perceives as the relative decline or lack of prominence of its country in global affairs to a loss or lack of faith in whatever religious principles it espouses.

3. Each contemporary fundamentalism has designs on state power and has, in one form or another, adopted contemporary political structures (e.g., political parties, youth organizations, modern communication techniques) to attain that end. In some cases they seek control over established nation-states, whereas in others they wish to establish their own, independent states.

4. All insist that although converting others to their world view is a central goal, believers should keep themselves separate from nonbelievers.

5. Each makes and has a strong appeal to young people, particularly college students, and has developed organizations to reach them.

6. Although each has attempted to reach its goals by socially approved methods, each has a militant segment, such as Hizbullah in Lebanon, Operation Rescue in the United States, and Gush Emunim in Israel, that challenges the power of the secular state by disobeying secular law with violent and/or nonviolent means in what they claim is a call to a higher law.

7. Most religious fundamentalisms stress the importance of the family in social life, claiming that the family as an institution has been undermined by the secular nation-state. Some place a striking emphasis on the duty of women to embody tradition, with the home being for men a sanctified retreat from the world of work, where they can relax and assert their authority.

8. Although none of the fundamentalisms has a well-developed economic agenda to replace the corporate libertarianism of capitalism, they do have in common certain criticisms of it. They feel that capitalism has replaced the fraternal atmosphere of the premodern economy with ruthless economic competition and bitter competition over public resources (Kuran 1993:290–291). They all believe that the economic problems of today are caused by moral degeneration. Modern economics, they say, sees human wants and consequently human demands as unbounded; the supply can never catch up with demand. Most fundamentalisms reject this amoral approach, seeing human wants not as unbounded but as a problem of modern civilization's ability to control individual acquisitiveness. Individuals can be persuaded against pursuing an immoral lifestyle (Kuran 1993:295).

The redistribution of wealth is a common theme in religious fundamentalisms, although not all deal with it in the same way. All encourage the wealthy to aid the poor, but none insists on full equality. Islamic fundamentalists encourage the state to enforce traditional Qur'anic rules on a religious tax whose proceeds go to help the poor. Christian fundamentalists are generally opposed to economic redistribution, advocating instead the end to transfer programs, arguing that obeying God's commands will alleviate poverty and inequality.

Islamic Fundamentalism

Islamic fundamentalism gained international prominence with the Iranian revolution, Iran's transformation into an Islamic state, and the return from state-imposed exile of the Ayatollah Khomeini in 1979. The media has paid much attention to the fundamentalist resurgence, as have the leaders of nation-states with sizable Muslim populations. There has also been much media attention to so-called Islamic terrorist organizations, attention that has often bordered on bigotry. Thus, when the Oklahoma Federal Building was blown up by American militia sympathizers in 1995, the media first reported the presence of "Middle Eastern–looking" men in the area of the blast. There has also been a tendency in the Western media to assume that the beliefs, goals, and organizational methods of Islamic fundamentalists are everywhere the same, thus ignoring important local differences.

The general thrust of Islamic fundamentalist belief is that Muslims have strayed from the moral life that the Qur'an dictates and that true Muslims must return to a life of piety and faith. Fundamentalists believe that the early success of Islamic civilization was because of their faith and that the decline of Islamic influence over the past centuries is a result of their straying from that faith. If Muslims can return to their previous religious idealism, they can eliminate the social, political, economic, and moral problems afflicting the Muslim people and create an ethical order on Earth (Sachedina 1991:406).

Muslims attribute the decline of Islamic piety to the influence of the West on their societies in general, and on colonial and economic domination and the rise of Western secular influence in particular. Islamic fundamentalists are not opposed to modernization; rather, they argue that the Qur'an could provide the foundation for appropriate social institutions and social ethics in a modern, technical age. Islamic fundamentalists see a conflict between the religion that God ordained and the historical development of the world He controls. Consequently they have tried to prevent further erosion in what they see as the true faith, at the same time resisting what they see as alien domination in any form over Muslim societies.

Islamic fundamentalists in different countries attribute the ills of their country—poverty, loss of influence, conflict—to a straying from true Muslim belief and behavior and to some degree blame the West, or modernization in general, for their political, economic, and social problems. In Egypt, for example, fundamentalists believe that their defeat at the hand of Israel in the Six Days War in 1968 was a sign from God that they had strayed from the true faith. National good fortune, however, is attributed to maintenance of the faith; the discovery of offshore oil in Malaysia, for example, was attributed by Muslims to their faith.

Although Islamic fundamentalists in different countries share certain beliefs and goals, there are significant differences among them. In Egypt, for example, fundamentalists believe that creating an Islamic society will help people compensate for the loss of family relationships incurred as people find it necessary to leave villages and become more independent of their families. For that reason, suggested Andrea B. Rugh (1993), the most militant are the young people, especially those who, despite having college educations, can find no jobs and who consequently see in Islam a non-Western alternative. The dominant feature of Islamic fundamentalism in Malaysia is the *dakwah* movement. The *dakwah* is a small religious group or commune that separates itself from the larger society to lead lives that members believe are based on Muslim law as given in the Qur'an. Manning Nash noted that *dakwah* is a youth movement of largely university-educated men and women. Members of *dakwah* express discontent with what they see as the modern, urban, pluralistic, and secular world. They see it as sensual, corrupt, neurotic, and trivial (Nash 1991:695). They read Islamic literature, carefully evaluating their behavior according to passages from the Qur'an. Women wear ankle-length dresses and, in public, the *chador* or a version of it. Members of the *dakwah* try to maintain small businesses or stalls or bake items to sell locally. Another unique feature of Islamic fundamentalism in Malaysia is its ethnic character and its appeal to Malays as opposed to other ethnic groups, such as Indians and Chinese. To some extent, it is a nationalist protest against the influence of Indians and Chinese who gained economic prominence in Malaysia during the British colonial period. It also relies heavily on anti-Western, antimodern rhetoric. The West, wrote Nash (1991:731),

> [i]s seen primarily as the threatening "other," personified variously by the United States and Western Europe—a chaotic power, lacking in discipline, in morality, and indeed in simple human decency. Thus, for most dakwah organizations, the West remains the principle enemy, an aggressor who through its educational systems and its mastery of science has been successful in implanting atheism, materialism, and moral decadence in the heart of Malaysian Islam.

Islamic Fundamentalism in Iran.   The Islamic revolution in Iran has all the characteristics of an antisystemic movement. Iran was controlled by core states—Russia, Great Britain, and the United States—for more than a century. The secular government of the shah was put in power by an American CIA-engineered coup in 1953 against an elected government and was rapidly industrializing, led by the sale of its plentiful oil supplies to core nations. The Islamic revolutionary government quickly acted to reverse what they saw as the imposition of a foreign culture on their own. It's important, therefore, to understand the social and historical background of this revolution.

Iran was the center of the Ottoman Empire that began to rise to prominence in the Middle East in the sixteenth century. As the Ottoman polity began to break up in the nineteenth century, both England and Russia inflicted military defeats on Iran and gained concessions to exploit various resources such as tobacco. But the tobacco concessions so angered merchants and the Islamic religious leaders, the *ulama,* that they forced the government to rescind the concession to the British. A leader in this revolt was Jamal al-Din al-Afghani, who preached against Western imperialism and became one of the central figures in Islamic resurgence at the turn of the twentieth century in both Iran and Egypt. Thus, the protest against Western influence hardly began with the overthrow of the shah in 1979; it extends well back into the nineteenth century.

The British gained economic control over Iran when the Russians withdrew after the Bolshevik revolution in 1917. Because of the weakness of the Iranian central government there were various revolts, the most serious being the Jangali revolt of 1917–1921 led by Kuchik Khan—referred to by one English writer as the Robin Hoods of the Caspian Marshes—who financed their revolt by stealing from wealthy landlords (Munson 1988). Reza Kahn defeated the Jangali by gaining the support of the merchants and the army. Reza wanted to establish a republic but the *ulama* objected, so Reza had himself declared shah and established the Pahlavi dynasty. With the support of the British, he rapidly secularized the country, clearly trying to Westernize it; he forced men to wear European clothes, including brimmed hats, and forbade women from wearing the *chador* or veil, analogous to requiring European women to go bare breasted. Public protests followed. More importantly, trade and commerce under the shah was monopolized by Europeans.

The gradual withdrawal of the British from Iran after World War II allowed the *ulama* to regain some of their authority and led to the democratic election in 1951 of Mohammad Mosaddeq as prime minister. One of Mosaddeq's first acts was to nationalize the Anglo-Iranian Oil Company. He also banned a militant religious group, the *Fada'iyan-e Islam,* led by Ayatollah Kashani. These two acts ultimately led to his downfall in a coup arranged by the American CIA to install the son of Reza Kahn as shah. After the coup, the shah banned the parties that had helped put him in power and began the period of American domination of Iran and continued the Westernization of the country. When the shah announced that women would be allowed to vote there was a religious protest in Qum, the religious center of Iran, to which the shah responded by attacking the seminary. With the help of the CIA, the shah set up a security apparatus, SAVAK, to suppress domestic opposition.

The revolution of 1979 that overthrew the shah and brought Ayatollah Khomeini to power represented a joining together of the *ulamas,* the merchants, and the intellectuals in reaction to the shah's policies, the repressions, and the killings. The stage was set for the return of Khomeini on February 1, 1979, aboard a jet from France.

We can see in this history the interplay between, on the one hand, British and American attempts to control political events in Iran and, consequently, the vast Iranian oil fields and, on the other hand, Islamic leaders who objected largely to the secularization of Iran that seemingly arose from British and then American influences. But the fundamentalist revolution in Iran was neither sudden nor surprising. There were many factors involved in the revolution, including the poverty of the majority of Iranian peasants, the violent repression of dissent led by SAVAK, and the economic excesses of the leaders who took great pains to flaunt the wealth gained by oil sales to the West. It also marked the continued resistance by many Iranians to the assimilation of their country into the culture of capitalism.

Protestant Fundamentalism in North America

Protestant fundamentalism has gained almost as high a profile in the United States as Islamic fundamentalism has in Arab and Southeast Asian countries. Although it is difficult to estimate precisely how many people in the United States are fundamentalists, it is clear that many people share the same beliefs. For example, 72 percent of Americans say the Bible is the word of God and 39 percent say the Bible is literally true. Two-thirds say that Jesus Christ rose from the dead, and 44 percent are creationists who agree that God created the world in pretty much its present form within the last 10,000 years (Ammerman 1991).

Protestant fundamentalism clearly has gained a strong voice in the political process in the United States, demanding that political candidates adhere to certain fundamentalist principles, including support for the banning of abortion, support for school prayer, and support for laws controlling what can appear in the mass media.

Foundations of Protestant Fundamentalism.   There are three basic tenets held by people who consider themselves to be Protestant fundamentalists. First, they are evangelicals, that is they begin with the fact that they are saved. Not all evangelicals are fundamentalists, but this is one point on which evangelicals and fundamentalists agree. Second, they believe in the inerrancy of the Bible; they believe the Bible to be true, even when it says things they don't like. Furthermore, they believe it provides an accurate view of history and science, as well as God-given moral guidelines. Theologians may argue about what different passages mean, but through prayer and study the truth evident in the Bible will be revealed. Third, they believe in premillenialism, the doctrine of rapture. Fundamentalists, like other Christians, believe in the end times, a point in history when the present world ends and the thousand-year reign of Christ on Earth begins. But fundamentalists also believe that prior to that, Jesus Christ will appear and to the blare of heavenly trumpets lift his bride, the (true) church, up to heaven. This is the rapture. Then begins the tribulation, a seven-year period when all unfilled Bible prophesies are fulfilled, when God, Satan, Christ, and anti-Christ meet in the final battle of Armageddon in Israel, and when Christ returns with his army of believers to begin his millennial reign on Earth. Christians have no role in the playing out of these events, and nothing that anyone can do will change the date of the rapture; that date was set by God at the beginning of time (Harding 1991:61). However, it is possible, through careful observation of world events, to predict the coming of the rapture.

There are some variations in Protestant fundamentalist belief and practice, but the essentials are relatively consistent. The question is, *what was the stimulus for the rise of Protestant fundamentalism, and how can we account for its recent resurgence?*

The Emergence of Fundamentalism in North America.   Fundamentalist belief began to form in the mid-nineteenth century, largely in reaction to the modernization and secularization of Protestant churches and as a response to the challenge to religion of nineteenth-century science, technology, and culture. Darwin's theory of evolution was one of the most threatening scientific developments, but others, such as sociologist Émile Durkheim's ideas about the power of social forces to shape individual behavior, Sigmund Freud's theories of sexuality, and the works of anthropologist Franz Boas that attacked ethnocentrism and absolutism, struck at some of the basic beliefs and the truth of the Bible. Fundamentalists were particularly offended when biblical scholars turned a scientific eye to the Scriptures, claiming the Bible is neither unique nor the "word of God" and comparing biblical stories with the myths of other societies.

But it was not only the work of academics who threatened the inerrancy of the Bible that triggered a fundamentalist reaction, there was also the change in American culture itself. There were new attitudes and values that accompanied the shift from a primarily agrarian society to an urban industrial society. From the end of the Civil War to the beginning of the twentieth century the industrial workforce quadrupled, and inventions such as the telegraph, electricity, and telephones were transforming the country. It was to science and technology that people began to look for improvements in their lives.

In addition, immigration and urbanization were changing where people lived and with whom they lived and worked. All of these changes prompted religious reactions. Some of those who were religiously inclined joined the Social Gospel movement, which sought to alleviate the ills caused by urban crowding and poverty; others became Adventists or Jehovah's Witnesses, carrying on the early nineteenth-century prophesies of William Miller and Charles Russell that the world was about to end. Or people became possessed by the Holy Spirit and joined Pentecostal movements. Those who were fundamentalists, however, differed in that they rejected any compromise with those who no longer saw the Bible as the word of God (Ammerman 1991:14).

Inerrancy of the Bible became the centerpiece of the fundamentalist movement in the early twentieth century. Theologians attacked the works of German scholars who claimed the Bible was an historic document composed by many authors. Fundamentalists argued that if the Bible claimed to be divinely inspired then, because it was the word of God, it must be inspired. Those trying to show that the Bible was in error, fundamentalists said, had to "prove" that a disputed fact was in the original texts—those unsullied by copying and transmission—and that it really meant what the critic said it meant and was really in conflict with a proven fact of science. Given such a standard, it was virtually impossible to prove the Bible wrong.

After World War I fundamentalists interpreted Germany's defeat as punishment for the work of German scholars trying to examine the Bible scientifically and for the acceptance of Darwin's theory of evolution, whereas they saw the League of Nations as the world government that they believed would appear just prior to the tribulation. Thus, as Christian fundamentalists do today, they interpreted world events in terms of their religious beliefs.

Early twentieth-century fundamentalists focused their early protests on schools and the teaching of Darwin's theory of evolution. There is some misunderstanding about fundamentalist objections to Darwin's theory of evolution. Most theologians had little problem accommodating Darwin's theory to religious doctrine. The problems were created by two implications of Darwin's theories. The first was that if evolution operated through random beneficial variations and the destruction of the weak, then, by implication, the God of Darwin acted randomly and cruelly. Darwin could not accept that and became an agnostic (Larson 1997:17). The second implication was that the social world operated on the same principles as the natural world and that these principles (e.g., natural selection) could be used, as many were, to justify laissez-faire capitalism, imperialism, and militarism. Furthermore, the application of Darwin's theories to the workings of society legitimated the then very popular doctrine of eugenics, the idea that the state should enact laws to ensure that only the "fittest" bred. This, of course, further imposed human will on a divinely guided universe.

The protest over the teaching of evolution in American schools may never have received the prominence it did had not William Jennings Bryan volunteered to prosecute John Scopes, a Tennessee high school teacher charged under Tennessee law with illegally teaching the theory of evolution. Bryan was a major American figure, three-time presidential candidate, advisor to presidents, crusader for women's rights, and defender of the Bible. To counter Bryan the American Civil Liberties Union sent a team of lawyers headed by Clarence Darrow to defend Scopes. Darrow, in his way, was as imposing a public figure as Bryan, and probably the most famous lawyer of his time. He had also worked for Bryan in his presidential campaigns and shared much of his social philosophy.

The Scopes trial has been depicted in theater, movies, and literature as a battle between science and rationality on the one side, and religion and superstition on the other. Lost in that depiction of the struggle was a genuine antisystemic sentiment, particularly on the part of Bryan. Bryan had voiced his objections to Darwin as early as 1904. In one speech he said,

> The Darwinian theory represents man as reaching his present perfection by the operation of the law of hate—the merciless law by which the strong crowd out and kill off the weak. (cited Larson 1997:39)

For Bryan, who had built his career denouncing the excesses of capitalism and militarism, this was unacceptable.

Darrow, however, succeeded in turning the case into a science versus religion contest, forcing Bryan to defend a literal interpretation of the Bible, and the issue of using the theory of evolution to interpret social history and human behavior never received a hearing. Bryan won the case; Scopes was convicted. But the public ridicule of fundamentalist arguments of the inerrancy of the Bible resulted in American public opinion overwhelmingly supporting Scopes.

After the Scopes trial and the public reaction to it, Protestant fundamentalists were convinced that American culture had come under the sway of "secular humanism," a godless view of the world that substituted human action and wisdom for divine action and

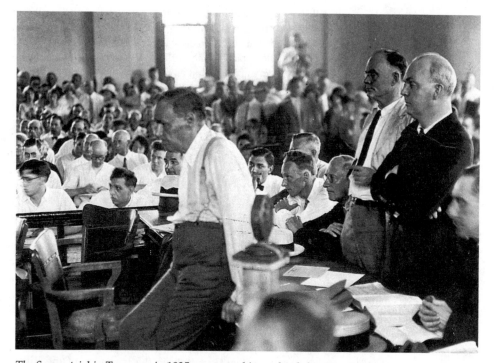

The Scopes trial in Tennessee in 1925 was turned into a battle between religion and science by Clarence Darrow (standing in front of the table) in his defense of John T. Scopes (seated behind Darrow, in a white shirt and staring straight ahead).

guidance. Because they could not transform society, they turned to saving individual souls. Most fundamentalist churches broke away from their parent churches and formed their own organizations, such as the American Council of Christian Churches founded in 1941 by Carl McIntire. Fundamentalists joined missionary organizations, and there was enormous growth in Bible colleges and institutes as well as expansion into publishing and radio and television broadcasting. Charles Fuller's "Old Fashioned Revival Hour," which appeared in 1934, became one of the most popular shows on radio, followed on television by the enormously popular Oral Roberts and Rex Humbard.

There was also a growth in political radicalism; Gerald Winrod wrote in his journal of seeing the end times, a Jewish anti-Christ, and a Jewish conspiracy to rule the world. In the 1950s, fundamentalists took up the banner of anticommunism, with Carl McIntire arguing that the Revised Standard Version of the Bible was a communist plot, and that Jews and Blacks constituted the main threat to White Christian civilization. But it was the revolution of 1968, the civil rights movement, the feminist movement, and the antiwar movement with its slogan "question authority" that seemed to provide evidence for fundamentalists that society was disintegrating and the rapture must be near.

Burned-out hippies and disenchanted liberals, along with other seekers who had failed in the 1968 revolution to transform society, began to join fundamentalist churches. As one hippie-turned-fundamentalist said (cited Ammerman 1991:39),

> [o]ne person tells you to do one thing, and the next person tells you to do the opposite. "Get a job, get a haircut." Or "Turn on, tune in, drop out." Or "Support the President," and someone else says "Impeach Nixon" or "Stop the War," or whatever it is, you know. It makes you crazy. What do you do? It's typical of the world. You're in confusion. In the Lord the Word shows you what to do, and you can rest in it. You don't have to be gray.

Fundamentalists were also concerned about America's role in the world; in spite of their condemnation of what was happening to American culture, America was still the fundamentalists' "city on a hill"; moreover, America's military strength and economic influence provided the entree into other countries for fundamentalist missionizing; there was a fear that "the light of the gospel might go out because it would have no great chosen nation to carry it" (cited Ammerman 1991:40).

Finally, there were a series of changes that seemed to be challenging fundamentalists to come out of their political isolation. Among them was the Equal Rights Amendment (ERA) to the Constitution; fundamentalists feared it would prevent women from fulfilling their biblical role as submissive wives. They saw laws promoted by governmental and private social agencies that sought to define the limits of a parent's right to punish their children as an attack on parental authority as it was defined in the Bible. They saw the extension of the civil rights movement to homosexuals, whose lives seemed to fundamentalists grossly immoral, as a direct attack on biblical injunction. They fought against the prevention of prayer in school. And, finally, they saw behind *Roe v. Wade* and the legalization of abortion all the forces that were trying to destroy the family and Christian morality.

The defense against the scientific attack on the inerrancy of the Bible did not go away; it resurfaced in the doctrine of scientific creationism, the use of the tools and language of science to prove that the world was indeed created in 4004 B.C. But where the inerrancy of the Bible was the major issue one hundred years ago, today the focus of fundamentalist interest is the protection of the traditional family—a legally married man and woman with their children preferably supported by the husband's work—as the basic unit of society (Ammerman 1991:45). From this flows the fundamentalist opposition to gay and lesbian rights, the Equal Rights Amendment, and laws designed to protect abused wives and children. And at the centerpiece of this agenda is the opposition to abortion.

With these agendas, and the active participation of Protestant fundamentalists in politics, there has been a resurgence of fundamentalist influence in American life. One of the clearest indications of this is the enormous growth in church schools and home schooling. From 1965 to 1983 enrollment in evangelical schools rose sixfold, and the number of schools approached 10,000. As many as 100,000 fundamentalist children were being taught at home. This pattern is evident also at the college level. For example, enrollment in the ninety-eight evangelical colleges in the United States represented by the Council for Christian Colleges and Universities increased almost 50 percent from 1990 through 2000, as opposed to about 10 percent of all other colleges and universities in the United States (Council for Christian Colleges and Universities 2001).

Some of these positions have served to unite fundamentalists with other groups with whom they have, at one time or another, been vehemently opposed. Their opposition to abortion with Catholics; their opposition to pornography with the feminist movement; their opposition to the ERA with Mormons; and their support of Israel with Jews. But it has also created splits with those who decried such alliances.

Variations in Doctrine.   There are also new variations of Protestant fundamentalist belief, most markedly the Christian reconstructionists, probably the most clearly antisystemic fundamentalist group. Christian reconstructionists seek to replace the "modern bureaucratic state" with a Christian state modeled after the Bible; their ideal is the seventeenth-century Puritans of Massachusetts. They argue that people must submit to the rule of God and follow a doctrine they call "theonomy."

The economics of Christian fundamentalists are more complex and varied than generally supposed (Iannaccone 1993; Kuran 1993). Most people associate Christian fundamentalists with support of the free market economy, opposition to government redistribution programs, defense of private property, and opposition to any form of socialism. Yet little is made of economics in the writings of most Christian fundamentalists, and many fundamentalist colleges or universities do not even have economics departments. Jerry Fallwell is the most outspoken of the Christian fundamentalist leaders when it comes to the defense of the free market, but the Christian reconstructionists are the only group to systematize a conservative economic agenda, arguing that the Bible dictates that private property should be regulated only by the family and the religious community, not by the state. The Bible, they say, imposes a flat tax of 10 percent and argues against any kind of centrally planned economy. Metallic currency is the only kind permitted, and income redistribution violates the eighth commandant, "Thou shalt not steal," and is simply institutionalized theft.

There is also an evangelical left that argues that the Bible teaches that God is on the side of the poor. Best represented by the writings of Jim Wallis (*Agenda for Biblical People,* 1984), they draw attention to the vast disparities in wealth that exist in the modern world and argue that "overconsumption is theft from the poor," that the wealth of the core comes only at the expense of the poor of the nonindustrial world. The biblical solution, they argue, is redistribution. Christians should consume less, they say, and contribute more to the poor. Influenced by the secular left, the counterculture of the 1960s, and communitarian Christian groups such as the Amish, Mennonites, and Hutterites, said Laurence R. Iannaccone (1993:350), the evangelical left argues that

> [t]he system which creates and sustains much of the hunger, underdevelopment, and other social ills in the world today is capitalism. Capitalism is by its very nature a system which promotes individualism, competition, and profit-making with little or no regard for social costs. Its puts profits and private gain before social service and human needs. As such it is an unjust system and should be replaced.

"TERROR IN THE MIND OF GOD"

Religion, as we mentioned previously, has always had a revolutionary dimension. Most (if not all) religious movements began at a moment of dissatisfaction, if not despair, and sought to reorder or revitalize a world that its members found wanting. In addition, virtually all the major religions of the world contain texts detailing violent battles between the forces of good and the forces of evil. They all have what Mark Jeurgensmeyer (2000:158) refers to as "shadowy foes," "thems," "strangers," and such who dwell in the

> shady edges of known civilizations.... They represent what was chaotic and uncertain about the world, including those things that defied categorization altogether.

The Book of Revelation of the New Testament with its description of the forces of Satan and the ultimate battle between good and evil provides one of the best (and most violent) metaphors of war and redemption in Western literature.

Characterizing one's enemies as "Satanic," as Elaine Pagels (1995:xix) points out in her book *The Origin of Satan,* lends a moral and religious meaning to conflict in which "we" are God's people, and "they" are God's enemies, an interpretation which, as Pagels notes, has been extraordinarily successful in justifying hatred and mass slaughter.

Therefore, it should not be surprising that religion is used by some as a justification for violent acts. The juxtaposition of religion and violence has become more common since the attacks on the World Trade Center and the Pentagon on September 11, 2001, and has focused added attention on radical religious groups. Attempts to understand the motivations and rationales of religious violence, however, have tended to underestimate the deep religious convictions of religious group members. It would be a mistake to dismiss them as "cultic," or "irrational," or "alienated." Followers of these movements believe that the religious forms they follow are the ones with the deep historical roots; they are the "true" Christianity," the "true" Judaism, the "true" Islam, and so on. In addition, it would be a mistake to neglect the political aspects of religious violence. Religion provides a framework for viewing events and interpreting experience. When followers of Christianity, Judaism, Sikhism, Buddhism, or Islam commit violent acts in the name of God or some spiritual mission, they are acting in response to some social, political, or economic griev-ance. When Reverend Michael Bray set fire to abortion clinics in the name of a heavenly mandate, he was convinced that the United States government was undermining individual freedoms and moral values; his acts were directed at the nation-state as much as at the clin-ics themselves. Osama bin Laden sought the establishment of an Islamic state, but clearly his acts were as much political as they were religious. The Israeli occupation of Palestinian territories, the stationing of U.S. troops in Saudi Arabia, the U.S. support for oppressive governments in the Middle East were as much reasons for his acts as anything religious (see Guardian-Observer 2002). It is common for the media to see so-called "suicide bomb-ing" as motivated solely by religious (usually Islamic) "fanaticism." Yet, as Robert A. Pape (2003) notes in his study of suicide bombers, of the 188 incidents he documented from 1980 to 2002, 75 were instigated by the Tamil Tigers in Sri Lanka, a Marxist-Leninist group whose members adamantly oppose any religion. Thus, whether religion provides the motivation for political violence or is simply an additional justification for it remains an open question.

Regardless, given the deep religious convictions common to many members of all societies, it would be a mistake to underestimate the power of believers to project social, political, and economic grievances onto a religious or spiritual framework. The questions we need to ask are, *how do people explain their use of religion as a justification for violent acts, and how do we explain the conditions under which such justification occurs?*

Some Examples of Religious Violence

The Militants of Protestant Fundamentalism.   The militant groups of Protestant fun-damentalism include Operation Rescue and the Army of God, both dedicated to, among other things, halting abortion. Randall Terry began Operation Rescue in Binghamton, New York, in 1988. Its goal was to protest legal abortion by barricading abortion clinics, block-ing women's access to clinics, confronting women entering and leaving the clinics, and ha-rassing them verbally and physically, even following them or tracing their license plate numbers and calling them at home. Operation Rescue picketed clinics and the homes of clinic physicians, sent threatening letters, and made threatening phone calls. By 1990, Op-eration Rescue reported that 35,000 of their protesters had been arrested, whereas another 16,000 risked arrests in what the group called "rescues" (Ginsburg 1993).

The ultimate goal, however, was more than simply stopping abortion. Rather, they intended to use the opposition to abortion, in the words of evangelical Protestant leader Francis Schaeffer (cited Ginsburg 1993:558), "as a way for evangelicals to challenge the entire legitimacy of the secular modern state, withholding allegiance until the nation re-turns to its religious roots in matters like public prayer and religious education." As Faye Ginsburg (1993:558) noted, the opposition to abortion is the means protesters use to return America to "traditional Christian values."

Operation Rescue was not the first group to use violence to protest abortion. The Right to Life movement goes back to the 1973 Supreme Court ruling in *Roe* v. *Wade* that recognized a woman's right to abortion. Some groups had already adopted confrontational tactics of blocking the entrances to clinics and harassing abortion providers. The National Abortion Federation keeps a record of "violent incidents" against abortion providers that includes invasions of clinics, vandalism, murders, death threats, bomb threats, bombings, assaults, arson attempts, arson, and kidnapping attempts. From 1977 through 2003 they have documented a total of 4,120 violent incidents including 7 murders, 41 bombings, 169 cases of arson, 82 cases of attempted arson or bombings, and 373 cases of invasion. They have also documented 33,830 arrests of abortion protesters (see National Abortion Federation 2003).

The state's official reaction to the violence has been ambiguous. In an influential anti-abortion essay in 1983, President Ronald Reagan, an opponent of abortion, said the increase in attacks on abortion clinics did not constitute terrorism because they were not carried out by an organized group; he reversed himself in 1985, speaking out against these "violent anarchistic activities."

It is clear that Randall Terry's agenda is to refashion what he sees as a godless society according to the beliefs and values of his version of Christian fundamentalism. Thus, as Ginsburg (1993:579) said, it is a mistake to look at Operation Rescue only in the context of the abortion debate; rather, its intent is to impose on American society its version of Christian culture: "For 'rescuers,' fighting abortion is simply a first step in reversing America's 'moral decline,' much as opposition to the teaching of evolution was considered a way to fight secularization in the 1920s."

A more militant Christian fundamentalist group is the Army of God. Its doctrine was outlined in an underground manual, *Army of God,* whose authorship is attributed to the Reverend Michael Bray (see Juergensmeyer 2000:21). Regardless of whether Bray was the author, he clearly sympathizes with its sentiments. Bray was convicted in 1985 of setting fire to seven abortion clinics on some of which were found the initials AOG. He is also the author of the book *A Time to Kill,* which defends his own actions as well as the killing of abortion providers. He was also a friend and defender of the Reverend Paul Hill who was convicted and executed for killing Dr. John Britton and his bodyguard, retired Air Force Lieutenant Colonel James Herman Barrett. According to Bray, Americans live in a state of "hidden warfare," comparable to that of Nazi Germany, and a dramatic event, such as an economic collapse, would reveal the demonic role of the government, at which point the people would take up arms in a revolutionary struggle and establish a new moral order based on biblical law. Until then, Bray believes, he and others must have the moral courage to resist, particularly by defending unborn babies and killing those who threaten them. Bray justifies his acts by drawing on the work of theologians, such as Reinhold Niebuhr, who, trying to come to grips with when it is permissible to use force, argued that force could be used moderately in the cause of justice.

Jessica Stern (2003:150) asked one young member of the Army of God how he became involved with the group. "I am a Christian," he said, "and therefore opposed to abortion. Unborn babies are dying by the millions, and I feel compelled to help." For members of the group, killing abortion providers is "justifiable homicide."

The organization even has developed an operational strategy designed to escape electronic detection by U.S. law enforcement officials. They call it "swarming," in which many, semi-independent networks converge rapidly and stealthily on chosen targets. One member described his vision of a swarming operation:

So we have the Army of God, which in the future will organize and coalesce like those of Europe who had centuries of underground work, and there will be skilled assassins and skilled saboteurs after the abortion industry, which is not only the abortionists but also the people on top of them, including Supreme Court judges. Now Paul Hill has called for the Supreme Court judges to be killed and also for chemical and biological weapons, and we support this call, at least I do (cited Stern 2003:151–152).

Terror in the Holy Land.   Perhaps there is no better example of violence over contested space than Israel and the Palestinian territories, an area sacred to three of the world's major religions—Judaism, Christianity, and Islam. And perhaps there is no greater symbol of this contestation than the Qubbat as-Sakhra, housing the al-Aqsa mosque that encloses the Dome of the Rock. The mosque was built by the Caliph Abd al-Malik and completed in A.D. 691. The rock at the center of the structure is one of the holiest places in Islam. According to tradition, the Prophet Muhammad ascended to heaven from the rock at the end of his Night Journey. In the Jewish tradition this is the Foundation Stone, the symbolic foundation on which the world was created, and the place where Abraham was preparing to sacrifice his son Isaac when an angel of God told him to stop. It is also the site of the *Beit Yahweh* (Temple of Jerusalem) destroyed by the Romans in A.D. 70 and the holiest place of worship in Judaism.

The contest for control over the Holy Land is, of course, centuries old, but it is the Arab–Israeli conflict of today that has more recently fueled religious violence. For that reason it is necessary to understand something of the history of the conflict (see Smith 2000; Cohn-Sherbok and el-Alami 2002).

Very briefly, in the nineteenth century the often virulent anti-Semitism in Europe persuaded many Jews of the need for a Jewish homeland in Israeli, the biblical origin of Judaism. From this emerged the Zionist movement that began to raise money from wealthy patrons (e.g., the Rothschilds) to fund Jewish settlements in Palestine. In the middle of the nineteenth century there were already some 10,000 non-Zionist Jews in Palestine, but by 1914, with the influx of Zionists, there were some 90,000 compared to some 500,000 Arab Palestinians. At that point Palestine was part of the Ottoman Empire controlled by Turkey. But after World War I and the defeat of Germany and her allies—including Turkey—the Ottoman Empire was disbanded and Palestine was assigned as a protectorate to Great Britain. With European Jews lobbying for a Jewish homeland, the British Cabinet, in consultation with Zionist leaders, issued a letter in 1917 from Arthur James Lord Balfour to Lord Rothschild making known their intent to establish a Jewish homeland in Palestine. The interpretation of the Balfour Declaration became a center of dispute for the next forty years.

With the defeat of the Germans and the Turks in 1918, the remaining population of Palestine consisted of 66,000 Jews, 512,000 Muslims, and 61,000 Christians. Arab hostility to the influx of Jewish immigrants, however, led to riots in 1920 and 1921 when as many as forty-seven Jews were killed. Jewish immigration increased in the 1920s and 1930s as Russia permitted more Jews to leave and as many Jews fled Germany in the face of Nazi persecution. The increased conflict between Jews and Palestinians led to the formation of armed Jewish groups, such as *Haganah,* the first Jewish defense force. A more militant group, the *Irgun* (*Irgun Tsvai-Leumi* or "National-Military Organization"), was regarded by the British as a terrorist organization. Jewish protest against both the Palestinians and the British increased in the late 1930s and the British hung a Jew for attacking an

Arab bus. The *Irgun* responded by exploding land mines in Haifa, killing seventy-four people. In 1937 the British issued a white paper (the Peel Commission) suggesting a partition of the Palestinian protectorate into Jewish and Arab sections, and then they issued another in 1939 that recommended the protectorate be declared an independent Palestinian state but with the rights of Jews protected. This satisfied neither the Palestinians nor the Jews.

The beginning of World War II added complications to British-run Palestine because neither the Jews, intent on establishing a Jewish state on their ancestral homeland, nor the Arab Palestinians, intent on establishing an independent Palestinian state, recognized the legitimacy of British rule. After the war, during which the Jews allied themselves with the British and the Arabs with the Germans, and after the full extent of the Nazi holocaust was known, the British insisted on implementing the 1939 white paper, resulting in an armed uprising by the Jews against the British, fanned in part by messages over the illegal Voice of Israel radio station. The *Haganah* blew up the Palestinian railway system and the *Irgun* bombed the King David Hotel, the site of British offices, killing close to one hundred people. In 1948, the *Irgun* and another Jewish group, the *Lehi,* massacred men, women, and children in the village of Deir Yassin and entire Palestinian villages fled (Cohn-Sherbok and el-Alami 2002). Following these incidents, the British withdrew their mandate, and David Ben-Gurion, the first prime minster of Israel, declared the independence of the state of Israel, which was quickly recognized by both the United States and the Soviet Union. At this time, the United Nations called for a partition of Palestine into Arab (the West Bank) and Jewish sections; Arab forces invaded Israel and within three months were turned back by Israeli forces.

Beginning in 1948 there were intermittent hostilities between Israel and its Arab neighbors (wars in 1957, 1967, 1973), and, as a consequence of the wars, Israel occupied areas that had been Palestinian land, and proceeded to establish Jewish settlements in violation of various U.N. resolutions. Militant Palestinian groups, such as the Palestinian Liberation Organization (PLO), Black September, Hamas, and Palestine Islamic Jihad, emerged in response to Israeli exploitation and oppression of the Arab population and with their own nationalistic aspirations. Black September claimed responsibility for the kidnapping and killing of Israeli athletes at the 1972 Olympics in Munich, Germany, whereas Hamas and Islamic Jihad have taken responsibility for hundreds of attacks on Israeli civilians and military targets. Israel responded with increasingly violent repression, particularly after the Palestinian uprising (*Intifada*) in 1987. In 1993, both sides were brought together in Oslo, Norway, and the Israeli prime minister Yitzhak Rabin signed a peace treaty with Yasser Arafat, head of the PLO, to end hostilities. The Oslo Accord recognized the Palestinian Authority as a governing group and gave it civil authority in Palestinian-occupied areas (the West Bank and the Gaza Strip). But radicals on both sides refused to accept the agreement, and, in November 1995, Rabin was assassinated by a right-wing Jew, Yigal Amir, who defended himself by saying, "I acted on God's order and I have no regrets." As the Oslo Accord stalled and as Israeli settlements on the West Bank grew, violence on both sides increased. When the accord collapsed in 2000 with the election of the Likud Party, a second Arab *Intifada* began. In 2002 and 2003 Palestinian attacks increased as Israel allowed more and more Jewish settlers into what had been Palestinian territory, increased military operations within occupied territory, and began the building of a wall intended to separate the Jewish and Palestinian populations, while, at the same time, Israeli politicians spoke openly of the "ethnic cleansing" of the Palestinian population.

Religion clearly plays a major role in the conflict, in spite of the obvious political and economic factors, not the least of which is the annexation of Palestinian land and territory by Israel. Jewish settlers, regardless of where they come from, justify their taking of land held by Palestinians for decades by reference to the Old Testament creation of the land of Israel. Palestinians justify their resistance by reference to the Koran, as well as by U.N. resolutions that condemn the Israeli takeover.

In 1990, a Jewish messianic group known as the Temple Mount Faithful, announced their intent to lay a 4.5 ton cornerstone at the site of the ancient Temple of Jerusalem and the Haram al-Sharif. Palestinians reacted to the threat to the Haram al-Sharif with massive riots. One member of the Temple Mount Faithful, Yoel Lerner, a Brooklyn-born, MIT-trained mathematician, was imprisoned for a plan to blow up the Dome of the Rock to make room for the rebuilding of the Temple of Jerusalem (Stern 2003:86). For Lerner, no one has the moral right to give up any territory that comprised the ancient state of Israel. Furthermore, the rebuilding of the temple is necessary for people to practice their religion; the Torah, he says, has 613 commandments and 240 of these require worship at the temple. Thus, for almost two millennia, says Lerner, Jews have not been able to practice their religion. The assassination of Rabin, says Lerner, was completely justified because by signing the Oslo Accord Rabin was stealing Jewish property. "The land is a sacred thing," he says, trying to justify Amir's decision to kill Rabin (Stern 2003:91). As Jessica Stern (2003:92) put it:

> The biblical promise of Eretz Israel, The Land of Israel, to God's chosen people, makes the concept of land a key component of religious doctrine to fundamentalist Jews, who believe that possession of the land of Israel is part and parcel of the Jews' covenant with God. Accordingly, relinquishing or dividing any part of the land promised by God to the children of Israel would constitute a breach of the Covenant.

Lerner was also a follower of Rabbi Meir Kahane who was assassinated in New York City in 1990 by a Muslim. Kahane was radically anti-Arab and founded the Jewish Defense League and the organizations Kach and Kahane Chai, both of which were declared terrorist organizations by the Israeli Cabinet in 1994. One of its members, Dr. Baruch Goldstein, a Brooklyn-born Jewish fundamentalist, walked into a mosque in Hebron in 1994 and massacred more than thirty Palestinians as they prayed. Goldstein remains a hero to right-wing Israelis.

While Jews commit violence in the name of reestablishing the Jewish ancestral homeland, Palestinians kill in the name of Islam and the establishment of an independent Palestinian state. One of the groups prominent in the Palestinian resistance is Hamas. In 1999, Mark Juergensmeyer interviewed Abdul Aziz Rantisi, who, after the Israeli assassination in March of 2004 of Hamas founder, Sheik Ahmed Yassin, was selected as the leader of Hamas. Rantisi was then assassinated one month later by Israel. Juergensmeyer asked Rantisi the meaning and significance of suicide bombings. Rantisi explained that it is called "self-chosen martyrdom" because that doesn't carry the connotation of impulsive or deranged individuals. In response to the question of why Hamas targeted innocent civilians and bystanders, Rantisi replied that the bombings were moral lessons. "We want to do the same thing to Israel as they have done to us," he said. It was necessary, he added, for the

Israeli people to actually experience the violence before they could understand what the Palestinians had gone through (Juergensmeyer 2000:74).

As Jewish fundamentalists justify their violence and the seizing of Palestinian land by reference to Judaism, Islamic fundamentalists justify their violence as a defense of Islam. Egyptian writer Abd al-Salam Faraj, whose writings have great influence among Islamic fundamentalists, argued that the Qur'anic concept of *Jihad,* or "struggle," was meant to be taken literally and not allegorically. Muslims, wrote Faraj, have neglected their sacred duty of targeting for Jihad enemies of Islam as well as apostates within the Muslim community. A true soldier of Islam, he argued, is permitted to use any means to achieve a just goal (Juergensmeyer 2000:81). These ideas and similar ones by other writers circulate in Islamic universities and among Muslim clergy. Thus, the contest in Israel between Arabs and Jews is placed in the larger context of defending the integrity of Islam.

Armageddon in a Tokyo Subway.   On March 20, 1995, five members of the Aum Shinrikyo movement, all with scientific training, walked into the Tokyo subway and with sharpened umbrellas, punctured plastic bags filled with deadly sarin gas killing twelve people and injuring more than 5,500, some permanently. When Mark Juergensmeyer spoke to members, they explained that Aum Shinrikyo represented for them a critique of Japanese religion and of the hierarchical Japanese social system that did not exemplify principles of justice, fairness, and freedom (Juergensmeyer 2000:105). The movement was founded by Shoko Asahara in the belief that a world catastrophe would occur, a World War III or "Armageddon," in which the forces of good and evil will confront each other, but members of Aum Shinrikyo would survive. The question is, *how does one find justification for killing in Buddism?* Juergensmeyer points out that Buddism, as in other religions, has a tradition of conquest and empire, generally in the name of routing infidels. In the case of Asahara, he found justification for his act in Tibetan Buddism.

Instead of focusing on the effect that killing has on the killer's moral purity, this doctrine focuses on the one who is killed and the merit that comes after death. As Juergensmeyer (2000:114) explains it,

> The concept of *phoa*—that consciousness can be transferred from the living to the dead to elevate their spiritual merit—was extended by Asahara to imply that in some cases people are better off dead than alive. According to Asahara's interpretation of this Tibetan principle, if the persons killed are scoundrels, or are enmeshed in social systems so evil that further existence in this life will result in even greater negative karmic debt, then those who kill are doing their victims a favor by enabling them to die early. Their early deaths would be a kind of mercy killing, allowing their souls to move to a higher plane than they would otherwise have been able to achieve. (Juergensmeyer 2000:114)

Understanding Religious Violence

As we mentioned, it is tempting to dismiss religious violence as the work of irrational fanatics or worse. But that would be overlooking the varied backgrounds and motives of people such as the Reverend Michael Bray, Dr. Baruch Goldstein, Shoko Asahara, Osama bin Laden, Timothy McVeigh, or Abdul Aziz Rantisi. In addition, in no case was the violence arbitrary. In all cases there were specific grievances that the violence was intended to address. The question then is, *under what conditions do people seek to justify violence through religious means?*

Mark Juergensmeyer (2000:146) suggests that locating a struggle on a cosmic scale elevates its importance beyond local concerns and, instead, invokes legendary battles between good and evil. Michael Bray defended the need to kill and, if necessary, die over the issue of abortion. There is a great cosmic war going on, he said, a confrontation between good and evil, but it is unseen because the enemy has imposed control. Osama bin Laden justifies violence by projecting the struggle as that between the forces of Islam and those trying to destroy it. The rhetoric of wars of good versus evil has even entered the U.S. political mainstream with terms such as *axis of evil.*

There is real power, suggests Juergensmeyer, in elevating a political conflict to a cosmic war. "To live in a state of war," says Juergensmeyer (2000:154–155)

> is to live in a world in which individuals know who they are, why they have suffered, by whose hand they have been humiliated, and at what expense they have persevered. The concept of war provides cosmology, history, and eschatology and offers the reins of political control. Perhaps most important, it holds out the hope of victory and the means to achieve it. In the images of cosmic war this victorious triumph is a grand moment of social and personal transformation, transcending all worldly limitations. One does not easily abandon such expectations. To be without such images of war is almost to be without hope itself.

The next questions are, *when does violence call for religious justification, or why do real-world struggles involve religion?* Juergensmeyer (2000) suggests three reasons: First, when the struggle is perceived as a defense of basic identity and dignity, religious justifications are needed. "To die as a suicide bomber," said Abdul Aziz Rantisi, "is better than to die daily in frustration and humiliation." Baruch Goldstein justified his killing of Muslims because he believed that Jews were being humiliated by the Israeli government's protection of Arab Muslims. At the point when members of religious movements see the struggle as a defense of entire cultures, rather than of individuals, the conflict becomes a cultural war with spiritual implications. The conflict in Northern Ireland between Protestants and Catholics, for example, became spiritualized when the Reverend Ian Paisley interpreted the Catholic demand for independence from Great Britain as an attack on Protestants, and the Palestinian struggle took on a religious aura after a significant number of sheiks and mullahs interpreted it as a defense of Islam. Second, suggests Juergensmeyer, the political confrontations adopt religious justifications when losing the struggle would be unthinkable. For Yoel Lerner, a failure to rebuild the Temple of Jerusalem would threaten the very foundations of the Jewish religion. Finally, if the struggle is blocked and cannot be won in real time, suggests Juergensmeyer, it is more likely to be reconceived on a sacred plane where victory is in God's hands.

CONCLUSION

We began this chapter by asking to what extent religious movements have been expressions of antisystemic sentiments and how they have served as a means of protest against the expansion, both in the core and in the periphery, of the culture of capitalism. It is clear, we believe, that in the case of small-scale religious protests, such as the Ghost Dance, the cargo cults, and the attraction of Western religious movements such as Zionism, participants are responding to the effects of the expansion of the culture of capitalism. It is less clear, however, in the case of the various fundamentalisms that have gained popularity in the latter part of the twentieth century whether they represent antisystemic movements. These cultural movements oppose what they call modernization, secular humanism, or, in the periphery, Westernization, seemingly synonyms for capitalism. Yet they contain elements, particularly in their views of women, the family, and opposition to alternative lifestyles, that suggest that they are more reactions to the antisystemic revolution of 1968 than protests to capitalism.

It may be fruitful to look at instances of religious protest, particularly its violent manifestations, as protest over the decline of social and political capital, an unraveling of social compacts and feelings of marginalization, and both symbolic and geographic isolation. The rhetoric of religious violence that we examined is certainly filled with images of contested spaces and cultures; it is no accident that the objects of terrorist violence are laden with symbolism of the market.

Regardless of the object of their protest, in seeking to transform capitalism by using the Qur'an, the Old Testament, the New Testament, the teachings of Buddha, or some other cultural alternative, fundamentalisms represent, with the exception of small-scale secular and religious movements, the only viable alternative to the culture of capitalism and, in the event of a global economic collapse, the only cultures prepared, politically and ideologically, to replace it.

CHAPTER THIRTEEN

CONSTRUCTING THE CITIZEN-ACTIVIST

Our task is no longer one of creating countercultures, engaging in political protest, and pursuing economic alternatives. To create a just, sustainable, and compassionate post-corporate world we must face up to the need to create a new core culture, a new political center, and a new economic mainstream. Such a bold agenda requires many different kinds of expertise, working at many levels of society—personal, household, community, national, and global. It requires breaking the bonds of individual isolation that leave us feeling marginalized when in fact we may already be part of a new majority.
—David Korten, *The Post-Corporate World: Life After Capitalism*

Among the privileges enjoyed by rich, fat, superpower America is the power to invent public reality. Politicians and the mass media do much of the inventing for us by telling us stories which purport to unfold a relatively simple reality. As our tribal storytellers, they shape our knowledge and ignorance of the world, not only producing ideas and emotions which influence the way we lead our lives, but also leaving us dangerously unaware of the difference between stories and reality.
—Russell Baker, "The Awful Truth"

WHAT ARE THE REAL DANGERS?

The extent of active resistance to the expansion of capitalism is evidence of something wrong. The difficulty, of course, is isolating the problem and fixing it. *Is the problem the exploitation of labor? Is it the economic and social marginalization and suppression of women and minorities? Is it the excessive power of corporations or the widespread distribution of deadly armaments? Or is it the assault on the environment or the decline of community and religious values?* Anthropology suggests that even our perceptions of the risks and dangers we face can be culturally and socially determined. That is, the way in which our society or culture filters our experience and sense of the world may dictate what we most fear. Thus, whether your greatest concern is environmental destruction or financial collapse, a nuclear holocaust or disease, the power of witches or God's damnation, crime or societal disintegration, it may be as much a function of your society, culture, and personal experiences as it is of any "real" or "objective" dangers (see Douglas and Wildavsky 1983). This does not mean, of course, that some, if not all, of these threats are unreal, but our view of the world does determine our sense of or lack of urgency concerning them. The questions are, *can we articulate effectively the sources of global problems and gain some consensus regarding their urgency? If so, what are the chances that there is the will to make a change? And finally, even if there is a will to change, what are the specific things that need to be changed?*

Hunger; poverty; the spread of disease; environmental degradation; exploitation of women, children, and minorities; and global conflict and militarization are not imaginary dangers or problems. Their effects are felt daily by billions of people. Our analysis suggests that the root of these problems is the central and unarguable tenet of the culture of capitalism—the need and desire for perpetual economic growth. Each of the major elements of this culture—the consumer, the laborer, the capitalist and the nation-state—has a vested interest in the production and consumption of ever more goods and services. As we stated earlier, and as we examined in the first four chapters, this is not "natural." If acquiring material things were a dominant instinct or value, it should not be necessary for producers to spend some $500 billion a year to persuade people to buy stuff or devise advertising images that promote desires by appealing to people's longing for love, acceptance, and contact with nature.

Objecting to perpetual economic growth, however, will not win many friends. Capitalists require it for their profits; laborers for their wages; consumers for the "stuff" they are convinced they need; and nation-states for their power, revenue, and legitimacy. Although people organize to resist capitalist expansion, argue for alternative forms of governance, or propose a different distribution of resources, rarely will they articulate any objection to growth itself. The need for economic progress is deeply entrenched in our culture.

Perpetual economic growth, however, occurs at great costs to our environment, to our ability to control our own lives, and to the patterns of social relationships that sustain us. Ensuring economic growth requires the creation and enforcement of rules and regulations that affect our lives in a myriad of complex ways. It can lead to the marginalization of people and violent protest. Consequently, before we address possible ways of addressing global problems, we must ask how economic growth has come to play the role it has in our society; examine how perpetual economic growth is accomplished; critically examine the direct impact it has on our lives; and then ask whether it is possible to reduce such growth without inviting economic, political, and social ruin.

The GNP and the Construction of the Doctrine of Perpetual Growth

Imagine the leader of a major industrial country giving her or his state of the country address. "We have had," he or she says, "a wonderful year. Floods in the eastern part of the country destroyed thousands of homes, requiring millions of dollars to rebuild. Water pollution has necessitated everyone purchasing bottled water. Because of an increase in crime, the sale of security systems is skyrocketing, and the country experienced its highest divorce rate ever. As a result of increased social and economic anxiety, doctors have prescribed a record amount of stress-relieving drugs. A flu epidemic filled hospitals and required millions of injections of flu vaccine and, because of increased global conflict, sales of our armaments are booming."

What, you might ask, would a country's leader find to celebrate in that news? The answer is an increase in the country's gross national product (GNP). All of these activities require the expenditure of more and more money, and, in the culture of capitalism, that is the primary indicator of a nation's well-being.

As we discussed at the beginning of this book, the GNP (or, as it is now called, the gross domestic product [GDP][1]) is the single most important statistic in our culture. The GNP is simply the total of money spent or invested in goods and services by households, governments, and businesses. The GNP emerged from the long-standing efforts of national governments to measure the progress of their economies. In the seventeenth and eighteenth centuries, for example, governments were interested in taxable wealth, which at that point was largely agricultural. In the nineteenth century a nation's measurable wealth was taken to include its manufacturers and, finally, the price of things. This was a significant jump. It meant that to have any worth, something had to have a price. Thus, such things as family or community activities and the natural habitat, because they were outside the price system, had no value (see Cobb et al. 1995).

Then, in 1932, when the United States was in the throes of the Great Depression, the U.S. Commerce Department asked a young economist by the name of Simon Kuznets to develop a uniform way of representing national accounts. Kuznets's efforts gave birth to what was to become the GNP. Progress was to be measured in terms of how much money people spent. The development of the GNP had two important consequences: It catapulted economists into their present role as the ultimate authorities on public policy issues and, in the eyes of the government, turned consumers into the engine of economic progress.

The problem is, as Eric A. Davidson (2000) has put it, "you can't eat GNP." That is, what counts for the calculation of GNP needn't represent a positive contribution to the life of the nation. The GNP includes money paid for marriage licenses, but it also includes lawyers' fees for divorce and the separate residences divorce produces. It includes spending on food but also on diet drugs and programs, as well as medical treatment for obesity. It includes the costs of producing weapons as well as the costs for cleaning up the damage they produce. The conversion of forest into wood products is counted completely as economic growth without depreciating the environmental loss that it entails. Cleaning up the environmental damage we create, if it creates profits for someone, is counted as growth. Manufacturing that contributes to the degradation of water resources counts toward GNP, as does the sale of bottled water to a populace wary of its publicly funded water supplies. Standing forests have no value in the national accounts until they generate revenue. As Clifford Cobb, Ted Halstead, and Jonathan Rowe (1995) put it,

[1]In 1991 the GNP was turned into the GDP. With GNP the earnings of a multinational firm were attributed to the country where the firm was owned and where the profits would eventually return. With the gross domestic product, however, the profits are attributed to the country where the factory or mine is located, even though the profits won't stay there. Thus, GDP excludes overseas profits earned by U.S. firms but includes profits earned in the United States by foreign firms. Although it makes little difference in the index of economic growth in core countries, this accounting shift has raised the measure of economic growth in the periphery. However, it hides the fact that profits extracted from the periphery are generally going into the core.

By the curious standard of the GDP, the nation's economic hero is a terminal cancer patient who is going through a costly divorce. The happiest event is an earthquake or a hurricane. The most desirable habitat is a multibillion-dollar Superfund site. All these add to the GDP, because they cause money to change hands. It is as if a business kept a balance sheet by merely adding up all "transactions," without distinguishing between income and expenses, or between assets and liabilities.

Economist Herman Daly (1996:41) tells the story related to him by a physician about doctors at a tuberculosis hospital who wanted to measure the progress of their patients. They placed microphones at beds to record the number of times people coughed, reasoning that the fewer times patients coughed, the more they were improving. The nurses, who were being evaluated by the success of the treatment, reacted by giving more cough-suppressing codeine to patients, and they coughed less. Unfortunately, because they were coughing up less congestion, more were dying. After a time the cough index was abandoned.

The cough index failed because people began manipulating the index rather than the condition that the index was supposed to measure. As was the cough index, the GNP is not only a mismeasure, but, says Daly, also a distorter of what it purports to measure. By assuming that economic growth as measured by GNP is a good thing, and by promoting policies for free trade, tax subsidies to corporations, and increased consumption to increase GNP, we "are reducing the capacity of the earth to support life, thereby literally killing the world" (Daly 1996:145).

But how can economic growth be detrimental? It creates jobs, products, profits, and dividends. It is supposed to promote democracy, end poverty, and lead to greater social equality. However, what seems to be largely hidden is the fact that GNP growth does not come out of thin air.

As we noted in the introduction to Part I of this book, perpetual economic growth requires the constant conversion of nonmonetary capital into money (see Figure I.3, p. 12).

In other words, the growth of economic capital (or power or wealth) can take place only by converting nonmonetary forms of capital—such as natural, political, and social capital—into money. Nonmonetary forms of capital represent savings (albeit in a nonmonetary form) as much as a bank account represents monetary savings. Viewed in this way, economic growth involves spending our savings, and counting it as income, squandering capital, and calling it growth. The question we need to ask is, *what are the rules by which these conversions occur? How are we doling out natural, political, and social capital to bloat our economic accounts?*

The Depletion of Natural Capital

Much like money in a bank, natural capital consists of those features of the natural world that human beings and all other living things draw on for their maintenance and survival. In the culture of capitalism we draw on the environment for our food, shelter, travel, communication, and virtually every other activity. Clearly, the growth of GNP is dependent on the environment. Freshwater, for example, is part of our natural capital. Whenever we use water, we are withdrawing some of that capital. Globally 10 percent of those withdrawals go to household usage, whereas some 90 percent is used by global industry, and 65 percent of that for global agriculture and meat production. According to the United Nations, however, there are 1 billion people who lack access to fresh drinking water. Furthermore, in the interests of economic growth, industry expects to double its consumption of freshwater in the next twenty-five years, leaving about two-thirds of the world's population with a severe water shortage. In the United States alone, users are depleting the High Plains Ogallala aquifer, which stretches from Texas to South Dakota, eight times faster than nature can replenish it (Barlow 1999).

There seems, now, to be little doubt that we are running out of clean water; finding places to dispose of toxic waste is becoming more and more difficult, and resource depletion is running well ahead of our ability to find substitutes for those resources (see Samat 2000). Each year each person in the United States dumps twenty-five metric tons of waste into the environment, while each person in Japan dumps eleven metric tons each year. If we add in the waste created by the production process—for example, soil erosion, mining waste, and so on—the amount of waste increases to eighty-six metric tons per person in the United States and twenty-one metric tons in Japan (Matthews 2000:xi).

The Ecological Footprint analysis developed by Mathis Wackernagel and William E. Rees (1996) provides a tool that estimates the resource consumption and waste assimilation requirements of a specific human population in terms of a corresponding land area. For example, based on an estimate of the amount of usable land in the world, each person would have approximately 4.2 acres (1.8 hectares), but the global average used is 5.4 acres (2.3 hectares). Furthermore, citizens in some countries use far more than the average. For the United States the average footprint is 25.4 acres (8.4 hectares); in Canada each person requires19 acres (7 hectares) to meet consumption and waste needs. In China the footprint is 3 acres (1.2 hectares) a person, whereas in India it is 2 acres (0.8 hectares). Those persons in countries whose lifestyle requires the use of more than 4.2 acres (1.8 hectares) are overspending the global amount that they are allocated (see Table 13.1)

The question is, *what are the rules by which natural capital is converted into economic capital and growth in the GNP?* The answer lies in some interesting bookkeeping tricks regarding what we count and what we don't count in our accounting.

Every product or service that we consume, that is everything on which we spend money, has at least four sets of costs; however, for the most part, our system of national accounts considers only one of these: (1) the costs that manufacturers pay to get something produced and distributed, costs that are then reflected in the prices people pay. Costs not assumed directly by manufacturers or consumers—that is, not included in the retail price—include (2) environmental costs associated with the production of products, (3) environmental costs of the item's use, and (4) environmental costs of the product's disposal.

Computers provide a good example of the rules that allow us to externalize costs. Computer makers must spend money to purchase computer components or the raw materials to make them, purchase machines and pay the labor to design and make their products, pay interests on loans and dividends on stocks, and pay shippers—truckers, railroads, shipping companies, and so on—to distribute their product. These costs are generally reflected in the price of the computers and all contribute to the GNP. However, there are a whole range of costs, many of them environmental, that are externalized; that is, passed on to the general public or to future generations. It begins with the silicon chip, the basic component in

TABLE 13.1   The Ecological Footprints of Nations: Ecological Footprint in Relation to Landmass

	POPULATION IN 1997	ECOLOGICAL FOOTPRINT (IN HECTARES PER CAPITA)	AVAILABLE ECOLOGICAL CAPACITY* (IN HECTARES PER CAPITA)	ECOLOGICAL DEFICIT (IN HECTARES PER CAPITA)
WORLD	**5,892,480,000**	**2.3**	**1.8**	**–0.5**
Iceland	274,000	9.9	2.5	–7.4
New Zealand	3,654,000	9.8	14.3	4.5
United States	268,189,000	8.4	6.2	–2.1
Australia	18,550,000	8.1	9.7	1.6
Canada	30,101,000	7.0	8.5	1.5
Ireland	3,577,000	6.6	8.3	1.7
Japan	125,672,000	6.3	1.7	–4.6
Russian Federation	146,381,000	6.0	3.9	–2.0
Denmark	5,194,000	5.8	2.1	–3.7
Sweden	8,862,000	5.8	7.8	2.0
France	58,433,000	5.7	3.8	–1.9
Netherlands	15,697,000	4.7	2.8	–1.9
Argentina	35,405,000	4.6	3.8	–0.8
Germany	81,845,000	4.6	2.1	–2.5
United Kingdom	58,587,000	4.6	1.8	–2.8
Italy	57,247,000	4.5	1.4	–3.1
Malaysia	21,018,000	2.7	1.7	–1.0
Brazil	167,046,000	2.6	2.4	–0.1
Mexico	97,245,000	2.3	1.4	–0.9
Philippines	70,375,000	2.2	0.7	–1.5
Indonesia	203,631,000	1.6	0.9	–0.7
China	1,247,315,000	1.2	1.3	0.1
Egypt	65,445,000	1.2	0.6	–0.5
Ethiopia	58,414,000	1.0	0.9	–0.1
India	970,230,000	0.8	0.8	0.0
Pakistan	148,686,000	0.8	0.9	0.1
Bangladesh	125,898,000	0.7	0.6	–0.1

*All expressed in world average productivity, 1993 data.

Data taken from Mathis Wackernagel, Larry Onisto, Alejandro Callejas Linares, Ina Susana López Falfán, Jesus Méndez García, Ana Isabel Suárez Guerrero, Ma. Guadalupe Suárez Guerrero. Ecological Footprints of Nations (http://www.ecouncil.ac.cr/rio/focus/report/english/footprint/).

See also Mathis Wackernagel and William E. Rees. 1996. *Our Ecological Footprints: Reducing Human Impact on the Earth.* Gabriola Island, BC: New Society.

computers. There are 220 billion chips manufactured each year that contain highly corrosive hydrochloric acid; metals such as arsenic, cadmium, and lead; volatile solvents such as methyl chloroform, benzene, acetone, and trichloroethylene (TCE); and a number of supertoxic gases. A single batch of chips requires on average 27 pounds of chemicals, 9 pounds of hazardous waste, and 3,787 gallons of water requiring extensive chemical treatment. Silicon Valley in California has the largest number of Environmental Protection Agency's (EPA) superfund sites (29) and researchers have detected more than one hundred contaminants in the local drinking water. None of these environmental costs of cleaning up the waste or despoiling resources (or for that matter, the health costs that may result) are included in the price of the computer.

Also not included in the price consumers pay are disposal costs. By the year 2007, experts estimate that we will have more than 500 million obsolete computers in the United States, many destined for landfills, incinerators, or hazardous waste sites in the periphery. "If everyone threw them out at once," as one person put it, "we would have a one mile high waste mountain of junked computers the size of a football field." Computers are not benign waste; those 500 million computers represent 1.2 billion pounds of lead, 2 million pounds of cadmium, 400,000 pounds of mercury, 1.2 million pounds of hexavalent chromium, to name a few of the toxic substances from which they are made. Yet the cost of cleaning up these substances are not included in the cost or price and so must be assumed by the general public. Any legitimate accounting system would deduct that cost from what computer sales contribute to the economy or internalize the cost that is passed on to the consumer. Instead, we count computer sales as additions to the GNP and ignore the environmental costs. In other words, using our current rules for national accounting, there is no economic deficit involved in using up our natural capital. Yet, clearly that makes no sense, from an economic or any other point of view. However, from the narrow prospective of consumers, capitalists, and laborers, it is beneficial to continue to externalize costs; it keeps production costs down, consumption and wages up. Yet in the long run, of course, it encourages the continued conversion of natural capital into economic capital (money).

Another set of rules that intensifies the conversion of natural capital into economic capital has to do with how we create money. Money, as we examined in the introduction to Part I, has changed over the past century. When money was tied to gold there were limits on the amount of money that could be issued. But with money tied to nothing of value, and banks and other lending institutions free to add money to the economy in the form of debt in an almost limitless fashion, all restrictions were off. Thus, although money—a symbol of the value of resources—can grow infinitely (and must grow infinitely in a society of perpetual growth), the things that it represents are finite. In other words, our timber resources are finite, but there is no limit to the money that can buy timber. The consequences of this are not easy to grasp, but, simply put, it means that if there is no limit on the amount of money that can be created, there should be no limit on those things that money represents. As Herman Daly (1996:38) puts it,

> Too many accumulations of money are seeking ways to grow exponentially in a world in which the physical scale of the economy is already so large relative to the ecosystem that there is not much room left for growth of any thing that has a physical dimension.

Conventional economics would solve or even ignore the problem by increasing the value of resources as they become scarcer, thereby enabling the continuous growth of money and GNP. But how high can one push the price of clean air, water, and other resources, and what price would be placed on them when they are gone?

The rule by which we create debt money encourages the conversion of natural capital in another way. In Chapter 3 we examined the problem of global debt and how countries borrowed heavily to promote economic growth. But to pay for that growth, and pay back the debts incurred to promote that growth, countries in the periphery must cut down their forests, accept toxic waste, and attract polluting industries. In effect they are converting their natural capital into money to repay debts and add to their GNPs. In the process, however, they are mortgaging the future of their citizens and leaving a ruined living space.

The Depletion of Political Capital

In the 1991 Human Development Report, the United Nations issued its "freedom index," an attempt to measure the existence and effectiveness of democratic institutions among the countries of the world. Among the some thirty-nine items considered were freedom to travel, freedom of association, freedom of expression, various measures of freedom from arbitrary persecution, measures of political freedom, and measures of freedom of access to information. In that survey, countries were assigned a number from 1 to 40, 40 being the highest level of freedom (see Table 13.2).

The Human Freedom Index captures part of the essence of political capital. A society rich in political capital enables its members to have a say in decisions that affect their lives. Political capital is measured by the extent to which each person can signify by a vote or other means their satisfaction or dissatisfaction with the state of things. It can be measured by the degree of access people have to those responsible for decision making. At one extreme are

TABLE 13.2 Human Freedom Index (Based on Conditions in 1985)

THE TOP TEN COUNTRIES WITH HIGHEST FREEDOM RANKING	POINTS	THE TEN COUNTRIES WITH LOWEST FREEDOM RANKING	POINTS
Sweden	38	Zaire	5
Denmark	38	Pakistan	5
Netherlands	37	Bulgaria	4
Finland	36	South Africa	3
New Zealand	36	USSR	3
Austria	36	China	2
Norway	35	Ethiopia	2
France	35	Romania	1
West Germany	35	Libya	1
Belgium	35	Iraq	0

Data from Michael Wolff, Peter Rutten, and Albert Bayers III, eds., *Where We Stand*. New York: Bantam Books, 1992.

those societies in which individuals have virtually no say in their own fate, such as the state of slavery. The other extreme is the society that operates on consensus in which each and every person can affect collective decision making. Examples would be small-scale, gathering and hunting societies or a small group of friends deciding on which movie to see. Things that detract from political capital, but that may add to monetary capital, are authoritarian regimes, the application of deadly force, the undermining of democratic institutions, and economic debt.

The question is, *how is do authoritarian regimes promote economic growth?* There is no overall consensus. Studies done in the 1970s and 1980s indicated that authoritarian political regimes had higher rates of economic growth than did more democratic regimes. Other studies claim that the more democratic the regime, the higher the rate of economic growth (see e.g., Scully 1995). Most recently, Robert J. Barro (1996:2), in a cross-cultural empirical study of determinants of economic growth, concluded that

> At low levels of political rights, an expansion of [democratic] rights stimulates economic growth. However, once a moderate amount of democracy has been attained, a further expansion reduces growth.

The key question is, *why should increased democratization inhibit economic growth?* Barro suggests that democratization retards growth because, as growth increases, citizens become more concerned with economic inequality and social justice and demand social programs and income redistribution, neither of which are conducive to the uninhibited accumulation of monetary capital. But the relationship was perhaps best expressed by a J. P. Morgan currency strategist commenting on the establishment of a democratic government in Indonesia in 1998: "Democracy," he said, "is a desirable form of government, but it's not necessarily the most efficient form of government" (Arnold 1999). What he meant, of course, is that authoritarian governments are better for business, and hence for economic growth, than democratic governments. That is, rules that encourage the centralization of power and the depletion of political capital also allow for greater accumulation of economic capital. Authoritarian governments are better able to suppress labor organizing, put down resistance to environmental destruction, confiscate property, offer generous tax benefits to investors, and cut back on social and education programs, all actions that encourage economic growth.

The rules now in existence in the global economy that permit the concentration of power in the hands of multinational corporations provide another example of how political capital can be converted into economic capital. As we noted earlier, of the world's one hundred largest economies, half are internal to corporations. The sales of Mitsubishi Trading Corporation are larger than the GDP of Indonesia, a country with the world's fourth-largest population. The combined sales of the world's top 200 corporations are equal to 28 percent of total world GDP (Anderson and Cavanagh 2000).

Nation-states, to further economic growth, have allowed and encouraged corporations to accumulate enormous economic and political power. CEOs can assign or withdraw resources at will; open and close plants, change product lines, or lay off workers with no recourse by persons or communities that are affected. The culture of capitalism, in the interests of increasing GNP, has transferred planning functions from governments accountable to their citizens, to corporations accountable only to their shareholders.

The consolidation of power and money in fewer and fewer corporations continues virtually unabated. Half of the top 200 corporations represent only five economic sectors—trading, automobiles, banking, retailing, and electronics. In automobiles, the top five firms account for 60 percent of global sales; in electronics, the top five control more than half of global sales. The top five firms in the areas of air travel, aerospace, steel, oil, computers, chemicals, and media control more than 30 percent of all global sales (Anderson and Cavanagh 2000). The ten largest corporations in each sector controlled 86 percent of the telecommunications industry, 85 percent of the pesticides industry, 70 percent of the computer industry, 35 percent of pharmaceuticals, and 32 percent of commercial seed. In the interests of economic growth we are moving rapidly toward ever greater consolidation of this unaccountable corporate power. Since 1992, the total value of corporate mergers has increased 50 percent a year in all but one, and most mergers are accompanied by massive layoffs.

The U.S. nation-state permits the erosion of political capital also through the rules that regulate (or fail to regulate) campaign financing. As corporations have gained more and more power, they are able to translate economic power to political power through massive donations to the country's elected representatives. Few politicians would disagree with the fact that, at the very least, money gains a hearing before our government officials, and that, in many cases, influences legislation. Market exchanges are surrounded by a lot of rules, rules concerning union organization, free trade, and the environment, and these rules are determined by a political process that is shaped by money donated to political candidates. The automotive industry has given candidates and parties in the United States more than $55 million since 1990. The senator who is also chairman of the U.S. Senate Appropriations Transportation Subcommittee has collected more than $74,000 from the automotive industry overall since 1995 (Public Campaign 2000).

Globally, we can see the diminution of political capital and its conversion into economic capital in the nondemocratic regimes of the WTO and IMF, and in trading agreements such as the North American Free Trade Agreement (NAFTA) and the Free Trade Area of the Americas (FTAA). These agreements represent a transfer of power from largely democratically elected governments accountable to their citizens, to nondemocratic institutions, controlled largely by multinational corporations and accountable to no one, except perhaps their stockholders. The panels empowered by these agreements can challenge environmental, health, labor, and social laws and regulations established by legislative bodies. These panels can, in secret and with no possibility for appeal, make decisions that may run counter to the wishes of the citizens of member countries. Thus, even if citizens in the United States wished to pass legislation to protect the environment or individual health, the WTO arbitrators could impose a severe economic penalty if the legislation was deemed to be a restriction of trade.

The expansion of armament production and distribution poses an additional danger to political capital. The production of armaments generates enormous wealth. As we saw in Chapter 4, in 1999 nation-states spent $852 billion on weapons. Much of this wealth comes at the expense of political freedoms crushed by these weapons. American "security aid" has contributed at one time or another to the establishment and maintenance of dictatorial governments in Guatemala, Haiti, Chile, the Philippines, Indonesia, Iran, the Congo, Brazil, Argentina, and Nicaragua, to name only a very few. Governments use these weapons primarily to maintain control over their citizens; they contribute to state terrorism and killing. In fact, the arms expenditures of developing countries reached a high in 1999 at

$245 billion. And, as we saw in Chapters 4 and 9, even the more democratic among nation-states use force to suppress dissent and limit democratic prerogatives.

Debt, which contributes to the depletion of natural capital, also encourages the generation of rules that require indebted countries to sacrifice their autonomy and the political rights of their citizens to the nondemocratic regimes of the IMF and WTO. Thus, against the will of citizens, indebted nation-states are forced to cut necessary social programs, devalue currency, or permit the takeover of services or property by corporations or foreign investors.

There are other areas in which our political capital is converted to economic growth, such as the increased concentration of media sources in the hands of fewer and fewer people. The media is able to control what sorts of information we get and to whom we listen. In the United States, the media has the power to choose the political candidates and the range of political positions to which people are exposed. But perhaps the greatest danger in the erosion of political capital is that it may reach the point that so little is left, that it becomes impossible to offer any resistance to its continued conversion into wealth.

The Depletion of Social Capital

Economic growth and development also require the expenditure of social capital. The depletion of social capital has received more recent attention through the work of sociologist Robert Putnam (2000). Putnam's work documents what he considers the measurable decline in social capital in America, a decline captured in the title of his book *Bowling Alone*. For Putnam (2000:19)

> social capital refers to connections among individuals—social networks and the norms of reciprocity and trustworthiness that arise from them. In that sense, social capital is closely related to what some have called "civic virtue."

Social capital allows people to acquire benefits through their memberships in social networks, to resolve problems, and make decisions collectively. Social capital bonds people together in groups enhancing trust and the conviction that others will "do the right thing." Social capital is evidenced in what anthropologists call *generalized reciprocity*, the giving of things to others with only the understanding that at some time in the future something will be received in exchange.

Social capital needn't be a positive thing. Strong social bonds among members of powerful groups may be used to deny resources to the poor or any nonmembers. Men's associations and clubs, while perhaps rich in social capital, may be used to deny access of economic resources to women. It is likely that the Ku Klux Klan was rich in social capital, but it was capital that was used to disenfranchise others. Thus social capital may have its "dark" or "perverse" side (see Putzel 1997; Rubio 1997).

Nevertheless, social capital can improve our lives by making people aware of how our fates are linked while building social networks that help people fulfill individual goals. In U.S. communities that are rich in social capital, persons serve in local organizations, attend public meetings, vote, spend time working on community projects, visit friends frequently, entertain at home, and feel that "most people can be trusted," or agree with the statement that "most people are honest."

In *Bowling Alone* Putnam (2000:287) measures the evolution of social capital in America over the past century and concludes that, "By virtually every conceivable measure, social capital has eroded steadily and sometimes dramatically over the past two generations."

Putnam attributes the decline of social capital to some four factors. About half of the decline, he says, is a result of the slow, steady, replacement of a long "civic generation" by a generation of their less involved children and grandchildren, and about one-quarter to the advent of electronic entertainment, particularly television. The rest of the decline he attributes to time and money pressures on two-career families and the increase of suburban sprawl that creates communities with no centers.

It is significant, of course, that most of the factors Putnam identifies as contributing to the decline of social capital also contribute to economic growth. That is, we have converted social capital into economic capital by enacting rules and regulations that encourage suburban sprawl that, while reducing contact among people, creates new and larger homes, more expenditures on household items, more road and bridge construction, while creating a dependence on automobiles and all the expenses they involve. Two-income families exchange time that might be spent in family activities for increased monetary exchanges and income, while television watching, which further reduces family interaction, nevertheless exposes people to thousands of hours of advertisements and media images that create new consumer needs and offer happiness through goods. It is noteworthy perhaps that in an earlier study, Putnam (1996) named television as the main culprit in the decline of American social capital.

There are other ways, however, that we convert social capital into economic capital. To a great extent the economic growth in core countries of the past fifty years has been produced by transferring social, capital-rich functions, such as child care, food preparation, health care, entertainment, and maintenance of physical security, from households or communities, where they did not count in GNP figures, to the market where they did count. Of course, this is not an entirely new phenomenon. The process began with the first act of trade, but its acceleration over the past few centuries has completely transformed our social environments. When families gathered to collect food or slaughter game or livestock, multiple social interactions ensued. In the modern economy those interactions are replaced by a simple exchange of money at the grocery checkout counter.

We squander social capital in the name of economic growth, also, by the creation of and increase in social inequality. Social inequality creates unnecessary boundaries between people; increases mistrust and resentment; necessitates the creation of ideologies that attempt to justify social differences as natural differences; and, in the extreme of poverty, devastates individuals, families, and communities.

As GNP has risen in the United States, so has inequality. The gap between rich and poor has grown so wide that the richest 2.7 million Americans, the top 1 percent, will have as many after-tax dollars to spend as the bottom 100 million. This ratio has more than doubled since 1977, when the top 1 percent had as much as the bottom 49 million (Shapiro and Springer 2000).

Globally, the situation is similar. Although the United States is enjoying its greatest economic expansion in history, no fewer than eighty countries had a lower per-capita income in 1998 than they did in 1989. The gap between the average incomes of the richest 20 percent and the poorest 20 percent in the world increased from thirty to one in 1960 to sixty to one in 1990. In 1999 the gap widened even further to seventy-four to one. At this rate, the disparity could be one-hundred to one before 2015 (UNDP 1998). There is nothing mysterious about this trend toward greater inequality nationally or globally. Public policymakers at national and global levels create rules that are designed to give the rich more disposable incomes through tax cuts, while pushing down wages to increase production, profits, and consumption. In that sense, inequality is good for GNP, regardless of what it does to people and societies.

Perhaps one of the best examples of how economic growth and development destroys social capital can be seen in the movement of corporations from one country to another. In their search for greater profits, they leave behind broken communities and declining social capital, while creating virtual slums for low-paid workers, isolated and removed from the families in which they once lived. Yet companies will always move to areas in which decision makers are willing to sacrifice environmental, political, and social capital for an increase in GNP.

Capital and Public Policy

The process by which we diminish natural, political, and social capital is a relatively transparent one. When a policy decision is made by a government, a multilateral institution, or virtually any organization from a large corporation to a local school, that decision will almost always favor economic growth even if it requires the squandering of natural, political, or social capital. The decision of a government, with the support of an agency such as the World Bank, to build a huge dam may result in widespread environmental destruction, be dependent on and reinforce the power of an authoritarian government, and destroy the social capital of hundreds of communities built up over centuries. The decision will also produce wealth for a few while impoverishing many. Yet as we have seen time and again, the choice will be to build the dam.

The policy choice needn't involve huge construction projects to have an effect on the depletion of noneconomic capital. For example, our town has an oratorio society that each year presents a holiday concert at our college. In the past, after the concert, members and friends would prepare cakes and cookies for a reception for the audience. It was a nice conclusion to the event, promoted community interaction, and gave members of the oratorio group the satisfaction of creating a commensal meal. Even cleaning up afterward created a sense of shared purpose and community. A few years ago, however, the college signed a contract with a major food corporation to provide campus food services. The contract contained a provision requiring that any food served on the campus be supplied by the company. In doing so, of course, the policy decision resulted in the depletion of the social capital that had been created by the communally oriented activities of those who, at their own expense, provided the refreshments and labor. Unfortunately, the oratorio society does not have the funds to pay for the food, and the after-concert gathering has been cancelled.

The policy decisions to build the dam or transfer food services to a large corporation were not necessarily "bad" decisions. The dam created power for industry and homes, jobs for some, and irrigation facilities for food production. The policy decision to have a corporation provide the food was not a "bad" one; the provision in the contract likely reduced food costs to students and provided a few student jobs for those paid to prepare and serve the food and clean up afterward. It also contributed to the profits of a large corporation and added, imperceptibly in this case, to the GNP. But when almost all of the millions of policy decisions made by hundreds of thousands of decision makers all favor rules that promote the accumulation of monetary capital at the expense of nonmonetary capital, the result is a society rich in money but poor in almost everything else.

The intent of the previous analysis is not to dismiss the need for healthy economies. The issue has to do with the rules and regulations that nation-states and the culture of capitalism itself create to ensure economic growth, rules and regulations that take very little consideration of other areas of our lives. It is the economic reductionism of the sort we discussed in Chapter 6 that creates our obsession for greater and greater monetary wealth and has created consumption expectations well beyond what is reasonably required.

We need to be mindful also that any consideration of the conversion of one type of capital into another must recognize (1) the complexity of the interactions between our economic, natural, political, and social capital accounts and (2) the nature of the capital conversion rules that are in place. For example, measures to decrease environmental pollution that increase industrial costs may result in smaller manufacturers going out of business, resulting in greater centralization of corporate power and depletion of political capital. Increases in social capital, instead of sacrificing economic growth, may contribute to economic well-being. Thus, anthropological studies of poverty reveal that impoverished conditions may lead to the formation of close, interlocking, cooperative groups that ensure economic and social support in times of need (see e.g., Stack 1973). Further, it is possible to convert economic capital into natural, political, and social capital. For example, gift giving is the simplest way of converting economic capital into social capital. Clearly, then, the range of changes and the interrelationships among them must be carefully considered in any effort to rethink public policy.

Regardless, however, we need to realistically recognize that any effort to rebuild our stocks of natural, political, and social capital will require a significant cultural change and some sort of economic devolution, if only because economic growth can no longer be our sole priority. The question is whether there is the possibility for changing our misplaced sense of priorities that would sacrifice virtually everything else, including, as it does now in parts of the world, human lives, for perpetual economic growth. For example, *is it possible to add to our personas of consumers, laborers, and capitalists the persona of citizen-activist whose interests lie in building natural, political, and social capital even if it comes at the expense of economic growth and GNP? And, if we could, can we create policies and rules that would allow economic growth to be reversed, stopped, or even slowed without creating massive social and economic devastation?*

CONSTRUCTING THE CITIZEN-ACTIVIST

In November 1999 thousands of citizen-activists—labor leaders, environmentalists, indigenous peoples, nongovernmental organizations (NGOs), and religious groups—gathered in Seattle, Washington, to protest against the WTO. The WTO is, in many ways, the perfect symbol of the growth-at-any-cost paradigm. It has proved more than willing to penalize countries for enacting environmental, social, health, and labor legislation that in any way restricts the rights of corporations to make and sell anything they want, in any way they want. As we noted earlier, the WTO makes its decisions in virtual secrecy, with little or no accountability to the citizens of the countries that it comprises.

The protest did succeed in disrupting the meetings, and protests against the World Bank and the IMF in Washington, DC, and in Prague, Czechoslovakia, focused additional scrutiny on these multilateral institutions.

The protests may have also alerted others, who share the same concerns, that they are not alone. Paul Ray and Sherry Ruth Anderson (2000) claim that there are some 50 million people in the United States, 60 percent of whom are women, whose reported values are supportive of environmental reform, social justice, building helpful relationships, psychological and spiritual development; and distrustful of the power of corporations and media. Ray and Anderson distinguish between these "Cultural Creatives," as they call them, and the "Moderns"—those who accept the commercialized, urban-industrial world, desire to make a lot of money, and so on—and the "Traditionals"—those who adhere to traditional values regarding religion and gender and family relations, and are willing to accept authoritarian rule to maintain social order. From their research, Ray and Anderson conclude that Moderns represent 48 percent of the U.S. citizenry, Traditionals some 24.5 percent, whereas Cultural Creatives represent about 26 percent.

Although Cultural Creatives represent a significant portion of the population, say Ray and Anderson, they are generally unaware of their numbers, assuming that there are far fewer who share their values than really do. Furthermore, Cultural Creatives share many values in common with Traditionals. If they were able to consolidate their influence, they have the potential to redefine the political landscape and promote social change. Assuming, then, that it were possible to create a social or political movement to promote change, *what sort of goals might such a movement articulate?*

Indices and Goals for Well-Being

We do not lack indices with which to measure our quality of life in other than economic terms. The Human Development Index (HDI), published annually by the United Nations, for example, ranks nations according to their citizens' quality of life rather than solely on economic criteria. It considers factors such as life expectancy, adult literacy, school enrollment, gender equality, food, and income security, as well as GNP (see Table 13.3) Clearly, economic factors are important, but they are not the sole indicators of the quality of life.

Redefining Progress, a nonprofit public policy institute, proposes that we assess the state of a society through the Genuine Progress Indicator (GPI). The GPI takes household consumption as a base figure, and then adjusts it by adding factors such as the value of housework and parenting, value of volunteer work, and so on, while subtracting for such things as cost of environmental pollution, crime, noise, family breakdown, loss of leisure time, all factors that would contribute to GNP. Subtracting items that diminish our quality of life, rather than adding them, as does the GNP, we find that as GNP has risen over the past few decades, the GPI has declined (see Figure 13.1).

In addition to the existence of alternative ways of measuring quality of life, and evidence of citizen support for social change, there are program proposals by governments and international institutions and agencies. For example, the IMF, the Organization for Economic Cooperation and Development/Development Assistance Committee (OECD/DAC), World Bank, and U.N. issue a set of international development goals (see Table 13.4).

TABLE 13.3   Most Livable Countries Based on the Human Development Index, 1998*

1	Canada	9	Japan	17	Luxembourg	25	Greece
2	Norway	10	United Kingdom	18	Ireland	26	Hong Kong, China (SAR)
3	United States	11	Finland	19	Italy	27	Malta
4	Australia	12	France	20	New Zealand	28	Portugal
5	Iceland	13	Switzerland	21	Spain	29	Slovenia
6	Sweden	14	Germany	22	Cyprus	30	Barbados
7	Belgium	15	Denmark	23	Israel		
8	Netherlands	16	Austria	24	Singapore		

*Data from United Nations, *Human Development Report 2000*. Oxford: Oxford University Press; see also
http://www.undp.org/hdro/statistics.html.

The U.N., under a program called the "Global Compact," has brought together some forty-four multinational corporations and banks—including DaimlerChrysler, Unilever, Deutsche Bank, BPAmoco, Novartis, Ericsson, and Nike—a couple of labor confederations, and NGOs—including the International Confederation of Free Trade Unions, Amnesty International, the World Wildlife Fund—to embrace policies supportive of human rights, labor, and the environment (see Table 13.5).

The goals established by various agencies to solve some of the problems that we have examined are certainly admirable. Yet given the fact that past efforts to remedy global problems have done little, it is difficult to be optimistic that the very agencies responsible

FIGURE 13.1   Gross Production versus Genuine Progress, 1950–1998

Copyright 1999, Redefining Progress (http://www.rprogress.org/progsum/nip/gpi/gpi_main.html). Reprinted by permission.

TABLE 13.4   International Development Goals

TARGET	YEAR
For economic well-being	
Reduce by half the proportion of people in extreme poverty	2015
For social development	
Achieve universal primary education	2015
Eliminate gender disparities in primary and secondary education	2005
Reduce by two-thirds the mortality rates for infants and children under five and by three-fourths the mortality rates for mothers	2015
Provide access to reproductive health services for all individuals of appropriate age	2015
For environmental sustainability and regeneration	
Implement national strategies for sustainable development	2005
Reverse current trends of loss of environmental resources globally and nationally	2015

Data from International Monetary Fund et al. 2000. *A Better World for All: Progress Towards the International Development Goals.* http://www.paris21.org/betterworld/home.htm.

TABLE 13.5   A Compact for a New Century

HUMAN RIGHTS

- Principle 1   Support and respect the protection of international human rights within their sphere of influence
- Principle 2   Make sure their own corporations are not complicit in human rights abuses

LABOR

- Principle 3   Freedom of association and the effective recognition of the right to collective bargaining
- Principle 4   The elimination of all forms of forced and compulsory labor
- Principle 5   The effective abolition of child labor
- Principle 6   The elimination of discrimination in respect of employment and occupation

ENVIRONMENT

- Principle 7   Support a precautionary approach to environmental challenges
- Principle 8   Undertake initiatives to promote greater environmental responsibility
- Principle 9   Encourage the development and diffusion of environmentally friendly technologies

Data from United Nations, 1999. *The Global Compact.* http://unglobalcompact.org/gc/unweb.nsf/content/thenine.htm.

for the global domination of the economic-growth paradigm could be capable of significant change. For example, in 1992 150 nations negotiated the Kyoto Protocol, a treaty designed to reduce the release of carbon dioxide and other greenhouse gases responsible for global warming. The latest projections are that global temperatures will rise four to eleven degrees Fahrenheit over the next century, bringing the average temperature of the earth to a level unseen since the era of the dinosaurs. In November 2000, nations met to try to reach agreement on each nation's responsibility to reduce carbon emissions. However the meetings collapsed as industrial nations, particularly the United States, tried to negotiate standards that would have removed any obligation for a significant reduction. In part, the United States is reacting to efforts of groups such as the Global Climate Coalition and the Greening Earth Society made up of power and coal companies that have spent millions of dollars to convince legislators and the public that global warming is "theory" and not "fact" or that global warming is a "good thing."[2]

The Means and Prospects for Change: Attaining Zero Economic Growth

If the obsession with economic growth and the GNP is the ultimate deciding factor in public policy decisions, whether at the international, national, institutional, local, or household level, then, if the previous analysis is accurate, we can expect little to change. We will simply continue to create and enforce rules and regulations that deplete natural, political, and social capital. The effects of this depletion will not be felt by all people at the same time. Indeed, many are already suffering, whereas others are hardly aware of the problems. But sooner or later, all will confront the consequences of these cumulative decisions. Clearly, any meaningful action will require a challenge to public policy analysts in the social sciences, humanities, and sciences to devise a coherent plan to reallocate different types of capital with the least possible economic, social, and political disruption. The question is, *what sorts of measures do we need to consider to effect this type of change?* The following represent some actions that could be considered and that have been proposed by others. Each would have to be examined by public policymakers in terms of how it relates to other proposals. Nevertheless, they reveal that we are not without concrete measures to remedy the problems that we, collectively, have created.

Rebuilding and Maintaining Natural Capital

Any action to rebuild natural capital must, at a minimum, not demand more from the ecosystem than the ecosystem can sustain. This, according to Herman Daly (1990), can only be accomplished when three conditions are met:

1. Rates of use of renewable resources must not exceed the rates at which the ecosystem is able to regenerate them.

---

[2]You can find out all about the supposed benefits of global warming at the Web site of the Greening Earth Society at http://www.greeningearthsociety.org/ or the Web site of the Global Climate Coalition at http://www.globalclimate.org/index.htm.

2. Rates of consumption or irretrievable disposal of nonrenewable resources must not exceed the rate at which renewable substitutes are developed and phased into use.
3. Rates of pollution emission into the environment must not exceed the rates of the ecosystem's natural assimilative capacity.

There are many actions that can promote environmental sustainability and that have been advocated by environmentalists. Here are a few of the major ones.

- Stop counting the consumption of natural capital as income. Consumption, if it is to be called income, must leave intact the resources to produce the same amount next year. We must stop treating natural capital as a free good. For example, the sale and export of lumber must be treated as a sale of a capital asset that not only generates income but also reduces future income and productivity.
- Tax labor and income less and tax resource throughput more. Our current system of energy taxation encourages energy usage by requiring governments to subsidize throughput—energy, water, fertilizer, and even deforestation. Rather than allowing producers and consumers to externalize costs, we must build those costs into our pricing system.
- Maximize the productivity of natural capital in the short run, and invest in increasing its supply in the long run. For example, we must price a nonrenewable resource (e.g., oil) the same or higher than a renewable substitute (e.g., wind). To do otherwise encourages the further depletion of nonrenewable resources and discourages investment and development of renewable resources.
- Devise a "garbage index" (see Korten 1998:47) to reduce to zero the amount of waste we pour into the environment that is not recyclable.
- Place a holding fee on money to provide incentives to hold real (e.g., trees) rather than virtual (e.g., money) assets. In our present way of doing things, trees (or any other noninterest bearing commodity) generate no income, and may even require the payment of taxes. It makes sense, then, as a member of the Malaysian government suggested, to cut down and sell all the forests reasoning that the money earned would gain interest, whereas the standing forest generated no income.
- To maintain national or local control over resources, move away from the ideology of global economic integration by free trade, free capital mobility, and export-led growth. Create rules to encourage a more nationalistic orientation to develop domestic production for internal markets as the first option, developing international trade only when it is clearly much more efficient in preserving natural capital.

As Herman Daly (1996:93) points out, by erasing national boundaries we weaken the communities that alone are capable of devising policies for the common good. If nations, or localities for that matter, have no control over local resources, they are in a poor position to defend them.

Restoring Political Capital

How is it possible for people to restore control over their lives? Obviously, for some it is an easier task than for others. Given the military power of peripheral countries, it is, as we have seen, difficult for people to reassert their control. However, one might take heart at how a relatively small group of indigenous peoples in Chiapas, as we saw in Chapter 10, could force a highly militarized nation-state to negotiate to allow greater freedoms.

For some, however, the real danger to democracy is not from nation-states but from the increasing power of corporations. For David Korten (1998, 1999), it is corporations that deplete natural capital by strip-mining forests and marketing toxic chemicals; they deplete social capital by maintaining substandard working conditions, by breaking up unions, bidding down wages, and uprooting plants, leaving devastated communities in their wake; and they deplete political capital by subverting governments to subsidize their costs and weaken environmental, health, and labor standards.

Korten (1999) proposes the following concrete measures to limit corporate power and influence:

- End the legal fiction of corporate personhood. This 1886 Supreme Court ruling (by essentially one judge) that granted corporations the same rights as persons changed American history.
- Exclude corporations from political participation. It is clearly not fair to allow corporations with billions of dollars in financial resources to lobby elected legislators in ways not open to individual citizens.
- Implement serious political campaign reform to reduce the influence of money on politics.
- Eliminate corporate welfare by eliminating direct subsidies and recovering other externalized costs through fees and taxes.
- Implement mechanisms to regulate international corporations and finance. The Tobin Tax (named for Nobel Laureate economist James Tobin), if implemented, would place sales taxes on cross-border currency trades (which amount to about $1.8 trillion a day). The benefits include discouraging short-term currency trading that can leave nations devastated by the rapid withdrawal of money, while raising about $100 to $300 billion a year to fund urgent international priorities such as debt relief.
- Use fiscal and regulatory policy to make financial speculation unprofitable and to give an economic advantage to human-scale, stakeholder-owned enterprise.
- Encourage responsible spending and investing that enables consumers and investors to assert some degree of power over what is produced and the conditions under which it is produced. Work to ensure that as many people as possible are aware of corporate and government practices that promote oppression (e.g., sweatshop labor) and encourage them to redirect spending and investing accordingly.

Korten agrees also with Herman Daly that we should disband institutions such as the WTO and IMF. The culture of both is imbued with the policy assumption that all problems can be solved through economic growth. Instead, says Korten, we must devise policies that return economic power to local communities. For example

- Tax short-term capital gains substantially higher than earned income. This will discourage financial speculators from disrupting local and national economies by the sudden withdrawal of funds.
- Encourage the use of local currencies. This encourages local businesses and encourages local investments.

- Make the creation of national currencies a public function, rather than allowing banks and other financial institutions to increase the money supply through debt.
- Restore the concept of community banking.

In general, says Korten (1998:20), we must work to return the power that we have yielded to institutions of global finance to local institutions and communities.

Rebuilding Social Capital

Finally, we need to establish policy initiatives that would rebuild social capital. Economist Herman Daly (1996:203) recommends that we begin by reducing the gap between the rich and the poor through a maximum and a minimum income. This maximum and minimum, he says, should be limited by a factor of ten. In the United States this would involve a return to a pre-1960 situation. In 1960 the after-tax average pay for corporate chief executives was about twelve times that of the *average* factory worker; by 1974 the factor had risen to thirty-five. In the late 1990s, chief executives earned 135 times the amount of the *average* (not the lowest) factory worker.

It may be time, says Daly (1996:206–207), to reconsider the biblical limits on capital accumulation in which the limit was what one could accumulate in fifty years, at which point resources were redistributed. We must put aside, says David Korten (1998:30), the illusion that economic growth will end poverty.

As we must do to rebuild natural and political capital, to rebuild social capital we must rebuild local communities. We can begin, suggests Korten (1998:57–58), by trying to determine how rich our own communities are in social capital. Ask yourselves the following questions about your community:

- Do people prefer to shop in small local shops run by merchants they know by name or in mega–shopping malls and large retail chain outlets? Do they favor the farmer's market or the supermarket?
- Are farms small, individually owned, and family operated? Or are they controlled by huge corporate enterprises and worked mainly by itinerant landless laborers?
- Are there local noncommercial print, radio, and television media where members of the community can express a diversity of ethnic, social, political, and cultural views where they will be heard by most of the community? Or is the majority of community news and needs filtered through commercially controlled media?
- Do people devote their free time to Little League baseball, community gardens, local theater, community choirs, community centers, and school boards—or to watching commercial TV?
- Are there credit cooperatives and local banks committed to supporting local enterprise or only branches of large urban banks engaged in channeling local deposits into their global financial operations?
- Do residents consider the area their permanent homes or are working and professional people largely itinerant?
- Do most households feel secure in their basic sustenance or do they depend for their survival on poorly paid temporary work?
- Are productive assets owned locally or by distant corporations?

- Are forests harvested selectively and sustainably by local firms to provide material for local industry? Or are local forests stripped bare every forty to sixty years by global corporations and the raw timber exported to distant lands?

The answers to these questions predict the sense of dignity, freedom, responsibility, prosperity, and security of individual people and the extent to which relationships are characterized by trust, caring, and cooperation.

The role of women, says Korten (1998:62–63), is critical in the rebuilding of social capital. Hence, there must be policies that create incentives to provide multiple economic, political, and social options for women. Among these are the following:

- Create an economic policy that allows a household to subsist on one income. This need not return women to their traditional roles; rather, it provides families a choice regarding the division of labor for traditional family tasks.
- Reverse the structural adjustment policies of the World Bank and IMF to give priority to the needs of local enterprise and the creation of good wages over the repayment of foreign loans.
- Extend to household workers and volunteers the same benefits as paid workers.
- Issue measures of the amount of social capital and contributions of unpaid labor.
- Assure women equal rights and access to land and shelter.
- Encourage political participation by women.
- Sustain a community media system.

These, then, are concrete policy suggestions through which we can begin to alleviate some of the problems we have explored. Certainly, we have the means through which we can improve peoples' quality of life, return political control to local areas, and sustain the environment. There seems to be a significant number of people, perhaps even a considerable majority, who would welcome the implementation of some, if not all, of these measures. The question is, *what would provide the impetus to action?* We are, after all, talking about a significant cultural change, not entirely unlike those promoted for the periphery by core governments and institutions, such as the World Bank. Most of the measures proposed have existed for some time, but clearly national priorities have not veered from the promotion of economic growth regardless of the consequences. *What, then, would make people, particularly those in power in either the core or periphery, significantly change their priorities?*

CONCLUSION

Solving the problems reviewed in this book will require change in both patterns of everyday individual choices and in the way we view the world.

Every day we make choices that reduce, maintain, or add to our natural, political, or social capital. When we choose to purchase an item at a large-scale chain store, we may save money, but we may also take away business from local enterprises whose success supports our neighbors. By purchasing the item, we may tacitly support the exploitation of cheap labor and add to the economic power of multinational corporations whose power can then be used to sway or control the policy decisions and legislation of local and national governments. By choosing to purchase an item or not purchase an item, we add, perhaps imperceptibly, to pollution and waste. Individual decisions themselves, of course, may have little impact. But when millions, following some cultural imperative, make the same choice, the results can be either destructive or constructive.

Meaningful change, therefore, will only occur when cumulative decisions and the rules that dictate those decisions change. However, it is hard to conceive of individuals altering these choices when their view of the world and of others is essentially materialistic. Over the past three centuries we have evolved a cosmology that assumes that the creation of the universe was essentially accidental and that the evolution of life consisted of millions of random occurrences. Those of us (including the author) who reject any sort of divine or spiritual intervention in the creation of life have a difficult time attributing any special significance to living things or to other members of our species for that matter. But this view creates a dilemma because this view of the world is not one that would inspire anyone to want to save it.

In January of 1990 at a meeting in Moscow of the Global Forum of Spiritual and Parliamentary Leaders, a group of well-known scientists organized by Carl Sagan presented "An Open Letter to the Religious Community" to encourage a common cause to save the earth. Its text states

> As scientists, many of us have had profound experiences of awe and reverence before the universe. We understand that what is regarded as sacred is more likely to be treated with care and respect. Our planetary home should be so regarded. Efforts to safeguard and cherish the environment need to be infused with a vision of the sacred. At the same time, a much wider and deeper understanding of science and technology is needed. If we do not understand the problem, it is unlikely we will be able to fix it. Thus, there is a vital role for both religion and science.[3]

The letter led to a meeting in May of 1992 in Washington, DC, hosted by then-U.S. vice president Al Gore. The conference brought together scientists, including Sagan, Stephen Jay Gould, and Edward O. Wilson, and a few religious leaders with the goal of crafting a joint statement in support of environmental sustainability. Economist Herman Daly attended the conference and asked whether scientists were recruiting religious leaders to provide a moral imperative lacking in science, while, at the same time, dismissing these religious leaders for their "distorted" view of reality. For science the universe is largely random and meaningless; as Steven Weinberg (1999), winner of the Nobel Prize for physics, said, "The more the universe seems comprehensible, the more it also seems pointless."

Apparently, some religious leaders had the same thought and wondered how a change toward sustainability could take place without a conviction that the universe carries meaning or that it is the "unfolding of a promise." As theologian John F. Haught (quoted in Daly 1996:19) put it,

---

[3]The letter is available on the Web at http://earthrenewal.org/open_letter_to_the_religious.htm.

A commonly held sense that the cosmos is a significant process, that it unfolds something analogous to what we humans call "purpose," is, I think an essential prerequisite of sustained global and intergenerational commitment to the earth's well being.

Stephen Jay Gould (1991:14) expressed this dilemma well when he said that,

We cannot win this battle to save species and environments without forging an emotional bond between ourselves and nature as well—for we will not fight to save what we do not love.

But from where does this "love" come? Where is this spirituality supposed to originate? There is a disconnection in the idea that scientists can use love as a tool for saving what for them is an accidental and pointless universe. In the words of Daly (1996:21),

There is something fundamentally silly about biologists teaching on Monday, Wednesday, and Friday that everything, including our sense of value and reason, is a mechanical product only of genetic chance and environmental necessity, with no purpose whatsoever, and then on Tuesday and Thursday trying to convince the public that they should love some accidental piece of this meaningless puzzle enough to fight and sacrifice to save it.

Environmentalists who utilize indigenous spirituality and a supposedly mystic tie to nature are guilty also of trying to appropriate religious values to lend legitimacy to sustainability. Like the scientists, they are trying to inculcate some sort of religious legitimization into an essentially materialist agenda.

Yet there seems also to be a realization that without some moral, religious, or spiritual imperative, the kinds of changes that are required to solve the questions we have addressed in this book, cannot be addressed with any sort of urgency, if at all. In the history of social movements in America, only a few, such as the abolitionist movement and the civil rights movement, have succeeded in joining political and religious agendas in the cause of change. The efforts, however, highlight the question of whether there must be some philosophical or religious foundation to impel us to restore our waning natural, political, and social capital. Herman Daly (1996:201), I think, sums up the prospect for change well when he says that significant change will require

[a] change of heart, a renewal of the mind, and a healthy dose of repentance. These are all religious terms, and that is no coincidence, because a change in the fundamental principles we live by is a change so deep that it is essentially religious whether we call it that or not.

REFERENCES

Abu-Lughod, Janet L. 1989. *Before European Hegemony: The World-System* A.D. *1250–1350*. New York: Oxford University Press.

Africa 2000. What Is N.S.S.M. 200…? And Why Do Western Leaders Care So Much About Population Control? http://www.africa2000.com/INDX/nssm200.htm.

Ahmad, Nik Nazmi Nik. 2003. The State Under Seige. *Asia Times,* December 25.

Allen, James (editor). 2000. *Without Sanctuary: Lynching Photography in America*. Santa Fe, NM: Twin Palms.

Alpert, Bracha. 1991. Student's Resistance in the Classroom. *Anthropology and Education Quarterly* 22:350–366.

Amin, Samir, Girovanni Arrighi, Andre Gunder Frank, and Immanuel Wallerstein (editors). 1990. *Transforming the Revolution: Social Movements and the World-System*. New York: Monthly Review Press.

Ammerman, Nancy T. 1991. North American Protestant Fundamentalism. In *Fundamentalisms Observed,* edited by Martin E. Marty and R. Scott Appleby (Fundamentalism Project, volume 1). Chicago: University of Chicago Press

Anderson, Sarah, and John Cavanagh. 2000. *Top 200: The Rise of Global Corporate Power.* Corporate Watch. http://www.globalpolicy.org/socecon/tncs/top200.htm.

Arnold, Wayne. 1999. Foreign Investors Express Concern About Indonesia's New President. *New York Times,* October 27.

Baker, Brenda J., and George Armelagos. 1988. The Origin and Antiquity of Syphilis. *Current Anthropology* 29:703–721.

Baker, Russell. 2003. The Awful Truth. *New York Review of Books,* November 6.

Bales, Kevin. 1999. *Disposable People: New Slavery in the Global Economy*. Berkeley: University of California Press.

Barlow, Maude. 1999. *Blue Gold: The Global Water Crisis and the Commodification of the World's Water Supply*. International Forum on Globalization. http://www.ifg.org/bgsummary.html.

Barnes, Barry. 1974. *Scientific Knowledge and Sociological Theory*. London: Routledge & Kegan Paul.

Basch, Linda, Nina Glick Schiller, and Cristina Szanton Blanc. 1994. *Nations Unbound: Transnational Projects, Postcolonial Predicaments, and Deterritorialized Nation-State.* Amsterdam: Gordon and Breach.

Basu, Amrita. 1995. Introduction. In *The Challenge of Local Feminisms: Women's Movements in Global Perspective,* edited by Amrita Basu. Boulder, CO: Westview Press.

Basu, Indrajit. 2003. India's Growing Urge to Splurge. *Asia Times,* August 22.

Bauman, Zygmunt. 1998. *Globalization: The Human Consequences*. New York: Columbia University Press

Beal, Merrill D. 1963. *"I Will Fight No More Forever": Chief Joseph and the Nez Percé War.* Seattle: University of Washington Press.

Beard, Charles (editor). 1959. *The Enduring Federalist.* New York: Frederick Ungar.

Beaud, Michel. 1983. *A History of Capitalism 1500–1980*. Translated by Tom Dickman and Anny Lefebvre. New York: Monthly Review Press.

Beeman, William O. 1997. Revitalization Drives American Militias. In *Conformity and Conflict: Readings in Cultural Anthropology,* 9th ed., edited by James Spradley and David W. McCurdy. New York: Longman.

Belk, R. W. 1988. Possession and the Extended Self. *Journal of Consumer Research* 15:140–158.

Bello, Walden. 1998. The End of a "Miracle": Speculation, Foreign Capital Dependency and the Collapse of the Southeast Asian Economies. *Multinational Monitor,* 19.

Berthelsen, John. 2003. Asia's Consumer Revolution Deepens. *Asia Times,* November 26.

BGH Bulletin. 2000. BHG Bulletin: News of Lawsuit Exposing Media Coverup of Suspected Dangers in Milk. http://www.foxbghsuit.com/.

Bidwai, Praful. 2003. Editorial. *Daily Star* (Bangladesh) November 7.

Binswanger, Hans. 1994. *Money and Magic: A Critique of the Modern Economy in the Light of Goethe's Faust*. Translated by J. E. Harrison. Chicago: University of Chicago Press.

Birdsall, Nancy. 1994. Government, Population, and Poverty: A Win–Win Tale. In *Population and Development: Old Debates, New Conclusions,* edited by Robert Cassen. New Brunswick, NJ: Transaction.

Blondet, Cecilia. 1995. Out of the Kitchens and onto the Streets: Women's Activism in Peru. In *The Challenge of Local Feminisms: Women's Movements in*

Global Perspective, edited by Amrita Basu. Boulder, CO: Westview Press.

Bodley, John H. 1990. *Victims of Progress,* 3rd ed. Mountain View, CA: Mayfield Publishing.

Boserup, Ester. 1965. *The Conditions of Agricultural Growth.* Chicago: Aldine.

Boserup, Ester. 1970. *Women's Role in Economic Development.* New York: St. Martin's Press.

Bourdieu, Pierre. 1986. The Forms of Capital. In *Handbook of Theory and Research for the Sociology of Education,* edited by John G. Richardson. New York: Greenwood Press.

Bourgois, Phillipe. 1995. *In Search of Respect: Selling Crack in El Barrio.* Cambridge: Cambridge University Press.

Bradsher, Keith. 1997. License to Pollute: Light Trucks, Darlings of Drivers, Are Favored by the Law, Too. *New York Times,* November 30. http:www.nytimes.com.

Braudel, Fernand. [1979] 1982. *Civilization and Capitalism 15th–18th Century: Vol II, The Wheels of Commerce.* Translated by Siân Reynolds. New York: Harper and Row.

Business Week. 1997. Gen X Ads: Two for Me, None for You. August 11.

Calder, Lendol. 1999 *Financing the American Dream: A Cultural History of Consumer Credit.* Princeton, NJ: Princeton University Press.

Caldwell, John C. 1982. *Theory of Fertility Decline.* New York: Academic Press.

Carneiro, Robert. 1978. Political Expansion as an Expression of the Principle of Competitive Exclusion. In *Origins of the State,* edited by Ronald Cohn and Elman Service. Philadelphia: Institute for the Study of Human Issues.

Carrier, James G. 1995. *Gifts and Commodities: Exchange and Western Capitalism Since 1700.* London: Routledge.

Caufield, Catherine. 1996. *Masters of Illusion: The World Bank and the Poverty of Nations.* New York: Henry Holt.

Chase, Allan. 1977. *The Legacy of Malthus: The Social Costs of the New Scientific Racism.* New York: Alfred A. Knopf.

Chen, Shaohua, and Martin Ravallion. 2000. How Did the World's Poorest Fare in the 1990s. Development Research Group, World Bank. http://www.globalpolicy.org/socecon/develop/pov90.htm.

Chossudovsky, Michel. 1996. Dismantling Former Yugoslavia, Recolonizing Bosnia. http://groundwork.ucsd.edu/bosnia.html.

Chossudovsky, Michel. nd. *Global Falsehoods: How the World Bank and the UNDP Distort the Figures on Global Poverty.* http://canadianliberty.bc.ca/relatedinfo/globalpoverty.html.

Chua, Amy. 2003. *World on Fire: How Exporting Free Market Democracy Breeds Ethnic Hatred and Global Instability.* New York: Doubleday.

CNN. 2001. Congress Looks to Shield Economy. September 15.

Coale, Ansley. 1974. The History of Human Population. *Science* 231:40–51.

Cobb, Clifford, Ted Halstead, and Jonathan Rowe. 1995. If the GDP Is Up, Why Is America Down? *Atlantic Monthly,* October.

Cohen, Joel. 1995. Population Growth and the Earth's Carrying Capacity. *Science* 269:341–346.

Cohen, Lizabeth. 2003. *A Consumer's Republic: The Politics of Mass Consumption in Postwar America.* New York: Alfred A. Knopf.

Cohen, Mark. 1977. *The Food Crisis in Prehistory: Overpopulation and the Origins of Agriculture.* New Haven: Yale University Press.

Cohen, Mark. 1989. *Health and the Rise of Civilization.* New Haven: Yale University Press.

Cohen, Mark. 1994. Demographic Expansion: Causes and Consequences. In *Companion Encyclopedia of Anthropology,* edited by Tim Ingold. New York: Routledge.

Cohen, Mark. 1998. *The Culture of Intolerance.* New Haven: Yale University Press.

Cohen, Roger. 1991. For Coke, World Is Its Oyster. *New York Times,* November 21, D1.

Cohen, Roger. 2003. Iraq and Its Patron, Growing Apart. *New York Times,* December 21.

Cohen, Ronald, and Elman R. Service (editors). 1978. *Origins of the State: The Anthropology of Political Evolution.* Philadelphia: Institute for the Study of Human Issues.

Cohn-Sherbok, Dan, and Dawoud el-Alami. 2002. *The Palentine–Israeli Conflict: A Beginners Guide.* Oxford: One World.

Coll, Steve. 2004. *Ghost Wars: The Secret History of the CIA, Afghanistan, and Bin Laden, from the Soviet Invasion to September 10, 2001.* New York: Penguin Press.

Colley, Linda. 1992. *Britons: Forging the Nation 1707–1837.* New Haven: Yale University Press.

Collier, George A., Jr. 1994. Roots of the Rebellion in Chiapas. *Cultural Survival Quarterly* 18:14–18.

Collins, Jane L. 2000. Tracing Social Relations in Commodity Chains: The Case of Grapes in Brazil. In *Commodities and Globalization: Anthropological Perspectives,* edited by Angelique Haugerud, M. Priscilla Stone, and Peter D. Little. New York: Rowman & Littlefield.

Comaroff, Jean. 1985. *Body of Power, Spirit of Resistance: The Culture and History of a South African People.* Chicago: University of Chicago Press.

Connell, K. H. 1965. Land and Population in Ireland, 1780–1845. In *Population in History: Essays in Historical Demography,* edited by D. V. Glass and D. E. C. Eversley. Chicago: Aldine.

Conrad, Joseph. [1902] 1972. *Heart of Darkness.* New York: W. W. Norton.

Cook, Sherburne Friend, and Woodrow W. Borah. 1960. The Indian Population of Central Mexico, 1531–1610. *Ibero-Americana 44.* Berkeley: University of California Press.

Cooley, John. 2002. *Unholy Wars: Afghanistan, America and International Terrorism.* London: Pluto Press.

Cordell, Dennis. 1994. Extracting People from Precapitalist Production: French Equatorial Africa from the 1890s to the 1930s. In *African Population and Capitalism: Historical Perspectives,* edited by Dennis Cordell and Joel W. Gregor. Madison: University of Wisconsin Press.

Council for Christian Colleges and Universities. 2001. Enrollment Continues to Surge at Christian Colleges. http://cccu.org/news/newsID.84,parentNav.Archives/news_detail.asp.

Crosby, Alfred W. 1986. *Ecological Imperialism: The Biological Expansion of Europe, 900–1900.* Cambridge: Cambridge University Press.

Daly, Herman E. 1990. Towards Some Operational Principles of Sustainable Development. *Ecological Economics: 2:*1–6.

Daly, Herman E. 1996. *Beyond Growth: The Economics of Sustainable Development.* Boston: Beacon Press.

Danner, Mark. 2003. Delusions in Baghdad. *New York Review of Books,* December 18.

Davidson, Eric A. 2000. *You Can't Eat GNP: Economics As If Ecology Mattered.* Cambridge, MA: Perseus.

Dettwyler, Katherine. A. 1994. *Dancing Skeletons: Life and Death in West Africa.* Prospect Heights, IL: Waveland Press.

Dobyns, Henry F. 1983. *Their Number Become Thinned: Native American Population Dynamics in Eastern North America.* Knoxville: University of Tennessee Press.

Douglas, Mary, and Aaron B. Wildavsky. 1983. *Risk and Culture: An Essay on the Selection of Technical and Environmental Dangers.* Berkeley: University of California Press.

Drèze, Jean, and Amartya Sen. 1989. *Hunger and Public Action.* Oxford: Clarendon Press.

Driscoll, David D. 1992. *What Is the International Monetary Fund?* Washington, DC: International Monetary Fund.

Dubos, Rene. 1968. *Man, Medicine, and Environment.* New York: Mentot.

Dubos, Rene. [1952] 1987. *The White Plague; Tuberculosis, Man, and Society.* New Brunswick, NJ: Rutgers University Press.

Dunaway, Wilma A. 1996. *The First American Frontier: Transition to Capitalism in Southern Appalachia, 1700–1860.* Chapel Hill: University of North Carolina Press.

Dunlap, Albert J. (with Bob Andelman). 1996. *How I Saved Bad Companies and Made Good Companies Great.* New York: Time Books.

Durning, Allan. 1992. *How Much Is Enough: The Consumer Society and the Future of the Earth.* New York: W. W. Norton.

Earle, Duncan. 1994. Indigenous Identity at the Margin: Zapatismo and Nationalism. *Cultural Survival Quarterly* 18:26–30.

Edgerton, Robert B. 1989. *Mau Mau: An African Crucible.* New York: The Free Press.

Edwards, Michael, and David Hulme. 1995. *Non-Governmental Organizations—Performance and Accountability: Beyond the Magic Bullet.* London: Earthscan Publications.

Ehrlich, Paul R. 1968. *The Population Bomb.* New York: Ballantine Books.

Ehrlich, Paul R., and Anne H. Ehrlich. 1990. *The Population Explosion.* New York: Simon & Schuster.

Eisenstein, Zillah. 1997. Stop Stomping on the Rest of Us: Retrieving Publicness from the Privatization of the Globe. In *Feminism and Globalization: The Impact of the Global Economy on Women and Feminist Theory,* edited by Alfred C. Aman, Jr. *Indiana Journal of Global Legal Studies,* Spring (special issue).

Ember, Carol R. 1983. The Relative Decline in Women's Contribution to Agriculture with Intensification. *American Anthropologist* 85:285–304.

Endelmann, Mark. 1987. From Costa Rican Pasture to North American Hamburger. In *Food and Evolution: Toward a Theory of Human Food Habits,* edited by Marvin Harris and Eric Ross. Philadelphia: Temple University Press.

Ensminger, M. E. 1991. *Animal Science.* Danville, IL: Interstate Publishers.

Erasmus, Charles J. 1972. *In Search of the Common Good: Utopian Experiments Past and Future.* New York: The Free Press.

Evans-Pritchard, E. E. 1940. *The Nuer.* Oxford: Oxford University Press.

Ewald, Paul. 1993. The Evolution of Virulence. *Scientific American* 269:86–93.

Falk, Richard. 2003. *The Great Terror War.* New York: Olive Branch Press.

Farmer, Paul. 1992. *AIDS and Accusation: Haiti and the Geography of Blame.* Berkeley: University of California Press.

Farmer, Paul. 1999. *Infections and Inequality: The Modern Plagues.* Berkeley: University of California Press.

Fernández-Kelly, María Patricia. 1983. *For We Are Sold, I and My People: Women and Industry in Mexico's Frontier.* Albany: State University of New York Press.

Fey, Harold, and D'Arcy McNickle. 1970. *Indians and Other Americans: Two Ways of Life Meet.* New York: Harper & Row.

Finkel, David. 2000. Few Drugs for the Neediest HIV Patients. *Washington Post,* November 2.

Fintan, O'Toole. 1998. "The Masked Avenger." *The New York Review of Books,* XLV, Number 131, 21.

Firdausy, Carunia Mulya. 2000. The Social Impact of Economic Crisis on Employment in Indonesia. Centre for Economic and Development Studies—Indonesian Institute of Sciences. http://ismea.org/asialist/Firdausy.html.

Firth, Raymond. 1959. *Social Change in Tikopia: A Re-Study of a Polynesian Community After a Generation.* London: Allen & Unwin.

Fishman, Charles. 2003. The Wal-Mart You Don't Know. *FastCompany* 77, December, 68. http://www.fastcompany.com/magazine/77/walmart.html.

Fjellman, Stephen M. 1992. *Vinyl Leaves: Walt Disney World and America.* Boulder, CO: Westview Press.

Flannery, Kent V. 1972. The Cultural Evolution of Civilization. *Annual Review of Ecology and Systemics* 3:339–426.

Flannery, Kent V. 1973. The Origins of Agriculture. In Siegel, Beals, and Tyler, eds., *Annual Review of Anthropology* 2:271–310.

Forbes. 2000a. Forbes World's Richest People. http://www.forbes.com/tool/toolbox/billnew/.

Forbes. 2000b. Global 500. http://www.fortune.com/.

Foster, John Bellamy. 1993. "Let Them Eat Pollution": Capitalism and the World Environment. *Monthly Review* 44:10–11.

Frank, Andre Gunder. 1998. *ReOrient: Global Economy in the Asian Age.* Berkeley: University of California Press.

Fratkin, Eliot. 1997a. Pastoralism: Governance and Development Issues. *Annual Review of Anthropology* 26:235–261.

French, Hilary. 2000. *Vanishing Borders: Protecting the Planet in the Age of Globalization.* New York: W. W. Norton.

Fried, Morton H. 1967. *The Evolution of Political Society: An Essay in Political Anthropology.* New York: Random House.

Gardner, Gary, and Brian Halweil. 2000. *Overfed and Underfed: The Global Epidemic of Malnutrition.* Worldwatch Paper 150. Washington, DC: Worldwatch Institute.

Garrett, Laurie. 1994. *The Coming Plague.* New York: Farrar, Strauss & Giroux.

Geertz, Clifford. 1963. *Agricultural Involution: The Process of Ecological Change in Indonesia.* Berkeley: University of California Press.

Gellner, Ernest. 1983. *Nations and Nationalism.* Ithaca: Cornell University Press.

George, Alexander. 1991. *Western State Terrorism.* New York: Routledge.

George, Susan. 1999. A Short History of Neo-Liberalism: Twenty Years of Elite Economics and Emerging Opportunities for Structural Change. Address to the Conference on Economic Sovereignty in a Globalising World, Bangkok, March 24–26.

Gibbons, S. David, and Kasim Sukor. 1994. *Banking on the Rural Poor.* Dhaka: Grameen Bank.

Ginsburg, Faye. 1993. Saving America's Souls: Operation Rescue's Crusade Against Abortion. In *Fundamentalisms and the State: Remaking Polities, Economies, and Militance,* edited by Martin E. Marty and R. Scott Appleby (Fundamentalism Project, volume 3). Chicago: University of Chicago Press.

Gleissman, S. R. 1988. Local Resource Use Systems in the Tropics: Taking Pressure off the Tropics. *Tropical Rainforests: Diversity and Conservation,* edited by F. Alemeda and C. M. Pringle. San Francisco: California Academy of Sciences.

Goodenough, Ward. 1963. *Cooperation in Change.* New York: Wiley.

Gossen, Gary H. 1994. Comments on the Zapatista Movement. *Cultural Survival Quarterly* 18:19–21.

Gould, Peter. 1993. *The Slow Plague: A Geography of the AIDS Pandemic.* Cambridge: Blackwell.

Gould, Stephen Jay. 1991. Unenchanted Evening. *Natural History,* September.

Goulet, Denis. 1971. *The Cruel Choice: A New Concept in the Theory of Development.* New York: Atheneum.

Graeber, David. 2001. *Toward an Anthropological Theory of Value: The False Coin of Our Own Dreams.* New York: Palgrave Macmillan.

Gray, John. 2003. *Al Qaeda and What It Means to Be Modern.* New York: The New Press.

Greenhouse, Steven. 2000. Foreign Workers at Highest Level in Seven Decades. *New York Times,* September 4.

Greider, William. 1997. *One World Ready or Not: The Manic Logic of Global Capitalism.* New York: Simon & Schuster.

Guardian-Observer. 2002. Full Text: bin Laden's "Letter to America." http://observer.guardian.co.uk/worldview/story/0,11581,845725,00.html.

Guha, Ramachandra. 1990. *The Unquiet Woods: Ecological Change and Peasant Resistance in the Himalaya.* Berkeley: University of California Press.

Gunaratna, Rohan. 2003. *Inside Al Qaeda: Global Network of Terror.* New York: Berkley Books.

Guttmann, Myron. 1988. *Toward the Modern Economy: Early Industry in Europe, 1500–1800.* New York: Alfred A. Knopf.

Guttmann, Robert. 1994. *How Credit-Money Shapes the Economy: The United States in a Global System.* London: M. E. Sharpe.

Halweil, Brian, and Lisa Mastny. 2004. *State of the World, 2004: Special Focus, The Consumer Society. Worldwatch Institute.* New York: W. W. Norton.

Handwerker, W. Penn. 1989. *Women's Power and Social Revolution: Fertility Transition in the West Indies* (Frontiers of Anthropology, volume 2). Newbury Park, CA: Sage.

Hanson, F. Allan. 1993. *Testing, Testing: Social Consequences of the Examined Life.* Berkeley: University of California Press.

Hardin, Garrett. 1968. Tragedy of the Commons. *Science* 162:1243–1248.

Hardin, Garrett, and John Baden. 1977. *Managing the Commons.* New York: W. H. Freeman.

Harding, Susan. 1991. Imagining the Last Days: The Politics of Apocalyptic Language. In *Accounting for Fundamentalisms,* edited by Martin E. Marty and R. Scott Appleby (Fundamentalism Project, volume 4). Chicago: University of Chicago Press.

Harris, Marvin. 1971. *Culture, Man, and Nature.* New York: Crowell.

Harris, Marvin. 1986. *Good to Eat: Riddles of Food and Culture.* New York: Simon & Schuster.

Harris, Marvin. 1987. *The Sacred Cow and the Abominable Pig.* New York: Touchstone.

Harris, Marvin, and Eric B. Ross. 1987a. *Death, Sex, and Fertility: Population Regulation in Preindustrial and Developing Societies.* New York: Columbia University Press.

Harris, Marvin, and Eric B. Ross. 1987b. *Food and Evolution: Toward a Theory of Human Food Habits.* Philadelphia: Temple University Press.

Harris, Ron. 1989. Children Who Dress for Excess: Today's Youngsters Have Become Fixated with Fashion. The Right Look Isn't Enough—It Also Has to Be Expensive, *Los Angeles Times,* November 12.

Hartmann, Thom. 2002. *Unequal Protection: The Rise of Corporate Dominance and the Theft of Human Rights.* New York: Rodale Press.

Haas, Robert. 1999. Poet's Choice. *Washington Post,* September 5.

Haugerud, Angelique, M. Priscilla Stone, and Peter D. Little (editors). 2000. *Commodities and Globalization: Anthropological Perspectives.* New York: Rowman & Littlefield.

Hobsbawm, Eric J. 1959. *Primitive Rebels: Studies in Archaic Forms of Social Movement in the Nineteenth and Twentienth Centuries.* New York: Frederick A. Praeger.

Hobsbawm, Eric J. 1975. *The Age of Capital: 1848–1875.* New York: Charles Scribner's Sons.

Hobsbawm, Eric J., and Terence Ranger. 1983. *Inventing Tradition.* Cambridge: Cambridge University Press.

Hodder, Kathryn. 1999. *Annual Survey of Violations of Trade Union Rights.* ICFTU International Confederation of Free Trade Unions. www.icftu.org.

Howell, Nancy. 1979. *Demography of the Dobe !Kung.* New York: Academic Press.

Hudson, E. H. 1965. Treponematosis and Man's Social Evolution. *American Anthropologist* 67:885–901.

Iannaccone, Laurence R. 1993. The Economics of American Fundamentalists. In *Fundamentalisms and the State: Remaking Polities, Economies, and Militance,* edited by Martin E. Marty and R. Scott Appleby (Fundamentalism Project, volume 3). Chicago: University of Chicago Press.

IBRD. 1950. *The Basis of a Development Program for Colombia.* Baltimore: Johns Hopkins University Press.

Ignatiev, Noel. 1995. *How the Irish Became White.* New York: Routledge.

International Center for Technology Assessment (ICTA). nd. The Real Price of Gasoline: Report No. 3, An Analysis of the Hidden External Costs Consumers Pay to Fuel Their Automobiles. http://www.icta.org/projects/trans/realpricegas.pdf.

International Confedation of Free Trade Unions. 2003. *Annual Survey of Violations of Trade Union Rights.* http://www.icftu.org.

International Labor Organization. 2003. *Global Employment Trends.* Geneva: ILO. http://www.ilo.org/public/english/employment/strat/download/trends.pdf.

International Confedation of Free Trade Unions. 2000. *Annual Survey of Violations of Trade Union Rights.* http://www.icftu.org.

International Monetary Fund, United Nations, World Bank, and Organization for Economic Cooperation and Development. 2000. *A Better World for All: Progress Towards the International Development Goals.* http://www.paris21.org/betterworld/home.htm.

Jaimes, Annette M. 1992. Federal Indian Identification Policy: A Usurpation of Indigenous Sovereignty in North America. In *The State of Native America: Genocide, Colonization, and Resistance,* edited by M. Annette Jaimes. Boston: South End Press.

James, C. L. R. 1963. *The Black Jacobins: Toussaint l' Ouverture and the San Domingo Revolution,* 2nd ed. New York: Random House.

Johnson, Paul E. 1978. *A Shopkeeper's Millennium: Society and Revivals in Rochester.* New York: Hill & Wang.

Jubilee. 2000. Jubilee USA Network. http://www.j2000usa. org/index.html.

Juergensmeyer, Mark. 1993. *The New Cold War? Religious Nationalism Confronts the Secular State.* Berkeley: University of California Press.

Juergensmeyer, Mark. 1996. The Worldwide Rise of Religious Nationalism. *Journal of International Affair* 50:1–20.

Juergensmeyer, Mark. 2000. *Terror in the Mind of God: The Global Rise of Religious Violence.* Berkeley: University of California Press.

Junas, Daniel. 1995. Rise of Citizen Militias: Angry White Guys with Guns. *Covert Action Quarterly,* Spring:22–25.

Kanogo, Tabitha. 1987. *Squatters and the Roots of Mau Mau 1905–1963.* Athens: Ohio University Press.

Kanter, Rosabeth Moss. 1972. *Commitment and Community: Communes and Utopias in Sociological Perspective.* Cambridge: Harvard University Press.

Kearney, Michael. 1991. Borders and Boundaries of State and Self at the End of Empire. *Journal of Historical Sociology* 4:58–74.

Kearney, Michael. 1996. *Reconceptualizing the Peasantry: Anthropology in Global Perspective.* Boulder, CO: Westview Press.

Kemp, Amanda, Nozizwe Madlala, Asha Moodley, and Elaine Salo. 1995. The Dawn of a New Day: Redefining South African Feminism. In *The Challenge of Local Feminisms: Women's Movements in Global Perspective,* edited by Amrita Basu. Boulder, CO: Westview Press.

Kennedy, Paul. 1993. *Preparing for the Twenty-First Century.* New York: Random House.

Kenyatta, Jomo. 1962. *Facing Mount Kenya.* New York: Random House.

Kincheloe, Joe L. 1997. McDonald's, Power, and Children: Ronald McDonald (aka Ray Kroc) Does It All for You. In *Kinderculture: The Corporate Construction of Childhood,* edited by Shirley R. Steinberg and Joe L. Kincheloe. Boulder, CO: Westview Press.

Klugman, Jeni, and Jeanine Braithwaite. 1998. Poverty in Russia During the Transition: An Overview. *The World Bank Research Observer* 13(1).

Kopytoff Igor. 1988. The Cultural Biography of Things: Commoditization as Process. In *The Social Life of Things: Commodities in Cultural Perspective,* edited by Arjun Appadurai. Cambridge: Cambridge University Press.

Korten, David C. 1990. *Getting to the Twenty-First Century: Voluntary Action and the Global Agenda.* Hartford, CT: Kumarian Press.

Korten, David C. 1995. *When Corporations Rule the World.* Hartford, CT: Kumarian Press.

Korten, David. 1998. *Globalizing Civil Society: Reclaiming Our Right to Power.* New York: Seven Stories Press.

Korten, David. 1999. *The Post-Corporate World: Life After Capitalism.* West Hartford, CT: Kumarian Press and San Francisco: Berrett-Koehler.

Kowinski, William Severini. 1985. *The Malling of America: An Inside Look at the Great Consumer Paradise.* New York: William Morrow.

Kroeber, Alfred L. 1939. *Cultural and Natural Areas of Native North America.* Berkeley: University of California Press.

Kuletz, Valerie. 1998. *The Tainted Desert: Environmental and Social Ruin in the American West.* London: Routledge.

Kumar, Radha. 1995. From Chipko to Sati: The Contemporary Indian Women's Movement. In *The Challenge of Local Feminisms: Women's Movements in Global Perspective,* edited by Amrita Basu. Boulder, CO: Westview Press.

Kuper, Leo. 1990. The Genocidal State: An Overview. In *State Violence and Ethnicity,* edited by Pierre L. van den Berghe. Boulder: University of Colorado Press.

Kuran, Timur. 1993. Fundamentalisms and the Economy. In *Fundamentalisms and the State: Remaking Polities, Economies, and Militance,* edited by Martin E. Marty and R. Scott Appleby (Fundamentalism Project, volume 1). Chicago: University of Chicago Press.

Landes, David S. 1969. The *Unbound Prometheus: Technological Change and Industrial Development in Western Europe from 1750 to the Present.* Cambridge: Cambridge University Press.

Landes, David S. 1998. *The Wealth and Poverty of Nations: Why Some Are So Rich and Some Are So Poor.* New York: W. W. Norton.

Lappé, Marc. 1994. *Evolutionary Medicine: Rethinking the Origins of Disease.* San Francisco: Sierra Club Books.

Larson, Edward J. 1997. *Summer for the Gods: The Scopes Trial and America's Continuing Debate over Science and Religion.* New York: Basic Books.

Lasch, Chistopher. 1977. *Haven in a Heartless World: The Family Besieged.* New York: Basic Books.

Leach, William. 1993. *Land of Desire: Merchants, Power, and the Rise of a New American Culture.* New York: Pantheon.

Leacock, Eleanor. 1983. Interpreting the Origins of Gender Inequality: Conceptual and Historical Problems. *Dialectical Anthropology* 7:263–283.

Leacock, Eleanor. 1986. Women, Power, and Authority. In *Visibility and Power: Essays on Women in Society and Development*, edited by Leela Dube, Eleanor Leacock, and Shirley Ardener. Delhi: Oxford University Press.

Leaf, Murray. 1984. *Song of Hope: The Green Revolution in a Punjab Village*. New Brunswick, NJ: Rutgers University Press.

Lears, T. J. Jackson. 1983. From Salvation to Self-Realization: Advertising and the Therapeutic Roots of the Consumer Culture, 1880–1930. In *The Culture of Consumption: Critical Essays in American History, 1880–1930*, edited by Richard Wrightman Fox and T. J. Jackson Lears. New York: Pantheon.

Lee, R. B., I. DeVore, et al. 1969. *Man the Hunter*. Chicago: Aldine.

Lewellen, Ted C. 1992. *Political Anthropology: An Introduction*, 2nd ed. South Hadley: Bergin and Garvey.

Lincoln, Bruce. 1989. *Discourse and the Construction of Society: Comparative Studies of Myth, Ritual, and Classification*. Oxford: Oxford University Press.

Little, Peter D., and Catherine S. Dolan. 2000. What It Means to Be Restructured: Nontraditional Commodities and Structural Adjustment in Sub-Saharan Africa. In *Commodities and Globalization: Anthropological Perspectives*, edited by Angelique Haugerud, M. Priscilla Stone, and Peter D. Little. New York: Rowman & Littlefield.

Livi-Bacci, Massimi. 1992. *A Concise History of World Population*. Cambridge: Blackwell.

Lloyd, Cynthia B. 1994. High Fertility at the Level of the Family. In *Population and Development: Old Debates, New Conclusions*, edited by Robert Cassen. New Brunswick, NJ: Transaction.

Lohr, Steve. 2003. Discount Nation; Is Wal-Mart Good for America? *New York Times* December 7. http://query.nytimes.com/gst/abtract.html?res=F1071EF839590C748CDDAB0994DB404482

Low, Patrick. 1993. *Trading Free: The GATT and US Trade Policy*. New York: Twentieth Century Fund Press.

Lutjens, Sheryl L. 1994. Remaking the Public Sphere: Women and Revolution in Cuba. In *Women and Revolution in Africa, Asia, and the New World*, edited by Mary Ann Tétreault. Columbia: University of South Carolina Press.

Maddison, Angus. 2003. *The World Economy: A Millennial Perspective*. Development Centre of the Organization for Economic Co-operation and Development, Paris.

Malthus, Thomas Robert. 1826. *Essay on the Principle of Population*. London: John Murray.

Mamdani, Mahmood. 1972. *The Myth of Population Control: Family, Caste, and Class in an Indian Village*. New York: Monthly Review Press.

Mamdani, Mahmood. 2004. *Good Muslim, Bad Muslim: America, the Cold War, and the Roots of Terror*. New York: Pantheon.

Manning, Patrick. 1990. *Slavery and African Life: Occidental, Oriental, and African Slave Trades*. Cambridge: Cambridge University Press.

Marx, Karl. 1972. *Ireland and the Irish Question: A Collection of Writings*. New York: International Publishers.

Marx, Karl. [1844] 1970. *Critique of Hegel's "Philosophy of Right."* Translated by Annette Jolin and Joseph O'Malley. Cambridge: Cambridge University Press.

Marx, Karl, and Frederick Engels. [1848] 1941. *Manifesto of the Communist Party*. New York: International Publishers.

Matthews, Emily. 2000. *The Weight of Nations: Material Outflows from Industrial Economies*. Washington, DC: World Resources Institute.

Maybury-Lewis, David. 1997. *Indigenous Peoples, Ethnic Groups, and the State*. Boston: Allyn & Bacon.

McCay, Bonnie J., and Louise Fortmann. 1996. Voices from the Commons. *Cultural Survival Quarterly* 20:24–25.

McCracken, Grant. 1988. *Culture and Consumption: New Approaches to the Symbolic Character of Consumer Goods and Activities*. Bloomington: Indiana University Press.

McNeal, James. 1999. *The Kids' Market: Myths and Realities*. Ithaca, NY: Paramount Market.

McNeil, Donald, Jr. 2000. Drug Companies and the Third World: A Case Study of Neglect. *New York Times*, May 21.

Mead, Margaret. 1961. *New Lives for Old*. New York: New American Library.

Meade, J. E. 1967. Population Explosion, the Standard of Living, and Social Conflict. *The Economic Journal* 77:233–255.

Meggitt, Mervyn. 1962. *Desert People: A Study of the Aalbiri Aborigines of Central Australia* London: Angus and Robertson.

Merari, Ariel. 1993. Terrorism as a Strategy of Insurgency. *Terrorism and Political Violence*, (Vol. 5, pp. 213–251).

Mintz, Sidney W. 1985. *Sweetness and Power: The Place of Sugar in World History*. New York: Viking.

Mooney, James. 1965. *The Ghost-Dance Religion and the Sioux Outbreak of 1890*. Chicago: University of Chicago Press.

Munson, Henry, Jr. 1988. *Islam and Revolution in the Middle East*. New Haven: Yale University Press.

Nag, Moni (editor). 1975. *Population and Social Organization*. The Hague: Mouton.

Nagengast, Carole. 1994. Violence, Terror, and the Crisis of the State. *Annual Review of Anthropology* 23:109–136.

Nash, George. 1988. *The Life of Herbert Hoover: The Humanitarian (1914–1917)*. New York: W. W. Norton.

Nash, June. 1994. Global Integration and Subsistence Insecurity. *American Anthropologist* 96:7–30.

Nash, Manning. 1991. Islamic Resurgence in Malaysia and Indonesia. In *Fundamentalisms Observed,* edited by Martin E. Marty and R. Scott Appleby (Fundamentalism Project, volume 1). Chicago: University of Chicago Press.

National Abortion Federation. 2003. Incidents of Violence and Disruption Against Abortion Providers. http://www.prochoice.org.

National Abortion Federation. 2001. Incidents of Violence and Disruption Against Abortion Providers; http://www.prochoice.org/.

Nations, James D. 1994. The Ecology of the Zapatista Revolt. *Cultural Survival Quarterly* 18:31–33.

Needleman, Joseph. 1991. *Money and the Meaning of Life*. New York: Doubleday.

Nerfin, Marc. 1986. Neither Prince nor Merchant: An Introduction to the Third System. *IFDA Dossier* 56:3–29.

Newman, Lucile F. (editor). 1990. *Hunger in History*. Oxford: Basil Blackwell.

Nigh, Ronald. 1994. Zapata Rose. *Cultural Survival Quarterly* 18:9–11.

Nigh, Ronald. 1995. Animal Agriculture for the Reforestation of Degraded Tropical Rainforests. *Culture and Agriculture* 51–52:2–5.

Noriega, Jorge. 1992. American Indian Education in the United States. In *The State of Native America: Genocide, Colonization, and Resistance,* edited by M. Annette Jaimes. Boston: South End Press.

Nye, Joseph. 2003. *The Paradox of American Power: Why the World's Only Superpower Can't Go It Alone.* Oxford. Oxford University Press.

O'Brien, Jay. 1994. Differential High Fertility and Demographic Transitions: Peripheral Capitalism in Sudan. In *African Population and Capitalism: Historical Perspectives,* edited by Dennis Cordell and Joel W. Gregor. Madison: University of Wisconsin Press.

Oduol, Wilhelmina, and Wanjiku Mukabi Kabira. 1995. The Mother of Warriors and Her Daughters: The Women's Movement in Kenya. In *The Challenge of Local Feminisms: Women's Movements in Global Perspective,* edited by Amrita Basu. Boulder, CO: Westview Press.

Omran, Abdel R. 1971. The Epidemiological Transition: A Theory of Epidemiology of Population Change. *Milbank Memorial Fund Quarterly* 49:509–538.

Ong, Aihwa. 1987. *Spirits of Resistance and Capitalistic Discipline: Factory Women in Malaysia.* Albany: State University of New York Press.

Ong, Aihwa. 1990. Japanese Factories, Malay Workers: Class and Sexual Metaphors in West Malaysia. In *Power and Difference: Gender in Island Southeast Asia,* edited by Jane Atkinson and S. Errington. Palo Alto, CA: Stanford University Press.

Ong, Aihwa. 1997. Strategic Sisterhood or Sisters in Solidarity? Questions of Communitarianism and Citizenship in Asia. In *Feminism and Globalization: The Impact of the Global Economy on Women and Feminist Theory,* edited by Alfred C. Aman, Jr. *Indiana Journal of Global Legal Studies,* Spring (special issue).

Opensecrets.org. nd. Retail Sales: Top Contributors. http://www.opensecrets.org/industries/contrib.asp?Ind=N03&Cycle=2004.

Oved, Yaacov. 1988. *Two Hundred Years of American Communes.* New Brunswick, NJ: Transaction.

Paddock, William, and Paul Paddock. 1967. *Famine—1975.* Boston: Little, Brown.

Pagels, Elaine. 1995. *The Origin of Satan.* New York: Vintage Books.

Pape, Robert A. 2003. The Strategic Logic of Suicide Terrorism. *The American Political Science Review* 97: 343–361.

Pera, Lee, and Deborah McLaren. 1999. *Globalization, Tourism, and Indigenous Peoples: What You Should Know About the World's Largest "Industry."* Rethinking Tourism Project. http://www. planeta.com/ecotravel/resources/rtp/rtp.html.

Pimentel, David, O. Bailey, P. Kim, E. Mullaney, J. Calabrese, L. Walman, E. Nelson, and X. Yao. 1999. Will Limits of the Earth's Resources Control Human Numbers? *Environment, Development, and Sustainability* 1:19–39.

Pimentel, David, and Marcia Pimentel. 1979. *Food, Energy and Society.* New York: Wiley.

Platt, Anne E. 1996. *Infecting Ourselves: How Environmental and Social Disruption Trigger Disease.* Washington, DC: Worldwatch Institute.

Polanyi, Karl. [1944] 1957. *The Great Transformation.* Boston: Beacon Press.

Polgar, Steven. 1972. Population History and Population Policies from an Anthropological Perspective. *Current Anthropology* 13:203–211.

Polgar, Steven. 1975. Birth Planning: Between Neglect and Coercion. In *Population and Social Organization,* edited by Moni Nag. The Hague: Mouton.

Population Reference Bureau. 2000. *2000 World Population Data Sheet.* http://www.prb.org/pubs/wpds2000/.

Posey, Darrell A. 1996. Protecting Indigenous Peoples' Rights to Biodiversity. *Environment* 38:6–13.

Posey, Darrell A., John Frechione, and John Eddins. 1984. Ethnoecology as Applied Anthropology in Amazonian Development. *Human Organization* 43:95–107.

Power, Samantha. 2002. *"A Problem from Hell": America and the Age of Genocide.* New York: Perrennial Books.

Presley, Cora Ann. 1992. *Kikuyu Women, the Mau Mau Rebellion, and Social Change in Kenya.* Boulder, CO: Westview Press.

Preston, Julia. 1998. Feuding Villages Bring Mexican Region to Brink of War. *New York Times,* February 2. http://www.nytimes.com.

Public Campaign. 2000. *The Money Trail: Automobile Industry Campaign Contributions.* http://publicampaign.org/articles/automoneytrail.html.

Putnam, Robert D. 1996. The Strange Disappearance of Civic America. *The American Prospect,* no. 24, Winter.

Putnam, Robert D. 2000. *Bowling Alone: The Collapse and Revival of American Community.* New York: Simon & Shuster.

Putzel, James. 1997. Accounting for the "Dark Side" of Social Capital: Reading Robert Putnam on Democracy. *Journal of International Development* 9(7):939–949.

Rahman, Aminur. 1999. *Women and Microcredit in Rural Bangladesh: Anthropological Study of the Rhetoric and the Realities of Grameen Bank Lending.* Boulder, CO: Westview Press.

Ramos, Alcida Rita. 1995. *Sanumá Memories: Yanomami Ethnography in Times of Crisis.* Madison: University of Wisconsin Press.

Ray, Paul H., and Sherry Ruth Anderson. 2000. *The Cultural Creatives: How 50 Million People Are Changing the World.* Nevada City: Harmony Books.

Reagan, Ronald. 1982. Proclamation 4908—Afghanistan Day. http://www.reagan.utexas.edu/resource/speeches/1982/31082.htm.

Reed, Richard. 1997. *Forest Dwellers, Forest Protectors: Indigenous Models for International Development.* Boston: Allyn & Bacon.

Restad, Penne L. 1995. *Christmas in America: A History.* Oxford: Oxford University Press.

Rich, Bruce. 1994. *Mortgaging the Earth.* Boston: Beacon Press.

Rifkin, Jeremy. 1992. *Beyond Beef: The Rise and Fall of the Cattle Culture.* New York: Dutton.

Robbins, Richard H. 2001. *Cultural Anthropology: A Problem-Based Approach.* Belmont, CA: Wadsworth.

Robbins, Richard H. 2000. The Political Economy of Twinkies: An Inquiry into the Real Cost of Things. In *Globalization and Community: Canadian Perspectives,* edited by J. L. Chodkiewicz and R. E. Wiest. University of Manitoba, Anthropology Papers 34. Winnepeg, MB: University of Manitoba, Department of Anthropology.

Ross, Eric. 1980. *Beyond the Myths of Culture: Essays in Cultural Materialism.* New York: Academic Press.

Rowbotham, Michael. 1998. *The Grip of Death: A Study of Modern Money, Debt Slavery and Destructive Economics.* Charlbury, Oxfordshire: Jon Carpenter.

Rubio, Mauricio. 1997. Perverse Social Capital—Some Evidence from Colombia. *Journal of Economic Issues* 31(3):805–816.

Rugh, Andrea B. 1993. Reshaping Personal Relations in Egypt. In *Fundamentalisms and Society: Reclaiming the Sciences, the Family, and Education,* edited by Martin E. Marty and R. Scott Appleby (Fundamentalism Project, volume 2). Chicago: University of Chicago Press.

Rummel, R. J. 1994. *Death by Government.* New Brunswick: Transaction.

Ruskin, Gary. 1999. Why They Whine: How Corporations Prey on Our Children. *Mothering Magazine.* http://www.mothering.com/SpecialArticles/Issue97/whine.htm.

Ryan, John C., and Alan Thein Durning. 1997. *Stuff: The Secret Lives of Everyday Things,* NEW Report No. 4, January. Northwest Environmental Watch, Seattle, Washington.

Sachedina, Abdulaziz A. 1991. Activist Shi'ism in Iran, Iraq, and Lebanon. In *Fundamentalisms Observed,* edited by Martin E. Marty and R. Scott Appleby (Fundamentalism Project, volume 1). Chicago: University of Chicago Press.

Sachs, Wolfgang. 1999. *Planet Dialectics: Explorations in Environment and Development.* New York: Zed Books.

Sacks, Karen. 1979. *Sisters and Wives: The Past and Future of Sexual Equality.* Westport, CT: Greenwood.

Salamon, Lester M., and Helmut K. Anheier. 1996. *The Emerging Nonprofit Sector: An Overview.* Manchester: Manchester University Press.

Sale, Kirkpatrick. 1991. *The Conquest of Paradise: Christopher Columbus and the Columbian Legacy.* New York: Alfred A. Knopf.

Samat, Payal. 2000. *Deep Trouble: The Hidden Threat of Groundwater Pollution.* Worldwatch Paper 154. Washington, DC: Worldwatch Institute.

Sanderson, Stephen K. 1995. *Social Transformation: A General Theory of Historical Development.* Cambridge: Blackwell.

Sauvy, A. 1969. *General Theory of Population.* New York: Basic Books.

Scheper-Hughes, Nancy. 1992. *Death Without Weeping: The Violence of Everyday Life in Brazil.* Berkeley: University of California Press.

Schmidt, Leigh Eric. 1995. *Consumer Rites: The Buying and Selling of American Holidays.* Princeton: Princeton University Press.

Schneider, Jane. 1989. Rumpelstilskin's Bargain: Folklore and the Merchant Capitalist Intensification of Linen Manufacture in Early Modern Europe. In *Cloth and Human Experience,* edited by Annette B. Weiner and Jane Schneider. Washington, DC: Smithsonian Institute Press.

Schneider, Jane, and Peter Schneider. 2002. The Mafia and al-Qaeda: Violent and Secretive Organizations in Comparative and Historical Perspective. *American Anthropologist* 104: 776–782.

Schuler, Sidney, and Syed M. Hashemi. 1994. Credit Programs, Women's Empowerment, and Contraceptive Use in Rural Bangladesh. *Studies in Family Planning* 25:65–76.

Schusky, Ernest L. 1989. *Culture and Agriculture: An Ecological Introduction to Traditional and Modern Farming Systems.* New York: Bergin and Garvey.

Scott, James C. 1985. *Weapons of the Weak: Everyday Forms of Peasant Resistence.* New Haven: Yale University Press.

Scott, James C. 1998. *Seeing Like a State: How Human Schemes to Improve the Human Condition Have Failed.* New Haven and London: Yale University Press.

Scully, Gerald W. 1995. *Multiculturalism and Economic Growth.* National Study for Policy Analysis, Policy Report Number 196. http://www.ncpa.org/studies/s196/s196.html.

Sen, Amartya. 1990. Food Entitlements and Economic Chains. In *Hunger in History,* edited by Lucile F. Newman. Oxford: Basil Blackwell.

Service, Elman R. 1975. *Origins of the State and Civilization: The Process of Cultural Evolution.* New York: W. W. Norton.

Shalom, Stephen R. 1996. The Rwanda Genocide: The Nightmare That Happened. *Z Magazine,* April. http://www.lbbs.org/zmag/article/april96shalom.htm.

Shapiro, Issac, and John Springer. 2000. The Not-Rich Are Getting Not-Richer. *Los Angeles Times,* October 9.

Shiva, Vandana. 2000. Poverty and Globalization. *BBC Reith Lectures,* 2000. http://news.bbc.co. uk/hi/english/static/events/reith_2000/lecture5.stm.

Shor, Juliet B. 1993. *Overworked American: The Unexpected Decline of Leisure.* New York: Basic Books.

Silverblatt, Irene. 1988. Women in States. *Annual Review of Anthropology* 17:427–460.

Silverstein, Ken, and Alexander Cockburn. 1995. Major U.S. Bank Urges Zapatista Wipe-Out: "A Litmus Test for Mexico's Stability." *Counterpunch* 2 (3), February 1.

Sinclair, Upton. [1906] 1971. *The Jungle.* Cambridge, MA: R. Bentley.

Singer, Peter Warren. 2003. *Corporate Warriors: The Rise of the Privatized Military Industry.* Ithaca, NY: Cornell University Press.

Sisci, Francesco. 2002. Risky Business: Exporting the Amrican Dream. *Asia Times,* March 15.

Skaggs, Jimmy M. 1976. *Prime Cut.* College Station: Texas A&M University Press

Sluka, Jeffery A. (editor). 2000. *Death Squad: The Anthropology of State Terror.* Philadelphia: University of Pennsylvania Press.

Smith, Adam. [1776] 1994. *The Wealth of Nations,* edited by Edwin Cannan. New York: Modern Library.

Smith, Anthony D. 1995. *Nations and Nationalism in a Global Era.* Cambridge: Blackwell.

Smith, Charles D. 2000. *Palestine and the Arab–Israeli Conflict.* New York: St. Martin's Press.

Stack, Carol. 1973. *All Our Kin: Strategies for Survival in a Black Community.* New York: Basic Books.

Steele, Jonathan. 2003. A War That Can Never Be Won. *The Guardian.* November 22.

Stern, Jessica. 2003. *Terror in the Name of God: Why Religious Militants Kill.* New York: HarperCollins.

Stone, Lawrence. 1976. *The Family, Sex, and Marriage in England 1500–1800.* New York: Harper & Row.

Sutherland, Daniel. 1989. *The Expansion of Everyday Life: 1860–1876.* New York: Harper & Row.

Tambiah, Stanley J. 1996. *Leveling Crowds: Ethnonationalistic Conflicts and Collective Violence in South Asia.* Berkeley: University of California Press.

Tardieu, Vincent. 1999. The Economics of Disease Remedies. *Le Monde Diplomatique.* September.

Taussig, Michael. 1977. The Genesis of Capitalism Amongst a South American Peasantry: Devil's Labor and the Baptism of Money. *Comparative Studies in Society and History* 19:130–155.

Taussig, Michael. 1987. *Shamanism, Colonialism, and the Wild Man: A Study in Terror and Healing.* Chicago: University of Chicago Press.

Taylor, Bron. 1995. Earth First! In *Ecological Resistence Movements: The Global Emergence of Radical and Popular Environmentalism,* edited by Bron Raymond Taylor. Albany: State University of New York Press.

Tétreault, Mary Ann. 1994. Women and Revolution: A Framework for Analysis. In *Women and Revolution in Africa, Asia, and the New World,* edited by Mary Ann Tétreault. Columbia: University of South Carolina Press.

Thompson, E. P. 1967. Time, Work-Discipline and Industrial Capitalism. *Past and Present* 38: 56–97.

Thoreau, Henry David. [1854] 1957. *Walden.* Boston: Houghton Mifflin.

Thornton, John. 1992. *Africa and Africans in the Making of the Atlantic World, 1400–1680.* Cambridge: Cambridge University Press.

Tsing, Anna Lowenhaupt. 1993. *In the Realm of the Diamond Queen: Marginality in an Out-of-the-Way Place.* Princeton: Princeton University Press.

Twitchell, James B. 2002. *Living It Up: Our Love Affair with Luxury.* New York: Colombia University Press.

Twitchell, James B. 2004. A (Mild) Defense of Luxury. In *Talking Points on Global Issues: A Reader,* edited by Richard H. Robbins (pp. 9–17). Boston: Allyn & Bacon.

UNAIDS. 2003. *AIDS Epidemic Update, 2003.* http://www.unaids.org/en/Resources/Publications/Corporate+publications/aids+epidemic+update+-+december+2003.asp.

United Nations. 1993. *Development Programme, Human Development Report.* New York: Oxford University Press.

United Nations. 1998. *Revision of the World Population Estimates and Projections.* http://www.popin.org/pop1998/.

United Nations. 1999. *The Global Compact.* http://unglobalcompact.org/gc/unweb.nsf/content/thenine.htm.

United Nations. 2000. *Human Development Report 2000.* Oxford: Oxford University Press.

United Nations. 2003. *World Economic and Social Survey.* http://www.un.org/esa/analysis.

United Nations. 2004. *World Economic Situation and Prospects,* 2004. http://www.un.org/esa/policy/wess.

United Nations Development Programme. 1997. *Human Development Report 1997: Human Development to Eradicate Poverty.* http://www.undp.org/hdro/e97over.htm.

United Nations Development Programme. 1998. *Human Development Report.* http://www.undp.org/hdro/e98over.htm.

United Nations Population Fund. 2000. *The State of the World's Population, 2000: Lives Together, Worlds Apart: Men and Women in a Time of Change.* http://www.unfpa.org/swp/swpmain.htm.

U.S. Bureau of the Census. 1990. *Statistical Abstract of the United States: 1990,* 110th ed. Washington, DC: U.S. Government Printing Office.

U.S. Bureau of the Census. 1992. *Statistical Abstract of the United States: 1992,* 112th ed. Washington, DC: U.S. Government Printing Office.

U.S. Bureau of the Census. 1993. *Statistical Abstract of the United States: 1993,* 113th ed. Washington, DC: U.S. Government Printing Office.

U.S. Bureau of the Census. 1994. *Statistical Abstract of the United States: 1994,* 114th ed. Washington, DC: U.S. Government Printing Office.

United States Department of Agriculture. 1992. *Census of Agriculture.* http://www.nass.usda.gov/census/census92/agrimenu.htm.

U.S. Department of Agriculture. 1999. *Expenditures on Children by Family: 1999 Annual Report.* Center for Nutrition Policy and Promotion. http://www.usda.gov/cnpp/Crc/crc1999.pdf.

U.S. Department of Agriculture. 2000. *Agricultural Fact Book 2000.* U.S. Department of Agriculture. Office of Communications. http://www.usda.gov/news/pubs/fbook00/factbook2000.pdf.

U.S. Department of State. 2003. *World Military Expenditures and Arms Transfers, 1998.* http://www.state.gov/www/global/arms/bureau_ac/wmeat98/wmeat98.html.

United States Energy Information Agency. 2000. *Energy Use and Carbon Emissions of Selected Countries 1998–1999.* http://www.eia.doe.gov/emeu/cabs/contents.html.

United States Federal Reserve. 2004. Federal Reserve Statistical Release: Historical Data. http://www.federalreserve.gov.releases/h6/hist.

van den Berghe, Pierre. 1992. The Modern State: Nation-Builder or Nation-Killer? *International Journal of Group Tensions* 22:191–208.

Vaughn, Megan. 1987. *The Story of an African Famine: Gender and Famine in Twentieth Century Malawi.* Cambridge: Cambridge University Press.

Wackernagel, Mathis, and William E. Rees. 1996. *Our Ecological Footprint: Reducing Human Impact on the Earth.* Gabriola Island, BC: New Society.

Wagar, W. Warren. 1991. *The Next Three Futures: Paradigms of Things to Come.* New York: Greenwood Press.

Wahid, Abu N. M. 1994. The Grameen Bank and Poverty Alleviation in Bangladesh: Theory, Evidence, and Limitations. *The American Journal of Economics and Sociology* 53:1–15.

Waits, William. 1992. *The Modern Christmas in America: A Cultural History of Gift-Giving.* New York: New York University Press.

Wallace, Anthony F. C. 1966. *Religion: An Anthropological View.* New York: Random House.

Wallace, Anthony F. C. 1987. *St. Clair: A Nineteenth-Century Coal Town's Experience with a Disaster Prone Industry.* New York: Alfred A. Knopf.

Wallace, Ernest, and E. Adamson Hoebel. 1952. *The Comanches: Lords of the South Plains.* Norman: University of Oklahoma Press.

Wallace, Mike. 1985. Mickey Mouse History: Portraying the Past at Disney World. *Radical History Review* 32:35–57.

Wallerstein, Immanuel. 1989. *The Modern World-System III: The Second Era of Great Expansion of the Capitalist World-Economy, 1730–1840s.* New York: Academic Press.

Wallerstein, Immanuel. 1990. Antisystemic Movements: History and Dilemmas. In *Transforming the Revolution: Social Movements and the World-System,* edited by Samir Amin, Giovanni Arrighi, Andre Gunder Frank, and Immanuel Wallerstein. New York: Monthly Press.

Wallerstein, Immanuel. 1997. Ecology and Capitalist Costs of Production: No Exit. Keynote address at

PEWS XXI, "The Global Environment and the World-System," University of California, Santa Cruz, April 3–5. http://fbc.binghamton.edu/iwecol.htm.

Wallis, Jim. 1984. *Agenda for Biblical People.* San Francisco: Harper San Francisco.

Ward, Martha C. 1996. *A World Full of Women.* Boston: Allyn & Bacon.

Weatherford, Jack. 1988. *Indian Givers: How the Indians of the Americas Transformed the World.* New York: Fawcett Columbine.

Weatherford, Jack. 1997. *The History of Money: From Sandstone to Cyberspace.* New York: Crown.

Weber, Eugen. 1976. *Peasants into Frenchmen: The Modernization of Rural France, 1870–1914.* Stanford: Stanford University Press.

Weber, Max. 1947. *The Theory of Social and Economic Organization.* Translated by A. M. Henderson and Talcott Parsons, edited by Talcott Parsons. Glencoe, IL: The Free Press.

Weber, Max. 1958. *The Protestant Ethic and the Spirit of Capitalism.* Translated by Talcott Parsons. New York: Scribner.

Wedel, Janine R. 1998a. *Collision and Collusion: The Strange Case of Western Aid to Eastern Europe, 1989–1998.* New York: St. Martin's Press.

Wedel, Janine R. 1998b. The Harvard Boys Do Russia. *The Nation,* June 1.

Wedel, Janine R. 1999. U.S. Assistance for Market Reforms: Foreign Aid Failures in Russia and the Former Soviet Bloc. *Policy Analysis, No. 338,* March. http://www.cato.org/pubs/pas/pa338.pdf.

Weinberg, Steven. 1999. *No to Cosmic Design.* Presentation at the "Cosmic Questions Conference," April 15, unpublished text.

Weisbrot, Mark, Robert Naiman, and Joyce Kim. 2000. *The Emperor Has No Growth: Declining Economic Growth Rates in the Era of Globalization.* Center for Economic and Policy Research, Briefing Paper. http://www.cepr.net/images/IMF/the_emperor_has_no_growth.htm.

Weiss, Thomas G., and Leon Gordenker (editors). 1996. *NGOs, the UN, and Global Governance.* London: Lynne Rienner.

White, Benjamin. 1973. Demand for Labor and Population Growth in Colonial Java. *Human Ecology* 1:217–236.

White House Conference on Child Health and Protection. 1931. *The Home and the Child: Housing, Furnishing, Management, Income, and Clothing.* New York: Arno Press.

Williams, Jonathan (edited). 1997. *Money: A History.* New York: St. Martin's Press.

Willis, Paul. [1977] 1981. *Learning to Labor: How Working Class Kids Get Working Class Jobs.* New York: Columbia University Press

Wilson, Edmund. [1931] 1961. *The Shores of Light ("An Appeal to Progressives").* New York: Vintage Books.

Winters, Jeffrey A. 1996. *Power in Motion: Capital Mobility and the Indonesian State.* Ithaca, NY: Cornell University Press.

Wittfogel, Karl A. 1957. *Oriental Despotism.* New Haven: Yale University Press.

Wolf, Eric. 1967. *Peasants.* Engelwood Cliffs: Prentice-Hall.

Wolf, Eric. 1969. *Peasant Wars of the Twentieth Century.* New York: Harper & Row.

Wolf, Eric R. 1982. *Europe and the People Without History.* Berkeley: University of California Press.

Wolff, Michael, Peter Rutten, and Albert Bayers III (editors.) 1992. *Where We Stand,* New York: Bantam Books.

World Development Report. 1996. *From Plan to Market.* Oxford: Oxford University Press.

World Economic Outlook. 1999. The World Economic Outlook (WEO) Database September 2000. International Monetary Fund. http://www.imf.org/external/pubs/ft/weo/2000/02/data/index.htm.

World Health Organization. 1995. *The Tobacco Epidemic: A Global Health Emergency.* http://www.who.ch/psa/toh/Alert/apr96/index.html.

World Health Organization. 1995. *World Health Report.* http://www.who.ch/whr/1995/xsum95_e.htm.

World Health Organization. 1997. Fifty Facts of Health. *World Health Report.* http://www.who.int/whr2001/2001/archives/1997/factse.htm.

World Heath Organization. 2003. *World Health Report.* http://www.who.int/whr/2003/en/Annex2-en.pdf.

World Investment Report 1999. *World Investment Report.* New York: United Nations Publications for UNCTAD.

Worsley, Peter. 1968. *The Trumpets Shall Sound: A Study of "Cargo" Cults in Melanesia,* 2nd ed. New York: Schocken Books.

York, Geoffrey. 1999. "A Deadly Strain of TB Races Toward the West. *Toronto Globe and Mail.* March 24.

Zollo, Peter. 1999. *Wise Up to Teens: Insights into Marketing and Advertising to Teenagers,* 2nd ed. Ithaca, NY: New Strategist Publications.

NAME INDEX

PLACE AND CULTURE INDEX

SUBJECT INDEX

■ ■ ■ ■ ■ ▬▬

CREDITS

p. 5, © Warner Bros./Photofest; p. 7, © John Gillmoure/CORBIS; p. 15, © Anthro-Photo File; p. 23, © AP/Wide World Photos; p. 29, © Bettmann/CORBIS; p. 32, © David Ball/ Index Stock Imagery; p. 40, © Craig Strong/Getty Images; p. 46, The Granger Collection, New York; p. 57, © Keith B. Richburg/Reuters; p. 68, © Bettmann/CORBIS; p. 86, 93, The Granger Collection, New York; p. 115, North Wind Picture Archives; p. 117, © Russell D. Curtis/Photo Researchers, Inc.; p. 131, © John Jonik, reprinted with permission; p. 150, © Alain Le Garsmeur/CORBIS; p. 155 left, © AP/Wide World Photos; p. 155 right, © Ira Kirschenbaum/Stock Boston; p. 167 left, © Bruce Paton; p. 167 right, © Kindra Clineff/Index Stock Imagery; p. 185, © Bernard Bisson/Corbis Sygma; p. 192, © Sean Sprague; p. 203, © Gilles Saussier/Gamma Press; p. 213, Culver Pictures; p. 225, © Kathy McLaughlin/The Image Works; p. 237, © Sean Sprague; p. 253, © Estate of Leah Melnick; p. 257, © Sean Sprague/Stock, Boston; p. 263, © AP/Wide World Photos; p. 271, The Granger Collection, New York; p. 289, © Thierry Orban/Corbis Sygma; p. 319, 322 left, © Bettmann/CORBIS; p. 322 right, © Jacques Torregano/Gamma Press; p. 331, © Bettmann/CORBIS; p. 334, © John Filo; p. 348, © Bettmann/CORBIS; p. 363, © Julio Etchart; p. 371, Culver Pictures.